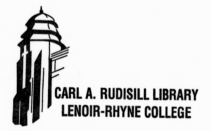

Also by Gabriel Kolko

ANATOMY OF A WAR:
Vietnam, the United States,
and the Modern Historical Experience

CONFRONTING THE THIRD WORLD:
United States Foreign Policy, 1945–1980

MAIN CURRENTS IN MODERN AMERICAN HISTORY

RAILROADS AND REGULATION, 1877–1916

THE TRIUMPH OF CONSERVATISM:
A Reinterpretation of American History, 1900–1916

WEALTH AND POWER IN AMERICA:
An Analysis of Social Class and
Income Distribution

GABRIEL KOLKO

THE POLITICS
OF WAR

THE WORLD AND UNITED STATES
FOREIGN POLICY, 1943–1945

With a New Preface and Epilogue by the Author

PANTHEON BOOKS   NEW YORK

Copyright © 1968, 1990 by Gabriel Kolko

All rights reserved under International and Pan-American
Copyright Conventions. Published in the United States by Pantheon Books, a division of Random House, Inc., New York.
originally published in different form by Random House, Inc.,
New York, in 1969. First paperback edition published by Vintage Books in 1970.

Library of Congress Cataloging-in-Publication Data

Kolko, Gabriel.
    The politics of war : the world and United States foreign
policy, 1943–1945 / Gabriel Kolko ; with a new preface and
epilogue by the author.
        p.   cm.
    Reprint. Originally published: New York : Random
House, © 1968.
    Includes bibliographical references.
    ISBN 0-679-72757-4 (pbk.)
    1. United States—Foreign relations—1933–1945.
    2. World politics—1933–1945. 3. World War, 1939–
1945—Diplomatic history.
    I. Title.
E744.K65   1990
327.73—dc20   89-43238

Manufactured in the United States of America

Pantheon Paperback Edition

TO JOYCE

ACKNOWLEDGMENTS

Solely as a form of literary convenience, throughout this work I refer to the "United States," "Americans," "Washington," "London," "Moscow," and the like. In fact what is meant is the leaders or rulers of these abstracted nations, the men who made decisions taken as a collective entity after they had settled their own differences. Where a specific group, faction, or agency is involved, I so indicate, but in no case should it be thought I am referring to the entire people of a nation. In the conduct of wartime grand diplomacy the people of all the major nations were the object of worried attention, manipulation and, in many places, physical restraint, but nowhere were they consulted on the contours of the policy of any state.

MY debts to those who have made possible this and subsequent volumes on the history of United States foreign policy since 1943 are too great to acknowledge sufficiently, not the least because research materials were gathered over years and on three continents with the aid of archival workers and librarians who tolerated much and gave yet more. Some of these libraries are cited in the footnoted sources, and for those not acknowledged my appreciation is no less. The Social Science Research Council generously made possible a year's research and the Committee on Regional Studies of Harvard University provided me with helpful assistance during that time. The Penrose Fund of the American Philosophical Society gave me a grant to continue research and visit various archives, and I am grateful for its support. The John Simon Guggenheim Memorial Foundation made possible a year's freedom for writing, for which I am especially indebted. The Institute for Policy Studies made the final preparation of the text infinitely easier for me in every way. Needless to say, none of the above foundations and organizations assumes any responsibility for the views contained in this book, much less the quality of the research. It is for the author alone to accept responsibility for his words, but also to observe that careful research takes much time and money, and I am deeply grateful for what I have received and to those who have helped make this volume possible.

N. Gordon Levin, Jr., made valuable suggestions for improving the text, and both in his *Woodrow Wilson and World Politics* (New York, 1968), and in Arno J. Mayer's *Politics and Diplomacy of Peacemaking* (New York, 1967), the reader may discover the grand themes of American and world diplomacy that make even more comprehensible the events he will find described in this volume.

To some very great measure this book would have been very different without the prodding, questions, and encouragement of Barrington Moore, Jr., and whole sections of it are responses to his critical commitment to seeking truth regardless of conventional fashions. If this book satisfies at least some of his questions in our running dialogue on the role and application of reason in history it will be reward enough. And if others perceive the character and reality of history as something beyond ideology and soothing illusions, I shall be totally satisfied.

Above all, without the continuous aid, insights, and sustenance of my wife, Joyce, this book would not have been written. All that follows is in every sense a reflection of her commitments and scholarship as well as my own, and the product of our joint labors.

GABRIEL KOLKO

CONTENTS

PREFACE TO THE
1990 EDITION

THE MEN who initiated World War II, just as had those who unleashed World War I, began their venture with false expectations regarding its duration and costs. This was not surprising given that the visions and goals of both Japanese and German leaders during the 1930s were syntheses of ideological fantasies and a grandiose desire for power, which they then merged with profound illusions about the weaknesses of their adversaries. What is surprising is how totally unprepared the aggressor nations proved to be when their overly sanguine expectations of early victory were not met and the war took on its ultimate dimensions.

Japan was the first to learn, in regard to China, how far off its initial premises about fighting a war could be. A strong militarist faction among those Japanese officers and civilians stationed in northern China and Korea had long advocated integrating north China into an economic empire that would include Manchuria and Korea. When a trivial altercation between Chinese and Japanese soldiers occurred on the Marco Polo Bridge outside Peking on July 7, 1937, this faction used the "incident" to initiate a military campaign to advance its imperialist objectives, thereby inadvertently setting in motion the chain of events that was to produce World War II in Asia. Their audacity was possible because their nominal superiors in Tokyo were in consensus with them on the fundamental goal of imposing Japanese hegemony over East Asia, if not always on the means to attain it.

Most of Japan's leaders expected that the north China aggression would be over in a matter of a few months, as had been the case with the annexation of Manchuria six years earlier. Only the navy warned that the war might spread to China's coastal cities as well. But rather than accept defeat and come to terms, as Tokyo had naïvely assumed they would, the Chinese Nationalists under Chiang Kai-shek retreated into the interior, allowing the Japanese to capture a vast amount of territory but inflicting on them a very high price: 140,000 Japanese dead and over a half-million wounded during 1937–1938. Chiang was confident that in due course the war would be internationalized, and that eventually Japan would find itself spread too thin to prosecute its China ambitions. By 1938 a large part of the Japanese army was mired permanently in China, and the "China Incident" that had proved to be a major, if not the decisive, cause of World War II in Asia became as well a major cause of Japan's eventual military defeat. What had been envisioned as a minor effort had grown into a monumental, debilitating sustained campaign and became a serious drain on Japan's limited resources—one it could scarcely afford after it added the United States and the British Commonwealth to its list of enemies.

Once the China adventure became a Pacific war, it developed its own logic and momentum, and Japan's leaders, notwithstanding deep differences among themselves on means, pursued their goals with a fatalism that revealed how precious little rational calculations informed their conduct. Tempted by the collapse of the European colonial system in Southeast Asia in the wake of Hitler's victories after 1939, and convinced that eventual success in China also required their establishing economic hegemony over the colonies south of it, Japan's rulers merged optimism and a desperate need for material resources with an essentially irrational faith in their own destiny to justify embarking on a course that led, ineluctably, to their decision the following year to go to war with the United States.

Japan's leaders had, in fact, been given an accurate assessment of what would be the nation's long-term weaknesses in industrial output, and in its gravely inadequate access to petroleum, should the war go on for a number of years. As important, in the summer of 1940 Japanese experts estimated that if access to the Dutch East Indies were cut off, Japan would have sufficient fuel and resources to fight the Americans for a year or two at most. The navy was therefore able to prevent the army from embarking on a northward strategy against the Soviet Union, but it was less successful in convincing the government to win the war in China before moving southward to conquer Southeast Asia's riches.

By September 1941 Japan had no illusions that it could ever compel the United States to surrender. But still it hoped that the combined impact of its projected initial naval triumphs, the new material power it would have once East Asia was conquered and integrated into the Japanese sphere of influence, and the competing demands on American resources by Germany's victories in Europe would force the Americans to accede to a Japanese-dominated status quo in Asia. Even the most militant advocates of the war, those who dominated Tokyo's policy, expected victory in this sense only. It was generally understood that the longer the war went on, the more Japan's inherent economic liabilities would weigh against it, making even this more limited goal unattainable. Pessimism suffused estimates of the Japanese navy during the weeks before Japan's attack on Pearl Harbor. Their adventurism, mystical fatalism, and imperialist consensus notwithstanding, Japan's rulers also respected facts sufficiently to share a profound uneasiness about the grave course on which they had embarked.

This Japanese clarity regarding the material balance of forces reflected basic realities that always were factored into their estimates of the future, if not into their final political and military decisions. The Nazi leaders, by contrast, thought they could easily compensate for the weight of the economic power and size of the armies that would eventually be arrayed against Germany by the skillful use of mobile military forces applied selectively and surgically against an Allied cause divided on basic diplomatic and political issues.

But it is instructive to look at just how great the discrepancies were. The United States accounted for 32 percent of the world's industrial production in 1936–1938, and together with Great Britain and the U.S.S.R. the figure rose to 60 percent. American output was ten times that of Japan, three times that of Germany. In fact, the three major Axis states combined had only 17 percent of the world's industrial production. The Allies' airplane output in 1940 was 2.3 times that of the Axis, and during 1941–1945 their tank output was nearly 5 times that of their enemies. During 1941–1942, Great Britain alone outproduced Germany, often by a huge margin, in all crucial forms of military equipment. Given the facts, both Japan and Germany had to score quick, decisive victories or the war would become one of attrition, the inevitable result of which would be an Axis defeat. But long wars impose incalculable social and political as well as human costs on all the nations involved, and it was in this domain that the leaders of all the contesting nations had only the vaguest vision of what the future contained for them.

That Hitler embarked on war in Europe without taking sufficient heed of the potential weight of the vast resources that would be arrayed against Germany reflects his romantic penchant for substituting his desires for a realistic assessment of the factors that would decide success or failure for each belligerent. But the Allies share some of the blame for Hitler's overconfidence. The fact that Hitler helped Franco impose fascism on Spain while the French and British remained passive, that he annexed Austria in March 1938 without significant world opposition, and finally that in September 1938 he obtained Anglo-French acquiescence at Munich to his dismantling of Czechoslovakia caused him understandably to conclude that his enemies' vacillation and disunity would permit him to fight a sequence of small, quick wars at the times and places of his choosing, thereby never calling into play the overwhelmingly decisive economic power of a united Allied response. Moreover, given the anti-Soviet consensus that existed in the West, he doubted he would ever see the emergence of the sort of effective alliance against him between Britain, the U.S.S.R., and the United States that later did in fact come into being.

And so he ignored the warnings expressed in August 1939 by his navy as well as his army leaders that Germany was unprepared for a war of long duration. He gave even less attention to the arguments of some of his officers that a war involving Britain would last years. Instead, on September 1, 1939, he attacked Poland, achieving a stunning, instant victory. His daring and his blitzkrieg strategy proved successful, even though he had no coherent war organization at home, a stockpile of raw materials sufficient for less than six months of conflict, and a labor force still geared to peace. Hitler was genuinely surprised when Britain and France declared war two days later. Still confident that he had not triggered a replay of the war of attrition World War I had become before its end, he continued vast civilian projects close to his heart that he had initiated before the war's outbreak. He refused to put the economy on a war footing after the official outbreak of World War II in Europe, and although military outlays increased greatly, civilian spending also remained virtually constant until 1944. The astonishing ease with which Germany destroyed the armies facing it on its western front in May and June 1940 only strengthened Hitler's conviction that relatively low-cost and brief blitzkriegs would suffice for him to achieve his goal of dominating the whole of Europe and the Middle East and North Africa beyond it.

When the British in 1940 committed themselves to continue the war without their French ally, Hitler turned to the task of first conquering the Soviet Union and then compelling the British to capsize before the United States, with its still unknown but huge and potentially decisive resources, could enter the war on England's side. Most German generals also shared the supreme self-confidence with which Hitler embarked on the Russian campaign, their earlier skepticism toward his strategy having disappeared as his promised quick successes had been easily attained. Germany planned on a war against the U.S.S.R. that would last five months, but in early June 1941 Hitler confided to Japan's ambassador that he expected to attain victory within two to three months after Germany's initial assault. Although the Nazis had an accurate general impression of the extent of Soviet military manpower and equipment, they attached little weight to these statistics because they firmly believed that the U.S.S.R., like France, would disintegrate politically and socially almost immediately upon being faced with the reality of modern war as the German blitzkrieg had redefined it.

In fact, overweening self-confidence caused Hitler and his generals to initiate the war in the East wholly unprepared logistically for the vast spaces and poor roads, and even less for the prospect of a terrible winter requiring resources the German army simply did not possess. Output of weapons and munitions was increased somewhat before the attack began on June 22, 1941, but Hitler's planners reduced it again after Germany's first spectacular successes. But even before the winter cold paralyzed their efforts, the Nazis had bogged down owing to insufficient spare parts, a lack of reserve troops, and the weakness of their basic field strategy. When, at the beginning of December 1941, unusually severe winter weather immobilized the poorly clothed Nazi forces and froze their equipment, and the Soviet army counterattacked, it was clear that the defeat of the U.S.S.R. would be no simple matter. Over 830,000 German casualties by the end of the year mocked Hitler's earlier optimistic assumptions. By the end of 1941, anyone who chose to look at the facts could see that the second world war would be a war like the first—protracted and draining. It would be a test of the abilities of the leaders to mobilize their societies and to direct internal political forces so as to help their populations survive the searing ordeal that was to last over three more years.

For Germany's ad hoc improvisations to change the course of events, Germany had to pull off a series of quick successes. Speedy victory was also essential for the Japanese. But while the Japanese stoically embarked on a course they sensed would lead to tragedy, the Nazis repeatedly proved to be naïve and frivolous, a quality of analytic mindlessness rooted in Nazi romanticism and its concept of racial supremacy.

Hitler's early optimism regarding the Russian campaign nonetheless had some justification. As a result of Stalin's purge of most of the Red Army's senior officers after 1936 and the consequent lack of experience within the Russian command structure, chaos ruled the Red Army in early 1941. But notwithstanding its serious organizational problems, the Red Army had begun to acquire large amounts of new, increasingly advanced tanks and other equipment before June 1941, and Soviet aircraft output in 1940 was equal to Germany's. The U.S.S.R.'s principal initial weaknesses were less its limited military and economic resources than Stalin's total unwillingness to believe the extremely detailed, accurate intelligence he received on German war preparations, down to the anticipated time of attack, and his failure to take precautions accordingly. Out of fear of provoking a Germany attack, Stalin refused to implement the Red Army's operational plans before the German assault began, even though local commanders tried to improve troop readiness in various ways. Up to the day of its attack, Germany was still receiving shipments of the goods and resources the Soviets were obligated to send them under the terms of the August 1939 Soviet-German Nonagression Pact, including those essential for the imminent war between the two countries. The Soviet Union survived the awful last half of 1941 by the narrowest of margins and only by virtue of the fact that Hitler's current blunders exceeded Stalin's earlier blunders by a decisive margin, and perhaps also because the winter was colder than usual. The Soviet dictator unquestionably was chastened by near defeat.

BUT more important, Hitler's misplaced confidence led him to believe that the war could be fought and won without great disruptions of German civilian life. Vast economic exactions from France and other occupied countries and the utilization of forced labor from those countries to work principally in war industries mitigated, to an important degree, the war's strain on the German society and economy. From 1.1 million in May 1940 to 3 million a year later and over 6 million in 1943, more than one-fifth of Germany's workforce at the end of 1944 consisted of foreigners. Although nearly 1.5 million German women were employed as domestics, joined by nearly 500,000 Ukrainian women, here too there was no substantial societal disruption. On the contrary, Hitler refused to allow German women to assume the new wartime tasks women were performing in all the Allied nations. Partly owing to overconfidence and partly to the Nazi belief that women belonged in the home, but also because of his fear of upsetting the comfortable world of good burghers, Hitler limited women's work largely to housework for the rich.

Hitler's refusal to mobilize fully before the course of the war had tilted irrevocably against Germany was neither haphazard oversight nor the consequence merely of underestimating the enemies' capabilities. Nor was it only the result of making too much of one's own racial prowess. Nazi unwillingness to allow German women to work in the same roles or to the same extent as women did in wartime England and as they had done in the Soviet Union since the revolution, or to greatly prolong the working hours of German male civilians, reflected Hitler's deep consciousness of the nation's dangerous World War I experience, when the German homefront was exhausted before its armies were defeated. And that experience also goes a long way toward explaining the Nazis' policy of exacting enormous financial and human resources from conquered states while showing great leniency toward their own people.

Yet, to a crucial degree, it was the cruelty of these Nazi impositions that defined for Europe's civilian populations the social and human impact of the war. And it was also this cruelty that provoked in great measure the emergence of powerful resistance movements during the war and the political radicalization of the populations of various countries once the war ended.

One must ask why Germany after 1939, but especially after May 1945 when there was no brutal Nazi terror to inhibit it, did not produce the radical and regenerative political movements that had so profoundly challenged its conservative politics after 1917. And no less crucial is the question why France, which after World War I had returned fairly smoothly to essentially its prewar political mold and was spared the profound political upheavals that shook Germany, was now to produce a powerful Communist Party and labor militancy. Variations of this question are relevant also for many other European nations. The radicalizing economic and social forces that the war produced impinged on politics directly, thereby creating those disputatious issues of power and society which were to shape profoundly inter-Allied relations and diplomacy both during and especially after the war. Such trends were partially to impose boundaries on what the Allies were free to do insofar as the social effects of the war on various nations were to define, at least to some vital extent, its political outcome in Europe—and above all in Asia. For the impact of World War II on the rhythm of the daily experience of people throughout the world and on their consciousness was to shape its consequences for years to come even more than the visible immediate successes or failures of armies.

World War I impoverished the German working class, and it was not until 1928 that it regained its 1913 standard of living. From 1913 to 1917, for example, real wages fell by half for printers and nearly as much for miners and skilled railway labor as well as for workers in civilian goods industries. The entire working class suffered in some fashion, a fact that was reflected during the postwar decade in its unprecedented militancy— strikes, local revolts and military mutinies, and the growth of the Communist Party. As Albert Speer, Hitler's head of war production, later recalled, "Hitler and the majority of his political followers belonged to the generation who as soldiers had witnessed the Revolution of November 1918 and had never forgotten it. In private conversations Hitler indicated that after the experience of 1918 one could not be cautious enough." Forced to choose, the Nazis therefore preferred to risk depriving the war effort to possibly alienating the workers and seeing them driven once again to political action in its various forms, including slowdowns and sabotage. Real weekly income in Germany grew dramatically from 1932 to 1941, and even in 1944 it was only slightly less than it had been at its peak 1941 level.

The net result of Hitler's great gamble was that the Nazis succeeded both in forestalling further internal upheavals in Germany and in co-opting the working class functionally if not psychologically.)There were those—principally some young people and former Socialist or Communist activists—who retreated to personalism and retained a silent opposition or skepticism toward the Nazi system. The enlisted army, unlike the officer corps, remained wholly disciplined until the end, and a socially relevant popular opposition did not emerge to threaten the war effort, or to transform postwar German society or politics. But Hitler's success in this domain seriously, perhaps even gravely, reduced the potential resources he might have utilized for his military efforts, and this lenient social policy at home was to a great degree responsible for the eventual collapse of his mad dreams of European domination.

The most profound dilemma for any nation waging war in the twentieth century is that if the state is serious about attaining victory, it must implement economic and political measures that may risk alienating large numbers of its own people, thereby provoking domestic social trauma. As protracted war increasingly absorbs civilians, extending in some manner the sacrifices of the battlefield to the homefront, a transformation of mass consciousness also occurs. In this manner the breakdown of capitalism since the late nineteenth century (which Marxists had once assumed would be an autonomous, nationally self-contained economic process) has been inextricably linked in its final stages with those vast, complex interacting economic, social, and human events associated with wars. Indeed, until now the potential for revolution in this century in the more industrially developed nations, as well as in China, Vietnam, and part of the Third World, has been indissolubly linked to the very process of war and its effects. World War II confirmed the critical significance of how in our century the price the general public pays to continue a war inevitably becomes intertwined with previously existing social tensions and crises to exacerbate and bring them to fruition and generate yet others, becoming integral to the dynamics of modern change.]

Ironically, Germany, with its policy of taxing heavily the nations it captured rather than its own population, emerged from the war less radicalized than most of the rest of Europe. In this regard, therefore, it transferred the principal social and political costs of its war to those it had conquered, and ultimately—a further irony—to the victors, protecting the pre-Nazi social hierarchy against internal challenges. That a generalized economic breakdown usually foretells a rise in leftist politics does not argue against the influence of other factors also in promoting popular radicalization. Still, the material causes of the growth of the Left in all of postwar Europe cannot be minimized. Seemingly stale data on inflation, real income, and such do provide a means, however limited, by which to measure the human condition in wartime and remain useful if one is to draw comparisons, notwithstanding a certain listlessness inherent in all numbers.

But it is even more important to attempt to enter into the minds, with their fears and inspirations, of those many hundreds of millions of people caught in the great vortex of that terrible war if one is to fully comprehend the determination of those who survived that a return to the old must never happen again.

One sees these forces at work in France, to take one of the clearer examples. World War I was very destructive in the battlefield area along the French-Belgian border, but the region of intense physical wartime damage after 1939 was at least twice as large. But more important, the German occupation of so much of France in 1940 allowed Gemany to tax it ruthlessly for almost five years, apart from the fact that the Nazis deported to Germany over a million and a half French workers and captured soldiers. The Nazis wore down the entire French economy with their exactions; while real income in France during the war of 1914–1918 remained relatively stable, by 1943, to take one example, real income in Paris was about one-third less than it had been in 1938. As would be expected, the working class suffered from such changes far more than any other social class. It was this long night of economic hardship, combined with the traditional elite's collaboration with the Nazis via the Vichy regime, that was to result finally in that entrenched mind-set of non-cooperation among the French masses indispensable to the growth of an armed and fighting Resistance, of which in this case the Communists were the single most important component. For those who refused to obey Nazi orders, including the orders deporting them as labor to Germany, the choice was very simple: they escaped to the maquis in the forests and mountains. What began as an almost inchoate mentality founded on the daily responses of average people, largely expressed spontaneously, was to evolve into clear political and social aspirations that in turn made profound social change inevitable. Especially on the part of the organized Resistance, which had close to half a million mobilized members by July 1944, these responses would translate into a demand to take power. In most of Western and Southern Europe it was above all the physical and mental toll of the war, rather than the efforts of organized parties, that radicalized the masses initially and produced their potential for action.

People in arms or ready to employ them became an altogether new reality on the world scene, one that had never existed before to such an extent or over such a broad area. In this process, the initial existence of significant Communist parties was irrelevant, for it was the war itself, with its combination of external oppression and internal conflict between competing sectors, that galvanized the process of opposition. Eventually the trauma of war stimulated the organization of a Resistance that became part of World War II's fundamental political outcome—and its most enduring legacy in the immediate postwar period.

In Yugoslavia, for example, widespread incidents of fighting occurred spontaneously in many areas, and at the inception of the struggle the Communists sought mainly to provide those already engaged in the Resistance with needed leadership. In China especially, the war preceded by many years the emergence in much of the country of a strong Communist Party. As with the Nazis, Japanese-created dislocations and property requisitions traumatized Asian society and life profoundly. Even the Soviet Union's nominal hegemony over a world Communist movement was to be decisively challenged in due course as the presence of "Marxism-Leninism" in vast new areas soon transcended Moscow's ability to dominate it.

It was above all the transformation of China, which I detail in this book, that became the single most important political and human outcome of World War II, revealing how fundamental the war's social consequences were to its most significant political results. Chiang Kai-shek's strategy of allowing Japan's army access to China's vast space in order to bog it down and exhaust it helped greatly to defeat Japanese militarism. But it also allowed the war to traumatize so much more of China, both physically and, eventually, politically. The time Chiang and his administrative apparatus gained by this strategy was used to exploit China's few resources for their own political and private gain, further adding to the stresses that would soon rip apart the traditional Chinese economic and social order.

The enormity of the Chinese tragedy still defies all efforts to describe it. The decline in the standards of living of its population was uneven; in certain regions hyperinflation wrecked the economy and imposed a monumental human toll. While landowners suffered least of all, those who worked for them saw their real incomes fall by as much as one-half between 1938 and 1944. Labor in general suffered even more. By 1943 government officials were earning about one-eighth of their 1938 income and were forced to turn to corruption in order to survive. Soldiers' salaries were one-twentieth of their earlier level. Attempts to compensate for the breakdown of the economy, with its labor conscription and forced taxes collected in the form of grain, and the need of the utterly demoralized army to live off the population led to disasters in China that reached a scale of tragedy far exceeding our imagination. The Honan famine of 1942–1943, the result of Chiang's policies, most seriously affected 5 million people, the majority of whom died, while millions more were uprooted from their homes. Over time, comparable calamities occurred elsewhere with growing frequency.

WORLD WAR I was pre-eminently a European conflict and did not alter Asian politics and society dramatically. Its principal immediate outcome in Europe was the transformation of Russia into a Bolshevik state, followed by the unleashing of a crisis in European society which was later to produce fascism as conservatism's alternative solution to those offered by Marxism and parliamentarianism. World War II was, by comparison, a truly global war, the ramifications of which were ultimately even greater in Asia than in Europe. The demise of European colonialism in the wake of Germany's aggression and Japanese imperialism's subsequent dislocating impact on all of East Asia metamorphosed international politics and upset the balance of forces within it, producing radical and national liberation struggles—the results of which increasingly defined the major postwar world issues confronting the United States.

In the end World War II became an interlocking global event, and it can be understood adequately only with this interwoven set of linkages and repercussions in mind. Indeed, one cannot comprehend the events that took place in any one nation or during any one crisis without carefully studying the relationship of these events to the dynamics of power in its largest context—a redoubtable task for anyone, including scholars and leaders. There is no such thing, for example, as an exclusively East European question set in isolation during the war, but rather a general European problem impinging on the affairs of the entire continent and even, in due course, on Japan. Such complex webs of interrelated and multifaceted issues arose continually, and just as Allied leaders never permitted each other to ignore such linkages, neither can we. The weakening of Europe after 1939 had great implications for Japan's ability to attack Asia and to set loose a chain of forces that was to continue well after 1945. Similarly, the changed social, economic, and political dynamics within those nations involved in the transformation of the world after 1939 would have great implications for the reconfiguration of the world order from one dominated largely by the nations of Europe to one with many centers of power, but with a United States believing it ought to involve itself in the affairs of all these new centers.

These internal dynamics within various countries remain still dimly understood and scarcely appreciated in traditional histories and analyses. And during the war itself such changes were to define what was not negotiable between the Great Powers in ways that were increasingly to aggravate relations between them. The imperatives of space and war, which decentralized economic and political life within nations from Greece to China, and so made it possible for autonomous local forces of opposition to emerge, also guaranteed that the Great Powers during and after the war would not be able easily to reimpose their wills on recalcitrant constituencies, ranging, to name but a few, from local warlords in China to armed nationalists in Indonesia or leftist guerrilla bands in Yugoslavia and the Philippines. For the second world war galvanized the peoples in far more nations than had the first into seeking to define their own destinies by themselves and for their own interests. And to the extent that the United States failed to understand the causes of such changes or refused to accept their consequences, and instead attributed their origins to Soviet initiatives, it missed comprehending the richly textured, infinitely complicated web of factors that had gone into producing the postwar international order. To a crucial degree this lack of perception and comprehension laid the foundation for the postwar confrontation between Washington and Moscow.

These local sources of change which immediately posed challenges to the United States and its allies, only to present others within a few years to the Soviet Union in Yugoslavia and China, began most obviously with the rise of nationalism throughout Europe, Asia, and the Middle East. Indeed, they greatly exacerbated Washington's relations with Great Britain and France as well. Psychologically and intellectually, the experience of war unleashed a seemingly unlimited skepticism among the masses toward the legitimacy and pretensions of the prewar constituted orders, and the intensity of this negativism was almost proportional within each nation to the extent to which the war had tormented that nation. For those people who had suffered most, their rejection of traditional power groups' ideological and political legitimacy was greatest. Men and women had discovered that even when they tried to avoid political engagement they still paid greatly in their daily lives for the failures of traditional politics, and the consciousness of vast numbers of people was colored profoundly thereby—generally benefitting leftist parties. Politics no longer remained an abstract avocation for ambitious men or literate intelligentsia; for millions it became a means for their eventual deliverance from the causes and consequences of a world gone mad with destruction and terror. To an unprecedented extent, countless people throughout the world lost their fear to act, and they learned to do so in innumerable ways that gravely threatened the traditional order. This reality profoundly affected the political outcome of the war, producing many of the great political and social challenges the United States was to confront long after the fighting ended.

No less critical than the collapse of conventional wisdom's near monopoly over the way society ought to be organized was the sheer magnitude of the war's physical dislocations, ranging from the loss of life to the destruction of means of livelihood. Barriers to innovation in the prewar status quo collapsed because that system was either being destroyed physically or being transformed by high state taxes and expenditures to build the sinews of war. The very process of war necessarily socialized the economies of the major contestants, most notably that of the British, as the issue became whether their benefits would serve private or public ends. Further afield, peasants in China and the Philippines had seen the war shatter their customary relationship with landlords, and from World War II onward, the issue of land reform emerged prominently in many nations as the one that was to shape their politics most deeply—a reality that continues to our day. The combination of innumerable internal factors such as these, and their deep intellectual, economic, and political roots, guaranteed that continuous sources of upheaval and change in nations throughout the world would emerge during and after World War II, with all the destabilizing implications this might have for the United States in its relations especially with the Soviet Union, but also with France and Great Britain.

GABRIEL KOLKO

THE

Politics of War

INTRODUCTION

THE HISTORIAN may attempt to abstract the essentials of a reality, but the realities of World War II defy description. Yet without an appreciation of the quality of existence for the people of Europe and Asia from 1939 through 1945 one cannot understand the ultimate significance of the battles which were fought, the dispatches issued, or the more obvious externals of human behavior which are the stuff from which histories are composed. The primary condition of World War II, the crucial background for understanding *all* else, was the unprecedented human pain and misery, the millions upon millions of deaths, the widespread tragedy and suffering transforming the existence of the peoples of Europe and Asia, tragedy and torment the depths of which no one, however sensitive, can plumb. The war swept away all the institutions and relationships that anchor man to his society: the home was shattered, the family destroyed, work was gone, hunger and danger were ever more pressing as ever-growing millions wandered over lands in search of safety and security, or as enemies or governments forcibly wrenched them from their environment. Man became degraded and uprooted, and having lost his commitment to and interest in conventional ways and wisdom, he sought to redeem himself and his society in order to save himself. For no civilization can indulge in two terrible and prolonged wars in twenty-five years and emerge untorn.

The impact of World War II on the individuals who experienced and fortunately survived it was the motor of political and social change, the creator of mass movements and parties, the catalyst that made men act, that destroyed constituted orders everywhere. All who wished to survive accepted in principle the currency of violence and repression, for it was the reality that had transformed their existence and one which they could not deny. Both reactionaries and revolutionaries quickly accepted this premise, in theory if not in practice, and this too became an essential quality of the politics of a war-torn world. War therefore carried with it the ever-present possibility of shaping the actions of men of power, or of generating social revolution—and eventually World War II devastated the established societies far more thoroughly than any of the upheavals following World War I.

Most historians still tend to think in noncataclysmic categories appropriate to the pre-1939 period, if not the nineteenth century, but World War II and its aftermath witnessed the definitive smashing of a world political and economic order that began tottering after 1917. Germany ceased to be a Great Power, Eastern Europe was no longer a hotbed of potential conflict and entered into a period of internal preoccupations, the balance of power in the Far East shifted away from Japan in a manner that permitted revolutionary changes, colonialism began to die, and England assumed a lesser role in regulating the world scene. In brief, everywhere the war and the suffering of men transformed the political and social landscape drastically, even decisively, to define the preconditions of world politics over the subsequent decades.

THE human condition the war created also produced the larger backdrop for diplomacy, battles, and the multifarious immediate events that were expressions of conflict between enemies and allies alike—and the reader would do well to fix this essential ingredient firmly in his mind. When turning to the overwhelming and bewildering succession of events, historians have treated them simplistically, as evidence of the naïveté, good faith, or malice of one nation or another, or as singular occurrences unconnected with the entire fabric of the war, much less with the events of the post-1945 period.

To understand the role of the United States in World War II one must also understand that the American government had a series of immediate objectives, centered first of all around the desire to win battles and defeat the Axis, and an elaborate and highly sophisticated set of economic and political goals it defined as urgently desirable war aims. The interaction between the larger objectives of the United States and the world as the military and political leaders of the United States perceived it formed the vital context of the politics of World War II.

In considering World War II, and especially the years 1943–1945, there are three major issues, or themes, which subsume many, if not most, of the concerns of those in Washington who thought about the problem of American war and peace aims. First was the question of the Left, which is to say, the disintegration of the prewar social systems and the growth of revolutionary movements and potential upheaval everywhere in the world.

Next was the problem of the Soviet Union, which at times appeared very much connected with the issue of the Left. Finally, there was the issue of Great Britain, invariably set in the context of the future of the world economy, and its present and future relationship to the United States. No facile dissection of these three elements is possible, and no priority or weighting is useful as a general rule. All three themes interacted so that a change in one area often affected policy and conditions in another, lowering the significance of one factor at one moment, posing new dimensions at another. Yet the reader must recall these intertwined components again and again, or else the events of the war will appear discrete and disconnected, and the politics of the war bewildering and confused. Moreover, the contemplated problems of the peace and the military realities of the war meshed with each other with increasing frequency as the war wore on.

War in the twentieth century has become a necessary precondition for the emergence of a powerful Left, and for the first time since 1919 the Left, both in Europe and Asia, issued forth from the shadow of political defeat and impotence to the very center of world politics. War has come to mean not just the defeat of armies or the change of borders, but frequently the destruction or disintegration of social systems. Internal class conflict ripened to complicate the more traditional issues of international political, economic, and military conflict. In China, Italy, Greece, France, and Eastern Europe there were in varying degree real or disguised civil wars taking place at the very time of the war against Germany and Japan. Germany for its part saw the significance to the Allied camp of the movement toward the left and ultimately, in the last moments before defeat, attempted to play on the fears of the West in a manner that profoundly shaped relations among the Allies and the contours of postwar politics.

In Europe the form of the armed Resistance, the phenomenal growth of the Communist parties in Western Europe, and the rise of Soviet power as the tide of the Red Army moved relentlessly toward the West all typified the problem of the Left for the United States. The Resistance and the growth of the Italian and French Communist parties, however, were not the result of the presence of Soviet troops, as was the case in much of Eastern Europe, but of the collapse of the Old Order during the war and its alliance in many nations with fascism. To this extent, therefore, the potency of the threat of the Left did not reflect support from a broken Russia, but from the momentary collapse of European capitalism and, in the Far East, colonialism or oligarchy.

The United States and Britain could see powerful Communist movements emerging throughout Western and Southern Europe and the central role of the Communists in the leadership of the armed Resistance. The Resistance attracted men and women who exhibited the courage and abandon of nationalist revolutionaries. They developed appropriate leftist ideologies, and might in time become social-revolutionary actors as well, to purge not only the foreign invaders but also those domestic forces of conservatism that had collaborated with fascism and made its victory so easy. Would the Resistance act, would the Communists take power? If historians have hardly examined the internal world of these movements in relation to global politics, it is also a fact that the American and British leaders at the time similarly failed to perceive them clearly and correctly, for there was seemingly no alternative but to prepare for the worst or face a possible effort to wrest from the West the political victory that was the objective of their military sacrifices and triumph.

Given the collapse of the prewar power of the social forces that had contained the Left after 1920, the question confronting the United States and Britain was how to fill the vacuum and what to do with the traditional parties of conservative order. Between 1943 and 1947 the Western Allies developed, at first haphazardly and then with deliberate consciousness, a coherent policy toward this dilemma save, as in China, where they frankly acknowledged the magnitude of the undertaking to be beyond their capacity.

The vast upheavals in Europe and Asia invariably impinged on relations with the Soviet Union, for suspicion of Communism in Europe inevitably confirmed the conventional belief that international Communism, presumably Moscow-directed, could turn the revolutionary forces of Europe and Asia on and off at will. Western-Soviet diplomacy therefore was contingent on developments beyond the control of the Soviet Union insofar as no nation could undo the nearly universal social and political consequences of the war, even when the U.S.S.R. was quite willing, indeed anxious, to attempt to do so. Yet in Eastern Europe, where Soviet presence gave it the power to define events, the United States could perceive policies which only confirmed its worst fears and violated the American definition of an ideal world order. Relations with the U.S.S.R. therefore subsume the problem of revolutionary upheaval in Europe and Asia, especially in Eastern Europe, and the bearing of military strategy on the more obvious political issues dividing the Allies. At the same time the United States defined for its own purposes the preconditions for Russia's return to the family of nations after twenty-five years of isolation, preconditions that vividly illustrate the nature of the world which the United States hoped might emerge from the war.

The nascent rivalry between the United States and Russia was not the only critical broad area of concern in Washington. To the extent that the United States articulated clear political and economic objectives for the postwar world—and much effort went into such a definition—it came into direct conflict with Great Britain. The Americans saw the problem of the prewar and postwar world economy primarily as a problem of British policy in conflict with American goals, and the entire issue of postwar political alliances raised the issue of the British desire to ally itself with France to create a Western European bloc quite independent of both the United States and the U.S.S.R., much less a United Nations system as the Americans envisaged it. The problem of France is not only a question of the threat of the Left, even less of the personality of De Gaulle, but also of France's postwar political and economic commitments. Much the same was true for Italy, Yugoslavia, and Greece, where the United States had to think not merely of the potential domination of the Left, but also of the domination by Britain. Indeed, even the question of British diplomacy toward Russia was a source of dispute, and in the Middle East prewar antagonisms were rekindled as the two Western Allies found themselves working against each other in Saudi Arabia and elsewhere. And as military allies, fighting side by side at all times, the differences in military strategy were exacerbating and often serious. Without the even greater common problem of the Left and the U.S.S.R. many of these disagreements between the United States and Britain would most certainly have led to sharper, more serious clashes. As it was, the problem of Anglo-American relations during the period 1943–1945 and thereafter is the key to comprehending a whole spectrum of issues and America's definition of its unique postwar political and, above all, economic aims.

Taking into account the conditions which the war, the Left, the Soviet Union, and Britain created, the United States had to balance its desire for an ideal world system against its perception of a more complicated economic, military, and political reality, and to merge the two insofar as it was possible. In considering the postwar world political order, and especially the United Nations as a forum for the resolution of future problems, the United States had to shape its position to adjust for its Western Hemispheric policies and needs, its desire for military security via bases, and its rapidly growing spheres of interest elsewhere. It expressed the synthesis in a distinctive form of internationalism quite compatible with American interests, but obviously elusive insofar as the existing international political system was merely a tentative world coalition unified only in that it shared a common enemy. On an economic plane the United States had to weigh its objectives against the fact that the war, and the depression preceding it, had dangerously undermined world capitalism and would compel the United States to seek its goals in a seriously altered strategic and economic context. The attention and energy which the Americans devoted to meeting these objectives during the war, in the framework of the problems of the Left, the U.S.S.R., and England, is the key to the problem of the politics and diplomacy of World War II.

. . . .

ONE must study the development of United States political policy in the context of the kind of world that emerged from the chaos of World War II, and I will refer to that vital background again and again in this work. For I have written this book as much to describe the actual condition of the world during World War II as much as the way the United States defined and quite as often misconceived the course of global realities. Yet what can be said about the seeming variability of a national policy that to the professional, much less the casual observer, has often seemed chaotic? To the extent that any system is haphazard or improvised, of course, no single theory or explanation will cover the phenomenon, and the fashionable tendency to believe that men of power are the victims of errors rather than the creators of them—and that perhaps reason or pressure by reasonable men will bring them back to the truth—has reinforced this homily. This assumption, so crucial to the premises of liberal political theory, implies that "democratic" power structures are not merely poorly informed but innocent, and that a true dialogue between virtue and power is possible. Such an image, postulating behavior as a series of bumbles, ignores the possibility that policies which are dangerous, destructive, or even do not work are very often quite consistent and necessary in forwarding interests or holding the line in defensive situations.

In attempting to appraise the conduct of policy one does not have to assume that history is determined or made up of repeated accidents. It is sufficient to study its pattern of functional behavior, to comprehend the assumptions formulated in response to challenging situations, and to perceive a policy and pattern that in some sense makes future responses predictable and in this sense inevitable. And quite beyond rhetoric are the institutional forces that do or can influence policy and power. If rhetoric is confused with reality, the banalities of speech writers, platitudes, and the convenient transformation of words into useful symbols rather than truth all become the basis of analysis and a substitute for comprehending action, clear definitions, and institutional imperatives. A description of functionally defined goals and consistent actions, whether or not someone has consciously defined and explicitly acknowledged them, reveals the motives and consequences of any nation, the United States included, in specific and general cases. The reader will soon discover that policy-makers usually explicitly acknowledged these de facto principles as immediate objectives relevant as a basis for action in specific situations when they had to consider concrete national interests, and usually the leaders of American foreign policy articulated them into a coherent, long-term world view. Illusion and mere rhetoric are plausible only when an environment for action never breaks down; in times of crisis, which is to say for the major part of the period after 1939, policy requires a meaningful basis of action for sheer survival, and American leaders often articulated it in private and in public as well. It is not difficult to focus on underlying patterns and concrete events that illustrate them. In doing so one must evaluate two levels of political crisis: precise causes, such as who did what first, and who was responsible for escalating specific, relatively minor crises into major ones, and why. Throughout this study I will refer to broad patterns as well as to actual events that especially illustrate them.

We live in the shadow and with the consequences of World War II, and a reassessment of the meaning of that war is crucial to an understanding of our own decade and the sustained foreign policy crisis that has engaged the United States for over twenty-five years. The events at the beginning of that critical period are all largely contemporaneous with present confrontations —indeed, their very genesis. To separate these events from a continuum, in the hope that decision-makers will apply reason in one case and not in others, is to do violence to the history of the great shifting and reintegration of the world political system that occurred between 1943 and 1949, and to the magnitude of the issues involved. By understanding the meaning of that period we comprehend our own decade in microcosm and the challenges we face in breaking the paralyzing grip of a thirty-year-old crisis in international relations over the future of all mankind. In viewing the genesis of the challenge of our time we hold a mirror to ourselves, the problems we confront, and the source of our malaise.

BOOK ONE

TO THE YALTA CONFERENCE: FROM 1943 THROUGH JANUARY 1945

1

THE POLITICS OF
STRATEGY IN EUROPE

A HISTORY of the politics of World War II can both conveniently and legitimately begin with the year 1943, because only then was the tide of German military success stopped and turned, and only then did the military exigencies of the war become less pressing and politics again move to the foreground. There was precious little, however, in the earlier diplomatic relations between the Great Allies that augured well for their ability to accommodate politically once they had met the necessities of war. The nature of the immediate prewar diplomacy was such that it raised very real questions in the minds of the leaders of the coalition born of necessity. For it was German foreign policy that created the wartime alliance, and once that external threat was removed there is nothing surprising in the disunity that followed.

During the prewar years the so-called Allies lived, in varying degrees, in mutual distrust and divisive fear of one another. One cannot measure cynicism, but surely it must have been pervasive after the utterly compromised role of the European powers in the face of Axis expansion after 1935. England and France went to war to save Polish reaction—not Czech democracy—after refusing to form an alliance with the Soviet Union for fear of opening Eastern Europe to Russian predominance. The Czechs themselves willingly surrendered, after England and France deserted them, rather than accept the destruction inherent in fighting alone. The U.S.S.R. signed a pact with Germany that made Nazi aggression possible elsewhere rather than against the Soviet Union, and in the process extended Russian power toward the West, but only after it appeared likely that Britain preferred a Nazi-Soviet war as the lesser evil. The United States, removed from the immediate scene, nevertheless endorsed the diplomacy of appeasement from the Spanish Civil War through Munich, urging the Czechs in September 1938 to negotiate rather than fight. In brief, the West and the U.S.S.R. dribbled into a war they had not wanted, and it was unclear whether any of the Allies retained any principles, in the positive sense of that term, much less had decided who were their true enemies. When Hitler forged the Allied system by creating the necessity for it, none of the prewar considerations disappeared, and the political leaders and tendencies responsible for these policies were also still largely in the major seats of power. Indeed, going back to the years after 1917 and the intense hostility of the Western nations toward Bolshevism, it is clear that the coalition between England, France, the United States, and the Soviet Union was the exception to the basic trends in international affairs after World War I, and that any temporary alliance would be fragile at best.

The Second Front and the Test of the Alliance

War determined the possibilities for politics, which might become more or less important as the pressure of mutual defense against the common enemy defined the limits of one's diplomacy. "We had to fight in unison, which was the only way to shorten the war," Anthony Eden, the British Foreign Secretary, later recalled. "Consequently, our relations with Soviet Russia seemed to be a swaying contest between what common sense declared we ought to do and what experience proved practicable."[1] "The antifascist coalition . . . ," Soviet Deputy Premier Nikolai A. Voznesensky observed in 1947, "arose in the flames of war for the purpose of crushing the armed forces of fascist states."[2] Beyond that, all the Allies had different objectives. Or, as George Kennan wrote to the State Department from Moscow in September 1944, in ascribing to Russia the ultimate objective of dominating Eastern and Central Europe: "Until June 1944, however, all such Russian aims had to await the exertion of a real military effort by the western powers. Without that effort, not even Russian victory was assured."[3]

Until that Anglo-American sacrifice in blood was made, the alliance meant considerably less to the Soviet Union than it might have. Hitler, of course, dictated the moment of contact with the Soviet armies, thereby giving the British and the Americans the luxury of choosing the time and place of combat, with all that choice might mean politically to the nature of the coalition and the consequences of the war. As that outcome seemed ever more certain, political considerations could move even further to the fore than they had been between the oppressive days of 1941 and the stalemate of 1943, by which time it was clear that Germany and Japan at the worst could not win the war. By late 1944 every movement of men, every action by an ally, was fraught with political significance and consequences. Once the troops became victorious politics could reign supreme, and the physical position of these troops might ultimately determine the bargaining power of the Allies when they made the final political reckoning.

For the Russians, however, until military victory could be assured the pressures of military necessity were infinitely greater than motives of politics. As Kennan suggested in 1944: "The second front was a paramount requirement of all Russian policy. The suspicious Russian mind naturally exaggerated the danger of Russia's being left in the lurch by her western Allies. To offset this danger the Kremlin was prepared to go a long way to meet the requirements and the prejudices of the western world."[4] The question of the second front in Western Europe, which is to say, direct military assistance and sacrifices in blood, therefore became the primary and critical test of the hastily formed alliance. That alliance might fail even if the West met the Russian demands for aid, but it certainly could not succeed if it did not.

The Soviet Union desired military aid from the West, primarily in the form of an invasion of Western Europe, but anywhere if necessary. No theme studs the correspondence of Stalin, Roosevelt, and Churchill during 1942 and 1943 more than this one. High-level diplomatic conferences considered no question more thoroughly. The Soviet pressure for a second front was incessant, because in no other manner could its alliance with the West benefit it more than by sparing Russian men and resources from the brunt of the German onslaught. In the months after the German attack on the U.S.S.R. on June 20, 1941, Stalin did not conceal from Churchill the fact that the German sweep had "confronted the Soviet Union with mortal danger."[5] Russia's need had never been greater, and though Stalin admitted "the difficulty of establishing such a front . . . it should be done, not only for the sake of our common cause, but also in Britain's own interest."[6] When the Americans entered the war the Soviets besieged them with similar requests, and because of the radically different American view of a desirable European military strategy, the details and justification of which are found later in this chapter, the United States offered the U.S.S.R. more hope of support.

When Molotov visited Washington in May 1942, Roosevelt promised a second front, but without designating its location. What the Russians desired was a drawing off of at least thirty to forty German divisions from the eastern front, and a military operation of that magnitude was not forthcoming during 1942. Still, the West implied, if it did not promise, such a front, and in July 1942, Stalin, in a message to Churchill that he was often to repeat, could "state most emphatically that the Soviet Government cannot tolerate the second front in Europe being postponed till 1943."[7] It was not for Stalin to act, however, and he was compelled to bear the bitter disappointment—and the losses. But the West gave Stalin every reason to believe that they would invade along the Atlantic coast sometime during 1943. On February 9, 1943, Churchill unequivocally informed Stalin that such an invasion would begin in August or September of 1943, but on March 11 Churchill notified him that "the actual situation can only be judged nearer the time and in making, for your own personal information, this declaration of our intentions there I must not be understood to limit our freedom of decision."[8] On June 4 Roosevelt told Stalin that the press of military activities elsewhere compelled a postponement of the invasion of Western Europe until the spring of 1944. "Need I speak of the dishearteningly negative impression that this fresh postponement of the second front . . . will produce in the Soviet Union—both among the people and in the Army?" the Russian replied.[9] To Churchill, Stalin was even more outspoken. At no time, as a result of Soviet triumphs, were the military conditions in Europe more promising.

> You say that you "quite understand" my disappointment. I must tell you that the point here is not just the disappointment of the Soviet Government, but the preservation of its confidence in its Allies, a confidence which is being subjected to severe stress. One should not forget that it is a question of saving millions of lives in the occupied territories of Western Europe and Russia and of reducing the enormous sacrifices of the Soviet armies, compared with which the sacrifices of the Anglo-American armies are insignificant.[10]

Later, at the end of October, during the Foreign Ministers' Conference in Moscow, Stalin quipped that Churchill preferred to leave the difficult tasks to the Russians. But when Molotov asked Eden whether the Anglo-American plans for OVERLORD—the invasion of France—still held, Eden could reply in the affirmative with the contingency that "this decision, however, is not a binding legal contract."[11] Then at the Teheran Conference during the last days of November 1943, Stalin asked Churchill the same question, since he knew that the Americans were by now insistent on the invasion: "Do the Prime Minister and the British Staff really believe in 'Overlord'?"; to which Churchill replied, "Provided the conditions previously stated for 'Overlord' are established when the time comes. . . ."[12] Despite this very serious doubt as to what might ultimately occur in the West, and their grim resignation to the possibility that Western pledges for the future might prove as hollow as those of the past, the Russians agreed to coordinate their own massive spring campaign with OVERLORD to relieve the pressure on the western front—a commitment they kept.

The Russians suggested one other option, open to the British and later to the Americans, provided they were willing to pay the price in lives: fighting on the eastern front. During 1941–1942 the Russians barely avoided defeat. The Germans overran a vast area containing 45 percent of the prewar Soviet population which accounted for one-third of its industrial output and 47 percent of its agricultural lands. Soviet industrial output between June and November 1941 fell to "less than half" according to Soviet accounts.[13] The Russians wanted aid—anywhere—in the form of men and munitions, and in the process of asking for them offered the West an almost certain opportunity to stave off the Soviet predominance over Eastern Europe it so feared. In July 1941 Stalin suggested to Churchill that England return to the Continent by opening a front in France. By late summer he suggested something else as well: on September 3 he confided that "the way out of this more than unfavourable situation . . . is to open a second front this year somewhere in the Balkans or in France. . . ." Ten days later he was more precise: "It seems to me that Britain could safely land 25–30 divisions . . . for military cooperation with the Soviet troops on Soviet soil. . . ."[14] The British, of course, had no intention of sending their men to die in what appeared to be a losing situation, and despite some support for the proposal in the Cabinet, Churchill thought the suggestion a "physical absurdity."[15] Molotov pressed the request for several months and then let it drop. In June 1942, when England offered six RAF squadrons to work out of the Murmansk area to protect British convoys, Stalin gratefully accepted. Such token forces subsequently required more resources and time than they were worth, and the Russians later discouraged them. But as long as they needed the aid they retained a lively, often friendly, and never hostile interest in Western attempts to open a Balkan front via two British plans: Turkish entry into the war, toward which the Russians cooled by mid-1944, and a British thrust into the Balkans via northern Yugoslavia, a scheme that never lost Soviet support.

The Turks, for reasons I will discuss in detail later, wanted no part of the war against Germany during 1943, and indeed had been pro-German during the first years of the war, both for historic reasons and because of their intense anti-Communism. When Churchill, much to the irritation of the United States, opened his campaign in late 1942 to bring Turkey into the war, Stalin expressed skepticism about the possibility of success but authorized Churchill on February 6, 1943, to inform the Turks that the U.S.S.R. would meet them "half-way" in improving relations.[16] By the Moscow Foreign Ministers' Conference in late October 1943, however, the Russians were willing to meet the British all the way, and only the United States and, of course, Turkey, eventually vetoed the scheme. "Turkey's participation is needed now," V. M. Molotov is paraphrased in the State Department's records; "later it will not be necessary . . . therefore Turkey should be asked to come into the war now."[17] Although doubtful that the Turks would agree, the Russians nevertheless proposed that the Three Powers request that Turkey declare war on the Axis. Going a step further, the Russians agreed to declare war against Bulgaria should that Axis satellite respond to Turkey's entry into the war by a declaration of its own.

The British interpreted Russian interest in their proposal, at a time when Soviet victories were rolling back the Germans, as a reflection of Russian desire to end their own suffering despite the obvious political consequences. The British effort was unsuccessful, and at Teheran, a month later, Stalin told Churchill, "I am all in favour of trying again," but Molotov indicated that such approval was contingent upon the Turkish affair not delaying OVERLORD.[18] The British again tried, failed, and the U.S.S.R. lost interest, and like the Americans began to fear that the English were attempting to drain forces from OVERLORD. During July 1944 the Russians informed their allies that it would now be best to leave the Turks to their own devices, for they had little to add to the tide of victories for the Allies everywhere.

At the end of 1944 the British gave the Russians one last opportunity to pass on their desire to send Western troops into the Balkans. On October 12, when Churchill was in Moscow, Stalin raised a plan for the encirclement of Germany that involved sending ten Allied divisions north through Austria to aid the Red Army's advance through Hungary. Churchill told Stalin that he wished to consider military matters later. The following week Eden was still in Moscow and Churchill instructed him "to find out what the Russians really feel about the Balkans" by obtaining their opinion of another British plan to open their own theater of war in the region.[19] The scheme, somewhat different from Stalin's, involved landing on the Dalmatian coast, moving along the shore to Fiume, and then striking north through the Ljubljana Gap toward Austria and perhaps Hungary. "For political reasons," Churchill predicted, "the Russians would not want us to develop a large-scale Balkan strategy," but they had raised no objections when he first proposed the Turkish strategy, and perhaps there was reason to hope for their consent.[20] Much to Churchill's delight the Russians did not oppose the idea, perhaps knowing that the Americans most certainly would, and that Tito did as well. During January 1945 Churchill proposed another variation of this plan, involving a thrust from Italy to Vienna, and Churchill was pleased when the Russians not only raised no objection, but indicated that they had no immediate plans to move into the area which the British aspired to conquer. Again, defeat of the scheme came from both exigencies and American opposition.

In brief, when given the option between immediate military aid designed to relieve her frightful suffering and long-term political gains by way of maximum conquest of territory, the Russians chose military aid. Russia entered a military coalition with the West to save its very existence, and it was to be a long time before ideological considerations would replace the trauma of the German attack and the material and human imperatives it created.

Despite the delay in opening a second front, on July 12, 1943, the Russians launched the longest sustained offensive in military history along a 1,500-mile front, driving a maximum of 650 miles at the widest point. On January 5, 1944, four months after the Anglo-American forces invaded the Italian mainland, Russia penetrated prewar Polish territory and left Soviet soil for the first time. As 1944 proceeded the colossal Soviet military machine developed an awesome superiority over the Germans in manpower, aircraft, and especially artillery. By February 1945 Stalin could report that his offensive was employing 230 heavy artillery weapons per kilometer and destroying the German armies at an unprecedented rate.

The beginning of 1945 also marked the peak German resistance to the Anglo-American and related armies of the war. At that time the Russian army confronted only 58 percent of the German divisions, though for most of the war that figure wavered around 70 to 75 percent of the German army. When OVERLORD began, the Western armies met only twenty-seven of the eighty-one German divisions allocated to the western front as a whole—at a period when 181 German and a third as many satellite divisions were in the East.[21]

During later years the United States and the Soviet Union debated in an inconclusive manner the question of how significant American Lend-Lease aid was to the Soviet military success; the Russians claimed that it accounted for a mere 4 percent of total Soviet armaments, while American estimates ran as high as 15 percent. More recent Soviet discussions have been somewhat less penurious, and it seems likely that about one-tenth of Russian military needs in all forms came from the Allies. However, Soviet military successes were unmistakably based primarily on the efforts and sacrifices of the Russians themselves, and not on such external aid as the United States gave to them. Certainly American Lend-Lease efforts, to the British, Russians, and all Allies did not represent a significant loss of American wartime output. During 1943 and 1944, respectively, the United States lend-leased only 15 and 13 percent of its munitions output to *all* the Allies, as opposed to 9 and 8 percent of its food for the same years. In 1944 the United States lend-leased only 4.6 percent of steel and iron output, and 5.4 percent of tires and tubes. The Russians were therefore most irritated in March 1943 when the American ambassador to Russia, Admiral William H. Standley, informed American correspondents in Moscow that the Kremlin failed to acknowledge to the Soviet people that they were fighting the war with massive American aid, a comment which contributed to Standley's being asked to leave his post, but which pleased W. Averell Harriman, his successor, and those who felt that the Russians had "kicked around" America on this and other matters.[22] The Russian reaction, of course, reflected the fact that many Russians—the final count reached twenty million—were to die in World War II to defeat Germany, seven million of them soldiers. In comparison, the Americans lost 405,000 soldiers, the British 375,000. American living standards, after the grim decade of the depression, had never been higher, and as the official United States Army history of the war concluded, the United States fought World War II with a "guns and butter" policy that only a prolonged war against Germany might have jeopardized.[23]

The Americans were spared that inconvenience, but at a political cost that only a mutually beneficial political agreement with all their allies might minimize. The West's failure to initiate a second front until Germany was on the defensive must certainly have raised very serious question in the Kremlin about the ultimate value and reliability of the coalition. And since in the end the Soviet armies captured more territory than its allies did, and the West refused to pay the price of conquest in blood, it was imperative for the West that the principle of possession as the determinant of the political future of a nation not be permitted to become a precedent. If the Anglo-American allies acted cynically when they believed their vital interests to be involved, the Russians might as well do the same. As it was, the failure of the West on the second-front issue struck at the very basis of the tenuous Allied collaboration, which was a mutual necessity that had not been mutually beneficial. The West might redeem this inequality of sacrifice only by moving more circumspectly on other vital, essentially political issues, if the United States and Britain wished to test the possibility of postwar collaboration with Russia fairly before accepting the very obvious consequences of failure.

The American Strategy in War as Politics

The British and American military staffs agreed, even before December 1941, that they would fight the war on the basis of "Europe first," and that the United States would take primary responsibility for the lesser commitment in the Far East. In the eyes of the British, after Churchill's visit to Washington in December 1941, "The Americans have got their way and the war will be run from Washington. . . ."[24] As much as possible they attempted to mitigate that fact. Despite the objections of the United States Navy, which wanted more emphasis on the Pacific war, the United States always committed the greater part of Army and Air Force resources to the European theater of war. Beyond this global priority, however, the British and American military and their political leaders agreed on little else; they hammered out the grand strategy of the war in Europe in a series of often bitter disputes that ultimately satisfied no one and made Anglo-American strategy a synthesis of grudging compromises.

The American political and military leaders almost unanimously agreed that they did not wish to fight a war in the Mediterranean area, much less North Africa, but until 1944 the Mediterranean was their main theater of war. Ideally the United States hoped to marshal its resources for a vast cross-Channel invasion of Europe, if not in 1942 certainly in 1943, which would take the war to the heart of the enemy's empire. The United States regarded every diversionary operation elsewhere as an example of British unwillingness to open a second front in Western Europe. The Americans saw the Mediterranean as part of the British political sphere of influence, if only for the moment, and in North Africa the Western Allies bitterly disagreed on policy toward the Vichy French authorities in power there. All the architects of the American strategy shared a consensus on these points.

The Americans attempted to obtain a definite British commitment to a cross-Channel invasion as the primary strategy of the war, and therefore reluctantly conceded to what were supposed to be carefully restricted and timed operations in the Mediterranean preparatory to OVERLORD. These operations, beginning in North Africa in November 1942, merely permitted the British to incorporate the Americans into ever grander and escalating campaigns. The British and the Americans repeatedly scrapped agreed-upon manpower and resources ceilings as the critical battles of Libya, Anzio, and elsewhere compelled the Americans to send in ever greater power or risk defeats. Once the British obtained American agreement to the North African campaign, in the summer of 1942, they moved, via similar arguments and implied threats in regard to OVERLORD, to get the Americans to cooperate in conquering Sicily and then southern Italy. At the Casablanca Conference in January 1943, much to the alarm of Secretary of War Henry L. Stimson, who regarded Roosevelt as a weakling in front of Churchill, the British overwhelmed the American strategists and Roosevelt into a Sicilian escapade that delayed OVERLORD another year.[25]

The ultimate American justification for the invasion of Italy, other than the limited use of resources until OVERLORD could begin, was that the political impact of knocking Hitler's main ally out of the war might overflow to the other satellites, and that in any event it would help if the strategic Air Forces could use the bases around Rome against southern Germany. The Americans did not intend to go beyond Rome, but even this concession to the British deeply alarmed Stimson and others in Washington who were unable to prevail upon Roosevelt. For the British leaders, the Italian campaign was essentially a political matter, and they all treated it as such. Eden was particularly anxious to go beyond Rome and move Western forces into the Balkans, and a controversy with the Americans over this strategy raged until the end of the war. For the Americans, and especially for Stimson, the British proposal "was another diversion in the interest of the British Empire and contrary to our American instincts."[26] Yet the Allies ultimately went beyond Rome, and even if the United States did not accept the British view in full, its deeply politicized orientation influenced American strategy and the American view of their role vis-à-vis not only the Russians but the English as well.

The State Department, and particularly Ambassador to Russia Harriman as well as Stimson were among those in the Administration who realized what these concessions to British strategy and a delay in OVERLORD could mean to long-term relations with the U.S.S.R., and it must be added, the political outcome of the war insofar as the location of troops determined it. Stimson wrote Roosevelt in August 1943: ". . . the British theory . . . is that Germany can be beaten by a series of attritions . . . and that the only heavy fighting which needs to be done will be done by Russia. To me, in the light of the postwar problems which we shall face, that attitude towards Russia seems terribly dangerous. . . . None of these methods of pinprick warfare can be counted on by us to fool Stalin into the belief that we have kept that pledge."[27] "The Soviets accepted the explanation of our military plans," Harriman wrote Roosevelt in November, "but our whole permanent relations depend in a large measure on their satisfaction in the future with our military operations. It is impossible to over-emphasize the importance they place strategically on the initiation of the so-called 'Second Front' next spring."[28] If the Russians do most of the fighting, Stimson observed during May 1943, "I think that will be dangerous business for us at the end of the war. Stalin won't have much of an opinion of people who have done that and we will not be able to share much of the postwar world with him."[29]

The British too realized the consequences of Western military passivity to the alliance, though they attempted to argue the matter for different ends. In January 1942 Eden wrote the Foreign Office that, given the eclipse of German and French power at the end of the war, "Russian prestige will be so great that the establishment of Communist Governments in the majority of European countries will be greatly facilitated. . . ."[30] That prestige would be linked to the fact that the Russians had defeated the Germans. As South African General Jan C. Smuts, of whom Churchill said "our minds were in step," explained it in August 1943: "Surely our performance can be bettered and the comparison with Russia rendered less unflattering to us. To the ordinary man it must appear that it is Russia who is winning the war. If this impression continues, what will be our post-war position compared with that of Russia?"[31] But unflattering comparisons or not, the Western Powers formulated strategies, however diverse, that attempted to take into account the political consequences of the massive Russian presence in Europe.

Anglo-American disagreements were deep-rooted, even personal among the generals, and continuous joint consultations at every level did not succeed in overcoming them; but such discussions did permit a common Western policy on certain issues, which only exacerbated relations with the Russians. Eden understood the dangers of such a joint front. All factors being equal, and they rarely were, he preferred tripartite consultations, for he understood that bilateral talks would not reconcile many very real differences with the United States. He wrote at the beginning of 1942:

> If it came to a direct conflict of policies and we had to choose between the United States of America and the Soviet Union, we should no doubt decide that Anglo-American co-operation is more indispensable and the more natural because it rests on broader and older foundations than Anglo-Russian co-operation. . . . we shall have to consult the United States Government in all our discussions with the Soviet Government. . . .[32]

In practice this often meant joint or obviously coordinated communications to the U.S.S.R., frequently on matters of very great substance which presented the Russians with the option of accepting a *fait accompli* or confronting its two allies together. By 1943 this joint front had become standard procedure for handling problems. "My thought," Roosevelt explained to Secretary of State Cordell Hull in March 1943 on the obviously critical issue of how the Allies would run Germany and Italy in the first months after the war, "is if we get a substantial meeting of the minds with the British that we should, then, take it up with the Russians."[33] Hull chastised the British from time to time when they wandered from this principle. "Please impress upon Mr. Eden and the Prime Minister," he wrote American Ambassador to England John G. Winant in August 1943, "the importance we attach to reaching prior agreement. . . . for the British Government to approach the Soviet Government singly with regard to matters under discussion between the British and United States Governments may give the Russians the impression that the British Government is seeking the role of intermediary. . . ."[34]

This advance cooperation between the British and Americans on questions of vital concern to the Russians appeared to the Kremlin as something less than a true alliance, and they let it be known they resented the procedure. The British ambassador to the U.S.S.R., Clark Kerr, notified the American embassy during August 1943 "that the Soviet Government felt that the American and British Governments first consulted together and arrived at a decision and then simply communicated that decision to the Soviet Government for its information."[35] "It is clear," Harriman cabled Roosevelt three months later, "they never like to be faced with Anglo-American decisions already taken."[36] Insofar as the British and the Americans could agree, and the containment of Bolshevism was assuredly one of the few questions on which they were unanimous, in reality there were two coalitions fighting the Axis: the first, between Great Britain and the United States, was a true alliance in the sense that both countries shared certain larger fundamentals, which did not, however, prevent conflicts of a serious nature; the second was between the Anglo-American bloc, when the two nations acted in concert, and the U.S.S.R. In this sense the world was already fractured in a manner that became obvious to all after the defeat of the Axis Powers.

For the course of the war, however, the conflict within the Western bloc was often to be of greater significance. The British could act unilaterally, but naturally wished the United States to help them fight the war according to British reasoning, and the United States in important ways also acted alone. The question of the unconditional surrender policy was one such instance. With Churchill by his side, Roosevelt announced on January 24, 1943, before a conference of reporters at Casablanca, that the Allies would compel Germany, Italy, and Japan to surrender unconditionally. He had not warned Churchill, much less Stalin, that this was joint policy, and under the circumstances the Briton had to contain his surprise. At that time, of course, any surrender imposed on Germany would have had to be largely as a result of Russian bloodshed, and Stalin argued that the "unconditional surrender" slogan only solidified the German ranks and suppressed dissension that might lead to a negotiated surrender. Churchill's opinion was similar, and in the end, of course, none of Germany's allies surrendered unconditionally, and Germany also was able to negotiate contingencies of great significance. Roosevelt had not even warned the State Department, which had not recommended such a policy prior to 1943. Hull remained opposed to the policy, as did General Dwight D. Eisenhower, and in the end the Allies backed away from the doctrine, but not before giving the German propaganda machine ammunition with which to fortify German willingness to resist to the bitter end.[37]

Anglo-American differences on the conduct of the war extended to less consequential matters of glory associated with the military chain of command of the Western theater, though at times these issues also impinged on vital questions of strategy. Superficially it usually revolved around the issue of whether an American or English general would command the Italian and later the Western European campaign, but ultimately the issue was one of where to fight the war in the West. By 1944 the American troops in Europe far outnumbered the English and the United States wished a command responsibility proportionate to the commitment, and in August 1943 Churchill himself proposed that the Americans command OVERLORD, shifting, however, the Italian command from Eisenhower to an English general. Later, during November, the British proposed that they place the command of the entire Mediterranean theater, including the Balkans, under one commander empowered "to transfer forces from one part of the area to another in order to take advantage of fleeting opportunities."[88] Although the Americans were gratified at the British concession on the command of OVERLORD, they well realized that the British wished to postpone that plan indefinitely, and they demanded something tangible. The Americans asked to have one commander-in-chief for both the Mediterranean and Western European theaters, who, presumably, would be an American.

Each side vetoed the other's plans, and during the month of November the policy and personal relationships between the British and American generals declined to such a point that Churchill angrily informed his Chiefs of Staff that he was inclined to tell the Americans: " 'All right, if you won't play with us in the Mediterranean, we won't play with you in the English Channel.' And if they say, 'All right, then we shall direct our main effort in the Pacific,' to reply, 'You are welcome to do so if you wish.' "[39] "If . . . the Supreme Command were given to a United States officer and he pronounced in favour of concentrating on 'Overlord' irrespective of the injury done to our affairs in the Mediterranean, His Majesty's Government could not possibly agree," Churchill informed his Chiefs of Staff at the end of November.[40] By the last months of 1943 fundamental differences in strategy, irritations which had emerged in the course of the brief joint occupation of Italy, and the lesser, personal resentments that are a by-product of men who work together but see the world and their role in it quite differently were all factors straining the alliance. Thereafter mutual doubts and suspicions plagued the Anglo-American alliance.

Having conceded to an important phase of the British Mediterranean strategy, by 1943 every important American military leader, as well as Harry Hopkins, Roosevelt's closest adviser, and Hull, was convinced that the British were attempting to renege on OVERLORD. Despite subsequent British disclaimers, which deal with Churchill's defensive statements rather than the basic thrust of his strategic argument, the American view was correct, as any careful reading of the Churchill memoirs will reveal. Churchill saw the entire war after 1943 in purely political terms, whether it was a Soviet thrust in the Balkans or an American campaign in Burma. His memoirs are entirely explicit on these points, despite his attempt to show his exaggerated prophetic insight into the Bolshevik menace during the war. He was a realist, in that he understood the limits of British power, and a great diplomat in the Machiavellian sense, attempting to accomplish through words what he could not attain by force of arms. In light of his political understanding, his letters to Stalin, full of feigned warmth and solicitude, reveal the extent of his duplicity. Where he had the advantage in power, which had now been reduced to Britain's relations with the small or weak states, such as Greece, he used it ruthlessly. Not merely the Americans were thrown off course by him, but Stalin too exhibited a confidence in the man's words that only Roosevelt exceeded.

Until OVERLORD and June 1944 Churchill's diplomacy attempted to shift the thrust of American military power from France to the Balkans via two means: first, by continuing and accelerating the Italian campaign into Yugoslavia and Austria; and second, by involving Turkey in the war, thereby bringing non-Russian troops into the Balkans. Throughout 1943 the British pushed for the first course, though clearly the second was more promising and it eventually secured the greatest British efforts.

Churchill's only hope for winning the Americans to the first strategy depended entirely on Roosevelt, for with the exception of Harriman in Russia and Robert Murphy in Italy, virtually every American leader of consequence opposed a Balkan invasion with American or British troops. Churchill on the other hand had the backing of Eden and his Chiefs of Staff, with the exception of Sir Alan Brooke, who did not regard an Aegean campaign as militarily feasible. A few weeks before the Teheran Conference, Roosevelt informed Stimson that the United States would not intervene in the Balkans without Soviet approval, and when Stimson suggested that it would be best to drop the Balkan idea under all circumstances, Roosevelt evaded this position as well. Then, at Teheran, Roosevelt shocked Hopkins by mentioning the possibility of an Adriatic drive to reach Rumania. "Who's promoting that Adriatic business that the President continually returns to?" Hopkins asked Admiral Ernest J. King. "As far as I know it is his own idea," King replied.[41] Roosevelt's typically impressionable reaction to Churchill's pressures also made it necessary for his advisers, as always, to bring him back into line with dominant opinion. When the British Chiefs of Staff presented a memorandum to the Americans shortly before Teheran, calling for an intensification of the war in the Mediterranean, adding in regard to OVERLORD: "We do not . . . attach vital importance to any particular date or to any particular number of divisions in the assault and follow-up . . . ," the American military quickly beat it down.[42] At Teheran, Stalin too pressed for going through with OVERLORD as planned and with a troop strength obviously incompatible with British proposals.*

Far more promising for Great Britain during 1943 was the Turkish strategy, for here the Russians acquiesced to the British efforts, at least in principle, and all that remained was to win over the skeptical Americans, and of course, the Turks. Everyone understood Turkish entry into the war to mean a Balkan campaign, and the British ultimately attempted every

---

* During September 1943 the British greatly irritated Roosevelt, Stimson, and the Joint Chiefs by opening, with small detachments of men, a campaign to capture Rhodes, Cos, Samos, and Leros, islands off the Turkish coast with virtually no strategic value. The undertaking was an immediate disaster, and Churchill pleaded with the Americans for substantial aid that threatened, as the Americans saw it, to escalate into a major campaign for objectives of no consequence, perhaps endangering OVERLORD as well. Among themselves, Roosevelt and Stimson were furious and they refused to make any move to prevent the British forces from eventually being wiped out. [See Churchill, *Closing the Ring*, chap. XII; Stimson Diary, October 12, 15, 1943, HLS Mss.]

form of persuasion to beg, cajole, and threaten the Turks. In June 1943 Lord Beaverbrook, Lord Privy Seal, made very explicit to Harry Hopkins that Turkish involvement at that stage would result in a delay in OVER-LORD, precisely the British intention.

The Turks were much more concerned about Russia than Germany, and until the end of 1942 were openly pro-German in their sentiments and economic policies. German military successes only encouraged this tendency, just as their defeats moved the Turks closer to a position of true neutrality. The army was especially anti-Soviet, and later the prospect of Soviet penetration into the Balkans struck terror in the hearts of Turkish leaders. Ideally the Turks wished to see the Germans and English working together to contain Soviet power and they did not take well to the proposal that they join the Allies, though as flexible politicians they also appreciated the value of being on the winning side. During January 1943 Churchill and Turkish President Ismet Inönü met secretly in Turkey and the Turks frankly revealed their anxieties. The primary problem was the Soviet Union, Inönü made clear; also, the war should end promptly by Britain concluding peace with Germany. In any event, the Turks argued, even if the war continued they would put off entry until the last moment, not simply because they were unprepared but also, they tried to reason, an exhausted Turkey would be of no use in balancing Soviet power in the Balkans after the war. At the least they would not enter the war until the British attacked the Balkans, for they had no intention of risking the possibility of having the Russians liberate them. It was at this point that Churchill successfully attempted to obtain vague Soviet assurances regarding their future relations with the Turks. The State Department was also fully informed of the Turks' political fears concerning Soviet power and ambitions in the Balkans. Everyone knew that the Turks were interested in the postwar Eastern European blocs directed against Russia that the London Poles were plotting, and perhaps even that they were attempting, as late as the summer of 1944, to create a Balkan Federation to contain the spread of Russian power.[43]

The Turks then cleverly imposed a firm precondition requiring the Allies to supply them with 180,000 tons of highly specialized equipment as well as Western air squadrons to enable them to defend their homeland and contribute to the war effort in an active manner—a quantity so obviously large that the needs of OVERLORD made it impossible. From that point on the Turks merely left the timing of their entry into the war to the West. And since the Russians wanted immediate Turkish aid or none at all, they too made the British dilemma insoluble. The Americans consistently refused to give Turkey the equipment it demanded, though a trickle of Lend-Lease continued for much of the war, and in effect vetoed the Turkish project.

In December 1943 Churchill again saw Inönü and attempted to pressure the Turks by threatening to throw them to the Russians if they did not enter the war immediately and implying British support for greater Soviet rights in the Turkish Straits. In February 1944 the British Military Mission left Ankara, and London ordered the British ambassador to break all social contacts with the Turks, leaving Hull to wonder during July if such rough tactics might result in pushing the Turks closer to the Russians, a misplaced fear indeed. By that time the incessant Western pressures, plus their impending victory, convinced the Turks that it was time to make some gesture without Western arms, though by this point the Allies had lost interest. On August 2, 1944, the Turks broke off diplomatic and commercial relations with Germany, but did not declare war until after the Yalta Conference.[44]

BY August 1943 the United States resolved to go ahead with OVER-LORD in 1944 even without the British, provided, of course, there was access to English bases. Despite Stimson's fears that the British were determined "to stick a knife in the back of Overlord" and the irritation of the American military at the British suggestion of possible disaster if German forces exceeded certain force levels, the Americans were not to be thrown off their course.[45] Yet one critical point must be made about American as compared to British grand strategy: if the British proposals were based on deeply political premises so were the American. The areas of disagreement reflected differences in political views and assessments of national interests, and as the Americans prepared for OVERLORD they too thought constantly of politics.

Stimson, as I have already mentioned, was not alone in comprehending the political consequences of the U.S.S.R.'s winning the war in Europe, both from the viewpoint of the West's prestige in the world and of violating a strategic compact of great consequence to the Russians. This compact had yet to deliver all the assets the Americans sought from it, because Soviet entry into the war against Japan, for pressing reasons I will discuss later, was still a prime objective of American policy vis-à-vis the U.S.S.R. American failure in Europe might lead to a similar Soviet response in the Far East, a factor that did not enter into British calculations at all. Beyond this, and much more significant, was the American belief that Western possession of France and Germany would be far more consequential to the future of world politics than control of the Balkans. If one had to choose— and Western inability to fight on both fronts at the same time necessitated this choice—then there was a kind of higher realism in the American position that deserves greater consideration.

On March 30, 1943, General George C. Marshall, Chief of Staff of the Army, prepared a memo for Roosevelt, with the unusual designation of "super secret," dealing with the postwar political consequences in Europe if the Western and Soviet military offensives did not keep pace. Only two weeks before, while discussing the possibility of Germany or Europe going Communist, Roosevelt suggested to Hopkins, as he recorded, that "we should work out a plan in case Germany collapses before we get to France."[46] "United Nations troops," the President commented at the end of August, had "to be ready to get to Berlin as soon as did the Russians."[47] Marshall, Stimson, and Secretary of the Navy James Forrestal were not alone in these thoughts; Roosevelt, later that November, thought "There would definitely be a race for Berlin," and "We may have to put the United States divisions into Berlin as soon as possible." Hopkins proposed that "we be ready to put an airborne division into Berlin two hours after the collapse of Germany."[48]

Since the Americans were not even in southern Italy when these questions first arose, much less in a position to reach Germany, they formulated a remarkable and entirely politically conceived plan entitled RANKIN to solve the dilemmas of Soviet military domination of Europe in case Germany collapsed or was defeated before OVERLORD. Much of the planning for RANKIN was later useful for OVERLORD and the occupation of Germany as well, and so critical was it that its logistics were continuously revised on the basis of intelligence reports, while the Combined Chiefs of Staff reviewed its status once a month. Naturally the British supported the plan, and at the Quebec Conference of August 1943 the Combined Chiefs worked it out and approved it in detail. And quite as naturally the Russians read about it only years later. Alternative RANKIN schemes were initially based on three different assumptions: a partial collapse of Germany permitting Anglo-American forces to land in Normandy earlier than June 1944; or, a more substantial collapse permitting larger landings throughout France; and, in the case of total or near complete German collapse, a general invasion of all Western Europe and an armored and airborne rush into the Rhineland and northwest Germany, including paratroop occupation of the major public buildings of Berlin. The United States held special troops in readiness for RANKIN for three months after D-Day, June 6, 1944, when the military further modified the plan.

By the Quebec Conference of September 1944, to which the United States and England had not invited Russia, the spectacular Anglo-American advance through France, with the concomitant slowing of the Russian momentum, opened the possibility of a deliberate German collapse in the West only. By this time Western officers worked RANKIN into a plan called "Operation Talisman," later "Eclipse," and modified it to assume the need for a quick assault on Hamburg, Berlin, and the northern coast of Germany. The contingency plan received the general approval of all political and military leaders of England and the United States who knew about it. It was never applied, because the Germans did not collapse in the manner RANKIN predicated, and when they did fall there were rather different pressing strategic and political factors to consider. But even as late as Easter 1945 America kept its paratroopers in readiness for implementing a variation of this strategy.[49]

The significance of RANKIN was in its mere existence, for it reflected a political sophistication no less intense than that of the English, and it indicated the political importance that the Americans attached to the possession of German soil rather than the Balkans. If the United States refused to go along with British pleas for a Balkan strategy after OVERLORD it was not because it was unconcerned about the alleged danger of Bolshevism, but only because it differed on how and where to meet it. By the end of 1944, and certainly by the early part of 1945, to the United States and Britain every Soviet military advance took on, in varying degrees, the aspect of a political threat. RANKIN was only one index of that political sensitivity, and the final battles of the war and the movements of troops were ultimately to become another.

To the Russians it appeared that the West was making politics while Russia made war. Other than reconsidering the coalition after so many broken promises in regard to a second front, the Russians must no doubt have realized that Anglo-American delays, whether intended to do so or not, were weakening them materially, and that this would also affect their relations with the West at the end of the war. What was also certain to the U.S.S.R. was that Anglo-American temporization had also weakened the force of its own obligations to its allies. By the Yalta Conference the military experiences of the Grand Alliance had done nothing to mitigate the political differences that were to appear during the course of 1943 and 1944.

THE PROBLEM OF THE LEFT AND ALLIED COOPERATION IN EUROPE

The Threat of the Left

AS THE AMERICANS and British contemplated their return to Europe during 1943 and 1944 they also had to consider the problem of the political and social systems that might emerge within nations wracked by war. Everything they saw in this regard disturbed them, for throughout Western and southern Europe the political tides were blowing strongly toward the left and challenging the one unifying and fundamental premise both the Americans and English shared: anti-Communism. Inevitably the problem of the Left spilled over to the question of current and postwar political relations with the U.S.S.R., because it seemed impossible to divorce the two issues.

When the intelligence information on the rise of the Left flowed in to London and Washington the problem indeed seemed awesome. There is an almost inverse correlation between the actual and impending location of Soviet troops and the strength of the Communist parties, which were virtually nonexistent in most of eastern Europe save, of course, in Yugoslavia and Czechoslovakia. Taken together, however, Communism, either in the wake of Russian troops or powerful Western European parties and the movements they controlled might, if that were their intention, blanket Europe.

Moving from east to west, the statistics on the rise of the Communist parties from the depression decade to 1944–1948 simply show that war and stability were incompatible with the Old Order. In Austria the Com-

munist party grew from 16,000 members in 1935 to 150,000 in 1948. In
Czechoslovakia membership increased from 60,000 in 1935 to 1,159,000
in 1946, when the Communist party obtained 2,500,000 votes in an honest
election. The Finnish Communist party increased its electoral power between 1930 and 1945 from 1.0 percent of the votes to 23.5 percent. In
Greece the Communist party, which had received a peak of one-tenth of
the votes during the 1930's, now greatly enlarged its prestige, and much the
same was true in Yugoslavia, where the Communist party received a high
of 12 percent of the vote in the 1920 election and now had a vast army at
its command. In Italy the party had a mere 12,000 members in 1924,
402,000 in July 1944, and 2,068,000 by the end of 1946, obtaining 19
percent of the vote in the 1946 election. In other parts of Western Europe
the situation was the same. In 1937 the French Communist party had a
peak of 328,000 members, 1,034,000 in 1946, receiving 29 percent of the
vote in the November 1946 election. The Belgian party vote increased
from 125,000 in 1939 to 301,000 in 1946, its percentage more than
doubling to 13 percent, the party itself growing over tenfold. The Norwegian Communists increased their vote from almost zero in 1936 to 12
percent in 1945, the Danish party from 2.4 percent to 12.5 percent from
1939 to 1945. And between 1937 and 1946 the Dutch party tripled its
vote to 10.5 percent.[1]

Yet the problem of the Left did not end with the figures, as troublesome as they were, but in the new character of a Left encompassing many
more elements than the Communist parties, and the critical position of the
Communist parties in Resistance movements that had, during 1943–1945,
more tangible power in the form of arms in hand. Other left parties in
many nations were no less powerful, and were frequently more militant
than the Communist party. During 1944–1945 the dominant current
among the now radicalized prewar Social Democratic and Socialist parties
was in favor of a United Front of *all* the Left to defeat fascism and build a
new society, for the failure of the Left to collaborate more fully in the
1930's nearly led to its total physical demise before the onslaught of reaction. The Communists too accepted the concept of the United Front,
making their political potential all the more credible and frightening in
areas where democratic freedoms existed.

The role of the Communist parties in the Resistance posed immediate
problems of physical security which could not wait for time or evolution,
for the Resistance movements everywhere attracted men who were exhibiting the courage and abandon of revolutionaries, advocating corre-
spondingly radical social theories, and who might in time become revolutionary actors as well. Everywhere they looked the Americans and British
saw political dangers on the left, and they had to prepare for the worst or
else risk political defeat after their military triumphs. Perhaps the Left and

the Resistance would be moderate, but no one could tell, much less risk a mistaken assumption. Later chapters dealing with specific countries will illustrate the dynamics and content of the Western response.

The existence of Soviet troops had little to do with the emergence of the Left, for they were not needed, at least at that time, for the masses of Europe to express repugnance over the condition to which the Old Order had forced them twice in their lifetime—the hunger, the decadence, the terror which had wrenched their lives apart. And the major recruiter for the Resistance and guerrilla movements was the occupying powers' brutality and humiliations, forcing men to choose sides and act, or die. This was especially true in France, Yugoslavia, Italy, and China during the war, and in Greece and Vietnam in later years. Would these men act—when, and how? In fact, as we shall see, there was a catalytic agent in the form of a merger of circumstances that did lead men to revolt in the cities, but only when it was too late to gain power. What were the characteristics of the Resistance? of the followers as well as the leaders? what were their goals? and could the West work with them? To answer these questions in specific countries in the context of concrete problems is not merely to show to what extent the Soviet Union was responsible for the Left, but also why mass social movements in modern times emerge in the context of nationalism and revolution, and perhaps also why men act and how their aspirations are aborted.

The fear of Communism and social revolution, given the power vacuum that existed in each European country as a result of the eclipse of the Right and prewar forces of order, could not help but create serious doubts and suspicions in the minds of the American and British leaders about the role of the U.S.S.R. Belief in the hegemony of international Communism, with its seat of power in Moscow, was not a discarded prewar bias, though all acknowledged the critical importance of the breakdown of the prewar social structure. This tendency to associate the U.S.S.R. with the Left created problems for which there were no easy solutions, for so long as the West opposed revolution it was compelled to regard the Soviet Communists with distrust. The United States and England could not undo the war, but only try to redirect its consequences. If, indeed, the Left was monolithic, perhaps the Russians might help to contain it, and their willingness to do so might be a critical index of their ultimate political objectives. Evidence of the Left's activity the Western Powers might regard as hostile Soviet behavior.

The American and British consciousness of the problems which the Left posed, and the U.S.S.R.'s relation to it, was entirely explicit. RANKIN and the British strategy for the Balkans mirrored this awareness. During March 1943, before the Resistance movements of Europe had emerged in full strength, Hopkins, Hull, and Roosevelt considered the problem that "either Germany will go Communist or out and out anarchic state would set in; that, indeed, the same kind of thing might happen in any of the countries in Europe and Italy as well."[2] Specific plans for occupation administration, which I will discuss later, and the diplomacy dealing with various countries and questions reflected such attitudes. The State Department and all major agencies in Washington followed the political events on the Left with rapt interest, and by February 1944 its Division of Eastern European Affairs, the major specialists on the problems of Communism, could report "that in all the countries [of Europe] studied except Poland . . . Communist elements have built up the strongest political group in the nation and hope that they will be in *de facto* control of many of the areas at the time of liberation." The division understood, with great clarity, that not merely the Communists' United Front strategy but also their ardent nationalism had won adherents to their cause. No less significant was their leading role in the armed Resistance, and "their espousal of a more active resistance than preached by the Governments-in-exile," and the support of those "who are not communist sympathizers but who are disgusted with the conservatism, political bickering and passive resistance policies of the exile governments."[3] Eisenhower too, in his war memoirs, referred to the problems these "dissident elements," who "had long served in the underground" and "did not easily adapt themselves again to the requirements of social order," created for the occupying powers.[4] ". . . the postwar world all around the globe is going to trend irresistibly toward social liberalism (if it does not go much farther and actually swing to a Communistic base)," Senator Arthur H. Vandenberg predicted in January 1945. ". . . the capitalistic system will *not* survive . . . unless we meet 'social liberalism' with forward-looking 'capitalistic liberalism.' "[5] "The main tendency was to the Left," British diplomatic specialist on Bolshevism R. H. Bruce Lockhart concluded in discussing early 1944, "and eagerness to raise the banner of revolution in Europe was widespread."[6] ". . . the issue," Churchill wrote Eden in May 1944, "is, Are we going to acquiesce in the Communisation of the Balkans and perhaps of Italy? . . . we are approaching a showdown with the Russians about their Communist intrigues. . . ."[7]

Churchill was convinced that the U.S.S.R. was largely responsible for such intrigues and Washington generally supported this reasoning at the time. Since the Russians were not fully convinced cooperation with the West would succeed, the State Department's Eastern European Affairs Division wrote in February 1944: "They are, therefore, fostering a rather extensive, pure Soviet, supplementary policy through the Comintern apparatus."[8] They considered the dissolution of the Comintern in May 1943 a myth, and it "still is used primarily as an instrument of Soviet foreign policy. . . ."[9] American diplomats in Latin America sent back anxious reports about the size of Soviet embassies and the alleged financing of local Communist parties, all of which reinforced the will to see Moscow as the manipulative center of the entire world's revolutionary ferment.

Such critical evaluations impinged on Anglo-American predictions of Soviet intentions after the war and deeply colored that estimate. Eastern European questions were ultimately to be at least as important in defining America's view of its ability to adjust to Soviet power after the war, but during 1943, before the Red Army crossed Russian borders, these issues were abstract. The State Department's Russian experts warned during the first months of 1943 that Soviet commitments had been unreliable in the past, and that this was a bad augury for the future. Ambassador Standley in the Soviet Union was basically suspicious of the U.S.S.R.'s postwar plans, though he admitted that the United States was receiving a good press. ". . . present Soviet policy is based upon the principle of maintaining a completely independent position at least until the end of the war and of avoiding any commitments which would prejudice a later determination of Soviet aims."[10] Harriman, his successor in October 1943, for the rest of the year was "a confirmed optimist" in this regard.[11] Hull took a rather more petulant position, in part because he felt that the Russians were not interested in his plans for the postwar world economy, but also, as he put it to Eden in March 1943, because there was widespread American apprehension "that Russia is saying almost nothing about her future plans and purposes and that, in fact, Russia will at the end of the war do as she pleases, take what she pleases and confer with nobody."[12] Later that October, while meeting with Molotov and Eden in Moscow, he frankly told the Soviet Foreign Minister that "one of our difficulties had come from the efforts to promote communism in the United States from abroad and also the question of religion in the Soviet Union," to which Molotov smilingly replied that there was no danger of Communism's being imposed upon America.[13]

References to the need "to convince them [Russia] they will have to drop their 'Comintern foreign policy' if they want our aid and cooperation after the war," appear in varying forms with greater frequency in State Department documents after the Teheran Conference.[14] By September the Eastern European issue and a myriad of others had convinced Kennan, Harriman, and those the Administration relied upon to report on Soviet policy that Russia was bent on dominating Eastern and Central Europe, though not necessarily through Communist governments. At the same time Harriman could report that Stalin and his advisers, even within the context of an aggressive Eastern European policy, "place the greatest importance and reliance on the newly won relationship with the British and ourselves. . . ."[15]

These rising apprehensions were well known to the Russians, for the Americans made slight effort to conceal them. Several significant Soviet gestures indicated that the Kremlin understood that the West identified the mushrooming Communist parties with Soviet foreign policy, and that the U.S.S.R. would have to pay the political price, including that of postwar collaboration with the United States and Britain, should the European Left move too far and too fast. Ambassador Standley at the beginning of 1943 warned the Soviet ambassador to the United States, Maxim Litvinov, "that the Comintern was one of the greatest problems in the relations between the Soviet Union and the U.S." Then, when Hull saw Czech President Eduard Beneš on May 18, he stressed that immediate Soviet prohibition of Comintern activities throughout the world "would go further than all else to restore the most agreeable friendly relations between the people of Russia and other nations."[16] On May 22, 1943, the U.S.S.R. dissolved the Comintern, since, as Stalin explained to Reuters on May 28, "It exposes the lie of the Hitlerites to the effect that 'Moscow' allegedly intends to intervene in the life of other nations and to 'Bolshevize' them." Communists, Stalin now stressed, had to make the social demands of the Left secondary to antifascist unity, and Hull praised the announcement as "welcome news" promoting "a greater degree of trust among the United Nations," but no one in Washington believed that the Russians would end their alleged subversion abroad.[17]

Then, early the following spring, Molotov publicly announced that Communist governments in Europe were not an objective of Soviet policy, though they favored political freedom for Communist parties everywhere.[18] Stability in Europe was, in brief, a prerequisite to stability in the alliance so long as that was a Soviet objective. Prior to OVERLORD this was surely the case, and there is much evidence that it remained a goal thereafter as well. For the Soviets would not go beyond their essential security interests in Eastern and Central Europe, where there was a powerful Left in only a few nations, if only because they were aware by mid-1944 of numerous Anglo-American acts of resistance to the Left, actions which I will discuss in subsequent chapters. To sacrifice the Left elsewhere appeared a small price, but it was not entirely within Soviet capabilities. The Russians had not created the Left and they ultimately could not stop it, though they might try and in the process eventually fractionate it. The Americans and British saw the emergence of the Left as related in some vital way to Russia rather than to the collapse of capitalism and colonialism throughout the world. Ironically, and it cannot be overemphasized, where the Russians could control indigenous, powerful Communist parties, they served an essentially moderating and conservative function, compelling the world Communist parties to choose between obedience and success. The two genuinely popular Communist parties to take power—in Yugoslavia and China—did so over Soviet objections and advice, and were the first to break the hegemony of the world movement. Without Soviet policy the Left might—it is speculation to state "necessarily"—have moved into the economic and political vacuum that existed in the major countries on the Continent and created noncapitalist societies. However, the Left's failure to exercise its option to take power was not only due to the policy of the U.S.S.R., but at least as much to the character of the Communist parties, the Resistance, and especially their leaders, but both dimensions of the problem warrant intensive exploration. No one of consequence in Washington by the end of 1944 regarded the relationship between the Russians and the world Left as conservative. No one saw the ironic possibility of Bolshevism helping to save capitalism. Yet such understanding would not have altered their reaction, for the United States and Great Britain opposed all revolutionary movements on principle, and whether or not they were Moscow-controlled was of lesser consequence than their fundamental relationship to a status quo which the Western leaders wished to see preserved.]

Great Power Collaboration and the European Advisory Commission

Wracked by doubts and uncertainties about the political future of Europe, enemy and vanquished nations alike, the British and Americans held their own counsels as to how they would occupy the territory they were soon to conquer. In the context of their concern over the Left and Bolshevism the question of occupation policies was in reality primarily political, deeply involving relations with the Soviet Union and Western peace aims.

The War Department first assigned the problem of civil affairs in occupied countries to special military divisions considered adjuncts of the military commanders. Both Britain and the United States created special schools to train these officers, mainly former civilian specialists with skills suited for the function. By the end of 1942 the American school in Charlottesville, Virginia, was under fire in the press for being predominantly composed of conservatives, a charge that Roosevelt quickly dismissed at Stimson's behest. Yet by December 1943 the United States based its civil affairs directives on the need, insofar as was possible, "that local laws, customs, and institutions of government be retained," as well as local officials and police, save where these practices conflicted with the aims of the military government.[19] During early 1943 both Roosevelt and Hull felt that they should work out plans for the occupation of Italy and Germany with the British before presenting them to the Russians, and in fact they followed this course. That the Russians would look askance at such a procedure was not difficult to predict, and Ambassador Standley reported intimations of Soviet displeasure to Hull at the end of July. Standley felt "obliged to point out the great importance of everything feasible being done . . . to avert developments which would give the Soviet Government plausible ground for believing or affirming that a sufficiently cooperative attitude had not been shown toward the Soviet Government."[20]

Then on August 22, 1943, Stalin sent Roosevelt and Churchill a rather stern protest, taking the Anglo-American surrender negotiations with the Italians as the occasion to suggest the creation of a Three Power political-military commission to deal jointly with Axis surrender problems and related questions involving common enemies. "To date it has been like this," Stalin wrote: "the U.S.A. and Britain reach agreement between themselves while the U.S.S.R. is informed of the agreement. . . . I must say that this situation cannot be tolerated any longer."[21] Churchill responded by suggesting a representative commission with nominal powers that could not interfere with the Allied Commander in Chief, and Roosevelt proposed the Russians, perhaps along with the Greeks and Yugoslavs, send an officer to Eisenhower's headquarters, with no powers implied. But Stalin would not be put off; he wanted a commission that would deal with Italy first and then with the other Axis countries and a host of subsequent political problems which most certainly would arise in the wake of victory. Although the Allies had not solved any of the disagreements on the functions of the commission, which were obvious from correspondence, Stalin showed the importance he attached to the scheme by appointing A. Y. Vishinsky, the Deputy Commissar for Foreign Affairs, as the Soviet representative. The Soviet proposal as such was seemingly innocuous, but it brushed on so many sensitive issues of Allied collaboration that the United States and Britain had to accept it as a form—"since we are in fact rejecting [the] Soviet proposal," Churchill wrote Roosevelt—intending to debate the content at the Foreign Ministers' Conference in Moscow at the end of October.[22] Washington was hostile to the idea from its inception and insistent that the military authorities—at the time Eisenhower—retain all decision-making powers. China, and perhaps Brazil, the State Department suggested, might water down the membership to reduce the significance of the body. Churchill was quite frank: "We cannot be put in a position where our two armies are doing all the fighting but Russians have a veto and must be consulted. . . ."[23]

On September 14 the Russians proposed that they permit the new "Political-Military Commission" to approve the participation in the occupation of local personnel sympathetic to the Allied cause—which implied, among others, the Communists. On this point the Americans would not compromise, insisting that the military authorities should have jurisdiction over such matters and decide when normal politics might resume. At the Moscow Conference, Molotov tried to pin Eden and Hull to a definite timetable for the restoration of civil control over Axis nations, with joint Russian participation on a political level. He also submitted a seven-point political reconstruction program, the sixth point of which—"The creation of democratic organs of local government"—Roosevelt and Eden especially designated as being entirely a matter for the military to determine.[24] More significantly, he emphatically stressed, according to State Department records, "that as Italy was the first country to surrender to the Allies, new problems in this connection were arising which affected very directly the cooperation between our three countries. . . . there was no need to emphasize the great political significance which the acceptance of the Soviet proposals would have. . . ."[25]

It is worth dwelling on the implications of the Soviet proposal for a moment. By October 1943 everyone expected the Russians to conquer the three other German satellites in Eastern Europe as well as much of Germany itself. Italy did not augur well for future Allied collaboration if mere conquest permitted the military authorities to control local political affairs in an essentially unilateral and totalitarian manner, extending to unfriendly political parties. Italy too had fought on the Russian front, and the Anglo-American attitude ignored the fact that the Italian campaign was possible because they had delayed OVERLORD and left Russia to face the brunt of the land war in Europe. The precedents, as we shall see repeatedly in detail, were ominous, for the Russians forgot nothing.

The results of the Moscow meeting ultimately satisfied no one. There the Allies created three organizations. One, the Advisory Council for Italy, was, as its name suggests, strictly advisory to the Allied Commander in Chief and the Allied Control Commission, of which he was president. Members of the council, including the three Great Powers, France, and eventually Yugoslavia and Greece, remained in isolation in Algiers during the war. The Russians were not at all pleased with the impotent council, nor did it salve their ruffled feelings at being excluded from Italian affairs and being left, they claimed, in ignorance. The terms of the Italian surrender, which the Russians ratified at Moscow, created an Allied Control Commission for Italy, though the formal Russian relationship to it was vague and it was clearly to be an Anglo-American body. The Allied Control Commission became the political arm of the military government and the effective ruling body in Italy. The third organization was the European Advisory Commission, with its seat in London, which would be a tripartite body to consider the terms of Axis surrender and related issues. Essentially a British plan, the Moscow Conference only vaguely specified the European Advisory Commission's powers and functions and both the Russians and the Americans, for very different reasons, looked at it skeptically. To the Russians the European Advisory Commission was no substitute for their original proposal or normal diplomacy, despite British assurances that the commission met their demands; to the Americans it seemed even worse.

When Hull returned to Washington after the Moscow Conference he discovered that Roosevelt, Hopkins, and Stimson, among others, were completely hostile to the idea of a European Advisory Commission, as nebulous as were the functions of that organization. In common with the English they were hostile toward the initial assumptions behind the Soviet proposal, but they believed that a commission centered in London, as Stimson explained it to Roosevelt, "would assume additional powers which the British were so evidently anxious to give it and that as the war went on it would tend, rightly or wrongly, to center the attention of the world upon London as the seat of the direction of the war."[26] So far as occupation problems were concerned, Stimson felt, the Civil Affairs Section of the United States War Department could handle the job. At this time, of course, United States-British disagreements over command jurisdiction and military strategy reached a most sensitive, if not breaking, point. The Americans saw the European Advisory Commission as another British ploy to "give orders" to Eisenhower, and worse yet, preempt American political supremacy in the postwar world.[27]

John J. McCloy, the Assistant Secretary of War, summed up the deeper political issues in a memo prepared immediately after Hull's return from Moscow. The effort on the part of the British to transfer as many decision-making bodies as possible to London could "be a development that may affect the attitude of the U.S. toward all post-hostility policy." The British failed to realize that the locus of world power had shifted from Europe to the United States, which had twice rescued Britain in European conflicts. The United States could never become isolationist, and "It is essential that the people of America become used to decisions being made in the United States." In the future,

> European deliberations must be made in the light of the concepts of the new continent because that continent has now, for better or for worse, become a determining factor in the struggles of the older one. . . . All this and more can be said against the spirit which motivates the London tendency. One cannot control the shift of power (if that is the heart of the matter) by such artificial devices in any event.[28]

McCloy's reasoning prevailed when the State Department appointed John G. Winant, the American ambassador to England, representative to the European Advisory Commission and asked him to rely primarily on the already overworked embassy staff for the very limited tasks which the department permitted him to consider. He had no power to initiate discussion on important issues of any sort, and Hull instructed him to restrict the functions of the European Advisory Commission to minimum technical questions on the German surrender and occupation that did not impinge on political matters. Winant understood that the European Advisory Commis-

CHAPTER

3

ITALY AND THE
RESTORATION OF ORDER

BETWEEN 1943 and the end of the war Italy was a perfect microcosm of the European political situation as fascists, monarchists, liberals, leftists, and opportunists vied for power in endless Byzantine intrigues. After the invasion of Sicily on July 10, 1943, and the mainland itself on September 3, British and American tensions fed on each other, further complicating local politics. Then the Russians persisted in adding to the burgeoning maze by entering the scene directly and through the agency of the Italian Communist party. There was, at one time, war and cold war between foes and friends alike.

Initially the British and Americans had hoped, even planned, to have it otherwise. Well before the invasion of Sicily they negotiated, then debated back and forth, the question of civil and political control and the responsibility of each power. At Casablanca, Roosevelt, pliable as always, agreed that the Mediterranean was primarily within the British area of interest and that they would bear the senior political responsibility in Italy. Upon his return to Washington, however, Roosevelt confronted the solid opposition of Hull, Stimson, and Eisenhower on this point. The Italian operation, Eisenhower predicted in February 1943, "will inevitably establish precedents far-reaching in scope and importance and will set the pattern for later operations in Europe."[1] The political implications were so clear to the American military that they insisted that the civil affairs responsibility be joint and equal, at least in principle. The two nations designated Eisenhower Supreme Commander in the Mediterranean, a title which the American kept only until the end of the year when British General Sir Harold Alexander was put in charge of the Italian campaign. Taking this as their starting point, Eden and Churchill during March and April 1943 pressed the Americans to recognize them as the "senior partner in the military administration of enemy occupied territory in that area." "For either government to assume primary responsibility," Eisenhower warned, "could invite undesirable speculation with regard to imperialistic intentions. . . ." Hull and Roosevelt, however, now felt that the Italians were more pro-American, and that they should exploit this psychological advantage: "The administration should be so organized that in its relations with the local population the greatest emphasis possible is given to the American character of the undertaking." The British and Americans did not resolve the controversy but left it hanging, only to have it emerge again later in an aggravated form once they had invaded Italy. From that time on the British dominated the key political and economic posts, especially after Washington gave them formal military command of the entire Italian campaign at the beginning of 1944 and "the American element in the administration," as McCloy reported in June 1944, "was rather submerged. . . ."[2]

The issues that unified the two allies were greater during mid-1943, and so they were able to postpone the question of relative jurisdictions. There was, of course, the common danger of combat. More important was a very real consensus on the political situation in Italy and the alternatives to the existing regime. Neither the Americans nor the British had identified Mussolini totally with Nazi Germany. During the last days of the Munich Conference, Roosevelt urged Mussolini to mediate to prevent a European war, and it was no secret that Mussolini opposed the German plans for attacking Poland; however great his opportunism, it did not prevent Mussolini from again urging European mediation in November 1939. During April and May 1940 Roosevelt appealed to Mussolini to remain neutral, and only on June 10 did he bring Italy into the war. Italy never directly attacked American interests and Roosevelt and his party never forgot the Italian-Americans' political significance. As Churchill later put it in his memoirs:

> He was, as I had addressed him at the time of the fall of France, "the Italian lawgiver." The alternative to his role might well have been a Communist Italy, which would have brought perils and misfortunes of a different character both upon the Italian people and Europe. His fatal mistake was the declaration of war on France and Great Britain. . . . Had he not done this, he might well have maintained Italy in a balancing position, courted and rewarded by both sides and deriving an unusual wealth and prosperity from the struggles of other countries. Even when the issue of the war became certain, Mussolini would have been welcomed by the Allies.[3]

The Allies were to treat, instead, with Mussolini's former friends.

By the end of 1942 it was apparent to most of Italy's fascist and military leadership that they had chosen the losing side, and the members of the ruling elite hatched plots and cabals as King Victor Emmanuel, who had cordially supported fascism from the inception, took a neutral stand. On July 25, 1943, the Fascist Grand Council, monarchists, and officers, led by Marshal Pietro Badoglio, the conqueror of Ethiopia, deposed and arrested Mussolini. Equivocating with the Germans, who were able to move divisions into Italy and liberate Mussolini during the interim, the Badoglio government immediately sent secret emissaries to negotiate a satisfactory peace with the Allies. These representatives made it clear, as Churchill told Roosevelt on August 5, "There is nothing between the King, with the patriots who have rallied round him . . . and rampant Bolshevism." Roosevelt needed no prompting, for at the end of July, when the possibilities in Italy became clear, the United States and Britain agreed upon a joint political strategy in regard to certain fundamental political questions that would unite them for much of the remainder of 1943. "There are some contentious people here who are getting to make a row if we seem to recognize the House of Savoy or Badoglio," Roosevelt wrote Churchill on July 30. ". . . we have to treat with any person or persons in Italy who can best give us, first, disarmament, and, second, assurance against chaos. . . ." "My position," Churchill responded the next day, "is that once Mussolini and the Fascists are gone, I will deal with any Italian authority which can deliver the goods. . . . Those purposes would certainly be hindered by chaos, Bolshevisation, or civil war. . . . I should deprecate any pronouncement about self-determination at the present time. . . ."[4]

The way was now clear, and for both military and political reasons the Western Allies were ready to negotiate with a disaffected section of the Italian ruling class begging the West to save it from the Left. The Italian officer class supported Badoglio, but his opportunistic fishing for terms from both the Germans and Allies during August permitted the Germans to consolidate their military power in Italy in a way that shunted the thoroughly demoralized Italian military aside and deprived the Allies of important strategic gains. On September 3, as Allied forces landed in Italy, Badoglio agreed to a secret armistice in the hope the Allies would land a major force north of Rome and save his government and the king. When he learned such a rescue would not occur he desperately attempted to call off his bargain with Eisenhower, who cut short the matter on September 8 by broadcasting news of its existence. The next day the hero of Abyssinia, his king, and a small retinue deserted Rome for the southeast tip of Italy, leaving most of Italy to the Nazis. They thereby deprived the Allies of their hoped-for military coup and made them heirs to a reactionary political authority which on September 29 unconditionally surrendered what was left of the Italian navy and an army it no longer controlled. In return for Badoglio's agreement to sign the secret so-called "long-terms" surrender, the Allies promised that they would support the king's authority until the end of the war, when the Italian people could determine the fate of their political order. And once Italy declared war against Germany, which it did on October 13, the Allies would recognize it as a cobelligerent, and presumably Italy would begin its way back to eventual independence and equality. For the duration of the war, however, the Allied armies on the scene would run Italy according to military exigencies, with such economic and political conditions or concessions as they might care to make in the future to the Badoglio government.[5]

Roosevelt announced on July 28 that the United States would in no way cooperate with fascism in Italy and resolved the dilemma which working with Badoglio and the king posed by deciding that they were not fascists after all. Eisenhower reached this conclusion in regard to Badoglio after meeting him on September 29 and immediately reported the change to Washington. "It would be a mistake," Stimson warned Roosevelt only nine days earlier, "for us to try to impose from outside too hastily a modern democracy upon a government which has had such a history of free parliamentary government."[6] Stalin approved the surrender, ignoring the political complexion of the government called upon to implement it, and Churchill's consistent position until 1944 kept Badoglio and the king in power until the Allies were in Rome and might form a "broad-based" Italian government.[7] For a brief time, at least, all was well, until the Italians themselves began intruding into affairs, ultimately driving wedges into the superficial Allied unity.

On the surface the Italians seemed overly fractious in wanting to remove Badoglio and the king from a power that was largely fictional as a result of the stiff surrender terms, but those two gentlemen, and especially the king, were universally regarded as remnants of the equally widely hated fascist order. From the moment they signed the "long surrender," until the end of the year, opposition to the Badoglio government grew in intensity as part of the sustained political crisis that characterized Italian politics for the next two years. Both Right and Left condemned him. Prefascist Foreign Minister Count Carlo Sforza, especially close to Washington after years spent in exile in the United States, leveled an attack on Victor Emmanuel that initiated a running controversy between himself and Churchill, who, with much justification, came to view the returned leader as an American ploy. More significant, the Committee of National Liberation, organized in the south by six parties ranging from constitutional monarchist to Communist, refused to join the Badoglio Cabinet so long as the king or his son remained on the throne—remaining unyielding on this point until late April of the following year. The Badoglio government, composed of so-called "technicians" who represented no one, therefore accelerated the total economic, political, and moral collapse in Italian life which followed in the wake of fascism and war.

The Badoglio government had the unique distinction of alienating everyone. The leaders of the Committee of National Liberation, such as Benedetto Croce and Arancio Ruiz, much less Sforza, were by no means radical. Sforza himself favored representative monarchy and wished the king's grandson to take the throne to wipe away the taint of fascism associated with it. The Committee of National Liberation agreed to enter the Badoglio Cabinet if it implemented this formula. But the king was adamant, and it became increasingly apparent to the American representatives in the area that the existing political arrangement, however much Badoglio himself claimed he was creating "continuity without a radical change" for the Allies, was not confronting the most serious problem facing the Anglo-American forces: the rising strength of the Left, moving to fill the vacuum in Italian life. The Americans had not objected to Badoglio before, and they were not overly hostile even in November, but given the critical political tasks at hand he was no longer useful; loss of the king and an offense to the British preference for monarchies appeared to be a small price to pay for an effective non-Communist government. During mid-November 1943, at Eisenhower's suggestion, the State Department formulated a position in favor of tolerating the king, who refused to abdicate, and a Badoglio government without broad-based support only until the Allies reached Rome, which they expected to do in the very near future. In the meantime the United States expected Badoglio to work with the Allied Control Commission and continue to try to reach an accord with the Italian parties. The State Department also authorized Eisenhower, should a military justification warrant it, to compel the king to abdicate.[8]

Washington then permitted the matter to rest, in the belief the conquest of Rome would soon lead to urgently needed changes. However, they were not to conquer Rome until June 4 of the following year, and so the American policy, in effect, only perpetuated a status quo utterly incapable of stemming the growth of the Left. When the new realities became apparent by the beginning of 1944, a political crisis of the first magnitude was in the offing, involving Anglo-American conflicts, their joint fear of the Soviet Union, and the dangers an ever more powerful Left posed to their mutual objectives.

The Resistance: 1943 to Early 1944

After almost two decades of fascism the Italian Resistance was late in organizing, and this critical fact also explains why it eventually failed. Small antifascist groups existed well before 1943, of course, but action was virtually nonexistent. The only manifestations of resistance prior to the toppling of Mussolini from above were the Communist-led workers' strikes in northern Italy during March 1943. Until the Allied invasions and the coup the Resistance did not exist save as an abstraction, and, of course, as a fear in the minds of the Italian elite and Anglo-American leaders. For all knew the Italian masses were disaffected, and as a result of the hardships of war, deprived—and these are necessary, if not sufficient, conditions for a revolution. During the fall of 1943 small terrorist groups, mostly Communist led, began to wreak revenge on the Germans, and in September the Communists, the Action party, and then shortly thereafter the Socialists (PSIUP) and other groups began organizing Partisan groups under political auspices. These organizations often included apolitical ex-soldiers who had deserted or had nowhere else to go, or young men whom the fascists were about to draft or the Nazis to deport, but political bands under political leadership always comprised the vast majority of the Resistance groups in the center and the north. Perhaps a better indication of the Left's strength is the fact that during the late winter of 1944 strikes in the north, lasting as long as eight days in Turin, well over a half million and perhaps closer to a million workers participated despite the presence of German and fascist guns. In March 1945 the United States Office of Strategic Services (OSS) estimated that there were about 182,000 Partisans in the occupied area, with as many as 500,000 potential recruits.

Although there had been manifestations of resistance in the south—a spontaneous mass uprising liberated Naples in the days before Allied entry —the movement was preeminently the "wind from the north." All the more ominous, because by August 1944 the Allied armies reached only as far as Pisa and Florence and went only slightly farther by April 1945, leaving the power and potential of the Resistance unaffected. The Resistance was perhaps more disturbing as a threat than as a physical reality, but until the Allies reached the north they could not tell which form it would take.

The British Special Operations Executive (SOE) and the American OSS had agents in the north to report such information as they might obtain, and Resistance leaders visited Allied intelligence officials outside Italy. The Allies sent little aid north during the winter of 1943–1944, in part because, where possible, the British opposed large-scale underground armies and wished aid merely in the form of sabotage and intelligence, and also because they relied heavily on Badoglio's intelligence agents, who sought out the small number of monarchist resistants and ignored the rest. But the American OSS reports from Switzerland at the end of 1943 regarded the developments in the north as "revolutionary" and political rather than military events. The Communists led the largest group of the organized Resistants, other leftist parties most of the rest—and nearly all were of working class and peasant origins. Early in 1944 they created the Committee of National Liberation for Northern Italy (CLNAI).[9]

There was no single Resistance ideology because the CLNAI was an amalgam of rather independent groups working together via a central co-ordinating body. There were only positions, and the Communists, the largest party within the CLNAI, determined the functional, ideological objectives, which were ultimately to prove sufficiently conservative. On a lower level the Resistance, as in France, was a euphoric and promising idealistic experience for those independent leftists and intellectuals in search of a new radical creed. The Old Order had decayed and was now falling apart, and power would fall to the men of ideas who were also men of action with guns in hand. A radical transformation of society seemed not merely necessary but possible, and in the course of 1943–1945 they considered and debated every suggestion, with strong libertarian strains quite as powerful as any. Even the small monarchist bands in the north affirmed their belief in "the radical reconstruction of the political, moral and social life of our country. . . ."[10] Would this redeeming movement liberate Italy, or would it be stillborn? More than any other group the Communists were to answer this question. At the beginning of 1944 the Americans and British also watched anxiously for an answer.

The Italian Political Quagmire

If the Western Powers were to meet the rising challenge of the Left during the first months of 1944 they would have to do it with the aid of a fragile king and government devoid of any support from the center or left parties. The Americans were fully aware of this weakness as were, increasingly, many of the British military and political leaders in Italy. Badoglio could not prevent the movement toward the left, much less meet the insistent demands of the six parties in the Committee of National Liberation for greater civil liberties and a thorough purge of key fascists in government. By the end of January, Hull strongly urged Roosevelt to agree to the immediate removal of the king and reconstruction of the government, even if this required a public break with the British. Churchill, despite the now general opposition of the British military, was uncertain of what would follow Badoglio's and the king's departure, and consistently denigrated "the worn-out débris" leading the Committee of National Liberation, and especially Sforza. For the moment only, as "a temporary reprieve" and also because some in Washington wished to maintain unity with the British during the military crisis of late winter, Roosevelt agreed on February 11 to tolerate the existing government until the military situation improved.[11]

The incipient conflict between the English and American governments over Italy reflected both the clash of political ambitions and radically different objectives for the postwar world economy, for which Italy set a precedent. Although Roosevelt in early 1944 was willing to grant Great Britain primary leadership in occupied and postwar Italy, his advisers did not share his generous indifference and they were to prevail. For general reasons they wished at least parity with England in the definition of internal Italian affairs, although both governments shared a more primary antipathy toward the threat of the Left which kept them in political unison on most fundamental, immediate questions. No less consequential, especially in the State Department, was the fear that British hegemony in Italy would add yet one more nation to a British-dominated world economic bloc hostile to the comprehensive plans they were then working out in detail in Washington. Even if Washington had yet to define a policy for Italy which gave the United States a predominant influence in Italy after the war, its political and economic objectives required that both Britain and Russia be denied such a role, and given the economic dependence of Italy this ultimately required American domination over the essential thrust of Italian affairs in the world scene.

The reprieve did not last long. At the beginning of March, Roosevelt let Churchill know that military conditions no longer required maintenance of a government unable to function with local political support; now was the time to discard the king and, if the Committee of National Liberation could not work with him, Badoglio as well. As these matters moved toward a decisive resolution and Badoglio's days seemed numbered, the neofascist regime and Churchill found new allies: the Soviet Union and the Italian Communist party.

Whether the Soviet exchange of diplomatic personnel with Italy at the beginning of March would give de jure or de facto recognition, an "ambassador" or "representative," was not entirely clear, but what is certain is that the Russians gave the neofascists a new lease on life. Why?

Stalin supported the West's surrender policy in Italy, and at Teheran he avoided taking an unequivocal position against the king of Italy, being far more interested in getting part of the captured Italian fleet assigned to the U.S.S.R. But obviously the Russians strongly felt they had a right to be represented in the Allied control of Italy, hence their proposals during August through November 1943 for a Political-Military Commission and certain reforms in Italy itself. In November the matter of Allied cooperation on Italian political matters came up when Vishinsky arrived with two senior officers to take his place on the Advisory Council and the British feared he might arrogate executive functions to himself. What was the Soviet status to be? Allied authorities in Italy referred the matter to Washington and London, where policy-makers on the highest levels carefully considered it, and the United States accepted the "British formula." They would give the Soviet representative "token representation" on the Allied Control Commission, but he would be excluded from the actual operational structure itself—"a kind of superior 'liaison officer,'" as Hull explained to Roosevelt.[12] The Russians accepted the "formula" without much enthusiasm, but carefully noted the arrangement for future reference and as a precedent.

For the rest of March 1944 the U.S.S.R.'s intrusion into Italian affairs, and the implications of Russian action for the future of United States-Soviet relations, became far more important to Washington than the inability of Badoglio and the Committee of National Liberation to unite, a dilemma for which no solution seemed to be available anyway. The United States had to consider three major questions. Why had the Russians taken the step? What did it presage for future diplomatic relations and how should they handle the issue in this context? What did it mean to Italy?

The reason the Russians entered into direct relations with the Badoglio government was self-evident to American analysts: ". . . it would seem to reflect," American chargé in Algiers Selden Chapin immediately wired Hull, "Soviet impatience at the not inconsiderable barrier to unhampered Soviet activities in Italy presented by the machinery of the Allied Control Commission and the Advisory Council."[13] Washington generally accepted this analysis, and when Harriman complained to Vishinsky in Moscow on March 13 the Soviet diplomat offered it as an explanation. For a short time the State Department considered recommending a change in the Allied Control Commission structure to meet what they begrudgingly recognized as a legitimate Soviet complaint, but the Allied headquarters in Italy had them drop the proposal.

The State Department nevertheless considered the recognition crisis a serious one for other reasons. Harriman wrote Hull:

> The Soviets should be made to understand that they have made an error in procedure which if continued will have serious repercussions on over-all collaboration. We have a long and perhaps difficult road while the Soviets learn how to behave in the civilized world community. Effective results can I believe be obtained by taking a firm position when they take improper steps. . . . If we don't . . . with each incident we may well look forward to a Soviet policy of playing the part of a world bully.[14]

In strong terms Washington admonished the Russians to work through the Advisory Council, which by now was a fiction without any power, and not to forget that the Allied military commander held supreme authority. On March 25, Molotov informed Harriman the Soviet government did not believe the recognition matter in any way impinged on the rights of the military authorities, but for the most part the Russians concentrated on the immediate political issues in Italy. These were perhaps a better indication of what the future might hold.

The British and Americans severely reprimanded Badoglio and clearly and unceremoniously told him that any diplomatic agreement would have to be with the permission of the theater commander, but he received a new political lease on life as a result of the Russian action, and he understood this fact immediately. On March 19 Soviet Ambassador Andrei Gromyko handed Hull a memorandum which explained what the Soviet action meant for Italy. The division between the Badoglio government and the Committee of National Liberation, both described as anti-Nazi, was hindering the war in Italy. The Badoglio government had been unable to unite the anti-fascist parties, and it received the support of Britain and America even on the question of the king's abdication. It was important to fight the war and to unite for that purpose, and therefore "the Soviet Government proposes to the governments of Great Britain and the United States to take steps toward the possible union of all democratic and anti-fascist forces of liberated Italy on the basis of appropriate improvement of the Government of Badoglio."[15] But how? The British and the Americans unsuccessfully interfered in Italian affairs for six months with precisely this objective in mind, and during the following months did so with even greater energy. The difference between Soviet and Western efforts was in the relationship of Russia to the Left. On March 26 Palmiro Togliatti returned to Italy after nearly two decades of exile in the U.S.S.R. to direct the Italian Communist party. Whoever controlled the Left controlled Italian politics, and the Communist party was the key to the Left.

The dimensions of this incident reveal much about the nature of the Allied alliance, the intentions of its members, and the role of power in the world by 1944. The British and Americans excluded the Russians from the critical political decisions arising out of the reconquest of the first European as well as Axis power, but the Russians had decided to make their presence felt and then withdraw. The Russians released a press statement in Moscow on April 14, calling for the unity of the Left and Badoglio for an anti-Nazi crusade, and the U.S.S.R. quietly followed Western leadership from that point on. The Communist party thereupon reflected Soviet intentions insofar as they were an accurate gauge. At the same time the West made it clear they regarded Italy as their sphere of active interest, at least for the duration of the war, and this was the obvious burden of their policies in regard to the Allied Control Commission and the notes to the Russians from September 1943 to March 1944. It is important to recall again that Soviet troops entered Poland for the first time on January 4, 1944, and on April 2 invaded Axis Rumania. In each case, as the British predicted, they had significant precedents to follow both in regard to collaboration among the Allies on political matters arising out of military occupation and in the reorganization and control of local political affairs.

The British promptly interpreted the Soviet policy toward Badoglio, which reflected both the immediate Soviet priorities and its latent power, as a clear warning to the Left to do nothing to detract from the war effort. In his arguments with the Americans over Badoglio, Churchill was glad to have Soviet backing, and he used it ruthlessly as a debating point. Yet he too worried about the very fact that the Russians had the power to intrigue in Italy and elsewhere, and ultimately this was his greater concern. The Americans shared this view. They did not like Badoglio, partly because he had been ineffectual in blocking the growth of the Left, and now, using a reactionary, the Left was able to become a decisive factor in internal Italian politics. What they did not appreciate was that the Communists were now also able to become the critical factor only because they were moving toward the right and had eschewed sectarianism for Cabinet politics. In the process the Communist party strengthened both the forces of order and itself. Would the Communists continue?

As if by magic the insoluble political problems of the last half year began moving toward a resolution for the West. The State Department's decision to act decisively on the king's future helped somewhat, but Togliatti helped even more. At the beginning of April, Roosevelt called Robert Murphy, his personal representative in Italy, to Washington and instructed him to move energetically for the king's abdication. Since the British military could not neutralize Churchill's inconsistent monarchist enthusiasms—for they saw no point in political paralysis aiding the Left—Murphy pressured the king into agreeing to abdicate to his son the day the Allies captured Rome, leaving the ultimate question of the monarchy as an institution for the Italians to decide after the war.[16]

The next step was up to Togliatti, a rather remarkable, urbane, and literate personality, who was most welcome on the scene. A former poet of sorts, he rose to the leadership of the Communist party as a result of an unswerving loyalty to Stalin during the internecine Bolshevik disputes of the 1920's and by accommodating himself to the intricacies of the Comintern line thereafter. His main function as leader of the Communist party in the 1930's had been to defeat the militant Communists who wished to follow a separate revolutionary course and break entirely with the moderate Socialists in Italian politics. Of all the important Western European Communist leaders, Togliatti was at this time one of the most obedient to every Soviet desire, the perfect caricature of a "Moscow agent." During the previous August he informed his party colleagues in the north of Italy, from the remoteness of Moscow, that they were to make all traditional party objectives secondary to the goal of driving out the Germans and winning the war. To Togliatti, the Resistance was not a step in the direction of social revolution, but a means of combatting Germany and its allies. And to the Russians, as one Allied representative reported Vishinsky to have declared in December 1943, "this parochial communism as merely likely to be a nuisance at this stage since it had no real background or purpose."[17]

Then, on April 1, a few days after he returned, Togliatti delivered a policy statement to a party conference in Naples that revealed the basic line the Communist party was to pursue for well over a year. It called for political collaboration among antifascist parties and asserted the question of the monarchy as an institution could wait until the end of the war, even if the king remained on the throne. The Communist party would cooperate with Badoglio and after the war would operate within the context of a democratic, republican, and parliamentary Italy. The task at hand was to subordinate all partisan goals to the need to defeat Germany. Essentially, Togliatti merely repeated the March 19 Soviet memo on Italian politics, with which he was certainly familiar. This defection of a key party profoundly agitated the Committee of National Liberation, and many Resistance members in the north found the statement intolerable. Badoglio flattered Togliatti himself for his "seriousness and objectivity" and also praised his subsequent utterances for the family and religion.[18] To the king, "Togliatti . . . has spoken as an Italian. . . ."[19] And thereafter Robert Murphy found him "an agreeable dinner guest" who added "a piquant touch to gatherings."[20] More significantly, he gave definite political assurances about the Communist party's role to British General Noel Mason-MacFarlane, which slightly assuaged Anglo-American apprehensions. On April 21, on the basis of Murphy's compromise on the monarchical question and Togliatti's nonpolitical program, the Committee of National Liberation gave allegiance to the Badoglio government, and Sforza, Croce, and other Committee of National Liberation leaders entered his Cabinet. Togliatti, Murphy reported Badoglio as saying, "had proved the most effective collaborator throughout the negotiation with the Party leaders."[21] He even vetoed the appointment of a Communist as War Minister.

Togliatti, with his polished, witty repartee, was one thing, but the hungry, often armed men who flocked to the banner of the party and the Communist-led Resistance were quite another. Quite unconsciously at first, an important dichotomy between the leaders and followers emerged, and Anglo-American leaders' distrust of the latter increased in intensity because they could never accept the phenomenon of armed mass movements. The spectacular growth of the Communist party itself continued to cause the greatest alarm to both the English and the Americans, who, if they agreed on nothing else, always feared the potential of the mass party of the Left. Between the end of 1943 and July 1944 the party's membership quadrupled, as it did again over the next year and a half. The developments of March, Allied Control Commission headquarters reported, strengthened both Badoglio and the Communist party. Long lines formed in the streets to join the party, Sforza reported to Murphy, and they included many members of the middle classes. The party, surely, was the best organized and financed in Italy, both north and south. No longer intransigent and sectarian, its very reasonableness made it the most important political factor in Italy, for it could attract more conservative leftists as well as radicals still unwilling to go elsewhere. All these thoughts Murphy and others communicated to Washington, including the possibility, as one Control Commission report stated it, "More than twenty years ago a similar situation provoked the March on Rome and gave birth to Fascism. We must make up our minds—and that quickly—whether or not we wish to see this second march developing into another 'ism'."[22] Even Togliatti and Moscow might not have the power to prevent that fate, and while the Communist party might be safe in politics for the moment, perhaps even longer, there was always the threat of the armed Partisans in the north, and of course, the other parties of the Left, who might win ascendancy over the leftist masses.

These other parties, primarily the Action party and the Socialists under Pietro Nenni, were consistently more troublesome than the Communist party. For one thing, they were not under Moscow discipline, which was now a moderating factor. The Socialists were powerful in the cities among the workers, and although intellectuals and professionals with a strongly radical bent led the Actionists, they managed to organize about one-quarter of the Partisans in the north. In the broadest terms their joint positions during 1943 and 1944 called for prompt elimination of the monarchy, immediate land and economic reforms of the most far-reaching nature, a socialist republic rather than a parliamentary fiasco of the nineteenth-century variety, workers' control, and a new society based on the structure of the Committee of National Liberation at the grass-roots level. Libertarian and Left—whenever there was a political crisis these two groups were invariably in the opposition, and when in the government they threatened to resign at any moment. Until the end of the war they always proved more troublesome than the Communist party, and only the Nenni party's passionate desire for a United Front on the Left—which meant the Communists—eventually kept it from posing a very real threat to Anglo-American plans during 1945. Smaller Communist groups, by virtue of their growth no longer mere sects, also confused and worried occupation authorities. These included the Catholic Communists and the neo-Trotskyist *Movimento Communista Italiano*. When American authorities asked Togliatti about these parties he only denounced them and gave assurances that "he is the head of the only Communist party in Italy with nationalistic and patriotic tendencies."[23]

The Occupation Government

The Americans and the British did not wait until the end of the war to hedge against future political contingencies, and however much they disagreed on specific political questions, or the issue of who should control the

Italian occupation government, they fully agreed on what should be the essential relationship of the occupation to the Left. In a sense the imbroglio of Italian politics was an illusion, save insofar as the Communists managed to become its arbiters, for the Anglo-American military ran that part of Italy not under Nazi control and they quickly determined not to allow the Left to take over. Politics existed by suffrance of the occupation authorities, and they were not inclined to be generous.

"No political activity whatsoever shall be countenanced during the period of military government," Eisenhower publicly proclaimed in July 1943, and banned all publications or public meetings without the consent of AMGOT, the military government.[24] Yet the Italians complained bitterly about these proscriptions, especially after they became cobelligerents against Germany, and applied very great pressures to modify the rules. During December 1943 the Committee of National Liberation unsuccessfully attempted to hold a public convention in Naples, and riots between students or political groups attempting to hold meetings and police were common. The occupation continued to prohibit meetings and the somewhat greater freedom of the press did not eliminate the constant threat of military censorship. The matter was a source of continuous embarrassment and concern to AMGOT. When Vishinsky attended the January 1944 Advisory Council meeting in Algiers he pointedly asked why many antifascists were still in prison and why AMGOT had permitted so few political liberties. The Combined Chiefs of Staff in January authorized the military in Italy to allow more internal political freedom as conditions warranted, but they used this prerogative sparingly. The Communists did not press for such liberties as forcefully as the Action party, which warned the military that they would merely ignore a ban on political activity when Rome was taken.

While the Committee of National Liberation pressed for greater freedom and began breaking Allied injunctions, the Badoglio government, after a brief period of ambivalence, urged the Allies to censor all criticism of the king, the government, and the army. ". . . any signs of political activity in the forward areas are at once suppressed," military authorities reported in January 1944, and during February more rigorous press censorship was imposed after the Committee of National Liberation called for noncooperation with all bodies of the Badoglio government.[25] The British, anxious to strengthen Badoglio and largely in charge of such questions, informed Washington that "no agitation calculated to disturb the military situation will meanwhile be tolerated."[26] Then, when three Committee of National Liberation parties in Naples moved to call a strike at the beginning of March, General Wilson, the British commander, banned it and Roosevelt was then inclined to warn Churchill, for the first time, that to use force against the anti-Badoglio groups would be ill advised. For the Committee of National Liberation generated pressures which reinforced American policy.

The basic premise of American occupational planning prior to the conquest of Italy was to maintain existing governmental structures, laws, and even official personnel so long as they did not conflict with military needs or ultimate political objectives. Despite some internal criticism, Washington did not alter these assumptions, which required, in effect, that all factors being equal they would preserve the status quo. In Italy this meant, as the Pentagon instructed the theater commanders in mid-October 1943, "it is expected that the *carabinieri* and Italian Army will be found satisfactory for local security purposes. . . ." To have an antifascist administration "while using the old framework of machinery and local government" would be desirable but the first objective must be to get and "keep a local government working smoothly so as to relieve the Commander-in-Chief of all trouble and anxiety as regards civil population." The Old Order fully understood the meaning of this. ". . . the machine cannot be broken up or Fascist influence eliminated in a day," AMGOT directed. ". . . it will not be possible to remove or intern all members of the Party. This would merely cause a breakdown. . . ."[27] First in Sicily, and then in Italy, the British and Americans increasingly relied on existing fascist institutions, and save in the most blatant cases, fascist personnel. The commanders disbanded fascist organizations themselves, but retained their useful institutions and personnel. Later, they promised, when military exigencies were less pressing, they would effect a more thorough purge.

The Badoglio government and the king also strongly opposed any serious dismissal of the fascists and spent most of their time purging the army of antimonarchical elements. Predictably the Committee of National Liberation vigorously complained that the Badoglio government was carefully appointing ex-fascists to security and military posts. But such ex-fascists were politically reliable from the viewpoint of the military occupation, and after twenty years of organizational responsibility, very useful for military efficiency. For, as a Control Commission report stated: "the bulk of officials were and had to be Fascists to earn their daily bread. The appointment of an efficient man [by the Allied Control Commission] nearly always means the appointment of a Fascist in some degree, with resulting criticism. . . ."[28] The criticism continued, and the occupation authorities suspected the Communists instigated the frequent local riots against fascists, but they also initiated a "defascistization" program that presumably differentiated the hard-core fascists from the opportunists. Review boards dismissed fewer than 5 percent of those brought up for epuration from their posts, and criminal penalties were quite rare. When asked about it during May 1944, General Mason-MacFarlane admitted that since "Marshal Badoglio's former Cabinet was too weak to take a resolute stand on this subject, the purge program had proceeded somewhat slowly in the past."[29] Later the government assigned Sforza and a Communist assistant the ministry in charge of epuration, and the results were identical.

In nominal ways related to Italian prestige the Allies moderated the terms of the surrender throughout 1944 and 1945, and in October 1944 dropped the term "Control" from the Allied Control Commission's title. Then in February 1945 Roosevelt and Churchill announced that they would grant the Italians much greater management of their own affairs, including aspects of foreign policy, "subject to effective maintenance of law and order."[30] The contingency was by no means casual, but reflected a very deep concern in Washington as to what the future might hold once they withdrew their troops.

The Italian Imbroglio After Rome

If the Americans and British agreed on the manner of responding to the Left, they agreed on very little else. All of the incipient controversy, reflected in interminable bickering, smoldered until the summer of 1944, when the conflict became sharper. For on June 4 the Allied troops entered Rome and the king's moment to abdicate to his son arrived. To add to their problems, the Anglo-American leaders soon discovered that the Central Committee of National Liberation in Rome, under the chairmanship of a moderate former Prime Minister, Ivanoe Bonomi, refused to cooperate with the Badoglio government. Bonomi was a conservative in the spectrum of Italian politics, and a believer in constitutional monarchy, and the Americans were glad to support him. Churchill was furious at "Badoglio's replacement by this group of aged and hungry politicians. . . ," more because the Italians had not first consulted Britain, rather than because he had any confidence in Badoglio.[31] He even had Stalin join him in questioning the legality of the matter under the surrender terms, but to no avail. Despite the backing of the Communists, the Committee of National Liberation excluded Badoglio from the new Cabinet, with American sanction. The United States finally beat the British in the game of Italian politics, but the British successfully insisted on vetoing the appointment of Sforza to the post of foreign minister, trying to score against America's closest friend. "He has always seemed to understand our position and I believe we could depend on him to keep us fully informed. . . ," Chapin consolingly wired Hull on June 10.[32] For the first time the Americans began to assume the lead over the British in Italian affairs.

The United States and Great Britain now entered a period of tacit competition for the predominant role in Italy. The Foreign Office urged Churchill to see the matter in the light of the much more serious threat of Communism, and not merely the future of monarchy, and at the end of

August, Churchill visited Bonomi in Rome and came away ready to work with him, but not with Sforza. From this point onward Churchill could only accommodate to a reality the United States increasingly controlled.

The fall of 1944 was a good time for America to be generous, for the November presidential election involved Italian-American voters in a significant manner, and the Administration publicized in the eastern cities of the United States all that transpired in Italy up to the first of November. Churchill and Roosevelt met in Quebec at the end of September, and over Churchill's protest the President insisted that they announce to the press a whole range of political and economic concessions to Italy. The Allies would relax military controls to an unspecified extent, grant United Nations Relief and Rehabilitation Administration (UNRRA) aid, and extend diplomatic recognition—and promised postwar aid in reconstruction. They did not mention the term "reparations," and they immediately granted a $100 million United States credit as well. The American largesse delighted the Italians and Bonomi informed Alexander C. Kirk, the American representative on the Advisory Council, that "Italy looked for guidance more to [the] United States than to any others."[33] He felt this even more strongly when Churchill decided to renege on full diplomatic recognition of Italy, causing the United States to take the step alone.

At the end of November the Bonomi government was itself in a Cabinet crisis as a result of the departure of the Nenni Socialists and the Action party over the ineffectual defascistization program, the growing role of the monarchy, and a host of pent-up issues. The Communist party remained passive throughout the crisis. More significantly, the Action and Socialist parties complained that Bonomi permitted the British to extend too great an influence over domestic affairs, and much to Washington's chagrin the once friendlier Bonomi now obeyed British dictates in organizing a new government. Churchill and the Foreign Office unsuccessfully tried to exclude Sforza, the symbol of American involvement in Italian affairs, from Bonomi's new Cabinet. Churchill regarded him as "an intriguer and mischief-maker of the first order," and Eden refused to receive communications from him for many months.[34] Kirk deplored the British intervention in the strongest terms, especially given the joint Anglo-American military operations in Italy. Edward Stettinius, the Acting Secretary of State since Hull's resignation at the end of November, instructed Ambassador Winant to remind the British that the internal affairs of Italy were not their responsibility if the new government met Italy's formal commitments. In this case, the State Department complained, the British had taken a "unilateral" step "in an area of combined responsibility." On December 5 the State Department issued a press statement saying that it did not oppose Sforza, that Italy was indeed "an area of combined responsibility," and that they expected it to work out its problems "without influence from outside."[35] Having publicly rebuked Britain, they were unwilling to go further at the time, though nine days later, after the British protested bitterly, they issued a statement of "accord" with the British over the new government.[36] Kirk, less sanguine, wired back that while the elimination of the nuisance Action party was a gain, the fact that Togliatti had become Vice-President and gained several new ministries for the Communist party would make the situation more dangerous in the future.

The British won a skirmish but lost their dominant role in Italy once and for all. The turning point came not when Sforza was the nub of the controversy, but when the Italian government acknowledged at the end of September that American economic power was critical to its immediate and postwar needs. In this area the British were simply not in a position to compete, and clever diplomacy was no substitute. The United States contributed four-fifths of the civilian relief supplies shipped to Italy, gave an enormous credit to it only a year after it left the war, and promised even more via UNRRA, for the Americans financed over two-thirds of that organization. Hull invited Italy to attend the July 1944 Bretton Woods Conference on postwar economic policy, and only British opposition prevented its participation. During the winter of 1944–1945 the Bonomi government sent an economic mission to the United States that ended in pledging support for United States peace aims for the world economy, which, as we shall see, were sharply at variance with British policies, save insofar as they expressed a preference for capitalism over socialism. In principle the United States reintegrated the first defeated Axis power into its plans for a new world economy and thereby attained an important war aim. In fact, unless Italy was prepared to go Left it could only turn to the United States for substantial postwar aid, and this Bonomi understood. In summarizing their basic policy toward Italy at the end of 1944, preparatory to the Yalta Conference, State Department planners rejected the basic assumption of British policy and formulated premises incompatible with the triumph of the Left:

> The United States does not accept the theory of economic and political "spheres of influence." While, for geographic reasons, this country's interest in Italy may not be as great as that of certain other powers, it has, nevertheless, very real interest in the development of normal and mutually profitable trade relations, in the protection of American property and investments in Italy and in insuring that Italy becomes a positive force for peace and cooperation in the post-war world.[37]

Winds from the North: The Resistance, 1944–1945

The Resistance during the last half of 1944 and beginning of 1945 created both a threat and an attraction to the Anglo-American military leaders. Armed and in Allied-controlled areas they posed a threat, and here the Allies followed a definite policy of disarmament. In the north, however, their ever-growing ranks offered very real military advantages, and the two allies pursued a policy of selective aid, political negotiations, and planned control upon liberation. When it became clear the Partisans could no longer aid the Western forces, the Anglo-American leaders imposed decisive controls, and political considerations became the almost exclusive criterion of Western policy. Despite great anxieties among the British and American political officers, they implemented their entire strategy with surprising ease.

To the Allied soldiers reaching the Rome region the experience was strange indeed. Armed Italians, often in red shirts, waving revolutionary banners, greeted them, frequently after they had set up their own local administrations. The Allied armies pushed some Partisans aside, and even threatened them with the firing squad; they arrested many and threw them into prisons. "The problem is a novel one and is bound to be met with in further intensity the further north the advance goes," one political officer reported in June, and whether these men were elected or not, Anglo-American officers decided, the Partisans would have to place themselves under occupation authority. The basic policy urged "tact and sympathy" but the Partisans were to surrender their arms; if possible, employment was to be found for former "patriots," as the military authorities preferred calling them. Indeed, the Occupation followed the carrot and stick policy, those Partisans refusing to hand in arms facing prison, those cooperating being given special food rations and, if available, jobs, though not usually in the army and rarely in the police. Unemployed, the Partisan was a "menace," armed a danger: "One thinks of the troubles of Yugoslavia and Greece in this connection," one regional commander observed to his colleagues. By September 1944, however, Western experts decided that the Partisans were returning an insufficient quantity of arms—the amount outstanding was unknown—and that "a firmer attitude must be adopted."[38] At the same time, they acknowledged widespread ex-Partisan dissatisfaction with rations and employment as justified, and made greater efforts to satisfy their needs.

The problem of the Resistance, the Western leaders understood by the end of summer 1944, was not in controlling that small part of it liberated in the Rome area, but in reducing the potential danger that the very much larger groups still on Nazi-held territory posed. Throughout the summer they sharply reduced the quantity of arms dropped to the Resistance, which had never been substantial in the first place. For purely military reasons—the Resistance was tying down as many as fourteen Axis divisions at one time—the Anglo-American authorities renewed sending in a somewhat greater quantity at the end of September, but OSS agents in Partisan territory were able to have non-Communist Partisans receive first priority. Then, when the Allied military decided the Italian campaign had gone as far as it might for the winter and should not detract from the war in Western Europe, it was possible to regard the problem of the Resistance as mainly political. With constant references to Greece, Yugoslavia, and the threat of Bolshevism everywhere, the military authorities embarked on a Resistance policy that was both military and political in its dimensions.

On November 13, General Alexander, Supreme Allied Commander in the Mediterranean, broadcast a message to the Resistance urging them, in light of winter conditions, not to engage in large-scale military operations, to save their supplies and await orders, and restrict their activities to smaller operations. To the Germans it was a notice that the Allies would not initiate a winter campaign, freeing the Nazis for other tasks, including greater efforts in wiping out the Partisans. The Resistance was demoralized and significantly only the Communist leaders in the north attempted to paint the best possible face on Alexander's message. The Germans and fascists were now in a position to consolidate their power, and a widespread hunt resulted in an unprecedented elimination of Resistance leaders and members. Defections, death, and reprisals were everywhere.

The announced Allied policy was essentially political, because it was *not* followed by a reduction in arms and supply drops to the north, which, on the contrary, increased after mid-November. Then why did Alexander free the Germans from doubt about Allied intentions? Perhaps it was merely innocent stupidity, but one can hardly ignore that its consequences were purely political and fit neatly into an effort to bring the Resistance into line. The CLNAI, the political arm of the Resistance in the north, was now under terrific military pressure; it was desperately in need; the Allies and the Badoglio government were willing and able to help it, but at a very stiff political price.

The political advisers on the Allied Commission understood that the CLNAI would become "a separate independent government" upon liberation, and that it was crucial to "allow both AMG and the Italian Government absolute freedom of administrative and political action on the liberation of this area." This question, in fact, was the one most likely to move the Resistance to act to take power, especially if there was a speedy German withdrawal and the CLNAI was able to take administrative reins before Allied troops entered—"a situation not unlike that which exists in Greece today."[39]

Until December 1944 the CLNAI never resolved its relationship to the government and the Bonomi government treated it merely as the directing organization of the Resistance in the north. The Action and Socialist parties, however, wished the CLN to form the basis of a reconstructed political order, the local CLN's to name local officials—a form of workers' councils. Throughout 1944 the CLNAI leaders debated these issues, which were reflected in the Bonomi Cabinet crisis of November 1944, and the Communists consistently avoided endorsing the radical position.

On December 7 the representatives of the hard-pressed CLNAI and the Allied Commission met in Rome and signed a secret agreement, "the Protocols of Rome," that makes the subsequent tale of the Italian Resistance almost anticlimactic. In return for the promise of financial subsidies, food, clothing, and arms, the CLNAI agreed to subordinate itself to the Supreme Allied Commander, not to appoint a military head of the CLNAI unacceptable to him, to hand over power to the Allied military government upon its arrival in the north, and to follow the orders of the military government before and after liberation. "At one point we asked ourselves if we should sign," one of the Resistance delegates recalled. "But we signed."[40] The Allies obtained assurances from the Resistance that it would not create a revolution.

Later in the month the still unsettled issue of the precise relationship of the CLNAI to the Bonomi government arose as well, and on December 26, after the British threatened a total break, the CLNAI agreed to recognize the political supremacy of the Rome government and act only as its military "delegate" and representative in occupied territory. Having brought the Resistance into line in principle, the Allies now moved to weaken it in fact, for they never trusted the CLNAI and the Protocols were merely a starting point for destroying it. The Communists, though now comprising over a majority of the Partisans, of course received only two-fifths of the delivered funds. Robert Murphy and his British counterpart, Harold Macmillan, at the end of January 1945 stressed that, agreements aside, "Speed in getting ourselves firmly established is the essential factor: without this there is real danger of extreme Communist elements taking control. . . ."[41] How to take physical possession of northern Italy was to become one of the most critical problems facing the Anglo-American leaders, for revolution in the wake of fascism was for them merely the prospect of a Pyrrhic victory.

FRANCE: AMERICAN POLICY AND THE AMBIGUITIES OF REALITY

NO POLITICAL QUESTION proved as divisive to the Anglo-American alliance as that of France. Deprived of political content, the issue of whether to support the Vichy government in France, Darlan and Giraud in North Africa, or De Gaulle in preference to them all, [historians have invariably interpreted as a disagreement with the British over military expediency or the unique personality of De Gaulle himself. In reality it was a question of whether France should be weak or strong after the war, and how it would align itself in the world power structure.]

The United States, Vichy, and Great Britain

When France fell in June 1940, the political composition of the government the Germans tolerated in Vichy under Marshal Henri Philippe Pétain was right wing and anti-British, and so anti-Soviet as quickly to become pro-German. It could hardly have been otherwise, given Germany's war with England and its military ability to conquer the rest of France at will. In return the Germans permitted the forces of the French Old Order around Pétain, composed of most of the military and an important sector of the banking and industrial community, to rule southern France and the French overseas possessions free from the specter of the United Front of the Left and the chronic instability of republican politics.

The British were at war with Germany and at near war with Vichy France. During 1940 and 1941 they blockaded North Africa and imposed trade controls in a manner that irritated the State Department and especially Admiral William D. Leahy, the United States ambassador to Vichy until April 1942. The Americans insisted on the right to export to French North Africa, under the governorship of Admiral François Darlan, and in February 1941 Robert D. Murphy, the State Department's specialist on France, concluded an agreement with Vichy—the Murphy-Weygand Agreement—that gave America a distinctive position in the French North African economy for the first time. The British could only protest any such aid to a tacit ally of Germany, however carefully defined in its use, and well before United States entry into the war or the appearance of De Gaulle as an influential figure, the British and Americans went their separate ways on France. Leahy formed a favorable impression of Pétain and Darlan, and especially of Maxime Weygand, the anti-British former hero of World War I. He and Murphy believed they could work with Vichy, and Leahy's special, intimate relationship to Roosevelt, especially after he became the chief of staff to the President, was always significant in the determination of subsequent policy. During mid-1941 the United States courted Weygand, not only because he wished to keep France from becoming a more active ally of Germany, which would have meant open war with Britain, but also as a possible future charismatic leader of Vichy and all France—and an alternative to the obviously rising star of Colonel Charles de Gaulle in London.

A prime objective of both United States and British policy was, of course, to keep France out of the war, and at the beginning of 1942 Roosevelt informed Vichy, as William L. Langer's official account puts it, "that the President was about the best friend the French had, and that one of his most cherished wishes was to see France restored to the splendid position she had enjoyed throughout history. This meant also the French Empire."[1] Cooperation with the Axis implied risking all this. Vichy realists did not need Roosevelt's messages to understand it was safer to remain neutral than attempt to rally a disaffected, hostile French nation to a course that might only lead to revolution. During the first ten months of 1942 Vichy remained loyal to its treaty of cooperation with Germany and studiously avoided as much offense as possible to the Americans. The British, by contrast, still regarded all of Vichy's leaders with contempt.

In the fall of 1942 the United States' Vichy policy became a matter of central concern as it prepared for the invasion of French North Africa at the beginning of November. Would the French military forces there resist, cooperate, or remain neutral? Darlan, whom Leahy described as "a complete opportunist," was nominally Vichy's representative in North Africa, but in reality fully capable of deciding his own policy.[2] Darlan had been a passionate Anglophobe since the Washington Disarmament Conference of 1922, when he believed the British attempted to subordinate French naval power to their own. He cooperated with the Nazis as much as any Vichy leader save Pierre Laval. During October and early November—the invasion of North Africa began November 8 with only the assured aid of the local underground—American General Mark Clark and Murphy in secret negotiations with various Vichy leaders moved to win the acquiescence, if not the support, of the French military in North Africa. Among others, they approached General Henri Giraud, a former military hero in hiding in the south of France, and obtained his legitimation of the invasion as a foil to Darlan, should he refuse to cooperate. The Americans obtained Giraud's cooperation without consulting the English—in return for the promise that the invasion would involve only American troops, and would include southern France as well as North Africa. The United States chose Giraud for the role, although he had no legal authority whatsoever, in order to create a political hero capable of offsetting the now ascendant figure of De Gaulle. They only vaguely defined his immediate duties.

Winning Darlan's backing was more difficult, despite Murphy's pledge of future American support for the empire. If the French authorities in North Africa did not resist the Anglo-American invasion neither did they make efforts to prevent the Germans from taking Tunis and Bizerta, and only on November 19 did they begin attempting to stop the German advance. Darlan watched the war for over two weeks, then negotiated terms with the Americans, and on November 22 signed an agreement to support the Allied cause in return for their respecting his civil authority and officials in North Africa and outfitting his military forces. Had they not concluded such an agreement, as Washington publicly rationalized the "Darlan Deal," they would have had to fight the French as well, a justification based on the assumption the French soldiers could and would fight for the Nazis. By early October, however, American military authorities privately operated on the well-founded supposition that the French were not going to resist, and the Allies were to treat them as friends.

The British were delighted the Americans had assumed primary land responsibility for a campaign that was British in conception, but despite the random citations that the defenders of the Darlan policy offered to the contrary, Britain wanted no political arrangements in North Africa which detracted from the authority of De Gaulle's French National Committee in London. The Foreign Office silently viewed North African political developments with distaste, for Darlan "was incurably anti-British," just as De Gaulle was a "British-sponsored leader," according to Leahy. Eden described Darlan and Giraud as ". . . turncoats and blackmailers."[3] During September and October the British and the American OSS recommended greater cooperation with De Gaulle and the Free French, but the matter was blocked because the State Department and Joint Chiefs of Staff treated De Gaulle as a British ploy. In the end De Gaulle learned of the invasion over the radio. Giraud, and perhaps Darlan, provided the Americans with an alternative.

Darlan, however, was assassinated on December 24, hardly a month after his agreement with the Americans. Now the allegedly right-wing assassin, who was hastily put to death before his motives might have been thoroughly explored, solved somewhat the question of alternatives to working with the representatives of Vichy. When the Vichy-appointed Imperial Council met to designate Darlan's successor they passed over their preferred candidate when Eisenhower, acting on instructions from Roosevelt, insisted they choose Giraud instead. The American-sponsored leader of France was now in power and master of the French overseas empire not in Axis hands. But the regime that Darlan created and Giraud continued proved strikingly unsuccessful in winning the allegiance of Frenchmen. Even after his treaty with the Americans, Darlan considered his authority derived from his relationship with Vichy and Pétain, and he considered himself, as did the majority of his subordinates, a part of Pétain's "National Revolution." "Even the Kingpin [Giraud]," Eisenhower reported to the Joint Chiefs in mid-November, "who has been our most trusted adviser and staunchest friend . . . clearly recognizes this overpowering consideration and has drastically modified his own ambitions and intentions accordingly."[4]

The Darlan and Giraud regimes, therefore, were neofascist in character, supported by the colons and the local bankers and industrialists. At first their internal policies deeply disturbed the Joint Chiefs who along with the Office of War Information asked Eisenhower why "Fascist organizations continue their activities and victimize our former French sympathizers some of whom have not yet been released from prisons," and "French soldiers [were] being punished for desertion because they tried to support the Allied Forces during the landing."[5] The Giraud regime kept anti-Semitic laws on the books and arrested Gaullists, and outraged United States Psychological Warfare Branch members began leaking honest accounts to the press that gave the Germans much propaganda material. "The resistance movements in all the occupied countries. . . ," according to Bruce Lockhart, head of British Political Warfare, "were horrified. . . ."[6] Then, the following January, while Roosevelt was in Casablanca, the Algiers government announced that Marcel Peyrouton was returning to become Governor General of Algeria, and the allies of De Gaulle obtained the support of many new Frenchmen in North Africa. To Giraud, Peyrouton was a representative of order, but he had also been the Vichy Minister of Interior in charge of political arrests and enforcement of anti-Semitic laws. The State Department approved the appointment, and Eisenhower and Murphy obtained Roosevelt's support as well. Eisenhower's private justification revealed the basis of American policy: ". . . there is a great paucity of qualified men to fill the highly specialized posts. . . . Abrupt, sweeping or radical changes, bringing into office little known or unqualified administrators, could create serious difficulties for us." He could not make decisions "on the basis of prejudice or past political affiliations in France," but "Any Gaullist was considered as impossible, being regarded as too extreme by leaders of the French armed forces." Besides, Eisenhower concluded, "The only active dissatisfaction may be presumed to be among the Gaullists and left wing groups which in North Africa however plentiful do not constitute an organized body capable of running a government."[7] Try though it might to change its image, such policies soon lost the Giraud government its major backing in North Africa, save from the Americans.

Most American historians of this period have never studied Giraud except in the context of his pro-Americanism. But the subtleties of the man's ideology reveal something of the larger politics of the region and period as well as the reasons for Eisenhower's eulogy of him. Was Giraud merely a convenient accident, a general beyond politics?

The essence of Giraud's position might be stated as "Vichy without Germany." Giraud was the leading spokesman for a group of conservative officers and industrialists who were both strong nationalists and opposed to the undisciplined politics of prewar France. They approved of Pétain's "National Revolution," with its idealization of the state and its chief, and Giraud publicly defended Pétain and Vichy but hoped they would also fight if Germany invaded Vichy France. Some of his important supporters were anti-Vichy, or more particularly anti-Darlan, but since the entire tendency was committed to a thoroughgoing Anglophobia they refused to cooperate with De Gaulle. Reactionary and antirepublican, Giraud naturally saw his regime in North Africa as a refinement and continuation of Vichy. He and his followers viewed international Communism as the great postwar danger after the desired defeat of Germany, and therefore they soon oriented themselves toward the United States. By being anti-British and anti-German, as well as opposed to the Left, Giraud was a most useful ally for the United States. But since he represented the traditional French Right, which had barely any future in 1943 even with American backing, it was not long before French conservatives considered De Gaulle, who also shared many of the ideological tenets of antirepublican nationalism, as a more viable opponent to the rising Left.[8]

Giraud's politics were well known to many of the Americans working with him, and they regarded him as a useful antidote both to the British-dominated De Gaulle and the Left. Eisenhower was aware of his devotion to Pétain and Vichy, and Hopkins noted "he is a Royalist, and is probably a right-winger in all his economic views. . . ."[9] A French industrialist, Jacques Lemaigre-Dubreuil, who was a leader of *Giraudisme* and had been in close contact with Robert Murphy since 1940, carried on the crucial preliminary negotiations with Giraud for Murphy.

The United States found ample reason to fear De Gaulle, and even as late as February 1944, Leahy advocated leaving Pétain as head of France after D-Day. De Gaulle's relations with the Communists, while perhaps more correct than cordial during the period 1942–1943, nevertheless posed difficult questions. Would the Communists use De Gaulle, or could he bend them to his own purposes? This distinct anxiety was not rooted out until after D-Day, and several feeble but carefully noted discussions between De Gaulle and various Russian diplomats before 1944 only heightened it. Much more important, in the eyes of the Americans, was the certain fact De Gaulle was a British tool.

By January 1943 it seemed to Washington that De Gaulle was apparently going to become stronger before he became weaker, and the Americans formulated their policy for the next year amidst a rising tide of support for the head of the National Committee. All of the major underground parties in France endorsed the committee, and the vast majority of French soldiers and citizens in North Africa, and a growing number of colons, were pro-De Gaulle by mid-1943. "But we must realize that the British Foreign Office will persist in its buildup of General de Gaulle," the United States embassy in London informed Hull at the beginning of January. "If de Gaulle is a 'symbol' to the people of France, he is also a 'symbol' to the British Government, a symbol of justification for its whole French policy since June 1940."[10] And, implicitly, he was also a test of the success of a very different American policy since 1940.

The split in United States-British policy on Darlan, Giraud, and De Gaulle almost immediately became a matter of widespread public discussion, and the British ambassador to Washington, Viscount Halifax, on January 5 approached Hull about the fact and its possible consequences. The British support of De Gaulle, Hull regretfully informed Halifax, "will soon create enough differences between our two countries. . . ." To the British, according to the American embassy, De Gaulle was a "Rightist" with sympathy from leftists.[11] Murphy in particular, perhaps because Harold Macmillan, the British political representative, informed him of the vast sums the British government provided the penniless De Gaulle, saw the problem as one of containing the British use of the general, "Britain's chosen instrument."[12] To solve the problem he and Eisenhower devised a formula to merge the Imperial Council in Algiers and the London Committee, with De Gaulle and Giraud as joint heads. Under terrific pressure from Churchill to meet with Roosevelt, and Giraud and himself at Casablanca at the end of January, De Gaulle—with the secret backing of the Foreign Office—refused the terms and would only consent to pose with Giraud before photographers. With time working for him, De Gaulle could wait.

By May 1943 the United States, Britain, and De Gaulle could no longer leave this tension unresolved. De Gaulle had been increasing his following in North Africa, agitation and intrigue was rampant, and at the end of March, when De Gaulle attempted to meet Giraud to negotiate an agreement that was clearly going to be more advantageous than Murphy's earlier proposal, American authorities refused him entry into North Africa. Eden, while in Washington during mid-March, had attempted to talk amicably to Hull and Roosevelt about the matter, but instead they quibbled over who should administer French territory after liberation. "It seemed to me," Eden recalled, "that Roosevelt wanted to hold the strings of France's future in his own hands so that he could decide that country's fate."[13] Washington had the same suspicion of British intentions, and by this time Hull detested De Gaulle, an attitude he held as long as he was Secretary of State. Any merger between De Gaulle and Giraud, Hull warned, would have to avoid taking on the appearance of a government-in-exile that De Gaulle might then impose on France after the war.

Then, in early May, Churchill came to Washington and debated the French crisis at length, with growing acrimony. ". . . the conduct of the Bride," as Roosevelt wrote Churchill in a contemptuous note on De Gaulle, "continues to be more and more aggravated. His course and attitude is well nigh intolerable. . . . he has the Messianic complex." And then, pointedly, Roosevelt held the British responsible. "Unfortunately, too many people are catching on to the fact that these disturbances are being financed in whole or in part by British Government funds." Yet Hull demanded an even stronger protest to the British. ". . . the French situation has come to a head and we must take a definite position that will determine the future of this controversy which, although outwardly between two French factions, may, if permitted to continue, involve both the British and American Governments in difficulties. I say this because the issue at stake is not only the success of our future military operations, but the very future of France itself." De Gaulle "has permitted to come under his umbrella all the most radical elements in France."[14] He was agitating in North Africa. The British could stop it all by cutting off De Gaulle.

Hull had an opportunity himself to present these thoughts to Churchill, and the Prime Minister for a moment seemed receptive. He praised the American policy toward Vichy, claimed personally to be utterly disgusted with De Gaulle, and then feinted back by urging the Americans not to support Giraud to the point "of engaging in a quarrel with De Gaulle and the British."[15] Hull concluded he had not made any special impression on Churchill, and urged Roosevelt to consider a total break with the British on the question and to support Giraud in every way.

Hull had impressed Churchill, however, and the gravity of American warnings caused him, at least for several days, to balance the value of the alliance with the United States against British policy toward Europe. But Eden and the Foreign Office quickly got him back into line, for, as we shall see, the Foreign Office especially considered De Gaulle to be worth the risk of a split in the alliance.

As a result, De Gaulle and Giraud then resumed the stalled negotia-

tions, on June 3 they announced the formation of the French Committee
of National Liberation (CNL), with themselves as co-presidents, to manage
French participation in the war. In fact the new committee also assumed
the powers and structure of a government-in-exile. De Gaulle, Churchill
consoled Roosevelt, will be in a minority in the committee's leadership,
and for the next several weeks he and Halifax moved to reassure the
Americans that they would reduce their very substantial subsidies to De
Gaulle. Yet De Gaulle only regarded his agreement with Giraud as a
starting point for replacing Vichy in North Africa altogether. While Churchill attempted to soothe, De Gaulle openly plotted, and since most Frenchmen were with him he was in a position to press his advantage. Roosevelt
was furious: "I am fed up with DeGaulle," he wrote Churchill on June 17,
"and the secret personal and political machinations of that Committee in
the last few days indicates that there is no possibility of our working with
DeGaulle."[16] To Eisenhower he cabled that no one could question the
supremacy of his authority, that he should give no arms to any military
bodies not recognizing it, and in the future not permit "any Government or
Committee" to rule France over the Allied military government until such
time as the French people elected it.[17] The obliqueness of the reference
was not very subtle, and for the next month Churchill continued to urge
Roosevelt not to upset the Giraud-De Gaulle agreement, which most surely
would control the enthusiastic General's impulses. At the beginning of July
the State Department invited Giraud to Washington to be ostentatiously
feted as the leader of Free France, and on the last day of the month De
Gaulle reorganized the CNL by giving Giraud an impressive new title
totally devoid of power and assuming for himself effective control of the
CNL as a political body. Giraud was increasingly isolated as De Gaulle
altered the structure of decision-making in the CNL, and on November 10
he resigned and withdrew from politics entirely.

The State Department and Roosevelt watched these later developments
in distress, quite powerless to sway either the resolute British or De Gaulle.
The British, seeking to consolidate De Gaulle's power vis-à-vis the United
States, attempted to extract "recognition" of the Algiers body, but Roosevelt preferred "limited acceptance" of its civil authority in various colonies
on a temporary basis. "After prolonged discussions of a laborious character," Churchill dolefully reported from the Quebec Conference at the end
of August, both governments agreed to choose their own wording and
intention in recognizing the CNL on August 26.[18] "At some moments the
conversation had become a trifle sharp. . . ," Hull later recalled.[19] They
became even sharper later, as the full magnitude of the issues involved
became more apparent.

A Western European Bloc

Why was Great Britain willing to alienate its most powerful ally on behalf of a man who was at the time totally dependent on whatever aid and sustenance England chose to give him, a man whose manners and illusions even Churchill found difficult to tolerate? Conversely, why should the United States risk so much to build an alternative to De Gaulle, even if it meant working with semifascist governments and groups? [Neither simple military expediency nor the clash of personalities reveals the only explanation which would satisfy the major actors in the drama,] who could only obliquely refer to the realities at the time for fear of revealing a fundamental split in the alliance over the type of postwar world each wished to see evolve, and their disagreements on the political objectives of the war.

Since 1942 Eden and the Foreign Office, the very group in British politics that several times kept Churchill from accommodating himself to American policy toward De Gaulle, had been considering the role of British power in the postwar world. There was no question in Eden's mind at that time, or later, that Britain's future in global politics would depend on the situation in Europe, but that Great Britain alone could not equal the influence and power of the United States or Russia in Europe or elsewhere. ". . . it will give us more authority with the other great Powers if we speak for the Commonwealth and for our near neighbors in Western Europe," he told the House of Commons in September 1944. "In the company of these Titans, Britain apart from the rest of the Commonwealth and Empire, could hardly claim equal partnership," Halifax, Ambassador to the United States, had stated earlier that year. ". . . Western Europe, as never before, will look to her for leadership and guidance."[20] [As part of a Western European bloc, of which Britain would naturally be the leader, the United Kingdom might speak as an equal to anyone in the postwar world. To implement such a policy it needed friendly governments in Western Europe willing to cooperate, and France was the crucial link in the entire project.]

The smaller Western European governments-in-exile were enthusiastic proponents of the Western European bloc concept, and Norwegian Foreign Minister Trygve Lie and Belgian Foreign Minister Paul Henri Spaak from 1942 on publicly made such an alliance, referred to as a military and economic union at times, the objective of their policy as well. The Dutch also agreed, and European Social Democrats especially favored the scheme.

The assumption of this bloc strategy in relation to America was, as Eden wrote in July 1942, that "we should always consult the U.S. Government, but our object should be to bring them along with us. They know very little of Europe and it would be unfortunate for the future of the world if U.S. uninstructed views were to decide the future of the European continent." In brief, the Foreign Office explicitly detailed, Britain would follow a Europe-first policy. As Eden wrote a year later after a bitter debate in Washington over De Gaulle, and much had transpired in regard to the Americans:

> These arrangements will be indispensable for our security whether or not the United States collaborate in the maintenance of peace on this side of the Atlantic.
> Our whole policy toward France and Frenchmen should therefore be governed by this consideration. . . . In dealing with European problems of the future we are likely to have to work more closely with France even than with the United States, and while we should naturally concert our French policy so far as we can with Washington, there are limits beyond which we ought not to allow our policy to be governed by theirs. . . .
> Europe expects us to have a European policy of our own, and to state it. That policy must aim at the restoration of the independence of the smaller European allies and of the greatness of France. . . .[21]

The instrument for implementing this policy, a Western European bloc with vaguely defined economic and political functions, the British in fact publicly endorsed again and again, and any keen analyst could deduce the political logic of it at the time. In March 1943 Churchill publicly discussed the desirability "of groupings of States or confederations," later of a "Europe truly united," and Eden did likewise. De Gaulle fully subscribed to this policy no later than March 1944, when he publicly endorsed the "renovation" of the Continent via "a sort of Western European grouping," especially an economic one, and later he simply used the term "bloc."[22] De Gaulle understood very clearly that British advocacy of his cause was based on this diplomatic strategy, and he could not afford to forget it. In return England became the spokesman for the illusion of France being a Great Power in the hope of ultimately making it one, or at least bringing a restored France into the British orbit. Britain therefore became the ardent and consistent advocate of French equality in the United Nations, its rearmament, restoration of its colonies, a zone for France in Germany, and the like. France, in brief, was to serve Britain as China was to serve the United States—a ploy in the postwar world of alliances and blocs.

The Americans understood these implications, and therefore they hoped to stop De Gaulle's rise to power. When John Foster Dulles was in London in July 1942 on a semi-official tour, he told Eden the Americans would not welcome a bloc of lesser states concentrated around a Great Power. ". . . the British wanted to build up France into a first class power, which would be on the British side," Roosevelt observed on his way to

Teheran in November 1943, and the State Department certainly viewed the problem in this light as well.[23] Throughout 1944 the President accepted this understanding of basic policy differences on France as well as the future of Europe, and whether it should be strong or weak, which was to say pro-English or pro-American. Eden rightly felt the United States was "suspicious" of their bloc scheme, but during July 1944 he nevertheless informed Hull that Britain would initiate discussions with various Western Europe nations concerning matters of joint defense, discussions which obviously had deeper political and economic implications. When Eden, Spaak, Lie, and the Dutch Foreign Minister, Eelco van Kleffens, met to consider this matter, they did so with the growth of Soviet power in mind as well, and although the formal justification for a bloc was to prevent future German aggression, the Russian problem was an articulated consideration also. The result of the conference was that military and technical arrangements rather than a comprehensive treaty were accepted for the moment, with stress on rearmament, and they duly notified the Americans and Russians, always giving Germany as the vindication. Then, at the end of November, Spaak presented the British with a proposal for a "West European Regional Entente," and for the time Churchill and Eden decided to wait before pressing forward in even greater detail with their plan. At that point the three Allies were organizing the Yalta Conference and planning the United Nations Conference, and perhaps the results of those conferences might make superfluous something more elaborate than the existing Western European understanding. Moreover, relations with De Gaulle had taken a temporary turn for the worse at the end of 1944 as a result of Anglo-French clashes over predominance in Syria, though the General's loyalty to the scheme did not waver. For the moment, at least, the matter was held in abeyance.

The British had several other reasons for going more slowly with their plans. They clashed with the Americans over the prerequisite for such a bloc, a France led by De Gaulle, and during 1944 the Americans were suspicious of their intentions. In May 1944 the United States Joint Chiefs of Staff had considered the proposed bloc and rejected it, for fear it would lead the Russians to create one of their own—a thought that occurred to the pro-bloc British Joint Chiefs several months later—and set off a chain of events over which the Americans would have no control. The following November the United States moderated its position, favoring rearmament of the Dutch and Belgians for the postwar period, the possible Russian response becoming less of a consideration.[24] To the extent that a British-led bloc assumed the character of an economic alliance, the United States always opposed it. And to the extent that such a bloc appeared to be a common front by strong rather than weak states, Washington maintained grave reservations about the English plan. Later, when it became apparent that the weakness rather than the strength of the individual states was drawing the organization into being, the Americans were willing to consider moderating their opposition until, in the form of an American-dominated NATO, it became a pillar of anti-Russian policy.

Since the press had extensively discussed the matter, it was now necessary to ascertain Russian opinion of the project. Churchill wrote Stalin on November 25 that despite all the talk in the press about a Western bloc, "I have not yet considered this," assuring Stalin of his cordial friendship but also leaving the door open to future consideration.[25] The British ambassador in Moscow, Clark Kerr, also asked to see Molotov about the matter, comforting him by saying there was no truth to rumors the British planned to create a bloc as a balance to Russian and American power, the present discussions being only for mutual defense. Molotov asked questions and indicated his government took very great interest in the entire question. Shortly thereafter, when Stalin and De Gaulle met in Moscow, the Russians raised many pointed questions concerning the matter, and De Gaulle, like the British, was somewhat less than candid.[26]

There the matter rested preceding Yalta, with the British both seeking and hoping to restore their position of power in the postwar world of super powers. Whether the fortunes of French politics could or would allow the participation of that nation remained to be seen, but for years Britain struggled with America on behalf of a conception which revealed an alliance rent by conflicts and counterpressures.

De Gaulle versus the Left

It was painfully obvious by early 1944 that the American policy of support for Darlan and Giraud had failed, and that the real option in France was not between disaffected Vichyites and De Gaulle but between De Gaulle and the Left. The United States could work for Giraud so long as he could maintain some semblance of support, which by the end of 1943 was impossible, and as long as the game of French politics was abstract and did not involve real property, which in fact the Nazis and their associates controlled. As D-Day and June 1944 approached, the American military and political leaders had to make definite choices based on actual as opposed to desired options, for the problems of occupation and liberation were imminent. What were the choices?

Frenchmen opposed to Vichy may conveniently be divided into those outside France, such as the Free French forces and the army in Africa, and those in the interior, the French Forces of the Interior (FFI), or the Resistance. De Gaulle by mid-1943 had become the undisputed leader of the external forces, but the Resistance in France, with many tendencies, was deeply divided within itself and over De Gaulle, the most important friction being between the Communists and the non-Communists.]

Those surrounding De Gaulle were primarily military men, and their response to the Resistance within France ranged from indifference to hostility. They had no sympathy for the clandestine elements, regarded their activities as a waste of money and effort, and thought them to be of very minimal military value. Their view of war was professional, and they were convinced that an invasion based on regular military principles and tactics would liberate France, and until that moment Vichy might rule essentially undisturbed. When the time came for the invasion, De Gaulle and his associates thought, the Resistance might provide intelligence, perform acts of sabotage or the like, but they considered them too weak to play a significant military role.

Advocates of moderation, they looked with horror on the idea of a national insurrection. If this viewpoint was justified on technical grounds, it nevertheless had obvious political implications as well, for their hostility toward the Resistance ultimately reflected political considerations.

The Free French movement around De Gaulle in England, and in Algeria, was heavily drawn from patriotic officers disgusted by the defeatism of Vichy, former high functionaries in the Third Republic, and members of the upper occupational and social classes. There was no significant "Left" in this movement, but only a Center and a Right, bound together in a fragile unity the charismatic personality of De Gaulle himself cemented. Some offered purely military reasons for France's defeat, such as insufficient mobility and armor, but most had contempt for the effete politics of the Third Republic which had sapped the strength and unity of the state and paved the way for Vichy. Seemingly apolitical in this regard, [Gaullism was in reality the politics of patriotism and the state above parties, and this meant ultimately the cult of personality above partisanship.] De Gaulle's followers adored him as a man with a messianic mission to redeem France, and based their political style on a concomitant and inevitable emotionalism which made much of the "nation," "national independence," and similar traditionalist slogans of the Right. Gaullism would become a source of national renovation after the war, one that would cooperate with England in the world and work for the entire nation, above all classes, at home. The Gaullists ill concealed their hostility toward republicanism, but an advocacy of strong doses of welfarism for the masses and national economic planning usually tinged their economic ideas.

De Gaulle and his followers were strongly anti-Communist and deeply suspicious of the intentions of the U.S.S.R. in the postwar world. The British fully comprehended this, and used it to gain support for the French leader. As we shall see, De Gaulle spent much time warning the Americans of the danger of Russia, but out of necessity he worked with the Communists in France because they appeared ready to cooperate on his terms as long as he needed them. When their function ended, he quickly disciplined them. For all of these reasons—his nationalism, anti-parliamentarianism, and anti-Communism—De Gaulle from mid-1943 onward attracted many former Vichyites and silent collaborators with Vichy.[27]

Although precise figures do not exist, within France itself the Resistance groups that were Gaullist in ideology were always in a small minority. In many key parts of France they hardly existed at all. They were, for the most part, ex-officers and former rightists who had quietly watched the nationalist ideals of Pétain with some sympathy until about the end of 1942, and then turned to De Gaulle as a superior expression of their objectives. The transition in the ideas of this group ultimately made them somewhat closer to the Left than the Gaullists in exile, but they were never able to define the course of the Resistance in France itself. For most of the Resistance, De Gaulle was the leading symbol of opposition to Germany, but scarcely more than that.

The Socialists had been the party *par excellence* of the Third Republic, and their compulsive devotion to remaining in politics, even after Vichy, eventually resulted in the party's expelling two-thirds of its National Assembly members for collaboration and compromise. After 1941 the Socialists literally disappeared as a party, and only gradually began reconstituting their ranks in 1944. They were active initiators of the Resistance only in the north of France and elsewhere were secondary in importance. They soon divided on their relationship to De Gaulle, and although some of their members hoped to assume a more friendly policy toward the U.S.S.R. after the war, in France itself they early became chronic anti-Communists in a manner that did little to strengthen their following in the Resistance.[28] Unlike Italy, no Left alternative to the Communist party existed in France, and the Communist party was able to channel the trends in France toward the Left and toward the Resistance as well.

The Communists came a very long way from the period of the Hitler-Stalin Pact, when they condemned the war as an imperialist venture, to the time they were the largest and best-organized element of the Resistance. Since Vichy had already forced them underground, they entered their reformed role with an elaborate underground organization and a nucleus for expansion. Their new line was an immediate success: patriotism, if not chauvinism, merged with social reform and combined with an earnest desire to attain a United Front with all, an objective they did not waver from throughout the war and which caused them to modify their program to make it acceptable to as many Frenchmen as possible. The party ignored ideological criteria. It welcomed atheists and Catholics, and anyone else who cared to join. They were friendly to Giraud when he formed the Committee of National Liberation with De Gaulle, and even as late as May 1944 favored working with the impotent general, but they maintained an apprehensive yet essentially cooperative stance toward De Gaulle, for his hostile feelings were manifested in numerous attempts to impose control

over them via the various organs of the CNL. Ultimately they accepted his
authority, but only after much hedging and controversy.

The Communist-dominated Resistance organization, the *Francs-
Tireurs et Partisans* (FTP), was the largest and in its verbal style the most
aggressive of the various "fighting organizations," most of which did little
fighting at all until mid-1944. They were the most enthusiastic advocates of
action and deeds, and they deplored the *attentisme* so common among the
Gaullists in France. But they added one more dimension to the struggle—
the national insurrection at the critical moment as a tool of mass action.
This concept attracted many followers who saw in the FTP the most aggressive Resistance group, and many of these groups came from elements
in the south and southwest of France previously immune to Communism.
Indeed, it was not among the urban working class but among peasants and
hitherto untouched elements that the party attracted its fresh influx of
nearly 600,000 new members from 1937 until 1945. The Communist party
stressed resistance and action above divisive debates over economic and
political questions, and unity in the anti-German struggle above all. It
appealed for the support of the middle classes while its very name permitted it to retain the illusion of radicalism among the working class, it
endorsed a liberalized form of the empire in the postwar world, and became, like the Italian party, the movement that combined transcendent
nationalism and reform.[29]

The Communists did mention, when they talked about future reform at
all, the need for a regeneration of the parliamentary system, as well as a
more equitable economy and distribution of income, and of course they
strongly demanded a thoroughgoing purge of the Vichyites, but in fact they
were the party of rhetoric and the upholders of order. The Communists
participated in the Committee of National Liberation and its nominal Consultative Assembly. Technically, at least, the FTP, which was the military
arm of their *Front National,* was responsible to the command structure of
the CNL, which ultimately meant De Gaulle. This integration was essential
to the policy of a United Front, and though there was much quibbling over
the rights of the various component organizations of the CNL, the Communist party accepted the basic principle of responsibility to De Gaulle by
April 4, 1944, when the Communist party entered the CNL.

Aside from the Communists, who were the largest single faction, the
Socialists, and the major organized bodies, there were numerous smaller
groups and sects, and of course, the *maquis,* essentially unarmed noncooperators in southern forests and something quite apart from the Resistance. In fact it is essential to remember the Resistance in France was
beyond any single group, including the Communists, and what its participants held in common was ultimately more important than what divided
them. The Resistants shared a spirit of defiance toward the Germans and a
contempt for the corrupt Old Order that had brought France to collabora-

tion and defeat. The French suffered humiliation at the hands of invaders and their own leaders, their economy had broken down during the 1930's, and every Frenchman who was sensitive enough to have insight desired a thoroughgoing change in the Old Order and a purging redemption via resistance. It was not so much a question of defeating Germany, which was always critical, but of saving France, and of saving the humanity of France by building anew and smashing the shell of the old. The urgency of this feeling was so overwhelming that the French Resistance fought the war until 1944 with pens and printing presses rather than bullets. And the growing realization of their own impotence and the futility of words as the war was coming to an end in France ultimately had the greatest consequences when the Resistance in Paris, the heart and inspiration of the movement, sought to atone for its passivity and give meaning and life to its words and promises by acting in an essentially irrational and heroic manner.

There was, as French historian Adrien Dansette has put it, a mystique of the Resistance born of its secret life. The Resistants saw themselves as revolutionaries purifying their consciences, France, and justice. And so long as the Resistance concentrated on mysticism rather than politics, new bureaucrats and even some of the old could not brusquely shatter its dream in the underground. In a brilliant and prodigious press, written in the inimitable elegance of classic French style, articulate with ideas but relatively silent with guns before spring 1944, the Resistance possessed eloquence and pathos in its impotence, but it held out the promise, and threat, of action. France had known such action over half a century before—in the Commune—and the Resistance, even with only its press, struck the same terror into the hearts of the French elite as had the armed workers during the Commune in 1871, when respectable society worked with Germany as they did in 1942. At a critical juncture in French history the patriotism of the propertyless challenged the international solidarity of the Right. This class of Resistants justified itself by references to both the flag and equality, a tension that might lead to the necessity of choosing one or the other. The Communist party captured the preeminent position within the Resistance and channeled to itself this vast upsurge of new commitment. Now the question was whether the Resistance would act, and if so how.

The English and the Americans asked this question. So too did De Gaulle, for his control over the Resistance in France was insecure.

The United States and the Resistance, 1944

By the end of 1943 and beginning of 1944 the United States no longer had a coherent policy on French affairs, but only a series of impressionistic responses and hunches about the future which Leahy generally provided. Leahy at the end of 1943 managed to convince the always receptive

Roosevelt that there would be civil war in France upon liberation, probably between De Gaulle and Vichy, but perhaps between De Gaulle and everyone else, and that the rearmament of De Gaulle's army would only feed this vicious situation. "France is a British 'baby,'" Roosevelt impetuously declared. "[The] United States is not popular in France at the present time. The British should have France [as an occupation zone]. . . ."[30] His advisers immediately brought him back into line.

The questions the Americans and British had to resolve at the beginning of 1944 centered about rearmament and the projected occupational government after D-Day—whether an Anglo-American military government would rule France as they did enemy Italy—and the latter problem involved, in turn, the status of the Committee of National Liberation and whether the Anglo-Americans would permit De Gaulle to extend his control over France. The rearmament issue was straightforward. The United States favored the rearmament of the French army in North Africa when it was seemingly under the control of Giraud, but when De Gaulle took over, the Americans decided to delay shipments for fear De Gaulle intended to use the army merely to consolidate his power in France. During 1943 the British supplied the Resistance—the FFI—and the somewhat different *maquis*, though under carefully circumscribed conditions. The quantity and quality of arms dropped into France made it impossible for the FFI to plan for more than sabotage, and at no time did they supply the Resistance in urban areas in a way that would eliminate the possibility of later conventional military conquest of cities. The *maquis* in the south and southwest of France, which never attained a strength of more than 15,000 in each of its three major areas of operation—about 50,000 for all France in the fall of 1943—they supplied somewhat more generously, for this group was initially mainly nonpolitical. They were noncooperators rather than Resistants, chiefly youths who would not accept compulsory labor in Germany, various refugees, escaped prisoners of war, and the like. In isolated mountainous regions of no military or political significance, they were unable to acquire the rudiments of guerrilla warfare until many disastrous military experiences taught them better. The Communists had some contempt for the *maquis* until the end of the war, for the *maquis* was the least ideological and the least controllable for most of the war, when they too·began moving toward the left.[31]

By early 1944 both the British and Americans saw the question of supplying the Resistance in France itself as an issue of prestige, and on this basis the Joint Chiefs and State Department urged American drops as well. By June 1944, when the Western generals thought the estimated 200,000 FFI fighters in France would be of military value, the United States had become the major arms supplier, though never in sufficient quantities to permit large, independent Resistance operations. And they never knowingly sent arms to urban and Communist-controlled groups.

Occupation policy for liberated France was much more complicated, for De Gaulle urgently wished to have final American recognition of the CNL as the provisional government of France, thereby consolidating his power once and for all. The State Department and Joint Chiefs were quite prepared to use a French civil administration insofar as was possible, but under the final authority of the Supreme Allied Commander, Eisenhower. They quite rightly suspected the British of attempting to extend political recognition to the CNL as part of a civil affairs agreement, and as D-Day approached there was a flurry of efforts to weld the Allies together before the great trial by arms. De Gaulle and the CNL were entirely uncooperative, insisting that any agreement they make be with the Allied governments themselves—which implied recognition—rather than the Combined Chiefs and that they be free to dispose of their own forces "for maintenance of internal order." Washington would do no more than agree to work with the CNL on unavoidable military questions, and this remained the American position until after D-Day. At the beginning of May, Eden announced that his government would deal only with the CNL as the civil authority in France. A crisis of the first order was in the making.[32]

On May 15 the CNL voted to call itself the Provisional Government of the French Republic as of June 3, three days before OVERLORD. During all of May both the French and the Americans had declined to alter their positions substantially, and the United States refused to enter into British-sponsored negotiations on civil affairs, the question of the military cooperation of the French troops during the invasion not having posed a problem. Churchill pleaded, Winant urged a reconciliation, and Washington's vacillation continued to irritate Eisenhower, but to no avail. ". . . if anyone could give him a certificate proving that De Gaulle was a representative of the French people," Hull reports a petulant Roosevelt at the May 20 Cabinet meeting, "he would deal with him. . . ."[33] Churchill was now left with the responsibility of bring an obdurate De Gaulle back to London in the hope he would not seriously jeopardize the invasion by noncooperation. De Gaulle was officially informed of the invasion not earlier than two days before it occurred, and he immediately took exception to parts of Eisenhower's planned proclamation on D-Day, as well as the general civil affairs program. At first he refused to allow more than a handful of French liaison officers to land in Normandy, he then delayed in making a broadcast to the French people urging cooperation with the landing troops, and finally he denounced as "counterfeit" Allied franc currency printed without the consent of the Provisional Government. Churchill was furious, and the Americans were even more enraged. Then, a week later, De Gaulle returned briefly to a small corner of a liberated Normandy, where CNL authorities had begun to set up unauthorized civil administrations, and it was distressingly clear to Washington that De Gaulle would probably be able to produce a certificate of support from the French people. In mid-June, De Gaulle's representatives formally asked Washington for an invitation to visit America, and it was now obvious the United States would have not so much to reconsider its French policy as to formulate one.

There was one aspect of De Gaulle about which Washington was confident, however, and that was his position on Communism. De Gaulle himself went to great pains to get this information across, for he appreciated that the Americans might be willing to put up with a great deal to have a charismatic leader who could save France from the Left. The Americans worried about the Communists' being one of the parties of the CNL, and for this they criticized De Gaulle, but they had no doubts about the political safety of the man himself, save in relation to the British.

De Gaulle and his aides warned the Americans of the Soviet as well as the Communist menace from at least the spring of 1942 onward. De Gaulle told Winant in May 1942 that if the Russians won the war in Europe alone they would also be masters of the Continent. Under Secretary of State Sumner Welles received the thought from André Philip, De Gaulle's close adviser, that American support for Vichy risked throwing the Resistance to the Communists, a point De Gaulle sincerely believed. Murphy, one of the most sensitive Americans concerning Communism, reported to Hull in June 1943 that De Gaulle told him "the French Communist Party had by its resistance to Germany gained an important place in France and he feared that unless a capable French administration is built up in time to control the Communist element there would be grave danger of widespread violence in France after liberation. . . . in his opinion he felt he is qualified to control the French Communist Party."[34] The State Department received the same message from other observers as well, and it did not take them long to conclude that any relationship between De Gaulle and the Communist party would be strictly one of convenience and quite temporary.

The acid test of what De Gaulle would do as well as say was shown in his handling of the Corsican uprising of September 1943. The Italians garrisoning the island with 20,000 Germans had withdrawn from the occupation upon the Italian surrender, and the Communist-led local FFI attempted to take over. Soon they and French soldiers from Algeria were able to drive the Germans out and liberate the first occupied territory. On October 8, soon after the shooting had stopped, De Gaulle visited the island, pushed the Communists aside, and left his own administrators behind to run affairs entirely by themselves. By June 1944 the Americans and English needed someone who could repeat the Corsican precedent in France itself, for the FFI was in many areas on the scene before Anglo-

American troops could arrive. Many of the FFI were Communists, under the formal jurisdiction of the Provisional Government with which the Americans refused to treat. If the Americans did not like De Gaulle they preferred the Bolsheviks even less.

It was a difficult course for the Americans to follow, but there was no alternative, though they never relinquished the covert search for one. On June 8 Roosevelt confessed to Stimson that he was quite ready to hand the entire French occupation to the English, which would leave them with the problem of handling the imminent revolution Leahy kept predicting. The Secretary of War could only urge him "to think the matter over carefully," because it was "a very serious situation."[35] Stimson was anxious to inhibit Roosevelt from rash action, as he often had in the past, and had come to the conclusion De Gaulle was going to win in France and the United States could only try to make the best of it. He confided in his diary:

> . . . we really cannot stop it, and it is better not to run the risk of bickerings now which will serve not only to divide us from deGaulle but will divide us from the British who more and more are supporting deGaulle. It is this latter situation, namely the cleft between us and the British, which most alarms me. . . . This morning [June 14] a telegram came through from Marshall, King, and Arnold voicing in serious language Eisenhower's embarrassment and earnestly recommending that we and the British get together, but as yet nothing has been done to solve that deadlock. . . . Personally I have great distrust of deGaulle and I think that the President's position is theoretically and logically correct, but . . . it is not realistic.

Stimson then called Hull about the needed reconciliation with England, even if it required recognizing De Gaulle, but Hull would not hear of it, for "He hates deGaulle with such fierce feeling that he rambles into almost incoherence whenever we talk about him. . . ."[36] Roosevelt was becoming less truculent on this issue, but it was more important to win over Hull, and during the last days of June, shortly before De Gaulle himself arrived in Washington, Stimson worked on the State Department. De Gaulle was coming, he told Hull, and there was no point in swearing at him if he was willing to reach a working agreement. Above all, "we couldn't reveal to the world outside a deep cleft with the British. . . ." Hull was unmoved and could only repeat "that the whole problem of deGaulle was a British combination with him," for the postwar implications of a world of political or economic blocs disturbed Hull much more than anyone else in Washington. There the matter rested, with Stimson hopelessly trying to convince Hull that in return for United States cooperation on France we might "get a quid pro quo from U.K. in developing our policies elsewhere."[37]

It was De Gaulle himself who broke down Hull's antagonism when he arrived in Washington on July 6. "De Gaulle was now in a much more reasonable frame of mind," Hull recalled, and his conciliatory words smoothed over many difficulties.[38] Precisely what they said or promised is unknown; but on July 11 the United States recognized the CNL as the de facto civil government of France. Why the sudden change from intense hostility to somewhat more normal tolerance? It is quite possible that De Gaulle astutely discussed his relations to Britain and Russia in the same way he did when he met with Secretary of the Navy James Forrestal in Algiers on August 18. At that time the General suggested a French-American entente, since there were no conflicting or imperialist aims between the two powers, and the same could not be said of their relations with the British. Moreover, he argued, a strong France would be a barrier to the expansive designs of the Russians sure to follow in the wake of the war. Such a line, whether sincere or not—and it was not in regard to Britain— was calculated to work wonders with Hull. More likely was De Gaulle's presentation of his problems in regard to the French Communist party and the FFI and the options to his rule, for from this time until October 23, when the United States formally extended recognition to the Provisional Government itself, the United States thought of the problem of France not merely within the context of Britain but of the threat of the Communists and the Resistance, though with some idiosyncrasies and reservations. "Recognition," the American representative to the CNL told Hull, "would unquestionably strengthen standing of the Provisional Government with the populace and assist materially in its control over elements subversive of public order."[39]

The Summer of 1944

De Gaulle obtained partial recognition from the United States, and during the next few months he moved at last to obtain final obeisance from the Resistance and the various sectors of the FFI. Shortly before the invasion the Allies supplied arms to the units of the FFI in the west of France, sabotage of German supplies was widespread, and by the end of July the FFI tied down as many as eight German divisions in action, a far larger force than De Gaulle himself had in his own command. To succeed politically De Gaulle had to subordinate the Resistance to his CNL, and later, the Provisional Government.

Clandestine organizations are not easily centralized, especially if their membership ebbs and flows or is never really known. The French Resistance consisted of a series of loosely united groups, some small and a few large, and when efforts to centralize them into the National Council of Resistance (CNR) were begun in May 1943 its directors quickly discovered the CNR was hardly more than an amalgam of aspiring generals without their troops. The behest of De Gaulle's organization in London initiated the CNR, which included all the political parties in the London group and technically was subservient to it. A special bureau in London ostensibly directed the affairs of the CNR, but the professional officers who ran it had little faith in unconventional warfare and failed to develop a precise command structure over the Resistance groups to cover all contingencies. In reality the Resistance operated on the basis of its component organizations, of which the Communist-controlled FTP was the largest, or local and regional groups close enough to work with one another effectively. All, professedly, were ultimately responsible to the CNR, and above it, London, but excessive centralization was impossible because of the continuous threat of Nazi destruction of the Resistance via its crucial leaders. Decentralization was inevitable and desirable, but politically risky. At the beginning of 1944 De Gaulle and his associates moved to take over the Resistance in fact as well as theory, and by the spring De Gaulle, General Pierre Koenig, his leading military aide, and others devoted much effort to the task. The political necessity of attaining this objective before the Allies had proceeded very far was obvious, for De Gaulle did not wish to confront another government upon his return to France.

In March the CNR in exile restructured the Resistance and created a three-man committee of military action called COMAC to implement its directives within France itself. Since these three leaders, Villon, Valrimont, and Vaillant, were actually representatives of the major Resistance groups, for the next four months COMAC haggled with De Gaulle's representatives in Paris over the mutual rights and obligations of the Resistance to the CNL abroad. The issues involved were very much like those later confronting the Bonomi government and CLNAI in Italy, and so they referred them to London and the CNR in France many times. The exile group could also use the available pressures—a supply of guns and money—and the French Resistance needed both. They held over forty meetings until the matter was terminated.

COMAC immediately agreed it would fulfill all military tasks the CNL or the Allies assigned to it, but they insisted on the freedom to carry on their own operations at the same time. Soon the issue broadened to Koenig's right to appoint regional or local military commanders over the wishes of the local Resistance councils. COMAC in turn held out for more and immediate arms as well as Allied aid for the national insurrection which they hoped to organize as quickly as possible. Although such arms were never forthcoming, and those that were had value mainly for sabotage and small operations, COMAC always cited the CNL and then the Provisional Government as a source of its legitimate authority. The other power cited was the CNR within France itself, which in turn was responsible to the Provisional Government.

On June 14 Koenig issued his own orders directly to the Resistance, urging them to avoid large-scale operations and not to expect substantial arms drops, and COMAC responded by calling upon Resistants in the occupied zones to strike where the enemy was weak and to take over civil authority on a provisional basis. However, COMAC always emphasized preparations under hypothetical circumstances for a future national insurrection for which they never set a date. The critical contingency was the availability of sufficient arms, for which they continually and pathetically appealed but never received. By the end of June, though COMAC still continued to reject the centralization of all authority and activities under Koenig, they clearly had no will to act alone, and their pleas that an insurrection would have moral value could not sway De Gaulle. The only words that would persuade him were a part of an oath of obedience which was quite incompatible with action unless De Gaulle wished it, and in turn might convince the English and Americans to supply the arms.

At the beginning of July COMAC was ready to begin conceding to the demands of De Gaulle's spokesmen, and agreed that it would execute the orders of the Allied command, via Koenig, as requested. Since COMAC argued not for the Communists but with the backing of all the major Resistance groups, it was necessary for De Gaulle to seek out reliable internal supporters, and after mid-July COMAC was aware of efforts by agents of De Gaulle to recruit his own forces, especially among the police and former pro-Vichy officers in Paris and elsewhere. By that time the underground press was discussing the dispute, which made it in effect public knowledge. And having granted Koenig a first priority in orders, De Gaulle's representative then told COMAC a national insurrection was impossible and asked them to concede on all the outstanding questions: the appointment of regional officers and the application of all orders that the Allies isued via Koenig. Despite COMAC's major and growing concessions to the authority of Koenig, the Allies did not send arms to COMAC nor did they call for a national insurrection. Units of the FFI struggling against the Germans outside Paris, where the entirely unreal, theoretical debates were taking place, did so on their own initiative and usually with captured arms. Then, on August 14, when it was too late to exert its effective commandment, COMAC capsized and formally acknowledged Koenig as commander in chief of the FFI.[40] By this time it was clear that the liberation would not come from the purifying actions of France redeeming herself, but from the Anglo-American foreigners, who by now had broken out of Normandy and were moving toward Paris. The leaders of the Resistance had argued on principle, but in the end they had sacrificed even that.

The position of the Communist-dominated sections of the Resistance was fully predictable given the unwavering public position of the Communist party in favor of unity of all classes at any cost. This commitment to a national as opposed to a class uprising—a national uprising in the future rather than the present—and the repeated appeals of French Communist party secretary general Maurice Thorez's broadcasts from Moscow to aid the Anglo-American advance rather than preempt the need for it marked the Communist line throughout 1944. Unity, aid to the Allies, and an absolutely classless emphasis on moderation permeated all of Thorez's statements during the stormy summer of 1944 and thereafter, and by August, De Gaulle's political challenges rested not at home with the vast majority of Frenchmen in arms, but elsewhere—with the Americans and those they supported.[41] For the Communists had neither the inclination nor the power to impose their will on France. Only the colossal power of the American armies, buttressed by a now deeply rooted political hostility, might deprive him of ultimate success. It was to this greater danger that De Gaulle turned his attention in July and August of 1944.

Pétain and the followers of Vichy were certain their end was near, and in July, for the first time, they began openly disobeying German orders and exhibiting a patriotic fervor appropriate to the changed circumstances. In addition, or so De Gaulle was correctly convinced, various representatives of Vichy approached the OSS in Berne and learned "that Washington would favor a scheme that inclined to silence or set aside De Gaulle."[42] Via Leahy and Murphy, who had many contacts with such conservative French notables as Edouard Herriot, Henri Bonnet, Paul Faure, and lesser Vichy sympathizers, the Americans approved a plan to reconvene the National Assembly of 1940 in Paris, and in the name of the moribund Third Republic to pass power to the Provisional Government of De Gaulle in a manner designed to bind and then submerge him in the future. This project was actively under way no later than the first week of August, when leaders of Vichy, including Laval himself on the 8th, began returning to Paris to reconvene the Assembly. For the Germans too gave their approval to the scheme, having recognized their imminent need to leave Paris and preferring a form of Vichy to a strongly anti-German regime. Whether the precise allegations are true or not, McCloy had earlier warned Eden that Leahy wished to work with Pétain after OVERLORD, and many Frenchmen believed such rumors. Both De Gaulle and the Resistance were aware of the situation, for Vichy formally made the proposition no later than August 12, and this consideration became a catalyst to action—the need to take Paris before the Americans found an alternative to De Gaulle.[43]

De Gaulle also wanted to take Paris because of the uprising of August 19, and the nature and motives behind this event, the intentions as well as the effects, deserve some consideration.

The situation in Paris in the two weeks prior to the uprising was hardly propitious for a calculated revolt, but a grave condition existed which was perfect for a revolt by desperate, uncalculating men—a precondition for the very act itself. The war had entirely disrupted the food and fuel supply, and the shortage was critical, with the threat of famine if the last small trickles into the city ended. The FFI itself, which Colonel Rol-Tanguy of the Communist FTP, not COMAC, technically commanded, had little or no control over its forces, which were practically autonomous in greater Paris and had to be given orders largely by proclamations which might or might not be obeyed. In making an inventory of all their forces in Paris on the eve of the revolt the FFI counted 35,523 members, including those who had merely told friends they could count on them when the time came. This indeterminate group shared, as of mid-August, not more than 1,800 rifles, pistols, and weapons of every type, excluding what sympathetic police and gendarmerie might bring along, and the FTP accounted for approximately two-thirds of these arms. They never received guns from the Allies, who were correctly reported to be two weeks away and planning to bypass Paris and encircle it rather than engage in costly street fighting and then confront the task of supplying the population. De Gaulle himself, and Koenig as well, "considered it essential that the arms of France act in Paris before those of the Allies, that the people contribute to the invader's defeat. . . . Hence I ran the risks of encouraging the revolt without rejecting any of the influences that were capable of provoking it. It must be added that I felt myself in a position to direct the operation so that it would turn out for the best."[44] All anti-Vichy French leaders agreed upon the principle of an uprising, and only the timing was in question, for neither De Gaulle nor the Resistance wished to see the American-sponsored machinations of Vichy succeed, and the CNR had given full obeisance to the authority of De Gaulle.

Still, given Anglo-American strategy, De Gaulle was not in a position to take over Paris at the time, save by a revolt. In Paris itself an intense feeling of frustration had been building up, developing a climate for insurrection that can be meaningfully explained only in nonpolitical terms. All of Paris, excluding a few Vichyites, shared this mood to some extent. On July 14, Bastille Day, over 100,000 Parisians spontaneously demonstrated in the face of German guns, and on August 10 the railroad workers went on strike. A sense of euphoria among the local Resistance became ever greater as the Allied troops advanced. Now victory was imminent, they had yet to stop debating and to act, and soon they would lose the possibility of redeeming their integrity and commitment—and staking a moral claim—as a result of the *attentisme* they had denigrated around café tables and in living rooms. For coolly calculating men with only 1,800 guns and no supplies do not decide to initiate a permanent political revolution, and what followed in Paris, and the ease with which De Gaulle terminated and brought it under political control, indicates the Communists were never in search of power, and their leadership of the FFI was irrelevant to the events themselves. Even if they had taken Paris, it was apparent to everybody that they could not have held the city against the Germans or Americans. Paris revolted to save itself. If it appeared otherwise to Americans outside the city at the time, that reveals only something of the measure of the Americans and their political anxieties and values.

On August 7 Colonel Rol, effective head of the FFI in the Paris region, issued an order very much like those released in earlier months: struggle should continue in the form of guerrilla action, the only possible course at the time, and hopefully circumstances conducive to a general insurrection, of which they had talked for years, would arise. But on the 14th the FFI in Paris was permanently mobilized as it was swept along in a wave of spontaneous events it had not even predicted. Only two German divisions occupied Paris and when the Nazis moved to disarm the police, on August 14, three police organizations issued an appeal for a police strike the following day. The debate that went on between the leaders of the FFI in Paris and De Gaulle's military emissaries, Alexandre Parodi and Jacques Chaban-Delmas, they now resolved, as Parodi gave his blessings to new action. The reported machinations of the Vichyites only added to their sense of urgency.

On August 17 and 18 the subway, post office, and other workers went on strike, and for the first time the command of the FFI in Paris sent out a list of objectives to attack in the event of an insurrection, as well as detailed instructions on street fighting and tank destruction. On the morning of the 19th Rol issued a call for a general uprising "to open the route to Paris to the victorious allied armies and to welcome them there."[45] There was no mention whatsoever of social revolution in his proclamation, for none was intended or possible. What happened surprised even the leaders of the local FFI, for they had scarcely prepared for the 19th, and were to improvise as best they could. Given the police strike—for that became the critical source of arms—the leaders of the FFI had neither the power nor the inclination to stop the flow of events. They could now only join them.

Whatever their motives, the Germans chose not to defend Paris, much less destroy it as they were doing to Warsaw those very same weeks. Despite Hitler's August 22 orders to hold the city at all costs, the Germans had already begun to withdraw from Paris at the beginning of the month and regarded it only as one of a number of links in holding the Allied advance and as an evacuation center. They were resigned to losing it well before the 19th, for on the 9th various service units began leaving and by the 17th the national radio was closed down. German General Walther Model had already issued an order to prepare the general line of defense along the Seine north and east of the city, and he understood that street fighting in Paris was less important than keeping the Allies from advancing on a broad front across the Seine. The number of German units in Paris had already been reduced, and at the time of the outbreak he commanded fewer than 20,000 men of mediocre quality, relatively poorly equipped. It may be that the German commander of Paris, Dietrich von Choltitz, was a sentimentalist about the city or an opportunist about his own fate should he destroy it, or that he realized that the Allies and the Resistance might end up fighting each other. All of these recent speculations are less important than the facts: at a time when he had the artillery to destroy any building or center of resistance in Paris, Von Choltitz told his troops to act with prudence. He then opened negotiations with the Allies, via Swedish Consul General Raoul Nordling, to surrender the city under terms which permitted him to retain some nominal military honor, and to enter into a truce with the Resistance until the Allies might arrive. Representatives of De Gaulle in Paris, working through Nordling, arranged the truce itself, which was supposed to last until noon of the 23rd, while German troops withdrew to the east. Neither COMAC nor Rol recognized the armistice, but the CNR and other bodies debated the truce and threw the entire leadership into disarray, leaving the uprising in a state of near anarchy. Events were still moving quite beyond them, as the fighting resumed and more and more guns fell into the hands of Frenchmen. At this point a small number of representatives of the Provisional Government, who suddenly appeared, began taking over key buildings in their own name, and rumors of a transfer of control over the police to the Provisional Government were rife. At no time did the Germans make full use of their available weapons, contenting themselves with holding key buildings and arteries as well as they might and protecting their own security.

Both the radio and emissaries from Paris, whom the Germans permitted to leave with safe-conduct passes, kept the American military, De Gaulle, and Koenig fully informed of developments within Paris. Von Choltitz was quite willing to give the city to the Allied military, but not to the Resistance. The immediate thought at Allied headquarters was to parachute arms, which was actually scheduled for the 22nd and then called off, ostensibly because of weather conditions. But this would have been insufficient in any case, and it was then necessary to attempt to convince Eisenhower and his officers to alter their strategy and immediately head toward Paris. The arguments De Gaulle's men used were diverse: the fear of Communists, the need to prevent another Warsaw, the extreme ease of the operation from a military viewpoint, but also De Gaulle's threat to send his own troops on the 21st if Eisenhower would not do so. In fact, on the morning of the 21st General Jacques Leclerc of the 2nd French Armored Division, then a hundred miles from Paris, had sent a small unauthorized column speeding on its way to the capital. Yet this too was no solution, for the American forces were less than twenty-five miles away, and their actions would be decisive. On the evening of the 21st De Gaulle's officers swayed Eisenhower, and he sent the French 2nd Division and an American division toward Paris, where they arrived the morning of the 25th to take Von Choltitz's surrender and hand the military governorship to Koenig. While there is no doubt that the Americans feared a Communist takeover, and this was certainly Stimson's understanding of the reason for the decision to enter Paris, it is quite unmistakable that De Gaulle's motives were rather more complex.[46]

De Gaulle had to worry about the machinations of the Vichyites, who were involved in the surrender negotiations that Von Choltitz authorized, and above all, he had to establish himself in Paris and consolidate his Provisional Government so that there would be no question of Allied, and especially American, recognition of another government. On August 17 the United States Joint Chiefs of Staff considered the question of De Gaulle's visiting Paris, which they understood to have direct bearing on the recognition problems that plagued French-American relations for most of 1944. De Gaulle was fully aware of the Communist issue, but it did not bother him overly much, for he had brought them into line before the 19th and could do so again. He understood that the uprising was a chaotic, spontaneous action of all Paris—an event that made him proud. Indeed, he even regretted the truce, for it deprived Frenchmen of an opportunity for heroism. But to accomplish the critical political task of the Provisional Government he had to get to Paris quickly. When he considered the American refusal to take Paris, he regarded it as a political maneuver on their part to save Vichy.

De Gaulle moved to take care of the Resistance and Communist issue on the 24th, the day before his triumphal return to Paris. That night he could report that "Parodi has everything well in hand. Contrary to rumors, the capital is all right."[47] De Gaulle's representatives informed the FFI that the police were now under the direct jurisdiction of Koenig and Charles Luizet, whom De Gaulle had used to establish control over the Communists in Corsica. The leaders of the CNR and COMAC now morosely watched their glorious victory over the Germans turn to bitter gall. On the same day they discussed ways of better integrating the CNR into the war effort, considering, among other things, dissolution. The next day was one of abuse for the bewildered Resistance leaders. First De Gaulle did not permit them to sign the German surrender, and after much haggling Rol was allowed to attach his signature only to the French copy, which was in the name of the Provisional Government and not the Allies. De Gaulle managed to accomplish two feats in one gesture, but even this petty concession to the Resistance impressed him as being too generous. Then De Gaulle arrived on the heels of the troops to receive the almost hysterical adulation of the Parisian masses, "confirmed in my intention of accepting no investiture for my authority save that which the voice of the people would give me directly." The order of the day's ceremony he had thought out well in advance, and calculated the symbolic meaning of each act. The first stop for De Gaulle was the Ministry of War, for "I wished to establish that the state, after ordeals which had been unable either to destroy or enslave it, was returning, first of all, quite simply, to where it belonged."[48]

The leaders of the CNR and the Resistance were impatiently waiting for De Gaulle at the Hôtel de Ville, and only Parodi and Luizet's desperate pleading convinced him to stop there briefly after visiting the Prefecture of Police. At the Hôtel de Ville, De Gaulle refused to proclaim the restoration of the Republic when CNR head Georges Bidault asked him to do so, and merely informed him it had never died and that he, De Gaulle, was its president. Everyone felt the calculated chill, and the next day, when De Gaulle paraded through Paris to receive the accolades of the people, he pointedly kept the CNR leaders well to the rear and then shocked them by attending mass in Notre Dame presided over by pro-Vichy clergy. On the 27th De Gaulle consented to see the CNR and Resistance leaders at the Ministry of War, coldly thanked them for their efforts, and informed them they were hereby disbanded, the Consultative Assembly to take over political affairs and the police and army the problems of order and war respectively. The following day COMAC met, handed all of its functions over to Koenig, and dissolved itself. The CNR was no more, and the Resistance was officially dead.

Since COMAC controlled the Resistance in name only, De Gaulle had to confront the possibly far more difficult problems the Resistance posed elsewhere, particularly in the southwest of France, where they were moving into the vacuum the Germans left in their swift retreat. It was at this point the Americans decided to give up their opposition and intrigues, and to support De Gaulle in his suppression of the Left once and for all. American military and political experts, as well as their British equivalents, during August and September watched French developments with rapt attention. American troops landing in the south of France in August found the Resistance, including a preponderance of Communists, firmly in control of the civil administration. They had few specific complaints concerning the behavior of the Resistance, whose efficiency they rather admired, but their deep apprehension is revealed in their reports which are now in the military archives. The State Department also observed the Paris uprising, though it appreciated its spontaneous nature and begrudgingly acknowledged the cooperative attitude of the Communists. What particularly disturbed the Anglo-Americans was that arms remained in the hands of the estimated 200,000 armed FFI, and rumors were rife that the FTP was planning a revolution in the southwest, or that exiled Spanish Republicans in the Resistance were planning a march on Spain. Above all, the Resistance was shooting collaborators by the thousands—at least 11,000 were shot, and perhaps several times that number—and was showing some will to act.

[The endless American procrastination in regard to his authority in France stimulated De Gaulle's rush to Paris to exercise an authority that now could maintain the order that even the Americans desired.] On August 26 Eisenhower formally recognized De Gaulle's jurisdiction over civil affairs in France and even sent an American division to pass in review before De Gaulle several days later. From that time on he pressed Roosevelt to end the interminable bickering and recognize the French government under De Gaulle, which Roosevelt refused to do until the end of October. Even in September the President persisted in believing there would be a non-Communist revolution against De Gaulle, an attitude Stimson thought "almost ridiculous," and an increasing number of advisers warned him would open the possibility of a revolution from the Left.[49] By October, Roosevelt was willing to consider France in terms of the problem of the Left as well.

Prior to that time, however, De Gaulle and the Americans moved to take care of the disarmament of the Resistance, first by drastically cutting supplies to the FFI still in German territory. Since the FFI had called for a national army of the people, they encouraged their members to join the existing army in the hope the government might later organize it along more democratic lines. Eisenhower attempted to make available, as best he could, the equipment which enabled De Gaulle eventually to enroll 137,000 former FFI members into the army, the safest place to put them. Here the former Resistants were given a high proportion of outmoded equipment and assigned to the most menial tasks, many in isolated regions far from the fronts, bases which many bitterly dubbed "concentration camps." Eisenhower also transferred one French division to De Gaulle at the end of August expressly for the purpose of maintaining internal order, and when De Gaulle asked for two more divisions at the end of September to handle the Communists in the Toulouse-Limoges area, Eisenhower refused to take them from the front but assured De Gaulle and General Alphonse Juin that he would bring French troops from Africa and the front as soon as possible. "I explained to him that we were all in favor of maintaining order and that we wanted the French to do it, not ourselves."[50] Though De Gaulle made similar requests as late as February 1945, by the end of the year the armed FFI ceased to be a potential threat.

De Gaulle himself contributed much to the reestablishment of a stable social order in a society war and defeat had disarranged. His triumphant tour through France after mid-September, and his careful placement of men loyal to himself and his ideas in critical offices along the way, did much to neutralize the Resistance leaders who had taken key posts in local governments. His submission of the FFI to strict military discipline during September and October was also significant. If pure charisma ever saved a social order—for De Gaulle's speeches were platitudinous in their references to national renovation and social responsibility—this is certainly such an instance. But despite De Gaulle's success the Communist party grew during the last months of 1944, until at the beginning of 1945 it was the most powerful single party in France. Its development in terms of raw figures was spectacular. The party almost doubled its membership in the six months after December 1944, its Paris newspaper was the largest in the city, the Communists won a controlling position in the French trade union movement, but, above all, their role in the Resistance permitted them to stake the preeminent claim to the moral right to build a new France. It was, in its role in politics, in the economy, among intellectuals, the one party with sufficient power to consider defining the tenor and direction of France.

The position of the U.S.S.R. on French affairs throughout the latter half of 1944 was certainly crucial, for the Russians loyally followed the lead of the United States and Britain in regard to such matters as diplomatic recognition and the like. Stalin told Roosevelt and Churchill at Teheran that France was now a relatively minor power, though "charming and pleasant."[51] But he understood England's position on the matter and conceded to the myth of French equality among the Allies in the United Nations and Germany. The Russians inquired about the question of a French occupation government in March 1944, but they saw that the West would not give them any more rights in France than it had granted them in Italy, and Molotov informed Harriman several times in July, as the American reported it, "that the Soviet Government would take no action vis-à-vis the French at variance with the Anglo-American position. . . . it was the Soviet policy to leave the initiative in French policy to the British and ourselves."[52] That assurance was worth a very great deal to the West, and there is not the slightest reason to believe that it was not respected.

Maurice Thorez returned to France from exile in Moscow at the end of November 1944, apparently with the blessings of De Gaulle, who concluded that his arrival "would involve more advantages than drawbacks at the present moment." Yet the Communists were in the Provisional Government and remained there until May 5, 1947. De Gaulle believed that "once the Communists adopted preponderance in a parliamentary regime instead of revolution as their goal, society ran far fewer risks."[53] De Gaulle appreciated Thorez, who quickly ended the last illusions within the Resistance-based leadership that the party would make an attempt for power outside bourgeois legality. ". . . the best of the lot," Foreign Minister Georges Bidault quickly assured the Americans.[54] From the time of his arrival the party actively and successfully recruited on the basis of a moderate, reformist, and patriotic platform, for above all the Communist party was the party of France at war. Thorez disciplined the older, militant leadership around André Marty and Charles Tillon, whom he ultimately expelled; he banned strikes, demanded more labor from the workers, and endorsed the dissolution of the FFI. Every social objective he subordinated to the objective of winning the war. "The task of Liberation Committees is not to administer," he told the party Central Committee in January 1945, "but to help those who administer. They must, above all, mobilize, train, and organize the masses so that they attain the maximum war effort, and support the Provisional Government in the application of the program laid down by the Resistance." In brief, at the critical point in the history of French capitalism, the party of the Left refused to act against it. "The unity of the nation," Thorez never tired of reiterating, was a "categorical imperative."[55]

Later Thorez explained that the idea of pushing the working class toward "Blanquist" adventures and away from its United Front strategy was intended to isolate it from the broad masses and destroy the party. Somewhat more realistically, as an afterthought, he cited the example of Greece, and pointed out that "With the Americans in France the revolution would have been annihilated."[56]

Thorez's analysis may have been correct, but there is no doubt that the Communist party made a virtue of necessity and played a political game in which it had no chances, given Western troops. Furthermore, the party helped to disarm the Resistance, revive a moribund economy, and create sufficient stability to give the Old Order a crucial breathing spell—and later took much pride in its accomplishment. If the French and Western Communist parties in fact acted on orders from Moscow, which was widely believed and was very likely the case in at least an indirect manner, then what this revealed of Soviet intentions was extremely significant. In this case one must conclude that by February 1945 the U.S.S.R. was anxious to prevent social revolution in the Western nations. If the Kremlin did not order the Communist parties to follow this line, then the parties had on their own initiative become social democratic both in theory and practice. It is quite possible that both independently and on direction from the U.S.S.R. the French Communist party embarked on a moderate course, because the Resistance was not in the last analysis as formidable a threat as the Anglo-American soldiers and diplomats thought. Its rhetoric in France was never ferocious, its deeds even less so. As in Italy, the Resistance was slow to begin and quick to end. The Paris uprising was possible only when liberation and victory were almost certain, and the desire to revenge humiliation would not result in disaster for more than 1,500 Parisians.

. . .

EVEN though De Gaulle continuously warned American leaders through-out 1945 that he was the only alternative in France to the Communists, and of their need to resist Russian expansion, he did not enter into a comfortable relationship with Washington. For one thing, he continued to refer to some variation of a Western European bloc, which Washington most certainly opposed. For another, there were numerous petty irritations over such issues as France's refusal, after much delay, to sign the invitation to the first United Nations conference, its aggressive shipment of troops into Syria and the Val d'Aosta in northwest Italy, and its unilateral policy in its German zone. Stimson, by June 1945, "was coming to regard [De Gaulle] as a psychopathic."[57] France hurt itself thereby, because while America supported its claim to a restoration of Indo-China in mid-1945, in principle it also delayed making available the equipment to ship two French divisions to the Far East because of France's propensity to create needless crises. Yet in the end, from the last months of 1944 and for the rest of the war, the United States regretfully had to go along with French pretensions, in part because they certainly preferred De Gaulle to the Communists, and also because France had become a British protectorate and it seemed increasingly pointless to strain the alliance unnecessarily. No less important, as Edward Stettinius, the new Secretary of State, pointed out prior to going to Yalta, challenges to French-British policy had failed, and "It would seem the part of wisdom to accept the proposals now, when credit can be obtained for that action. . . ." American policy for the rest of the war was "to treat France in all respects on the basis of her potential power and influence rather than on the basis of her present strength."[58] France could have its glory in theory if not in fact, its pretensions and national prestige placated. The assumption was based on a myth, and did not eliminate the tensions between the states. And the principle of transforming a secondary power into a Great Power proved debilitating at Yalta and thereafter.

Belgium: Containing the Left in Western Europe

A situation similar to the Resistance problem in France developed in Belgium, and to a lesser extent, Holland, as Anglo-American troops moved into the northern Channel region after September 1944. The exile governments of both nations were singularly unpopular with those who remained at home, and the question was whether the English and Americans could control the Resistance and make it accept the exiles. In Holland they managed the problem with moderate ease, but in Belgium the situation was far more critical, and ultimately required a massive show of force to prevent what the English and Americans considered the threat of revolution.

The OSS and the British watched developments in the Belgium Resistance with great alarm. It was large, estimated at over 80,000 in a country much smaller than France, not centralized as was the FFI in France, and predominantly under the control of the Communist-dominated *Front de l'Indépendance* (FI). The Socialists, who like King Leopold III had largely been collaborators, gave the Communists a monopoly of the Left. On September 11 the Hubert Pierlot government arrived from London and quickly restored the monarchy in the form of the king's brother as regent. It gave local parties, including the Communists, various Cabinet posts, but the government was generally unpopular among virtually everyone left of center and most of the Resistance members held on to their guns. Given this hostility and the inability of the government to handle mounting food and fuel problems, by October the Allied military authorities and Eisenhower were seriously concerned about the imminence of anarchy. Eisenhower on September 29 urged the Belgians to hand in their arms, and by the end of October he was ready to make the order compulsory. Eisenhower himself visited Brussels on November 9 as a gesture of support for the government, which he assured would have his full backing in enforcing disarmament of the Resistance. On November 13 Pierlot ordered all arms returned by the 18th, and three days later two Communist ministers and one FI minister resigned from the Cabinet, suggesting that the government would do better to deal with the collaborators first. The FI on November 17 publicly refused to hand in their arms, and the Allied command prepared to aid in the full use of force that they urged the government to employ. The Allied commander, British General W. E. Erskine, at this point met with the resigned ministers and presented the alternatives, including his willingness to disarm them forcibly. His appeal to patriotism succeeded, and on the 19th the leaders of the Resistance announced that they would give their arms to the Allied military, not the discredited government, and work for victory over Germany. At that moment the leaders lost their followers.

The Resistance did not hand in most of the arms, and instead called a demonstration for November 25, to be held in the major Brussels square in the quarter containing the government offices. With Belgian forces in the square and British tanks and troops nearby, ready to aid if necessary, the mass of protestors confronted the Belgian police, who forbade them to enter the square. When they did so the police opened fire, dispersing the demonstrators and wounding thirty-five. The revolution now seemed imminent, for the FI then called a general strike for the 29th. At this critical juncture the leaders were able to reestablish their control and the strike failed, but had it not, Allied policy would have doomed it to failure in a swift repression, for the alternative, as Churchill told the Commons on December 10, would have been "a bloody revolution."[59] They were able to solve the problem because the Communists agreed to do everything for the war effort, a matter that became rather less abstract in mid-December when the German counteroffensive threatened all Belgium for a time. In February 1945, when the government slightly modified itself and appointed a new prime minister, the Communists returned to the Cabinet and loyally supported the regime.[60]

Belgium was important chiefly to Britain, which wished a friendly government to cooperate with it in the postwar world, in particular in a Western European bloc the Belgian conservatives and social democrats had championed. But with strong American approval the British implemented their entire policy of repression, which involved the deepest possible intervention into the internal politics of a nation whose government everyone granted to be conservative and ineffective. The lesson was not lost, and thereafter other powers might also find parallel situations to their own liking.

CHAPTER
5

EASTERN EUROPE, I:
THE CASE OF POLAND

ONE MUST CONSIDER Eastern Europe from 1943 to 1945 as a whole cloth and examine the reasons for the variable political developments in each nation with a view to why the evolution differed in each nation. What options existed for the Poles, Czechs, or Hungarians, and did the U.S.S.R. have a comprehensive plan for all of Eastern Europe in the postwar world, or did the policies of the existing governments merge in some critical fashion with Soviet intentions to define the outcome?

⌊For the United States and England the Polish question was the most sensitive index of Soviet intentions in Eastern Europe, and it was a major piece in the complex jigsaw of United States-Soviet relations⌋ It would be speculative to state that it was the most important factor in shaping the American view of the Russian problem, but neither should one minimize the role of the Polish controversy and the discussion of that nation's borders and its political and economic composition. For the United States the Polish imbroglio began in earnest as soon as it entered the war, and continued unabated thereafter.

For the Poles and Russians, however, the mutual suspicions and animosities preceded not just the war but the Bolshevik Revolution, for Poland's existence as a state had always been contingent on the expansive designs and power of its eastern neighbor. After the Revolution animosities were aggravated by the war between the two nations that finally terminated in the Treaty of Riga of 1921, which gave Poland most of its territorial claims but left unsettled a smoldering dispute over a vast border area the Russians never ceased to claim. So long as this issue remained outstanding, mutual hostility between the two nations was the basis of their relationship. The U.S.S.R. regarded the Polish government as incorrigible, especially after its flirtations with Germany in the mid-1930's and its refusal, in the months preceding the outbreak of the war, to conclude a treaty with the U.S.S.R. that would have permitted Soviet troops to fight against Germany on Polish soil. Poland's anxieties over Russia seemed fully confirmed when the Hitler-Stalin Pact assigned the Russians control over eastern Poland. There was no reason to believe that the nebulous Polish-Soviet Treaty of Alliance of July 1941 which the existence of a now common enemy made mandatory could solve any of the traditional conflicts and animosities, because it only invalidated the territorial provisos of the Hitler-Stalin Pact.

The men who signed the treaty with the U.S.S.R. and maintained the Polish government-in-exile in London were successors to the confused interwar legacy of Polish life and politics. That experience had been a failure of intrigues and alliances among the Polish elite—the gentry, bourgeoisie, and military—one that ultimately produced a military coup in 1926 that left Poland in the shadow of the more or less totalitarian regime of Pilsudski and Beck. One-third of the population in Poland was non-Polish, as a result of the Versailles and Riga treaties and the acquisition of a part of Galicia in 1923, and anti-Semitism and persecution of minorities, especially the Ukrainians, was a unifying element among all the major Polish parties. Economically, Poland stagnated and failed to recover from the effects of the World War I, as manufacturing output exceeded the 1913 peak in only one postwar year. They never solved pressing land-distribution problems even though the major opposition party, the Peasant party of Wincenty Witos and Stanislaw Mikolajczyk, ostensibly made this its prime concern. Instead their leaders sustained the Poles on a universally accepted program of anti-Semitism and expansive nationalist pretension, a pretension that led to cordial relations with Nazi Germany between 1934 and 1938, and resulted in Poland's invading the Czech area of Teschen after the Munich abdication. Poland regarded itself as a major, even a great, nation that might command a tier of diplomatically aligned Eastern European states in a decisively powerful anti-Soviet alliance.[1] The exiles in London, under General Wladyslaw Sikorski, shared this faith as well.

The Polish-Soviet Treaty of July 1941 barely patched over this essential hostility, for it solved none of the outstanding border disputes. The Russians, having made the defeat of Poland easier for Germany, permitted or forced about one million Polish refugees to enter Soviet territory, and as the Polish ambassador reported to Hull in September 1941, "the USSR has granted to our Armed Forces full rights of an independent National Polish Army, giving it likewise the right of opening its own schools, full cultural freedom and freedom of worship. . . ."[2] The Soviets were lenient because they desired to obtain the fighting aid of Polish troops during those desperate months, and when the Poles violated their repeated pledges and refused to participate, the Russians began cutting off precious supplies and reducing freedoms, an action which only corroborated the Poles' worst anxieties and led to their incessant complaining to the major friendly ministries of the world. When the Polish army under General Wladyslaw Anders requested permission in early 1942 to remove 75,000 troops and their families to Iran, the Russians gladly complied. Anders made the decision to leave Russia over the opposition of the London government-in-exile, and it was the first of a number of unilateral, unauthorized steps various Polish generals took, all of which had the greatest political consequences. For London knew that if Polish troops helped reconquer their homeland, their presence at a critical juncture might alter the shape of postwar Polish politics. Once this option was lost, the London Poles determined not to squander their overseas army or their underground Home Army, estimated to be about 300,000 strong, until the politically opportune moment struck. At the end of 1943, however, Churchill successfully insisted that the Polish Army, which had drained large British resources after leaving Russia, finally enter the Italian campaign.

The question of the treatment of the Poles in Russia was merely an irritating backdrop to the central problems of Soviet-Polish relations, with the border issue foremost. When Eden visited the Kremlin in December 1941, Stalin proposed that they reach a settlement on European borders, Russia demanding the Curzon Line as the approximate basis of the settlement in eastern Poland. The English demurred, though acquiescing on a number of less important subjects, but since the United States made it clear that it would not consider territorial matters until after the war, they recognized that any Russian-British consensus was meaningless. And the British immediately notified the Poles of the Soviet position.

The Curzon Line had no status in international law, and Poland, which had obtained far better terms at Riga, never legally accepted it. In origin it was the result of a five-nation commission the Paris Peace Conference of 1919 created and assigned the task of drawing up Poland's eastern border along ethnographically homogeneous lines, with a view to equity rather than political realities; in December 1919 the Supreme Council of Allied Powers under Georges Clemenceau endorsed the Curzon Line. On the basis of this proposal, which was admittedly vague on certain minor border lines but on the whole remarkably clear, Lord Curzon, British Secretary of State for Foreign Affairs, proposed it to the Soviet government as a foundation for a settlement on July 12, 1920. Curzon did so at the request of the Poles, then in rout before Soviet troops, but the matter was delayed and the line became merely the Allied concept of equity, though it was associated rather more closely with the English alone. The United States, however, endorsed it in its initial form.

In 1943, when the border issue became the reef on which Polish-Soviet relations broke apart, the Curzon Line meant Soviet acquisition of 70,049 square miles, with a population in 1931 of ten and a half million. Even the Polish census of 1931, the last made, indicated that this population was 50 percent Ukrainian, White Russian, or Russian, 40 percent Polish, and 9 percent Jewish.[3] During 1942 and 1943 none of the Polish leaders would for a moment consider accepting the Curzon Line.

They based their refusal on a larger Polish political strategy which was unquestionably even a much more difficult problem than the border, in itself seemingly insurmountable. The London Poles, as had Pilsudski and other nationalists before them, considered themselves quite capable of becoming a Great Power, able to determine the fate of Central Europe by halting Soviet expansion, and they were convinced that the global political situation at the end of the war would permit them to realize their destiny, for then Russia would be weakened and Germany crushed. This role, in turn, was contingent on obtaining the support of the United States, the one nation certain to emerge from the war able to define the direction of international politics. In this context, and so long as this dream was not shattered, the eastern border issue could wait and the present, minimal military power of the London Poles reserved to contain or limit Soviet power, hopefully with the aid of Anglo-American troops.

Both publicly and privately, from the very beginning of the war, the official representatives of the London Poles reiterated their intention of organizing an Eastern European "federation," "bloc," or "union" along this line, never sharply defining its extent but obviously dependent on the political inclinations of the other Eastern European powers. Turkey endorsed the scheme by the end of 1942. "Poland would be the anchor in the north and Turkey the anchor in the south," Polish Prime Minister Sikorski told Sumner Welles, the Under Secretary of State, in January 1943.[4] For this reason Poland opposed the Soviet-Czech Treaty of December 1943, since they considered Czech participation in their projected bloc indispensable. Sikorski explained the plan to Roosevelt as early as March 1941, and the President said nothing to encourage or dissuade him. Eden and Kerr discussed it at various times with the Russians, who wanted to know precisely what the purposes and extent of such an alliance might be, their suspicion being ill concealed. Sikorski was forever meeting with the small Balkan states and promoting grandiose Polish ambitions, Eden complained, and the Russians knew all about it. The London Poles reiterated the theme until Yalta, by which time their fate was sealed. Publicly, they usually explained the purpose of the confederation as a bar to future German aggression, but privately they invariably connected it to Polish discussions of their future relations with the U.S.S.R. No later than the Moscow Foreign Ministers' Conference of October 1943, the Russians stated that "the plans for federations remind the Soviet people of the policy of the

'cordon sanitaire', directed as is known, against the Soviet Union. . . ."[5]
But this consideration became a factor in Polish-Soviet relations well before the break in diplomatic relations on April 25, 1943.

The Poles did not permit their refusal to consider any alteration in the
eastern borders to conceal their desire to acquire, at the expense of Germany, additional new territories in the west, where they never clearly defined the extent of their ambitions. East Prussia, part of Silesia, greater
access to the Baltic, and the like, Polish officials marked out in public
pronouncements. If such ambitions were to succeed, it would have to be
with Anglo-American help, and the London Poles made no secret of their
desire to obtain it.

Polish appeals for American support were diverse in their nature.
When Sikorski talked to Welles in January 1943, he pointed to Poland as
the significant precedent in future Soviet-American relations, particularly in
regard to Eastern and southern Europe, suggesting that Poland was the
place to oppose and stop Soviet imperialism. Later that March the Polish
ambassador to the United States, Jan Ciechanowski, handed the State
Department condescending notes on "the intricacies of Russian mentality"
and Stalin's "peasant logic," suggesting that Western firmness would cause
the Russians to back down on their overbearing border demands.[6] The
Poles permitted such advice to get into their official press. "The war is not
yet finished," a Polish government organ stated in March 1943. "It will
still bring changes in the relation of forces. . . . Russia will not have the last
word. . . . An important role in determining the map of this part of Europe
will be played by Poland and her Anglo-Saxon allies. . . . Note the statement made by General Sikorski after his return from Washington where he
coordinated the principles of our foreign policy with the views of President
Roosevelt. . . ."[7] These public references to Anglo-American military and
political supremacy at the end of the war caused Eden to warn the American embassy, as it reported to Washington in March, "that the Poles must
bear some of the responsibility for their present state of relations with the
Russians in view of the indiscriminate talking in which they have been
indulging." By the following October the Poles were ready to request "the
American and British Governments for a guarantee of independence and
integrity of the Polish territory," and "To safeguard such a guarantee,
American-British troops . . . should be stationed on the territory of Poland
to prevent Polish-Soviet friction. . . ."[8]

The pressures the Poles applied were verbal, comprising discussions of
alleged Soviet imperialism, but at times the pressures were direct, involving
Polish control of actual forces. Although the Polish leaders alluded to the
Polish army and underground, they deliberately cultivated a policy of keeping it an unknown factor. Would it fight, and whom? Throughout 1943 this
question was never resolved. ". . . only firm and active American and

British support by means of effective interventions in Moscow," they told the State Department in March, would permit Sikorski "to maintain his undisputed authority" among the army and those in Poland.[9] The implications were ominous. By that month the Poles had already informed the Americans the underground Home Army might take action against the Germans "to forestall the entry of the Russians. . . ."[10] They might even, they explicitly stated, revolt at the time of Soviet entry into Poland despite the strength of the Germans, with the implication that this would lead to conflict with Russian troops. By March 1943 the Poles formulated a plan coordinated to a projected Western invasion of Europe, one that would keep the Germans from retreating from Poland or Russia until the Anglo-Americans could arrive. In brief, there was an unknown threat in the Home Army in Poland which might, the Poles hoped, stimulate the necessary decisive action by the West, and Eden and Hull were certainly reminded of the possibility of "a desperate self-defense" against Russia.[11] Before his arrival at Teheran, Hull summed up for Roosevelt the Polish threats as Stanislaw Mikolajczyk, who became Prime Minister after Sikorski's death in an air crash on July 4, 1943, outlined them: ". . . decisions taken without full consultation with the Polish Government upon which the underground in Poland stakes its hope would undoubtedly lead to a serious crisis in that quarter . . . and might have 'serious repercussions among Americans of Polish origin.' "[12] Both threats had a very real basis.

Katyn

The final break in Soviet-Polish diplomatic relations on April 25, 1943, merely formalized the deep-seated rupture that had existed for years. The pretext used, however, did nothing to assuage Polish passions and fears, which would soon unquestionably have precipitated a diplomatic crisis, though for other reasons. The incident is most significant as an example of the conduct of Polish diplomacy, which had lost touch with reality as a consequence of xenophobic pretensions of being a power that no longer had to make the best of its limitations.

On April 13, 1943, the German radio prominently announced that German troops had uncovered near Katyn forest the graves of about 10,000 Polish officers who were allegedly murdered by the Soviets as they evacuated the Smolensk region nearly two years earlier. Earlier the Poles had wondered about the disappearance of these officers and the information the Russians provided had hardly satisfied them. When the German announcement came, Polish diplomats in Washington immediately acknowledged it was part of a plot to fan disunity, even that "the entire story might have been concocted out of thin air. . . ."[13] Obviously aware of what it would mean to their relations with the U.S.S.R., the Poles on the 16th called for an International Red Cross investigation of the Katyn incident. Since the territory was German controlled, any investigation at the time would have been less than disinterested, as the British and the Red Cross immediately pointed out. Stalin warned Churchill of the impending break in relations several days before the event, and the Prime Minister rather prematurely told him Sikorski had called off the Red Cross inquiry, which in fact the Polish leaders personally refused to do, preferring on May 1, when it was too late, to have the Polish Telegraphic Agency indicate the request had merely lapsed. What can the observer, removed from the events by many years, make of this strange sequence of events?

The criminological evidence aside—for it is vast and has been used convincingly to prove the culpability of both sides—certain larger facts must be taken into account. Given the exacerbated condition of Polish-Soviet relations, the Poles were fully aware that a final break with the Russians would probably follow their Red Cross proposal. Sikorski himself privately confessed to Harriman on May 1 that the Poles made a great mistake. The mistake, of course, was to count on the affair's evoking a sympathetic response that would be reflected in Anglo-American policy, for the Russian response was predictable. At this point in the war, given Soviet impatience with the delay in the second front, the clumsy amateurishness of the London Poles horrified the Anglo-American diplomats. They were desperately and futilely to attempt to undo the damage over the succeeding months as Polish-Soviet relations continued downhill. As practitioners of a peculiar mode of diplomacy, the Poles evidenced a crudeness that merely alienated everyone.

There was a dimension to the Katyn affair which only the London Poles could appreciate, however, and which might have caused them to take such drastic steps. Millions of Poles were killed in German death camps throughout the war, and with considerably less sustained outcry from the London government. Indeed, only that very month the Germans were annihilating some 50,000 Jews in the Warsaw Ghetto rebellion, and far less was heard from London on this matter. Katyn was an infinitely more sensitive issue because the men killed there, as Polish underground leader Tadeusz Bor-Komorowski described them, "had been the *elite* of the Polish nation . . . ," that is to say, the friends and family of the exiles in London.[14] Whoever destroyed the officers at Katyn had taken a step toward implementing a social revolution in Poland, and on the basis of class solidarity, the London Poles felt one officer was worth many Jews or peasants.

Looked at from this viewpoint, the Russians had the political incentive to destroy the Polish officer class at Katyn, the Germans the military motive—and both were equally persuasive. Yet insofar as Soviet culpability is concerned, of the by now endless lists of complaints the Poles made about the treatment of their nationals in Russia, mass murder was not one of them. Indeed, the U.S.S.R. permitted a much more formidable Polish military force to organize with Soviet weapons, and then finally to leave, and no one ever attributed a similar incident to the Soviet Union in Eastern Europe during the period 1940–1945. German mass liquidation, by contrast, was a common occurrence. If the criminological evidence exhumed in this ghastly affair does suggest Russian guilt, or if the Russian defense is inconsistent on serious points, then it must be suggested that Katyn was the exception rather than the rule, and its relative importance in Polish-Soviet relations must be downgraded very considerably so that its subsequent useful propagandistic function in the Cold War does not distract from the fundamental causes of the breakdown in Polish-Soviet diplomacy. Without Katyn nothing would have been different.

On April 28 the hitherto unknown Union of Polish Patriots in Russia announced that the London Poles did not have a popular mandate or the support of all free Poles. The world press was full of rumors of a new government on Soviet soil, and Ambassador Standley predicted such a move in "the near future."[15] On May 4, after the British and Americans pleaded with the Russians to restore ties with the Poles, and at least scotch the reports of a new government, Stalin assured Churchill and the Americans that no one was contemplating such a government despite the "vast pro-Hitler following" around Sikorski. He did not rule out, he explicitly stated, the three Allies "taking measures to improve the composition of the present Polish Government in terms of consolidating the Allied united front against Hitler."[16]

Such a change did not occur in 1943, and the only shift in the London government came after Sikorski's accidental death in July, when a group generally considered less flexible and even more anti-Soviet replaced him. On August 15 the four major parties in Poland, the parties with which the U.S.S.R. would have to work, issued a political agreement which included war and peace aims that were to set the tone for future Polish-Soviet relations. Prominently placed were "A constant watchfulness concerning Soviet influence, which is becoming increasingly marked in the Allied countries and a ceaseless recalling to their consciousness of the latent danger in Russian-Communist totalitarian peace aims." And, "The securing to Poland of a Western and Northern frontier, which would guarantee to her a wide access to the sea, together with the integrity of her Eastern frontier, as well as suitable indemnities." Finally, "The formation of a confederation of states of which the Polish-Czechoslovak union might be the nucleus."[17]

The British and American Response

In this exceedingly inflexible context both the British and American governments throughout 1942 and 1943 tried their hand at straightening out the tortuous labyrinth of decades of mutual Polish-Russian grievances and hostilities. To the British the matter was one of prime interest, and the

Americans, while seemingly passive, nevertheless based their approach on a conscious policy that defined the limits of British diplomacy and their ability to influence the Poles.

Although the British leaders refused to discuss the Polish border problem in Moscow in December 1941, they quickly saw that the Curzon Line was the best Poland might obtain, and indeed, all it deserved. Churchill and the Foreign Office were chagrined, then horrified, at the heavy-handed tactics of the Poles and their failure to recognize their own limitations. The British position was "Curzon and compensation," the compensation to come from German territories. Much more important to the British throughout the greater part of the war was the kind of political and economic system within Poland itself, and on this point they were intransigent with the Russians at the same time that they chided, then berated, the Poles for their inflexibility on the border issue. Churchill, in brief, sympathized with the Poles but opposed their tactics, which more and more forced the Poles to make their plans on the basis of their estimate of American intentions and power.

Before Eden left for the Moscow Foreign Ministers' Conference in October 1943 he met Mikolajczyk and tried once more to sway him along the line of a "Curzon and compensation" formula. The Pole would not budge, for he feared that Russia merely wished to Communize his nation as a part of its plan for international domination. To the British, however, it was more apparent that such an attitude on the part of the Poles would bring about the very Russian domination they most feared, for if the Polish government greeted Soviet troops with hostility, the Russians could exercise the options that the physical possession of Poland might afford them. There was still time before the Russians reached prewar Polish territory, and now was the opportune, perhaps the last, moment. The Polish response, as Mikolajczyk presented it, was straightforward: he handed Eden a memo which suggested the Poles would reestablish relations with the U.S.S.R. *if* they did not raise the frontier question, and "only if the British and United States Governments would express their firm support of the Polish Government." In any event, the Poles were not merely "opposed to even temporary occupation of Polish territories by the Red forces," but "of any other eastern or southern European State . . ." as well.[18] The implications of this position, involving Russia's ending the war in the east, and temporary Polish preference for German occupation rather than Soviet liberation, were too far-fetched for Eden to take to Moscow, for the West was neither politically nor militarily ready to give the Poles what they demanded.

At Teheran, the following month, Churchill took up the Polish question with Stalin, perhaps in the hope he might then convince the Poles to follow him. Stalin readily acceded to the "Curzon and compensation" formula, even as far west as the Oder River, which was far into Germany. But this would not be sufficient, he also told Churchill in the course of their discussions, because Russian security and the integrity of its revised borders depended on good relations between the two nations, and he did not think this was possible with the openly hostile London exiles, whom he doubted anyone could reform.

Stalin did agree to modify the Curzon border to relinquish to Poland those areas that were mainly Polish, but he also requested a section of East Prussia containing Königsberg. On the basis of this Oder-Curzon compromise Churchill told the Russian leader he would urge the Poles to accept a very good bargain, though he also expressed skepticism that anything would satisfy them. In fact, of course, the Poles snubbed the offer despite Churchill's and Eden's enthusiasm. Therefore the matter remained abstract. Still, there were certain loose ends to the Churchill-Stalin talks. Stalin expressed his dislike of the London exiles, and many rather important fine points regarding the borders were left for the Allies to work out. Churchill, as well, favored some variation of the Polish plan for an Eastern European confederation, perhaps around the Danube River powers as a start. He told Stalin he did not wish to see separated and weak states in the region. Stalin would not acquiesce, for only the previous month the Russians had handed the English and Americans a note categorically opposing Eastern European alliances, strikingly similar to the prewar cordon sanitaire against the U.S.S.R., and Churchill waited for a more opportune moment to raise this question again.[19]

The British kept the American government fully informed of the Polish imbroglio, as did the Poles and Russians themselves. The Poles, in particular, made a point of alternately informing and pleading with the Americans, but not once throughout 1943 did they show the slightest sign of flexibility on the border controversy. Polish plans for an Eastern European confederation were also well known, and the State Department's position on this matter was, for the time at least, neutral, until it could study the issue more fully. State Department experts had carefully researched the eastern border problem and concluded that the area was, as the Russians claimed, primarily non-Polish. Despite this, during 1942 and 1943 it was the consistent American position to the British and Russians that the United States wished all questions of borders and territorial changes deferred until the end of the war, when the Allies might consider them at the peace conference according to the principles of the Atlantic Charter. Eden warned Roosevelt that such a policy might cause the Russians to become less cooperative on other issues since the conference was so distant, but Roosevelt would not endorse the Curzon Line. In reality, the Americans both consciously and unwittingly pleaded the case for the Poles. Before meeting Stalin at Teheran, Roosevelt told Hull, as the Secretary noted, that he "intends to appeal to him on grounds of high morality. . . .

The President thinks that the new boundary should, in any event, be somewhat east of the Curzon line. . . ."[20] If Roosevelt made the proposal to Stalin, it is likely he did not regard the idea cordially. In fact Roosevelt tried at Teheran, whenever Poland was brought up for discussion, to move to other topics.

By the end of 1943, and for most of the following year, the American position became complexly inconsistent. First, it did not wish to resolve the issue during the war. Secondly, Roosevelt persisted in referring to the desirability of vague Soviet concessions, and frequently mentioned Lwow and Wilno in this regard. Even when Mikolajczyk told American diplomats in October and thereafter of the possibility of "skirmishes in various sections of the country between the Russians and Poles," the Americans made no attempt to adjust their political position. They considered the Poles to be excessively excited, and when the London exiles attacked the innocuous Four Nation Declaration the Moscow Foreign Ministers' Conference issued, Hull initiated "informal efforts" to have the Poles "take a calmer outlook and not alienate public sympathy. . . ."[21] But at no time did America alter its positions on the border issue in a manner intended to curb the Poles, and in November, Hull assured the Polish ambassador "that as a friend of Poland I would continue to watch every opportunity to be of service to both Governments."[22]

Hull told Eden in October that he considered Poland to be "more of a British problem in view of their treaty relationships," but quite imperceptibly the Americans defined the limits of Polish willingness to negotiate their border problem.[23] United States insistence on postponing the issue meant a preservation of the 1938 status quo, which was all the Poles were asking for in the east. As Churchill pressured the Poles, the American position encouraged them to stand fast, for as overly sophisticated geopoliticians the Poles realized America would emerge from the war as the most powerful nation in the world and might then define the political outcome of the war. Until the Americans abandoned this stance the Poles remained adamant, but by then it was too late.

The Americans did not base their position on naïveté, but on a very real set of commitments. As a result, Roosevelt and the State Department tolerated some unusually blunt threats from the Poles, much condescending advice that was invariably offensive in tone, and a level of diplomatic conduct that was unusual. The Poles referred first of all to the Polish vote in the United States. On a local level their Polish constituents during 1943 and 1944 lobbied critical Senators, such as Arthur H. Vandenberg of Michigan, and in turn the lawmakers backed a tougher State Department line toward Russia. More significant, State Department experts gathered complete data on the nationality dimension of the eastern border problem, which sustained the Soviet claim, but privately the Americans did not want the Curzon Line, primarily because they wished to hedge against Soviet power in the future. Lwow province, for example, was only 35 percent Polish, but it contained oil the United States experts thought a strong and friendly Poland ought to have. In discussing the southern border the State Department's political experts "agreed that an effort should be made to keep the greater part of Eastern Galicia, including the line of the Carpathians, within Poland, on the ground that the extension of Soviet territory to the Carpathians would represent an insuperable obstacle to the creation of an East European federation."[24] From this viewpoint, American and Polish political objectives, and the preservation of the past gains of Polish expansionism, were identical. Hence they both had to preserve the status quo and defer diplomatic discussion.

They reasoned that Soviet power would have to be contained in the future, perhaps via a cordon sanitaire, which was all the London Poles were arguing for frenetically. Hull in February 1942 sent Roosevelt a memo emphasizing the importance of Soviet intentions: "There is no doubt that the Soviet Government has tremendous ambitions with regard to Europe and that at some time or other the United States and Great Britain will be forced to state that they cannot agree . . . to all of its demands. It would seem that it is preferable to take a firm attitude now. . . ."[25]

Poland, to many key Americans, seemed to be the place to take that stand. In April 1943, before the diplomatic break, Standley urged that the United States "intercede on behalf of Poland."[26] John Foster Dulles, at about the same time, publicly declared Poland was the test of future relations with Russia throughout the world and the place to draw the line. State Department experts observed with unconcealed anxiety the creation of the Union of Polish Patriots in April and Polish military formations in the U.S.S.R. later that year. Only the American ambassador to the Polish government, A. J. D. Biddle, Jr., urged Washington to pressure the Poles at least to negotiate with the Russians behind closed doors rather than in the press. Hull, with Standley's prompting, on June 29 formulated the basic American view of the Polish problem: the Poles and Russians should "resolve the dispute on a just and equitable basis without attempting to induce the Polish Government to accede to the Soviet request for changes in the Sikorski Cabinet." The dispute, however, at that time was primarily over the border issue, and on this, Hull insisted, when considering the controversy, "the Department's consistently held position that no discussion of frontier problems should take place at this stage of the war. . . ." should lead to every effort being made "to eliminate therefrom any question involving frontiers." The significance of the Polish question was much greater: ". . . one of the principal reasons which induced the Soviet Government to break with the Poles may have been the desire to make it clear to all neighboring governments that their continued existence will depend upon the degree of their willingness to accede to Soviet demands upon them and to adapt their foreign policies to those of the Soviet Union." Hull admitted that such a stand was not likely to lead to a resumption of Polish-Soviet relations, but it was the larger "settlement of the complex post-war problems on a just and equitable basis" that they now had to consider.[27]

When Molotov reassured Hull at Moscow, later that year, that the Russians wanted an independent Poland, but one "which entertained friendly feelings toward the Soviet Union and it was precisely this element which was lacking," the Secretary did not have much to say, for he had already formulated his policy, and on this he had Roosevelt's support.[28] Poland became a test case for future relations with the Soviet Union, above all in Eastern Europe, and the Americans never considered the merits of Soviet or Polish arguments, nor were the statements and annoying manners of the London Poles of any great consequence to the United States. A seemingly passive policy of postponing the issue and maintaining the status quo now gave the Poles room for hope, and set American, British, and Soviet diplomacy at mutual cross-purposes, while the Americans and Poles, for their own reasons, now shared the same assumptions.

1944: The Polish Suicide Complex

Advance patrols of the Red Army crossed the prewar Polish borders on January 4, 1944, and the mightiest land army then in Europe followed close behind. The futile bickering and entreatments of the past two years were now supplemented by the possibilities power made real. From this point onward the Russians might negotiate or they might merely take what was now physically theirs.

The Poles earlier threatened armed conflict with the Russians, but they reserved this option for a later time, since the Russians would obviously win any such engagement. On January 5 the London Poles issued a statement and Mikolajczyk went on the radio and identified the Russians not as allies but merely as "allies of our allies," with whom he had ordered the underground to avoid conflict. "Cooperation" would follow the resumption of diplomatic relations.[29] No conflict, no cooperation—a formula that pleased everyone in the Polish exile government, but not the Russians. "They are incorrigible," Stalin wrote Churchill several days later.[30] The U.S.S.R. officially retorted on the 11th, pointing out that the Poles were wrong in asserting the Russians had crossed Polish territory, for it was Russian land. The U.S.S.R. sought friendship with Poland, the announcement continued, but on the basis of the Curzon Line modified to exclude predominantly Polish areas, with compensation for Poland in the west and north. Perhaps most alarming to the Poles, the Russians prominently mentioned the Union of Polish Patriots and their army corps fighting with their troops, followed by the statement "The emigré Polish government, isolated from its people, proved incapable of establishment of friendly relations. . . ."[31] Such public exchanges became increasingly common in the weeks and months that followed.

The open split in the Allied camp made it doubly urgent for the English to attempt to mediate the impending crisis, and they now determined to exploit a possibility Stalin offered in his talks with Czech President Eduard Beneš in December. At that time Stalin specified certain important modifications in the Curzon Line that he would accept in return for the inclusion of several pro-Soviet Polish Cabinet members and military cooperation between Polish and Russian forces. The Poles would form a new government under Mikolajczyk excluding the unsuitable elements, but the Soviet Union would not interfere in Polish internal affairs nor attempt to Bolshevize it. Stalin declared himself ready to talk to the Poles, and solicited British aid in the matter. Despite the unpleasant developments of early January, Churchill was anxious to try again, but first he attempted to get the Poles to agree. They would not, despite the fact Churchill made it clear that the British would support the Curzon Line alone and in fact publicly endorsed it the next month. Great Britain, he informed the Poles, would not go to war to defend Poland's eastern frontier. On January 10 Beneš and Churchill met with the Polish leaders, and the Prime Minister asked them to accept the essence of the Russian plan as a basis of negotiation. The Polish response was twofold: first, they asked for American, British, and Polish troops to be sent into Poland to accompany the Russians; second, the Poles conferred and decided to ask the United States and Britain to indicate whether they would guarantee Poland's borders against the U.S.S.R. should it reach an acceptable agreement, which was by no means certain.

During these same weeks circumstances compelled the American diplomats to think again about Poland. When Beneš had notified Harriman in Moscow of Stalin's offer, the American could only repeat the official formula: as much as the United States wished to see a rapprochement, it could not mediate and could only ask that they defer the controversy until after the war. Within several weeks Harriman had serious reservations concerning the sterility of this position, and he wrote Hull "that the Poles can make a better deal now than if they wait living as they appear to be in the hope that we and the British will eventually pull their chestnuts out of the fire." It was important to tell them the limits of Western backing, on which they were counting, and urge them to negotiate now. On January 21 he informed Hull: "I believe the Soviets are sincere in their willingness to have a strong and independent Poland emerge providing, of course, that it is well disposed toward the Soviet Union." Bolshevism was not their aim. Yet Hull still saw the question in the larger context of a Soviet "doctrine of unilateralism," and hence it was necessary to resist their demands on Poland.[32]

When the Polish ambassador presented Churchill's proposal and his government's question concerning guarantees on January 26, Hull and Roosevelt begged off. The United States would not guarantee any territorial settlement, favored negotiations but not on any definite frontier assumptions, and reiterated the belief that considering all factors it would be best to wait until after the war. Churchill could not succeed on this basis, as the London Poles well realized, and on February 15 the Polish Cabinet resolved to paraphrase the American position: "Only after the war can the final results of conversations regarding frontiers be effected." Churchill knew of this impending development, and on February 6 called the Polish leaders to the Foreign Office for a blunt, unfriendly lecture, arguing that the Poles had no right to Wilno and other regions, and that "the Russians, in view of the blood they had shed, had a moral right to the security of their western frontiers." The Poles remained unmoved, insisting that the Russians sought not to revise the border but to Communize their nation. They would not concede on their eastern border. "In that case," Churchill warned in anger, "the situation is hopeless. No agreement could be reached on such a basis and the Soviets having occupied the whole of your country will impose their will."[33]

For the next months the Polish press continued to refer to the incipient conflict between the Russians and their allies that would ultimately cause the West to use their superior power to redeem Poland. This logic underlay everything the Poles did during this period, and Eden referred to it at the time as a "suicide mind." Jan Masaryk, the Czech Foreign Minister, told one American OSS official that "He had never seen a group of politicians . . . who could by their every act commit suicide with such professional thoroughness."[34] Only Washington came to different conclusions, and this merely served to reinforce Polish inflexibility, for Hull and the State Department's analysts regarded Soviet rather than Polish policy as responsible for the crisis. It revealed a Soviet policy of "self-interest" based on "hostility" toward capitalist nations. "Under the circumstances the only positive course that the United States Government could take to resolve this conflict, therefore, would be to abandon the Polish Government in exile and assist in forcing on Poland the Soviet territorial demands—a course of action which would expose this Government to the justifiable charge of violating the principles for which this war is being fought."[35] By defending continued Polish control of a non-Polish majority, the Americans were resisting Russia.

After the collapse of the debate the Soviet offer to Beneš had generated, Churchill attempted to save the political integrity of Poland despite its exiled government, a task that was doomed to failure from the beginning, for the Poles would concede nothing. But Churchill wished to prevent Poland from emerging as a total satellite of the U.S.S.R., irrespective of the strategy of the London exiles, and as in so many other instances, he could be sweet and tough to both sides at one time. He now became firm with Stalin in pleading Poland's case and tough with Mikolajcyk, attempting to beg and threaten him into seeing the merits of the Soviet position. For only in this manner could Churchill create a non-Communist Poland and legitimate Russian demands be met. He therefore sent his ambassador in Moscow, Clark Kerr, to see if he could obtain some new concession from Russia to move the Poles. He freely admitted to Stalin that the Poles were intractable, and told him of the many aggravations they had caused him, even presenting Stalin with the transcript of his unpleasant February 6 Foreign Office altercation with the Poles. This strategy of evoking Stalin's sympathy backfired, for after reading it he wrote to Churchill: "I am more convinced than ever that men of their type are incapable of establishing normal relations with the U.S.S.R." Now it was Churchill's turn to be tough with Stalin, and despite the fact he had publicly endorsed the Curzon Line the previous month, on March 21 he informed Stalin: "we now consider all questions of territorial change must await the armistice or peace conferences of the victorious Powers; and that in the meantime we can recognize no forcible transferences of territory."[36]

By spring 1944 the matter had come to rest in a perfect stalemate, with no hope of resolution.

THROUGHOUT the spring of 1944 Mikolajczyk sought an invitation to Washington to win Roosevelt even more closely to his side. In fact, behind the scenes the State Department had been complaining to the Russians concerning Soviet overtures in the direction of creating an alternative Polish government. When the Russians invited two Polish-Americans friendly to the Soviet position, Professor Oscar Lange and an obscure Catholic priest, Hull called Soviet ambassador Gromyko in on May 1 and roundly chastised him. Several weeks later, as Harriman prepared to return to his post in Russia, Roosevelt instructed him to ask Stalin to give the Poles "a break."[37] At the same time, the President finally granted the Polish Prime Minister's request to see him, and during the second week of June, Mikolajczyk had an opportunity to discuss the Polish question in detail with Roosevelt and Hull.

The Polish leader arrived and left Washington committed to no permanent concessions on the eastern border issue, and detailed his feelings on this matter as well as Polish plans for a regional confederation. He did, however, suggest the possibility of strictly temporary occupation zones for the Russians somewhere east of Wilno and Lwow, a suggestion that the Poles made earlier in the year, but he linked it to the same set of Anglo-American guarantees that they had attached to the plan before. For the sake of the future peace of Europe, and not as compensation for lost eastern land, he told Roosevelt, the Allies should meet the Polish demands on Germany. The response of Roosevelt and Hull was more significant. On the one hand Roosevelt told the Pole that he ought to talk to the Russians, who would give him fair treatment and truly desired an independent and strong Poland, and this Mikolajczyk was not anxious to hear. But soothing words were more abundant. According to Stettinius' record, "The President said he did not agree on the formula based upon the old Curzon Line." The Russians would prove willing to negotiate this, and Roosevelt might have added that Harriman was at that time urging Stalin to meet the Poles on the Lwow region and parts of East Prussia. The Pole then asked if he might have American "moral support" in his future discussions with Stalin. What did this mean? Whatever it was, he received it: "The President apparently found Mikolajczyk's approach to the many problems discussed to be objective," Hull noted, "and indicated to him that he could count on the moral support of the United States Government in any efforts that the Premier might make to reach a mutually satisfactory understanding with the Soviet authorities."[38] For good measure Hull told him that although the Russians did not have to recognize anyone, "The Polish Government's resistance to that [Soviet] dictation was based on a sound position."[39] Mikolajczyk, much to the irritation of the Foreign Office, left Washington pleased and even less willing to compromise, and Roosevelt wired Stalin to arrange a meeting, for the Polish leader was "a very sincere and reasonable man."[40]

Churchill also urged Stalin to agree to such direct talks, and the Russian reluctantly consented to see him at the end of July. Before leaving for Moscow, Mikolajczyk talked with Soviet diplomats in London during late June, but they broke off the discussions after futile dickering over the border and political issues, on which Poland would cede nothing. The British once more insisted that he be more flexible on border and political questions, but to no avail. Even before the Pole left London, American diplomats concluded that his discussions would prove fruitless, and despite Stalin's courtesy, which for a moment gave Mikolajczyk cause for mild optimism, they were correct. Not only would the Pole refuse to compromise on the border issue, but between July 21 and 25 the Russians announced that an obviously pro-Soviet group of Poles had organized the Polish Committee of National Liberation in Lublin to become the provisional executive power in Poland, and that it would administer civil affairs in liberated areas—in effect, a new government. Also on the 26th, as Soviet troops crossed the Curzon Line into Poland, the Russian press announced Russia had no intention "of altering the social system of Poland."[41]

The Warsaw Cauldron

As the Polish, Russian, and British leaders haggled and stood on legalisms, principles, or pride, the Home Army of Warsaw considered all the dimensions of their situation, both political and physical, and on August 1 rose in arms against the German invaders.

The uprising was in reality against both the Germans and Russians, and therefore doomed to failure from the beginning. It was a ghastly outcome of the logic which the Poles, both in London and in the Home Army, attempted to employ for years as a part of their diplomacy of grandeur. Sikorski and Mikolajczyk both threatened to use the Home Army against the Russians, or against the Germans in a manner intended to keep the Russians out. On this basis the Home Army laid its plans for Warsaw, Wilno, and Lwow as a part of a scheme called "Burza," or "Tempest," and then modified it to changing conditions. "The plan for this action had been prepared in detail years ago and constantly modernised," Bor-Komorowski, the leader of the Warsaw uprising recounts in his memoirs. By July 14 Bor and his locally based command determined that it was time to translate their words into deeds, "preparing the capture of the capital just before the Russians would enter it." The reasons they offered London were diverse, including the need to defeat the Germans, "deprive the Soviets of the spiteful propaganda argument of putting us into the category of silent allies of the Germans," and in order to rally those independent Poles who might revolt on their own and "fall under Soviet influence." If they could hold Warsaw for only twelve hours, Bor calculated, they could take over the administrative organs of the city and the pro-London Poles could "come out in their full part of host to receive the entering Soviet armies." Bor realized that the Germans had stubbornly fought for all Polish cities against the Soviet advance, but the Soviet tide across Poland was so swift that he was "certain that the struggle for Warsaw, with the help of an organised fight within, would be of short duration."[42] It would have to be short, because Bor's forces had food and ammunition reserves sufficient for only ten days when he made the decision to revolt. Any complication might lead to the destruction of the city.

Bor presented the plan to London and General Kazimierz Sosnkowski, Minister of War, who opposed it, for he believed the revolt would be doomed to failure if it did not have assured outside support, but the rest of the London leaders hedged, and it is still unclear whether Bor had sufficient authorization. On July 26 Bor received a message permitting the revolt "at a moment you will decide as most opportune," but Mikolajczyk later claimed ignorance of the matter.[43] The military factors on the 20th appeared ripe, for on that day the Germans began what appeared to be an evacuation of Warsaw in front of the massive Russian sweep that was grinding its way toward the city. The Russians had been on the offensive since the beginning of the year and had come three hundred miles over the past month, reaching the Vistula River and the last major natural barrier across Poland on the road to Germany. Their logistics and communications were overextended, their men tired, but by the 29th they had almost reached Praga, a suburb across the river from Warsaw. There were now only two factors that could bring about the destruction of Warsaw, and either one would be sufficient: German willingness to defend the city, or Russian refusal to continue their attack. On July 27 the Germans began mobilizing the Warsaw population to build fortifications, and fresh troops began pouring back into the city that day, with the elite Goering Panzer Division, the first of five new armored and SS divisions, arriving on the 30th. On the 28th Eden informed the London Polish leaders that Britain would not be able to supply extensively an uprising, and in the meantime Bor's men failed to make contact with Russian troops to determine what help they might expect, or even to inform them of the planned revolt. On the last days of the month the Polish Communist radio called on the residents of Warsaw, as they had over the past year, to revolt under the auspices of the Communist Resistance. There was "nothing new" in these declarations, as Bor later stated, but at the time he feared the Home Army might lose control of the unaffiliated local population. "I had to act by myself and to rely on my own estimate of the situation," Bor recalls, and he ignored the pleas of many of his aides that he wait two weeks before making a final decision on the adventure.[44] On July 31 he gave the order to revolt the next day, and 44,000 largely unarmed members of the Home Army obeyed. Sixty-three days later, when the last resistance died, Warsaw was the most devastated city in Europe: 166,000 Poles died, and almost half the buildings were demolished.

The Germans decided to defend the Vistula, and they proceeded to burn and shell the centers of revolt in the city. This meant the uprising was doomed to bloody failure. The small Communist Resistance in the city joined the revolt, but the Russians did not save the Poles from disaster. Why?

Churchill pleaded with Stalin to aid the Poles, for the RAF wanted no part of the logistically hopeless task. Stalin told him on August 5 he could not imagine that the Poles would succeed in the adventure, but for the next two weeks he was continuously pressured to give them support, for Warsaw was too far from the West for massive airdrops. Mikolajczyk was also in Moscow at the time, and Stalin confessed to him that they had planned to take Warsaw on August 6, but German resistance was much greater than anticipated.[45] Several days later Molotov informed Harriman that the necessary frontal attack on the city would be too costly, and it would take time to outflank the city. On the 16th Stalin reluctantly agreed to drop supplies to the Poles, but he made it clear "the Warsaw action is a reckless and fearful gamble" for which he would assume no responsibility.[46] Hull bitterly regarded Stalin's hesitancy and his refusal to allow British or American planes to shuttle from Soviet bases as purely political in motive.

The messages from the British to the Kremlin over the next month were among the sharpest of the entire war, and far exceeded even Hull's willingness to excoriate the Russians. The British alone risked the long flight to Warsaw a number of evenings; the sole American squadron was sent out on September 18. In all, 104 tons of Western supplies and 50 to 55 tons of Soviet supplies were dropped on Warsaw, most of which were destroyed, captured, or dropped outside the city. The Russians also permitted Polish Communist brigades, accompanied by Soviet troops, to cross the river at several new points, where they suffered losses as high as 70 percent. By the end of September the German troops were driving the Russians back from surrounding towns, and it was not until the following January 17, more than three months after the collapse of the revolt, that the Russians took Warsaw. Bor and his followers felt the Russians and the West alike betrayed them.[47]

For everyone concerned, the Poles most of all, the Warsaw uprising contained obvious political dimensions, and Soviet responses were in part certainly political. Yet Soviet consideration of the political aspects of the Warsaw problem were an afterthought, not a cause of their remaining on the eastern bank of the Vistula. The Russians were used to outflanking and isolating cities, which was the strategy the Americans hoped to use on Paris to prevent loss of manpower in costly street fighting. If the strict application of such strategy meant conservation of Soviet troops and the elimination of the Warsaw political opposition, that was a fortunate coincidence for the Russians which surely figured in their calculations, but it does not necessarily make the political consideration the causal factor. To have removed any political imputation from their actions would have required much Russian blood. Reinforced German troops and the exhaustion of the Soviet forces by that stage of the war is a fact military historians with few political motives accept, and when Stalin and Harriman had a long, relaxed dinner in mid-October, the Russian explained the logistics in detail. The Red Army ran ahead of its supplies, and to outflank the city it needed many more divisions than it had. To engage in a frontal attack from Praga, which was on lower ground than Warsaw, would have been unjustifiably costly. So the Russians waited, probed slightly, were repulsed for a significant distance, and regrouped.[48] But above all the Russians were unable to take Warsaw until three months after the Polish defeat.

Bor's gamble failed, and the murderous reprisals the Germans took against the Warsaw Ghetto uprising of April 1943 should have warned him of the possible monumental cost to the city and its population. Yet had the revolt succeeded, and had Bor greeted the Russians with the government buildings under his control, absolutely nothing would have changed, for the Russians could merely have thrown his exhausted forces out. The Soviet troops that later entered Bucharest and Prague had no difficulty whatsoever in removing the successful Resistance, just as the Americans and English removed the occupants from liberated public buildings in Rome and all of northern Italy. That Bor should have ignored predictable future realities on behalf of some symbolic gesture which cost Warsaw its very life is certainly one of the saddest tales of a very tragic war, reflective as well of the complete lack of realism which permeated the Polish leadership. Once the Germans had decided to resist, which was apparent before the Home Army formally ordered the revolt, only a successful assault by the Red Army could have saved the million Poles in Warsaw from disaster, and that would have ended the political dreams of Bor and his colleagues, for the Russians were not likely to tolerate an armed Resistance in Poland any more than the Americans and British were willing to do elsewhere in 1943 and early 1944.

The Slovak Uprising

The Soviet military operations were largely based on nonpolitical considerations at this point in the war, and there is no reason to believe that had the Warsaw leaders been Communists the Russians would have sacrificed their own manpower to the indefensible cauldron. The most important basis for evaluating the motives of Soviet conduct at this stage of the war can be seen in the Russian response to the Slovak uprising during the very same months.

Isolated Czech and Soviet Partisan detachments, Resistance groups, and defectors from the Slovak army initiated the Slovak uprising in the eastern portion of Czechoslovakia in what was then the Nazi-sponsored Slovak Republic. Intense guerrilla action throughout late July and early August by Partisan units ultimately resulted in the liberation of much of central Slovakia. The commander of the Slovak army at the beginning of August opened what proved to be unsuccessful negotiations to switch sides. On August 29 the Resistance formally proclaimed the national uprising, followed several days later by a manifesto that was distinctly radical in content. Prominent Slovak Communists were the most important leaders of the revolt and various brigades were named after Stalin, Alexander Nevsky, and other eminent Bolshevik heroes of the day. By the beginning of October, 60,000 partially armed Partisans were locked in battle with German and puppet Slovak forces. At the time of the uprising the Russian army was eighty to a hundred miles from the main revolutionary forces, and within easy flying distance. Czech Foreign Minister Jan Masaryk appealed to all the major Allies for aid, since he did not regard the political composition of the leadership as reason for passivity.

The Russians had received advance warning of the event, but watched it indifferently for the first week until they could no longer ignore the dimensions of the uprising. During the next six weeks the Russians sent a trickle of supplies and some 2,800 men, despite the relative ease of using airfields for landing them or even sending them in by land. The Czech also sent pleas for aid to the British and American Chiefs of Staff, who declined with the excuse that the area was within the Soviet sphere of military operations, although the Combined Chiefs of Staff had decided on September 7 "that this would not be a reasonably feasible operation for American or British aircraft" even if the Russians approved.[49] But the Russians saved the West the political embarrassment by refusing to expedite the question. The West sent a few token flights, amounting to less than the trivial fifty tons of supplies—about what they sent the Warsaw Poles—flown in by the Russians themselves. At the end of October, as the Germans began wiping out the main centers of fighting, Masaryk again appealed to the United States for aid, and the Americans permitted over three weeks to lapse before sending back a routine rejection. The Russians and their allies watched with indifference as the Germans liquidated the nearly successful uprising along with 25,000 patriots.[50]

Since the Communists controlled and led the uprising and the Czech government-in-exile under Beneš hailed it as a glorious event in Czech history and pleaded for its support, the Russians had no political reasons for refusing to aid it. Their reasons were quite certainly purely military and reflected a commitment to an overall strategic plan that they applied literally and at minimum loss to Russian manpower. If one looks at the Russian response to the Slovak situation, then the military explanation for their behavior before the gates of Warsaw becomes much more convincing. Politics they relegated to a place behind military exigency.

The Poles Unmoved

If Warsaw proved nothing else to the London Poles, it convinced many of them that the West would not casually rush to their aid at the critical moment of need. The myth of the power of the Home Army was buried in the ruins of Warsaw. Time now seemed to be running out, but in fact it was already too late.

For Mikolajczyk especially the situation appeared more and more futile. His experience in Moscow had been personally flattering, if not pleasant. He met the mysterious Boleslaw Bierut and members of the Committee for Liberation, and while they were completely unknown to him from prewar politics, they extolled him and offered him the prime ministership of a government they would control. And not all of their ideas seemed unrealistic. Molotov and Stalin had been almost cordial, and Molotov found the Prime Minister to be "a wise man." Mikolajczyk was suspicious, the small number of posts offered to the prewar parties was absurd, and he conceded nothing, save a few posts to committee members, but they were running Poland and he was not. When he returned to London he and his Cabinet argued bitterly over a new proposal to the Russians, and finally decided on one by the end of August. The Communist PPR (*Polska Partia Robotnicza,* Polish Worker's party) would receive one-fifth of the seats in the War Cabinet, all foreign troops would leave Poland at the end of hostilities, and insofar as border matters were concerned, a vague formula was proposed which raised more questions than it solved. The Poles "cannot emerge from this war diminished in territory," but "In the east the main centres of Polish cultural life and the sources of raw materials indispensable to the economic life of the country shall remain within Polish boundaries."[51] What did this include? If the statement was vague, at least there was something to talk about. Churchill for once had a proposition to take back to the Russians, and at the end of September, when the London Poles eliminated Sosnkowski and several figures especially obnoxious to the Russians from the Cabinet, which they had irately refused to do earlier in the year, the British Prime Minister resolved once more to attempt to redeem Poland before it was too late.

Who Stands for Poland?

The Poles in London claimed to represent Poland on the basis of their prewar party mandates and the dubious 1935 Constitution produced after a military coup d'état. They stood, in brief, for the Old Order and social forces that managed to exist within the framework of an illusion that had not been torn asunder by a war that destroyed six million Poles and physically uprooted and tortured an even larger number. Russian military power had placed the Poles in Lublin who were actually running the nation behind Soviet lines, but they claimed to speak for the same masses as the Poles in London. What was the truth of these assertions, and what had the war done to the nation that probably suffered most from World War II?

Whole classes were destroyed by the end of the war. The military, so critical in prewar Polish politics, was now virtually gone, the economic power and connections of the upper bourgeoisie and capitalists wiped out and turned into rubble. These two facts alone, as careful OSS reports let Washington know, would make the structural position of prewar reaction the very weakest. Yet all of the inherited prewar problems remained, and the terrible impact of the war only compounded them. Anti-Semitism existed everywhere at the same time that the Germans were destroying the Jews, even among the underground groups and conspicuously in the Polish army abroad. The land problem remained unsolved, a vast proportion of the peasantry still restricted to small plots, with two-thirds of the land holdings under twelve acres and most of these less than five. By 1943 local contacts had fully informed the London Poles of the existence of two overwhelming postwar problems they would have to face. The first was the vast national minorities whom the Poles had ruthlessly persecuted after 1918, and whom London was fighting to retain behind their postwar borders. "If our aim is to defend the Polish frontier of September 1, 1939," one Polish diplomat reported from Washington during the war, "we should try to get the support (if it is not too late) of all our minorities. . . ." This meant the Ukrainians, the Jews, the Lithuanians, the Czechs, and the indigestible one-third of prewar Poland. Another problem the underground at home reported back to London was: "The PPR [Communists] has its task simplified by the growing desire among the Polish masses for radical social reforms. In spite of the radicalization of the Polish masses, resentment of the Soviets is formidable—but fear of the Red Army is considerable, too."[52] Which way would the radicalized Polish people go?

Only a rather general hatred of Russia kept the Communists from gaining additional adherents, but that the Poles were ready to desert their old leaders was certain. Beneš told Harriman during June 1944 that the London Poles appreciated that there were many in Poland who wished to give up Great Power aspirations and the virulent anti-Russian emphasis and get down to the more essential tasks. The PPR, by virtue of its association with the U.S.S.R., had only 20,000 members in 1944, but it was split into factions, the nationalist wing led by Wladyslaw Gomulka emerging more from the ideological tradition of Rosa Luxemburg than Stalinism; this group was able to present a United Front policy for the party that by May 1944 attracted a large group from the powerful prewar Socialist party and other, smaller leftist organizations. It was this merger that resulted in the creation of the Committee for National Liberation in July 1944 around a vague reform program, with a place for private initiative, that mentioned neither "Communism" nor "socialism" and was typical of the United Front tactics of the Communists everywhere. Of the fifteen members of the executive of the CNL, only seven were known Communists. In this new guise, only the pro-Curzon Line policy of the CNL kept it from becoming a truly mass party of the Left.

But there was no doubt that the shift in Polish politics was naturally and inevitably toward radical reform, and given the strange mixture of passions and prejudices characteristic of the Poles, this probably meant away from both London and Moscow and toward a radical, nationalist synthesis that was never given the freedom to emerge in this decade.[53]*

---

* Although the Home Army was by far the largest group, with 100,000 to 300,000 members, the small Communist underground was very active, and in October 1943, the militant Socialists opposed to both formed a Resistance organization. All fought in Warsaw. The large Jewish underground was overwhelmingly Socialist, but all save the Communists persecuted it. A powerful rightist group, the NSZ, went into the Home Army in March 1944, but later reappeared to fight the Communists.

EASTERN EUROPE, II: DIVERSE PATHS TO SECURITY

POLISH-SOVIET RELATIONS were not the only index to Russian policy and intentions in Eastern Europe from 1943 until the end of the war, for a multiplicity of situations and possibilities emerged during those decisive years. The critical question is not merely why the Soviet Union pursued a hostile policy toward the Polish government-in-exile, but also why it had excellent relations with the Czech exile government, or why its conduct toward Finland, Rumania, and the other Eastern European nations was, each in its own way, different.

Beneš and the Czech Bridge

Czechoslovakia had been the victim of Munich as well as French and English unwillingness to respect a binding treaty obligation to defend its integrity. Despite the near certainty France would not cooperate, only the U.S.S.R. during the Munich crisis offered to enter a war against Germany should the French and the Czechs agree, and their joint unwillingness to do so resulted in the first major imperial triumph for Nazism. Beneš vowed never again to permit his nation's fear of Russia to lead to its defeat, and he set out on a new course.

Munich occurred, Beneš concluded, because the West feared Russia more than it hated Germany, and Hitler's knowledge of this fact gave him the freedom to embark on a course that eventually made war inevitable. Czechoslovakia shared this Western faith and ended in disaster, and Beneš was certain that unless the mutual hostility between Russia and the West was bridged, they would repeat the disaster. "It was clear to me that this, *the real world catastrophe,* could only be prevented by devoted work for a firm and *permanent* agreement between the Anglo-Saxons and the Soviet Union—that it was our chief task in this situation to work for such an agreement. . . ."[1] The Czechs would base their diplomacy on the need to end the hostility and would lead the way in creating a link between East and West.

Nothing in Czech relations with the U.S.S.R. from 1941 through 1942 discouraged this vision. In July 1941 Russia was the first major power to recognize the London exile government without reservations as to its pre-war frontiers, and although the English and Americans quickly followed with recognition, they were not bound to any borders. The distinction, to the Czechs, was critical. Then in June 1942 Molotov told Beneš that Russia recognized Czechoslovakia's pre-Munich borders as binding save by mutual consent, and that the U.S.S.R. had no intention of meddling in Czech internal affairs. In return the Russians made it clear over the year that they expected Czechoslovakia not to align itself with the Poles in an Eastern European federation directed against the U.S.S.R. During the same period the Russians treated Czech soldiers exiled in the U.S.S.R. well and reorganized them into exclusively Czech fighting units. By early 1943 the Czechs in London were ready to become active proselytizers for their new concept of European politics.

The peace of Europe, Beneš notified the English, would depend on the West's willingness to recognize a radically new power situation in Eastern Europe and to work with the Russians. The Soviet Revolution, he maintained, had become a permanent factor in the world and its success in resisting and then driving back Germany established its influence once and for all. He was anxious to pioneer in *"systematic and definite cooperation between Western* and Eastern Europe," and in the spring of 1943 he began to seek both Soviet and Anglo-American support for the undertaking.[2] In March 1943 Beneš asked the Russians whether they would be willing to sign a treaty similar to the Anglo-Soviet Pact of May 1942, modified to include noninterference in Czech internal affairs, with the Czechs remaining aloof from any anti-Russian blocs in Europe. He frankly told the Russians their response would reveal to the West their intentions in Eastern Europe as well. On April 23 the Russians replied favorably to all his questions. Beneš then sought to obtain American and British endorsement for the endeavor.

Beneš reached the United States on May 12 and met with Roosevelt, Hull, and various State Department officers. The American records of the visit are not available to the historian, but Beneš states in his memoirs that he went "to explain our whole policy towards Germany, Poland and the Soviet Union" and to win American support for it.[3] The only available

State Department document indicates "much of the conversation concerned in one way or another the relations with the USSR."[4] In addition to advancing various Czech claims, Beneš outlined his concept of future Czech neutrality and covered a host of Eastern European problems with Roosevelt and the State Department. Although Roosevelt and Welles appeared friendly, and Beneš tried to convey this impression in his memoir, in fact they were elusive on the critical problems of Poland, and Roosevelt asked Beneš to inform Stalin of American unwillingness to recognize the annexation of the Baltic states officially. From Hull he got the impression that he was "chiefly interested in getting guarantees that Russia will not interfere in their interior affairs and will not deliberately support communism and communistic programmes."[5] Beneš' many public speeches and statements while in the United States reflect the essence of what he told to official Washington. These merely detailed his earlier position. "To my mind," he declared in New York, "the Soviet Union is bound to play her full and rightful part in the post-war settlement" and should "not be isolated again." The Czechs would sign a treaty similar to the Anglo-Soviet Pact, and would coexist with the institutions of the Soviet Union in return for its respecting those of Czechoslovakia. "We shall not indulge only in a pro-Eastern policy, or a pro-Western, but in a world and European policy. We have no secret politics, nor any secret diplomacy. And because we have acted so, our position is secure. We must continue in this policy because Soviet Russia will not be isolated after this war."[6]

The American stand on the treaty was unfavorable, and they so informed the Czechs. ". . . such a treaty would be a step backward in our efforts toward international understanding. . . . We have no reason to suppose that either the Secretary [Hull] or Mr. Welles at any time have had any 'favorable reactions' to the project," the only available State Department account relates.[7] The British response was identical, and we have more information on their motives. Masaryk and Czech officials, Beneš recalls, were "occupied in Great Britain and America chiefly with efforts to neutralise and overcome these difficulties."[8] Both the British and Russians had similar agreements under discussion at the time with Greece and Yugoslavia respectively, but Eden suddenly informed Beneš of an accord he had reached with Molotov the year before not to sign bilateral treaties with small nations. Though the Russians at first could not recall such an agreement, and Eden later reduced the nature of their commitment to an "impression" he obtained from the Soviet ambassador in England, they obliged the British and delayed the matter until the Moscow Foreign Ministers' Conference the following October.[9]

Before his proposed visit to Moscow, Beneš offered to sign an identical treaty with the British, but they refused and the hapless Czechs were stymied. Actually the British Foreign Office decided to make friendly

Czech-Soviet relations a reward to the Russians for greater cooperation on Poland, and they told Beneš they did not want to leave Poland isolated. Moreover, it would mean the end of a possible Eastern European confederation based on a Polish-Czech alliance along the lines the Poles sought. The Polish-Czech federation was certainly the first fatality of Beneš' policy. Molotov told him in July 1942 the Russians did not like the Polish scheme, nor was Beneš overly enthusiastic, not only because of Russian opposition but also because he felt such alliances were the wrong way to begin creating a stable Europe. First, he stated in early 1943, all the irredentist controversies and frontier issues that had divided Eastern Europe had to be solved among the independent states or any federation would soon fall apart. But, more importantly, Beneš reasoned that unless Poland was willing to reach an accord with Russia, it was unthinkable that the Czechs could enter into a close bloc with their northern neighbor. If they could solve all these problems, however, in principle the Czechs favored an Eastern European confederation that was not explicitly aimed against the Soviet Union. In fact, however, the Czechs had reason to be more apprehensive about the Poles than the Russians, for the London Poles indicated no willingness to relinquish Teschen or to give up imperial pretensions, aspirations only Russia could inhibit. On this question, therefore, the Czechs saw their interests were with Russia, and Beneš always remained intolerant of the politics of the Polish émigrés.

These circumstances compelled Beneš to bide his time until the British and Americans moderated their opposition. Since the Russians had a general idea of the reasons for the sudden failure of their friendly negotiations with the Czechs, on October 24, at the Foreign Ministers' Conference, Molotov tried to pin down the British objections. After hedging, Eden finally withdrew his opposition to Beneš' trip to Moscow, for he no longer objected to the treaty itself. Several days later Harriman advised Hull that the United States should publicly dissociate itself from the contemplated treaty. It "appeared to be part of the same pattern in present Soviet policy to extend Soviet predominance over eastern Europe and the Balkans," one of his assistants wrote.[10] The British, whose hostility had hardly subsided, also told Beneš to be wary. They too did not want the Czechs to fall into the "Soviet orbit," as yet still nonexistent, but a decades-old fear in the minds of Western diplomats.

Beneš shared this anxiety with Eden and Harriman, but he also saw that the way to prevent a "Polish response" by the Russians was to meet them halfway. He also worried about another problem, the position of the Communists in Czechoslovakia after the war, for Beneš appreciated that the mood in Europe was toward the left and he wished to redefine that development to his own convenience. Furthermore, there was the question of a civil affairs agreement during the impending Russian occupation of

Czech territory, which might determine the fate of his nation. The Russians would be of value in this regard as well, and he was delighted to arrive in Moscow on December 11, 1943, to test his grand strategy. The Russians in turn were on their very best behavior, and Stalin was especially charming and pleasantly frank. They doted over Beneš, treated him royally, and he was happy to agree when Stalin requested his help in unfreezing the Polish problem. The Czech Communists, who had a peak of 13 percent of the vote in the 1925 election but were growing rapidly throughout the war, agreed to take only one-fifth of the seats in a new government, and since Beneš and most of his followers were in favor of extensive nationalization and social welfare, they quickly agreed upon an interim postwar program.

The twenty-year treaty of friendship the Czechs signed with the Russians was unobjectionable, and like the treaty they had with England. Czechoslovakia and Russia agreed to remain aloof from any alliances directed against either nation, which implied opposition to the cordon sanitaire. Privately, however, Stalin pledged support for the return of Teschen to the Czechs, and they decided to resolve the question of the Ruthenian area bordering the U.S.S.R. later. The German and Hungarian minorities were to be "transferred," or sent back home. He promised again not to interfere in Czech internal affairs, to send Czech troops back with the Soviet military, and to transfer civil administration to the Czechs as quickly as feasible. Harriman reported Beneš was "elated," and had told him Russian nationalism had replaced the desire to Bolshevize Europe. Peace between the Great Powers was possible, and between the Czechs and Russians certain.[11] Beneš always regarded the trip as a vindication of the "great success of our policy," and he immediately informed Churchill of his triumph. The English leader was visibly impressed, thought his Polish compromise plan "most useful," and regarded the Russians "quite agreeable" in all respects, including the minor Ruthenian border alterations. He quickly notified Roosevelt of his favorable impressions of Beneš' voyage, and Churchill never ceased to regard the Czech as a man who "In all his thought and aims . . . consistently sustained the main principles on which Western civilisation is founded. . . ."[12] As Beneš saw it at the time: "We are . . . a link between Western Europe and the East."[13]

If Churchill was convinced, and if indeed both he and Eden˙ were impressed by the good Beneš' trip had accomplished in regard to Poland, there is no indication that the general direction of Czech affairs pleased either Britain or the United States. Only the relative unimportance of the nation kept it from having a more significant impact on Western thought and diplomacy. When during mid-March 1944 the Czechs asked the three major Allies to sign civil affairs treaties, the United States and Britain failed to do so, not because they thought the nation was within the Soviet sphere, but due to a combination of outright opposition and a mistrust of Czech civil authority, the political reliability of which they might evaluate later as the need arose. The Western nations realized that Russian troops might enter Czech territory before the end of the war, which in fact occurred. Only the Russians agreed, on May 8, a month after reaching the Czech border, to meet all the Czech demands on the issue. The Czechs, the American embassy in Moscow reported to Hull, were "expressing deep satisfaction," and the Russians gave unusual attention to the civil affairs treaty in the leading article in the May 9 *Izvestia,* pointing to it as a stellar example of Russian respect for the independence of liberated nations. Subsequent American diplomatic dispatches in 1944 soon portrayed Czechoslovakia as a Soviet-style "friendly" country which illustrated Russian expansionist intentions.[14] Many occasions arose over the next three years for the United States to declare with conviction that Czechoslovakia had fallen into the Russian orbit, until it eventually did so and Beneš' illusion that the Western Powers would permit him to build a bridge was shattered.

The "Italian Formula" for Rumania

Italy was the first member of the Axis bloc to surrender and Rumania was the next to follow suit, ending hostilities on August 23, 1944. Throughout 1944, however, the United States and Great Britain watched almost helplessly the developments in that nation, unable to intervene, since not only the distance of their own troops separated them from the scene but also the precedents they had created in Italy. The result intensified the already deep fear of Soviet intentions in Eastern Europe and caused new tensions within the alliance over the nation that actively joined the German attack on the Soviet Union from June 1941 onward.

Rumanian peace overtures began during the early part of 1944, and the United States attempted to define a preliminary position on what they might expect there. The State Department realized the Russians would cite the Italian precedent to take Rumania's surrender on behalf of the Allies, for "its forces have borne the brunt of the fighting," though it hoped they would include nominal Anglo-American representation. By March the State Department felt it desirable to freeze all discussions of territorial changes the Russians might propose and to reaffirm Rumania's future existence as an independent state. It rejected the British position that Rumania was primarily a Soviet affair. The State Department's political experts suggested that the United States and Britain "should maintain their interest in that country and should apply to Rumania the general principles underlying our conduct of the war. . . ."[15] By March, Rumania was making various peace offers directly and solely to Anglo-American political and military representatives, with the objective of excluding Russia from the surrender terms and hopefully obtaining Anglo-American occupation forces. The Western position on these gestures was always correct: the Axis states must surrender to all three powers, but the Russians found the responses clumsy and worried American diplomats, who saw the Russians working for exclusive control over surrender negotiations. The United States Joint Chiefs of Staff submerged such fears by deciding at the end of March that Russian participation in the Italian surrender had proven "impracticable," and the same would probably prove to be the case with Anglo-American involvement in Rumania.[16]

On April 2 the Russians crossed the Rumanian border and issued a declaration "that it is not pursuing the aim of acquiring any part of Rumanian territory, or of changing the existing social order. . . ."[17] By "Rumanian territory," the Western Allies discovered a few days later, Russia meant the frontier they acquired as a result of the Hitler-Stalin Pact. Yet much to Washington's surprise, at Churchill's request the Russians immediately withdrew such major territorial demands until the peace conference, but these twists in their position only increased apprehension in Washington. By intrigues of every variety the Rumanians under King Michael and Marshal Antonescu pleaded with the British and Americans to take their surrender and send their troops in to stop the "unrestrained introduction of Communism into Southeast Europe," upsetting the European balance of power and leading to the "Slavization of Rumania."[18] In return the Rumanians would join a Balkan federation and establish political and military collaboration with the West. They did not approach the Russians themselves, and in August, as the Red Army broke through German lines, four anti-German Resistance groups in Bucharest, including one Communist group, moved to drive out the Nazi collaborators and take over the government. On August 23 fighting terminated and the armistice proposal followed a week later; it was based essentially on the Russian April terms, eased even further in regard to indemnities and a free zone for the government seat. Churchill, at the end of September, thought these conditions showed real "restraint" on the part of the Russians. Well he might, for the Soviets fixed reparations at $300 million over a six-year period, restored Rumanian civil administration thirty-one to sixty-two miles behind the front under ultimate Soviet military control, and promised the return of all or part of Transylvania.

The American response to the proposed armistice stipulations—much to the State Department's irritation the Russians rejected their draft—concentrated on the provisions for reparations and an Allied Control Commission, both of which were ultimately incidental to the type of political and social system that would emerge in Rumania, but critical to United States-Soviet relations. For the Russians the reparations issue was straightforward: the Rumanians had done far greater damage to the U.S.S.R. and the proposed sum was no more than a fifth of that amount. The terms, which Churchill felt were lenient, appeared to Harriman to "give the Soviet Command unlimited control of Rumania's economic life," and the Russians would do no more than agree to set that figure as a maximum demand. Hull formulated the United States position with the German reparations problems explicitly in mind. The armistice terms should give no fixed figure, but in any event, he strongly emphasized to Harriman, "you should make it clear that this Government does not consider its action in agreeing to the Russian reparation demands on Rumania as setting a precedent in any way. . . ."[19]

The Control Commission problem was of critical significance and deserves careful consideration, for it set the tone for future relations with the Russians not only in Rumania, but in Hungary and Bulgaria as well.

The armistice conditions did not mention an Allied Control Commission, and on September 6 Harriman and Clark Kerr together saw Molotov about this issue. Harriman informed him the United States expected to have a political representative in Rumania, and Molotov responded by implying it would have to be through the Control Commission. Above all, "Molotov said that he wanted it understood that the Control Commission in Rumania would operate in the same way as the Control Commission in Italy." On the basis of this, Harriman reported back, "It seems clear that the Soviet Government intends to keep a tight rein on Rumanian affairs during the period of military operations."[20] But under the circumstances there was not much Hull could do, and perhaps it was his hope that the Russians would be more generous to the Americans in Rumania than the West had been to the Russians in Italy. The next day he accepted Molotov's dictum without protest, content that there was at least no squabble over the commission itself.

The British were not at all happy with the arrangement and refused to sign the armistice until they knew what their functions would be on the commission. The executive functions, Molotov replied, would belong to the Russians, just as, he might have added, they had belonged to the Americans and British in Italy. "He stated," Harriman reported, "that the task of the other representatives on the Control Commission would be analogous to the position of the Soviet representative on the Allied Control Commission for Italy. . . ."[21] Yet the Italian analogy offered one loophole in the existence of a political representative independent of the commission, which both the British and Americans now requested. The Russians consented almost immediately, and pressing the analogy even further, allowed the British and Americans precisely the same number of representatives on each innocuous control Commission subcommittee that they had doled out to the Russians in Italy. And, as in Italy, only the political representative could communicate directly to the Rumanians. The Americans could hardly reject living in a structure precisely like the one they had built elsewhere, and so they grudgingly accepted this state of affairs. In effect, the three Eastern European members of the Axis fell to the Russians as Italy had to the West. Would the Russians persist in pressing their literal comparisons all the way? If so, the Americans could only consent or insist that two standards for occupation governments should now become the rule.

To foretell, by Yalta the American representatives in Rumania were chafing under the restrictions the Control Commission arrangement imposed, and the irritations deeply colored their evaluations of Soviet conduct and intentions, as well as the reports they sent back to Washington.[22]

Yugoslavia: Communism versus Balkan Nationalism

Yugoslavia by 1944 had become a cockpit with four nations pursuing different policies based on radically different assumptions and objectives: the British, attempting to separate Tito from Russia; Russia, seeking to harness Tito's expansionism and keep him from damaging larger Soviet interests; the Americans, passively hostile toward all the other powers and working for and within the prewar status quo; and Tito and his Partisans, trying to gain power for themselves. By the fall of 1944 all that would occur during the next four years had begun to take shape in microcosm, and the participants had confronted all the issues.

Until 1943 none of the major Allies had shown any interest in Yugoslav affairs, and the royal government under King Peter in London became largely peripheral to the civil struggle within Yugoslavia itself between Peter's virtually independent Minister of War, General Draza Mihailovic, and the Communist-led Partisans under Josip Broz Tito. The split between the two forces was in part ideological, but primarily ethnic, with Mihailovic's Chetnik guerrilla army reflecting the interests of the urban and well-to-do Serbs, and Tito's a much broader, dynamic South Slav pannationalism encompassing all of Yugoslavia's numerous minorities. Tito's leadership was initially Serb as well, but it successfully assimilated many diverse elements and avoided discrimination within the upper echelons of the Partisan movement. The two movements used different tactics: Despite horrible German reprisals Tito wished to fight, in part because those frightful reprisals sent swarms of new men into the mountains to join his forces in the hope of escaping German retribution. Mihailovic, in contrast, fought little, and then only against the Germans in Serbia and never the Italian occupation army, and he soon lost the leadership of the Resistance to the far more dynamic Partisans. By early 1943 their relations with the Italians entirely compromised the Chetniks, who were, at the least, supplying information on the Partisans to the Germans and were preoccupied with fighting and containing Tito's growing power.

Although all the Allies had diplomatic relations with the Yugoslav government-in-exile, the Partisans' military significance was too great to ignore, for by October 1943 they had tied down twenty-five German and eight Bulgarian divisions in the Balkans. In May 1943 the British established their first agents with the Partisan forces, to supplement those with Mihailovic, and in June the British military decided "the Chetniks are hopelessly compromised in their relations with the Axis. . . ." The following month Churchill took the unusual step of appointing a representative to the Partisans—Fitzroy Maclean, whom he regarded as a "daring Ambassador-leader."[23] Maclean parachuted into Yugoslavia in September, when the Italian surrender permitted the Partisans to replenish their arms and increase their number to about 200,000 full-time combatants. No ordinary intelligence operative, Maclean was a Conservative member of Parliament with Foreign Office training—an important man for an important mission, for given his massive armed power, it was apparent that whoever controlled Tito controlled the south Balkans. Before the end of 1943 the British made this a formal assumption of policy. They nevertheless continued to recognize the London exiles, but mainly as a lever on Tito, for they knew the king could not unify the nation after the war and would at best find himself in a nominal position.

At the end of 1943, therefore, British interest in Yugoslavia made them the predominant Ally in the area, and they took it upon themselves to attempt to influence Russian and American policy toward Yugoslavia as well. The British, in October 1943, first encouraged the Russians to take a more formal interest in the area by urging them to send Soviet missions to both Tito and Mihailovic, hopefully to moderate Tito's position if they could. The Russians denied that they were aiding Tito, and during 1943 neither the British nor the Americans doubted this. In fact, only the British were in a position to know.

British interest in Tito did not diminish when he set up a new government in Bosnia at the end of November and banned Peter's return until the Yugoslavs determined the future of the monarchy after the war. They merely used the existence of the London government to attempt to extract political concessions from Tito, and Tito's existence to discipline Peter, who quickly concluded he needed to seek a more durable friend elsewhere. By January 1944 the British determined to resolve their ambivalent posture by supplying only Tito with arms, whether or not he cooperated with the king, discontinuing all aid to Mihailovic, and continuing to recognize Peter's government. That the policy made Tito stronger the British recognized, but it was also compatible with their grand strategy. Ultimately, during 1944, the British pleaded the case for both rebel and king.

The British knew, moreover, that if they were ever to mount their cherished military campaign in the Balkans it would have to be through

Croatia or Dalmatia, where Tito's forces dominated. So long as there was some thread of hope for this grand strategy, Tito's friendship held out far greater promise of political and military rewards.

The British were convinced that Tito was a nationalist first and a Communist second, and in defining Yugoslav policy before the Commons in February 1944, Churchill said as much: "The Communist element had the honour of being the beginners, but as the movement increased in strength and numbers, a modifying concept and unifying process has taken place and national conceptions have supervened."[24] And, Churchill might have added, there was no evidence of a Russian presence. Certainly the British widely shared this view at the time. Maclean, who left Churchill's son behind as an aide, was back in London briefly during the spring, and he informed British leaders that only 5 percent of Tito's army were Communists, many of the officers were non-Communists, and Tito was a nationalist with popular, mass backing whom they should not compel to rely on Soviet support. For the rest of the year Maclean urged that Tito be given sufficient means to become independent, so he would not become a Russian puppet. Throughout the better part of 1944 the British aided Tito, pressuring King Peter to repudiate Mihailovic and liberalize his reactionary government in order to lay the basis for an agreement with Tito. Forlorn, Peter finally agreed to do so in mid-May.

The United States watched these events with growing misgivings. The British had military responsibility for the area and were able to influence the Americans temporarily to withdraw part of their military mission to Mihailovic when they cut off all supplies and recognition to him at the beginning of 1944. But an exclusively American mission remained with Mihailovic until after November 1944, by which time virtually all admitted his full collaboration with the Axis. The reasons for keeping a mission, as the State Department and OSS understood it, were entirely political, as was their attitude toward Tito's Partisans. From early 1944 the State Department saw Tito as a danger to the development of democratic government, though they did not regard Peter and Mihailovic as such a threat, and the State Department merely ignored the detailed reports of Mihailovic's repression against the Partisans. They acknowledged that the Russians did not appear to be aiding Tito, but they saw the situation as one of Britain and Russia competing for Tito's favor, and the United States did not care for Tito. Therefore the Americans permitted the British to represent them to the Partisans in conjunction with the large British mission and established their own new mission to Mihailovic in spring 1944, a decision which Roosevelt approved.

The State Department regarded this as a nonintervention policy, and concluded that "both the Russians and the British may have interests in the Balkan and Mediterranean area which we would prefer not to support."[25]

To both Mihailovic and the London exile government, however, it looked as if the United States was supporting them, which, whether intended or not, was the case. Maclean talked to Robert Murphy about the possibility of Tito's being independent of Moscow if given the opportunity, and both the State Department and OSS reported that Tito had the backing of a majority of the population, including even the Serbs. The consideration which entered State Department discussions more often than Russian domination or an undemocratic state after the war was the danger of the preeminent role of Britain in shaping Yugoslav and south Balkan affairs.

The State Department in spring 1944 wanted to make it clear to the British that military unity in Yugoslavia under Tito was strictly a British, not an Allied, concept. In July 1944 the State Department insisted on continuing the arms drops to Mihailovic and attempted to see if they could find some way to keep Tito's forces from entering Serbia, which "would work an injustice on certain large and deserving groups among the Yugoslav population, whose major offense appears to be their opposition to Partisan domination." Then, in August, the Joint Chiefs of Staff, the State Department, and Leahy attempted to reiterate the American policy of noninterference by ascertaining the truth of rumors that American arms were being sent to Tito in violation of standing orders. "The Department has made it clear," a State Department memo to Hull indicated, "that we disapprove of any plan for building up the Tito forces at the expense of the Serbs. . . ."[26]

In late spring, when a German offensive smashed Tito's forces and compelled him to take refuge under British protection on the Adriatic island of Vis, the British decided to extract some political concessions by forcing Tito to negotiate with Ivan Subasic, the new Prime Minister of the exile government. On July 7 the two factions announced a unified Yugoslav government, with Subasic to be Prime Minister and Foreign Minister, leaving virtually all of the details of the relative strength of the parties and the future of the monarchy for the people to determine after the war. The State Department was cool toward these developments. Tito "is much more under British influence and control," was its first response, and Hull regarded the agreement as "essentially an arrangement between the British and Tito, representing an almost unconditional acceptance of the Partisan demands. . . ."[27] In fact, however, what it meant was subject to additional negotiations, but the Americans never ceased to hope that Tito, the British, and the Russians would all fail in their plans, for the success of British strategy meant the primacy of British influence in the south Balkans. They therefore continued their modest support for Mihailovic, and abandoned this policy well after it appeared too absurd to succeed. In practice, a consistent opposition to the only plausible alternatives left in Yugoslavia, rather than positive proposals, characterized American policy.

By the summer of 1944, however, the British had very serious doubts about the success of their tactics, and in mid-August, Churchill met Tito in Naples and attempted to pin down his postwar political commitments and shore up the position of Subasic and the king. Tito conceded nothing on the issue of the monarchy, agreed only to make a declaration that he would not unilaterally introduce Communism, and was reticent about everything else. He left hanging nearly all questions about the future internal political structure of Yugoslavia, and by mid-September Churchill had deep misgivings about the assumptions he had operated under throughout 1944. Maclean and Macmillan urged Churchill not to cut off Tito, but to leave him the option of pursuing an independent course. When Churchill discovered at the end of September that Tito had secretly flown to Moscow, it indeed seemed that his policy had failed.

Tito went to Moscow because his relations with the Russians were also in disarray, a fact he passed along to Maclean before leaving, who in turn also let the Americans know, but this information had no impact on their analysis of the situation. In reality his relations with the Soviet Union had never been cordial and nothing in the unique character of Yugoslav Communism was intended to endear it to Moscow. At the beginning of 1942 Tito's beleaguered Partisans had asked the Russians for military aid and had been refused. Instead they got advice which violated a deep-seated political radicalism, and they found the Russians entirely unsympathetic. The Russians would not even read proclamations over the Moscow radio when they received such requests from the Partisans. They told the Partisans their rhetoric was sectarian and urged them to develop a United Front line that minimized Communism and merely stressed the need for antifascist unity. More significantly, since Russia understood an independent line in Yugoslavia would alienate their allies, from whom they were expecting a great deal more than Tito might offer, they refused to break with Peter's government-in-exile or Mihailovic. The Soviets informed Tito in the fall of 1942 that they would send a military mission to Mihailovic along with matériel, and they even studied joint radio programs. So Tito fought without Soviet aid, and despite an abstract feeling of loyalty to Russia, by 1943 the Yugoslavs were beginning to act with their own future and welfare in mind. It was during this period that a telegram Stalin received from the Partisans which began, "If you cannot send us assistance, then at least do not hamper us," profoundly shaped his impression of Tito. Georgi Dimitrov, the leading Bulgarian Communist, reported that Stalin "stamped with rage."[28]

The Russians had other reasons besides alienating the Allies to fear Tito, since they perceived the very roots of Yugoslav Communist success. Tito had won the mass backing of the larger part of all Yugoslavs, whether Serbs, Montenegrins, Macedonians, or Croats, because he appealed to a

Pan-Slav nationalism, federal principles, and equality which promised a unified nation and social progress for the first time. The attraction was irresistible, and by its very nature applicable to much of the south Balkans. There was a potential expansionism, perhaps even imperialism, in Titoism which the Russians instantly recognized as a challenge to whatever position —passive or dominant—they would define for themselves in the area. By 1943 and early 1944 it was fairly certain to the Russians that Tito was more of a threat to their possible hegemony in the region than an asset. No later than April 1944 the Yugoslav Communists spoke of a Balkan federation that would include Bulgaria and Albania as a start, and they had vaguely talked of autonomy for Macedonia within a federal state, which would also include a portion of the population of northern Greece with the same ethnic background as well. All Yugoslavs at this time, from right to left, demanded the return of the Istrian peninsula and Trieste, and Tito made it explicit by early September 1944 that he would fight for Trieste if necessary. And in the same month he entered claims on parts of Thrace and Macedonia, which were part of Greece. But it was the Macedonian question in particular that must have disturbed the Russians, for no later than January 1944 the Yugoslavs were attempting to define the politics of the Bulgarian Communist party as a preliminary to establishing a federal state with Bulgaria that more and more took on the aspect of Tito's domination. The Russians, it now seems certain, by the end of 1944 were instructing the Bulgarian Communists not to agree to the Yugoslav plans for a South Slav federation in the Balkans. In brief, the pannationalist key to Tito's success threatened to absorb much more than the territory of Yugoslavia, and to challenge Russian preeminence in southeast Europe. Aside from this, his will to succeed, even by working closely with the British and opening the door to their influence, probably disturbed the Russians as much as it did the Americans. Since the Soviets did not initiate his movement, perhaps they might not be able to stop it, in which case their interests too might be at stake. Thus, the fulfillment of Tito's aspirations threatened to create a unified, powerful southern neighbor which, whether Communist or not, would be less amenable to pressure than fragmented smaller powers.

Therefore the Russians did not work for the success of Titoist Communism in Yugoslavia, and the roots of the later split in the Communist bloc originate in this period. At Teheran, when Eden urged the Russians to send a mission to Tito, Molotov responded by asking, according to the record, "whether it would not be better to have a mission to Michaelovich [sic] rather than to Tito in order to get better information."[29] When Tito created his new government in November 1943, he did not first inform the Russians, and they told Tito's representative in Moscow that Stalin "is extremely angry. He says this is a stab in the back of the Soviet Union and the Teheran decisions."[30] Stalin did not recognize the new government in the mountains. Instead he told Beneš, who promptly passed the word along, that Peter should improve his government and that the Russians in any event would not meddle in his country's internal affairs. Earlier, Soviet officials went to pains to dissociate themselves from aid to, or leadership of, the Partisans. When the Russians did send a mission to Tito, Churchill relates, they discouraged the introduction of Bolshevism in Yugoslavia.

By mid-1944 Tito and the Russians were on extremely cool terms, and when Milovan Djilas, then one of Tito's closest associates, saw Stalin about that time, he learned Stalin was dismayed by almost everything Tito was doing. Stalin insisted that the Yugoslavs not frighten the British into thinking that they planned a Communist revolution, not merely in the sense of hiding the intention, but in prohibiting it. As a start he angrily suggested that the Tito forces take the red stars off their uniforms: "By God, stars aren't necessary!" He then warned Djilas that they had to find a compromise with Subasic, which probably helped lead to Tito's half-hearted attempts in that direction.[31] When Tito secretly went to see Stalin in Moscow, after confiding the purpose of the trip to Maclean, it was to keep Russian troops out of Yugoslavia if possible (they were then approaching Belgrade) or at least to restrict their forces and powers, and then schedule their withdrawal.

The meeting with Stalin was a disaster, for Stalin advised Tito to take back Peter. "The blood rushed to my head," Tito recalled.[32] It was no better when Stalin warned him that the Serbian bourgeoisie was too powerful to be pushed aside. The two went over old telegrams and grievances and the tone of the meeting caused the other Russians to gasp at Tito's refusal to defer to Stalin's wishes. But Tito at least obtained the civil affairs agreement Stalin gave to Beneš with much more grace. The Russians helped take Belgrade, treated the population with contempt and petty violence, and left an even deeper chasm in Yugoslav-Russian relations. Unknown to Tito, shortly after this confrontation, Stalin encouraged the British to think again about marching through the Ljubljana Gap and Yugoslavia. That move, at least, would have served both Churchill's and Stalin's purposes.

In fact, by October 1944 the British were as close to Tito as any major nation, which is, in a fashion, a way of stating that Tito had begun to embark on an independent course which only the British had anticipated and were willing to make possible. The expansionist peasant nationalism of Titoism, which the United States regarded as merely an extension of Russian imperialism, again alienated the Americans and British in the Trieste crisis of 1945–1946, which all might have predicted with precision well before the event, and then the Russians in 1948. This too the United States might have anticipated.

Tito was the only Eastern European Communist with an organized as opposed to a potential mass base, and it was precisely because he was independent of the U.S.S.R. and the most militant and autonomous in Eastern Europe that he determined to create a Communist society immediately. He was also the only Eastern European Communist willing to override the Soviet Union and to cooperate with the West during 1944–1945. The lessons of the experience made little difference in Washington, but the Russians sensed the worst for their interests.

Finland

The Finnish experience presents another dimension in the variegated pattern of Soviet policy in Eastern Europe before Yalta. That nation waged war against the Soviet Union from the first day of the German attack, and Britain joined the war on Finland in December 1941. The United States, on the other hand, continued diplomatic relations with Finland until June 30, 1944, and maintained a sympathetic interest in the fate of that nation. At the Teheran Conference, Roosevelt raised the Finnish problem with Stalin, asking if he, Roosevelt, might help to get Finland out of the war. A general fear in Washington that Russia intended to annex all of Finland along with the Baltic states prompted his suggestion, and Churchill also voiced British concern over this possibility. Stalin attempted to reassure him that the Soviet Union would settle for reparations and territory protecting the approaches to Leningrad, where the Finns had attacked them. The territorial changes were quickly agreed upon, for the Americans and British did not find them unreasonable, but the reparations question caused Churchill some anxiety, and he reiterated the British desire to see an independent Finland after the war. Since the Finns wished to continue fighting, the Allies could settle only broad principles of an agreement. They remained deeply apprehensive as to what the Russians might do.

The Finns quickly confessed their fear of being Bolshevized and tried to convince the Americans to intervene to save them. By mid-February 1944, when it then appeared certain that the Russians would win the war, the Finnish government consented to discuss Russian armistice and peace terms, which the Soviets did not base on unconditional surrender but followed the general pattern of the Teheran understanding. The British press considered the terms "reasonable and generous," as *The Economist* phrased it, but the Finns preferred fighting and broke off discussions at the end of April.[33] It was at this point that the United States decided, after British and Russian pressures, to waver from Roosevelt's unconditional surrender formula for Axis satellites.

At the end of June, Russian troops penetrated the Karelian Isthmus, and after several Cabinet upheavals, the Finns in September consented to meet the Russians and sue for peace. Although the United States expected the peace terms to be far more onerous than the March offer, the Russians instead relaxed them very substantially. The Finns did not have to intern German troops, the terms halved reparations to $300 million, and both sides accepted the territorial changes agreed upon at Teheran. The Finns were even to remain neutral for the remainder of the war and independent of hostile alliances thereafter. The Soviets demanded occupation of various bases for the duration of the war, but not the occupation of the entire country, and the Finns accepted all these terms on September 19. Churchill praised the armistice as characterized by "restraint," and the English press again noted the unrepentant nature of the new Finnish government.[34] In the March 1945 elections the Communists received 23.5 percent of the vote, a trend that only filled the Western Powers with great apprehension about the future of the small nation despite the sanguine reports the State Department received from its representative in Helsinki. The election was honest, the Finns pro-German, and the peace terms were admittedly very moderate, but the realities of the Finnish situation, and the light it threw on Soviet policy, the West considered less important than the situation in Poland.

BY October 1944 the Soviet Union was pursuing a pluralistic policy in Eastern Europe based on the specific political conditions in each country. No single nation, whether Czechoslovakia or Poland, revealed the overall intentions of the Russians, nor could anyone say the Russians had embarked on a final course. Yugoslavia exposed its desire to subsume the impulses of the local Communists within its more conservative global and military policies, revealing an inability to impose monolithic discipline on an indigenous, powerful party. Rumania disclosed a Soviet desire to apply an Italian formula to a situation that was as yet uncrystallized, and Finland indicated its willingness to trade neutrality for easy annexation. Czechoslovakia showed the Russians' cordial enthusiasm for a reintegration with the West within a non-Communist framework if nonalignment provided for the ultimate question of military security. And Poland lay bare the fact that the U.S.S.R. would be implacably hostile toward those seeking to reimpose prewar diplomacy on new realities.

Despite this pluralism and diversity the tension and suspicion in the Western capitals mounted, for these relations were not final and each carried important elements of doubt, depending upon ultimate Soviet purposes in regard to its own role in Europe and the kind of economic and political relations it wished to establish in Eastern Europe. By October both Britain and the United States were ready to chart their own policies toward Eastern Europe and to seek anew assurances of Russian intentions.

CHAPTER
7

EASTERN EUROPE, III:
"WITH BOW AGAINST BEAR"
(OCTOBER 1944
TO JANUARY 1945)

B Y OCTOBER 1944 the Eastern European situation had all the ap-
pearances of a political vacuum, with emerging problems exceeding options and possibilities, but to Churchill and the British still within the
realm of control. And since all the Allies now acknowledged the principle
that military victory would define local politics, Churchill set out to do with
words what he could not do by force of arms: to stop the Bolshevization of
Eastern Europe. In the last months of 1944, after a period of obsessive
concern over the spread of the Red Army and a realization that there was
no way of gaining American support for a Balkan invasion, Churchill
embarked on an active policy of frank discussion and accommodation with
the Russians in the belief that the U.S.S.R. was not yet inflexible on the
future of Eastern Europe and that Britain, in any event, had no other
option at the time in the face of growing Soviet power. Churchill regarded
this recognition of necessity as a respite and first step in the containment of
Bolshevism. The United States agreed on the danger of Communism but
not the tactics for stopping it. The British pursued an active policy of grand
diplomacy while the Americans passively created obstacles to the attainment of their objectives. During October, Churchill traveled to Moscow to
negotiate spheres of influence in Europe that were less a creation of new
realities than a formalization of the status quo.

The division of Europe into Soviet and Western spheres had been taking place since mid-1943. Contributing to the partition were the policies of the English and Americans in Italy, the Allied rejection of the attempt to create a truly all-European system in a potent European Advisory Commission, Molotov's recognition of Western dominance in France, Anglo-American acceptance of an "Italian formula" in Rumania, the embryonic Western European bloc, and American supremacy in the Far East. Now all that was left was to legitimize reality with an explicit understanding. To undo that reality was impossible without infinitely greater Western military superiority and sacrifice.

Could it have been otherwise? In August 1943, when Stalin was pressing for the creation of a European political-military commission to hammer out a unified policy and unified control over the defeated Axis nations, the Soviet Ambassador to England, I. M. Maisky, went to see Eden about the long-term implications of the problem. There could be spheres of influence, he pointed out, or cooperation. If the West excluded the Russians from Mediterranean or French affairs, the Soviets would claim the same rights in the East. The alternative, which both Maisky and the British Foreign Office avowed they preferred, was to admit the rights of each power in every part of the continent. When during the remainder of 1943 the West formally excluded the U.S.S.R. from the Italian problem, the implications were not lost on the Russians. At the October Moscow Conference, both Molotov and Litvinov declared Russia was not interested in creating spheres of influence in Europe, but Litvinov scotched a proposed British self-denial declaration because it excluded non-European areas. Much changed to Russian advantage before the English raised the topic again.

By May 1944 Churchill and Eden were more deeply concerned about the growth of the Left in the Balkans and most especially in Greece, an obsession for the Prime Minister which over the summer blanked out references to Germany, and Churchill saw the Left threatening the "Communisation" of Europe as far as Italy. He then decided to confront the "brute issues" with the Russians.[1] On May 5 Eden posed the problem to the new Soviet ambassador, Fedor T. Gusev, and asked him if the Russians would support the British in Greece if Russia could count on British backing in Rumania. The Russian referred the question to Moscow and on May 18 responded favorably, but asked Eden if they had requested the Americans to give their consent to the arrangement. At the end of the month Halifax went to see Hull with the proposition and Churchill wrote Roosevelt. At first Churchill assured the President it was just a military compact for the duration of the war only, without prejudice to the peace settlement. But the English leader explicitly considered the bargain political and permanent and soon revealed these dimensions of the settlement. Hull categorically opposed the arrangement, as did Roosevelt initially.

By June 8 the English also mentioned Bulgaria and Yugoslavia as subject to division between the two European allies, and Halifax told Hull that American acquiescence was only logical given the fact "we follow the lead of the United States in South America as far as possible. . . ." Churchill reiterated that he did not have spheres of influence in mind, but made it perfectly clear he wished to stop Bolshevism. With this formulation, and over Hull's subsequent objections, Roosevelt agreed to Churchill's proposal on June 12 after the Prime Minister added that they would consider it a temporary three-month experiment. Churchill made it plain that the purpose of the understanding was to prevent the "slithering to the Left, which is so popular in foreign policy," and on this Roosevelt agreed, but the bilateral discussions between England and Russia disturbed him and he soon let Churchill know of his displeasure on this count.[2] On July 1 Gromyko presented the entire matter to Hull and asked for a definite American opinion, and the United States approved the three-month agreement formally on July 15. That the Russians would not have comprehended the anti-Communist motive of the arrangement is difficult to believe. It is likely the Russians were quite ready to leave the Greeks and Yugoslavs to their own fate, for they had not aided them in any event. Also clear is the fact that the Russians thought any agreement that excluded the Americans was not worth very much.

Churchill hoped before October 1944 to contain the expansion of Russian power in the wake of war by a number of grand diplomatic designs which reflected the ingenuity of his mind as well as his desire to compensate for the limits of British power. For Churchill was the master of nineteenth-century diplomacy and its techniques, and balances, and hidden meanings, and all the subtleties in the relation of present arrangements to future developments he anticipated, the grand architect of a classical diplomacy. He hoped to place the troops of his American ally in the Eastern European theater, but an American realism that struck him as shortsighted thwarted his design. He attempted to create a Western European bloc, but it was too soon to determine whether this would be efficacious or sufficient, or even whether he could patch the small Western European powers together into a controllable alliance. Finally, toward the end of 1944 Churchill realized he had begun to lose control of those Eastern European political elements, intransigent and obstinate, capable of serving as the keystone of his most ambitious hope, an Eastern European confederation which he publicly described as a cordon sanitaire against Germany, but in fact was primarily directed against the Soviet Union.

At the end of 1941, and again in spring 1942, Eden broached the subject of an Eastern European confederation centered around Poland, but with vague limits and functions which caused the Russians to express apprehension. At the end of 1943, first at the Moscow meeting and then at Teheran, the British raised the subject once more, and Churchill asked

Stalin if he wished to see small, disunited, and weak states in Eastern Europe. It was during these conferences that the Russians categorically tabled the proposal because it resembled the old cordon sanitaire of the prewar Western European anti-Bolsheviks, though with the word "premature" added to their admonitions so that the British retained some slight hope.[3] Without Poland, however, the plan was chimerical, and so the British saw their dreams fade, although not disappear. During May 1944 Churchill continued to devise schemes for various European blocs, councils, and the like, plans that met the hostility of his allies and even, at times, his War Cabinet. At the beginning of 1945 he again proposed a Balkan federation, perhaps to include Turkey.

Churchill's creativity was brilliant, his subtlety unquestionably far exceeded that of Stalin's, much less Roosevelt's, and his designs were ingenious in their appearance of serving many functions for many people. He survived the trials of the war in an impulsive manner, living on his nerves and often exhausted and ill. Many of Churchill's intimates regarded him as a "child," and as he grew more tired he became less and less interested in subtleties and complexities.[4] By September 1944 he was very tired indeed. His plans lacked realism, for Great Britain did not have the power to implement them, and most of Churchill's associates recognized this as Churchill did himself by the fall of 1944. There was no alternative at that time to directly confronting the Russians and reaching an agreement if possible, though not one that excluded new options in the future.

By the end of September 1944, as Churchill described it, "Communism raised its head behind the thundering Russian battle-front. Russia was the Deliverer, and Communism the gospel she brought."[5] It was necessary to go to the anti-Christ himself, Stalin, and induce him to accept the restraints of true religion.

If Churchill indeed believed the Russians were bent on the Bolshevization of Europe, it is difficult to understand why he went to Moscow, unless it was to lull the Russians into a disarmingly false sense of security through agreements he could then ignore when power and the initiative had shifted away from the Russian sphere. If this was his logic, and it seems likely it was, Churchill chose to talk to the wrong man. Stalin, if nothing else, was a consummate realist who based his action on a keen awareness of the limits and possibilities of real power in being. He rejected Trotsky's "adventurism" in the 1920's, when Russia was weak; he ruthlessly disciplined the peasantry and workers to make Russia strong; he liquidated and then pampered his military leaders; and he had no illusions about the value of British pledges after repeated broken promises of a second front had forced Russia to depend on its own resources. Britain had prestige, it had a persistent leader, but Stalin knew it no longer guided the destinies of the capitalist world and he certainly had no illusions about Churchill's attitude toward Bolshevism. Any agreement that excluded the United States could not be worth much, and England's word was less than sterling where Communism was involved. Stalin could therefore politely agree to see the British leader, but he could assume Russia would have to define its own essential interests in Eastern Europe. How it would do so was already shown in the conduct of Soviet diplomacy up to the fall of 1944, and Churchill sought to press this seeming reasonableness of phases of Soviet policy to his own advantage. With or without a discussion concerning spheres of influence, Stalin was not likely to waver from the course he had chosen for himself.

Churchill, for complex reasons I will discuss in the next chapter, was especially alarmed over the emergence of the armed Resistance in Greece, where British interests were far greater than in Yugoslavia and there appeared to be at least some option to the Left, and he was convinced only Russia could contain it or grant him the freedom to do so. Stalin could hardly refuse to see him in Moscow, and so, with scarcely a week's warning, on October 9 Churchill and Eden arrived in Moscow. By virtue of American policy, they were to arrive disarmed.

When Roosevelt learned of the impending meeting his first response was far more critical than the already hostile policy toward Churchill's June spheres-of-influence scheme. After some debate with Hopkins he informed Stalin that every political and military question he and Churchill might consider was of interest to the United States, and only Roosevelt's personal participation would bind America. Harriman could sit in on sessions only as an observer, unable to commit the United States on any question. "It is important that I retain complete freedom of action after this conference is over," Roosevelt wired Harriman in Hopkins' words.[6] Stalin replied somewhat bewilderedly, for Churchill gave him the impression he was coming to Moscow "in keeping with an agreement reached with you at Quebec."[7] Forewarned, Stalin was aware his discussion with Churchill would mean little, if anything, even if he could trust the Englishman. Churchill too was aware of his limited freedom and powers in regard to the Americans. Any agreement was bound to be worthless.

There is therefore little significance to the memorable and dramatic passage in Churchill's autobiography recalling how he and Stalin divided Eastern Europe the very day he arrived in Moscow.

> The moment was apt for business, so I said, "Let us settle about our affairs in the Balkans. Your armies are in Rumania and Bulgaria. We have interests, missions, and agents there. Don't let us get at cross-purposes in small ways. So far as Britain and Russia are concerned, how would it do for you to have ninety per cent predominance in Rumania, for us to have ninety per cent of the say in Greece, and go fifty-fifty about Yugoslavia?" While this was being translated I wrote out on a half-sheet of paper:

Rumania	
Russia	90%
The others	10%

Greece	
Great Britain	90%
(in accord with U.S.A.)	
Russia	10%

Yugoslavia	50–50%

Hungary	50–50%

Bulgaria	
Russia	75%
The others	25%

I pushed this across to Stalin, who had by then heard the translation. There was a slight pause. Then he took his blue pencil and made a large tick upon it, and passed it back to us. It was all settled in no more time than it takes to set down.

Of course we had long and anxiously considered our point, and were only dealing with immediate war-time arrangements. All larger questions were reserved on both sides for what we then hoped would be a peace table when the war was won.

After this there was a long silence. The pencilled paper lay in the centre of the table. At length I said, "Might it not be thought rather cynical if it seemed we had disposed of these issues, so fateful to millions of people, in such an offhand manner? Let us burn the paper." "No, you keep it," said Stalin.[8]

Stalin's "tick," translated into real words, indicated nothing whatsoever. The very next day Churchill sent Stalin a draft of the discussion, and the Russian carefully struck out phrases implying the creation of spheres of influence, a fact Churchill excluded from his memoirs. Eden assiduously avoided the term, and considered the understanding merely as a practical agreement on how problems would be worked out in each country, and the very next day he and Molotov modified the percentages in a manner which Eden assumed was general rather than precise. The duration of the understanding was later a subject of controversy, but the discussions had been extremely cordial and Harriman noted Stalin's conciliatory and almost effusive manner.

The Russian leader retained a tolerant sense of humor throughout his meeting with the British leaders, even when Churchill on October 11 placed the significance of his presence in a brutally frank ideological context. "If we manage these affairs well we shall perhaps prevent several civil wars . . . ," he notified Stalin. If the decisions would not be binding until after Roosevelt met with them, or at the final peace table, Churchill explained, agreement now could stop the tide toward the left. England had "certain relations of faithfulness" with the monarchies of Greece and

Yugoslavia, the two main areas of British concern. "However," he told the former agitator and son of freed serfs, "besides the institutional question there exists in all these countries the ideological issue between totalitarian forms of government and those we call free enterprise controlled by universal suffrage. We are very glad that you have declared yourselves against trying to change by force or by Communist propaganda the established systems in the various Balkan countries."[9]

Stalin surely must have been in good humor to retain his cordiality during Churchill's descriptions of the prewar clericalist and pro-Nazi dictatorships as based on universal suffrage, much less his imputation that a preservation of these regimes in preference to pro-Soviet states was desirable. In fact he had agreed to nothing because Churchill could deliver little and the United States was not willing to sanction anything. Above all, the nations traded were not Churchill's or Stalin's to give, for the people of those lands had their own aspirations, goals the heads of state had not defined and were powerless to eliminate. He was merely as polite as Churchill was deceitful, Soviet policy would be carried on as before, and it was this incident that showed Stalin as the greatest master in the art of diplomacy. As Churchill left Moscow on October 19, Stalin presented him with a vase, ironically entitled "With Bow Against Bear."[10] It was the only thing he took home that was tangible. In fact the exhausted and ill Churchill himself vacillated on the implications of his agreement, alternately denying the Russians were out to Communize Europe, and grateful that their vast human sacrifice alone had made possible Britain's return to Europe, and firmly convinced England and America had no greater duty than stoutly to offer joint resistance to the Soviet Union. This ambiguity continued for several more months, until he finally resolved it.

Harriman kept the American government fully informed of the proceedings at Moscow. But only Harriman favored reaching some serious agreement with the Russians, on the assumption that "the longer the situation drifts the more difficult a solution becomes."[11] Roosevelt himself would not endorse the understanding, and Stimson and Leahy found it outright objectionable. The duration of the arrangement was vague; Churchill used the term "interim," and also mentioned three months.[12] Winant pointed out that Churchill intended the entire discussion to save British interests around the Mediterranean—Greece, and Yugoslavia in particular —and "Eden was having his pants traded off" elsewhere.[13] Washington did not think this would do American interests in, say, Bulgaria, any good, and it might very well set the pattern for postwar settlements. Leahy and various State Department analysts merely regarded the whole scheme as an incipient conflict for power between England and Russia, excluding due recognition of American interests, and the State Department refused to endorse it. When Churchill quite erroneously wrote Roosevelt that Stalin agreed at least in principle to a Danubian federation after the war, the State Department concluded that this or a Balkan federation, to which Churchill referred again, might polarize Eastern European affairs away from United States interests. The Americans were now to define those interests with great clarity as a result of the Stalin-Churchill conference. Finally, Stimson pointed out at the end of the year, if the United States endorsed Britain's principle of a cordon sanitaire or alliances, the Russians might themselves apply it first to build a bloc of friendly nations on its borders.[14] Both policies, for reasons that became clear later, appeared equally unacceptable in Washington.

Churchill's effort failed, for he could not modify the de facto realities with secret understandings when he was unable to alter them by force of arms. Therefore British resources, materially weakened by the war, and their own definition of security imposed limits on their conduct. By October circumstances fully revealed the dimensions these assumptions might take. Yet Churchill attempted to apply the October formula as a permanent solution where it was to England's favor, and temporarily elsewhere, and the matter came up repeatedly as a criterion for evaluating Soviet conduct and intentions.

Eastern Europe before Yalta

Churchill also used the Moscow meeting to consider the specific internal problems of various Eastern European nations, especially Poland and Yugoslavia, and it is worth surveying the development in these areas as the United States attempted to define an extensive policy for the region and again assess and predict Soviet diplomatic and political intentions in the existing and postwar world.

Poland

Churchill went to Moscow not merely to solve his problems in Greece or Yugoslavia, but also because the Polish exile government in London, for the first time in years, had given a slim indication of willingness to at least discuss borders and even the inclusion of Communists in their postwar government. Perhaps he might still be able to do something at that late hour to redeem Poland from the freedom and provocation the Russians had to impose on it a government more to their liking.

Stalin agreed to see Mikolajczyk while Churchill was in Moscow, and so they brought the Polish leader to the Kremlin for the purpose, along with the Lublin Polish leaders. On the 13th Mikolajczyk, Churchill, and Stalin met in Harriman's presence, and the two heads of the Great Powers immediately lined up behind the Curzon Line. When Molotov indicated that the United States also supported this territorial settlement, Harriman silently noted the statement, as did Mikolajczyk, who resolutely refused to compromise on any border changes. Stalin attempted to reassure him that "Communism does not fit the Poles. They are too individualistic, too nationalistic. . . . Poland will be a capitalistic state." But the Pole found ominous meanings in Stalin's declaration that "there are certain people—both Left and Right—that we cannot allow in Polish politics."[15] They resolved nothing, and the Russians shrugged and passed the matter over to the British for a day.

Churchill resorted to his by now unsuccessful strategy of firmness to both recalcitrant Poles and determined Russians, and Mikolajczyk's vivid description of the confrontation indicates how desperate Churchill was to salvage a future for the uncompromising and legalistic Poles.

Mikolajczyk. I am not a person completely devoid of patriotic feeling, to give away half of Poland.

Churchill. What do you mean by saying "you are not devoid of patriotic feeling?" Twenty-five years ago *we* reconstituted Poland although in the last war more Poles fought against us than for us. Now again we are preserving you from disappearance, but you will not play ball. You are absolutely crazy.

Mikolajczyk. But this solution does not change anything.

Churchill. Unless you accept the frontier you are out of business forever. The Russians will sweep through your country and your people will be liquidated. You are on the verge of annihilation.

Eden. Supposing that we get an understanding on the Curzon Line, we will get agreement on all the other things from the Russians. You will get a guarantee from us.

Churchill. Poland will be guaranteed by the three Great Powers and certainly by us. The American Constitution makes it difficult for the President to commit the United States. In any case you are not giving up anything because the Russians are there already.

Mikolajczyk. We are losing everything.

Churchill. The Pripet marshes and five million people. The Ukrainians are not your people. You are saving your own people and enabling us to act with vigor. . . .

Churchill. You are no Government if you are incapable of taking any decision. You are callous people who want to wreck Europe. I shall leave you to your own troubles. You have no sense of responsibility when you want to abandon your people at home, to whose sufferings you are indifferent. You do not care about the future of Europe, you have only your own miserable selfish interest in mind. I will have to call on the other Poles and this Lublin Government may function very well. It will be *the Government.* It is a criminal attempt on your part to wreck, by your "Liberum Veto," agreement between the Allies. It is cowardice on your part.

On the remarks of Mikolajczyk that Churchill may set forth to Stalin his declaration as his project, toward which the Polish Government will confine itself to sheer protest, *Churchill* replies: I am not going to worry Mr. Stalin. If you want to conquer Russia we shall leave you to do it. I feel like being in a lunatic asylum. I don't know whether the British Government will continue to recognize you.[16]

This wild session did not move the London Poles and when Churchill met the Lublin representatives he quickly fell back into a milder stance, urging the exiles only to compromise on their borders to save their political integrity. Mikolajczyk considered his dilemma and on the 16th went to Harriman for information on the American position on the Curzon Line. Harriman had already informed Molotov that Roosevelt did not support the Curzon Line, and he now told the Pole the same thing. Personally, however, he warned Mikolajczyk the time would never be more propitious for him to settle his future relationship with the Lublin Poles. With this assurance on the borders, however, the classic Polish strategy of relying on the United States again moved to the fore, and subsequent meetings between Mikolajczyk, Stalin, and the Lublin Poles proved fruitless, with no agreement on either border or political issues. Churchill wired Roosevelt he could get majority control of a future Polish government for the London exiles "if all else is settled," and that Mikolajczyk would attempt to convince his associates the situation required a compromise.[17] This the Pole attempted to do upon his return from Moscow, but on October 26 he also appealed to Roosevelt "to throw the weight of your decisive influence and authority on the scales of events."[18] He then cleverly asked the British if they would guarantee Poland's independence within new frontiers, as well as for clarification of Poland's borders in the west. When the British declined to give ironclad assurances on independence, which could conceivably lead to war with Russia, the Poles in London hesitated. The Polish ambassador posed this question to the State Department on November I I, which then formulated a speedy and essentially satisfactory response to Mikolajczyk's plea of October 26. Harriman, the Department told the Polish leader on November 17, would ask Stalin to give Lwow province to Poland, though the United States still preferred postponing all border questions until after the war, and in no instance would guarantee any settlements. Alterations before peace should be by "mutual agreement," including those in Poland. One other factor may have weighed heavily with the Poles. The new American ambassador to the London exile government was Arthur Bliss Lane, a bitterly anti-Soviet diplomat who saw Roosevelt on November 20 and urged him to take a strong position for Polish independence, for the United States was now a strong military power and later might be weaker. Roosevelt refused to alter his stand, and Lane felt the President had much too much confidence in the Russians.

It is certain, however, that America's uncompromising policy was cru-

cial to the London Poles, who reconsidered the entire matter in the light of
the possibilities it posed. They determined to continue to hold fast, and on
November 23 Mikolajczyk told Winant that the London Poles had rejected his compromise program of reconciliation with the Lublin Poles,
weak as it was. The next day he resigned as prime minister. The reasons
Mikolajczyk gave Winant were not complex, but the assumptions they were
based on were out of date. The London Poles insisted on postponing all
border questions until the end of the war, precisely the American position
until that time. If they could not reach a compromise alternative soon, the
ex-Prime Minister now claimed, Poland would definitely go Communist.
He implied he would attempt, alone, to provide it, though the chances were
now slim. He would not leave politics, it was clear, but his resignation
spelled the doom of the London exile government. That one man who
listened to Churchill's advice only at the final moment could change the
course of events seemed too improbable at the time.

The American and British policy toward Poland was now irrelevant, and
the solidly anti-Russian, anti-negotiations bloc that took over the London
exile government did nothing to aid it. The English immediately recognized
the dilemma, and the Lublin Poles indicated they would cooperate with
Mikolajczyk on their platform only. Everyone considered imminent Soviet
recognition of the Lublin group almost certain. On December 13 Stettinius informed Harriman that United States relations with the London
Poles would remain nothing more than "correct," but that the ambassador
was to discourage Soviet recognition of the Lublin group. In brief, the
United States policy toward Poland not only floundered, but helped to
create the impasse. ". . . the Polish question," Stettinius notified Roosevelt,
is "much more difficult and acute."[19]

Throughout December, Stalin hinted to Churchill and Roosevelt that
Soviet recognition of the Lublin Poles was at hand, and as England and the
United States scurried about for a new policy, mutual recriminations
followed quickly. On December 15 both Churchill and Eden addressed the
Commons on the Polish question. For the London Poles, Churchill had
only words of condemnation, for they had dissipated all opportunities to
gain independence and Soviet friendship as well. As a futile gesture he
urged the London Poles to reach agreement with the Russians before it was
too late, but he admitted the opportune moment had passed. "I find great
difficulty in discussing these matters," Churchill obliquely chastised the
American role, "because the attitude of the United States has not been
defined with the precision which His Majesty's Government have thought it
wise to use." He made unkind reference to Polish-American voters. Eden's
words were something in the nature of a post-mortem, consisting of a
survey of the sequence of British attempts and failures to save an independent Poland. "That is the reason why we took this risk, and, if you like,
burnt our fingers. . . ."[20]

In direct response to British pessimism and criticism, on December 18 the State Department released another policy statement exactly like its previous one: border changes should be held in abeyance until the end of the war, save by mutual consent. It was precisely this policy that led the British to despair. For the remainder of the month Roosevelt urged Stalin not to act on the Polish matter until the Great Power conference at Yalta, and he stressed this was "of the highest importance."[21] Churchill joined in making similar pleas, but to no avail. On December 31 the Lublin Committee transformed itself into the Polish Provisional government, and on January 4 Russia recognized it.

[Stalin's formal justification for the new government was that the new Arciszewski Cabinet in London was entirely anti-Russian and that its underground was engaging in terrorism against the rear lines of the Red Army.] The Soviets repeated the arguments many times and their significance requires only a few words. The new exile government was assuredly not going to work with Russia on any basis that made sense to England, and continued, along with the Home Army, to threaten to fight the Russians if necessary. It seems almost certain, in the light of these warnings and later terrorist activities of much greater magnitude, that at least isolated and small bands, both for personal and political reasons, engaged in armed attacks on Russian troops and Polish administrators. In fact, segments of the Home Army had much more significant plans than the relatively petty events the Russians could conjure up, but at the time Stalin's excuse was feeble.

The Western Allies refused to recognize the pro-Soviet Polish government, and they urged Stalin to defer matters until Yalta, when the Allies might find solutions together. But throughout January 1945 the American government thought about the question, and failed to originate a new policy. For the rest of the month neither Stalin, Churchill, nor Roosevelt discussed the controversy with one another, and the Poles in London added no new possibilities for accommodation. In suggesting a Polish policy for guidance at Yalta the State Department determined to attempt to win the province of Lwow for Poland, but also to keep it from obtaining excessive compensation from Germany, especially along two alternative Oder-Neisse lines. But they finally decided to make the entire border issue secondary to the creation of an independent Polish government, one that included all major sections of the population and especially "liberal democratic groups." Who were they? The State Department frankly admitted within its own ranks that possibly both the London and Lublin Poles were unrepresentative, and OSS reports were even more emphatic on this point. The Peasant party of Mikolajczyk, which the OSS found most amorphous and therefore capable of flexibility and growth, was especially designated as the key party to receive American support and take a leading role in future Polish affairs.

The United States belatedly recognized the British position that politics was more consequential than territory, but the American border position still contained those elements that undercut the British and reinforced the uncompromising attitude of the London Poles. Until they could make these two positions consistent, therefore, there was nothing radically new in the American policy shortly before Yalta. The American decision to support Mikolajczyk was also inconsistent in light of a confessed ignorance as to who really represented Poland, but it made sense in the context of the larger American definition of Eastern European policy discussed at the end of this chapter. There was no reason to suspect that the modified American view would succeed where the old one had failed, or that they had created or found any new options.

On January 20 Harriman saw Maisky, who was now Assistant People's Commissar for Foreign Affairs. The Russian said Mikolajczyk had not shown himself a strong leader, and that the London government had dissipated all its opportunities. Russia saw nothing ahead save the "Lublin Poles," who were now in Warsaw. Harriman said little, "except to emphasize its importance as an issue that must be settled, and its effect on our relations."[22] These events were an evil omen of things to come.

Yugoslavia

At their October meeting in Moscow, Stalin was especially agreeable in approving Churchill's requests on Yugoslavia, granting at least equal influence with the U.S.S.R.—a concession, ironically, that could mean equal exclusion as well. The British were pleased with the ease with which Stalin satisfied their interests. The accord was to unite the Yugoslav peoples in a federation, and Stalin, with somewhat more gusto than usual, justified British concern in the nation by virtue of its mineral concessions and Mediterranean lifeline and commerce. He even suggested the British send armies through the northern Yugoslav area, even though Tito had warned him only shortly before he would use his troops against such an intrusion. Stalin, as Churchill may have suspected, was giving away property he did not own, and there is good reason to believe that the Russian may have preferred someone other than Tito even at this time. "If a King can be more useful in waging war against [the] enemy and maintaining stability after victory," Stalin was quoted as saying, "he would prefer him to a makeshift Republic."[23] Churchill was relieved.

For the next four months Churchill attempted to give political direction to Yugoslavia, quibbling with all the Yugoslav factions save Mihailovic's, whose intimate association with United States agents managed to isolate the Americans from the question. Churchill's suspicions of Tito increased and waned as the difficult negotiations proceeded, and only the Russians cooperated fully with his project. His purpose was to insert substance and meaning into the nebulous Tito-Subasic agreement which in principle merged the London exile government and Tito's Antifascist Council of National Liberation, in control of that part of Yugoslavia not in German hands.

On October 27 Tito's forces held a victory parade near Belgrade at which Tito declared the Yugoslav nation had already earned its own independence as an equal of its great Allies, and would in the future be the puppet of no one. During these final days of October, Tito and his followers were locked in secret negotiations with Subasic to determine the composition of a future Yugoslav government. Subasic, who had not been back to Yugoslavia for many years, was impressed, as Kirk reported to Washington, that "the whole of the country including Serbia was behind Tito. . . ."[24] Under the circumstance there was not much he could do alone, and Subasic turned to Britain and Russia for backing, nevertheless delighted with Tito's numerous concessions. At the end of October all he had to show was a secret and still vague framework for a future government, one based on the exclusion of King Peter until a plebiscite might be held, and a democratic, federative government the Yugoslavs would form on the basis of nationality representation. A Regency Council would exercise royal power during the interim, and they did not inform Peter of the arrangement. Tito was to be Prime Minister, Subasic the Foreign Minister, and a small minority of ministers would be Communists.

Churchill saw King Peter about the new arrangement on November 21, when Subasic was in Moscow, and Peter refused to sign an agreement equivalent to abdication, even threatening to denounce Subasic. Churchill reminded Peter that Tito controlled the country, and that he ought to make the best of the situation before taking rash steps. Unpleasant words were exchanged, and Churchill's conduct made it evident the British were not supporting monarchy as a principle but only for their own political interests.

Subasic heard kinder words in Moscow, for Stalin expressed abhorrence of any Yugoslav experiments in Bolshevism and restrictions imposed on free speech. Since Tito controlled the country, and the British were delighted with the impending arrangement Subasic had reached, Soviet acquiescence now cleared the way for recognition of the new regime. Stalin urged it, Churchill quickly concurred, contingent on a few minor clarifications, and Subasic was very pleased. Tito on December 7 readily signed an agreement that established full civil liberties prior to an election for the Constituent Assembly, with the Antifascist Council wielding legislative power until that time. The British then raised extraneous issues that delayed a final political arrangement for a time only.

Tito's forces had been especially rude to various British military personnel in Dalmatia, and the incidents were trivial save insofar as they were the beginning of later, similar events involving national prestige and authority that were first to color Yugoslav relations with the West and later the Russians. Tito had utter contempt for the Americans in Yugoslavia due to their country's dealings with Mihailovic, and he made slight secret of the fact. Later Washington confused such exuberance on the part of the Yugoslavs with Bolshevik maliciousness. But in December the British did not appreciate such behavior from a virtual ward whose political interests they were fostering, and Churchill sent Tito a note on December 8 that was strongly worded and threatened retaliation unless the Yugoslavs showed more courtesy. Perhaps equally disturbing was Tito's refusal to accept food and relief supplies if observers accompanied it. His representatives assured Anglo-American officers in Italy that they were equitably distributing food without political bias, which independent sources corroborated as true. Since the food shortage in Dalmatia had reached critical proportions, the Yugoslavs blamed the West for raising the question of political criteria. Tito won on this point. In fact, as Maclean admitted, the observers were intended to serve a political role in regard to inhibiting Communist willingness to act. All of these issues were minor in nature, and by the end of December the British forces noticed they were being paid new deference, but the less involved Americans drew the political moral: "While it can be argued that many of the current excesses should be ascribed to early revolutionary exuberance and to inexperience," Kirk wrote Stettinius, "we should not close our eyes to potentialities of a revolutionary and authoritarian regime inseparable from one of the most dynamic and courageous of the European resistance movements. . . ."[25]

The English worked out the political problems at the same time to everyone's satisfaction save that of King Peter and the Americans. New agreements between the two Yugoslav factions made during early December left the Communists with only seven of twenty-five government ministries, but these, everyone observed, were all critical. Stettinius informed the American ambassador to the Yugoslav government-in-exile, Richard C. Patterson, Jr., that the United States found the terms of the Tito-Subasic agreement too general to comment upon. They also told the British the United States would be unwilling to endorse the agreement, even if Tito's movement "should have found at least temporary popular acceptance," a fact that could no longer be denied. The British and Russians advised Tito, Subasic, and Peter on these matters, and Stettinius darkly referred to "understandings between the British and Soviet Governments" as the basis of their intrusion into Yugoslav domestic affairs.[26] To Patterson, however, Stettinius indicated the United States opposed "any foreign influence" on the Yugoslavs, and it was clear the failure of American policy in regard to Mihailovic was not going to lead to acceptance of the British strategy of winning Tito over to neutralism.[27] The United States notified Peter of its policy as well, and he now realized that any hesitancy on his part would coincide with American policy.

On January 10 King Peter denounced the Tito-Subasic agreement, and the following day Churchill proposed to Stalin that they "simply bypass King Peter II," obtain the agreement of the Americans not to oppose them, and recognize the Tito government.[28] Stalin immediately agreed, and Churchill delayed and decided to give Subasic one last chance to convince Peter. Stalin then pressed for action, but Churchill indicated Peter's consent might be critical to the elimination of the American opposition to their joint strategy, and on January 18 Churchill proved his loyalty to Stalin by publicly endorsing the Tito-Subasic agreement.

It was now Peter's turn to save himself from Churchill's strategy, and on January 23 he dismissed the Subasic government-in-exile. The British immediately responded by blandly informing Peter that they intended seeing the Tito-Subasic agreement implemented and would take the Subasic government back to Belgrade as soon as it chose to leave. Churchill asked Stalin for his aid in recognizing the new, merged government and in pressuring the Americans to withdraw their opposition. Stalin consented and Subasic and Peter then conferred. The first American response was to ask the British to delay implementing their policy, but when the State Department on the 28th wired Patterson not to assume any responsibility for the crisis, and in effect to remain neutral, the king relented, and the following day transferred royal power to the Regency Council. To the British, Winant made it clear America refused to endorse Anglo-Soviet policy.

The United States lost its veto power over Yugoslav politics and before Yalta was still as isolated on Yugoslav affairs as it had been on Polish problems. It would concede nothing to Russian or British interests in the area, much less to Tito, who the State Department was sure would be the direct beneficiary of the Tito-Subasic agreement. The Americans first placed their hopes on Mihailovic, then backed Peter. They acknowledged Tito had the support of the majority of Yugoslavs, and his nationalist and independent character was obvious, but to the Americans he stood for foreign influences and the Left, and Washington never critically questioned the nature of America's opposition to Yugoslav desires.[29]

The Three Former Members of the Axis

The United States and England reluctantly agreed to accept the organization of an Allied Control Commission in Rumania precisely modeled on the one they established in Italy, and the Russians compelled them to do the same in Bulgaria and Hungary as well. The political events in those countries caused the United States to have serious misgivings about having accepted a single standard for Great Power relations with the defeated Axis satellites, and by Yalta it had reconsidered the entire question.

Rumania

Rumania was the most important of the three Eastern European friends of Germany, not merely to the West but to Russia as well. Two constants characterized Rumanian foreign policy after World War I: militant anti-Bolshevism in the context of a strategy of creating a cordon sanitaire, and an orientation toward one or another Great Power. During the 1920's England and France served that function, and later Germany played the role. The Rumanians fought long and hard on the Russian front, and when defeat was imminent, they attempted to surrender to the West and reenter that orbit.

The Rumanian Communist party had never been important, and when the Russians arrived this fact and certain political realities confronted them, realities to which they almost immediately accommodated themselves. No one knew whether the Rumanian masses still followed the leaders of the prewar parties, who were, as some thought, "generals without armies," but they had credentials that were unimpeachable by prewar canons. The OSS ran an inventory of the various groups in December 1944 and concluded that the Peasant party, nationalist, monarchist, and "not inclined to show much concern in practice for minority rights," was the largest. The Liberal party, the representative of Rumanian business and in power most of the time between the wars, was corrupt and "widely distrusted." Both parties were strongly anti-Russian. The Communist-dominated Democratic Front was a United Front typical of those the Communists created elsewhere in Eastern Europe, and included the Socialists, the Ploughman's Front, and other smaller groups with rather different aims. The Democratic Front stood for limited land reform; it was neutral on the question of the monarchy, and the Communists were the most conservative members of the alliance, advocating reforms "involving no immediate threat to capitalism."[30] The OSS acknowledged that most Rumanians were cynical toward all the political groups. In fact, the Ploughman's Front, an antifascist, non-Communist group that originated in the 1920's among poor peasants, was the fastest-growing political organization during this period.

Until November, therefore, the United States could only watch Rumania apprehensively, for it had other, nonpolitical reasons to complain to the Russians. These involved American oil property in Rumania, for when the Russians entered the country they dismantled much of the local industry to replace their own destroyed equipment and to supply themselves with oil for war. The English worried also, for their prewar holdings in Rumanian oil were great, and Russian officers were not bothering to differentiate the owners according to nationality. The problem was further complicated when British and American bombers attacked Rumanian fields, for they too failed to make distinctions, and no one knew precisely what remained from the prewar investments, much less who the legal owners were in every situation. Before the American government found cause for complaint about politics, a mood of hostility and criticism colored its perspective.

At the beginning of November, George Kennan, the chargé in Moscow, went to see Vishinsky about the problem.

> I said I expected that this property would be returned and restored to its former condition at once and that the Soviet military authorities in Rumania would be instructed to take no further unilateral action affecting property in which American nationals or companies were interested. In conclusion I told him that I thought this was a serious matter. . . . I expressed the earnest personal hope in the interests not only of our property owners but also of American-Russian collabora- tion in general with respect to former satellite countries, that the Peo- ple's Commissariat would give immediate and favorable attention to the matter. . . .

Washington endorsed this policy, and the Russians heard much of the bewildering matter, for the battlefronts and war-torn nations were not ideal places for an orderly inventory. More important, Washington had long before decided that its national interests and private economic hold- ings were synonymous, and this assumption became a critical element in Eastern European policy from the inception of liberation. The Russians, for their part, attempted to offer justifications, and admitted in principle that American and English properties were "inviolable," but to no one's satisfaction.[31]

The oil-removal issue impinged on political problems. The State De- partment's observers concluded in November that the Russians were more interested in getting Rumania to "pay through the nose for its past trans- gressions" than Bolshevizing it.[32] In fact this estimate was correct, though Kennan worried about its consequences to the political and economic "sta- bility" of Rumania and Central Europe, on the assumption that stability had existed or might be brought into being. The Russians denigrated the leadership of the Peasant and Liberal parties, but these groups functioned and dominated the government, and the Russians were no less contemptu- ous of the weak Communist party. Both the Moscow embassy and the OSS concluded that "the Communists have not been given the official blessing of the USSR."[33] For they had no power among the masses and could not promise stability.

On November 4 the Rumanian Cabinet reorganized itself after the Liberals and the Peasant party became less defensive about their position, resulting in their taking ten of seventeen ministries, including placing a violent anti-Communist in the critical Interior Ministry. The Communists protested vainly, and at the end of the month, when the king attempted to create a new Cabinet of "technicians," they strove to obtain a greater share of power. The traditional parties proposed a new government under General Nicolae Radescu, former Chief of Staff, the Democratic Front refused to enter the government without having control of the Interior Ministry, but when Vishinsky instructed them to do so, they agreed. The Democratic Front obtained seven of the sixteen posts in the government, but Radescu ran Rumania. The Russians were full of praise for the general, who was at best a mild reformer whose main function was to create stability and a constitutional structure. The Russians saw this as the prerequisite to industrial production and economic recovery, leading to payment of their reparations debt. Vishinsky came to Bucharest during the political crisis, chastising King Michael in terms that made him fear for his future; but later the king told Burton Y. Berry, the American representative in Rumania, that "Vishinsky had talked to some of the more viperous Communists and had advised them against stirring up trouble." Indeed, Vishinsky told Michael he could expect Russian support along with the backing of the Radescu administration, for Russia did not want a Communist state but "a neighbor which was friendly."[34] The king was pleased.

Despite this series of relatively sanguine events the Americans and British were apprehensive, for it was obvious that the Russians had the power to change the conservative regime for one less palatable to the West any time they chose to do so. The Control Commission, therefore, became the focus for American plans to balance Russian power. And here the Soviets isolated and offended the American and British representatives who then were receptive to appeals from conservative prewar Rumanian political leaders who sought them out in the belief that only Anglo-American support could end Soviet predominance. Iuliu Maniu, prewar Peasant party leader excluded from the November Cabinet reorganization, was particularly effective in convincing Berry and the State Department of the imminent possibility of Communism's spreading and the need for Western help to stop it, and they considered his interpretation almost as credible as the events themselves. Despite the obvious coloration of Maniu's reports, his strategy of making Rumania a factor in inter-Allied conflict ultimately proved successful.

Before Yalta, therefore, due to the paucity of specific complaints about Rumanian politics, the United States showed most concern about its economic position in that nation and was very apprehensive about Russia's capabilities of shaping Rumanian politics to suit its own ends.[35]

Bulgaria

Elements similar to those in Rumania appeared in Bulgaria during 1944, but Russian power there also proved overwhelming. The Bulgarian rulers initially hoped to arrange a separate surrender with the West to save themselves from Bolshevism, but the historic friendship of the Bulgarian people for Russia undermined this position, as well as the fact that Bulgarian border claims were at the expense of Yugoslavia and Greece, both more likely to obtain Western backing than Bulgaria. Not until September did Russia declare war against Bulgaria, however, and until then Bulgarian diplomats fished about for the best terms possible. They did not obtain them. When Russia declared war on September 5, the Bulgarians responded four days later by requesting an armistice and declaring war on their former ally, Germany. The Russians were too popular among the people to fight against them.

Neither the British nor the Americans appreciated the Soviet declaration of war against Bulgaria after months of discussions concerning their exclusive war with that poor country. But the Russians finally realized they could not participate in the peace terms without declaring war. With Russian troops now entering their land, the Bulgarians attempted to be as agreeable as possible. On September 10 they reorganized the government so that one-third of the membership would be Communist, the remainder being disposed to work with Russia for both pragmatic and historic reasons. The Russians entered Sofia at the end of the month and announced they were liberators rather than invaders, proclaiming they would not impose Communism and would permit the Bulgarians to develop any form of society they desired. The Control Commission, as in Rumania, was in the hands of the Soviet military, and since the British acknowledged Soviet predominance in Bulgaria, they quickly began championing Greek reparations demands on that nation, demands that only drove the Bulgarians into greater dependency on Soviet favor.

The Bulgarian Communist party had always been powerful, especially in the Macedonian area of Bulgaria, and the presence of Soviet troops now made it more audacious. The American representative in Bulgaria, Maynard Barnes, at first saw the ruling Fatherland Front as a mere tool of the Communists, but later he came to appreciate important splits in its ranks, especially with the Agrarian party. He then realized the "Russians appear to be exercising a restraining influence on the Communists . . . primarily because Bulgarian communism, ideologically and with respect to methods, is still of the 1917 vintage."[36] Given the collapse of Bulgarian society and politics in the interwar years, which Barnes acknowledged, even Russian restraint would not ultimately keep the Communists from power, for their armed militia, he had heard, was the determining factor in the countryside. Barnes, as was also the case with American diplomats in other former Axis satellites, was deeply committed to the need for America and England to stop the flow of events toward Communism. His virtual isolation in Sofia left him susceptible to rumor and he responded to Soviet rudeness with hostility. His dispatches to Washington throughout 1944 portrayed the imminence of a Communist Bulgaria.

In defining policy toward Bulgaria, therefore, the United States appreciated British indifference, its own lack of any economic or political interests, and the political vacuum which made a Communist victory probable. The State Department decided in the weeks before Yalta to press for greater United States powers via the Control Commission, though it did not expect equality with the Russians. If the question of oil largely shaped American policy in Rumania, in Bulgaria alleged Soviet rudeness and questions of protocol colored it.[37] In fact the United States had no significant interests in the country.

Hungary

Hungary was the last European satellite of the Nazis to surrender and the last the Soviet troops reached, finally crossing the border during late October 1944. Hungary's rulers had been violently anti-Semitic, intensely anti-Bolshevik, and internally reactionary, especially in regard to the semi-feudal land ownership. Their affinity to the Nazis was perhaps greater than any of the other Axis Powers. As the end of the war seemed certain, during September 1944 Hungary's rulers desperately and unsuccessfully attempted to surrender to the Americans and English only, and then pleaded for Western troops to accompany those from Russia. During October a new government opened armistice discussions with the Russians.

American interest in Hungary was rather more substantial than it had been in Bulgaria and Rumania. First, there were important American oil properties owned by Standard Oil of New Jersey. Secondly, the State Department wished to break with the Italian and Rumanian precedents for representation on the Control Commission. And finally, in Hungary the State Department related the problem of reparations to the question of economic recovery and stability in Central Europe in a rather more sophisticated fashion than it had done in earlier instances.

Oil was always a clear-cut question, and Hull notified Harriman to tell the Russians that American oil rights were substantial and that he should guard them, but he neglected to mention that in 1941 he blocked Standard's attempt to sell its Hungarian property to I. G. Farben. In working out the reparations treaty with the Hungarians, the State Department energetically insisted on unequivocal protection of American oil. Next the United States determined to make the character and quantity of reparations secondary to the restoration of normal trade in Central Europe, and not to permit reparations arrangements to hinder recovery. The Russians initially demanded $400 million in reparations, then lowered it to $300 million over a six-year period. Despite Harriman's defense of the reasonableness of the sum the State Department instructed him not to approve the agreement, which in fact the United States and Hungary blocked until June 1945, by which time the Russians found a government willing to meet their demands.

The Control Commission was a matter of prime importance for the Americans and they fought vigorously on this question. Hull told Harriman in mid-October that equality on the Commission was necessary, especially on policy matters. The Russians refused to compromise on this, insisting on following the Italian arrangement down to freedom of movement for Commission members. The affair left an unpleasant aftertaste for the Americans.

In summarizing American policy toward Hungary preparatory to Yalta the State Department determined that the United States required both economic and political equality in Hungary, and that unlike the Bulgarian situation it could not receive a secondary position. Oil holdings were ample justification for economic equality and the anticipated future development in this area. The State Department had no complaints as yet concerning the political nature of the provisional government organized at the end of December, but it felt, in considering the former pro-Nazi dictatorship, that "It is also in our interest that free elections be held and that Hungary be left to manage its own internal affairs as soon as possible." Above all, "We do not, however, consider that the Soviet Union has any special privileges or dominant position in Hungary."[38]

At no time after December 1944 did the events of Italy, France, Belgium, or Greece affect American analysis of what the Russians might wish to do in applying the same reasoning and policies to the defeated Axis satellites. By Yalta the State Department, in considering Rumania, Bulgaria, and Hungary, determined that "Following Germany's surrender the United States would like to see the Control Commissions become genuinely tripartite in character, with all three Allied Governments having equal participation."[39] It said nothing of Italy.

The American View of Soviet Intentions and Postwar Eastern Europe

⌈Soviet foreign policy in Eastern Europe was probably the most critical American index for evaluating Russian intentions in the postwar world, a dark mirror of the future of the Alliance.⌋ There were others too, such as the belief that the Moscow-disciplined Communist parties controlled the Left, which in turn threatened United States interests. And, as we shall see, they also asked themselves to what extent the Russians would collaborate with American plans for postwar international political and economic organizations. But none of these concerns exceeded in significance the place of Eastern European events in American expectations for the future, and this view in turn reflected the nature of American commitments and objectives—in brief, the foundations of United States policy.

The impact of Eastern European crises was cumulative, and no single event shaped or reflected the American mood of growing apprehension and hostility. Indeed, one can only arbitrarily divorce Eastern Europe from the American fear of the Left and the Comintern everywhere, or even the position of the Russians on Christianity, which especially colored Hull's and Stimson's opinions. These problems weighed heavily on Washington from the beginning of 1943, when they were entirely abstract, and built up to a crescendo before Yalta, when the preoccupation with Russia's intentions and its future in the world became obsessive as the issues of war were progressively transformed from military questions to problems of pure politics. Any survey of high-level opinion on Russian motives in the two years prior to Yalta discloses the remarkable continuity in these American forebodings and opinions.

Eden visited Washington during March 1943, and he discussed numerous future grand diplomatic themes with Hull, Roosevelt, Hopkins, and others. Hull described his first meeting with Eden in a manner that revealed his own concerns:

> We both agreed on the extreme importance of ascertaining Russia's probable future course with respect to Europe and the world situation. I inquired whether, in his opinion, there was any alternative course Russia might pursue in addition to the possible course of isolation on her part after lopping off certain territory along the boundaries of Europe, accompanied by the maintenance of heavy armament, or whether in her own best interests, economically and otherwise, she might not decide to be a part of the world and to meet all of her responsibilities under a sane practical policy of international cooperation in all essential respects.[40]

If "lopping off" territory was a criterion, however, Washington viewed Russia's actual course with trepidation. Eden assured Roosevelt that the Russians would expect to take at least the Baltic States, and the President predicted this would meet with American resistance. These issues remained abstract only for the remainder of 1943. At the Moscow Foreign Ministers' Conference, Hull confronted Molotov concerning the dangers of exporting Communism and the intolerance toward religion within Russia, and Molotov passively acquiesced on both points. On a more serious military level, Harriman concluded, the Russians had been most cooperative, but they insisted on a friendly Poland and an end to the concept of the cordon sanitaire on their borders; they would, however, attempt to establish friendly relations along lines that did not preclude a Western role. But Harriman, applying American standards, could report almost no progress on outstanding political issues, since in his view the Russian attitude on Eastern Europe was "rigid."[41]

By the beginning of 1944, as more and more areas of disagreement appeared, Harriman was less sanguine, and State Department advisers urged a much tougher line toward Soviet use of Communists to further their aims. During February, Hull warned of impending difficulties with the Russians due to "Soviet determination to deal unilaterally with the problems of Eastern Europe. . . ." If they continued, it would indicate that "the Soviet Government is not disposed to play a constructive part as a full and equal member of the family of nations . . . ," and would "do irreparable harm to the whole cause of international collaboration." Over the next several months Hull saw a confirmation of his worst expectations in Eastern Europe, and at the end of March admonished the Soviet ambassador in Washington for "the rising hostility to Russia on account of these small acts on her part which are being interpreted as a movement toward unilateralism." Harriman predicted the Russians would maintain good relations with the West, but not at the expense of their basic principles, and from September 1944 he and Kennan sent extremely pessimistic analyses of Soviet intentions back to Washington. Kennan applied his lively literary talents to portraying, in historical tense, backward glances at Soviet diplomacy that the Russians had yet to implement. Western concepts of collaboration, he suggested, were "strange" to the Russians, for their objectives in Eastern and Central Europe "are directed to only one goal: power. The form this power takes, the methods by which it is achieved: these are secondary questions. It is a matter of indifference to Moscow whether a given area is 'communistic' or not. All things being equal, Moscow might prefer to see it communized, although even that is debatable. But the main thing is that it should be amenable to Moscow influence, and if possible to Moscow authority." The sources of this conduct, and the justification for it, he never examined in detail. Instead Kennan cited "contradiction," "xenophobia," and the like, as he saw the mystical Russian soul gravitating toward "a rigid police regime" to the exclusion of international cooperation.[42]

By mid-September 1944 these apprehensions regarding Russia were so pervasive that Roosevelt was convinced he should meet with Stalin and Churchill to discuss the vast backlog of disagreements and conflicts that had emerged since their cordial conference at Teheran in November 1943. A more critical factor, though, was that American policy was isolated and failing almost everywhere in Europe. After October it was even more urgent, for conferences such as those between Stalin and Churchill were side-stepping American aloofness from actual political decisions, which only created obstacles to British and Russian policy. The election of 1944, however, forced Roosevelt to postpone the meeting, and in the last months of 1944 the United States became even more apprehensive about Russian aspirations.

Soviet policy deeply disturbed most of Washington and now American

decision-makers attributed to it the most nefarious motives. Secretary of
the Navy James Forrestal saw Russian ambitions as almost limitless. Harriman suggested in October that Soviet reparations and economic policy in
Eastern Europe was something of a purge of those unreliable political
elements who would not be able to maintain order and would also stem the
rise of pro-Communist forces: "a certain amount of economic distress
would have [a] tendency to contribute to the establishment in power of
groups entirely friendly to the Soviet Union."[43] Kennan ascribed the same
motives to their advocacy of the arrest and speedy trial of pro-Nazis.
Perhaps the Russians might still cooperate, Harriman speculated at the end
of September, but their expansion in Eastern Europe, with all that implied,
was certain. "If the policy is accepted that the Soviet Union has a right to
penetrate her immediate neighbors for security, penetration of the next
immediate neighbors becomes at a certain time equally logical." Harriman
was "not optimistic" about arriving at an understanding with the Russians
on such matters. Still, there was no harm in trying, for the Russians wanted
to maintain their new alliance with the West, and "I believe we should
make them understand patiently but firmly that we cannot accept their
point of view and that we are prepared to take the consequences if they
adhere to their position. In such cases, I am satisfied that in the last
analysis Stalin will back down."[44] The specific disputes over Poland, Yugoslavia, and elsewhere illustrated what Russia would offer and what
America would demand.

Before Yalta there was widespread belief in the United States that the
Eastern European situation warranted a harsher posture toward Russia,
and Senator Vandenberg became the leading legislative spokesman for this
view. His words were superfluous, for the Administration had reached the
same conclusion much earlier.

Russia and Eastern Europe—Ideology and Natural Interests

The problem of estimating Russia's intentions began when the Americans failed to make a distinction between the U.S.S.R. as a state and the
internationalist Bolshevik ideology to which Russia gave obeisance, and
about which Communists spoke on May Day. All the Western fears of
revolution, now personified in the dynamics of an emergent new Left and a
Resistance, they projected on the Russians. The 1917-vintage Bulgarians
and the Partisans in the Croatian mountains all seemed mysteriously linked
to the Kremlin and responsive to it. With this view, of course, the Americans confused any small nation's act of friendship toward the Russians with
an oath of fealty, and they might dismiss neutral leaders, as they did Beneš,
as having been lured by the sirens of Moscow.

There was much in the heritage of Stalinism—its flexible opportunism and dialectic inconsistencies—that made Russian policy a source of doubt as well as hope for the United States. There was no imaginable ideological position that the U.S.S.R. had not taken in the interwar years, but in the conduct of foreign policy it acted circumspectly, and unsuccessfully, to integrate itself into an anti-German security system. As relevant as the question of Soviet intentions was, more important was what the U.S.S.R. would do in the light of its unsuccessful past experiences with a Western diplomacy that was quite as Machiavellian as the most cynical Leninism.

During the war the Soviet Union was a model of sheer pragmatism, and despite the availability of seminal descriptions of these tendencies, official Washington failed to generalize the implications of this trend and its effects on future Soviet policy. In September 1943 Stalin restored the Holy Synod and rehabilitated the Greek Orthodox Church. Throughout the war the Soviet press and radio made only slight reference to ideology but much to the nationalist and Slav sentiments of the constituent nationalities. Anti-religious and Marxist training became negligible, the officer corps was given all the perquisites and symbols of their caste. Why such capitulation to the legacies of an older order? Stalin himself suggested the roots of Soviet conduct at this time on November 6, 1944: When it came time to recognize a government, the Soviet Union's policy was "a businesslike one." Was the nation anti-German? If so, the U.S.S.R. recognized it. Stalin came to the same conclusion about his possible support at home for the desperate struggle for survival. He now accepted all that aided the war, and if kings helped more than Partisans or Resistance armies, he clearly implied he would work with them as well. ". . . the alliance between the Soviet Union, Great Britain and the United States," however, "is founded not on casual, short-lived considerations but on vital and lasting interests."[45] Could Stalin's rhetoric be believed? Did in fact the permanent international crisis of the post-World War I period, and the threat the possible breakup of the present alliance posed, cause Stalin to restate the consistency of Soviet dedication to permanent world cooperation? If so, it would have to be cooperation among true equals, for Russia was proud in its belief it had earned its own way across Europe's bloody battlefields. How it expressed its policies in specific situations would be the test of Soviet intent.

I have found no evidence that important American leaders seriously considered such questions, much less assimilated their answers into functional decision-making. No one formulated a larger interpretation of Eastern European events which suggested that the Soviets based their policy on pluralistic, nonideological responses always colored by local circumstances they did not always control. American leaders did not understand that the United Front strategy of the Communists throughout Europe inhibited decisive action by the local leftists, giving the Old Order a breathing spell to reassert itself. Careful assessment of Russian policy would have required close study of Beneš' success and rationale, the London Poles' greater failure, and Russian indifference toward the social order of a neutral Finland. Stalin declared he wished friendly and independent states on Russian borders, and he did not consider the openly rightist complexion of Eastern European prewar politics irrelevant to Russian security. Weak neighbors were more tolerable than strong ones, even if they called themselves Communist, as did Tito, or, it must also be noted, Mao. If they were willing to abjure grandiose schemes and alliances, he could suffer any and all.

Ultimately, however, the central question was whether American objectives in Eastern Europe could be reconciled with Russian security criteria, and what structural and political assumptions were implied in those relatively few articulated basic formulations which were continuously reflected in American policy. The answer would have told whether a meeting at Yalta on Eastern Europe would bear fruit.

Toward the Definition of an American Policy

The Americans did not articulate their Eastern European policy extensively until the months shortly before Yalta, when the subject became a matter of prime concern. Yet a fairly consistent policy existed, for under the guise of aloofness the United States constantly attempted to block both Soviet- and British-sponsored forces and strategies, first in Poland and then in Czechoslovakia and Yugoslavia. Where the United States worked with local political elements, they were invariably prewar centrists of the more conservative variety. If American policy seemed passive in that it appeared to consist of broad policy statements of objectives to be specifically defined and obtained with minimum discussion and compromise after the war, in fact it was active in creating obstacles to the immediate resolution of the Polish and Yugoslav imbroglios, and it made Beneš' plans insecure at best. Now it was time to articulate these impulses and tendencies into systematic policy.

During October the reparations question and the Polish crisis triggered the formalization of American policy in a manner that was essentially economic. The Hungarian reparations discussion led the State Department to reiterate that it wished to see "a speedy restoration of international trade on a liberal basis," "liberal" meaning with a minimum of tariff and state economic barriers. American investments, small in volume but enormous in principle, warranted informing the Russians that reparations "should be scheduled in such a way as to interfere as little as possible with normal trading relations."[46] Implicitly Eastern Europe's prewar economic relations became the model for recovery, and the United States placed a higher priority on their restoration than they did on Russian security and, as we shall see, local demands. Hull saw very clearly, as he told Roosevelt, that "The future economic pattern of Europe will be largely determined by policies and procedures established during the period of reconstruction." The objective was to prevent bilateral trade agreements, autarchy, and trade restrictions—to create the "liberalization of trade and investment." In Poland, for example, it was acknowledged there would be a "strong Russian influence," and "In this situation, the United States can hope to make its influence felt only if some degree of equal opportunity in trade, investment, and access of sources of information is preserved."[47] Even if Russia sought an exclusive position in Poland it would not have the economic power to aid Polish reconstruction, and via loans and credits, Hull suggested, the Polish economy would at least be accessible to America.

In defining "United States Interests and Policy" in Eastern Europe, Stettinius, Hull's successor, at the beginning of November outlined the basic American position for an always receptive Roosevelt:

1. The right of peoples to choose and maintain for themselves without outside interference the type of political, social, and economic systems they desire. . . .

2. Equality of opportunity, as against the setting up of a policy of exclusion, in commerce, transit, and trade; and freedom to negotiate, either through government agencies or private enterprise, irrespective of the type of economic system in operation.

3. The right of access to all countries on an equal and unrestricted basis of . . . press, radio, newsreel and information agencies. . . .

4. Freedom for American philanthropic and educational organizations. . . .

5. General protection of American citizens and the protection and furtherance of legitimate American economic rights, existing or potential.

6. The United States maintains the general position that territorial settlements should be left until the end of the war.[48]

The dimensions of this policy, which became the basic formulation of United States objectives in Eastern Europe, ignored the conflict between the implications of the first point and the others that followed, much less the fact that United States interference in the internal affairs of France, Italy, and elsewhere was well established by this time. Indeed, as Stettinius suggested in his fifth principle, Americans could make future investments only within the context of a capitalist economy at least some of the Eastern European nations might not wish to continue; and the settlement of territorial questions, in addition to resisting British and Russian policy, ignored the equity of self-determination implied in the first point. The inconsistencies of this formulation were less significant than the tangible demands for an open door to the Eastern European economies.

United States policy at Yalta, therefore, was primarily economic in content, calling for "the early return of trade to a multilateral basis under the freest possible conditions," "equality of opportunity," the freedom to invest and help in reconstruction.[49] The United States acknowledged the inevitability of Russian political predominance, but carefully defined it in such a manner as not to alter economic opportunities or involve a radical change in prewar internal or external economic relations. To some, such as Joseph C. Grew, Under Secretary of State, Russian precedence could not involve regional blocs that they might mobilize against other states nor could they interfere with the internal autonomy of the states within their zone. In brief, the United States divorced the political dimensions from their more fundamental economic context, and by so doing hoped for a continuation of a political status quo essential to its economic assumptions.

Inevitably, therefore, the Americans oriented their political definitions toward a concept of the nearly mythical "center" in Eastern European politics, one with a long prewar history, and it was unlikely that either the Russians or the now radicalized or apathetic Eastern European peoples themselves would accept it. Yugoslavia, for example, expressed self-determination in its own fashion, and those in Washington admitted the fact, but politically it was objectionable. The London Poles probably stood for no one but themselves, yet the United States supported them until the end of 1944, when they decided to back Mikolajzcyk, who had an amorphous prewar party behind him. The State Department officially recommended to Roosevelt that he propose at Yalta the creation of an "Emergency High Commission for Liberated Europe," consisting of the three major Allies and France, to run the former German satellites and liberated nations by maintaining internal order and setting up provisional governments composed of all democratic groups until such time as they could arrange free, supervised elections. It would "terminate when the functioning of popular and stable governments . . . removed the need for its activities."[50] How such a trusteeship organization would eliminate "outside" interference with local self-determination, the State Department advisers did not suggest in January 1945. The proposal was concerned primarily with the Polish and Greek situations, but Roosevelt failed to pursue the project.

The premises motivating the State Department's scheme postulated an emergent Anglo-Soviet rivalry which inadequately expressed, it felt, the true political mood of Europe, which was neither right nor left but "Between these two extremes. . . ." The High Commission plan presumably was to satisfy all sides, and the governments it chose would "be sufficiently to the left to satisfy the prevailing mood in Europe and to allay Soviet suspicions. Conversely, they should be sufficiently representative of the center and *petit bourgeois* elements of the population so that they would not be regarded as mere preludes to a Communist dictatorship."[51] But if the prevailing majority mood was toward the left, and they granted self-determination, how could American-stated objectives be reconciled with trusteeships that they would have to impose by force, at least on Yugoslavia? No matter, such a plan would unravel the Eastern European dilemma for America and even remove British power from a Greece that was in revolt at the time. But the State Department's official proposal reflected the lack of instrumentalities for implementing existing policy as well as its loss of contact with real possibilities. And this lack of meaningful options caused the United States to engage in a seemingly passive diplomacy which only thwarted the desires of England, Russia, and most Eastern European nations to resolve the political conundrums of the region. Washington could only ascribe the failures of its policy to the nefariousness of Russian, and occasionally British, intentions.

By the end of 1944 both the United States and Great Britain had intervened in the internal affairs of every major Western European nation in order to contain the Left and proscribe each other's influence, systematically restricting Soviet influence as much as possible while Russia fought the European land war in the theater of central importance. The United States could agree that the force of arms would ultimately define the limits of Eastern European developments, which potentially were strongly to the right, or it could destroy the last illusions as to the existence of a fragile union of powers with something more than a common enemy to unify them.

The type of politics the United States wished to see emerge in Eastern Europe assumed that the Eastern European masses would and should welcome back the prewar parties, and indeed that the holocaust of war had not gravely undermined and debilitated these parties. Moreover, the essential foreign policy of the prewar centrist parties had been anti-Soviet, irredentist, and expansionist. The Russians would not tolerate them, nor would the masses, who were not always Communist but very much for long-overdue radical social changes in one form or another. In fact the Americans appreciated this mood, but at no time did they bother to formulate a policy on the land problem so critical not only to the petite bourgeoisie but also to the larger majority that would unquestionably prevail either by a democratic vote or leftist totalitarianism. Throughout most of Eastern Europe the urban middle class was now a mere aspiration, for their irrational leaders had encouraged two wars which had resulted in the destruction of middle-class property. To suggest that social revolution in Eastern Europe was exclusively a product of Soviet intervention, much less that it was not needed, ignored the structural facts and accepted the argument of the advocates of a prewar status quo that was bankrupt and had perpetuated wide-scale misery far greater than that incident to sweeping social changes and broad internal economic and political development. The existence of Soviet power in Eastern Europe permitted more or less natural and indigenous forces to take their logical course, while in Western Europe, American and British power contained these forces directly or indirectly, a containment that became the preeminent unifying element in the Western alliance after 1945, and which also hindered postwar economic recovery. The mere fact that there was no serious internal opposition to the Communization of Eastern Europe, that is, no significant civil wars, reflected both the fundamental weakness of the Old Order (and suggests what kind of system they would have re-created without a mass base) and the flexibility and subtlety of the various Communist parties and the Russians.

Although it ruled together with England in the West with an iron hand, the United States called for free elections and self-rule in Eastern Europe at this time, but prewar precedents convinced the Russians that the West sought to create an anti-Soviet bloc. Unfettered democracy never existed in Eastern Europe outside Czechoslovakia; the prewar parties were venal, weak, or both; and the region needed a period of development on new social bases, with its dangerous nationalism contained, to prevent Europe from plunging into more irrational wars on behalf of the cause of Serbs, Macedonians, and the like. The American planners ignored these nationality questions, since they had no specific or new proposals to make. The Soviet role in shaping Eastern European politics may have been in the name of a cynical ideology, but Eastern Europe, it was clear by the end of 1944, was going to go right *or* left, into an anti-Soviet bloc, a pro-Soviet bloc, or true neutrality. The Russians would tolerate only the last two options, the United States only the first, and the British, with much twisting and turning, opted for neutralism more often than not. American diplomacy, in calling for the restoration of prewar politics and economics, worked for the Right, which quickly came to view the Americans as its last hope. Russia would not, and was not obliged to, tolerate this development.

The Americans had to work for the restoration of the London Poles, Mihailovic, and other conservatives because their economic objectives, which by the end of 1944 they clearly defined as primary, were incompatible with radical economic reform in Eastern Europe. Eighty percent of Eastern Europe's exports in 1938 consisted of raw materials, foodstuffs, and semifinished goods, and nearly three-quarters of it went to Western Europe.[52] To talk of the restoration of stability, normal trade, and the reintegration of Eastern Europe into the world economy meant, in effect, the continuation of the semicolonial economic relationship of that area to the rest of the world. Any alteration of this condition would have meant radical internal economic changes, and this in turn would have impinged on American freedom to invest and trade along traditional lines so central to its objectives in that area. If the United States chose to approach Eastern European problems from this viewpoint, it would find no satisfaction, for every important left-of-center group, Beneš' exile government included, favored far-reaching nationalization and economic reform. To make this the test of Eastern European friendship condemned the area to hostility unless it would restore the prewar politicians. And, as history proved, between the pressures of Western hostility and the final consolidation of Russian power in Eastern Europe after 1947, this policy spelled the end of Czech democracy. Nationalization and independent economic development along new lines became the critical gauge by which the Americans evaluated Eastern European trends, for politics was only the instrument for preserving and expanding America's unprecedented power and position in the European and world economy. When the State Department reconsidered and clarified its Eastern European policy before Yalta, in essence it defined a foreign economic policy.

CHAPTER

8

THE GREEK PASSION

THE GREEKS suffered much by 1943—from a pervasive poverty that defined the lives of the vast majority of the people, from their own leaders, and finally from their German, Italian, and Bulgarian conquerors. The prewar dictatorship of Ioannis Metaxas came to power in 1936 as a result of a coup designed to circumvent the threatened victory of an antimonarchical United Front, and it ruled with the blessings of King George II, who could assure him the loyalty of perhaps a majority of the army. Republicanism and constitutionalism became the cry of the opposition to the dictatorship, but after the death of Eleftherios Venizelos, the leader of the Liberal party, there was no serious, organized opposition to a regime that was pro-Nazi in sympathy prior to the Italian invasion of 1940. At that time the army and Metaxas resisted, though without the support of many leading generals, who preferred surrender. But the royal government, with its coalition of former Metaxists and right-wing Liberals, fled to London and spoke for a tortured Greece that hardly recognized it.

The Greek Prime Minister, Emmanuel Tsouderos, was outspokenly pro-British, anxious to anchor his nation to British power in the Mediterranean, and in return receive sustenance and reinforcement from England for a return to the homeland and for the recognition of long-standing Greek border claims that weighed heavily on the diplomacy of the Royal Greek government. The prewar experience, the problem of Greek territorial aspirations, monarchy versus republicanism, and the role of Greece vis-à-vis the Great Powers all intertwined after 1942 to make events in that nation insoluble and tragic. Greece was especially important from 1943 onward because it possessed the only armed Resistance that actually fought the West, and the precise reasons and causes for this struggle are critical to an understanding of the nature of the Left, the intentions of the Soviet Union, and the origins of the post-1945 crisis. But there are also distinctive and historic pre-Communist dimensions here as there were to every southeast European dispute of the period, with Bolshevik and anti-Bolshevik rhetoric concealing much more elemental and older objectives than social change. In Greece, as we shall see, this was true of both the Left and Right.

The Resistance in Greece was at first a spontaneous reaction to the fascist invasion. Concentrated mainly in the north it assumed a strongly nationalist, minority complexion it was never to lose in those regions. Largely apolitical, comprising chiefly true *maquis* who were later to find appropriate political expression, the always decentralized Resistance attracted at least a few traditional bandits who were later purged by the Resistance itself. But from its inception the Greek Resistance was marked by a lack of centralization and an unusual degree of local initiative. That quality was to prove crucial, for it critically minimized the ability of the Communists to control it.

The Metaxas regime drove the Communist party (KKE) underground; nevertheless, by September 1941 it was the best-organized and -disciplined party in Greece. In that month, after mass demonstrations in Macedonia made the need for an organization more than obvious, it initiated the National Liberation Front (EAM), which included five other parties and was then the only serious political group in the nation. Its allies were diverse, but the modest program of the EAM consisted essentially of a platform for constitutionalism and war against Germany, and so it attracted the vast majority of the republican political groups, including the Socialists, the left Liberals, the Agrarians, and others. In April 1942 the EAM created the People's Liberation Army (ELAS), which soon became the largest Resistance army and the only one to be found in all the major regions of Greece. By liberation the EAM's labor organization controlled the entire working class, and it helped lead strikes in occupied territories throughout the war; the EAM itself administered two-thirds to four-fifths of Greece and claimed one and a half million members out of a total population only five times that figure—a claim, even if exaggerated, that probably was not far from the unknown truth. By the end of 1943 the EAM administered most of the villages, collected taxes, supplied schools and relief, endorsed private property and even the churches to the extent of gaining much clerical support, and began to destroy the patriarchal village structure in a manner that won the fervent devotion of the youth and women. If the EAM was only a coalition—and it was a broad one—in this state within a state, it nevertheless introduced a degree of democracy hitherto unknown in Greek society.[1]

The fundamental bifurcation in Greek politics by 1943 was not between the EAM and anti-Communists, but between the traditionalist, monarchical factions, pro-Nazis and Anglophiles as opposed to the republicans, modernists, and the Left. The Communists were a powerful but very small minority of the EAM, about one-tenth of the membership. Of all the groups in the EAM the Communists were the most willing to submerge social objectives to the needs of a United Front and the only group willing to explicitly designate Greece, as early as 1943, as part of the general British sphere of influence after the war. In short, they were the most conservative faction of the EAM, but they were also badly split, for a significant group within the party was more committed to the cause of Greece than the dictates of Moscow. When in early 1941 Moscow instructed the Greek party to assume a passive role in opposition to the war the nationalist faction ignored the order. This independent element, within and without the Communist party, later became critical in Greek history.[2] Approximately nine-tenths of the ELAS consisted of peasants and workers, and the less timid non-Communist component of the leadership grew consistently. C. M. Woodhouse, the British commander of the Allied Military Mission in Greece at this time, and a staunch conservative, considered the Communists as "a tiny numerical minority," and London estimated nine-tenths of the ELAS was non-Communist. By mid-1943 the ELAS attracted many republican professional officers, and the military head of the ELAS was the prominent prewar officer Stephan Saraphis. When the EAM set up a provisional government in Greece in March 1944, its best-known leaders were outstanding prewar civil servants, intellectuals, and politicians who were, as Woodhouse begrudgingly admits, "some of the best of Greek democracy."[3] More properly, the EAM stood for democracy and against the old regime. Many of these men, of course, joined when the ultimate victory of the EAM appeared likely, and some would not later back a losing cause. Much the same had been true of Greek politics before the war.

The ELAS had anywhere from 20,000 to 70,000 members during 1943 and restricted its operations to sabotage and limited attacks. The other Resistance organizations were also pro-republican by 1943, but anti-Communism soon became their primary unifying ingredient. The largest was the EDES (National Republican Greek League), concentrated in the vicinity of Epirus in the northwest. Led by Colonel Napoleon Zervas it was busy with various nationalist causes, such as driving the Cham minority out of Greece, as well as resistance to the invader. Zervas later divided the organization because other leaders collaborated with the Axis. No group remotely equaled the power of the EAM and its military arm, the ELAS.

Within the EAM and ELAS the Communists occupied a critical position, especially in the command of political as opposed to the ultimately crucial military posts, but they did not by any means control either organization, whose mass base rested with its ability to articulate the pent-up grievances and needs of the vast majority of the Greek people. The most one can say is that the Communists played a role very much disproportionate to their numbers, but only because their program and politics were tailored to the mood of the Greek people. In fact, no one group controlled the ELAS or EAM. The organization was so vast that no well-disciplined elite could pull in all the threads of its decentralized, haphazard apparatus. The best the Communists could do was to assume a critical role in the not overly important central headquarters, but they could not initiate or stop action on a grass-roots level. In part this was due to a very deep split in the ranks of the CP itself over questions of political strategy, the importance of which emerged by the fall of 1944. More significant, however, was the extent to which diverse groups with objectives far different from the Communist or EAM program were attracted into the ELAS.

There were at least a few reformed bandits who decided to wrap their activities as guerrillas in ennobling political cloth. Much more crucial was the Macedonian nationality problem, on which the Greek Communists were, and remained, split. Tito's "Slav-Macedonian" propaganda in favor of an autonomous or independent Macedonian state attracted many Macedonians in Greece for purely nationalist reasons. This cause was decades old, but in 1943 such groups informally moved into the ELAS to create their own units. Tito's agents aided them in their plans and the EAM and Greek Communists resisted them throughout 1943. During early 1944 the EAM reluctantly permitted a Slav-Macedonian National Liberation Front (SNOF) to organize, but did not permit them to form units separate from the ELAS. By mid-1944 this issue reached a crisis point, and was later complicated when Macedonians oriented toward Bulgaria, as opposed to Yugoslavia, began operating in Greece. The ELAS military command wanted to destroy SNOF units, now growing and operating independently, and the Communists hoped to negotiate an end to their existence, sternly resisting all Macedonian claims on Greece. The Communists were overruled. During October the ELAS attacked the SNOF units and eventually permitted them to retreat to Yugoslavia.[4] The Macedonian issue had little to do with socialist ideologies, but indicated a revolutionary potential existed in Greece around traditional issues; and it also revealed how complex the Resistance was, and how far the Communists might or might not be able to control it.

The British and the EAM

This, then, was the labyrinthine situation confronting the British when they began to send military missions to Greece in the fall of 1942. These missions encouraged ELAS attacks on German railroads and shipping, with several spectacular instances of success, but events soon reduced the entire relationship to one of politics. The British wished to unite the various Resistance groups into a unified command, and to end conflicts be-

tween them that frequently ended in open warfare. In this they failed. The
Foreign Office also ordered British missions to "impress on such groups as
may be anti-monarchial the fact that the King and Government enjoy the
fullest support of HMG," and the Resistance should take no steps that
might promote disunity.[5] Since the ELAS, EDES, and tiny EKKA were all
republican, British admonitions also failed here. Ultimately, the British
decided by October 1943, they would give arms only to Zervas, for he was
the least objectionable politically and he also obeyed military orders. This
decision hardly hurt the ELAS, for it had never received more than a tenth
of its arms from the British.

The British were determined to support the monarchy and government-
in-exile as the only alternative to a Greece that might break away from the
British sphere of influence in the Mediterranean. The relationship was
reciprocal and mutually pressing. The exile government appreciated that it
could return to Greece only with British support, probably military, and it
had ambitious, long-standing territorial aspirations which it knew only the
Great Powers might satisfy. Britain was the only one interested. British
involvement in Greece was both economic and strategic, and since a "republican régime . . . in the past failed to produce anything but weak and
unreliable governments," as they informed the State Department in March
1943, they would opt for the prewar order. Their economic holdings left
them with control of the Greek treasury, via the interwar International
Control Commission on which they predominated. Strategically, Greece
was the key to the eastern Mediterranean and Suez. England did not intend
to lose it. For this reason full British political hegemony in Greece was far
more critical to English interests than the situation in Yugoslavia, where
they might attempt to transform the only politically serious option—Tito. In
return, the prewar Greek politicians hoped to claim Cyprus, which only
Britain could deliver, recoup the Dodecanese islands, restore the national
presence in the almost 2,000 square miles of northern Epirus now in
Albanian hands, rectify the western Thracian border with Bulgaria, and
perhaps bring Cyrenaica back to the classical heritage it lost when it fell to
the sons of Rome.

These border demands were of great consequence to the developments
in Greece, even as early as 1943, and they merely reopened counterclaims
by Greece's northern neighbors, titles political ideologies masked but which
dated back well before Lenin's birth. If aid to less ambitious, perhaps even
pliant, forces in Greece might save them from irredentist passions, or
extend those of their own, Greece's northern neighbors might aid the Left,
the Macedonians, Chams, or anyone else for that matter.

The British had little difficulty obtaining American support for their
position in mid-1943, carefully explaining to the State Department that
only the king could prevent civil war, tyranny, and bring stability after the

German departure. The United States informed the British in July that it hoped to see broader representation in the Greek exile government, but it "recognizes the present Greek régime . . . and acknowledges the necessity for continuity in government until the Greek people shall have had an opportunity to express their will. . . . It shares the confidence of the British Government in the friendly and loyal sentiments of the Greek King and Government. . . ."[6] The Greeks, however, did not share this trust, and the State Department decided that given the antimonarchist sentiments of Greek-Americans it might be best to remain slightly more aloof. The ELAS, EDES, and EKKA, for their part, traveled to Cairo during August 1943 to urge the king, the exile government, and their British sponsors that it would be undesirable for the king to return before the Greeks held a plebiscite, and they requested an immediate conference to bring the Resistance groups and other parties into a new government of national unity. They requested three seats for themselves. The British considered the matter, presented it to the State Department, and after obtaining its endorsement determined that the King of Greece would return to his recalcitrant subjects as soon as possible. They also denied the political demands of the three Resistance groups and unceremoniously ordered their representatives to leave Cairo immediately.

Since the Resistance, divided among itself but united against the monarch and government, would hold Greece when the Germans left, the British government decided at this point to withdraw all nominal aid from the ELAS. It knew that Greece would support the EAM, which was synonymous with Communism in Foreign Office parlance. The Italian surrender gravely aggravated the problem in early September, for their troops in Greece merely handed vast quantities of arms to the Resistance, mainly the ELAS. The British estimated that 35,000 to 40,000 well-armed ELAS Resistants might confront them. They now felt that sudden German withdrawal presented the danger and the British military and the Foreign Office proceeded to consider this potentially unpleasant contingency. Unless a large Allied force landed immediately after a German withdrawal, the military advised, the EAM would take over. This landing would involve "at least two divisions" which would have to remain as occupying forces. Such a commitment of over 50,000 men would be too large, given the military obligations elsewhere, and therefore the British decided not to invade Greece under any circumstances unless German evacuation compelled it, in which case it would really be an invasion of a Greek-held nation. In the event of sudden German withdrawal, however, London ordered a permanent force of 5,000 men with armor and high fire power and mobility to be held in readiness to enter and hold Athens immediately. Churchill approved the plan, which he agreed pertained to an "essentially political question. . . . Their duty would be to give support at the centre to the restored lawful Greek Government. . . . Once a stable Government is set up, we should take our departure."[7] Churchill also reluctantly acknowledged that his difficult task would be much easier if the king publicly offered not to return to Athens until such time as there was "a clear expression of the people's will" on the constitutional monarchy. In any event, the British told the king during November, to return to Athens immediately would cause him "to be associated directly with an administration bound to become unpopular and unable to accord all those freedoms associated with a constitutional monarchy."[8] It would be desirable during the interim to create a regency under Archbishop Damaskinos. The same month King George announced, in consultation with his government, he would now time his return to Athens in accordance with the "national interest."

The policy of discontinuing aid to the ELAS was hardly effective, for with relatively little violence the ELAS began disarming and isolating the EDES, which soon became primarily anti-EAM. And vague assurances as to the king's return or the future of the monarchy, much less the nature and composition of the government, only aggravated the relations between the British, their wards in Cairo, and the Greeks.

By the beginning of 1944 both the British and American governments viewed the question of Greece primarily within the context of the danger of Communism—which was synonymous with the EAM and the growth of Russian influence—and the Greek exile government assiduously played up this interpretation. All knew the Russians wished the various Resistance groups to unite and increase their struggle against the Germans, but lurking behind this aim, according to the American ambassador to the Greek exiles, Lincoln MacVeagh, was their desire to further "the spread of Soviet influence and prestige."[9] Indeed, the American officials concerned with the question soon saw the monarchical problem as incidental to whether it would increase Soviet influence. There the matter rested until March 3, 1944, when the EAM announced the formation of a "Provisional Governmental Committee" to run that part of Greece under their control. The committee, which technically was not another government but might easily become one, demanded representation in the Cairo government. The Cairo regime refused their request.

On March 31 a delegation of fourteen officers representing the large majority of the Greek army and navy in Egypt visited Prime Minister Tsouderos and asked for his resignation and the inclusion of the EAM in a new government based on republican principles. He arrested them. On April 3 Tsouderos' Cabinet forced his resignation, and until the end of the month, when they chose George Papandreou to replace him, the Greek government confronted a political crisis whose limits British soldiers defined. For from April 3 to 5 a large part of the Greek army in Egypt, including five ships of the navy, rioted and struck for a republican government and collaboration with the Governmental Committee in Greece. Army officers and nearly all of the navy's commanders, whom Churchill decided had been "contaminated by revolutionary and Communist elements," provided the leadership. "What is happening here among the Greeks," the British ambassador to the Greeks, Reginald Leeper, wired back, "is nothing less than a revolution." The Greek soldiers quickly took up arms and mounted defenses around their camps, and a number of ships also refused to obey British orders. On the 8th Churchill directed the British commander in Egypt to disarm them. He wired Leeper:

> Our relations are definitely established with the lawfully constituted Greek Government headed by the King, who is the ally of Britain and cannot be discarded to suit a momentary surge of appetite among ambitious émigré nonentities. Neither can Greece find constitutional expression in particular sets of guerrillas, in many cases indistinguishable from banditti, who are masquerading as the saviours of their country. . . . I have been planning to place Greece back high in the counsels of the victorious nations.

They would have to disarm the Greek dissidents in Egypt unconditionally. "Do not worry too much about the external effects," Churchill warned Leeper. "Simply keep them rounded up by artillery and superior force and let hunger play its part." ". . . without bloodshed," if possible, he had advised, "but brought under control it must be. Count on my support."[10] On the evening of April 23 the British forces moved against the starving Greeks in their camps and ships, and after brief shooting managed to obtain their surrender. They arrested their leaders and threw about 20,000 Greeks into prisoner-of-war cages.

Throughout this crisis the British sought and obtained the support of Washington. Lincoln MacVeagh, on this and numerous future occasions, was entirely uncritical, and convinced Roosevelt to be the same. He described the EAM as the cause of the mutiny, and behind the EAM stood Russia. The question, as the State Department understood it, was "whether Russia aspires to supplant Britain as the dominating foreign power in Greek affairs." Leeper, MacVeagh incredulously reported back on April 19, told him "The Russians could stop the trouble in a minute if they would." In this context Roosevelt gave Churchill a statement for public quotation declaring "I join in the hope that your line of action toward the problem may succeed in bringing back the Greeks into the camp of the Allies. . . ." The Greeks, he advised, should "set aside pettiness."[11] Both the British and Americans found confirmation of Russian responsibility for the crisis in critical articles the Soviet news agency sent out. Implications he was behind the revolt somewhat bewildered the Russian ambassador in

Cairo, and Molotov pleaded he had little information on the entire business, though he also instructed TASS to take greater care in its reports. All this seemed ominous, perhaps even more so when the EAM in Greece attacked the Egyptian mutineers. The British for their part resolved to purge the Greek army and navy thoroughly of politically unreliable elements favoring republicanism or the Left, and to take the matter directly to Stalin, the alleged ultimate cause of the trouble. They had already obtained American support, and via the spheres-of-influence agreement, already discussed in the preceding chapter, they set out to win Russian assurances of a free hand in Greece in return for Soviet freedom in Rumania.

The Greek army in Egypt acted on its own initiative, though the EAM was attractive to many Greek soldiers there as the solution to Greece's political and economic malaise. This did not, however, make the EAM the cause of the dissidence, which in fact the monarchy and extreme-Right exile government created. These elements were now the tools of England, which was resolved to apply the necessary force to maintain control of Greece. Stalin's approval was not a necessary preliminary to British repression, since the British had formulated their plans in September 1943 and applied them in part during the following April. That the British obtained Stalin's approval changed nothing in regard to their policy. The question was whether Russia could stop the EAM.

The Greek soldiers in any event demanded very little more than a reformed government, and Papandreou was pliable and perhaps even republican in his sentiments. There was no point in having a bloody conflict over small issues. On April 29, after his troops had laid the mutiny to rest, Churchill publicly instructed the new Greek Prime Minister to set partisan differences aside until the end of the war, when the Greeks would then be free to choose their own government. And during early May, while Churchill moved to get the Russians behind his policy, Leeper gathered the Greek exile leader and EAM representatives together in Lebanon to patch together a government compatible both with tranquility and British interests.

The Greeks haggled in the Lebanese mountains, with Leeper close by to give definition and direction to their deliberations. After much confusing debate, on May 24 they announced the formation of a Government of National Unity under Papandreou. The rest of the program involved disciplining the Greek army (Papandreou himself wished the leaders of the mutiny shot), unifying the Resistance under the exile government, termination of EAM rule in Greece, various border claims against Bulgaria and Italy, and a plebiscite after the war. On June 11, after the EAM insisted on a clear statement the king would not return before the plebiscite, Papandreou himself took such a position. But British and American support for the program did not convince the EAM delegates to endorse it immediately to the extent of agreeing to join the new government. They knew that unless the agreement established truly democratic politics their position would be perilous after liberation. They returned to Greece to consider the Lebanon agreement, and gave their full support only on August 19 in a manner intimately related to British efforts to reach an understanding with the Russians.[12]

The obscurity of the Russian presence in Greece was maddening to the English. The Soviet lack of interest appeared almost studied, and perhaps it was. Throughout 1943 there was absolutely no evidence of Russian contact with the EAM or ELAS, and Molotov at the end of the year took the position that he would say nothing on Greek internal affairs since he knew so little about the subject. Persistent ELAS requests to the Russians for arms were ignored. Radio Moscow in its New Year's Day broadcast of 1944 had even endorsed British appeals for Greek unity, and three days later agreed to a British request that Tsouderos be allowed to make a similar appeal in the name of the three major Allies. The Russians gave similar assurances to the Greek ambassador in Moscow during the first half of 1944, and Molotov had proven most agreeable to British suggestions during the April mutiny. If TASS called Tsouderos' government reactionary at that time, Molotov consoled the British, they would be more careful and would welcome any new information the British cared to provide. For a moment it seemed the events had shocked the Russians. In fact, the Russians always attempted to get their information on Greece through the British, and Eden felt they "had shown little interest" until spring 1944.[13]

It would be more precise to state that Britain attempted to cultivate and define Soviet interest in Greece in a way satisfactory to itself, for both the British and Americans saw a shadowy Russian hand in the cold mountains of Greece and the barracks around Cairo. At this time the British initiated the tenuous spheres-of-influence agreement with Russia, with Greece as the initial and principal objective of the British proposal.

During mid-July the Soviet ambassador to the Greek government left Cairo and did not return for sixteen months, and on July 26 the first Soviet Military Mission arrived at the ELAS headquarters. Escaped Russian prisoners of war had been with the ELAS earlier, but the alleged Communists treated them badly and eventually threw them into a concentration camp. The Russian Mission was openly unimpressed by the ELAS, who looked ragged compared to Tito's Partisans, but almost certainly the Russians' purpose was political, and this they quickly accomplished. Woodhouse did not find their presence discomforting, and it is entirely possible they were there at the suggestion or with the approval of the British, who had nothing to regret from their presence. In any event, on August 15 the EAM withdrew its objections to the Lebanon agreement, decided to send five representatives rather than the seven it previously demanded to the exile government, and to support loyally a program of national unity. The EAM was certainly deeply split on this issue at the time, for the non-Communists wished to hold out for more specific guarantees on the return of the king, amnesty for the soldiers in Egypt, and an acceptable replacement for Papandreou, with the CP taking a then typical position for wartime unity. Indeed, when the EAM delegation arrived in Cairo full of doubts as to whether to conform to their reluctant allegiance, the Soviet legation there instructed the two Communist members to enter the government immediately.[14] The first serious political division within the ranks of the EAM placed the Communists on the side of the conservatives and future British domination of Greece.

The Russians had finally visibly intervened in Greek affairs and helped the British to solve their problems, but would the Greeks themselves agree to play the role of pawn in the Great Power game? Churchill knew he could take no chances, and while the Soviet Mission busied itself trying to harness the EAM, Churchill laid specific plans for the British return to Greece, for he had no confidence in the EAM in or out of the government. Rumors of impending German evacuation of Greece aggravated the problem, and during the first week of August, Churchill embarked on a course to which the EAM might accommodate or fight. "Surely we should tell M. Papandreou he should continue as Prime Minister and defy them all," the British apostle of democracy wrote Eden. They could not throw him to "the miserable Greek banditti," for the issue was whether to permit "Bolshevism" or resist it. Churchill then ordered his military to prepare 10,000 to 12,000 men, plus "scrapings and combings from the 200,000 tail we have in Egypt," for a lightning descent on Athens and key areas, with a key group of parachutists to land in Athens within hours of the German departure.[15] It was in effect an Operation RANKIN for Greece, dubbed "MANNA." On August 17 the British asked Roosevelt to endorse the plan designed to keep "a tyrannical Communistic Government being set up," and Roosevelt agreed nine days later, even offering such American transport as might be available.[16] The British then moved Papandreou and his EAM-backed government to Italy as part of the plan "to strike out of the blue without any preliminary crisis," and on September 13 the British placed MANNA on forty-eight-hour readiness.[17] Papandreou himself warned the British at the end of August, and again on September 22, that unless they sent "impressive" forces to every major part of Greece the EAM would run the country where the British were not stationed.

The Restoration of the Ancien Régime

The Germans had been watching these events with much sophisticated attention, and even Hitler saw the advantages in a war between the ELAS and the English. On September 14 he ordered a withdrawal from Greece, designed according to German General Alfred Jodl, to "kindle and fan strife between Communist and nationalist forces."[18] Before they could do so the British Supreme Allied Commander for the Mediterranean met with the ELAS commander, Saraphis, and concluded the Caserta agreement on September 26. Both sides argued much over this agreement in subsequent months, and its contents deserve some description. At Caserta the ELAS agreed to place its forces under the orders of British General Ronald M. Scobie as the representative of the Allied High Command. They were "forbidden . . . to take the law into their own hands," "Security battalions will be treated as enemy organizations . . . or instruments of the enemy," "nothing is to be undertaken in regard to Athens except at the command of General Scobie," and all Resistance groups "have put themselves under the command of the National Unity Government of Greece." The EAM submitted to these provisions, according to the first article of the agreement, "in order to coordinate their activities in the best interest of the common struggle against the enemy."[19] When the British attempted to get Saraphis also to define his mission under the agreement "to restore law and order," he refused, making it clear the ELAS was consenting only to common military operations against the enemy, which meant the Germans.[20] Whatever else one may say about this agreement, it is not likely that an army about to embark on the Bolshevization of Greece would so readily agree to its binding terms. The fact that the ELAS signed it did not alter British plans.

At the beginning of October the Germans began a lightning withdrawal from Greece, leaving behind intact arms dumps which fell into ELAS hands. The ELAS quickly lost contact with the German rear guard, and merely filled in the vacuum they left. The British landed at Patras on October 3, and when the Germans evacuated Athens on the 12th, British parachutists landed the next day. As the small number of British troops proceeded slowly up the rest of the mainland, they found the approximately 50,000 to 75,000 well-armed ELAS troops in charge and the EAM administering Greece in the name of the national government. After the first few days of revenge on collaborators, during which time a small number of personal affairs were settled in the traditional manner, the EAM restored relative quiet. The EAM was running Greece with efficiency and order and the support of the majority of the population. The British interpreted the lack of an open opposition as proof of dictatorship, not considering that the major opposition had either collaborated or fled abroad, and that the EAM's political spectrum was broader than in many Western nations, much less prewar Greece. But the British were not to tolerate the EAM's monopoly on power, whether it was democratically based or totalitarian. The population, including the ELAS, was most cordial—the ELAS did not shoot a single British soldier, and the EAM did not proclaim a

Soviet republic. The last German soldier left Greece on November 10, and clearly the British remained not to fight the Nazis but to settle Greek political problems. Given the rampant starvation and economic disorganization, their task of moving the Greeks by reason to support the existing conservative government was hopeless from its inception. The British army would have to do the job, and Churchill seemed passionately eager to throw it into the fray. After his meeting with Stalin he was confident, as Leeper confided to MacVeagh on November 8, that "The Russians seem really to be keeping their hands off this country. . . ."[21] ". . . having paid the price we have to Russia for freedom of action in Greece," Churchill advised Eden on November 7, "we should not hesitate to use British troops to support the Royal Hellenic Government under M. Papandreou. . . . This implies that British troops should certainly intervene to check acts of lawlessness. . . . I hope the Greek [Mountain] Brigade will arrive soon, and will not hesitate to shoot when necessary." On the next day Churchill wrote he was convinced the "Communist elements in Greece . . . plan to seize power by force," and he ordered major reinforcements into Greece.[22] On the 15th Scobie commanded the ELAS to leave Athens, and they quickly agreed.

Leeper, who clearly saw a potential split in the EAM that would develop over time if Papandreou could stabilize conditions around Athens, did not share Churchill's nearly hysterical anxiety to open warfare against the ELAS. Moreover, the failure to act on the monarchical question, and treating the king's absence from the country as if it were merely a visit abroad, unnecessarily aggravated that problem and weakened Papandreou, who pleaded that he had no time to consider the obviously vital matter. For the same reasons, MacVeagh concurred with Leeper's estimate. The British energetically continued their military buildup throughout November (23,000 troops were there by the end of October), not trusting the quixotic Greeks to settle their affairs themselves.

What was the position of the Communists and the EAM during October and November, and were they on the road to power via arms? Was a political settlement possible?

Leeper knew that the EAM was deeply divided over what course to take, and he told MacVeagh on November 17 that he had "doubts as to whether the national leaders of the organizations are really able any longer to control their men."[23] This had always been the case, and it was a consequence of the democracy in the ELAS. Now that Greece was theirs and the people behind them, many ELAS and EAM members unquestionably were speculating, "why give it to the British?" As nationalists or as socialists, this logic persuaded many. It did not convince the Communists, and although they went to very great trouble to push the EAM on a parliamentary course, they too were split. George Siantos, the secretary general of the Communist party, at the beginning of November conspicuously endorsed "normal democratic solutions" to Greece's problems and the dissolution of the ELAS and all other armed groups into a national army which excluded Metaxist elements.[24] The official Communist program, in common with all Communist parties, stressed national unity against the Germans above all else. Throughout October the Communist party repeatedly appealed for public order, and its political manifesto of October 20 declared:

> It is everybody's primary national duty to ensure order and a smooth political life for the country. Avoid taking the law into your own hands, as the punishment of the collaborationists and other criminals rests in the hands of the United National Government. . . . Communists! You stood as the champions of the national and popular uprising. Stand now as the vanguard for securing order and democratic freedom. Patriots all, unite in the struggle for the completion of the liberation of Greece along with the ELAS and our allies under our United Government.[25]

The official EAM organ, *New Greece,* for the entire month of November called for maintenance of order to deprive the British of any excuses for intervening and restoring the monarchy. It urged support for the Papandreou government, a purge of collaborators and fascists, a quick plebiscite on the monarchy, social services within the context of a national economic plan, and continued private control of industry. As for foreign affairs, "Those who urge that Greece should orient her foreign policy towards only one of the great allied Powers are fifth columnists. . . ."[26] Northern Epirus, the Dodecanese, and parts of Thrace were openly coveted, and an intense nationalism, rather than a class orientation, permeated the entire journal. It was this nationalism that was to align the Greeks against Britain's control of their destiny.

The leadership of the EAM and the Communists were unquestionably committed to avoid armed conflict with the British, and the best evidence for this was their utter lack of preparation when England forced it upon them. That there were Titoist elements, various Macedonian independents, and as Churchill insisted on calling them after late December, "Trotskyites," does not alter the fact that no one has ever produced documented evidence to show that the EAM and Communists, or any part of them, prepared to seize power violently in Greece at the end of 1944. Nor has any serious student ever shown Soviet responsibility for the events of that period.

In fact, a concatenation of circumstances led to fighting, by far the most important being the intense desire of the British to impose control over a country which the wrong Greeks administered. On November 5

Papandreou and Scobie ordered the ELAS and EDES to disarm by December 10. At the same time, the British brought in the Mountain Brigade, composed of the archconservative, pro-royalist remnants of the Greek army in Egypt, and the Sacred Squadron. And nothing definite was done to clear up the problem of the Security Battalions which the German-sponsored Rallis regime organized in late 1943 to fight the ELAS. These men were Nazi collaborators, some were in prison, but many were also free and openly organizing to fight the EAM; Papandreou wished to eliminate them, but he had no power to do so and the EAM had to worry about them. MacVeagh considered that the return of the Mountain Brigade, "notably Rightist in sentiment," served "to strengthen EAM's nation-wide claim to represent Greek ideals of liberty and freedom from foreign control."[27] Their presence was in the nature of a provocation to the EAM, which could choose to fight, to capitulate, or to equivocate. To ask the ELAS to disarm in their presence was to ask them to risk destruction, and the British must have known the ELAS would resist. In fact the British prepared for violence as quickly as they could, bringing in air power, as many British and Indian troops as they could muster—all the while arranging public demonstrations of the Mountain Brigade and Sacred Squadron that served to outrage the large majority of Greeks and accusing the ELAS of terrorism. Yet such a direct confrontation with the EAM suited British purposes, for the Papandreou government ruled Athens only, and in a democratic situation the EAM was likely to take over Greece via legal parliamentary mechanisms. During November they administered most of Greece, and the British had to remove them quickly, even if that meant restoring collaborationists willing to work for a revival of the Old Order.

With a disarmament deadline hanging over them, the EAM then attempted to negotiate the problem with Papandreou, whom Scobie and Leeper constantly supervised. Up to that moment the EAM took the position that *all* groups should disarm and Greece should reconstitute a truly democratic national army, of which the former ELAS would be a part as individual members. In fact by this time the actual disarmament of the ELAS was well advanced, for many of its members, who were most powerful in the north, had already returned to their villages. During the last ten days of November the EAM and Greek Cabinet debated this issue in a manner that has yet to be fully explained, but the crucial developments, I believe, can be reconstructed. The EAM in principle favored general disarmament, and its Cabinet members reiterated that position again on the 22nd or 23rd. Papandreou on the 27th asked the EAM to draft an acceptable demobilization plan, and it is probable that the Communists took on this assignment. A draft came in the morning of the following day. Their plan, which elated Papandreou and greatly surprised Leeper, departed from their earlier position that all groups disarm and made an exception of the Mountain Brigade. The rest of the Cabinet immediately accepted it with important but complex modifications, and later that day the EAM thought once more, or perhaps for the first time as a collective group, about the problem, for it is likely that the drafters had not submitted the hasty text to the entire leadership of the organization and that the initial capitulation was the product of Siantos and his dominant section of the Communist party. The next day, the 29th, as the British and their allies continued to pour into Greece, the EAM submitted a revised plan in favor of disarmament along the lines of their previous plan for *all* groups to hand in *all* arms and reconstitute the army.* Papandreou and the British refused this revised plan on the basis that the Mountain Brigade was an official Allied unit, the ELAS a mere "private army." Papandreou then announced that a newly organized National Guard on December 1 would take over the arms of the EAM police, a proposal the EAM first accepted but in the light of the deadlock on the general disarmament issue now refused to agree to. On December 1 the EAM police held on to their arms and the six EAM ministers, only two of whom were Communists, resigned from the government.

It should be noted that of the EAM's two disarmament positions, neither postulated civil war. One involved a total elimination of the ELAS, and probably much terror against the Left. During the last ten days of November 5,000 troops were moved into Athens and Security Battalions' attacks against the EAM became more frequent. Therefore the EAM asked before and after November 28 that an essentially democratic and peaceful solution to the impasse be found; in effect, that the British acknowledge the EAM's now predominant role in Greek life as something more than the manifestation of banditti. And this in turn meant that the Greek Left, by asking for a position in politics roughly proportionate to its strength, was willing to digress from the pattern of the Left in Western Europe for two reasons. First, the Communists did not control the EAM, and especially the military leadership of the ELAS, well enough to prevent indigenous nationalist and radical protest from finding expression over the desires of the CP and Moscow. Secondly, Russia did not adequately dominate the Communists to make them of one mind when Moscow ordered a suicidal course. There were Macedonian and Titoist influences in the CP. The leadership, we now know, was split on the question of obedience to Mos-

* Sweet-Escott, *Greece*, 35; Churchill, *Triumph and Tragedy*, 248; Leeper, *When Greek Meets Greek*, 97–98; Woodward, *British Foreign Policy*, 140; Stavrianos, "The Immediate Origin of the Battle of Athens," 245; EAM, *White Book*, 34–39; FR (1944), V, 140–41, 148. The first two accounts assert the EAM plan of November 28 proposed reducing the ELAS to brigade size, with a continuation of the Mountain Brigade, Sacred Squadron, and a smaller EDES unit, but they fail to indicate Papandreou also added this was to be within the context of an integrated national army the EAM then expected would be stacked against them. Even if they are accurate, it would have meant the rightist military groups overpowering the ELAS.

cow's dictum to sacrifice all immediate issues to the war effort. Beyond this neither the EAM nor the Communists had a sufficiently tight grip on the Greek masses to allow the British policy of a showdown by force to prevail. After December 1 the people themselves were to act.

On December 2 the Papandreou Cabinet dissolved the ELAS, and the EAM asked for and was granted permission to hold a protest demonstration early the following Sunday morning in Athens, and also announced a general strike for the 4th. The government withdrew permission late that night, unquestionably aware of the very great difficulties in calling off a demonstration. Sunday morning demonstrators gathered about the city, including several thousand in front of the American embassy, cheering Roosevelt and the United States. The main group, however, headed toward Constitution Square in the center of Athens, where a large press corps watched as they reached the corner of the square near a police station and the police blocked their entrance, and then repeatedly fired on them for no apparent reason, killing twenty-four and wounding 150, including women and children. British troops were stationed nearby in case of need. Churchill warned his officers "I fully expect a clash with EAM and we must not shrink from it, provided the ground is well chosen."[28] The battle was on, and it was the only one like it during all of World War II.

ELAS units began moving toward Athens early the next day, but the British disarmed the first battalion of eight hundred without firing a shot, as if the Greeks were merely in peaceful protest; in reality they had definite orders to avoid conflict with British troops. The rest were more aggressive, and by the evening of the 4th the ELAS began getting the upper hand in savage battles throughout Greece and especially in most of Athens. On that day Papandreou attempted to resign, but the British Foreign Office immediately wired back their refusal to permit him to leave office. In the early hours of December 5 Churchill sent Scobie his instructions:

> . . . do not hesitate to fire at any armed male in Athens who assails the British authority or the Greek authority with which we are working. It would be well of course if your commands were reinforced by the authority of some Greek Government, and Papandreou is being told by Leeper to stop and help. *Do not however hesitate to act as if you were in a conquered city where a local rebellion is in progress.*[29]

To the House of Commons, which was gasping from the on-the-scene descriptions of the events and which several days later nearly defeated the government on the issue, Churchill announced "we shall not hesitate to use the considerable British Army now in Greece," and in this course England had "the support of an overwhelming majority of the Greek people." The alternative was "anarchy or a Communist dictatorship."[30]

The British rushed in troops as quickly as possible, but for the first several weeks 16,000 of them barely held on to the center of Athens. They were quickly isolated in the rest of Greece, sniped at in Piraeus, and on December 11, with food nearly exhausted and the ELAS making advances everywhere, Field Marshal Alexander predicted the possibility of "a first-class disaster."[31] The next day, with Greek victory near, an important Communist member of the EAM asked Scobie for his armistice terms, the Communists having first made a more general offer on the 8th. Scobie demanded immediate ELAS disarmament in Athens and Piraeus before opening discussions concerning the remaining issues. Four days later, while they still held military supremacy, the ELAS offered to withdraw their forces from the two cities as part of a general disarmament, and from this point on negotiations for an armistice continued along with the fighting, the British being saved from total defeat.

Although the British treated the ELAS response in Athens as part of a coup, no organized revolution ever opened discussions to terminate hostilities when it was obviously on the verge of success. Had they wished to do so, the EAM could have taken over Greece in early October, before the British returned, and they never rejected the idea of general disarmament. In mid-December they were quite able to defeat the British in open combat had they determined to apply greater force or hold on throughout Greece. The entire affair was spontaneous; the Communists later admitted the obvious fact that they were unprepared and that events had surprised them, and the Communists were the first to take the initiative in terminating the episode. The entire EAM obviously desired political legality, and they sensed that in the long run they might not be able to win a war. On December 22, with the massive influx of British might only beginning to take effect, the ELAS capitulated and offered to disarm in Athens and Piraeus in return for the formation of a new government before the armistice. At this point Churchill announced that he would himself come to Athens for Christmas to solve the impasse.

Throughout the fighting Churchill not only refused to treat with the EAM on a political level, but also with the remainder of the Greek politicians. Papandreou tried to resign, but Churchill "sternly discouraged," in Leeper's words, "any attempts among the Greek politicians to form a new Government." The leading Greek politicians were now no longer willing to serve in a British-sponsored government in any event, but again according to Leeper, "Mr. Churchill let it be known that while the British were fighting for Athens a change of Government was undesirable." In brief, Greece would find the solution to its problems in the streets or in EAM capitulation. "No peace without victory," Churchill wired Leeper. Indeed, the British ignored the protests of Papandreou and other anti-EAM Greek leaders who objected when Alexander and Leeper decided to revive their plan of late 1943 to appoint the Archbishop of Athens, Damaskinos, as regent. Leeper later recalled that he had no assurance that any substantial body of Greek opinion supported this course, but "what had to be done had to be done no matter what any local Gallup might have reported."[32]

When Churchill descended on Athens to impose a plan that he had outlined in principle and even in detail the year before, he had the assurance of both American and Soviet support or toleration, and so he proceeded with a free and heavy hand.

During the several days following the outbreak of fighting in Athens, American policy wavered and then came down solidly behind the British. Stettinius on December 7 told a press conference that he felt that the Greeks themselves ought to work out their own political future, obliquely rebuking Churchill. During these same days, of course, he had to deal with the Anglo-American disagreements over Italian and Polish affairs as well, and he was feeling generally piqued over the thrust of English policy when the comment was made. MacVeagh reinforced this critical mood in the State Department when he reported British policy was driving many patriotic Greeks to support the EAM merely on nationalist grounds, dangerously polarizing the contending forces. But Stettinius, who was not very influential in White House inner circles, did not define basic American policy. Hopkins and Forrestal quickly recognized the need to back the British, and congratulated Churchill for a speech he made to the Commons on a vote of confidence on the Greek affair most notable for its numerous abstentions. Then, on December 9, Churchill irately phoned Hopkins that the American commander in the Mediterranean would not allow his landing craft to transfer supplies to Greece. Leahy and Hopkins quickly had the order countermanded, citing Roosevelt's August offer to permit the use of American planes in Operation MANNA. Despite Stettinius' advice, on December 13 Roosevelt wired Churchill that "I regard my role in this matter as that of a loyal friend and ally whose one desire is to be of any help possible in the circumstances." If the United States did not take a public stand to this effect, he reassured Churchill, it was due solely to "the state of public opinion," which, he might have added, the numerous eyewitness newspaper accounts of the Greek events had aroused to a high pitch of criticism in England and America.[33]

For the remainder of December, Roosevelt sent pleasant notes of support to Churchill, and when the State Department summarized United States policy on Greece preparatory to the Yalta Conference it did not mention Greek political affairs and the events of December. That the United States supported the British on Greece at the same moment that they were bitterly disagreeing over most other problems pertaining to the future politics of Europe was entirely logical, for Greece at this time was the one nation where America had no independent position. It supported the British handling of the Greek mutiny, the plans for Operation MANNA, and was hardly more anxious than the British to see a Communist Greece emerge. Churchill could count on American backing.

(Churchill's other loyal ally was Stalin, and the Russian position might have been anticipated from the advice the Soviet Military Mission gave to the EAM the previous summer. No one heard a word of reproach of British policy in Greece from the Soviet Union throughout this bloody period, and Churchill appreciated it.)"I am increasingly impressed, up to date," Churchill wrote on December 11, "with the loyalty with which, under much temptation and very likely pressure, Stalin has kept off Greece in accordance with our agreement. . . . we shall gain in influence with him and strengthen a moderate policy for the Soviets by showing them how our mind works."[34] Since the Russians never favored an EAM revolt in the first instance, Stalin presumably traded toleration for Churchill's supposed reciprocation elsewhere as a result of their October "understanding," and Stalin assiduously cultivated this myth of a diplomatic exchange and held bloody Greece up to the West repeatedly over the next year. By comparison his hands were clean, but he learned much from British resolution to use guns and it only reinforced Stalin's natural anti-revolutionary instincts. One overt gesture in Churchill's favor, however, did come from Moscow during December, in addition to the instructive silence that impressed everyone. At the end of December, Vishinsky told the Greek ambassador in Moscow that the Soviets had appointed another Russian ambassador to the Greek government to replace the allegedly ill but conspicuously absent incumbent. This renewed recognition of the British puppet regime caused much consternation among the ranks of the EAM and ELAS, but it did not end their will to resist, for the vast majority stood only for themselves.

It would have been impossible for the Russians to have shared any responsibility for the rapid sequence of events between November 27 and December 4 without the fact being revealed to the British. The Russians had not organized the EAM and ELAS and they could not stop them, especially given their decentralized and therefore non-Bolshevik structure. Leeper, writing six years after the events, admitted that there was no evidence whatsoever for Soviet responsibility for the December uprising. Their complete lack of interest in Greek affairs even through 1945 impressed Woodhouse. Churchill too was aware of his freedom to impose his will.

At the time the ELAS offered to disarm in the Athens area, on December 22, they controlled four-fifths of Greece, and Field Marshal Alexander warned Churchill that he would not be able to reconquer more than the Athens-Piraeus area. To settle the problem politically was therefore urgent, and since the EAM obviously wished to opt for reentry into politics, they offered Churchill the possibility of exploiting both force and diplomacy to accomplish his end and prevent the Left's triumph. When Churchill arrived in Athens on Christmas Day, Alexander's basic respect for the stubborn military effectiveness of the ELAS had not diminished, and he again told Churchill that his forces could not eradicate them. Macmillan had also warned him that the longer the war, the greater was the danger of Macedonia's becoming independent. On the other hand, Ambassador Kirk in Italy wired Washington, "Macmillan added that the parties of the Right felt that this was the last chance to save Greece from terrorist dictatorship of the Left and that the Archbishop must be appointed at once as Regent. . . ."[35] Since Churchill refused to waver, the "Trotskyites," as he now dubbed them, would have to make whatever concessions might be forthcoming. Churchill saw the archbishop, about whom he had some reservations, but "He agreed to all that was proposed." He then met with Papandreou, Siantos, and other EAM leaders, telling them that the British had come to Greece to fight Germans and not Greeks, but in any case they had Stalin's support for the intervention, and the Communist contingent among the EAM leaders effusively thanked him. Their reference to England as "our great Ally" especially impressed Churchill.[36]

As the British proposed, Damaskinos was appointed regent, and Churchill subsequently assumed the task of convincing the Greek king to cooperate. With a supporting telegram from Roosevelt, who quickly obliged, Churchill and his chosen Greeks solved the regency problem almost immediately, promising a plebiscite in the future. The political and disarmament issue proved more difficult, for the British and their loyal Greeks wanted a caretaker government excluding the EAM, and ELAS surrender. These controversies were not solved during Churchill's stay, and fighting continued while both sides presented terms and counteroffers. On January 3 the regent appointed General Nicholas Plastiras prime minister, and his rightist views did not reassure the EAM. By the end of the first week of January, although the British had captured only Attica, the province containing Athens, nevertheless the ELAS ordered a general retreat. The EAM's main concern after this point was the question of amnesty and the fear of reprisals. On January 11 they signed a truce, with the ELAS surrendering most of the populous and strategic areas they controlled at the time. The truce reduced the arms the ELAS was to hand in to precise numbers, but gave them little of a political nature. The following day two of the EAM's constituent parties split from the coalition. Several days later Plastiras told the press that "The leaders and criminals of the Athens revolution will be severely punished."[37] To hedge against imminent vengeance some of the ELAS retained their arms and, according to their most likely executioners, took hostages as well.

Despite every sign of impending repression of the EAM and the Left,

the ELAS formally disbanded a month later when it signed the Varkiza
agreement on February 12. The agreement secured their promise to surrender their arms within two weeks, recognized the EAM and Communist
party as legal but not included in the government, promised elections and a
plebiscite within the year, guaranteed not to purge the EAM save for those
who violated "criminal" laws, and to remove the collaborators from all
branches of government.[38] Even before the ink was dry the agreement
broke down, for it alone would not successfully eliminate the Left, and for
the British there could be no respite. The Communists stopped the ELAS,
but they could not stop Churchill and the Right, and what had nearly been
the peaceful demise of a Resistance movement in the hands of the Communists was eventually to become the prelude to a revolution by men who
were ultimately compelled to fight to survive. By February 1945 the British
and their friends still retained the freedom to create the inextricable circumstances compelling that development.

CHAPTER

9

THE
POLITICAL CONDITIONS
OF MILITARY STRATEGY
IN THE FAR EAST

IN MARCH 1941 the American and British Joint Chiefs of Staff decided that any war against the Axis Powers would be a "Europe-first" undertaking, with the residual responsibility for Japan to fall primarily to the United States. They did not alter this priority throughout World War II. Yet the strategy of combat in the Far East was no less political in its assumptions and consequences than the war in Europe. The United States fought much of the early war in the Pacific from island to island, in difficult succession, if only because the political realities on the mainland of Asia closed the door on other strategic options. Those options involved the future of China, Russia, and Great Britain in the Far East, and the United States could not indefinitely avoid confronting the crucial question of the nature of Asia in the postwar world.

During 1942 to 1944 the Far Eastern war could not be fought in China, and since there was little military point to fighting in Southeast Asia as long as the United States could block the sea lanes to Japan, cutting off the mineral riches of the region, the Pacific war, as General Douglas MacArthur put it at the time, was "starved."[1] Beyond the limits imposed by political and military necessity, limits quite sufficient to stymie the expansion of the war, was Washington's belief that Europe would remain the locus of future world power, and that the political stakes there were greater by far. The American generals and especially the admirals in the Pacific chafed under the impositions limited resources and manpower allocations to their theater created, and MacArthur above all saw the Europe-Asia dichotomy as the prime reason for the neglect. "In continuing his criticism of Washington," Forrestal could write of a detailed report on MacArthur's views, "he said that the history of the world will be written in the Pacific for the next ten thousand years. . . . Europe is a dying system."[2] During World War II there was no one of consequence in Washington or London who shared this grandiose vision.

However, the United States still had to fight and resolve "the unknown war," as two official American historians describe the event.[3] And in the end its political significance involved the period during which the major political result of the war—the revolution in China—moved toward fruition. Hardly anyone in Washington perceived at this time the monumental and decisive long-term political implications the loss of Asia would entail to the future of world power over the next century. The United States was impotent to affect the course of that change, but it scarcely conceived of its cataclysmic implications during the wartime period. It only understood the marginal and immediate questions emerging from the upheaval—mainly the impotence of American power in a massive Asian land war.

For practical purposes, therefore, the Allies unanimously determined to fight World War II in and around Europe and to confront Asia subsequently. While they had varying estimates, both at the Quebec Conference of September 1944 and again at Yalta, the Anglo-American military leaders decided that the defeat of Japan would follow approximately eighteen months after the defeat of Germany, possibly earlier but perhaps later, an estimate that reflected their own priorities as much as the military and political realities in Japan. As MacArthur correctly perceived it, this timetable revealed the unwillingness of the Western leaders to commit immediately the manpower and matériel essential for an easy victory.[4]

The Role of the British in United States Planning

The leaders of the global American military theaters scrambled with each other throughout the war for the allocation of what they thought to be required resources, and the bitter relations with the British over the joint prosecution of the war followed the same pattern everywhere, but in Asia politics and not glory was the only consideration. Indeed, the question of how best to prosecute the war in the Far East matched the exacerbated controversies between the American and British leaders on how to fight the war in Europe. Since the Asian stakes struck both sides as less important, the tone of the disagreement was not as sharp as in Europe, but the principles were identical, and involved the preeminence of British as opposed to American power in Asia's postwar economic and political structure. By the end of the war, as the Americans gained the upper hand over the weakened defenders of the crumbling imperial system, they virtually excluded the British from the main theater of the war in Asia.

Their disagreements with the British on how to fight in Asia began almost as soon as America entered the war. Although the war in China had far-reaching implications about the justification and manner in which they would reconquer Burma from the Japanese, it was the least controversial aspect of the debate. The British economic mission sent to China in the fall of 1941 only confirmed the Foreign Office's opinion that the Kuomintang government was utterly corrupt, militarily ineffective, and beyond redemption. "The British military view," as the official history states it, "was that the diversion of resources on a large scale to China was not the best way to bring about the defeat of Japan. The Foreign Office also were not hopeful about the domestic prospects of General Chiang Kai-shek and the Kuomintang after the war." The British did not prefer the Chinese Communists, and indeed scarcely thought in terms of any solution to the myriad complexities of the situation, but they admitted that they did not want the emergence of an "aggressive nationalism on the part of the Chinese"—in brief, they wished China neither Communist nor too strong.[5]

British behavior toward China during the war confirmed this larger policy of neglecting the war in China, but the United States military leaders in China itself, even when they shared the same estimate and advice, were deeply disturbed about covert British intentions there. The British, they believed, maintained an extensive, even superior, intelligence network throughout China, and since it produced excellent data for the Americans as well, they probably were correct in assuming its size and efficiency. From this they concluded, however, that its real function was political. In the words of the official United States history of the theater, "Preparation for the postwar period and protection of the British stakes in China, such as Hong Kong, appeared to the Americans to be high on the list of British interests."[6] During 1945 most of the leading American political and military leaders in China shared this preoccupation with the long-term political implications of British involvement in China.

Since the Americans themselves were unwilling to make a serious military commitment in China, for reasons I will discuss, there was less conflict between functional Anglo-American policies over China than in any other Far Eastern area. But the total effect of this deep-seated American suspicion of British intentions precluded the possibility of depending on the relatively limited British resources to help resolve the Chinese military problem. In fact, the Americans merely inserted their apprehensions over Britain in China into their larger framework of distaste for the general British role in all of Asia.

[The bone of contention with the British in Asia was actually elsewhere, involving, as in Europe, where to fight the war, who would command it in each theater of activity, and the extent to which the Allies could employ British forces in Asian combat.]An outline will suffice to show the nature of the problem from 1943, when the Allies could finally think of passing from the defense to optional offensive strategies, until the end of the war. In a sense the problem was theoretical during 1943, involving the fact that, as Churchill summarized it, "Britain demanded a full and fair place in the war against Japan from the moment when Germany was beaten. She demanded a share of the airfields, a share of the bases for the Royal Navy, a proper assignment of duties . . . after the Hitler business was finished."[7] In short, Britain hoped to be included in the new distribution of Pacific power entailed in the defeat of Japan, and it was to the interest of the United States to exclude England, especially since the American military authorities in the Pacific were fully confident they could win alone, and with minimum challenges to the future growth of American power. The issue was abstract until 1945, however, for the British had limited resources and saw the critical stakes as still remaining in Europe, and even there relative English weakness permitted the Americans to define grand strategy. The British preferred allocating their resources to the European area, and later circumstances compelled them to choose during the critical months after Germany's defeat between acting as an imperial, expanding power in new areas or employing troops to consolidate British presence in the traditional colonies.

During the middle of 1943 the British hoped to confront these larger political problems by creating a combined military command structure in the Far East which would give the British military equality with the more numerous Americans. Before the Quebec Conference of August 1943 the two sides were locked in uncompromising dispute, the British insisting that the Combined Chiefs of Staff define grand strategic policy for the Supreme Commander, who was certain to be an American. The Americans, thinking of the European precedent, wanted a Supreme Commander who might actually control the operational activities of the military forces of both Allies. At Quebec they reached a compromise which created a separate Southeast Asia Command, pleasing the English, even though it ultimately restricted them to this region when they wished to expand into the Pacific area. The Americans, however, were able to define the next major step in Asian strategy—an intensified Burma campaign designed to open a southern route to China, break the Japanese blockade, and presumably keep China in the war and divert the Japanese.

British pleasure over the decisions at Quebec was short-lived, despite the award of the command of the new theater to Lord Mountbatten. The Burma campaign, especially the planned massive attack in the spring on the Bay of Bengal primarily with British troops, threatened to divert large numbers of landing craft and men from the European campaign. In particular it precluded the possibility of an attack on the Balkans, and this was of much higher political priority to Churchill. And given the growing belief of the American commander in China, General Joseph W. Stilwell, that all that was necessary and possible in China was to prevent its total collapse, the American military view that the Burma-India theater was a unique problem reinforced Churchill's now reluctant willingness to commit limited British resources. At the second meeting at Cairo, during early December 1943, Churchill used the Bengal campaign as a threat against the future of OVERLORD and won Roosevelt's consent to cancel the dubious Burmese venture. For at Teheran, Stalin again reiterated the Russian commitment to enter the war eventually against Japan, and to Churchill this warranted greater Anglo-American concentration on the critical European situation. From this time on the British showed little enthusiasm for such Burmese campaigns as the Allies initiated at American insistence.[8]

The British objective was to employ their very limited resources carefully in a global struggle at precisely those points where they might have the maximum political effect. Already overextended, they could not afford to squander men in difficult jungle battles, much less in defeating the Japanese in China. They were relieved that the Russians would handle the latter task on behalf of the three Great Powers. In early 1944, therefore, Mountbatten suggested that the South Asian campaign sharply downgrade Burma and concentrate instead on the reconquest of Malaya and the Dutch East Indies, especially Sumatra. Moreover, the surrender of the Italian fleet in September 1943 liberated a section of the British fleet for service in the Pacific, and Churchill in March 1944 now raised with Roosevelt the possibility of sending a British contingent to join the American fleet in the central Pacific area. The British had the latter plan in mind for many months, and when they first presented it to Admiral Ernest J. King, the United States Commander of the Pacific Fleet, he left Churchill with "the impression that he did not need us very much." In fact, King was openly discouraging, and in mid-March, Roosevelt added to the gloom by suggesting to the Prime Minister that "your naval force will be of more value to our common effort by remaining in the Indian Ocean." Since the Americans refused to cooperate with the proposed British land campaign in the former colonies in Southeast Asia, in effect there was no common effort and the British fleet had nothing to do. At this point, acknowledging the realities that the Americans imposed, Churchill decided that "We are therefore free to consider the matter among ourselves and from the point of view of British interests only."[9] There was no meaningful military coalition between the two nations in the Far East from this period on, save in the minor Burma campaign, and all the English could do was to fight a rearguard battle against unilateral American control over the larger Pacific and Far East military, and therefore political, situation.

The British understood the political consequences of this exclusion, and prior to the second Quebec Conference in September 1944 they resolved to attempt once more to obtain a full share, and reward, for their existing resources in the Pacific war. Before the conference Winant warned Hopkins of the probable British approach and he endorsed their desire, citing the unusual reason that the Americans later would resent the fact the British had not aided in the Pacific war against Japan. Precisely the reverse was likely to prove to be the case. At Quebec, Roosevelt proved more tractable than he had the previous spring. Churchill arrived full of resolve on the issue, ready to move much of the British fleet into the Pacific at the time, with the air force to follow later. When Churchill made his strong presentation to Roosevelt, offering aid in saving American lives, Roosevelt instantly and unequivocally accepted the proffer of the fleet to use against the Japanese mainland. But he was much more reticent about adding the British air force to the ostensibly too large United States Air Force, disliked the British strategy of taking Singapore, and was reserved on the Sumatra invasion, agreeing only to study the project. The Americans seemed interested in a revival of the Cairo Conference plan to capture Rangoon, which would have tied the British down. But by denying the Singapore campaign the Americans also denied what Churchill at the time admitted was "the supreme British objective in the whole of the Indian and Far Eastern theaters. It is the only prize that will restore British prestige in this region. . . ."[10]

At Quebec, Roosevelt overrode both the desires of the United States Navy to exclude the British from the major Pacific area and the British hope of United States support for a strategic view designed to maximize their own position in the region, but one which they were incapable of implementing without United States assistance. Yet the Americans did not need British aid, for they had sufficient power to win the Pacific war themselves, and only the Russians could provide the help they sought on the mainland of Asia. The political losses would be far greater than the military aid the English might provide, and so the British later confronted the fact that Roosevelt's advisers again had overridden his commitments. The United States Navy wished to restrict the British to the southwest Pacific area, and after laborious negotiations over the following winter the United States utilized the two small British task forces, both under United States command, in the Pacific region. Throughout this period the British understood that they were being excluded, and at the beginning of July 1945 their Chiefs of Staff again urged the Americans to permit them to help save American blood—implicitly granting Britain the political gains that might accrue for the sacrifice. Only at the end of the same month did the British formally grant final responsibility to the Americans for the entire Pacific campaign, though had the war continued another six months the British build-up in the Pacific might have been considerably greater. Until that time they would be committed to the supreme prizes in the colonies to the south, colonies by the end of the war in arms against their former rulers.

The British view of their strategic role in the Far East was entirely political, and they had no illusions about the real military value of their potential forces. The ever plastic Roosevelt did not define the American response on these questions of grand strategy. Rather, "The emergence of political consciousness among the Army staff during 1944," as their official historian phrases it, was the deciding factor, for Marshall "and his staff realized the political motivation behind the desire. The Army was as one with the Navy on the problem of keeping the Central Pacific an American affair and the Chief of Staff was content to let King argue the question of a British fleet under Nimitz."[11] Glory and prestige were also at stake for the Navy, which had little share in the European struggle, but in the last analysis politics was the core of the matter, and most certainly the lasting consequence of the dispute with the English.

In this sense, therefore, the Anglo-American alliance was essentially a European coalition, with the United States pursuing its own interests where it had nothing to gain from military collaboration. American power in the Pacific was expansive, and oriented toward the acquisition of postwar bases that were to loom large in political discussions. Conversely, where military necessity, as in the case of China, imposed collaboration—and there with the Soviets—they would pay the price, but they would give much attention to minimizing the political concessions and losses the Russians might extract.

The Condition of China

Though no one could prove it, at the end of World War II the Chinese army in the non-Communist and non-Japanese areas comprised 2,700,000 men in 290 divisions, approximately 50 divisions fewer than at the end of 1943. Their loyalty and efficiency aside, this army deserves the closest study and attention, for it was more an institution for taxing the peasantry than a military body; it rarely fought the Japanese or the Communists during the war—and it became a critical vehicle for breeding the revolution. The so-called Chinese army was probably no less consequential an instrument for oppressing the peasantry during the war than the Japanese, and probably a more significant factor because it persisted in the critical years after the defeat of Japan when it might otherwise have been the sole barrier between a decadent Kuomintang and the people.

The Chinese army was based on conscription. The rich could provide substitutes, the educated at the high-school level and above were exempt, as were only sons, and there were few physical disqualifications. At the end of his command of the American forces in China, General Albert Wedemeyer described his view of the conscription army in a remarkable memo to Chiang himself: "Conscription comes to the Chinese peasant like famine or flood, only more regularly—every year twice—and claims more victims.

Famine, flood, and drought compare with conscription like chicken pox with plague." As a system of direct and indirect physical liquidation only the Nazi terror surpassed it during the war. Press gangs conscripted peasants out of the fields, tied them, and transported them away. "Hoe and plow rest in the field," Wedemeyer wrote Chiang, "the wife runs to the magistrate to cry and beg for her husband, the children starve." If she could manage to pay for his release he was free until the following visit. In other instances the county magistrate would arrest ten men for each conscript needed and permit all but one to buy their freedom—if they could. "The conscription officers make their money in collaboration with the officials and through their press gangs." At the first stage the army was a vast traffic in human lives on an organized, legal basis depending on state power and the justification of national defense. In its macabre way it was the classic mandarin tax system of traditional China imposed on a disintegrating civilization. "So everybody is happy," Wedemeyer wrote, "except the conscript who soon will realize that he has been sold to something worse than death. . . ." At the next stage the army herded the new soldiers together for a long march with little or no food. Wedemeyer's description cannot be paraphrased:

> Later they are too weak to run away. Those who are caught are cruelly beaten. They will be carried along with broken limbs and with wounds in maimed flesh in which infection turns quickly into blood poisoning and blood poisoning into death. As they march they turn into skeletons; they develop signs of beriberi, their legs swell and their bellies protrude, their arms and thighs get thin. . . . From this point of view the conscripts' bodies have a great value. . . . A Chinese conscript's pay can be pocketed and his rations can be sold. That makes him a valuable member of the Chinese Army and that is the basis of the demand for him. Because of this demand, the journey has no end. Being sick, he has to drag himself along. . . . Dysentery and typhoid are always with them. They carry cholera from place to place. . . . If somebody dies his body is left behind. His name on the list is carried along. As long as his death is not reported he continues to be a source of income, increased by the fact that he has ceased to consume. His rice and his pay become a long-lasting token of memory in the pocket of his commanding officer. His family will have to forget him.[12]

Nearly every report the United States military authorities were ever to prepare on the subject corroborated Wedemeyer's statement to Chiang, which apparently did not move the knowledgeable Chinese ruler to action or sympathy. Americans in China compared hospitals there to Buchenwald, and on inquiring into the situation in one representative troop center an American military team revealed that "conditions proved horrible beyond imagination." One particular center carried 4,400 soldiers on the overhead charge, but only 2,000 were actually there. Of these, "One hundred per

cent were suffering from malnutrition, T.B., and other diseases, but no
medical care was being given." "One of the first things that strikes the eye
of an American in China," another officer reported, "is the physical condition of the troops dragging along the streets and highways. Their clothes
are old, patched, and tattered, but far worse is their physical condition.
Obviously they are suffering from every sort of disease and are just able to
walk."[13] This army would not and could not fight—against the Japanese,
the Communists, or anyone else. At the end of the war Wedemeyer estimated that only five of the approximately three hundred Chinese divisions
were effective military units, and American officers commanded three of
those in India.

The basic ration of the Chinese soldier consisted of an issue of rice and
salt, and at the end of 1944 a money allowance sufficient for a pound of
pork per month supplemented it. The Chinese troops rarely saw the money
and the ration was always much less than promised. To survive, the system
compelled the oppressed, sick mass of victims called the Chinese army to
live off the land by looting. The oppressed became oppressors, the system
of corruption and decadence pyramided. The Chinese army became the
vehicle for the further destruction of the peasantry and the corrosive and
sustaining ingredient of total collapse in China. Once that instrument and
victim of oppression disappeared, or switched sides to end its misery,
nothing stood between the rulers and those who had ample cause to seek
revenge and revolution.

In this context the Chinese army could not fight the Japanese, but
neither would anyone else. Internal transportation was entirely chaotic, and
the rail network was largely in Japanese-occupied territory. Trade between
occupied and unoccupied China was legal save for certain strategic goods,
but the KMT did nothing to enforce the ban and various entrepreneurs
shipped vast quantities of American drugs to Japanese-controlled Shanghai. The living conditions for the nearly 30,000 American troops in China
were already below standard, and without vast imports of most supplies a
new influx would have been impossible. There was no local petroleum
industry, and United States vehicles used a mélange composed three-quarters of local alcohol which destroyed bearings and crankshafts faster than
the Army could replace them. The supply problem in China was fabulously
expensive, requiring air transportation across the Himalayas from India, so
that even the small United States Air Force in China, the recipient of the
bulk of the transported goods, often operated at a supply level 40 percent
of normal. Taken together with the condition of the Chinese army, and the
repeated failure of the United States military authorities to reform it, the
sheer physical difficulties confronting the United States caused utter despair
among every military or civilian authority familiar with the problem.

At the end of November 1944 there were 28,000 Americans in the

Chinese military theater, and everyone believed at the time—and the reasoning probably was justified—that the economic conditions then prevailing in China made China the most expensive military operation of this scale anywhere in the world. To keep them operating, planes flew 1,200 pounds of necessities in for every man each month, at a tremendous cost. As expensive as this airlift was, it was still far cheaper than purchasing goods in China itself, for Chiang encouraged a catastrophic inflation, which, along with the army, ripped apart the entire Chinese social order and lay the conditions for the triumph of Communism. During the war it made any large-scale American military aid impossible.

Despite a vast increase in the open-market rate for dollars since 1937, the open-market purchasing power of the United States dollar had fallen five-sixths by the end of 1944. Worse yet, at least for the Americans, was the fact that the exchange rate the United States military received from the Chiang government was far less than the open-market rate. This situation quickly became the central controversy in American planning and diplomacy in China during the war, and all that can be done in this chapter is to give some essential details of the magnitude of the problem.[14] The implications for fighting a war in China will be quite apparent.

After 1937 China was in a state of dynamic, continuously rising inflation. Using an index of one for 1937 prices, by August 1945 prices in Chungking were 1,795, and 83,796 in December 1947. In 1944 alone retail prices in the fourteen major cities increased from a base of 100 in January to 321 in December. The black- or open-market value of the United States dollar in Chungking in 1944 increased from a low of 78 yuan in January to a peak of 645 in December, and was never less than 235 yuan during the last quarter of the year. Gold per dollar was three to four times more valuable. During the last quarter of 1944 the United States military authorities received 180 yuan per dollar, which represented a massive donation to the Chinese government. If the United States authorities purchased an American-made rubber tire in China in early 1944 it cost $1,000, and $75 for a spark plug. The general cost of installations and services in China was eight to ten times that of the equivalent in the United States. No one fully estimated the extent of the loss the disparity between the official and open-market rate created, but in April 1945 the United States Treasury calculated that of the $375 million paid directly to the Chinese government for goods and services, at least $200 million represented padding resulting from the currency situation.[15] The main beneficiaries, as everyone knew, were the most important leaders of the Kuomintang. This unceasing avariciousness soon reduced the question of United States presence in China—and military and political strategy—to one of monetary complexities, since all the wealth of the richest nation in the world was insufficient to fight a major war in China. For Chinese society itself the inflation was the undoing of whole sections of the educated bourgeoisie, small but critically placed, either unwilling or unable to succeed in the heady game of financial speculation which soon paralyzed all constructive Chinese economic activity. It soon divided the Chinese elite itself, leaving a fragile structure ready to collapse.

"Corruption, neglect, chaos, economy, taxes, words and deeds. Hoarding, black market, trading with enemy," were the adjectives Stilwell jotted in his diary when describing the Kuomintang.[16] Wedemeyer, his successor, shared his views. The Joint Chiefs of Staff, estimating Chinese capabilities at the end of 1943, concluded: "We feel that, at most, not more than one-fifth of the Chinese Army is currently capable of sustained defensive operations and then only with effective air support," air support only the Americans could provide.[17] This utter realism and contempt for the Chinese army never disappeared in Washington throughout the war.

But the American planners feared they might still have to fight a war on the Asian mainland. They had no assurance that the Japanese forces in China, and especially Manchuria, would surrender after the defeat of the homeland itself. "I contend," Stilwell warned General George C. Marshall in May 1944, "that ultimately the Jap Army must be fought on the mainland of Asia." The American command designed all of their operations in Burma and China to preclude this, but the total failure to improve the Chinese army left open the problem of who would destroy the Japanese in China, or keep them from returning to fight in Japan. The small China-Burma theater aided the forces fighting the Japanese in the central and southwest Pacific area, Marshall notified Stilwell, to draw Japan off and distract it: "Japan should be defeated without undertaking a major campaign against her on the mainland of Asia if her defeat can be accomplished in this manner."[18] If it could not, the cost in money and lives was certain to be very great. Stimson, perhaps more than any other man in Washington, was determined to avoid committing large numbers of men for Chiang's disposal, as he viewed it, to do what Chiang would not do himself. The desire to avoid war on the Asian mainland became the central limiting fact of American political and military strategy in the Far East during the last two years of the war—the reality that caused Americans to fight island by island rather than combat the greatly overextended and vulnerable Japanese troops in China. It is also the reason why they worked continuously to draw the Russians into the war against Japan.

If the Americans would not fight, and British aid would be small and politically costly, the Russians had to enter the war on the mainland. For Chiang it was a question of inability and unwillingness to fight. Chiang not only refused to engage in offensive operations, but he usually retreated before Japanese advances. The Americans could not ignore these facts, since they saw a land war in Asia as an endless sponge in which manpower rather than technology would be the price of victory. That fear was an almost constant assumption in the planning of American foreign policy during World War II and the following decade.

Chiang did not fight nor did he reorganize his army into a truly military organization, because that was not its function and it was improbable he had effective control over much more than a tenth of its divisions. In 1942 Stilwell suspected that Chiang was prepared to reach a détente with the Japanese in order to fight the Communists, and that he preferred a German victory over Russia to an even more powerful northern neighbor. While there is unquestionably documentary evidence to sustain these fears, in fact such policies may also have reflected Chinese weakness and a desire to make the best of what then appeared to be a losing war. But it is indisputable, no later than 1941, that Chiang truly believed "The Japanese are a disease of the skin. The Communists are a disease of the heart."[19] At the end of 1943 Patrick Hurley, after a mission for Roosevelt in China, warned the President he must take into account "the relative importance placed by the Chinese Central Government upon conserving its strength for maintenance of its postwar internal supremacy as against the more immediate objective of defeating Japan."[20] By the beginning of the next year no less than half a million Kuomintang troops—the best of the generally miserable lot—faced the Communists in the northwest. "For me the big problem is not Japan," a highly reliable French intelligence source quoted Chiang in 1944, "but the unification of my country. I am sure that you Americans are going to beat the Japanese some day, with or without the help of the troops I am holding back for use against the Communists in the Northwest. On the other hand, if I let Mao Tse-tung push his propaganda across all of Free China, we run the risk—and so do you Americans—of winning for nothing."[21] At the end of March 1944 Chiang admitted to Roosevelt that all he could do was to attempt to hold the line against further Japanese advances and "To prepare [China] for the day—may it not be distant—when Allied land and naval forces can be dispatched to the China coast and the Chinese Army can co-operate with them in consolidating our position in East Asia. . . ."[22] The American military and political leaders desperately sought to avoid for themselves precisely this imbroglio. They did not want to fight a war against Japan and a civil war at the same time, and Chiang was waiting for the Americans to save him from himself.

The Russians and the Far Eastern War

Due to the weakness of Chiang only the Soviet Union's eventual entry into the war against Japan could resolve the possibility of sustained Japanese resistance in China. Soviet supply lines, while long, were far shorter than the American route. The bases for a Russian attack were on the very frontiers of China, and the vast mass of the battle-hardened Red Army would be available after the defeat of Germany. If the Americans could obtain political guarantees from the Russians, so much the better. It was entirely logical, therefore, that they had a sustained and deep desire to involve the Russians in the war against Japan in China.

Throughout the latter half of 1943 the leaders in Washington were anxious to obtain Soviet agreement to enter into the Far Eastern war, the sooner the better. For their part the Russians hoped to get the Anglo-Americans to open a second front as soon as possible, and the Soviets always maintained the position that they were unable to combat more than one enemy at a time. But the Russians knew of the American eagerness long before October 30, 1943, when Stalin saw Hull in Moscow and on his own initiative made a statement of "transcendent importance" to Hull, pledging Soviet entry into the war against Japan after the defeat of Germany. Stalin, of course, authorized Hull to inform Roosevelt, "and he asked nothing in return."[23] Actually Stalin gave the West what he probably hoped would be a critical incentive to greater exertion on their part in ending the war against Hitler. He attached no timetable to the promise.

At Teheran, Stalin repeated his pledge to enter the war against Japan after the defeat of Hitler, but still did not assign a time formula. Roosevelt, on his own accord but after having earlier cleared the principle with Chiang, proposed that the Russians might have access to an internationalized port of Dairen in Manchuria, but Stalin wished to know if the Chinese would consent, and there the matter rested for the time. In fact the modesty of Stalin and the open-ended pledge delighted the Americans, the English, and even Chiang. By the end of 1943 the United States Joint Chiefs of Staff, despite the optimism of the Navy with its measurement of success on its own terms, were convinced that the Japanese army would fight hard on the mainland. The British were elated because they could now argue for the indefinite postponement of the Burma campaign and a sharp reduction of commitments in China and the Far East, and greater emphasis on the politically more critical European theater, on the assumption that eventual Soviet entry into the Japanese war radically improved the long-term strategic picture in the Far East. To the Chinese, no later than the spring of 1944, it meant certain outside aid and victory—if they could make the right political agreement in advance with the Russians—and the complicity of the Russians in permitting the Kuomintang to plan to spend all its resources containing Communism in China. Harriman in February obliquely asked Stalin when they might expect Soviet entry, but the Russian leader replied that his forces were too weak to risk a premature rebuff that might deprive them of essential bases later. In the spring of 1944 both Churchill and General Ho Ying-chin, Chinese Minister of War, wanted

Soviet entry into the war as soon as possible to divert Japanese efforts before China itself fought the decisive battles or suffered the decisive defeats.[24]

The Russians were fully aware of Anglo-American pressures to commit themselves and probably always correctly recognized that so long as they had such a large favor to grant they might obtain something in return. In fact, the American desire that the Russians fulfill their pledge repeatedly moderated American political policy on European issues for the remainder of the war. In May 1944, unable to deliver the carrot, the Russians decided to make it more attractive. The head of the Soviet news agency in Washington gave journalist Walter Lippmann more details on Russian plans and intentions in the Far East. When they entered the war they would seek American aid only in supplies, not troops, and they would definitely fight after the defeat of Germany. More important, Russia had no territorial ambitions in China, but merely hoped to obtain free access to Port Arthur. Above all, they carefully wished to make clear their desire not to Bolshevize East Asia. Lippmann immediately informed Joseph C. Grew, Under Secretary of State and former Ambassador to Japan, of the talk. The news was most welcome.

In stressing "The incalculable importance to the United States of the early entry of Russia into the war against Japan," General Marshall in August 1944, on behalf of the Joint Chiefs of Staff, raised considerations which remained constant assumptions of United States policy until the very end of the war. "China possesses at present but little military strength," and England, by virtue of its primary commitment to Europe, would not emerge from the war as a major military power in the Far East. Whether or not Russia entered the war against Japan, "the fall of Japan will leave Russia in a dominant position on continental Northeast Asia in so far as military power is concerned."[25] Its refusal to join the war would not alter this fact, and only Russia could make a major contribution against the Japanese army in a manner that would shorten the war and lessen American losses. It was in this context, in the fall of 1944, before the Russians submitted their timetable, that both Churchill and the Americans became increasingly impatient. Churchill wanted to press for a target date, and the United States Joint Chiefs of Staff decided to reconsider the entire issue of Soviet entry on the basis that the war with Japan would last at least twelve and probably eighteen months after the defeat of Germany. This assessment is of very great interest, for it defined the limits to which the Joint Chiefs thought the United States might go in resisting Russia on numerous other issues until the end of the spring of 1945. It made the military, not for the first or the last time, the most conservative group in Washington, fearing to risk a rupture of the scarcely minimal political relations with the U.S.S.R.

The Joint Chiefs recognized that they had always implicitly assumed that the United States could eventually defeat Japan without the aid of Russia, but also "the desirability, from our standpoint, of Russia's early entry into the war in order to add to the weight of force which may be applied to obtaining the earliest possible Japanese defeat." They also recognized that the Russians would not enter the war until it was to their interest to do so, and certainly not before they were sure of success. The key American objective was to prevent the Japanese from diverting troops from northern China and Manchuria to Japan during an American invasion, and also, if possible, to drain them toward the other direction. Maximum coordination would be highly desirable to effect these ends, for by holding down the Japanese army in China the Russians would spare the Americans a vast outpouring of blood. "We desire Russian entry at the earliest possible date consistent with her ability to engage in offensive operations. . . ."[26] And beyond this diversionary function, the American military also knew that the Russians might mop up a large Japanese force with an independent industrial and matériel base in Manchuria, a force the Chinese themselves would never defeat and which the Americans sought to avoid as well.

With these thoughts in mind the Americans approached the Russians again during the months before Yalta to encourage joint Soviet-American planning for the war in the Far East, intending merely to keep England informed. What they wanted, above all, was some timetable as to Soviet plans to enter the war after the defeat of Germany. In mid-October, Stalin suggested planning proceed on the assumption of Soviet entry two to three months after German defeat, but he specifically added that the date was not yet definite. Before Yalta the Joint Chiefs of Staff persisted in their strong desire to see the Russians enter the war, and the State Department, weighing the ideal for China against the necessities of war, recommended "this Government . . . lend no support to a policy by the Chinese Government which might impede Russian military action against Japan."[27] Toward this end Stimson, most aware of the military's desires, advocated a general quid pro quo with the Russians throughout the globe, one that would permit them to enter the war in the Far East while recognizing the primacy of American interests there in return for United States acceptance of the "buffer" principle in Eastern Europe.[28] So long as the Russians had something to give, the United States might recognize their presumed desires in return. The Americans did not wish to fight a war on the mainland of Asia, for they were not fully confident that they could overcome both Japanese resistance and Chinese apathy and costly corruption.

In the first weeks of 1945 all of these considerations and options took their place against other global questions in shaping American strategy toward the Yalta Conference and toward the future of China itself.

CHAPTER

10

THE EPIC OF CHINA

CHINA WAS a scene of epic proportions during World War II, a vast civilization in the last stages of decay, preparing the ground for an upheaval and transformation that was to become the most significant outcome of the entire war, and perhaps even of the century. The policy of the United States toward China was a synthesis of both realism and pessimism. It undertook almost everything it did in China with a foreboding, even knowledge of certain failure, and the few redeeming aspects of the Chinese political situation hardly compensated for the long-term consequences Washington understood would probably result from the defeat of American ends. Only the alternatives kept the Americans from deserting Chiang Kaishek and the Kuomintang government.

The Politics of Blackmail

Chiang based his strategy on his threatened surrender and defeat to extract vast American loans, which were really gifts, and as long as the United States wished to tie down Japanese troops in China, or to keep the Communists from replacing Chiang, he succeeded. A relationship without illusion and less and less without diplomacy, after Pearl Harbor it was soon based on blackmail.

Even before American entry into the war Washington generally felt that Chiang's associates in charge of finances were, as Secretary of the Treasury Henry Morgenthau described in April 1940, "just a bunch of crooks." Shortly before the Americans entered the war Chiang attempted to obtain a loan which at the end of December 1941 both he and the United States embassy in Chungking described as "political," one the embassy felt gave "no realistic consideration to the drastic domestic measures necessary to cope with the worsening economic situation." But Washington saw the loan as a way of stopping the Chinese "defeatists" who were ready to surrender, but since it and most subsequent loans went to "currency stabilization," and rested for long periods in United States vaults, the Treasury Department understood it to be an incentive to the ruling class to remain in the war in their own fashion. The United States eventually granted the February 1942 loan of $500 million to China, without binding terms and conditions, "to support the currency."[1] Under these circumstances the Chinese used it only to sustain the ruling clique of the Kuomintang. In addition, the artificial exchange rate for United States military dollar expenditures in China itself gave the government another continuous vast subsidy in the midst of the galloping inflation which it did nothing to stop and everything to aid. At the end of 1943 the Treasury estimated that the Chinese government had at least $300 million in dollars and gold, with the amount rising very substantially each month, with perhaps another $500 million in private holdings, much of which originated with the earlier United States aid. No one ever had any illusions about these facts.

The United States had undertaken to keep China in the war by making its involvement financially interesting, but it also hoped China would fight the war on a military level as well. In the end Chiang did the very thing he had been paid not to do—he stopped resisting the Japanese. In March 1942 the Pentagon sent General Joseph W. Stilwell to China with a small mission to improve the combat efficiency of the Chinese army. From its inception the Stilwell mission was constantly disappointed by the Chinese refusal to cooperate or fight. Stilwell was a brilliant general, irascible and frank. No one could have done better or worse at the task, for the regime's leaders themselves largely defined the condition of China and they eluded all Americans sent to aid the government. Nevertheless, Stilwell's utter contempt for Chiang and his government molded his first response to the never-ending frustrations he confronted in China. By July 1942 he regarded the Kuomintang merely as a form of "gangsterism," totally decadent.[2] He thought Chiang would sign a separate surrender with Japan when it was to his interest, and by the summer of 1943 was certain the Chinese would overthrow Chiang after the war. Throughout the first eighteen months of his service Stilwell realized that Chiang had reached an undeclared truce with the Japanese, perhaps even via secret negotiations, for every time they advanced the Chinese withdrew and then returned to their former positions when the Japanese voluntarily permitted them to do so. No less difficult, the provincial war lords, whom Chiang did not control, dominated a large, probably major portion of the "government" divisions, usually disregarding the desires of Chungking, and using them as private sources of income. Chiang in return attempted to restrict military supplies to his own divisions and loyal allies, leaving approximately one man in three in the army with a rifle. Virtually every scheme to reform the army that Stilwell ever devised failed because of Chiang's noncooperation. Feuding for limited supplies was the constant rule within the ranks of the United States military in China itself, most of whom were connected with the small air-base system in eastern China that hoped to destroy Japan with selective air strikes.

By October 1943 Stilwell concluded that there was no hope of improving the Chinese army and that it was more sensible to emphasize the Burma theater. In this context the Quebec Conference of August 1943 shifted support to the Burma campaign, and the Anglo-Americans earnestly sought Soviet entry into the war against Japan. Until the Western leaders made this decision, Stilwell defined the basic relationship between the United States and China. During the fall of 1943 the American government gave him new directions.

For one thing, Chiang intensely disliked Stilwell, who referred to the Chinese leader as "Peanut" and made no secret of his contempt for Chiang. And in November, Chiang departed for Cairo to see Roosevelt himself, the Chinese leader having just embarked on a program of full endorsement of many of Stilwell's proposed reforms. Perhaps there was hope. At Cairo the Allies made decisions to improve the fighting capacity of the Chinese army and to open a Burma campaign designed to supply it with needed imports, for China was almost wholly dependent on foreign arms and aid. Stilwell was skeptical, but the Allied leaders never permitted him to test their strategy in practice, for at Teheran, Stalin promised eventual entry into the war and Churchill succeeded in scuttling the Burma campaign.[3] At the beginning of December, Roosevelt told Chiang the bad news, and the Chinese ruler was spared the embarrassment of more unfulfilled promises. Better yet, he now had the vantage to obtain more money from the Americans.

Chiang responded on December 9. He expressed his deep sense of disappointment that the Allies deprived him of the opportunity to fulfill his pledge to fight the Japanese, but he was even more concerned over the impact of the news on the Chinese army and people. The collapse in morale might "cause at any moment a sudden collapse of the entire front. . . . The only seeming solution is to assure the Chinese people and army of your sincere concern in the China theater of war by assisting China to hold on with a billion dollar gold loan to strengthen her economic front and relieve her dire economic needs."[4]

The price was high, and the embassy in Chungking urged Washington not to pay it. Ambassador Clarence E. Gauss assured them that Chiang was bluffing, for he knew that surrender to Japan now in light of a certain Allied victory would endanger the lost territory the Americans pledged to return after the war. "They are just a bunch of crooks, and I won't go up [to Congress] and ask for one nickel," Morgenthau fumed.[5] The Chinese leaders merely stored the proceeds of the 1942 loan in banks, with no visible effect on the economy save to accelerate the already rampant inflation, and they were already manipulating the exchange rate to charge the United States military forces eight to ten times the cost of equivalent services in the United States. Morgenthau carefully documented the vast unpledged Chinese government funds in the United States, which he now estimated at $460 million and growing at the rate of $20 million a month, and the fact the government itself was selling its gold at fifteen times the official rate. ". . . insiders, speculators and hoarders" were benefiting from these schemes, which only aggravated the inflation.[6] Morgenthau gave this memo to Chiang, and throughout December, Chiang, his wife, and H. H. Kung, the Minister of Finance and Chiang's brother-in-law, sulked and threatened the imminent collapse of China. But given the indirect subsidy in the form of the artificially low exchange rate for United States expenditures, no one in Washington was ready to give Chiang his price. The United States refused the loan and henceforth there was a noticeable cooling in whatever shred of enthusiasm existed in Washington for the erstwhile idealism of the Kuomintang. Perhaps Chiang too sensed that he had overplayed his hand in attempting to drain the United States Treasury, for thereafter Roosevelt shared Stilwell's critical assessment of the Generalissimo and the President's previously benign feelings toward Chiang and his charming wife waned.

"Money is the root of all our trouble," one of the top American military leaders remarked early in 1944.[7] The Air Force devoted a significant number of its planes to carry in bales of currency to keep up with the inflation, the exchange-rate question was a source of interminable wrangling—for no sooner had the Chinese revised it than inflation made it grossly unfavorable to the Americans—and hostility toward Chiang grew by the month. In a sense money as the nexus of the relationship with Chiang accurately reflected the nature of the Kuomintang itself. It was surely to prove destructive to Chiang. At the end of March 1944, in the context of hassles over a spectrum of other issues as well, Chiang petulantly informed Roosevelt that his remaining task was "maintaining the various fronts" until the time "Allied land and naval forces can be dispatched. . . ." In fact, Chiang did nothing more throughout the war, and this statement destroyed the Americans' last illusions concerning the value of their aid and expenditures during the conflict. Amidst reports of planned military coups, growing peasant disaffection, and economic deterioration, Washington also had to consider Chiang's statement in light of a Japanese campaign against the American air bases in eastern China, one which met no significant Chinese resistance and continued into the summer. Roosevelt then threatened Chiang with the loss of future lend-lease goods, so laboriously flown over the Himalayas, unless he began to fight. "CKS will squeeze out of us everything he can get to make us pay for the privilege of getting at Japan through China," Stilwell wrote Marshall in May. The Joint Chiefs of Staff accepted his estimate by this time, and the State Department was no less gloomy.[8]

In this context Roosevelt decided in March to send his Vice-President, Henry Wallace, to China. Wallace had no special influence in Washington during the war, and his knowledge of China was extremely limited. Everyone knew that he was most impressionable, and there is no reason to believe that the Administration attached very great importance to the mission. Still, Wallace arrived at the end of June authorized to air American complaints and to ask Chiang to spend more time fighting the Japanese rather than guarding the Communists. Chiang for his part denigrated Stilwell and convinced Wallace of his own sincerity concerning postwar reform of the Chinese economy. When Wallace returned to Washington he recommended that Roosevelt replace Stilwell with someone who had Chiang's confidence, perhaps Wedemeyer, or supplement him with an independent presidential political representative.

During July the Joint Chiefs of Staff reacted against the imminent collapse of China and the certain loss of American air bases to the Japanese by proposing that the President appoint Stilwell a full general in recognition of his services and urge Chiang to place Stilwell in command of all Chinese armed forces. Roosevelt immediately accepted both recommendations, but the implications of the latter were so far-reaching that it is a measure of American desperation that they should have endorsed it without thinking through its consequences in the most unlikely event Chiang agreed. To hand the military power of China over to an American would have involved the United States in Chinese politics in the most intimate manner possible, for it would have made the last barrier to the overthrow of the Kuomintang a discretionary instrument of United States policy. The military, economic, and political defense of China implied in the obligation would have required a monumental commitment of American resources and ultimately would have necessitated American acceptance of, or more likely resistance to, Communism in China. Chiang most certainly appreciated this fact, but since he was ultimately committed not to saving the Old Order, but rather his own power, he failed to make an unconditional alliance with the only nation that might have saved China from vast revolutionary upheaval. Yet Chiang apparently entertained the idea, for when Roosevelt cabled the proposal to him on July 6 Chiang merely deflected it by referring to the necessity of a "preparatory period."[9] Roosevelt could only urge him to hasten that time, but meanwhile he appointed the headstrong, mercurial Patrick J. Hurley as his personal representative in China to work with Stilwell on political matters, and perhaps to ease relations between Chiang and Stilwell. He also sent Donald

M. Nelson, former chairman of the War Production Board, to try to salvage the Chinese economy before it was too late. Both men in fact had alienated too many in Washington to continue with their present responsibilities, and the China assignment removed them from their higher priority tasks. At the end of August, as China moved closer to the abyss of chaos and a group of war lords plotted a rebellion—which Stilwell secretly hoped would succeed—Roosevelt again urged Chiang to hand his army over to the American.

When Hurley arrived in China in August, after stopping in Moscow, the question of Stilwell's command of the Chinese army became the consuming diplomatic goal. Early in September, thinking Chiang had accepted the principle, he opened negotiations, and the Chinese ruler immediately observed that such an appointment would be nearly as political as military in nature. The obviousness of this fact passed the Americans by for the moment. Chiang then insisted that he would have to approve all projected arms shipments, not merely to the Communists, but to the majority of the army under the various war lords. Since Washington at this moment considered Chiang's position very shaky, though not yet critical, they obviously feigned obliviousness to the political dimension. The Americans agreed only that they would use the Communists militarily in the most restricted manner possible. But on general military questions Stilwell made it plain that "the Gmo [Chiang] would have to keep his fingers out of the pie."[10]

Chiang refused to accept such conditions, and Marshall and his staff on September 16 prepared a far-reaching document for Roosevelt to send to Chiang. The letter, virtually an ultimatum, began by warning Chiang that his military and economic position left him "faced in the near future with the disaster I have feared." The loss of eastern China would be "catastrophic." Only Stilwell's assumption of the command of China's army could stop the inevitable defeat.[11] Stilwell, however, on September 26 uncomfortably polarized the situation by hinting what he might do if Chiang gave power to him:

> Chiang Kai-shek has no intention of making further efforts to prosecute the war. . . . he believes he can go on milking the United States for money and munitions by using the old gag about quitting if he is not supported. . . . He himself is the main obstacle to the unification of China and her cooperation in a real effort against Japan. . . . I am now convinced . . . that the United States will not get any real cooperation from China while Chiang Kai-shek is in power. I believe he will only continue his policy and delay, while grabbing for loans and postwar aid, for the purpose of maintaining his present position, based on one-party government, a reactionary policy, or the suppression of democratic ideas with the active aid of his gestapo.[12]

At the end of September, Chiang categorically refused to accept Stilwell as his commander, and now demanded Washington recall him altogether. As the military leaders in Washington contemplated the new impasse, they determined to downgrade the China theater even further, and above all to avoid sending a large number of troops to China in the future. Roosevelt hesitated to take as strong a position as the military now urged upon him, and he toned down the drafts they prepared. At the beginning of October, Foreign Minister T. V. Soong submitted to Hurley a long and violent attack on Stilwell, blaming him for most of China's military losses. To Hurley the issue was now one of Stilwell or Chiang, and in this context the United States chose to recall Stilwell and appoint Wedemeyer in his place. It also made the decision to sharply minimize the possible military role of China, to refuse to accept the command of the Chinese army under any circumstances, and to separate the Burma-India theater from the Chinese. ". . . if you sustain Stilwell in this controversy," Hurley warned, "you will lose Chiang Kai-shek and possibly you will lose China with him."[13] Seen in this light Roosevelt believed he had no other choice, and the once-honored Stilwell, over the objections of the Joint Chiefs, returned to the United States, and according to his own account, the Pentagon isolated him and compelled him to keep silent on the realities in China.

The Options and the Gains

The United States might completely lack confidence in Chiang, but the Stilwell decision revealed that it would stick with him until the end even if it hedged on commitments. For along with the losses Chiang offered gains, and the alternative was totally unacceptable. Within this framework, and despite its accurate assessment of Chiang, United States policy in China during the years 1943 to 1948 remained entirely explicable. The only other option was the Chinese Communist party of Mao Tse-tung, which effectively foreclosed any debate.

During the 1930's all information the State Department by chance received on the Chinese Communists it automatically sent to the Eastern European office. Immediately before the war, however, it haphazardly attempted to gather additional details on Communist activities. Ernest Hemingway in August 1941 sent one of the first detailed reports to Washington, revealing the intensity of the division and the inevitability of civil war unless the United States called upon the Soviet Union to restrict the Communists. Hemingway reported Chiang's preoccupation with his internal problems in a more sophisticated fashion than the vast majority of accounts Washington received in subsequent years. In the spring of 1942 the OSS managed to interview Chou En-lai, who represented the Communists in Chungking at the time, and he presented a moderate picture of an ideal

China with parallel nationalized and private industry, full civil liberties, and political democracy. Such information never shaped the American estimate of the Chinese Communists. However, as long as Chiang sent half a million of his best troops to contain the Communists rather than fight the Japanese, the United States hoped to resolve the civil dispute in order to accelerate the war effort. For this reason alone the American interests favored a policy of peace between the Kuomintang and Communists, and later they explored ways of more effectively utilizing the substantial Communist forces in the common effort. American officials were pleased when Chiang in the summer of 1943 reopened political negotiations with the Communists, implying that he would negotiate rather than settle the division by force, but also inviting them to place their troops under his command. During November the American military attaché in Chungking reported that the Communists had a regular army of half a million men, an equal number of guerrillas, and perhaps a million militiamen. Such numbers could make the major difference for the war in the north. At the same time American officers continued to receive disturbing reports of Kuomintang troop movements toward the Communist border regions. They feared that outbreaks and renewed civil war were possible, perhaps even the defection of Chiang's troops to the Communists. Civil war therefore opened the door both to postponing the war against Japan and also the defeat of Chiang. To avoid these events was a prime objective.[14]

Stilwell and his staff were no less aware of the Communist problem, but the American general privately retained a rather strong admiration for the Communists' honesty and efficiency. His political adviser, John P. Davies, Jr., had as early as June 1943 advised sending a military mission to the Communist region, but Stilwell rejected the proposal. At the beginning of 1944 Davies again suggested that the mission might be opportune—before the Communists withdrew their welcoming offer—for reasons of military intelligence, but also to determine Russian intentions and if possible neutralize their influence among the Communists. During February, as Chiang was reinforcing his troops in the north and rumors of renewed civil war were circulating, Roosevelt asked Chiang to approve an American mission along the lines Stilwell now recommended. Chiang at almost the same time asked about his freedom to use Lend-Lease weapons against the Communists, and in March he categorically rejected the mission scheme. Roosevelt thereupon dropped the matter for many months, but his advisers feared the prospect of civil war, for Chiang might also lose. Throughout May and June the two sides contented themselves with more negotiations, Chiang renewing his demand that the Communists hand over their troops and control of their area, the Communists insisting on immediate civil liberties in all China and aid to their armies as part of the merger with Chiang's command. Not for the first or last time, such equally implausible demands consumed much time and accomplished nothing, and the details of the laborious debates will not be treated here, save where they involved the Americans.

Originally the military and the War Department initiated the effort for a détente between Chiang and the Communists, but by the spring of 1944 the State Department also took up the matter, in part fearing Russian intentions in China, but also because the nationalist dimension that permeated and modified Chinese Communism, especially among their troops, visibly impressed Davies and Foreign Service officer John Stewart Service. Service was one of the few Americans who saw the Communists emerging as the most dynamic force in China and he believed that it was especially critical to encourage their nationalist tendencies. With this trend in mind, and also fearing renewed civil war and defeat for the Kuomintang, the State Department in June determined to try to end Chiang's blockade of the north, have him mend his fences with the Russians as a step toward consolidating power over the Communists, and fight Japan. When Wallace arrived at the end of the month he made these proposals to Chiang, who refused to agree to concessions to China's Communists but eagerly welcomed American aid in improving his relations with Russia. In addition Chiang finally agreed to allow an American military mission to visit Yenan.[15]

The Communists received this mission most cordially, and at the end of August, Service had his famous and long-suppressed interview with Mao. The Communist leader made it plain that he wished to avoid civil war, but that only the United States could intervene to compel Chiang to accept a compromise. Such intervention was critical because without American aid Chiang would be unable to suppress the Communists forcibly. Civil war was "inevitable but not quite certain," but for the Americans finally to determine. In any event, Mao added, the Americans alone would have to liberate China from Japan, and at that point the aid of his armies would be crucial. The impact of the war would limit Russian help, both militarily and in the postwar period. He welcomed American investment in aiding rapid development, and pointed to his conservative land laws as an example of pragmatism. "We cannot risk crossing you—cannot risk any conflict with you," Service quoted him as stating.[16]

Concerned leaders in Washington read and generally ignored Service's eulogizing accounts, and inquisitive Congressional committees later misconstrued his own commitment to reporting facts honestly as aid to the Communists. By the summer of 1944, however, other than his accurate reports of statements Mao and others passed along to him, there was nothing in Service's or Davies' information on China that higher officials concerned with the topic did not generally know, and Service's advice was ignored. The question was never one of information but of policy and interests, and the United States did not regard it as in its interest in China or elsewhere to permit the Communists too much freedom to win by arms or ballots. In brief, even if nearly all of Washington did not regard Chiang highly, and many welcomed a plausible option, no one would ever designate the Communists as the alternative. Chiang perceived this reality, and at the end of August, via the rather uninfluential Gauss, urged Hull that

> China [Chiang] should receive the entire support and sympathy of the United States Government on the domestic problem of Chinese Communists. . . . The request that China meet Communist demands is equivalent to asking China's unconditional surrender to a party known to be under a foreign power's influence (the Soviet Union). . . . The United States should tell the Communists to reconcile their differences with and submit to the national government of China.[17]

Although his American advisers made many ingenious proposals in the summer of 1944, Chiang's approach to the Communist problem dominated official American policy as well, despite their hope that Chiang would agree to internal reform. When Stilwell and Hurley began their negotiations with Chiang and his aides in September they discussed the possible use of the Communist 18th Group Army under Stilwell's command, but the Chinese ruler was not interested in bringing Mao's party into the government. Americans had already approached the Communists during July concerning this possibility, and they appeared most receptive without committing themselves. Service thought such aid worth much, and Stilwell preferred to think only in terms of arming sixty Kuomintang divisions before supplying five Communist divisions, but he formally proposed the matter to Chiang's generals on September 23 in conjunction with a parallel moratorium on discussions of political matters between the Kuomintang and Communists until the end of the war. "This will knock the persimmons off the trees," Hurley approvingly wrote on the agenda when he saw it. He was right, for he later added "Too late."[18] Chiang was angry, and he established the principle that despite American freedom to restrain aid and commitments, he could define the outer limits of American political strategy in China—so long as his KMT remained the only acceptable option to Communism.

The International Quid Pro Quo—Chiang's Asset

Chiang was expensive, and Washington was completely realistic about his regime, but he was also useful. For Chiang was willing to trade his support on international questions in return for American backing within China itself, and for this reason the United States decided early to propagate the myth of China as one of the Four Powers.

By the end of 1942 Stilwell and Washington understood that China

could have a postwar international role only as a responsive, close friend of
the United States. If it emerged from the chaos of the war intact and
stronger, an American ally would regulate the affairs of the Far East, and
the United States would then assume primary responsibility for the security
of the Pacific. Stilwell informed the leaders of the Kuomintang of this
vision no later than December 1942. When Eden visited Washington the
following March, Roosevelt expounded the essentials of this strategy to
him, and Eden freely admitted that he didn't care to witness its success, but
the Foreign Minister was certain China was in chaos and its role as a
"great power" would be strictly verbal, and so he made no great point of
the matter. Since no one in Washington had any illusions about the reality
of China's future strength, Roosevelt observed to the Englishman, according to Hopkins' notes, "that China, in any serious conflict of policy with
Russia, would undoubtedly line up on our side."[19] A Mao-ruled China
would not, and the historian must understand this interrelationship as the
limiting factor in the American response to the nature and possibilities of
Chinese Communism.

The British were willing to tolerate this myth for the remainder of the
war in return for American concessions on France and in the United Nations, and from the end of 1943 channeled most of their communications
to China via the Americans. China was America's exclusive responsibility,
and Washington treated it as such on the international level, hardly consulting the British about the most far-reaching decisions involving its fate.
"That China is one of the world's four Great Powers is an absolute farce,"
Churchill wrote Eden in August 1944. "I have told the President I would
be reasonably polite about this American obsession, but I cannot agree that
we should take a positive attitude on the matter."[20] In fact the British
were convinced that there would be a vast upheaval in China and that all
they or Roosevelt might do there would come to nought. They were confident nothing would be lost or gained should the United States take the lead
in China.

No later than April 1943 the Chinese indicated that they would be
willing to play the American game when Kung informed the Treasury that
it could expect support from China in its struggle with England over postwar international financial reform. That August the Chinese asked that
England and the United States give them equal status on the various inter-
Allied bodies, but at Quebec the Western Powers decided not to do so. But
no sooner had they made the decision than the United States reversed it.
When Hull went to Moscow the following October and insisted that the
Russians accept China as part of the Four Power Declaration the Allies
were to issue, the Chinese ambassador in Moscow gave him carte blanche
approval to formulate any manner of declaration the Americans desired,
limply asking only that Hull send him those changes that he might make in

the name of China. [To the Russians, Hull insisted that China was really very concerned about becoming a member of the Big Four, and that failure to include it would have "the most terrific repercussions, both political and military, in the Pacific area."[21] The Russians decided not to make an issue of the matter, and henceforth they too went along with the American myth. It now became a permanent part of United States policy on China.

Before meeting Chiang at Cairo at the end of November, Roosevelt received a long report from Hurley concerning his discussions with Chiang. Chiang assured him that, in Hurley's words, "He will . . . follow your leadership on the diplomatic and political questions that will be considered in the impending [Teheran] conference."[22] When the two leaders met, Chiang was passively agreeable on the question of becoming a member of the Big Four and acceded to Roosevelt's wish that China consult with the United States before taking any significant decisions on Asia, a relationship that made China a useful lever for the postwar world. Roosevelt in turn promised the restoration of lost Chinese territory, including Taiwan and the Ryukyu Islands, and Chiang agreed to support the American desire for Pacific bases and offered some on the mainland as well. Korea, Indochina, and Thailand they marked for eventual independence, and Roosevelt sympathetically promised to consider Chiang's request for postwar economic aid. This comprehensive understanding, if fulfilled, would have left the United States as the major power in the Far East at the end of the war, for in dominating the international role of China, in large part through its internal economy, the alliance would have been critical in that area. Though elusive by virtue of China's weakness, to sustain Chiang and to succeed in this vision was worth a very great deal.

The United States had no illusions about its chances to succeed in making China the instrument of its Far Eastern strategy, but it was to attempt it nevertheless. In June of 1944 Hull strenuously insisted that the Allies place the Chinese on the projected United Nations Security Council, for reasons, he explained to Lord Halifax, that were "entirely psychological."[23] Since everyone knew that China was not going to fight Japan, these reasons were directly linked to the international role China played in American planning. When Lord Beaverbrook came to Washington the following month Hull admitted that the United States intended to prevent the triumph of Communism as well as Russian influence.

> I myself believe that China has only a fifty-fifty chance to reestablish herself as a great power. But if she's rebuffed now by the other major Allies even that chance might be lost, and the Chinese Government would tend to dissolve. In that case it's quite likely that the Soviets might have to assume responsibility for the whole situation—if they would.[24]

Hull was not going to take the chance, and the Chiang element in China knew that sustained American support depended on this fear. At the end of

August, during his precarious crisis with Stilwell, Chiang reminded Gauss, as the ambassador reported to Hull, that "In the matter of world problems, China is disposed to follow our lead. . . ."[25] In fact Chiang and his associates were entirely cynical about this arrangement and the realities of their own global power. Several months later T. V. Soong, Foreign Minister and also Chiang's brother-in-law, again stressed to Hurley the mutual advantages of a Chinese-American alliance in the postwar era, and also his complete cynicism about the pretensions of making China a Great Power. Such a chimera was in reality offensive to China because power was based on internal strength rather than external props and alliances. Perhaps someday, Soong confessed, China would arrive at that point.

In the meantime, however, both the Kuomintang and Americans would sustain the useful myth. The State Department recommended prior to Yalta "that we assume the leadership in assisting China to develop a strong, stable and unified government in order that she may also become the principal stabilizing factor in the Far East."[26]

Even as sordid descriptions of corruption and decadence poured into Washington and Stilwell entertained the possibility of a serious break with Chiang, the United States maintained this convenient invention which opened a Pandora's box of difficulties for the Americans. It encouraged Chiang's belief that he could succeed in his intransigence because the Americans still needed him. As a result the United States aided his downfall, almost certain in any event, and the conscious delusion led to the creation of a world organization based on a weak fiction of the moment that later created an insoluble obstacle to future Chinese recognition—when China in reality became a world power. The fiction of China as a Great Power provoked the cynicism of the other major Allies as to the American vision of a postwar world community based on United States predominance in the Far East and in the United Nations. However, since the great gamble depended on the frail reef Chiang offered, at least the British were certain the American design would fail. They were not disappointed.

American Policy in China Before Yalta

In the vast game of China the Americans in the fall of 1944 hoped they would not have to play their hand, for they feared they would lose. When General Wedemeyer arrived at the end of October to replace Stilwell the strategy was to hold on as long as possible within the same set of rules: support for Chiang, hedging where possible to reduce future losses, and chance. If this delicate combination succeeded, then the United States would emerge from the war with political mastery of the Far East.

To the American military, however, the critical objective was to win the war, and although Wedemeyer enjoyed far better personal relations with Chiang than Stilwell, his respect for the dictator's leadership was not much greater. During his first months as head of the China theater his intelligence sources reported to him that the unopposed Japanese advances toward the American bases in eastern China, which they soon captured, were possible because Chiang agreed to permit the Japanese to advance in return for their leaving him alone in southwest China. Since the Chinese generals in the area were not loyal to him, Chiang had certainly embargoed the shipment of arms to them, and at least Chiang's subordinates, if only on their own initiative, did reach an agreement with the Japanese. The American leaders suspected all this at the time, and after November 1944 Roosevelt rarely communicated with Chiang in contrast with the dozens of messages sent in the prior twenty-two months. In brief, the Americans abandoned all hope of reforming Chiang or replacing him, and froze their policy in the months before Yalta. They increased military aid only to prevent Chiang from collapsing, for preservation of the regime was implicit in maintaining the status quo. Wedemeyer's respect for Chiang's military prowess failed to rise.

On the assumption that negotiations were a preferable alternative to a civil war that would only strengthen Japan, Hurley undertook to end the prospect of combat within China and to create the basis for a renovated Chinese government capable of outflanking the Communists via reform. If possible, however, the United States wished to incorporate Communist forces into the war against Japan. The priority of American goals followed this order, and since they were only likely to attain the first, it had its own pacific justification even if they generally conceded that Chiang was not likely to agree to reform or to collaborate with the Communists.

In fact nothing in American policy required Chiang to do anything more than reenter into negotiations with the Communists, for throughout the subsequent maze of intrigue and banter Washington permitted Chiang to veto all aid to the Communists and at the same time to expect a growing level of United States support irrespective of his behavior. The United States alone could force Chiang to alter his course, and it decided not to do so.

At the beginning of November, Hurley flew to Yenan at the invitation of the Communists, and after several days of friendly haggling Mao approved a five-point program which accepted the unification of all military forces under a national government, a coalition of all political parties, which henceforth would permit full civil liberties throughout China. Hurley, delighted with the statement, showed it to Soong, who categorically turned it down as a program permitting the Communists to take over China: "The Communists have sold you a bill of goods."[27] The American thought Chiang might prove more tractable, but he was to be disappointed. Chiang proposed merely that the Communists agree to allow his government to reorganize and incorporate their forces under his sole jurisdiction, that they give full support to his government in return for legalization and the full restoration of civil liberties "subject only to the specific needs of security in the effective prosecution of the war against Japan."[28] Sun Yat-sen's "Three People's Principles," a vague paraphrase of Lincoln's Gettys-burg Address, would form the guiding basis of government and Communist cooperation. Although Hurley tried, he could not extract Chiang's consent to what he had obtained from Mao.

The Communists would not agree to Chiang's proposal, but instead thanked Hurley and assured him "we completely desire to continue to discuss with you and General Wedemeyer the concrete problems of our future military cooperation and to continue the closest contact with the United States Army Observers Section in Yenan."[29] Such thoughts had already occurred to Wedemeyer and Hurley, and during the end of November and beginning of December they formulated three different plans to supply arms and technicians to the Communists, all of which the Communists approved and Hurley permitted Chiang to veto. Chiang felt certain that he had nothing to fear from the Americans.

In thinking through the complex problems involved in the Communists proving friendly to the United States program while Chiang repulsed it, the Americans again had to make some basic political decisions. Davies and Service were both convinced that Chiang was not going to wipe out the Communists, and that quite possibly they would succeed him unless the Kuomintang took drastic steps to reform the regime. They now certainly estimated the Communists' strategic aid as much more significant than that of Chiang. These men considered and debated every option, including separating the Communists from the Russians as much as possible on the basis of their real Chinese nationalism. But in the end, fully aware Chiang would not reform until he knew the Americans might really cut him off, Davies in mid-November advised: "We should not now abandon Chiang Kai-shek. To do so at this juncture would be to lose more than we could gain."[30]

In this ambiguous context the Americans in China considered covert relations with the Communists, despite Chiang's opposition. The Communists' honesty, efficiency, and moderation profoundly impressed virtually all Americans coming into contact with them. The Army mission in Yenan immediately concluded that the Communist area was "a different country," and Yenan "the most modern place in China."[31] They described conditions there as far better than those under Chiang's regime. General Curtis E. LeMay, in memoirs written twenty years after the event, sympathetically recalls how Mao himself hauled and pounded rocks to improve the air field the Americans requested at Yenan, and reports how the Communists led downed pilots to safety as honored guests. The Americans noted Communist nationalism and pragmatism again and again, and during the fall of 1944 they considered the very real possibility of their ultimate triumph. Hurley during November concluded that the Communists were "the only real democrats in China," and Gauss thought it was now likely that they would eventually prevail.[32]

In this setting some of Wedemeyer's staff, in conjunction with the OSS, decided to propose to the Communists a plan to arm 25,000 guerrillas and many more militia (an idea Chiang's government rejected in mid-December). Special American units, they now added, would train and lead attacks on special points which Wedemeyer selected, and the entire Communist army would cooperate with him. The Communists not only approved, they asked to send Mao and Chou to Washington to confer with Roosevelt. Wedemeyer later claimed that he knew nothing about it at the time, but United States Naval Intelligence, the most conservative of all the intelligence groups and formally linked to Chiang's secret police, got wind of the plan and broke a version to all concerned, including Chiang. The Army was embarrrassed, disgruntled at the Navy's role as well as some of its own political machinations with Chiang, and both Wedemeyer and Hurley claimed to be ignorant of the entire exploration, but their denial was *pro forma* only. In fact both Hurley and Wedemeyer approved the principles of the plan in mid-December, but made it contingent on Chiang's consent.

During these same weeks Hurley tried to convince both Chiang and the Communists to negotiate a peace between themselves, but since Chiang rejected the five-point program Hurley helped to draft, the Communists were skeptical, as were many other Chinese observers, of Chiang's willingness to relinquish his one-party rule. At the end of December, Chou merely asked that Chiang prove his good faith by releasing political prisoners, establishing civil liberties, and ending attacks and blockades against the Communists. During the end of January, Hurley managed to get Chou En-lai to return to Chungking to discuss a new set of Kuomintang proposals which, while vague, would still leave Chiang entirely in control. Privately the Kuomintang leaders were entirely cynical about the possibilities of agreement, and the Communists preferred to stand on their five-point program. In the following weeks proposals and counterproposals masked the true estimates of the various sides, which only proved that words are also a mode of warfare. A tedious, tortured, and ultimately fruitless pattern of American mediation in China had begun.

After some private thoughts and perhaps even more private explorations of opportunities for working with the Communists whether or not Chiang consented, Hurley realized that Chiang had imposed an effective veto on real efforts for unity, reform, and collaboration with the Communists, and that American policy was still to sustain the Kuomintang while attempting to hedge against future losses. "In all my negotiations," he

explained to Stettinius at the end of December, "it has been my understanding that the policy of the United States in China is:" (1) To prevent
the collapse of the national government, (2) To sustain Chiang Kai-shek
as President of the Republic and Generalissimo of the Armies. . . ."[33] No
one ever denied the premise, and before Yalta the State Department felt
that "if any aid is to be given to the Communists by us this should be done
only through the National Government."[34] Therefore mediation was no
less contrived than the secret motives of the two disputants, for the impar-
tial chairman was present to guarantee that one side triumphed, and from
the volume of financial and military aid the United States granted the
Communists had no doubt as to whom the Americans would support.
Readiness to terminate this aid therefore became the test of American
intentions in reforming the Chinese quagmire or simply sustaining the
regime against ever-growing internal pressures. For Chiang would never
accede to serious and meaningful American demands unless it was to his
material advantage to do so. The aid continued, and eventually grew.

The Nature of the Kuomintang

In supporting the Chiang regime the United States had to evaluate its
postwar aims in China against the commitments to the Kuomintang and the
options its only likely successors to the north offered. The persistently
confusing statements of Chiang and his party on the kind of society they
wished to build had not made that task easier, and ultimately all the United
States could do was measure the reality of Nationalist China against its
ideology and hope for the best. There was not much cause for optimism.

The American criterion for its conduct in China was the Open Door
policy which the State Department had formulated at the end of the century to gain equal access for American commercial interests within the
structure of the European spheres of influence in China. In no sense did the
policy advocate equal opportunity for all nations, and not once did the
State Department think of it as a defense of, say, Belgian rights to trade,
nor did it defend Chinese national integrity. In 1900 the Chinese asked
when the Americans might apply the doctrine, and the State Department
made it contingent on Chinese "ability and willingness" to end their hostility toward Western nations, citing the Boxer movement in particular.[35]
For the United States was never cordial toward Chinese nationalism. In
1911 it supported the tyrannical Yuan regime against the Kuomintang of
Sun Yat-sen. Washington finally switched its support to Chiang's government at the end of the 1920's because it was weak, more independent of
the Japanese than were the northern militarists, and because Chiang made
a determined effort to woo the Western nations. His standing in Washington was never high, however, and both the State Department and the long

line of American ambassadors in China understood, though they did not support, Japan's desire to end the interminable division and chaos in a China Chiang never succeeded in uniting. The United States entered the war with the ambiguous legacy of hopes for a united, but weak and dependent China. The Americans never encouraged the emergence of Chinese nationalism and power as a balance to Japanese domination of the Far East. Least of all did the United States welcome the strong movement toward economic nationalism which during the 1930's advanced Chinese banking interests in their own homeland against the traditionally dominant Western firms. The nationalists created government-trading and -purchasing organizations and economic controls much like those many Western capitalist governments sponsored during the depression, but in conflict with United States concepts of multilateral trade.

In considering the future of the Chinese economy during a May 1939 discussion of a contemplated loan to that nation, Harry Dexter White, Morgenthau's close adviser, was typical in also seeing it as an opportunity to "get a firm foothold on future Chinese business and we will get the bulk of reconstruction work in China. . . . China under peace time conditions and a revitalized Central Government will make wonderful future market for American goods and enterprise."[36] If the attraction of profits soon wore off, the principle Washington would establish did not. Hull referred to the need for "the removal of economic and other maladjustments" in May 1941 when writing the Chinese Foreign Minister, and the 1942 loan agreement committed the two nations to "promoting mutually advantageous economic and financial relations" after the war.[37] Since the 1942 loan was really a gift which proved advantageous only to the Kuomintang, a fact everyone involved fully comprehended at the time, the American concern for principles where in fact it had no important interests is the significant dimension: insofar as the Americans based their foreign policy on expansive premises, such principles were critical and adequate as a foundation of contemporary diplomacy. Chinese trade and investment with the United States was small, but Washington assumed that it would grow and later prove vital. This belief in the economic potential of China, and especially Manchuria, became an important guiding premise in the definition of American interest in China, but since it had no relationship to immediate realities and possibilities until 1945, it became somewhat subdued, though never inconsequential. However, whether or not existing economic interests were large, the United States did not intend to permit an economic ideology alien to basic American war aims to predominate in China, and therefore the United States remained hostile toward Communism and suspicious of the formal ideology of Chiang and the Kuomintang. The United States wished to see a renovated China, but one open to economic penetration from the West.

The Americans worried, therefore, about the relationship of Kuomintang ideology to practice, the continuity between the party of Sun Yat-sen and that of Chiang Kai-shek, and the nature of the regime itself. Was it nationalist, or something less formidable? During 1943 no one in Washington felt quite certain, and even though Stilwell insisted Chiang favored a form of "gangsterism," most discounted this observation as a reflection of the general's colorful manner of expression. And while Kung in April 1943 claimed China would support the White plan for international financial reform, promises were hardly sufficient, especially those of the Chinese government.[38] For during the spring Chiang published two books under his own name, *China's Destiny and China's Economic Theory,* which caused such an immediate sensation among China specialists that Chiang withdrew, revised, and later released them in a more moderate version. As a result Chiang earned the reputation of still retaining an affinity for the anti-Western xenophobia of his youth. The volumes were strongly nationalist, antiforeign, and even anticapitalist in tone. They were also frankly authoritarian, based on a hierarchical and elitist theory of Confucian feudalism similar to that in vogue among many Asian reactionaries during this and later decades. The embassy in Chungking immediately summarized, translated, and sent them to Washington, where they caused much consternation in the State Department. For Chiang's theory implied an end to American war aims in the Far East. More disturbing than the contents was the fact that the real author was a close friend of P. L. Chen, Chiang's secretary, with a career as a Japanese collaborator attracted to a variety of fascist, romantic, and nationalist theories.[39]

Unless Chiang believed the book's message, which is most unlikely, he made a serious mistake, for it caused Gauss to warn Hull at the end of the year of the new "tendency in the formulation of plans and discussions in connection with a powerful and new China [which] shows a definite trend towards a closed economy . . . and veers distinctly away from those liberal principles set forth in the Hull . . . exchange of notes of May 1941 . . . and other expressions of our post-war objectives for a mutually beneficial world economy." Creating vast Chinese dollar reserves, he implied, would permit China to define its own postwar economic role independent of American pressures. ". . . without further delay," he recommended, "we should quietly put China on notice as to what we expect before policies are adopted by China . . . by opening negotiations for our commercial treaty, advancing our proposals in respect to the treatment of American commerce and American financial and industrial interests. . . ."[40] The United States had to stop "China's Destiny," but given the precarious political and military condition of the nation Washington preferred worrying to action, waiting meanwhile for an opportunity to impose and define its own objectives in China. China could not emerge from the war so powerful as to choose also to become independent.

Chiang's advisers apparently sensed the American suspicion, and at the

Bretton Woods Conference the following July, Kung reassured Treasury officials that China would not industrialize quickly, but rather that America would aid its development, for "you can get certain resources, raw materials, from China, and because there is a potential market in China."[41] Whether such soothing reassurances were true or false, the economic position of the government worried Washington for other reasons—the Chinese decision to cooperate would be optional. During October 1944 the Treasury prepared an inventory of the known Chinese dollar holdings and came up with a total of $1.2 to $1.3 billion, mostly in official funds, a large increase over the previous year. Since the Chinese holdings in hard currency and gold in other countries might be very large as well, China would not come hat in hand like England to accept American commercial principles as the price of a loan. Throughout the summer and fall the State Department and the embassy in Chungking anxiously described the growing number of KMT nationalist statements and gestures which appeared to pose a threat to the integrated world economy in which they hoped China would play a vital part. By the end of the year *Business Week* could pessimistically advise that "U.S. businesses should be warned not to rush into elaborate postwar contracts with China," for the Chinese wrapped the contracts and terms in mysterious contingencies having political implications no one could quite fathom.[42]

For whatever the reason, obviously by the end of 1944 Chiang was fully capable of paralyzing the Chinese economy, and only whether he did so for reasons of principle or private profit interested the Americans. That distinction was critical, for it foretold what "The Kuomintang . . . government representing the interest of the warlord, banker, landlord hierarchy," with its "feudalistic and authoritarian methods," as *Business Week* described it, might hold once the war was over.[43] The United States could deal more easily with a government if they could buy it, and that was their only hope.

During November, Stettinius moved to prevent the public release of contemplated Kuomintang postwar economic goals that he regarded as "at variance . . . with the liberal trade policies to which this Government is endeavoring to obtain general adherence." The State Department considered these much too protectionist and designed to exclude both desired American exports and investments, and at the beginning of December, Washington formally asked the Chungking government to postpone publication of any statement of postwar objectives until they harmonized them with those of the American government. Failure to do so, the message also warned, waving the carrot with the stick, "would make more difficult the negotiation of the proposed Sino-American treaty of friendship and commerce."[44] Before Yalta, however, the State Department was reasonably confident that it could make Chiang work with the United States if he could retain power. The United States was prepared to aid China economically in the postwar period, and the State Department ignored the limitations that Chiang's occasional ideological forays might have on the goal of working with China "within the framework of our traditional principles of equality of opportunity and respect for national sovereignty and the liberal trade policies to which this Government is endeavoring to secure general adherence." There was reason to believe that it could obtain a trade treaty "on the basis of unconditional most-favored-nation treatment and looking toward the elimination of all forms of discriminatory treatment."[45]

[By the end of 1944 and beginning of 1945 there were in fact almost no serious ideological underpinnings to the Kuomintang government's conduct, and Washington could trust Chiang and his circle not to deprive the West of access to China for principled reasons.] There was, however, the greater danger that he might destroy China with peculation and exploitation, excluding Western interests if only better to exploit China himself, opening the door to chaos or Communism.

Never in the history of this century was the ruling group of a nation so starkly corrupt as was the Kuomintang, and this fact is the key to analyzing the success of the revolution. For Chiang was a gangster, as indeed Stilwell perceived, and China and its misery was the racket of his clique and the political rivals he kept at bay with his bribes and benefactions. As Barrington Moore, Jr., notes in his discussion of Imperial China, "Gangsterism is likely to crop up where the forces of law and order are weak," leaving the local populations the helpless prey of war lords and their bandit accomplices.[46] Perhaps at no time in recent Chinese history had this decay of the traditional social order penetrated so deeply as after 1937. China in fact was in a state of advanced disintegration. There was sufficient information in mid-1944 to understand this, but Washington embarked on a policy of trying to buy Chiang. It is ironic that too much rather than too little financial aid immeasurably aided in the West's losing China.

[No serious account of China during the period 1942–1945 differs on the proposition that the corruption and venality of the ruling elite was its sole consistent characteristic.] The inflationary spiral was so rapid that only speculators could hope to survive. Service reported in June 1944:

> It does nothing to stop large-scale profiteering, hoarding and speculation—all of which are carried on by people either powerful in the Party or with intimate political connections. . . . The Kuomintang is a congerie of conservative political cliques interested primarily in the preservation of their own power against all outsiders and in jockeying for position among themselves. Economically, the Kuomintang rests on the narrow base of the rural-gentry-landlords and militarists, the higher ranks of the government bureaucracy, and merchant bankers having intimate connections with the government bureaucrats. This base has actually contracted during the war.[47]

. . .

In making specific studies of who actually profited, the Treasury and embassy clarified the nature of the corruption. Despite the later view that Chiang himself was a kind of moderator between the competing factions in the tiny elite, playing them off against one another, in reality he and his close family were probably the key benefactors, for they were the major insiders in the large transactions in American dollars and loans and best able to exploit the possibilities. Gauss was convinced that Mesdames Chiang and Kung during October 1943 purchased some $50 million in United States savings certificates and bonds when their government put some $89 million up for sale. In a detailed analysis of $43 million in such certificates various owners presented for payment, or one-quarter of a specific sale, 2 percent of the purchasers accounted for 70 percent of the total, the leading Kuomintang figures, their families and firms, composing nearly all of this group. T. V. Soong held $4.4 million, K. P. Chen $4.1 million, H. H. Kung $1.4 million, and so forth. "The Kuomintang," Mao Tse-tung correctly suggested in 1944, "is an amorphous body of no definite character or program. . . . Chiang is stubborn. But fundamentally he is a gangster."[48]

If one regards Chiang's actions as destructive to his personal control of China but not to his private fortunes, then gangsterism is a serious and fundamental basis for comprehending the nature of the Chinese situation at the end of the war, and the reasons why Chiang rather than the Communists made the Chinese revolution inevitable. For the Japanese did not impose the speculative inflation and chaotic financial structure on China, they did not require the officers to operate the army as an appendage to a vast system of human bodies exploited as part of an enormous racket, nor did they close all the options to an alternative to both Communism and the Kuomintang.

The Kuomintang based its brand of Chinese nationalism in the 1920's on the urban strata—intellectuals, professionals, the bourgeoisie. Chiang by the end of the following decade transformed the party from an oligarchy with vital roots in the social structure into a clique delicately balancing the centrifugal structure of the ruling elite and quickly corroding the former class base of the Chinese nationalist movement. Inflation split the classes that once had supported the Kuomintang into those who were speculators, and ready to use politics as part of their private business, and those who were not. This process destroyed the salaried classes, the intellectuals, the principled bureaucrats, and the advocates of national industrialism and capitalism who found economic development impossible amidst the wild inflation. The historical division between national capitalism and a comprador capitalism based on servicing the foreign concessionary and investment interests in no way describes the realities of China during the war. There were the speculators, an inherently small group, and all others, with the small but critically placed middle classes and even elite groups on the edge of ruin. Chiang lost nonspeculating elements, including most of the industrialists connected with China's nascent industrial sector, and removed the last political and ideological barriers to Communism. Neither American money nor troops could save Chiang's government under the conditions of endless greed, inefficiency, and corruption. Chiang ceased to represent any well-rooted element of Chinese society; he degenerated from the leader of a class to the ruler of a clique.

China was disintegrating when the Japanese invasion helped to create, as Chalmers Johnson has rightly suggested, a merger of nationalism and peasant radicalism, labeled "Communism," in relatively isolated areas that contained about one-fifth of the Chinese population at the end of the war. Yet there was no external reason to compel the Chinese peasantry outside of the Japanese-controlled regions to revolt to save itself, and only a full appreciation of the magnitude of the advanced social and economic disorganization in the non-Communist, non-Japanese area can explain that metamorphosis. The nature of the army and its impact is vital to any complete understanding. But even beyond this floating sea of tortured oppressors, no less horrifying to the masses than were the Japanese, was the impact of inflation on the peasantry. The Chinese landlord had always been exploitive, but the external pressures compelled him to transfer new risks and obligations to the peasantry, and many moved to the cities as even more ruthless men took their places. As these landlords incessantly manipulated crop prices, prices paid, and services rendered, hoarding, artificial shortages, and sudden gluts became more common. Inflation made the already great risks of peasant life totally unbearable to many, and for the poor masses in the south the impact of the war, even where there were no foreign invaders, was a great disaster. The process of disintegration spread throughout China at lightning speed even where the people failed to organize an opposition and there were no Communists to give them political direction. We can only comprehend the ease with which the nation fell by examining the collapse of the social system everywhere. Chiang and his coterie alone made that possible. Japan did not dictate these necessities because there was no real war against Japan, only a process of accumulation for Chiang's clique and the war lords within the non-Japanese areas not under Communist control. Any moderately honest government might have stopped the polarization of the political options between Communism or endless misery facing the urban and rural classes.[49]

The Soviet Union and China

The struggle between Stalin and Trotsky for the leadership and direction of Soviet Communism focused centrally on China, where Stalin's advice

to the Communists to cooperate with the Kuomintang led to a vast liquidation of the urban Communists, probably numbering over 100,000 in 1927–
1928. Stalin early marked out a course of furthering Russian state interests
and made all other considerations subsidiary. After the debacle of 1927 the
Chinese Communists decided their own strategy and never wavered from
their determination to achieve power. Throughout the following decade the
ties between the Chinese Communists and Russians were minimal but still
respectful. After 1938 the nationalist ingredient in Communism became
predominant. The Communists succeeded not only without the Russians,
but in spite of them.

Although the Russians appeared not to have any long-range policies in
the Far East, and at the end of the 1930's were unquestionably far more
concerned with European affairs, objectively their basic interest lay in a
weak neighbor to the south. This meant a minimum of foreign interference
in northern China and ultimately the elimination of Japanese influence in
China, but also a Chinese state unlikely and unable seriously to reopen the
question of the nineteenth-century victories of Tsarist imperialism in Mongolia and the western border regions. Chiang from this viewpoint might
possibly serve future Russian needs, though the problem did not have high
priority when World War II broke out. Chiang cooperated closely with the
U.S.S.R. before 1927, and even sent his son to Moscow for training, and
Sun Yat-sen increasingly oriented Chinese nationalism toward the Soviet
Union in the years before his death. From the Russian viewpoint there was
no reason to believe that Chiang was so inflexible as to be unwilling to
reenter into good relations with his northern neighbor, and thereafter
satisfy the Soviet desire for a weak China.

A weak China was one thing, a Japanese-dominated China another. To
maintain the pre-1937 balance of power in the Far East was very much in
line with Soviet interests, and the Chinese Communist movement might
upset this balance by further weakening Chiang in his struggle against
Japan. When seen in this light the Russians did not hesitate: by the end of
1939 they supported the Kuomintang government against the Japanese and
therefore against the Communists, for the arms Russia sent to Chiang he
would also use against Mao's forces. As the rest of the world hesitated for
fear of alienating Japan, Russia sent Chiang weapons. In the last two
months of 1939 almost two-thirds of the arms shipped to Chiang through
Rangoon were of Russian origin, and by July of the following year, when
Roosevelt asked Soong how he felt about Russia, Morgenthau recorded
Soong as being "very, very appreciative because all of their airplanes and
guns today came from Russia."[50] Russia gave Chiang's government vast
credits, amounting to well over $50 million by mid-1940, and at that time
offered to aid China further if they could arrange a triangular agreement
with the United States to sell up to $200 million in strategic materials. The

United States refused such an arrangement because of the dismal state of its own relations with Russia, but by the summer of 1940 K. P. Chen confidently informed Washington he knew that they would get such assistance as the Russians could afford, and the Soviet ambassador in Washington could report that "Our relations with China are very close, very friendly."[51] Altogether, the Russians eventually loaned Chiang a total of $250 million for arms purchases. It was no secret that Chiang used such aid as much to contain the Communists as the Japanese, and there is no evidence of Soviet military aid to the Communists.

Chiang, for his part, was quite ready to use the Russians as he did the Americans, but he apparently retained a deep suspicion of Soviet intentions, and as a nationalist unquestionably resented Soviet control of Outer Mongolia and various border regions. He could cite no proof of Russian aid to the Communists, but he suspected such help might eventually be forthcoming, and he knew that he had to head it off and win the solid support of the Russians in order to survive. That Russia was responsible for Communism in the north seemed quite as logical to Chiang as it was to the United States that this was also the case elsewhere. If Russia could turn that revolutionary force on it might also turn it off.

In the fall of 1943 the Chinese ambassador in Moscow sought Russian assurances concerning the Soviet relationship to the Communists. In November he reported to Harriman that the Russians told him that they wished to see a strong China united under Chiang's leadership, the regime liberalized, and the Communists permitted to function either as a party or a member of the government. Russia alleged to have no ambitions on Chinese territory, and in fact had recently withdrawn troops from the Sinkiang region, but it expected the Chinese to forego claims to Outer Mongolia. At Teheran, Stalin endorsed the agreement between Roosevelt and Chiang on the restoration of Japanese-conquered territories, with Dairen as a free port. He made no claims on China. In fact the matter was not very important to him at the time. During the same months Davies came to the conclusion the primary long-term Russian concern in the Far East was to consolidate the existing frontiers.

In March 1944 Chiang's forces clashed sharply with Russian soldiers along the Mongolian and Sinkiang borders, each accusing the other of trespassing. Both the embassy in Chungking and the State Department attributed fault to both sides, assigning Chiang the larger share of the guilt. His nationalist and expansionist aspirations were largely to blame, and the Russians provoked difficulties mainly in connection with Kazak nomads left behind when they had abandoned Sinkiang to Chiang's government earlier. This was the most serious dispute between the two nations during the war, though Chiang never ceased to exploit the ogre of Russian expansionism in his attempt to obtain greater United States aid. To reinforce their amicable intentions in the region, during the following May the head of TASS in Washington informed Lippmann, and through him the State Department, that the Russians desired neither territory nor Bolshevism in East Asia. Despite his mutterings Chiang actually came to the same conclusion. For he knew that an Allied invasion would be necessary to save his nation from Japan—he neither could nor would do it himself—and in May his Minister of War urged the United States to intercede with the Russians to invade Manchuria. Thereafter Chiang favored the principle of Russsian liberation of China with even greater and firmer concessions to his future control after they withdrew.

During the period 1943–1945 the Russian press largely ignored the existence and activity of the Chinese Communists. In the spring of 1944, for the first time, the Soviet press drew a careful distinction between Chiang and the rest of his government and thereafter frequently criticized the corruption and inefficiency of the latter. They maintained this dichotomy for some years, knowing of course that it was a fiction.[52] Useful to both Chiang and the Russians, this fiction permitted closer relations and allowed the Russians to hint that it was necessary for Chiang to pay greater attention to both the war and his northern neighbor. The utter ineffectiveness of his regime compelled Chiang to seek active Russian support in the hope that perhaps they could help him end the threat of revolution. The Americans were anxious to assist him in this task, and during the remainder of 1944 the United States acted as Chiang's powerful intermediary and ally in the undertaking.

In early June, Harriman discussed China with Stalin and Molotov, and the Russians complained Chiang was not fighting Japan but only the Communists, whom he took far too seriously on ideological grounds. "The Chinese Communists are not real Communists," he quoted Stalin as saying with a laugh. "They are 'margarine' Communists. Nevertheless, they are real patriots and they want to fight Japan."[53] When Harriman asked for his aid in arranging unity Stalin quickly demurred, for only America could influence Chiang and he again repeated that he acknowledged American supremacy in the affairs of the region. For this reason, as the TASS official told Lippmann, the Russians did not relish the prospect of entering Communist-controlled areas and giving the impression that they were out to Bolshevize China. But at the end of the month Chiang strongly urged Wallace to have the United States intervene to bring about a rapprochement between his government and Russia, and although the Vice-President declined to have America assume the role of mediator on a formal basis, by that time Washington concluded that perhaps the Russians might be able to find the solution to the Chinese problem that had so far eluded the Americans. If Chiang would not bend, perhaps the Russians could make the Communists do so. At least they would call upon the U.S.S.R. to help in the war against Japan, and their friendly intentions were more important than Stalin was willing to concede.

When Hurley stopped in Moscow on his way to Chungking at the end of August, Molotov repeated what he had told to Harriman, but now amplified it. He charted Russia's course in containing the Chinese revolutionary movement in the mid-1930's, since the Communists took Chiang prisoner at Sian and released him after Soviet intercession. Russia, he insisted, would bear no responsibility for any deterioration in relations with China, much less for internal conditions there. If Chiang and the Americans wished to eliminate the Communists, whom he again disparaged and for whom he explicitly insisted Russia had no responsibility, they would have to improve the condition of the Chinese people. Russia could not solve Chiang's problems and was not really interested in Chinese affairs. Again, Molotov stressed, it was a matter of American interest and leadership. The conversation impressed Hurley as frank and honest.[54]

Chiang for his part by the end of 1944 decided to win the Russians even more firmly to his side and thereby hopefully undercut local Communists with the aid of those in Russia. The Russian chargé in Peking in early November proposed a meeting between Stalin and Chiang, and now Chiang asked to send Soong to Moscow. Stalin agreed to the end of the following February—after the Yalta Conference—but no sooner had they made the arrangements than Harriman went to see Stalin on December 15 about Russian goals in the Far East. Stalin stood on the restoration of the Kuriles and Lower Sakhalin, to which Roosevelt consented at Teheran. Now he raised his desire to lease Port Arthur and Dairen, and when Harriman noted Roosevelt agreed only to international free ports in those cities Stalin indicated that his position was still subject to discussion. The Russians would also seek a lease on the Chinese Eastern Railroad in a manner that would not interfere with Chinese sovereignty in Manchuria, and ask the Chinese to recognize Soviet control of Outer Mongolia. While Stalin failed to mention the Chinese Communists, in fact his demands on China premised a weak nation willing to recognize Russian claims, and therefore Chiang. The State Department appreciated this assumption, for prior to Yalta it saw no evidence of Russian plans to encourage the Communists and did not object to Soviet claims if Chiang also consented. "The Russians," they decided, "primarily want a China friendly to them."[55] There was no evidence to the contrary.

For lack of any evidence that the Russians supported the Communist movement (and the latter might indeed be independent nationalists), Hurley and his military associates unsuccessfully attempted for the remainder of 1944 to convince Chiang that he ought to make a sincere attempt to work with the Communists. At the end of the year Hurley believed he had convinced Chiang "that the Russian Government does not

recognize the Chinese Communist Party as Communist at all and that
(1)   Russia is not supporting the Communist Party in China, (2)   Russia does not want dissensions or civil war in China, and (3) Russia
desires more harmonious relations with China."[56] Grew approved of the
plan to send Soong to Moscow, but assumed that the United States would
take no obligations as an intermediary, yet the very act of approval and the
realities of the previous two years belied the facts as Americans assumed
more and more responsibility for China's international relations.[57]

Had Chiang believed that the Russians were in fact willing to support
the Communists he might have been more tractable in dealing with them.
The Russian position, in effect, weakened the Communists' hand. But
Chiang needed allies because he had little else with which to save the
regime in its totally corrupt form. And he needed the Russians to liberate
China from Japan, for by mid-1944 it was clear that the Americans were
not prepared to send massive numbers of troops to China, at least at his
price. Perhaps the Russians could save him. Certainly they appeared willing to consider it.

Chinese Communism: The Structure and Reality

Did Stalin and Molotov speak the truth when they ridiculed the Chinese Communists as less than true Bolsheviks? Surely their record of un-
dercutting or betraying the Chinese Communists, as one chooses to see the
matter, is a matter of historical record. Molotov, Stalin, Service, and
Davies described them as radical nationalists with a popular base, certainly
not Russian agents and possibly quite independent of the U.S.S.R. Their
support was from the masses, their dynamism a result of the misery of
China. What in fact was the opposition to the Kuomintang?

The history of successful Communist movements everywhere has consisted of making a virtue of necessity. Lenin at first favored the centralized
party structure composed of professional revolutionaries, but later when
the mass workers' councils of the soviets spontaneously came into existence and promised success Lenin glorified them as the transitional means
to power. When he took power he abandoned democratic workers' control
as an "infantile disorder," thereby eliminating the only possible radical
opposition to the party. Where the will to power is sufficiently strong,
ideology can be doctored to needs and possibilities and ultimately becomes
irrelevant to strategy—save to justify it. The historian can only understand
the nature of a system and its functional ideology from its practice, as
opposed to its rhetoric, and should practice and rhetoric coincide, his task
is that much easier. But given the inconsistencies in the doctrine of any man
or party with a will to power, the structure of the social system they create
is a measure of their true commitments and limitations.

The Chinese Communists by the time of the Japanese invasion of 1937 had suffered bitter defeats and one of the most frightful liquidations of the twentieth century in the 1927 repression. Obedience to Moscow had proven calamitous, and by 1935 the Communists were ready to give their own interpretation to the basic United Front strategy the Communist International adopted, and to legitimize any tactic which brought or promised success. After the purges of 1937 the Communists under Mao's direction became tactical and then ideological opportunists, enamored with the rewards of conforming to necessity. Given the relative freedom physical isolation and Soviet indifference permitted, by the beginning of the war in Europe they had become self-guiding and pragmatic in their ways.

The United Front strategy of 1935 offered a useful instrument to the Communists, who in isolation in the north used it to appeal to the "national" as opposed to the "compradore" bourgeoisie married to foreign interests and concessions for their profit. They considered even the landlords capable of being incorporated into the movement of "China's national revolution."[58] If Mao in 1935 gave obeisance to the central role of the workers and peasants, the fact remains that the war with Japan prior to 1937 had galvanized only the urban bourgeoisie, which for decades had been the major group to respond to Chinese nationalism in a sustained manner. To work with them was a precondition for any movement. By 1937, when altogether new events opened the possibility for unprecedented successes, Mao cited dialectics to prove the relativity of historical processes and the inevitability of contradiction in knowledge and strategy as something both predictable and justifiable. Also at the beginning of 1937, Mao, who after purges of the previous year emerged as the undisputed leader of the Communist party, laid the basis for a Chinese strategy of Bolshevism, one whose distinctive character soon defined the nature of the party's ideology:

> Another group of people hold a second incorrect view. . . . They declare that it is enough to study Russia's experience of revolutionary war or, specifically, that it is enough to follow the guiding laws of the civil war in the Soviet Union. . . . if we copy them and apply them mechanically and allow no change whatsoever, it will also be like whittling down the feet to fit the shoes, and we shall be defeated.[59]

At the end of the following year Mao spelled out the practical meaning of the idealization of flexibility and tailoring strategy to Chinese conditions:

> Chinese Communists are Marxian internationalists, but Marxism must be expressed in a national form for practical realization. . . . It has become a problem which the entire country must understand and resolve, to make Marxism Chinese, to see to it that in every manifesta-

tion it bears a Chinese character, that is to say, that it is applied according to China's special characteristics.[60]

By 1937–1938 there was ample reason for Chinese Communism to seek its own road to power, for the impact of the Japanese invasion of the north opened vast new possibilities. Peasants spontaneously and independently formed armed organizations in those areas to resist the invaders, largely for reasons of survival and nationalism. As the Japanese responded to resistance with brutality they created a wave of reaction that grew into a vast guerrilla movement. While the Communists had experienced only fair success at best with the peasantry before this time, and the peasants had been largely immune to both the tides of nationalist ideology and the Kuomintang, they now saw that harnessing the dynamic new reality was imperative. The Communists gave the peasantry a program, coherence, and direction primarily by conforming to their impulses and molding Communism accordingly rather than redirecting them toward some fixed ideology. Henceforth the basic ingredient of the party was the appeal to nationalism and patriotism, to reform, and to the collaboration of all nationalist classes. This required a structure of political organization which incorporated peasant power but did not move reform so far as to sacrifice the United Front, yet far enough to win and hold the allegiance of the masses. It required a leadership that eschewed dogmatism and could attempt to strike the fragile balance. Mao, even before July 1937, was the man who could create the synthesis.

While the structure of Communist China is a topic too complex to be considered in detail here, it is important to note the setting in which Mao defined the nature of Chinese Communism and succeeded in holding and expanding power. Using the so-called "three-thirds" system, the Communists never controlled more than one-third of the government posts in their areas, and they allocated the remainder to elected and representative spokesmen of peasants, landlords, the bourgeoisie, and others. The assemblies they organized everywhere on this basis were open forums of criticism, which the Communists encouraged and heeded. The Communists easily forgave opposition if cooperation was forthcoming later. If the party's strength depended also on the army and mass organizations, it was because of the overall structure of control that the masses saw the Communists as having brought about a society far more democratic and equitable than anything they had ever experienced. They supported Communism.

The Communist army did not loot, but grew its own food and worked with the peasants. Its morale was high, its commitment great. The army was a political movement which educated its members, who in turn educated the masses. It treated its Japanese prisoners in much the same way, and many became Communists as well. There was inflation but no black market of consequence, and the Communists solved the basic problems of economic organization. No one ever saw the appalling sights of the Kuomintang areas in the Communist regions. Disease, hunger, and misery were uncommon where avoidable. The party lowered but did not abolish rent and interest. Land distribution was greatly improved. It permitted private capitalists to function, and encouraged them to do so, but also controlled their activity. At the highest levels of power the Communists ruled firmly but flexibly, and Mao was their leader. They had their factions, but ultimately Mao prevailed over all of them.[61]

Mao's ideology and strategy consisted merely of reifying the best tactical option of the moment, the only constant inspiration after 1940 being Chinese lore and folk wisdom, and even the Chinese classics, rather than Marxism, much less Stalin, to whom Mao rarely referred. Mao's goal and vision was to harness the energy and enthusiasm of many classes and reconstitute them into a stable but also developing society and social system, options the Kuomintang and Japanese had ravaged. In the end his approach was so moderate that the victory of Communism threatened only the speculators, Chiang's clique, and the war lords.

Mao made a virtue of the inevitable: decentralization. He feared "localism," but in fact permitted the regions much initiative, insisting only that they coordinate their work on basic problems and principles. During 1940 and 1941 he understood that "whoever can lead the people to drive out Japanese imperialism and carry out democratic policies will be the saviour of the people." The national bourgeoisie was flabby and prone to compromise, but it too had revealed "a revolutionary quality" during its history, and segments might ally with "the proletariat, the peasantry, the intelligentsia and other sections of the petty bourgeoisie in China [that] are the basic forces which decide China's fate." Together these groups would create "a new democratic republic," and "While different from the old European-American form of capitalist republic under bourgeois dictatorship which is now out of date, this new-democratic republic is also different from the socialist republic of the type of the U.S.S.R. . . ." Someday socialism might be created—Mao never said when—but there was no alternative to a new democratic republic in the present "historical period." While the Communists intended to nationalize the big banks and industries and distribute the land to its tillers, "the economic activities of the rich peasants will be tolerated," and "the sector of non-monopoly capitalism in our economy should be given the opportunity to develop. . . ."[62]

The Communists followed essentially this economic policy for the remainder of the war. "Give consideration to both public and private interests" was a major slogan. To stress either too much was dangerous. They encouraged private gardens. The party admonished the troops to support themselves by hard work, to help the communities they were in, to grow their own food, to reduce the peasants' rent while giving deference to the landlords' interests. Above all it was necessary in the base areas "to win the masses there by patient, conscientious and thorough work, and to share weal and woe with them."[63]

The ideological underpinning of this vast undertaking was antisectarianism, which in fact meant greater stress on the exclusively Chinese character of Communism as the means of reaching the vast masses.

> But our theoretical front [he wrote early in 1942] is very much out of harmony with the rich content of the Chinese revolutionary movement. . . . We have read a great many Marxist-Leninist books, but can we claim, then, that we have theorists? We cannot. . . . If we merely read their works but do not proceed to study the realities of China's history and revolution in the light of their theory or do not make any effort to think through China's revolutionary practice carefully in terms of theory, we should not be so presumptuous as to call ourselves Marxist theorists.[64]

By 1943 Liu Shao-chi, Mao's theoretical associate, audaciously suggested that "the Chinese Communist Party has in its twenty-two years passed through many more great events than any other Party in the world and has had richer experience in the revolutionary struggle."[65] The implications of this independent mood were far-reaching, for Mao obviously set his goal to become a leader and theoretician equal to any, including Stalin, and even Lenin. "In the course of its struggle," the Central Committee decreed in April 1945 in a statement ghosted by Mao himself, "the Party has produced its own leader, Comrade Mao Tse-tung. Representing the Chinese proletariat and the Chinese people, Comrade Mao Tse-tung has creatively applied the scientific theory or Marxism-Leninism, the acme of human wisdom, to China. . . ." Thereafter he was at least equal to Stalin, often cited alone as if Stalin had nothing to offer. In effect, Mao defined the ideological basis of a break with the Russians. To the Chinese party he was superior, for "Today, with unprecedented unanimity the whole Party recognizes the correctness of Comrade Mao Tse-tung's line and with unprecedented political consciousness rallies under his banner." That line at the beginning of 1945 inveighed against the "left" line, as it had since 1940; it favored working with the "middle peasants" and the "liberal bourgeoisie," "providing certain economic opportunities for the rich peasants and also enabling the ordinary landlord to make a living."[66]

What Mao called theory, with the intense vanity which made him manipulate the party into passing encomiums to him, was nothing more than tactics, tactics designed to lead a national revolution of a reformist character. What is less important than the superficiality of the thought is its intent—designed to make a coalition and victory politically possible. Mao was a great strategist and tactician in the acquisition of power, but in fact below even Stalin as a thinker. His ideology was derived, intellectually crude, and strictly relegated to his desire and passion to use the dynamics of China in chaos to attain power. He never rose to even Stalin's sterile level of generality and abstraction, or above homilies that took more from Sun Yat-sen than Lenin. He always knew what was right for the moment, and in this regard he was a genius.

Since the success of the Chinese revolution it is both easy and fashionable, even in China, to regard the Chinese Communists as dogmatists and highly principled. At the end of the war the party was not merely flexible with doctrinal inconsistencies, but a party which based its entire success and raison d'être on a strategy of coalition with anyone willing to work with it. Recognizing the limits of power and reality and molding itself to them, by 1945 the party was anxious to relate itself to the power of the real world—the Kuomintang, which it was sure would disappear, and also to the United States. It had an ideological structure which encouraged such collaboration, and successful experience in such efforts.

Mao found much more inspiration in the Chinese classics and folk allegories than in Marxism, and he cited them far more frequently as relevant to China and as the fount of wisdom. His obsession with being confirmed as the Great Sage made him dogmatic about a theoretical line so nebulous and pragmatic that it was always successful as a tactical armory. Mao channelized Chinese nationalism, and by stressing the national roots of radicalism he began moving toward Chinese chauvinism and, in his own role, authoritarianism. Along with Marxism and modernism there existed within this synthesis the possibility of the emergence of a renovated traditionalism appropriate to twentieth-century technology but grounded on anti-Westernism. The conflicting dimension of Chinese Communism and Maoism that eventually emerged depended in large part on the response of the West itself to the political and economic consequences of the volatile mixture.

CHAPTER

11

PLANNING FOR PEACE, I: GENERAL PRINCIPLES

WHAT KIND OF PEACE and world order did the leaders of the United States hope to attain after the war, and what type of world did they expect would emerge from the chaos and disintegration of the period? What did the Americans believe they were fighting for, and what were their peace aims?

There were two crucial aspects to American objectives. The first critical ingredient was economic—clear, explicit, and well outlined from 1943 onward. Indeed Washington's definition of its economic peace aims were by the inception of the war deeply established principles of American foreign policy, inherited almost completely from the world view of Woodrow Wilson. On the political level American objectives until Yalta were impressionistic and improvised with experience, but after February 1945 the policy-makers defined a firm American position on political peace aims. If Roosevelt and his advisers could disagree on political objectives and assumptions for the postwar period, though ultimately hammer out a unified position, there was strikingly little dispute over matters pertaining to the contemplated role of the United States in the world economy.

The Atlantic Charter Roosevelt and Churchill issued in August 1941 was the only statement of American peace aims with any pretense of formally indicating the objectives of the Anglo-American alliance and the alternatives it posed to fascism. The charter was a remarkably obtuse document referring to no territorial aggrandizement or changes without the consent of the people concerned; self-determination; free access of all states to economic opportunities, trade, and raw materials; freedom of the seas; disarmament; and "freedom from fear and want." One could make the broadest interpretation of its political meaning, for the charter said little concerning the procedures to implement its sweeping goals, save in the area of economic policy, where it was indeed quite clear. Roosevelt's public statements on war and peace aims in subsequent years were hardly more than vague homilies—"a decent peace and a durable peace" as he told Congress in January 1943—and the effective thinking on such matters was covert and subdued, and ultimately armies and diplomats meeting together at Moscow, Casablanca, or Teheran would hammer out such questions, at least on an abstract level.[1] Certainly the United States had not been isolationist during the interwar period, and it based its refusal to enter the League of Nations as much on its unwillingness to subordinate American power to a league in which the weak and strong alike were equals as on any other consideration. Everyone in Washington during the interwar years acknowledged American global interests, economic and strategic, and only the relative priority they assigned to this interest, as opposed to domestic problems, varied. American power existed, and the issue was less the basic role of the United States in the world than the conditions under which it would employ its power. When its interests were threatened, the United States had not hesitated to defend them, via diplomacy, occasional forays into Latin American nations, and finally entry into the massive global war. There was no chance whatsoever that the United States would isolate itself after the war, for that had been a physical impossibility for three decades. The question, rather, was what type of world strategy it would pursue.

Reflecting primarily on the lessons of World War I the United States began to plan for the peace in 1941 and by 1943 had a fairly coherent formulation of objectives—highly explicit in the economic field and less precise as to the political instrumentalities required—which it shaped into a well-articulated world view in the two years preceding Yalta. That the impact of the war would not be apocalyptic nor result in chaos and the radical transformation of the political and economic world system was the chief, if unspoken, axiom of American planning. Without this sanguine estimate rational plans for the attainment of functional goals would have been impossible. Even when the United States devoted increasing energy and time to restraining the pressures and disintegration the war in Europe and Asia created, it never expected that the operational basis of its planning would have to assume inevitable, widespread revolution in the world, revolution that might radically subvert the foundations of American policy. That realization, at least in part, came after the war ended, for during the war itself the obvious problems emerging from the breakdown of the Old Order seemed soluble—with patience, economic resources, and determination—to the men in Washington.

The basic responsibility for American political and economic planning for the peace befell the Department of State, which is to say Cordell Hull of Tennessee. Hull, Secretary of State longer than any other man in American history, was strong-willed and of firm convictions. That Hull was a minor figure under Roosevelt is a myth without basis in fact. It was Roosevelt's wont to take advice from many sources, even when contradictory and inept, and he often excluded Hull from the first round of such deliberations, even occasionally not informing him of their very existence. In the long run, however, Hull and the State Department made their full weight felt in subsequent discussions of foreign policy, and they more often than not prevailed by the time issues of policy were finally resolved. Due in part to the ultimate consensus on essential premises that everyone in Washington shared, disagreements were invariably over only means and tactics. Hull could often exploit this by lining up other powerful advisers behind his policies. Also Hull's tenacious manners created personal difficulties between himself and Sumner Welles, his Under Secretary, that undermined the influence of both. But by the fall of 1944, after Welles's departure, no one could doubt the State Department's active role in the definition and conduct of American foreign policy. And throughout the war Hull shared the basic responsibility for the formulation of economic peace aims, on which everyone in Washington agreed in principle, and of political objectives, on which there was more dispute and therefore many counterpressures to Hull's advice.

Hull was a disciple of Woodrow Wilson and the Wilsonian world view, which expressed in its essentials the foundations of American foreign policy. He recalled in his memoirs:

> But toward 1916 I embraced the philosophy I carried throughout my twelve years as Secretary of State. . . . From then on, to me, unhampered trade dovetailed with peace; high tariffs, trade barriers, and unfair economic competition, with war. Though realizing that many other factors were involved, I reasoned that, if we could get a freer flow of trade—freer in the sense of fewer discriminations and obstructions—so that one country would not be deadly jealous of another and the living standards of all countries might rise, thereby eliminating the economic dissatisfaction that breeds war, we might have a reasonable chance for lasting peace.

This theme was critical to United States policy, and Hull followed it with a literalness which gradually permeated all phases of American foreign policy. "It is the collapse of the world structure, the development of isolated economies," Hull declared in 1935, "that has let loose the fear which now grips every nation, and which threatens the peace of the world." This economic interpretation of the fascist challenge to the more conventional capitalist states led Hull later to write, "I kept hammering home the economic side of international relations as the major possibility for averting the catastrophe," and during 1938 he saw Nazi expansion as a simple

German desire for raw materials, resources that would be available "if the German Government decides to change its course and adopt our liberal commercial policy. . . ." Even when it became painfully obvious that Germany would not pursue this advice, in 1940, as Hull envisioned the postwar world, "I believed . . . that the trade agreements program should be retained intact to serve as a cornerstone around which the nations could rebuild their commerce on liberal lines when the war ended."[2] In the last analysis the solution to the world's political problems could be found in a rationally ordered world economy, and this guiding assumption colored United States response to specific problems in Europe, Asia, and Latin America continuously during World War II and thereafter. Even when they could not create the ideal world system, the model of it existed as a beacon toward which the Americans would attempt to strive.

There was an inflexibility in Hull's determined views that oriented his response to all specific political proposals and often led him to disagree with his peers in Washington, and most especially with Great Britain. But by the time Edward R. Stettinius replaced him at the end of November 1944, he had essentially defined American economic and political peace aims, and Stettinius, who was the son of a J. P. Morgan partner and himself a former vice-president of General Motors and president of United States Steel, was not inclined to alter this course. Roosevelt chose the affable, handsome, and always smiling Stettinius because his colorless past —"a curious blend of businessman and world social reformer," as one contemporary put it—had left him with fewer powerful enemies than James F. Byrnes, Hull's first choice as his successor.[3] Stettinius was an expert on internal administration within the State Department, and his major policy interest was in the creation of a United Nations organization which Hull and the rest of Washington had already outlined for him. During the crucial 209 days Stettinius spent in office, Joseph Grew served as Acting Secretary of State for 110 of them.

Toward a Reconstructed World Economy

The impact of the prewar world depression and the experience of the 1930's profoundly colored United States planning of its postwar peace aims. Hull unsuccessfully attempted to cope with that upheaval, and he and the other leaders in Washington were determined to undo its still pervasive consequences to the world economy, and perhaps above all, to prevent its recurrence. For this reason the United States did not simply wish to repair the prewar world economy, but to reconstruct it anew. There was a remarkable unanimity in Washington on this objective, and it was by far the most extensively discussed peace aim, surpassing any other in the level of planning and thought given to it. While the United States faltered for a time in regard to its postwar political objectives, it entered and left the war with a remarkably consistent and sophisticated set of economic peace aims.

The world depression had been cataclysmic, and if ultimately a consequence of the collapse of the European political order that World War I engendered, it nevertheless accelerated the emergence of fascism and Nazism and the new war. Hull for his part took an economic interpretation of the origins of World War II and saw the need to uproot their exacerbating potentialities in the postwar era. The breakdown of the world economy, to which the United States contributed so heavily in its high-tariff Fordney-McCumber Act of 1929 and refusal to commit itself to making a success of the London Economic Conference of 1933, affected the United States more than any other nation, for employment and industrial and economic activity declined more precipitously and for a longer time in the United States than in any other industrialized nation. American exports abroad, which had been $5.4 billion in 1929, declined to $2.1 billion in 1933 and $3.1 billion in 1938. American direct investments overseas stagnated and declined slightly during the decade. With the depression came the creation of exclusive trading blocs, the largest of which centered about the British sterling area, which progressively excluded American goods and threatened to tie up critical raw materials essential to a mineral-deficient American economy. This division of the world into increasingly self-sufficient blocs as much as any consequence of the world depression greatly alarmed the Americans.

Western European exports as a percentage of their national products declined sharply from 1929, and in the case of England from 15 percent in 1928 to 8 percent in 1938. Even more important was the fact that more and more of this lower volume of exports stayed within the sterling bloc or was bartered in bilateral exchange agreements that minimized the role of gold and dollars in world trade. By 1938 the sterling bloc accounted for one-third of world trade, depending less and less on United States imports and more on the products of other sterling-based economies.

To a very large extent such trade restrictions increasingly tied down essential imports in primary products—foodstuffs, agricultural raw materials, and minerals—that the United States had to have for a balanced industrial economy, and future growth. The exports of such primary products from the nonindustrial, usually colonial, economies grew by almost one-tenth in the decade after 1928, while exports from the industrialized nations dropped 15 percent. But since these nonindustrialized nations suffered the worst decline in the prices received for their goods, the depression compelled them more than any others to confine their foreign trade to barter, the sterling bloc, and various restrictions which increasingly excluded the United States from the global economy.[4]

Despite its own high-tariff policy and the existence of over a hundred legalized export-trade and price-fixing associations authorized by the Webb-Pomerene Act of 1918, the United States throughout the 1920's strenuously fought international price fixing and output-restriction agreements that discriminated against American industrial consumers, expecially in tin, rubber, and potash. The depression only accelerated the formation of such restrictive agreements and outright cartels, until 40 to 50 percent of the total world trade prior to the war was subject to some degree of their control. Dozens of the largest American corporations entered into comprehensive agreements with their powerful equivalents in Europe to stabilize world prices and restrict the output of literally hundreds of essential products, and to divide up marketing areas in a manner that ended competition among the industrial nations in numerous fields. Concomitant with such stabilizing agreements was stagnation in the world economy, especially its industrialized sector, and the retardation of America's recovery from the depression.[5]

Hull watched this development of a divided world economy with its exchange controls and barter arrangements and he vainly attempted to reverse the deep, if not primary, American responsibility for its development. The Trade Agreements Act of June 1934, which allowed for as much as a 50 percent tariff reduction for a reciprocating nation, was his sole victory throughout this period, but it hardly altered the much more fundamental trend toward economic autarchy, much less the collapse of American exports and investment abroad. Since Roosevelt's preference for emphasis on national economic recovery largely insulated from the problems of the world economy had not proven successful in restoring full employment, by the outbreak of the war Hull could embark on a redefinition of America's role in the world economy with a remarkable degree of support for his views, for events appeared to vindicate his belief that the collapse of the international economy had brought on the war.

The United States therefore planned for the peace on the basis of the experience of the depression and its relations with the United Kingdom on the economic plane. Given the critical importance of the sterling bloc, it seemed that the resolution of the problem meant winning England to the American viewpoint—and I deal with this phase of the question in more detail in the next chapter as well. Yet it had to formulate larger assumptions and attitudes apart from the problem of England and the sterling bloc, and these revealed the foundations of American policy and the outlines of the new world the United States hoped to create out of the rubble of the war.

In May 1941 Hull publicly enunciated the "few and simple" "main principles" of American foreign economic policy, principles that the United States did not essentially alter throughout the war. Indeed what is remarkable about this statement is not that the principles were precise, but that they were open to free interpretation if the circumstances required. "Extreme nationalism" could not be expressed "in excessive trade restrictions" after the war. "Non-discrimination in international commercial relations must be the rule," and "Raw material supplies must be available to all nations without discrimination," including the careful limitation of commodity agreements affecting the consumer nations, such as the United States. Lastly, in regard to the reconstruction of world finance, "The institutions and arrangements of international finance must be so set up that they lend aid to the essential enterprises and the continuous development of all countries, and permit the payment through processes of trade consonant with the welfare of all countries."[6] For the next four years United States planners merely moved from the general to the specific in defining the instrumentalities for implementing this constant set of principles.

The British avoided comment on these public statements of American peace aims, but since they desperately needed American intervention in the war they attempted to meet American pressures to endorse these goals by issuing the minimum and vaguest possible words. In the summer of 1941, while the British were negotiating in Washington for the American Lend-Lease aid that they required for survival, John Maynard Keynes frightened top officials of the State Department by hinting that the postwar era might compel Britain to resort to far more stringent and discriminatory trade control to save its depleted financial resources. As a result, Welles, Hull, and other American officials determined to obtain British endorsement of their sharpened economic peace aims as the price of American support during the war, thus compelling the Americans to define these aims even more explicitly. When Roosevelt arranged to meet Churchill off Newfoundland during mid-August 1941, Welles and other American leaders accompanying him came prepared to extract British support for what in effect was Hullian and official doctrine. This in fact became one of the stickiest and most unpleasant aspects of the conference, for the British, aware of American plans, came with their own vague and innocuous proposals for "a fair and equitable distribution of essential produce" which committed them to very little and infuriated the Americans. Welles immediately pointed out to Roosevelt that such pieties would alter nothing, least of all in the sterling bloc, and he offered his own amendment, categorically calling for "the elimination of any discrimination" and "access on equal terms to the markets and to the raw materials" of the world.[7] Churchill immediately rejected the proposal, indicating that a stroke of his pen could not eliminate the Ottawa Agreement on which the sterling bloc was based, nor were the members likely to alter it in any event. To Welles this was bitter medicine, and he recalls telling Roosevelt and Hopkins "that if the British and United States governments could not agree to do everything within their power to further after the termination of the war, a restoration of free and liberal trade policies, they might as well throw in the sponge and realize that one of the greatest factors in creating the present tragic situation in the world was going to be permitted to continue unchecked in the postwar world. . . ." When Roosevelt and his aides confronted Churchill with such reasoning he could only cynically recall "the British experience in adhering to Free Trade for eighty years in the face of ever-mounting American tariffs. . . . All we got in reciprocation was successive doses of American protection."[8]

Roosevelt and Hopkins shared the Hullian view, but during the Atlantic Conference they did not appreciate the argumentative and divisive problems the issue posed, and they were willing to accept a loftier and less legal-sounding compromise and depend on other occasions, under way in Washington at the very time in conjunction with the Lend-Lease negotiations, to cover the specifics. The compromise was the famous Article IV of the Atlantic Charter, the most carefully discussed of the entire document: ". . . they will endeavor," the statement read, "with due respect for their existing obligations, to further the enjoyment by all States, great and small, victor or vanquished, of access, on equal terms, to the trade and to the raw materials of the world which are needed for their economic prosperity."

The United States could not afford, however, to compromise on the essential principle of breaking down the sterling bloc, for that was the key to the reconstruction of the world economy after the defeat of the Axis. All concerned themselves with the issue, not only the State Department, whose well-supported Commercial Policy Division carried on the most sophisticated planning on the subject, but the Treasury and Commerce departments as well. Hull was "keenly disappointed" with Article IV, and Washington made sure that they included a more precise statement in the Master Lend-Lease Agreement with Britain that they ultimately signed on February 23, 1942.[9]

The British would not agree to Article VII of the Lend-Lease proposal embodying American economic aims, and both sides haggled over the matter until February. This was the only article of the Lend-Lease Agreement the British would not accept in essentially the form the Americans suggested, and they made it plain that they had no intention of giving up the imperial trade preference system to pay a debt. Hull, with the support of Washington, stood firm and when Churchill came to the United States in January 1942 he again argued for American flexibility. The final text was broad enough to convince both sides that they had won their points, but in fact it merely opened the door to future controversies.

> In the final determination of the benefits to be provided to the United States of America by the United Kingdom for aid furnished under the Act of Congress of March 11, 1941, the terms and conditions thereof shall be such as not to burden commerce between the two countries, but to promote mutually advantageous economic relations between

them and the betterment of world-wide economic relations. To that
end, they shall include provision for agreed action by the United States
of America and the United Kingdom, open to participation by all the
other countries of like mind directed to the expansion, by appropriate
international and domestic measures, of production, employment, and
the exchange and consumption of goods, which are the material foundation of the liberty and welfare of all peoples; to the elimination of all
forms of discriminatory treatment in international commerce, and to
the reduction of tariffs, and other trade barriers; and, in general, to the
attainment of all the economic objectives set forth in the [Atlantic
Charter]. . . .[10]

To the British, who immediately hedged on the meaning of the agreement,
it meant little more than immediate aid without massive postwar debts to
complicate their economic position. To Hull it was "a long step toward the
fulfillment, after the war, of the economic principles for which I had been
fighting for half a century."[11] The United States insisted that other nations
signing Lend-Lease agreements endorse provisos exactly or nearly identical
to Article VII of the British agreement.

There were so many other reiterations of such general statements of
economic objectives that it would be uselessly tiring to cite more than a
few. More to the point were the specific proposals that permit one to see
how the United States hoped to apply such principles, what they would
mean in practice for America and for the rest of the world, and the assumptions they revealed as to the nature of international conflict and
peace. In brief, it was not merely a question of what the United States was
willing to advocate for others, but what it was willing to do itself to
implement freer world trade, the breakdown of which the United States
greatly aided through its own interwar policies. For if the program was
merely for other nations to fulfill without specific guarantees from the
United States that it would go at least as far, the policy would be nothing
more than a lever with which to open the markets and resources of the
world to American exploitation.

What is most interesting about the more general American economic
statements after 1942 is not their content, but the relative importance
attached to their release. When Hull in July 1942 decided to make his first
major public address since October 1941 to discuss United States war
aims, and to give the press advance notice of its special importance, he was
again specific only on economic matters. Welles, Henry Wallace, the very
uninfluential Vice-President, Stimson, Hopkins, Roosevelt and, of course,
Hull again and again, privately and publicly, stressed this economic theme.
The future required American leadership in the world economy, "the oppo-
site of economic nationalism," or a new internationalism which many
American allies feared was synonymous with American hegemony over

the world economy. To the colonial nations Hull's often repeated words conveyed undertones of a new colonialism: "Through international investment, capital must be made available for the sound development of latent natural resources and productive capacity in relatively undeveloped areas." And the supreme role of the United States in this global undertaking struck many Allies as potentially damaging to their interests: "Leadership toward a new system of international relationships in trade and other economic affairs will devolve very largely upon the United States because of our great economic strength. We should assume this leadership, and the responsibility that goes with it, primarily for reasons of pure national self-interest."[12] Exactly this realistic theme aroused anxiety among the Allies.

The major allies of the United States heard about these problems often, for Hull never lost an opportunity to expound American postwar economic projects at various international conferences. At the Moscow Foreign Ministers' Conference he proposed that the Allies accept American doctrines and open systematic discussions for their implementation. The failure of the Entente during World War I to develop common economic peace aims especially obsessed Hull and Stimson, and they repeatedly cited the analogy. For, as Stimson typically commented after the Moscow Conference, "while these political arrangements are good, they haven't any grasp apparently of the underlying need of proper economic arrangements to make the peace stick."[13] Both Stimson and Frank Knox, Secretary of the Navy, felt such compacts were especially critical, for other than England, future American relations with the Allies in the postwar period would have to be limited "mainly to economic agreements in respect to (a) sound money; and (b) the prohibition of tariff obstacles."[14] The importance of this concept cannot be overemphasized.

Well before it formulated a coherent policy on political goals or the United Nations, therefore, the United States had reduced its postwar economic objectives to a precise form. The British too devoted much time and energy to this topic, and of course posed the largest single problem insofar as the implementation of United States policy was concerned. In Washington, however, the State Department and Henry Morgenthau's Treasury Department assumed the major responsibilities for postwar economic planning, with the Commerce and Agriculture departments also contributing specific reports and recommendations. This profusion of activity meant that the United States would have an elaborately constructed policy covering all phases of the world economy, for while it is true that on a personal and organizational level the Treasury and State departments were on especially cool terms, their practical functions were entirely complementary and essential to each other. The Treasury Department concerned itself with the reform of the international financial system, State with trade and raw materials policies; reform in one field was impossible without the other and all understood and accepted this fact. Both worked within the same set of assumptions, reflected in Hull's statements, and their cool personal relations did not detract from their parallel functions. Both defined American foreign economic policy in its larger sense for the war period, and it was of no special significance that Britain gave first consideration to the Treasury Department's rather than the State Department's proposals at the beginning of 1943.

The motives for advocating a reconstructed world economy were not at all deductive, based on the abstract premises of some logical theory, but reflected Washington's specific understanding of the problems that would confront the American economy after the war. The Department of Commerce in its first studies, published in 1943, pointed to the vastly increased industrial capacity that the economy would have to deal with during the period of transition to peace, and similar reports, many confidential, by other economic agencies followed. The War Production Board in April 1944 calculated that the termination of the war with Germany alone would free almost immediately five and one-half to six million workers, only two million being soldiers from a military force five times that size. They predicted peace with Germany would release some $27 billion worth of annual industrial capacity by fall 1945, at which time they still expected to be at war with Japan.[15] By spring 1944 the United States government financed three-quarters of the $20 billion in new industrial plant constructed during the war until that time, in addition to contracting for the construction of 2,700 Liberty ships to carry goods abroad. It was not merely a question of foreign trade, but how much they would need to maintain a reasonable level of employment, and the means by which they might obtain it. The State Department's "Special Committee on the Relaxation of Trade Barriers" in its interim report of December 1943 stated as its first "basic objective" that "A great expansion in the volume of international trade after the war will be essential to the attainment of full and effective employment in the United States and elsewhere, to the preservation of private enterprise, and the success of an international security system to prevent future wars."[16]

In this context the American economic war aim was to save capitalism at home and abroad. ". . . from a purely self-interested point of view," Harry C. Hawkins, the director of the State Department's Office of Economic Affairs stated on April 1944, "trade cooperation . . . will help us a great deal. As you know, we've got to plan on enormously increased production in this country after the war, and the American domestic market can't absorb all that production indefinitely. There won't be any question about our needing greatly increased foreign markets."[17] How great? At the end of the year Assistant Secretary of State Dean Acheson estimated $10 billion a year would be needed to add three million industrial jobs plus another million jobs for agriculture. Lauchlin Currie, deputy administrator of the Foreign Economic Administration, placed the figure at $14 billion a year for the immediate postwar period. The deluge of statements along these lines soon made it apparent that for the official government agencies it was not merely a question of saving the world from its prewar economic foibles, but the American economy from a recurrence of its depression. No other problem, without exception, received as much space in the *Department of State Bulletin* during 1944 and 1945 as postwar foreign economic policy. When Henry Wallace proclaimed his dream of international co-operation in July 1944 after returning from a celebrated tour around the world, the instrument of that destiny was to be "The American business man of tomorrow" who would understand that "The new frontier extends from Minneapolis . . . all the way to Central Asia."[18]

The United States not only would have to export goods, but investment funds as well, in part of course to make the exportation of goods possible, but also as a part of the new order of things. The State Department and National Planning Association (NPA) both gave much attention to the investment problem, and as Stacy May of the NPA explained to the House Special Committee on Postwar Economic Policy and Planning at the end of 1944, "We will have this big accumulation during the war in funds and War bonds and savings accounts and so forth. I think then there will be tremendous investment funds in the United States." Since the issue was not to add to the already overexpanded domestic industrial capacity, but to find some way of utilizing it, these investments would have to be shipped abroad, and both the NPA and State Department estimated that United States business could invest some $3 billion in private funds annually overseas with reasonable expectation of good returns and repayment. "The wise investment of United States capital abroad benefits the United States and the world at large," Acheson told the same House inquiry.[19] The government would have to protect the investor and the borrower of course, but as Herbert Feis, a leading State Department expert on such economic matters reasoned in a 1944 volume, *The Sinews of Peace,* which equated peace with the implementation of Hull's economic program, there could be no profitable investment without profitable trade which would allow the repayment of loans. The postwar situation would also require short-term and high-risk capital far in excess of $3 billion, both the State Department and NPA explained, and for all these purposes Acheson asked Congress to repeal the Johnson Act of 1934 banning loans to nations that had defaulted on United States loans after the World War I. The alternative to such vast capital exports, as Acheson carefully argued to Congress, would be grim from a domestic viewpoint:

> If you wish to control the entire trade and income of the United States, which means the life of the people, you could probably fix it so that everything produced here would be consumed here, but that would completely change our Constitution, our relations to property, human liberty, our very conception of law.
>
> And nobody contemplates that. Therefore, you find you must look to other markets and those markets are abroad.[20]

If the channels of world trade were reopened and reconstructed along the lines the State Department proposed, other essential American needs of a long-term nature would also be met. The United States required critical quantities of certain raw materials it possessed in short supply or not at all. "Our metals are running out," Charles P. Taft, the State Department director of the Office of Wartime Economic Affairs, explained in May 1944, "and so may our oil eventually. . . . Other essentials must come from abroad, and in 50 years, like the British, we shall have to export to pay for the things we need for life." Therefore it made sense to export goods and capital abroad now, not merely to solve the problems of reconversion, excess capital, and capacity, but to lay the basis for secure sources of raw materials. "But don't ever forget," Taft had suggested even earlier that year, "that they have to pay with their goods and raw materials. They can't pay with anything else. This is all a business proposition, not a handout."[21] "The doctrine of the open door long advocated by the United States is a sound though cavernous basis for general practice," Feis wrote in 1944. Save for certain commodity agreements for which the State Department was willing to make an exception, "This doctrine in its pure form would provide that the capital and enterprise of all countries should have equal opportunity (even with the capital and enterprise of the country in whose territories the resource existed) to participate in the ownership and development of natural resources. . . ." The practice of the closed door anywhere, including the colonial possessions, "would accentuate international separatism."[22] That the United States would energetically demand access to the world's raw materials would be unquestionable, especially if, to suit American convenience, they could now reinterpret so freely the doctrine of the Open Door, which originally meant only equality with the most-favored foreign nation rather than domestic interests.

As the agencies in Washington poured out vast quantities of speeches and studies on postwar economic policy, all precise and unequivocal, the identification of the interests of the world and the future peace with Hull's doctrines and American prosperity looked more and more like the classic pursuit of national self-interest in an ill-fitting wrapper of internationalist rhetoric. Would the allies of the United States see the posture as something other than a new imperialism?

The Instrumentalities of the Open Door

Businessmen and government officials alike considered virtually every measure intended to carry out these objectives. For an international free trade doctrine, the Hullian program, which in principle received the approbation of most business organizations and firms interested in the subject, seemed to rely much more strongly on the Federal government's active and continuous intervention than Adam Smith's invisible hand, but nearly a century of pragmatic business-government relations had determined the precedent. When the House Committee on Postwar Economic Policy asked businessmen to testify, the representatives of the National Foreign Trade Convention called for a continuation of government aid in finding export markets, a General Electric executive demanded United States underwriting of foreign credit sales, a United States Steel official endorsed legalization of the international steel cartel, the vastly enlarged merchant marine entered numerous pleas for government subsidies, and the convenient blending of public and private interests continued along its familiar path. This support of Washington's efforts to articulate general principles and outline a highly specific program to implement them meant that for all practical purposes few industrial and business interests at this time interfered with stated American economic peace aims. Their confidence was not to be misplaced.

The United States during 1943 and 1944 initiated two major and interrelated programs, one involving reform of the world financial and currency system, and other nominally dealing with food and relief in the postwar period but actually defining the principles of future trade as a central theme. Both projects revealed that Washington was not going to leave the detailed planning of peace aims for the world economy until the end of the war.

Washington first devoted its attention to the question of postwar finances, for at the beginning of 1942 the British informally submitted a plan Keynes prepared, which demanded an answer, but by the time that they concluded this discussion other necessarily related reforms were also far advanced. Harry Dexter White of the Treasury Department, Morgenthau's right-hand man, prepared the so-called White plan to counter the Keynes plan. Discussions and arguments between the two nations over the next two years modified the precise contents of both schemes, but their basic assumptions as to ends and control were rather different. The British wished to develop a world financial structure that allowed internal economic development, even on a moderately inflationary basis, without concern for the international liabilities that balance-of-payment problems or uncontrollable gold fluctuations imposed on a nation. They emphasized stability and reasonable trade expansion via an international stabilization fund that permitted countries in temporary difficulties to draw on vast international overdraft resources to meet deficits in balances of payments and exports. Under the British plan, control of the postwar fund would depend on a nation's prewar volume of trade, which obviously favored Great Britain.[23]

The Americans, by contrast, demanded an international banking fund which would expand trade and stimulate loans in a much more accelerated fashion, with special emphasis on its holding currencies in short supply, which is to say United States dollars, and they insisted that control of any cooperative organization be vested in proportion to contributions, which according to the White plan gave the United States a vote five times that of the next largest nation. Both agreed to make currency more convertible, to prevent the exchange controls that had frozen the world economy before the war, and to introduce a measure of stability in the world financial system. By April 1943 both nations were ready to release their respective proposals for the consideration of the other Allies, and from that time until the Bretton Woods Conference of July 1944 they continuously discussed the matter. Much of the time they spent on technical formulas designed to carry out the various plans. One of the most difficult problems proved to be American insistence during the fall of 1943 that future world bank loans would, as White explained, "doubtless need to be restricted in regard to the place of its expenditure." Both White and William L. Clayton, then of the Department of Commerce, carefully informed Keynes that Congress would hardly be inclined to contribute to the resources of a bank if borrowers were free to spend their loans in other countries. To Keynes "the [American] plan implied a tying of loans to trade."[24] It would guarantee American exports and little else.

Another British objection was that the White plan specified that loan funds were to be made available only to countries with a clear ability to repay them, a condition White thought elementary and essential. This linked repayment to ability to build up a favorable balance of trade, which required exports. Keynes saw the need to stabilize and reconstruct economies internally and raise the productivity of the borrowers, whether or not they stressed exportable goods. Quite predictably the British were intensely suspicious of any plan designed to link loans to exports, and they compelled White and his associates to revise their plans to meet this objection to some greater degree, but by no means to full British satisfaction. By the spring of 1944 the British were anxious to delay the international conference altogether. In its original form the American program looked very much like an export promotion and an attempt to assure a world raw materials supply capable of earning dollars and supplying United States needs.

The British and Americans reached general agreement on these matters prior to the Monetary and Financial Conference largely because the British attached sufficient contingencies to the American proposals to suspend them, but the International Monetary Fund (IMF) and International Bank for Reconstruction and Development that the Allies founded at Bretton Woods were far closer in their principles to the American scheme than any other. The IMF dedicated itself to the "harmonization of national policies" to promote a "multilateral system of payments" and the "elimination of foreign exchange restrictions which hamper the growth of world trade."[25] Members could modify exchange rates beyond a certain limit only by agreement with the IMF, and it carefully prescribed the entire process of altering and obtaining currencies. Since voting in the IMF was approximately in proportion to capital contributed, the United States and its immediate Latin American neighbors could exert a dominating influence. But the British insisted that the members be permitted to maintain exchange restrictions for five years, and during this critical period the IMF in effect would have to depend on more reliable and direct United States intervention to eliminate exchange controls.

The International Bank for Reconstruction and Development (IBRD) was even closer to Washington's desires, for while the bank gave obeisance to reconstruction loans it also emphasized its function "To promote private foreign investment by means of guarantees or participations in loans and other investments made by private investors," and also to give loans to nations to develop the necessary and unprofitable economic infrastructure of roads and utilities critical to later profitable private investment.[26] Dependent to a great extent on private sources of investment, the International Bank nevertheless permitted investors to move into the world economy with governmental backing, thereby obtaining far greater deference from the recipient countries. The control of the IBRD was also about proportionate to national capital invested, and this made it an American-dominated agency, always with an American president. Rather symbolically, both organizations maintained their headquarters in Washington, the seat of their power.

The importance of the Bretton Woods Agreement was less in what it accomplished than in what it promised, for everyone understood the agreement was not an organism for dealing with the problem of war debts and reconstruction, but rather a structure for a normal world economy the Americans envisaged would exist rather soon after the war. At that time there would be "a world in which international trade and international investment can be carried on by businessmen on business principles," as Morgenthau described the significance of the two new organizations. If there was no orderly mechanism, barter arrangements, exchange controls, and the like would quickly return, along with the "International monetary and financial problems [that] have been a source of conflict for a generation." ". . . the Bretton Woods proposals give us the opportunity to decide whether international trade and investment will be carried on through private enterprise on the basis of fair currency rules or through governments on the basis of bilateral agreements."[27] The United States had at least defined the Allied principles for a world financial structure.

The State Department welcomed the Bretton Woods Agreement as a necessary precondition to its trade program, and this too was Morgenthau's understanding of its ultimate function. As Feis, who became one of the leading theorists of the Hullian doctrine, analyzed it, "The United States could not passively sanction the employment of capital raised within the United States for ends contrary to our major policies or interests. . . . Capital is a form of power." The United States would not gratuitously use it to damage the interests of others, "But willingness on our part to subordinate the independent use of our financial power to joint decision must be limited and kept in step with the willingness of other countries to act likewise in other matters. . . ."[28] This would require an acceptance of the American program for world economic reconstruction not only in principle but in fact.

The Reconstruction of World Trade

While the Treasury Department assumed primary responsibility for the complex negotiations that led to Bretton Woods, during the same period the State Department moved to win Allied acquiescence to the closely related policies on postwar trade and exports. In doing so it had to consider the problems of food and reconstruction, the need of the United States for markets and raw materials, the impact of the war on the immediate postwar system insofar as reparations might replace normal trade, and the larger political significance of foreign economic policy in attaining strictly political objectives.

It lost no opportunity in obtaining Allied agreement to American economic objectives. In March 1943 the State Department took responsibility for organizing a United Nations Conference on Food and Agriculture at Hot Springs, Virginia, that they would convene during the latter half of May and early June. The formal invitation indicated that the conference would consider questions of food requirements and agricultural surpluses apart from the problem of relief, which it was not authorized to discuss. Instead it would consider the problem of world food output and "the attainment of equitable prices" for both producers and consumers, and the United States was, of course, included in both categories. The British thought that to discuss food without considering relief would strike many as artificial, if not crass. They soon learned, however, that the real purpose of the meeting was, as Hull wrote Halifax, "to relate the problems inherent in the production and exchange of food and agricultural products to the wider fields of trade and finance in general in the expectation that these would form, in due course, the subject of further discussions among the various nations."[29] Article VII of the Lend-Lease Agreement, the State Department told the British even later, would be an appropriate statement of principles to reiterate at the conference, and the State Department instructed the United States delegation to obtain some endorsement of these principles. The final conference document, in addition to mentioning the food problem in general terms, also endorsed the broad contours of Hull's trade program.

The conference, however, could not avoid the intimately related question of food for relief if only because it was obvious that the Allies would have to plan some measures in advance and the prospect of American food surpluses was beginning to weigh heavily on the Department of Agriculture. The Americans saw the organization of the United Nations Relief and Rehabilitation Administration (UNRRA) during the fall of 1943 as both a political and economic response to the immediate wartime dislocations, but not as a crucial tool in reconstruction, which only a permanent revision of the world trading and financial system could attain. UNRRA was therefore always an incidental aspect of American economic policy, but at times of great political value. Food had proven to be a critical political weapon after World War I, and during the discussions leading to the formation of UNRRA the obvious utility of its serving the same function came up again. Significantly enough the Polish exile government first raised the problem, and although Hull and Roosevelt denied UNRRA would serve a political function, Roosevelt also defined the standard for a nonpolitical policy: food would go to the people of the Allied countries in accordance with their needs. Any other criterion would obviously be political. Since the United States would contribute 70 percent of UNRRA's final cost of $3.5 billion, it followed that the United States would decide the ultimate nature of the program.

In fact as early as 1943 the American government was split on the precise function of UNRRA. Some officials advocated a wait-and-see policy until the world situation became clearer, and another group, which eventually prevailed, preferred to meet Soviet demands that UNRRA distribute its food to the needy Allies most active in resisting the Axis, which for the most part meant Eastern Europe. By early 1944 most of Washington shared Harriman's awareness "that economic assistance is one of the most effective weapons at our disposal to influence European political events in the direction we desire and to avoid the development of a sphere of influence of the Soviet Union over Eastern Europe and the Balkans."[30] In the end, of course, food became such a conscious political weapon, and except for the Ukraine the U.S.S.R. received nothing. Surprisingly, the Russians protested very little.

More important to United States policy during 1943 and 1944 was the

relationship of relief to America's anticipations of its food surplus at the
end of the war. American farm production in 1944 was 16 percent above
1940 output, despite the loss of agricultural manpower to the military
services. By mid-1944 Washington, and especially the Department of
Agriculture, officially assumed that there would be vast food surpluses
confronting the American economy at the end of the war. The invasion of
food-rich but unrepresentative Normandy in June 1944 reinforced this
policy, which required much greater attention to creating many complex
international commodity and marketing agreements and a deliberate policy
of reducing food stockpiles available to the United States. The United
States basically oriented policy to anticipating an excess rather than a short
supply of food, and after mid-1944 to using food as a political weapon, for
Washington made the Italians the chief recipients of UNRRA supplies.
"We are accumulating in stockpiles large quantities of food against contingencies that probably will not eventuate," James F. Byrnes, director of the
Office of War Mobilization warned Roosevelt in August 1944. At the end
of the war such surpluses would put terrific pressure on the agricultural
price support program, creating "a major farm problem more difficult to
deal with than any in our history."[31] Byrnes advocated removing sufficient
wartime restrictions to trim the growing farm surplus, and since a presidential election was coming up Roosevelt gladly consented and ordered the
new policy implemented so that he might mention it in a campaign speech
on September 23. Although Washington ostensibly called the Hot Springs
Conference to deal with precisely such problems, it ignored on behalf of
domestic needs the conference's resolution to cooperate in designing a
program to meet the problem of hunger after the war. No one in Washington of decisive influence asked at this time what the political consequences
would be if the sanguine American premises about food turned out to be
incorrect.

During this same period the State Department also had to confront
postwar commodity problems in a manner intimately related to American
agriculture's role as a producer of cotton and numerous other agricultural
commodities, and to American industry's role as a consumer of world raw
materials. The result was an uneasy and highly inconsistent balance that
raised obvious questions as to American intentions and the purpose of its
internationalism.

Washington determined not to repeat the costly and tense experiences
of the interwar years in regard to international commodity agreements,
most of which had raised prices and restricted supplies of numerous vital
goods and seriously aggravated relations with England, which dominated
many of the colonial nations involved. "Anticolonialism" was one mode of
expressing the [American belief that colonial raw materials ought to be
freely available without discrimination, but it was impossible to take a

radical position on colonialism, save on the economic level, since America already had plans for its own postwar trusteeships.] Moreover, many inter-war restrictive agreements were in large part the result of American firms seeking stability in their respective world industries, or American price fixing of its own agricultural raw materials. A consistent policy was there-fore impossible, and inevitably the United States created a dual standard that only increased Allied doubts as to the depth of America's sincerity in its stated postwar economic policies.

The State Department generally represented the needs of the raw mate-rials importers and the Agriculture Department those of American farmers who wished to maintain their prices and income. Many high-cost pro-ducers, attracted to new crops during the war, feared a collapse in inflated government-supported prices might prove disastrous. The Agriculture Department, with its powerful Congressional base, was able to stymie the State Department again and again during the wartime period and there-after. The Agricultural Act of 1935 made American agriculture one of the most highly protected in the world and provided for 30 percent of the gross customs duties to be used to encourage subsidized exports. No less signifi-cant were the tariff walls and import quotas on sugar and other commodi-ties. Yet without a solution to this problem, overseas if not at home, the State Department could not implement its program save in a manner grossly favorable to the United States, for at least one-third of the world's trade was in raw materials and another one-quarter in foodstuffs.

To get around this dilemma the State Department initiated interna-tional discussions, mainly and often exclusively with the British, dealing with price and output agreements of specific commodities, the most impor-tant of which were tin, copper, oil, and rubber, nearly all from the colonial and underdeveloped regions. Before Yalta the State Department actively sponsored such meetings on the assumption, as Feis put it, that "in the formulation of any plan, and in the control of its operation, consuming countries should have an adequate part," which was to say "The prices maintained . . . should seek adjustment of supply and demand on terms that encourage the growth of demand."[32] (I will consider the most impor-tant of these discussions, involving oil, in the following chapter.) The Americans soon made it plain to all nations they could not and would not work out a consistent practice before demanding the rewards of their new economic policy for themselves.

On cartel agreements, which strongly favored United States industry, the State Department confronted a situation which directly contradicted Hull's dicta, but had the support of existing law, precedent, and the vast majority of American industry. The National Foreign Trade Convention wished to see a federal review and legalization of approved cartels, but industries involved in such arrangements before the war continued to defend their utility. The first State Department program on cartels, prepared for official consideration in May 1944, criticized cartels but called for their international restriction rather than unilateral United States action. It made decisive action largely contingent on international acceptance of the remainder of the American trade program, and by the end of 1944 the State Department decided not to unequivocally oppose postwar cartels.

The other Allies carefully observed these specific expressions of American foreign economic policy, but they struck surprisingly few in Washington as inconsistent or as a legitimate cause for foreign concern because of their ambiguity. Hull continued to advocate general policies, which Roosevelt supported fully, and which progressively took on the character of an American export offensive without reciprocal concessions to the rest of the Allies. At the end of May 1944 Hull abbreviated the basic assumptions of American postwar trade policy for the President's consideration, and Roosevelt promptly endorsed them:

> (1) Policy of the Government of the U.S. to engage in a properly conceived program of foreign investment to aid in financing the reconstruction of war-torn areas. (2) This policy includes the elimination of unnecessary obstacles to the flow of private foreign investment and regulation of private foreign investment. (3) Adequate provision does not now exist for financing reconstruction and development programs which it may be anticipated will arise during the next year or until the United Nations Bank for Reconstruction and Development is established. (4) Reconstruction financing should take the form of loans with expectation of eventual full repayment.[33]

Nothing in this doctrine suggested a serious preoccupation with the problems of postwar reconstruction outside the context of a renovated world capitalist economy, and Washington's planning focused on its trade goals rather than emergency aid to a starving Europe that was fighting the war with far greater sacrifices than those of American businessmen, farmers, and exporters anxious over their future profit margins. These attitudes set the general tone for American thinking on numerous political issues with economic dimensions that arose during the remainder of the war, from Eastern Europe to Great Britain. Widespread starvation was a much more remote consideration than ripping down the accumulated prewar trade barriers and the special wartime licensing and governmental bulk buying practices that the British, French, and Russians threatened to continue in the postwar period. As defeat of the Axis appeared more certain and closer, the Allies' ability to resume a small amount of export trade took on an added measure of significance for the terms of trade and the markets obtained, mainly in regard to Britain. From July until December 1944 a special economic mission of United States government experts and important export-oriented businessmen toured North Africa, the Middle East, and Italy to "study in those areas conditions and controls which were holding up the return of trade to normal channels."[34] That they were also to uncover markets for American exports both the other Allies and Washington understood.

This policy of striving for business as usual was reflected by the end of 1944 in several developments of special consequence to the meeting at Yalta and the entire course of American foreign policy. The most critical by far was the American definition of a policy toward Axis reparations in conformity with larger American postwar economic objectives.

The United States hoped to find ample and profitable outlets in the postwar period for its exports and investments and in principle wished to see the markets and resources of the world available to all on equal terms, but most assuredly to the United States. Recovery and reconstruction was to proceed on this basis, with America playing a universally convenient and central role in the world economy. When the problem of reparations first arose during the Rumanian and Hungarian surrender negotiations, Washington formulated an immediate response that reflected these attitudes and required the articulation of a definite and practical policy on the subject. For if the Allies could reconstruct on the basis of reparations taken from the former Axis it would gravely minimize the American role in the postwar economy and remove the economies of the former Axis nations from the normal world trading structure.

In principle, at least, the Americans would not oppose reparations, for the Allies were certain to penalize the Axis nations. But they attached certain admonitions to the reparations terms discussed for Rumania and Hungary which had the greatest significance at Yalta, Potsdam, and thereafter. In the Rumanian situation—during the fall of 1944—Hull immediately advised leaving the settlement and amount "as open as possible."[35] He also wished the recipients to use payment in goods and materials solely for reconstruction, and not for reexport, for this would grossly alter the traditional control of Eastern European raw materials entering the world market. But above all reparations should "not be effected in ways which would unduly prejudice the resumption of normal commercial relations in accordance with the economic policies of this government." By this standard Russian reparations receipts could not be so large as to exclude American credits, which the State Department hoped the Russians believed would be forthcoming. ". . . a speedy restoration of international trade on a liberal basis," whatever that might mean, therefore became the first basis of American policy toward reparations, and in November 1944 the State Department notified the Kremlin that "reparation payments should be scheduled in such a way as to interfere as little as possible with normal trading relations."[36] This guiding principle dominated American thinking before Yalta even after Harriman assured Washington that the Russians merely wished to recoup their losses, if that were possible, and that they were not especially stern in their demands.

In the months leading up to the Yalta Conference the United States developed a highly detailed set of economic peace aims and the means for implementing them. It also moved to eliminate any organizational weaknesses in its policy-making structure dealing with the continuous problems of foreign economic policy. By Yalta the United States was better prepared to handle its contemplated problems of foreign economic policy than any other challenge it might confront.

The administrative processes of Washington left the various agencies working on foreign economic policy within the same policy framework but with different emphases, and personal rivalries of the usual sort that plague ambitious men of power led many times to a lack of coordination. The Treasury Department by the fall of 1944 was less interested in nonfinancial aspects of policy and wished to concentrate on the perfection of the Bretton Woods decisions. The Commerce Department under Jesse Jones played a relatively minor role in this wartime debate, but it advocated greater emphasis on domestic economic conditions as a prerequisite to the international trade it also favored with a by now pervasive passion. During the fall of 1944 the entire Washington organization dealing with these matters was centralized in the hands of William L. Clayton, the new Assistant Secretary of State. Clayton was a friend of Jesse Jones—both were Texans —and had Jones's warm support as the new chief of foreign economic policy. He was also by his own admission "an ardent, outspoken, and consistent advocate of Cordell Hull's philosophy regarding international economic matters."[37] He was the perfect man to provide continuity to Hull's policy after the Secretary's retirement.

Clayton's interest in foreign trade was personal as well as abstract, for he had been chairman of Anderson, Clayton & Company until coming to Washington in 1940, and he continued to hold 40 percent of the stock in the business, which with its six foreign subsidiaries was the largest cotton merchant firm in the world, with a gross income of $272 million in 1944. He was an obvious and continuous target for high-tariff Congressmen looking for a conflict-of-interest excuse for criticizing his policies, and as his star and influence rose they aired these charges again and again. There was no doubt that Clayton served to lose or gain personally by every policy he advocated, and although he insisted "I have tried . . . to keep out of any official discussions or actions relating to cotton," he also confessed willingness to "discuss the matter very informally" when necessary, and he also opened many doors to officials of his firm who actively sought to encourage sales.[38] Although Clayton retained a lively interest in cotton affairs throughout his career in government and gained much thereby, this hardly influenced American policy and its conduct, nor were his private relations at all unusual in Washington. Wilson and Hull had defined American policy with a nearly complete consensus well before Clayton appeared on the scene and he only implemented it with a higher degree of precision and sophistication, bringing the merger of American business interests and official policy together to create a policy said to be for the welfare of the entire globe.

When the Americans went to Yalta they had all of the experiences of the preceding years of discussion over foreign economic policy firmly in mind, and they intended to press the Allies to implement their pledge to Article VII of the Lend-Lease agreements during 1945. Certainly, the State Department advised, the moment was propitious to initiate the highest-level discussions and conferences to enact on a multilateral basis the terms of Article VII and the Bretton Woods Agreement, for without joint action "It is obvious' that the United States cannot reduce its trade barriers unilaterally. . . ." "If we delay too long," the State Department reminded, "the favorable opportunity which now exists may be lost, and the experience after the last war may be repeated."[39] Then why, if the economic objectives of the United States were so beneficial to the entire world, did not the other Allies rush to implement them as well? The failure to ask this question reflected the deeper assumptions of American policy.

THE major premise of the unusually sophisticated planning that went into United States economic peace aims was that World War II was an exceptional incident in the history of world capitalism, and not the beginning of its end after two suicidal conflagrations. The political assumption was that the great capitalist states and their prewar spheres of influence would re-emerge from the war as powers America could control and reform, and not that the war had irrevocably weakened the prewar order. The Americans envisaged these states, primarily Great Britain and Germany, as economic competitors but ideological allies, and expected that they would have to deal with their anticipated strength rather than their weaknesses. Emergency reconstruction and relief problems would exist, but they would be temporary and solved essentially as a by-product of the creation of a rational world economy, based on economic liberalism and the Open Door, that assumed the general interest of the world was synonymous with that of the United States.

Well before it could estimate the economic and political dislocations of the war or realistically appraise the long-term world economic situation, the American government insisted that all the Allies conform to the American statement of economic peace aims. The hard-pressed Allies did so out of necessity, only to find later that cooperation on American terms was impossible, and the attempt to do so aggravated their own problems, paving the way for innumerable controversies and breaches of faith which to the United States only revealed the ill will or nefarious motives of Britain and Russia. That these nations could not agree to commit economic suicide by accepting the American program was predictable in advance, but the suppositions and needs of American policy were such that the United States had to present the same demands in any case. Hull saw the problems of the postwar world in the light of the experience of the 1920's and 1930's and from the viewpoint of the problems and needs of American economic interests. Surplus rather than scarcity was the basic theme of this preoccupation, reflecting conditions unique to the United States, and every one of its specific proposals, cast in the context of inconsistent policies obvious to all, reflected this focus.

The United States set out to solve its own dilemmas through reorganizing the world economy, hoping that the sterling bloc, state-controlled economies, closed markets and sources of raw materials might all be pushed aside. In this manner new means—"multilateralism" and the Hullian rhetoric—that they had still to reconcile with American practice might save the Old Order. Less self-serving means of saving world capitalism, even at the expense of American plans, Washington simply could not harmonize with such objectives. If the other powers could not accede to this program, either because of their own imperial ambitions or desire to build economies along new, essentially socialist lines, or simply out of suspicion of the erstwhile selflessness of American purposes, conflict would surely be inevitable. For in no other area was the United States so determined to have its way in attaining its postwar aims.

The Politics of Peace

Hull regarded a postwar United Nations organization as an ancillary political instrument to attaining his much more important economic objectives, which he conceived to be the permanent, stable foundations of a lasting peace. He responded to every proposal in this light, and he opposed any hints of spheres of influence, alliances, or blocs in British or Russian postwar diplomacy and, given his single-mindedness, in American political strategy as well.

From the very beginning of the war the State Department assigned committees to begin planning for the numerous political and economic problems that America might expect to confront with the peace. These committees, composed of high-level officials and experts, patiently laid the groundwork for a postwar United Nations structure based on the premise of the United States as a major, even predominant, and active world power, but their views failed to filter through to Roosevelt until well into 1943, by which time it was clear there would be a synthesis of Hullian theory and

Roosevelt's own interpretation of America as a world power, leavened by the ideas of Hopkins, Stimson, and many others. Hull spent much time, therefore, attempting to redefine Roosevelt's impulses and preliminary enthusiasm for Britain's postwar proposals in a manner consistent with a world order that hopefully would move beyond power politics and that "natural economic principles" might determine. Roosevelt at the beginning of 1943 seemingly accepted the British outline for a postwar international system based on three or four regional blocs, with a minimum of centralized and universal authority in a United Nations organization. Briefly, a Western European bloc, a cordon sanitaire in Eastern Europe, and the like, were the core of British postwar strategy. Their initial plan for the European Advisory Commission assumed that body might become the political organ of the postwar United Nations for all of Europe. Hull saw this clearly, and did not like it. But the hard, realistic assumptions of this scheme attracted Roosevelt, for he knew that the United States would want to maintain its own spheres of influence elsewhere. Concentrated power existed, and Roosevelt for a time believed that the Allies must make it the basis of a world system that acknowledged its supremely defining role.

Hull, by spring 1943, disagreed with Roosevelt's commitment to this vision of a Four Power coalition to rule the world. Yet he could not fully overcome this trend in American thinking, which the anxiety over the role of the Senate in approving America's postwar commitment complicated more than Roosevelt. The final American political peace aims embodied only aspects of Hull's desire to see existing blocs destroyed and a world organization come into being that, while not active, prevented political impediments to a world economic structure that would in the last analysis be the best guarantor of peace. Ultimately the American government, through Roosevelt's efforts, wished the founding San Francisco Conference of April 1945 to create a United Nations organization that would acknowledge American political supremacy as unique in international affairs.

These alternative grand policy outlines remained in gestation until the fall of 1943, when the Moscow Conference and Teheran meeting gave firmer guidelines for the State Department, and Roosevelt developed his own views in greater detail. By this time his ideas had moved well beyond those of the British and he carried their logic of building a world around the Great Powers to its most consistent conclusion: a world built around the United States as the nation with a special position among the great nations. At Teheran the President outlined to Stalin a postwar organization composed of three tiers: an executive committee of the United States, England, Russia, and China, plus six other nations drawn from the various major regions and the British Empire, to deal with nonmilitary matters. Whether its decision would be binding on all nations remained to be determined, but Roosevelt did not think Congress would agree. There would also be an Assembly of all nations to discuss and recommend solutions to problems, implicitly nonbinding. Lastly, and at the top, there would be a body called "The Four Policemen," the three major Allies and China, to enforce order, by military intervention if need be, on any nation threatening the peace. Later at Teheran, Roosevelt suggested that the Four Policemen have access to bases, a theme on which Washington had definite ideas in regard to its own postwar objectives.[40] Since neither Russia nor Britain, as we shall see, expressed any enthusiasm for Roosevelt's proposals, the State Department again rethought and revamped the entire subject, but within the context of certain assumptions that were explicit in Roosevelt's Teheran proposition.

The President's ideas at Teheran were not meandering, but reflected certain deep-seated views to which Hull could now only accommodate. The concept of an alliance of the Great Powers, and the relative impotence of the smaller nations, was now a part of American policy. The policy hinted for the first time that bases have a special international significance for peacekeeping and should not be considered an adjunct of the question of colonialism. Most important, however, it suggested that China would be coequal with the three Great Allies, and this implied a special status for the United States among them.

The notion that they should treat China as an important world power struck the British and Russians as absurd, and Roosevelt and Hopkins knew this. Washington fully appreciated China's doleful performance in the war against Japan and its near anarchical internal condition. In March 1943 Eden explicitly stated to Roosevelt, Hull, and Hopkins that China was probably going to have a revolution after the war, and that in any event Britain did not wish to see it ever emerge supreme in the Far East. But Roosevelt based his reasoning on different considerations, for, as Hopkins explained it, "The President feels that China, in any serious conflict of policy with Russia, would undoubtedly line up on our side."[41] That China would do so became a certainty before Teheran, for Roosevelt had met China's ruler, Chiang Kai-shek, at Cairo immediately preceding Teheran and had received assurances that he would, as reported in the conference records, "follow your leadership on the diplomatic and political questions that will be considered in the impending conference."[42] Everyone in Washington acknowledged that Chiang could hardly cope with his monumental internal problems, much less play a world role, and the Generalissimo was quite content to trade his vote for American aid at home. He gave explicit pledges of this willingness again during 1944. This dependent relationship only filled the British and Russians with suspicion as to American motives, and Churchill contemptuously referred to "the United States with her fagot-vote China" dominating the United Nations executive.[43] Washington hardly consulted the Chinese about preliminary plans for the United Nations, and while the Russians were willing to grant it membership on the Security Council they were unwilling to permit China to attend the Dumbarton Oaks planning session at which the U.S.S.R. was present. The result was a division of the first conference into two sessions, one of seven weeks and the other of nine days, with the shorter part including China conducted with such haste and realistic acknowledgment of China's international unimportance that even the usually insensitive Chinese regarded it as an affront. In fact they merely called upon China to ratify what the Great Powers had already decided. From the very inception membership in the United Nations became the object of ulterior political manipulation, even within the highest body of that organization. England could respond in kind with France, which was hardly much stronger by 1944 than China, and such competition for special privileges guaranteed that the United States would have no difficulty in creating a veto principle as part of the United Nations voting system, if only to make its control over the world organization even more foolproof.

The Americans initially proposed the principle of a Great Power veto over United Nations decisions, though it is nearly certain the British and Russians would also have insisted on it. Roosevelt decided in February 1944 that the unanimity of the Great Powers within a United Nations Security Council—to include nations with "exceptional responsibilities" —be an essential principle, save when one of the four was directly involved in a dispute, when the charter would require it to abstain.[44] By April, however, Hull removed this last reservation in regard to nonprocedural questions to make it more palatable to Congress. Hull based his reasoning on the belief, common in the Senate after World War I, that a league of equals ignored the realities of world power and artificially bound the strong to the dictates of the weak, and the Congress of the United States to the unconstitutional dictates of foreigners. The distribution of power in the United Nations, as the United States envisaged it, granted special status to the strong, and the power to intercede on their own behalf. "We should not forget that this veto power is chiefly for the benefit of the United States. . . ," he explained to the Senatorial leaders.[45] Since the State Department itself was divided on the principle of the veto being suspended in the event of a controversy to which one Security Council member was a part, the United States soon reinserted it, only to complicate the very deep suspicions of the other major Allies.

By April 1944, therefore, after much polite but noncommittal discussion with the British and Russians on the proposed United Nations structure, Hull turned his energies to the Senate to avoid the debacle that befell Wilson in 1919. Hull especially sought to cultivate the goodwill of the key Republican Senatorial spokesman in foreign affairs, Arthur H. Vandenberg, and as a result of this intimate contact with United Nations problems

Vandenberg emerged as a leading figure in American foreign policy, always sanctifying Democratic policy with Republican approval in the name of bipartisanship which in fact was based on near unanimity that was natural rather than contrived. Vandenberg, however, did articulate the general but not so sharply defined Administration assumption that the United Nations would serve the role of an instrument of a "just peace."

Vandenberg's definition of a "just peace" reflected his intense hostility toward Russian policy in Eastern Europe, a position he sincerely believed in but which his very large Polish constituency, a considerable Finnish vote, and the like also cultivated. Hull did not have to cajole Vandenberg into being an internationalist, for the Senator had been a major architect of the Republican renunciation of alleged isolationism in the Mackinac Declaration of September 1943, and he, like Theodore Roosevelt's Republicans, saw the question as one of America's international role being polarized between a lone role abroad or cooperation with others on terms deferential to American interests and power. He was a strong advocate of a powerful postwar Navy and Air Force, but United Nations joint utilization of this might would depend first on containing Russia in Eastern Europe, and as a lesser consideration, British expansion in France, North Africa, and elsewhere.[46] A durable peace would be the foundation of true internationalism, and Vandenberg believed such a peace would have to be based on just political solutions, above all with Russian cooperation. If the United Nations could become an instrument of a just peace, as part of attaining acceptable and quick political solutions, rather than a neutral structure where nations could gradually consider such problems and possibly resolve them, it was to be a useful instrumentality of American policy. Since such a functional concept was also inherent in Roosevelt's view of China, the veto power, an exceptional position for United States bases, and the like, Vandenberg was to sharpen this trend in American thought on the postwar political structure.

After the beginning of 1944 Hull kept various members of the Senate Foreign Relations Committee apprised of his work on the United Nations, and on April 25 he called in eight leading Republican and Democratic Senators for the first of a series of intensive discussions preparatory to the international conference on the United Nations that was ultimately scheduled for August 1944 at Dumbarton Oaks, Washington, D.C. The first draft of the United Nations Charter he showed them included an absolute veto with no reservations on nonprocedural issues. Though Vandenberg took his time endorsing the proposal, privately he found the United Nations plan most agreeable. "The striking thing about it," he confided in his diary, "is that it is so *conservative* from a nationalist standpoint. It is based virtually on a four-power alliance. . . . This is anything but a wild-eyed internationalist dream of a world State. . . . I am deeply impressed (and surprised) to find Hull so carefully guarding our American veto in his scheme of things." Yet as attractive as it was, Vandenberg wished to make his formal support contingent on what would be done in regard to Russian and British expansion, and he insisted that politics precede organization. "It is my argument that we should go ahead and perfect a plan for collective security; but that we should make it wholly contingent upon a *just* peace (thus strengthening the hands of those who will be seeking a *just* peace)."[47] From its inception the Americans regarded the proposed United Nations organization as a forum and an instrument for furthering their specific political ends—Eastern Europe being the most important to Vandenberg—and on this point there was precious little disagreement in Washington.

Most other Senators on the "Committee of Eight" shared Vandenberg's views and apprehensions, though ultimately they endorsed a structure that seemed compatible on principles and which they hoped might serve their political ends in practice. Hull argued a great deal to convince Senatorial skeptics that such a reconciliation might be arranged. He even included the contrived observation that the Russians were at the time fighting the war in Europe alone and might sign a separate peace with Germany, leaving the West with a much more formidable task. He was far more optimistic with the committee in his observations on Russian intentions in the postwar world than he was in other private discussions, but since the Senators seemed to link the entire United Nations to the problem of Russia, Hull did what was required of him.

For their own reasons the British and Russians came to the same instrumentalist view of the United Nations' future as Vandenberg, his Senatorial allies, and those in Washington who saw it as a useful tool of American foreign policy. They too wished to see their political objectives attained, and this colored their every response to the United Nations proposals that the Americans insistently forwarded to them.

The British clearly defined their position, and America's stand on China only helped to reinforce it. Even when they patiently went along with American proposals in which they had slight confidence they never ceased to work for regional blocs and alliances based on classical modes of diplomacy and their own premises. ". . . the responsibility in any future world organization must be related to power," Eden told the Commons in May 1944, and that concept influenced the British response to every postwar situation, for power would respond to power, and this in turn required policies that could organize states into groupings.[48] If Britain failed in this undertaking it was only because, as its own definition implied, it was no longer equal to the task of dealing with two far stronger nations. Specifically the regional council system which Britain proposed—by early 1944 it reduced it to one for Europe, another for the Western Hemisphere, and a third for Asia—was always a useful first step toward a cordon sanitaire in one place, a restriction of American involvement in another, and the like. Churchill and Eden propounded random notions, variations of a regional strategy, and several schemes up to Dumbarton Oaks, but England's deepest commitment was toward its empire and Europe, and this was the basis of its policy. The rest was necessary for good relations with its American ally and Russia, though Churchill feared there was an ulterior motive behind many of America's proposals to transfer postwar social and economic functions to the United Nations, and for this the British also were glad to have a veto. Churchill wrote Eden in May 1944:

> As I see it, the Big Three or Big Four will be the trustees or steering committee of the whole body in respect of the use of force to prevent war; but I think much larger bodies, and possibly functional bodies, would deal with the economic side. You should make it clear that we have no idea of three or four Great Powers ruling the world. . . . We should certainly not be prepared ourselves to submit to an economic, financial, and monetary system laid down, by, say, Russia, or the United States. . . .[49]

Yet it was the prime American objective in a world political organization to break up precisely such regional and economic groupings as England hoped to create, or, what was much more objectionable, continue.

The Russian position was not unlike the British in replying to the persistent Americans who hoped by alchemy to transform China into an equal of the Soviet Union. When Russia proposed a political-military commission for Europe and its allies rejected it, the United States then asked the U.S.S.R. at Teheran to endorse a vast American scheme for postwar collaboration, presumably far more difficult to implement than the essential wartime test of mutual ability to work as equals. Stalin's response had hardly evinced enthusiasm, and he made it clear that China, which would be weak at the end of the war, had no place in European affairs. And he was obviously skeptical of any plan that would impose binding decisions on the members of the organization. He raised no objection, however, to the United States' acquiring bases, but staked no claims of his own. Indeed, prior to the meeting at Dumbarton Oaks in August the Russians showed no enthusiasm for the United Nations concept, as outlined in numerous drafts sent them, and they merely asked for clarification and held their counsel.

That clarification was essential because the United States had yet to come up with an unequivocal position on the application of the veto principle. The State Department first informed the Senate Committee of Eight that the veto was absolute in regard to all nonprocedural questions to which one of the Big Four was a party. For one thing, the State Department thought the Senate would regard a veto as greater protection of

American autonomy; for another, it was not considered worthwhile to persist with the theory of holding an uncooperative nation "before the bar of world opinion" over pointless issues on which there would not, by universal agreement, be freedom of United Nations action.[50] But the State Department gave the matter further thought, and by July reversed its position once more, permitting a party to a dispute to veto only in the case of a proposal to apply United Nations force. It again allowed Security Council discussion and recommendations. At Dumbarton Oaks, however, the issue came up in the form of a United States proposal not to permit a nation party to a dispute to veto a United Nations action. Moreover, the American position on regional groupings, unquestionably with Latin America in mind, wavered before the British pressures for such an arrangement. The State Department was then willing to permit vague powers to such regional groupings that might emerge. The resolution of these vacillations was deferred until Dumbarton Oaks, but Russian objections could be anticipated in their request on July 9 not to include the question of peaceful settlements of disputes on the agenda. The Russians had yet to develop their position, the Americans theirs.

The Dumbarton Oaks Conference opened August 21, getting off at once to an ominous start. The United States and England agreed to give France a provisional seat immediately and make it the fifth permanent member of the Security Council, upon Four Power recognition. Now the West had four of the five votes, making the veto privilege somewhat more precious to the Russians, and as if to emphasize the importance of this defensive principle, the United States asked that Brazil too be given a permanent seat on the Security Council. The suggestion of Brazil, which caught everyone by surprise, was an obvious effort to counter Britain's advocacy of France and its effort to gain recognition of De Gaulle's government. Although he did not press it too strongly, Roosevelt thought "the Brazilian matter was a card up his sleeve."[51] From this point on the Russians insisted on an absolute veto at every stage and never wavered from that position. When the question of who should sign the United Nations Declaration arose, the United States proposed including eight nations not at war with the Axis—six from Latin America. During this discussion of Brazil, the Russians, as if to suggest they could play the game as well, suddenly recommended that each of their sixteen constituent republics receive a vote, a suggestion which left Stettinius "breathless." Though the Russians dropped the proposal for tactical purposes during the remainder of the conference, to Hull and Washington it portrayed Soviet intentions in the worst possible light, and surely as qualitatively different from the Western effort to pack the Security Council and General Assembly.[52] It was an obvious Russian warning to the American effort not to press domination of the new organization too far, and a useful trading point.

The veto question proved insoluble and hovered about the discussions continuously, because it impinged on the issue of whether the Russians would permit the West via the Security Council to define for them a just position in case of the nearly certain controversies they might expect with, say, Poland or Turkey.] The Americans at Dumbarton Oaks could not convince the Russians to endorse the position that a party involved in a dispute should not be permitted to vote on a question—which is to say, exercise a veto. No amount of pleading could compel Gromyko to change his position on this issue, despite dire American warnings of its implications for future world unity. On September 8 Roosevelt appealed directly to Stalin concerning the issue, threatening that "public opinion in the United States would never understand or support" such a reservation, and the small nations would see it as an attempt to place the Great Powers "above the law." Stalin's reply again revealed his belief Great Power unity and collaboration were crucial to effective action, and no artificial mechanism, he implied, could serve as a substitute for a serious resolution of interests and viewpoints. This was the position Russia had taken since Teheran, and as if to reveal vacillations in the American position as the cause of the fault, he added "The original American proposal for establishing a special voting procedure . . . is, I think, sound."[53] The Soviet Union was not going to alter its stand.

Despite the State Department's effort to convince the Committee of Eight the Dumbarton Oaks Conference had resolved most of the outstanding problems, in fact it had resolved almost none of the crucial issues, in large part because American policy still wavered. The conference left hanging the question of regionalism and its role in the United Nations structure, and the delegates did not even discuss the trusteeship question, impinging on future American bases on former mandated islands, because of the opposition of the United States Joint Chiefs of Staff. Gromyko behaved very cooperatively at the conference, Hull concluded, but other than routine organizational matters, they had accomplished very little of substance. The British attitude was no less agreeable, but wise and aloof, for as Sir Alexander Cadogan, British Under Secretary of State, warned at the opening of the session, "we should not attempt too closely to define what is perhaps undefinable. . . . no machine will work unless there is, at any rate on the part of the Great Powers, a will to work it. . . ."[54] During the course of the conference Britain indicated it wished to see a Four Power agreement on basic political issues before voting on the final draft of a United Nations Charter. In effect England took the Russian position on the need to agree rather than expect formal organizations to solve problems automatically. For on the veto question the conference only brushed over the total deadlock on this crucial issue and decided to try to deal with the problem later.

The Geopolitics of the United Nations before Yalta

After Dumbarton Oaks the United States was compelled to reconcile its ambivalence and come up with a coordinated definition of a new world organization. The American concept of the United Nations was always entirely political in every objective, but structural proposals varied and Washington had yet to resolve certain key questions. Hull saw the United Nations as an instrument for breaking up world economic and power blocs and creating the preconditions for a single world economy, but he also expected the British and Russians to acknowledge the special prerogatives and power of the United States so that its very real predominance would raise America above that of the other major Allies. Hence he was anxious to have a veto, plus an additional vote via China, as well as a large pro-American membership in the General Assembly. Stimson and the military also wanted special recognition of American power, but had fewer illusions that the United Nations would serve as a substitute for classical diplomacy based on power, and they were especially interested in obtaining a special concession for American bases. The Joint Chiefs of Staff did not expect a postwar world order of equals, and in August 1944 predicted that "Both in an absolute sense and relative to the United States and Russia, the British Empire will emerge from the war having lost ground both economically and militarily."[55] Vandenberg and the Senate wished to use the United Nations as an adjunct to a peace settlement satisfactory to the United States and a means of handling the Russians. Roosevelt was able to synthesize most of these themes, being somewhat more partial than Hull to an organization that the United States unmistakably controlled. None of these factions planned for a neutral, unaligned structure of equal states. All saw the need for a special United Nations body of Great Powers, with the United States playing a predominant role among them. By the end of 1944 it was necessary to decide whether the United States would tolerate an absolute veto, or if the United States would now ask for special base rights as part of the transition from the League of Nations mandated islands to the United Nations, and whether the Western Hemisphere would be placed, for all practical purposes, beyond the jurisdiction of the other Allies.

Early in the discussions of a future United Nations organization the United States determined to link the question of the acquisition of American bases in the postwar world to the formation of a world organization. To make this position appear less predatory, they frequently joined the subject to the question of colonialism, which only aggravated the British, who wanted to hear nothing of the matter. The American position on colonialism was extremely cautious, and they frequently cited the Philippines as a model of desirable evolution elsewhere. Briefly, the imperial nations were to give the colonial people "protection, encouragement, moral support, and material aid" to prepare for independence, which the colonial powers would grant "progressively" and at the "practicable" moment. The only immediate change the United States wished to see in the colonies was in making their natural resources available to "the world as a whole."[56] Discussions of taking various colonies away from one power, such as French Indochina or Korea, invariably included the proposal they be given to another for this necessary transition period of as long as thirty years. "At no time," Hull later wrote, "did we press Britain, France, or The Netherlands for an immediate grant of self-government to their colonies. Our thought was that it would come after an adequate period of years, short or long. . . ."[57] This concept of trusteeship blended well with United States desires to acquire bases in the Japanese Pacific islands and elsewhere, for it was impossible to advocate granting total independence to former possessions and expect to continue to use them freely. [Hence the American discussion assumed an aura of moralism which struck the British as somewhat less than truly pious in its obvious concern for an immediate share of the economic spoils of colonialism.]

The leaders in Washington only seriously disagreed over how to obtain postwar bases, and also whether they should be trusteeships or outright possessions. During the first months of 1943 the State and Navy departments publicly declared American interest in "space in certain quarters of the world for sea and air bases," especially the Pacific.[58] Roosevelt discussed it with Chiang, with a view to obtaining bases in China, and he then raised it at Teheran, and Stalin did not object. In the months before Dumbarton Oaks the War Department and Joint Chiefs sustained a campaign to obtain bases "to maintain our power in the Pacific," and they privately lobbied Congress, hoping especially to obtain base rights in the Philippines before the United States granted independence.[59] At the behest of the Joint Chiefs the State Department forbade its delegation at Dumbarton Oaks to discuss postwar trusteeships, and when the Russians and others wanted to know why, they told them the matter would require consideration at some later date. By that obscure time the officials in Washington hoped a definite American policy would exist. By Yalta, therefore, the United States had claimed a special position in the Pacific, and the remaining question was how could it make the United Nations serve as an instrument of that policy, or should it, as Stimson urged, simply annex the desired former Japanese islands. To preserve the option to choose either policy, the United States continued its conservative position on freedom to dependent territories, adding that essentially independent regional advisory committees composed of the concerned powers represent the United Nations in the various areas where the United Nations established trusteeships.[60]

To hedge against contingencies that might arise at the founding of the

United Nations, the State Department, with Roosevelt's approval, energetically worked to increase the number of states qualified to be invited to the first United Nations Conference and amenable to American political direction. At Dumbarton Oaks the United States suggested inviting forty-four nations, including eight not at war with the Axis, to which the Russians retorted by proposing invitations to the sixteen Soviet "republics." Of these forty-four, twenty-three were obviously going to prove receptive to American advice, and after November the United States asked nonbelligerent nations to declare war against the Axis. The Americans sought British opinion of this strategy, but the Foreign Office demurred by stating that the problem was a peculiarly American one and not for them to comment upon. But whether the Allies permitted these nations into the United Nations or not, the United States determined to resist Russia's request for sixteen seats.

These American tactics caused the British leaders in late November to reconsider the veto question in light of emerging American domination of the United Nations, and they split on the controversy in a manner that consciously reinforced the chances of the U.S.S.R. to obtain an absolute veto power at Yalta. The defensive possibilities of an absolute veto obviously attracted Churchill in particular, and he argued that no matter what the formal structure of the United Nations, "The only hope for the world is the agreement of the three Great Powers."[61] Cadogan proposed several British strategies, preferring a compromise somewhere between the American and Soviet positions on the veto. Sir Stafford Cripps, Minister of Aircraft Production, urged outright acceptance of the Russian position, and in the end the War Ministry rejected the Cadogan proposals while Churchill now inclined toward the Russian position and refused to aid Roosevelt in pressuring them on this question before Yalta. In short, the British were not ready to trust an international body so obviously and aggressively under American leadership. The State Department by late October had melancholically concluded the Russian and British positions coincided.

The best the State Department could do to meet this obvious rejection of its persistent definition of a world organization was to introduce extremely complex veto procedures that failed to persuade the British and Russians that the Americans had done something to alter the substance of the controversy. Vandenberg, however, on the false assumption that everyone but Russia accepted the American veto proposal, only reinforced the State Department's intransigence, and in late November extracted Stettinius' agreement to a United Nations defined to include the right of nations such as Poland to come before the United Nations to plead, for example, for a return of the territory beyond the Curzon Line. ". . . under such circumstances," the Senator noted, "I would welcome the earliest possible organization of the League."[62]

The State Department managed to please the Senators anxious to "*really speak up* to Stalin," as Vandenberg put it, but Stalin could not be convinced.[63] On November 6 Stalin publicly declared that the way to resolve differences among the three Great Powers was to maintain the unity of interests—implicitly votes and force would not alter the situation. When Roosevelt sent Stalin the complex but inconsequential American modifications of the earlier veto principle, he also suggested to the Russian that the Soviet Union's selfless acceptance would increase the "moral prestige" of the Great Powers. Stalin only responded that such artificial devices in lieu of true unity would cause open and premature splits in the Alliance and unnecessarily complicate international affairs. The Russians, like the English, failed to comprehend American appeals to piety, especially in light of ill-concealed efforts to control votes in the future United Nations. In the month before Yalta the Russians made it clear that they would not welcome blocs in any form, even in the name of internationalism. For the first time, significantly, the Soviet press categorically attacked the concept of a Western European bloc. The problem of possible Western hostility in the future was beginning to weigh heavily on their minds, and they would not relinquish the veto.

The outright Russian refusal to meet the insistent American appeals on the United Nations veto, in the belief, as Harriman put it, that "The court . . . is packed against them," the United States interpreted as an ominous indication of Soviet unwillingness to cooperate in the future international security organization, and implicitly the world in general.[64] This sense of apprehension ultimately grew to proportions of outrage, as if the United Nations as the Americans created and defined it over Russian and English skepticism and objections could be identified with the true interests of the entire world. The other Allies, however, saw it as indistinguishable from American foreign policy, and for the moment, before Yalta, at least Stimson and Forrestal also understood it in this light. Stimson failed to comprehend the importance of the controversy over the veto principle, and told Roosevelt at the end of December that Stalin's concept of an absolute veto, in case "of our having a row with Mexico," might prove useful someday to American interests as well.[65] In any event, he warned Stettinius several weeks before Yalta, "fundamental problems should be at least discussed and if possible an understanding reached between the big guarantor nations before you endeavor to set up principles in a world organization which may clash with realities."[66] Such admonitions became ever more rare with each passing month.

The reader will note that I said nothing in the last dozen pages regarding the general political principles of American peace aims at this time. These were enunciated almost exclusively as part of an essentially organizational theory of internationalism in which American national interests became the foundations of the United States' concept of international welfare. Implicit in America's activity for the United Nations was its belief that it could organize the United Nations with American interests foremost in mind, and that the rest of the world would gladly welcome the world organization as part of an American-led century that would redound to the universal weal. There were no detailed stated political principles in this American policy, only an international system. The United States first proposed the veto concept to obtain Senatorial approval, but when the scheme failed to find Russian or British endorsement in the precise form America desired, it then regarded the veto as a sign of malicious intent and elevated it to a point of principle.

That the United States had to and would create a United Nations it could dominate was by Yalta apparent to all the Allies, who failed to understand that the moralism the United States now attached to its international plans was sincere, and therefore perhaps that much more dangerous. China on the Security Council, a packed Assembly, suspension of discussions on a number of matters of direct interest to the United States, a vagueness on regionalism that persisted until the formation of the United Nations itself —all these events served to disturb the other Allies. They only tolerated United States proposals and would have been quite as content to work apart from a new and complicating international organization that might now unnecessarily muddy the international scene and impede the practice of classic diplomacy, which would in any case be their final resort.

By Yalta the United States was well on its way to creating moral rhetoric around the United Nations that it used to set a standard of conduct for others, but which only obfuscated America's own intentions and the purposes of the organization. Since the other Great Powers could hardly agree to work within the context of a world organization one nation so clearly controlled, they were left only with the alternative of working outside it, presumably for their uniquely selfish purposes. Thus the United Nations, even before Yalta, assumed the role of an American moral bludgeon against others, but in the name of a world community that the United States was in fact to dominate at the level of United Nations representation. The belief that such a world system would succeed was sheer idealism only in the sense that it was unobtainable, and not in that it was selfless. If Washington was about to declare the American century, the Russians and British would resist. When the Americans took the United Nations problem to Yalta the possibility of the Allies' finding a solution to this dilemma was almost nil, and nothing in subsequent American policy on the United Nations or in the far more detailed statement of United States peace aims on an economic level reassured the Allies.

CHAPTER

12

PLANNING
FOR PEACE, II:
GREAT BRITAIN IN
THEORY AND PRACTICE

THE KEY to the attainment of American postwar objectives for the world economy was Great Britain, for prior to the war the sterling bloc and North America accounted for about one-half of the total world trade. If the two nations could agree, then the rest of the world would be unable to resist their power and would inevitably fall into line. To fail to reach a joint accommodation would thwart the United States in the achievement of its most important single war aim: reconstructing the world economy along Hullian lines. Throughout the war the planners in Washington correlated present problems to future goals, hoping to use the leverage of American power to convince, and if need be, pressure England into accepting American definitions of the desirable postwar world economy. The manner in which America implemented this policy toward England during the course of the war anticipated the postwar realities and the United States' functional interpretation of the world's economic welfare.

The British had to juxtapose their own theoretical preferences against the titanic economic problems emerging from the war and their beleaguered economic condition. They had substantially liquidated their vast overseas investments to pay for needed military matériel, in part because of the American cash-and-carry policy preceding Lend-Lease. They could therefore expect to enter the postwar world with drastically reduced foreign earnings from investments, and only a radical growth of their exports might prevent eventual impoverishment in the sort of world economy the United States envisaged. During the war Britain financed much of its effort by depending on the dollar and gold earnings of the other sterling-bloc members, which included the colonies and Argentina, Spain, Portugal, Turkey, and many other smaller nations producing raw materials and working through the United Kingdom Commercial Corporation. The result was a vast English debt to its fellow sterling-bloc members, and the creation of a potential new tool in the postwar period for tying up the sterling-bloc economies even more than in the prewar period.

Despite the temptation to use the sterling bloc to solve predictable postwar problems, it is fair to suggest that the principles of the American trade program appealed to the majority of British leaders, depending on how and when the United States would implement it. They were not willing to assign the Americans a blank check, and indeed insisted on escape clauses, due not only to their apprehensions concerning the possible gravity of their postwar economic plight, but to their unpleasant past experiences with the American interpretation of the Open Door as well as free trade. After all, the British had risen to world economic preeminence behind the banner of free trade at the end of the nineteenth century. Their attraction to the system caused them to sustain it in part after World War I despite higher American tariffs and aggressive American attacks on their Middle Eastern oil concessions and control over the prices and output of world tin, rubber, and other mineral raw materials. At the same time, the Americans systematically excluded them from Western Hemisphere oil, eventually controlling 82 percent of the world's critical oil production, and authorized their own price-fixing export associations. Meanwhile the United States demanded that Europe repay its war debts, which was only possible by dollar-earning exports to an increasingly protectionist United States. At the London Conference of 1933 the Americans embarked on a policy of national economic isolation, and from 1941 onward asked the world to do what they would not do themselves before that time, and had yet to give full evidence they would do in the future.

Within Great Britain prewar Liberals favored the principles of the Hullian program, and it especially attracted the Labour party, which saw it as some sort of anti-imperialism. Certain British trade interests saw that in the long run such a world economy might aid more than it could hurt British exports, and Keynes himself, the most important architect of the British position, while somewhat more concerned with maintaining stable employment and economic growth at home and the possibility of an American postwar depression, was cautiously willing to move in the direction the Americans advocated. Churchill, pragmatic as ever, was prepared to try it both ways, returning to a closed sterling system should the Americans show bad faith. Posed against them were the British industrial interests, centered about the Federation of British Industries, who wanted protection to export to the sterling bloc and defend themselves from cheaper American goods. They and a number of senior civil servants in the Foreign Office and Treasury reminded the government of the inconsistency of the American position every time an example of it arose, the first being in the autumn of 1941 when the Americans demanded Britain buy a minimum quota of high-priced American wheat on the world market.[1]

[For these reasons the British supported the basic theoretical assumptions of the Hullian proposals insofar as they stood for more than just American hegemony over the world economy, always insisting on the escape clauses that would permit them to save the sterling bloc as their major postwar crutch should that prove necessary.] They understood, as well, that the Americans would link the aid Britain so desperately needed to fight the war to their willingness to support this highly articulated American war aim, and that they could ill afford to reject the American position outright. The Americans for their part comprehended Britain's critical role in their economic plans, and the power that they exercised at the time over British planning by virtue of Lend-Lease and potential postwar credits and loans. Though America talked of multilateral world trade, in fact the attainment of its ends depended almost entirely on bilateral agreements between England and the United States which the Americans were determined to obtain. All of these considerations arose throughout the haggling over Article VII of the proposed Lend-Lease Agreement during the last half of 1941. Keynes and other British representatives threw all of the inconsistencies of past American policies in the faces of Ambassador Winant, who fully endorsed Hull's program, Assistant Secretary of State Dean Acheson, and others. Despite American alarm that the British might not sign the Lend-Lease Agreement altogether, they did so in February 1942 both out of necessity and conviction.

There was hardly an occasion during the next two years when the American government failed to attempt to consolidate and strengthen the British commitment to the American definition of the meaning of Article VII for the postwar world. By and large the British avoided discussions and further detailing of their commitments as much as possible, preferring for the moment to spell out the conditions that they might confront after the war. When Eden came to Washington in March 1943 he arrived unprepared to talk about such matters. The Keynes plan was so obviously lopsided in its deference to British interests, and the American rebuttal so much more unacceptable than the status quo, that the British hedged as much as possible. In sheer self-defense the aggressiveness of American plans and pressures forced them to respond in a manner intended to avoid as much offense and commitment as possible. The American government did not take any chances, for everyone of consequence in Washington was

convinced of the necessity of pinning the English down while the tools for
doing so were still in hand. That such bilateral talks would lead only to the
creation of a joint sphere of influence in the world economy struck no one
as incompatible with opposition to others' creating political spheres of influence.

Lend-Lease was the major leverage of American policy—not merely
the imprecise Article VII, but the program's actual implementation, leaving
the British economy ill equipped to resist American objectives at the end of
the war. On January 1, 1943, the State, Treasury, and War departments,
with the endorsement of Roosevelt and Henry Wallace among others,
unilaterally defined the administrative policy of Lend-Lease as being
such "that the United Kingdom's gold and dollar balances should not
be permitted to be less than about $600 million nor above about $1 billion."[2] Since their last known holdings at the time were $928 million, in
effect the Americans were going to hold the British to their existing position. Merely altering what they expected the British to pay for in dollars or
gold and what they would include in Lend-Lease could control this
balance. In addition the American government would ask Britian for raw
materials from sterling-bloc nations as reciprocal Lend-Lease for which the
Americans were paying dollars at the time. The Cabinet committee also
decided that since the British had available to them, if only as debts, the
dollar and gold holdings of the sterling bloc and empire, they would consider and treat the relationship of the British position to the empire as an
integrated economic proposition.

The implications of this policy were critical, and in short order the
British government correctly argued that its use of sterling-bloc dollars and
gold only represented postwar debts that would have to be repaid. [Accord-
ing to the reasoning in Washington, if Britain's postwar position were too
weak, presumably holding less than $600 million, necessity would compel
it to resort to stringent internal trade controls and embark on an aggressive
export program to remedy its plight—thereby damaging the implementation of the Hullian program. If it were too strong, however, presumably
holding more than $1 billion, it would not need postwar United States
credits, which would not only provide an important investment outlet, but
would also allow the United States to impose terms designed to consolidate
British support for American world economic objectives. It is not at all
clear how the experts arrived at these figures as a mythical balance point,
but in fact the United States administered the Lend-Lease program
throughout 1943 on this assumption, despite the eventual split in Washington over the ideal figure necessary to put the strategy into effect.]

What the United States expected the British to pay for under Lend-
Lease soon became intertwined with the problems of what and when they
would permit Britain to export before the end of the war, and the Ameri-

can desire to obtain sterling-bloc raw materials, for which they were paying about $200 million a year, as reciprocal Lend-Lease. The British quickly pointed out that their use of sterling-bloc holdings of dollars and gold represented a growth in their liabilities, which in fact had rocketed $2.6 billion since Lend-Lease began. Moreover, they resented the American insistence that they not increase exports abroad to earn gold and dollars, in part because they were hardly in a position to do so, but also because they publicly pledged in September 1941 not to export materials in short supply in the United States, incorporating materials received under Lend-Lease, or goods similar to those received under the program. The rest was their business, even if now abstract, and a slight on British honor. The British found the problem especially irritating, and in July 1943 submitted several *aides-mémoire* to the State Department concerning "an impression, however false, that there may be some desire on the American side to supplant British traders in the established and traditional markets, not only for the war period but permanently thereafter." In fact, as English businessmen had complained to their government, Americans had been quick to take over many British markets in Latin America, and the British now made emphatic that they "attach importance to the principle that no advantage in world markets shall accrue to either country at the expense of the other by reason of sacrifices made in the interest of the effective prosecution of the war."[3] If the United States, and especially Hull, persisted in asking for raw materials as free reciprocal Lend-Lease, State Department advisers warned that the British might also insist that America not reexport products using these materials. In September the British agreed to increase their reciprocal Lend-Lease in raw materials, but they demanded greater American sympathy for their reserve holdings, now passing $1 billion.

American righteousness nettled the British as the United States unilaterally made plans to keep them neither too weak nor too strong at the same time that it invaded prewar British markets and made direct efforts to break into the colonies. The most critical question of all, oil, as we shall see later in this chapter, was now moving inextricably to the foreground. On August 2 the British asked that the Americans reconsider the entire export question in light of mounting British deficits, and that the United States government agree to the policy in the Foreign Office's July *aide-mémoire* concerning the preservation of prewar markets. The State Department could only reply that the British proposal seemed "unduly restrictive," and they insisted that London tie this to essentially free, reverse Lend-Lease in raw materials, which in fact meant a reduction in British access to dollars.[4] By the fall of 1943 the interrelationship of Lend-Lease, prospective exports and the loss of prewar markets, and the American desire to maintain British dollar and gold reserves at a unilaterally fixed point meshed to create serious tension between the two nations and cast grave doubt on American willingness to treat Britain as an equal in the postwar world economy. British dollar and gold holdings sharply increased to well over $1 billion in late 1943, reaching $1.3 or $1.7 billion by the end of the year, according to British and American estimates respectively, and the British bitterly complained of the American intention to reduce it. Churchill, Hopkins, and Roosevelt discussed the matter no later than December 1943. Their sterling liabilities, the British insisted, were seven times their dollar-gold holdings, which in turn were only one-eighteenth of America's gold reserves, about one-third of France's, and only slightly larger than China's or Belgium's gold-dollar holdings.

The State Department was embarrassed, for it refused formally to agree to the British demands not to exploit their wartime export weaknesses, and at the same time they approved a policy which required a reduction of Lend-Lease by some $300 million to bring the British balances down. They also wondered whether a reserve limit of $1 billion was really sufficient. In any event the export issue, according to Acheson, "has produced friction between the two countries out of all proportion to any substantial question involved."[5] By November, Acheson could see the merit of the British position concerning their gold and dollar reserves, in part because the State Department made the decision to limit them without first consulting the British, thereby impinging on their control over their own economy in a rather blatant manner, but also out of fear that it would now drive the British to do the very thing which the State Department feared most—refuse to cooperate with the Americans after the war. He asked that Washington substitute a new formula, based on a six- or seven-to-one ratio of short-term liabilities to dollar and gold reserves, for a flat ceiling. The Treasury Department blocked any change, despite the fact that Morgenthau admitted there was some merit to Britain's position that American policy would jeopardize its postwar recovery.

During January and February 1944 Roosevelt again endorsed the Treasury position to keep British balances at no more than $1 billion, especially by reducing Lend-Lease civilian goods with a relatively long life, goods that America might want to sell later. British Treasury representatives in the United States emphatically warned Washington of the long-term implications of the roughshod treatment that they had received, and the State Department belatedly realized that it had predicated its earlier policy on an abstract reserve level which was patently incorrect. "If the British are to be able to cooperate with us in multilateral solutions of trade and financial problems," the State Department warned Roosevelt in February 1944, then "they must finish the war with enough assets to carry through such a program. Even as things stand now, it would be difficult for the British to consider unfreezing sterling at or near the end of the war, or giving up many of their other economic controls . . . we thereby reduce our chance to achieve the basic economic policy we want and need." During February and March 1944, when Roosevelt made the entire issue the primary responsibility of the Treasury Department, Roosevelt and Churchill had frigid exchanges on the matter, the acrimony remaining only slightly below the surface. "We have not shirked our duty or indulged in an easy way of living," Churchill reminded Roosevelt. "We have already spent practically all our convertible foreign investments in the struggle. We alone of the Allies will emerge from the war with great overseas war debts. I do not know what would happen if we were now asked to disperse our last liquid reserves required to meet pressing needs, or how I could put my case to Parliament without it affecting public sentiment in the most painful manner. . . ."⁶ Roosevelt was not moved.

American insistence on using Lend-Lease to further acceptance of Article VII among the members of the sterling bloc aggravated British suspicion of the purposes of the American policy. In this regard the problem of India was especially important for political and economic reasons. The character of any agreement with the representatives of the so-called Indian government, which was only fiscally independent, might imply a recognition of a greater degree of independence than the British thought desirable. Beyond this was the sheer economic importance of India to England as a result of the war. By February 1944 India had become a major creditor of Britain, to the extent of about $2.8 billion in sterling balances which the nature of the sterling bloc would ultimately compel India to liquidate in purchases within the bloc if bloc dollar earnings were too low to permit any other recourse. India as a member of the sterling bloc represented a closed door to American exports, and since the 1942 United States Mission under Henry F. Grady the Indians knew of American hopes to enter the Indian market. From that time on, breaking down the sterling barrier was the key to American penetration.

The Lend-Lease negotiations of early 1943 with the so-called Indian government impinged on all these political and economic questions, for the Indians were anxious to sign any document on certain minimum terms which implied a greater degree of control over their own affairs. Whatever industrial leaders existed in that land supported Indian nationalism because British low-tariff policy had stymied India's development in order to conserve it as a British market. They were therefore suspicious of Article VII's implied support for low tariffs and free trade, and William Phillips, Roosevelt's personal representative to India, reported "a growing sense of uneasiness in business circles with regard to American economic intentions towards India now and after the war." The State Department refused to remove Article VII, but gave the kindest possible interpretation to it, and Dean Acheson denied the validity of the impression the Indian Agent General in Washington reported to him "that the [Indian] Government, having won its fiscal independence from the British, was now compromising it by the agreement with the United States."[7] In the end the Indians refused to sign more than a cautious Reciprocal Aid Agreement, and later the United States government insisted that Britain, their debtor, guarantee certain of India's later silver loans, a position that greatly offended Indian nationalists. The British were not overly impressed when Hull assured Eden in March 1943 that the American government was in regard to Indian independence trying "to keep down the discussions here in every possible way. . . ." Since the Americans based their treatment of England's dollar and gold resources on the total holdings of the sterling bloc and empire, any crack in that economic system posed the gravest threat to the possible future deficits of an England now systematically drawing on all the resources at the bloc's command.

Since 1941 the United States had asked Australia, New Zealand, and South Africa, three of the most powerful members of the bloc, to conclude new trade agreements, and England actively obstructed American efforts. Hull in August 1943 asked Winant to pressure the British into ceasing their interference immediately, or else "the generally favorable present opportunity to negotiate worthwhile trade agreements will be lost. . . ."[8] The Dominions were willing, but their defection could only represent a major threat to the sterling bloc, and the British held the entire issue in abeyance. Before they would willingly give up their last economic fortress they would demand something tangible from the Americans in return. By the spring of 1944, when specific plans for postwar economic collaboration were at a much more advanced stage, the British felt that they had every justification in the light of merciless American conduct to be wary about American intentions and to insist on suitable protective loopholes.

British Second Thoughts

The issues at stake between the United States and England were raw materials, oil in particular, export markets, and the general structure of the postwar world economy. They barely concealed all of these divisive problems from the public, and the business press of both nations gave them much attention. "There will be no open break," *Business Week* reported in March 1944, "But the breach is already too serious to be ignored."[9] The necessity of fighting the common enemy would require preservation of a semblance of unity, but there was no doubt that the conflict was now corrosive and deep-seated. Britain, the highly influential *Economist* of London commented editorially in April, would agree to "the acceptance of about three-quarters of the American thesis both on currency and commercial policy," but they could not rush into hastily fulfilling it during the immediate transitional period after the war.[10] On April 21 Churchill addressed the Commons on postwar economic policy in a manner that now publicly revealed that the British would insist on sufficient contingencies to protect themselves from the risks of a world economy modeled on American desires. He "safeguarded the structure of Imperial Preference," Churchill recalled, and he reviewed the numerous clauses and contingencies that he insisted on inserting in the Atlantic Charter and Article VII:

> . . . we were no more committed to the abolition of Imperial Preference than the American Government were committed to the abolition of their high protective tariffs. The discussion as to how a greater volume of trade and a more harmonious flow of trade can be created in the immediate post-war years in agreement, leaves us, in every respect, so far as action is concerned, perfectly free.[11]

Churchill's comment, while true in theory, nevertheless ignored that the significance of Lend-Lease was not merely in Article VII, but in the effects its administration would have on Britain's functional postwar economic freedom as opposed to its theoretical preferences. If anything was designed to cause the Americans to intensify their effort to tailor the British financial condition to the point where cooperation on American terms would become an unavoidable necessity, such statements surely served that purpose.

Publicly the State Department insisted that the majority of British leaders endorsed the American position, but privately they rededicated themselves to making certain that the British would really do so. This meant renewed conversations, and of course, during the summer of 1944, finalizing the Bretton Woods Agreement. At the same time the insistent British need to export to increase their dollar and gold earnings threw a pallor over the entire course of Anglo-American relations on this issue. And at every turn, as we shall see, disputes over oil heightened the ill-concealed crisis in the two nations' joint postwar planning.

Of the Keynes and White plans for postwar monetary collaboration, the Bretton Woods Conference accepted the American plan in principle while it approved in fact the British suspension clauses on its implementation. The Americans based their scheme on the desire to grant the enormous credits which the new banks would raise on the American money market at substantial interest charges. The British plan was more inflationary, but neither based their calculations on the assumption of a total collapse in the world economy. In the end of course both arrangements hardly met the needs of the postwar world economy, but only those of their promoters. At this time Washington objected most to the British insistence on timetables that delayed the date when American plans would become operative. But so long as a flood of American goods was filling the British prewar export markets while England was devoting a much larger share of its industrial capacity to essential military production, the British could hardly plunge into commitments in a world economy that might be radically different from any they had known.

The British persistence in postponing the implementation of American plans was extremely irritating to the American leaders, but especially to Hull. When Richard Law, the British Minister of State, called on him at the end of July, Hull gave him a very stern lecture.

> I said that unless the businessmen in our two countries recognized that we had to turn over a new page in economic affairs . . . there would simply be no foundation for any stable peace structure in the future. On the contrary, there would be the inevitable seeds of future wars in the form of vast unemployment and hunger throughout the world. . . . if we postponed such a tremendous undertaking, many of its supporters would take entirely too much for granted and would become quiescent and inactive, which would be fatal. . . . it would be very hazardous to wait until the war was over. . . .[12]

So Hull insisted, believing that American power to define affairs by that time would have diminished with the decline of the unifying Axis menace.

"The success or failure of the United States and of Great Britain in harmonizing their trade policies and activities will affect decisively all other nations," Feis wrote in 1944.[13] It was one thing to urge the British to abdicate to the American proposals, quite another to make it safe for them to do so. The State Department by the fall of 1944 realized that the Lend-Lease policy of managing Britain's reserves was well on its way toward backfiring. America could seek advantages in the world economy, the department felt, for that was the purpose of the entire Hullian program, but it could not afford a Pyrrhic victory. The British, Hull advised Roosevelt in a long memorandum in September, could ultimately solve their problems only "by the adoption . . . of a liberal commercial policy. . . ." But the internal pressures on them not to do so would be strong and were increasing, and it was now vital that the United States relieve as much as possible the short-term British problems the war created to permit them to cooperate with the United States trade program. The United States should now permit Britain to export more to strengthen its reserve position, but not under circumstances which "will stir up the resentment of our export manufacturers and traders."[14] The Lend-Lease program, which had driven the British away from American objectives, Hull proposed now be reconstructed to fit the attainment of "our international economic program."[15] Now was the time to act, before it was too late. The State Department's position was easier to formulate than to put into effect, for in principle it too felt Lend-Lease mechanisms ought to pressure the British into supporting the American program. The department now disagreed only on the level at which the British would be neither too strong nor too weak to cooperate. Their solicitude for American economic interests abroad was at least as great as any other agency in Washington. The practical consequence of this ambiguous formula was that only the British were asked to do something tangible in support of Hullian objectives.

Since it was much easier for Washington to agree on what to ask the British than on what to give in return, the Americans compelled Churchill at the Quebec Conference of September 1944 to listen to more of their cajolery on the question, including a linkage of Lend-Lease to the German problem in a manner that proved both fruitless and irritating. Hopkins gave Roosevelt the cue:

> I think it important, in Quebec, that you tell the Prime Minister how strongly you feel about knocking down some of the trade barriers to get somewhere in terms of world trade. I have a feeling that the Prime Minister thinks that that is a pet hobby of Secretary Hull's. . . . I think it is essential to our future bargaining with Great Britain that you disabuse the Prime Minister's mind of this.[16]

The President duly informed Churchill, and for a brief period Hull's arguments impressed Roosevelt to the extent of seriously considering using Lend-Lease to provide important reconstruction aid to England in return for its unequivocal support of American economic objectives. Most of his advisers, including Stimson and Hull, thought this gesture went too far in meeting British needs, and the scheme soon died as did many of Roosevelt's first impulses.

At the end of September, Hull, ill and his retirement imminent, made a lengthy final plea to Roosevelt to pressure genuine British support for Article VII "as being . . . indispensable to conditions in which world peace could survive. . . . no collective system of security can be expected to work unless adequate measures are taken in the field of world economics. . . ." Hull's document is of great interest in revealing all of the elements and vacillations in American policy, even from week to week. Hull summarized the split that existed in the British Cabinet since April of that year over proceeding with discussions for the implementation of Article VII. "Naturally we don't know at this time the extent to which public opinion and Congress will support a program for the reduction of trade barriers," a point, he failed to mention, that was also a major reason for British hesitancy before they opened wide their remaining privileges to American penetration. "What is important, however, is that the British Government agree *now* that they will not be the obstacle if we are prepared to move along in that direction." In brief, the British had to trust America sufficiently to give a blank check on its good faith. But now Hull, contrary to his position earlier the same month, urged caution in using Lend-Lease to make it possible for England to join with America on trade matters. "My suggestion would be that we not proceed too rapidly with the implementation of plans for lend-lease aid . . . beyond the direct strategic needs of the Pacific war until we are able to ascertain a little more clearly the attitude of the British on these commercial policy questions. . . ." British policy in Argentina, where "we are not receiving that measure of British cooperation which is essential," warranted circumspection on Lend-Lease aid as well.[17]

Hull, like most American leaders, also appreciated the political dimensions of economic power, and although he wished Britain rebuilt as a major market and safe credit risk—only acceptance of his program could warrant the belief that it would attain that status—he was also willing to use economic power to extract political cooperation. For the rest of 1944 State Department advisers urged pinning the British down, and showed less and less sympathy for their economic plight as the British hesitated. Everywhere, from the Middle East and Latin America to direct conferences, any discussion of foreign economic policy with the British moved from bad to worse. "The combination of all these things," John D. Hickerson, the department's chief expert on Britain, warned in November, "may bring about an uproar which will result in a situation that will make U.S.-U.K. relations after World War I (and God knows they were bad then) look like a love feast by comparison."[18]

Hull's reference to Argentina impinged on the unpleasant controversy that was again emerging with Britain over its renewed desire to increase exports, which by mid-1944 was increasingly possible given the clear victory over Germany the military predicted for 1945 and the American desire to fight the Pacific war with minimal British aid. Moreover, British annual trade deficits continued to grow and the debts compounded, reaching 990 million pounds sterling in 1943 and over a billion pounds in 1944. Since May 1944, when leading British business organizations demanded an accelerated trade drive to recapture markets lost to the Americans and increase British reserves, the American business community and State Department watched the course of relations with apprehension. The British could cite the statements of American officials that "foreign trade must lean substantially on assistance from agencies of government," a fact Hull also explicitly accepted as compatible with his "free trade" program and which made any future American export drive that much more irresistible. State Department officials at times referred to these mutual fears of export drives as if they were unfounded, and like Charles Taft urged "we cooperate even in matters of mutual irritability," but given the total integration of the economies with war, all exports would by necessity represent intergovernmental problems for at least the duration of the conflict.[19]

Moreover, Lend-Lease terms controlled Britain's ability to export to a significant extent as well as its September 1941 pledge not to reexport Lend-Lease goods or articles similar to them.

In Argentina the United States and Britain were locked in a minor crisis over British economic relations with that nation. The United States considered the Argentine government pro-fascist, and the least that may be said is that it was not pro-Ally. More accurately, the Argentines were fully neutral but primarily anti-American, and internally their regime was no more and in some instances less tyrannical than many Latin American regimes fully acceptable to the United States. They carried on extensive trade relations with Britain, which was especially happy to preserve Argentina as a future market, one of the few the Americans were unlikely to penetrate so long as the Argentines had an option. Moreover, by spring 1944 Argentina piled up well over $1 billion in gold and foreign exchange reserves and represented a potentially vast export market for England. Since increased exports were ever more critical to the British, Argentina was in certain respects the best place to begin. In July 1944, when Britain prepared to sign a two-year meat contract with the Argentine government that would only have given Britain, in Hull's words, "petty commercial advantages of a long-term bargain with a fascist government," the State Department successfully undercut the economically binding proposal further linking Argentina to the sterling bloc.[20] Argentina for traditional nationalist reasons had always attempted to organize a southern alliance to challenge United States hegemony over the Hemisphere, which only infuriated Washington. British refusal to cooperate wholeheartedly largely neutralized the wartime trade controls Washington attempted to impose on Argentina in the name of antifascism. Everywhere in Latin America, American ambassador to Mexico George S. Messersmith reported, the British "are definitely tending toward the disruption of inter-American unity." If the British succeeded, he warned, they would close Latin American markets to United States exports.[21]

These irritating developments were only exacerbated by reports in American business journals that "hundreds of salesmen . . . have already left England to take orders for goods which will be delivered as soon as supplies are available."[22] In October the British government officially announced the resumption of woolen exports and a more inauspicious occasion could hardly have been chosen, for during November the American government reconsidered its future Lend-Lease grants to Britain in the context of the competitive export problem and British refusal to endorse American postwar foreign economic policy to the extent desired. The Americans reduced British and total empire requests for the first year following the defeat of Germany by $1.5 billion, or about one-half of the 1944 level. Moreover, as had been the case in the past, the United States could alter this program with changing circumstances. To compound American anxieties the British asked their agreement to a far-reaching modification of their September 1941 position concerning the reexport of Lend-Lease goods or domestic output of a similar nature, and now Morgenthau, Stettinius, and Leo T. Crowley, the Lend-Lease administrator, recommended that Roosevelt permit no changes whatsoever in the existing export prohibitions. They did suggest, however, that the United States then drop entirely from Lend-Lease whole categories of materials Britain ordinarily exported, thereby permitting the English to export those goods. To the British, Washington could explain this position, confusing to everyone at the time, as freedom to resume their export trade, and to American business as a measure to lower American foreign aid costs without seriously damaging export possibilities. So far as America was concerned it was not bound to sell to the British goods or materials for the export trade that the War Production Board defined as in "short supply," and it was explicitly understood Crowley would apply this definition in accordance with the true American policy, which Washington kept secret, of permitting only "certain minor British exports prior to V-E Day."[23] For at least the time being the American government could still regulate British reserves via Lend-Lease, ultimately making them contingent on British willingness to accept the American trade program even before Congress endorsed it or, as Feis advised Stimson at the end of November, on "the possibility of Great Britain giving us as a quid pro quo or a partial quid pro quo the right to exploit some of her Crown colonies."[24]

By the end of 1944, largely as a result of the nearly total collapse of mutual confidence in Anglo-American economic relations, sheer power in hand determined the future course of foreign economic policy. The new Lend-Lease arrangements and the obvious limits the Americans were attempting to place on their exports and recovery hardly pleased the British and a deep mood of alienation and suspicion cast its shadow on all future discussions. *The Economist,* which endorsed the essential outlines of the American postwar system for most of 1944, now surveyed the entire spectrum of Anglo-American political and economic affairs and asked:

> How can the ordinary Englishman be expected to listen without mockery to all the lofty moral generalities that are proclaimed in America, when he hears them against such a background? . . . Henceforward, if British policies and precautions are to be traded against American promises, the only safe terms are cash on delivery.[25]

These promises looked as if American economic goals for the world were hardly more than a hollow preliminary to a Pax Americana.

Indeed, when considering peace aims, many Americans who formulated American plans had a larger conception of the objectives of a policy that was increasingly imperial in its implications. Clayton made it a point to send the letters of Lamar Fleming, Jr., president of Anderson, Clayton & Company, to others in the State Department, with the admonition that they contained "a lot of good sense" and Fleming was "a very intelligent and very experienced man" in British affairs. Fleming argued that the "British empire and British international influence is a myth already." The United States would have to become its protector against the overwhelming Russian land power that would emerge at the end of the war. When that event came to pass, "it means the absorption into [the] American empire of the parts of the British Empire which we will be willing to accept."[26]

By the time the United States delegation traveled to Yalta they had considered all of these problems. The immediate task, however, required the premise that Britain was strong rather than weak, and they could reserve such thoughts as intrigued Clayton for future deliberation. Yet in principle there was no difference between using American economic power and the exigencies of the condition of desperate wartime allies to press acceptance of the Hullian doctrine, and a much more far-reaching implementation of American economic goals via a new empire that could exist as the preeminent factor in the world economy even without the formal political ties of traditional colonialism. The Americans acknowledged all of these options in considering peace aims, and only time and circumstance would tell which were relevant and feasible.

The Middle East: Opening the Door

The problem of oil was the most annoying and significant issue of the world economy to Anglo-American relations after 1943. There was ample precedent for the acrimony generated over this critical mineral. ". . . a review of diplomatic history of the past 35 years,'" a State Department trade analyst wrote in 1945, "will show that petroleum has historically played a larger part in the external relations of the United States than any other commodity."[27] Throughout the 1920's, when American companies controlled four-fifths of the world's oil output, British and American interests haggled for concession rights in the Middle East. In 1928, after much argument, they signed the so-called "Red Line" agreement granting American interests 24 percent of the output in a carefully restricted area of the former Ottoman Empire, which included Turkey and Iraq, made an exception of Kuwait and Egypt, and left open the question of Saudi Arabia and Iran. American interests shared equal control of Kuwait and had a monopoly over existing Saudi Arabian output and concessions. Marketing arrangements carefully circumscribed where the two partners might sell their oil, but the problem was largely academic until the mid-1930's, when Middle Eastern oil output increased dozens of times over. England's coal resources were rapidly being depleted, and its navy and a good part of its industry ran on oil. The issue in the final analysis was one of Britain's critical strategic power. The Americans in contrast had a powerful oil industry that successfully restricted excessive imports. As an oil reserve the Middle East was too distant to be reliable. Middle Eastern oil to the United States ultimately represented exports to Europe and a source of profit, and potentially an instrument to control the European economy. In the controversy that ensued after 1943 the British were battling for their very economic and strategic independence, the Americans for profits. Both sides were aggressive, both initiated new struggles, until the entire Middle Eastern question became a single, integrated problem. No other issue so vividly illustrated to the British the theory and practice of the new world economy the Americans said they wished to create.

Saudi Arabia was the first arena, in part because the Americans were so overconfident of their control there that the British were ready and able to prepare to move into the remaining concession areas. The California-Arabian Standard Oil Company handled all American relations with that feudal nation until 1941, and Washington did not even maintain a local diplomatic representative, assigning relevant questions to the minister in Egypt. In early 1941 the Saudi Arabian government pressed the American firm for increased loans on future royalties due to its reduced income from the disruption of pilgrimages to Mecca, and Standard attempted to convince Washington to take up the heavy demands as part of Lend-Lease, sparing Standard the expense and risks. In part they succeeded, but in a manner that the United States later regretted, for Roosevelt decided that the British ought to assume responsibility for King Ibn Saud's well-known extravagances, and this London gladly did. The Americans could permit the British to handle Saud's difficulties because the current American concession excluded them, but by 1943 there were growing suspicions in Washington over the reasons for British willingness to maintain such a seemingly disinterested and expensive role for so long. In May 1942, to get closer to the scene, they opened an American legation in Jidda.

By the beginning of 1943 Washington could no longer see the logic of aiding an American company via the British. The British were supplying Saud with Lend-Lease funds originating in the United States. ". . . we have thereby lost considerable prestige in the eyes of Saudi Arabians who have been given increasingly to feel that the British were their only friends in need," the American minister in Egypt reported in January 1943.[28] Oil company executives then advised that prolonged and exclusive British aid might tie the Saudi Arabians to the sterling bloc and threaten American concessions. Early in 1943, shortly after Roosevelt appointed Harold L. Ickes Petroleum Administrator for War, executives of the major American firms interested in Arabian concessions undertook to convince Ickes and the State Department that the richness and vast promise of the area warranted more direct government intervention. By February 18, when the

United States officially made Saudi Arabia a recipient of Lend-Lease, the oilmen had succeeded brilliantly in bringing the problem to the attention of most of the key leaders in Washington, starting with the President. In effect the American government was now solidly committed to protecting its interests, and henceforth oil became a lively issue of foreign affairs, for the wealth of the area warranted proportionately greater attention and protection.

Early in 1943 Hull had appointed a petroleum advisory committee under Feis, who suggested the appointment of Max W. Thornburg, then connected with a large oil firm, and at the end of the year a former independent oil producer, Charles Rayner, replaced him. In March, Feis's committee recommended that the United States create a Petroleum Reserves Corporation as a joint government-industry firm to develop reserves in Saudi Arabia, a measure that would have given the industry all the protection that it desired. Ickes and the Joint Chiefs of Staff immediately agreed, for the latter wanted to build reserves, but they quibbled over the extent of government participation, Ickes demanding majority ownership in the corporation for Washington, Hull preferring merely contracting for the output of the industry-controlled corporation. He based his opposition to Ickes' position, which soon escalated to total government control of the corporation, not merely on solicitude for private industry, though this was a factor, but his belief that Britain would respond in kind. "It will be recalled," Hull argued, "that in many conferences after the last war the atmosphere and smell of oil was almost stifling."[29] If possible they had to avoid a repetition of the situation.

Ickes prevailed for the moment, advancing plans in effect to loan the American companies $135 to $165 million to build a giant pipeline to the Mediterranean. Despite the fact that all these schemes came to nought by early 1944 due to opposition from domestic and internationally based oil companies, who had first cultivated government interest in the problem to gain backing for *their* control of the area, for their allies in Washington, and the British, the issue of British-American oil diplomacy was now brought to a head. For the Americans had refused the British pipes to build a much shorter pipeline from their Iraq fields, and American plans threatened their position in the marketing and output of world oil, all of which had been carefully regulated in the interwar years.

Quite apart from the pipeline issue American involvement in Saudi Arabia and the Middle East was heightened sharply by the middle of 1943, for preoccupation with oil was logical in light of American planning for larger postwar raw-materials sources. In part the local rulers themselves stimulated this renewed concern, both in Saudi Arabia, and as we shall see, in Iran, which later in 1943 reemerged as an additional factor in the Middle Eastern scene. Patrick Hurley visited Ibn Saud in June 1943 as Roosevelt's personal representative, and the following month the White

House invited the king to visit the United States. Hurley's special qualification for the mission, other than the President's special fondness for the man and his frank style, was his past experience as an important attorney for various American oil firms operating in the international field. Saud assured Hurley that his nation looked primarily to the United States for support, expressing distrust of British imperialism. "I found many manifestations in Saudi Arabia of Ibn Saud's confidence in America," Hurley reported, "and of his eagerness that American interests rather than those of any other foreign power, so often instrumentalities for political penetration, should assist the Saudi Arabian government in the development of the natural resources of the country."[30] Since there still were many concessions to grant, perhaps richer than any already in American hands, such assurances meant a great deal. Now in the fall of 1943 Washington was in the midst of defining a more comprehensive view of American interests in the Middle East, one deeply involving future relations with England. From August onward every British advance in Saudi Arabia, even down to the creation of branch banks, disturbed Hull and especially the Navy.

In the early summer of 1943 the British War Cabinet decided to try to head off this conflict by asking the Americans to agree to talks, not to persuade them to sacrifice their interests, but to convince them, as the official British history of the event describes it, "of the greater importance of the Middle East to the British Commonwealth and Empire. . . ."[31] The Americans delayed until the end of the year, by which time their own policy had taken firmer shape. It was expressed in different forms. ". . . we are for the first time developing some fundamental postwar economic interests of a long-term character in the Middle East . . . ," Harold B. Hoskins, the President's representative, reported in September.[32] If it did not take over British interests, and even if it became their junior partner, Hoskins suggested, Washington had now to recognize the substantial American oil position. In line with this thought he also recommended that the United States oppose Zionist claims, and in fact the attainment of control over oil now assumed top priority in American Middle Eastern policy. ". . . there should be a full realization of the fact that the oil of Saudi Arabia constitutes one of the world's greatest prizes," Hull told Ickes in November while disputing with him over the details of his proposed Petroleum Reserves Corporation.[33] Current British output would have to be kept to the minimum military necessity required, which meant that the Americans could not give them materials to expand Iraqi production.

In a somewhat blunter fashion Forrestal of the Navy Department phoned Byrnes at the end of December 1943 and informed him: "Well, it's one of the few things you can be sure—you can say today it is one of the great, important stakes for this country, and it is so important that what that President ought to do is delegate somebody—I mean one man—the threads of this thing. . . ." So far as Ickes' plan was concerned, "The private people, I happen to know, because of my contacts with business," would prefer no more than government backing for their aspirations. "But the main thing is that stack of oil is something that this country damn well ought to have and we've lost, in the last 90 days, a good deal of our position with this Sheik—Eben Sihudo, whatever his name is—and we are losing more every day. The British have now sent, under the guise of naturalists to prevent a locust plague, have got 500 people in Saudi, Arabia, for no other reason than to see what the hell we are doing and what we've got."[34] On the basis of these attitudes, as unformulated as they were at the time, the United States was prepared to forge a new role for itself in the Middle East.

THE United States was not only interested in extending control over Saudi Arabia's oil but that of Iran's as well, and with this new assumption the United States now moved to the offensive, laying the basis for subsequent crises in that nation with both Britain and Russia. Since 1911 Iran had hired American financial and technical missions for long periods of time to manage Iranian affairs in numerous government ministries. During the interwar years the Iranians sought an outside power capable of balancing British and Russian pressures, and when the American oil firms failed to overcome British resistance to their entry, preferring to concentrate their attention on the former Ottoman fields, the Iranian dictator, Riza Shah, increasingly aligned himself with Germany, which became the dominating power in Iranian economics. In July 1941 the Russians and English jointly demanded that the Shah, now virtually an ally of the Nazis, oust the large numbers of Germans in his country. When he refused, the British and Russians invaded Iran in August, replaced the Shah, and divided the nation into a northern zone of Russian occupation and a southern British zone. The three nations signed a treaty guaranteeing to evacuate all foreign troops within six months of an armistice or peace, and in October 1941 Churchill solemnly pledged "the faith of Britain" to Stalin that "we will not seek any advantage for ourselves at the expense of any rightful Russian interest during the war or at the end."[35]

When the United States sent its troops into Iran in 1942 to facilitate Lend-Lease shipments to Russia, they were followed by American advisers to the police and army who soon became critical in the operation of those agencies. At the end of 1942 a financial mission under Arthur C. Mill-spaugh, who years earlier had worked for the Iranians, arrived to take over the economic and financial affairs of the country, subject only to the Minister of Finance. The State Department believed Millspaugh was carrying out American policy, and until Iranian nationalists forced him out of office in February 1945 he was the most powerful man in Iranian economic affairs. Personally he did not believe Iran could ever be independent of one or another of the Great Powers or develop its own economy. He was there to open Iranian riches to the United States. From January 1943 onward, therefore, when the American government formulated an official policy of maintaining Iran's independence from Russia and Britain, it was in fact directing much of Iran's affairs. The Iranians for their part were delighted to have American protection, and they had no illusions either about their ability to survive the Great Power struggle or the role of the United States. "Dr. Millspaugh," the American ambassador in Iran, Louis G. Dreyfus, Jr., reported in July 1943, ". . . is a power to be reckoned with in Iran. He is gradually assuming control over the entire financial and economic structure of Iran. . . . He is perhaps the only man in Iran at present who can obtain passage of legislation by the Majlis when he desires to put on the necessary pressure. Frankly, politicians are afraid of him. . . ."[36] Millspaugh admitted in his memoir, "It may be doubted, however, that the British and American governments attempted properly and at the right time to induce the Soviets to participate in these inter-allied agencies."[37]

Briefly, the Allies were in the process of pulling Iran into one or another sphere of influence and were preparing the groundwork for another area of Allied conflict. At both the Moscow and Teheran conferences the three Great Powers failed to find common agreement on Iranian affairs, save for the most innocuous declaration of helping it with postwar economic problems and maintaining its territorial integrity and independence.

The inability of the Allies to agree on Iranian affairs was undoubtedly the result of intense British and Russian suspicion of American intentions in that country, not merely because of the power of the Millspaugh mission, which was public knowledge, but because of secret Iranian-American oil negotiations that were not fully known even to Washington until possibly as late as November 1943. In February of that year the Iranian commercial attaché in Washington secretly asked the Standard Vacuum Company if it was interested in an oil concession. The company replied affirmatively but wanted to wait, and in September specified certain areas of interest, especially around Indian Baluchistan, and asked permission to send their representatives to Iran. There is no direct evidence that Washington knew of this discussion, but it is difficult to believe Millspaugh did not, and the British soon learned of the impending American concession and immediately sent representatives of Anglo-Iranian Oil to Teheran to obtain the coveted area for themselves. At the end of October the Iranian government tentatively approved the American visit, but decided to determine whether the company would have official backing. Millspaugh and the American minister in Iran by this time were deeply involved in the question.

The Anglo-Soviet understanding not to scramble for privileges damaging to their mutual interests was not binding on the United States, but the American minister warned that any immediate American overtures for a concession, even though the Iranian government, which he might have added responded to Millspaugh's critical role, desired it, "would cause British and Soviets to suspect that our attitude toward Iran is not entirely disinterested and thus weaken our general position here." The day after Hull received this admonition he informed the Standard Vacuum Company "that, because of the importance of petroleum, both from the long-range viewpoint and for war purposes, the Department looks with favor upon the development of all possible sources of petroleum."[38] Now the State Department and Iranian government pressed the Standard representatives, who increased the area in which they would be happy to take concessions, to hasten to Teheran where the British oilmen were inopportunely offering terms.

The rivalry for Middle Eastern concessions was then on, for despite American suspicions of British intentions, the English had not yet made any overtures to obtain concessions in traditionally American areas. For the next thirteen years the consequences of the breakdown of Allied mutual toleration in Iran and the collapse of the laboriously constructed interwar oil agreements reemerged again and again to disturb the peace of the world. What the Americans tried to claim was the Open Door, to the British and Russians appeared much more like a rival imperialism. Was this an example of what Americans meant by postwar cooperation?

The Middle East: Model of the Future

The State Department could now take up the earlier British proposal to hold talks on oil affairs, for "There are indications that the British are utilizing present developments to achieve long-range ends"—in Iraq as well as Iran and Saudi Arabia.[39] In early December the Americans formally requested the British to agree to such conversations as promptly as possible, but now it was Britain's turn to procrastinate, giving Washington more time to define its own objectives and worry about British intentions while staking out American claims. The British first responded that the discussions ought to encompass not just the Middle East but the entire world oil economy, where of course the Americans were dominant. Hull refused to consider the demand, stating that they could discuss that phase of the problem later "in the light of the progress of the discussions on Middle Eastern oil."[40] In brief, if the British sphere of influence was settled to American satisfaction, Hull's position rather crudely implied, Washington might see its way clear to concessions elsewhere. Next, in mid-February 1944 the State Department told the British that "in view of the importance which the Government of the United States attached to the forthcoming discussions," Hull would be the chairman of the American delegation, Ickes the vice-chairman, with a suitable complement of undersecretaries, all to meet in Washington rather than London. Moreover, the subjects of Middle Eastern output quantities and concession rights would form main agenda topics. The British now expressed surprise, pleading they could not spare officials of ministerial rank for such matters, and assumed the talks would first be on a technical level. And they were loath to discuss concessions, which, they might have added, were a gross violation of the oft-stated American principle in favor of free access to raw materials for all. But by the end of February the issue moved beyond lesser diplomats and officials and into the hands of Roosevelt and Churchill themselves. The President insisted on discussing concessions, the State Department informed Halifax. "There is apprehension in some quarters here," Churchill wired Roosevelt, "that the United States has a desire to deprive us of our oil assets in the Middle East on which among other things, the whole supply of our Navy depends." Perhaps the technical experts might best meet first, Churchill counseled, for a conference that Hull led would turn the entire matter into one of "the first magnitude." "On the other hand," Roosevelt retorted, "I am disturbed about the rumor that the British wish to horn in on Saudi Arabian oil reserves." They had to reach a basic understanding soon, and that would require Cabinet-level guidance for the technical experts. "When I read the telegrams to the Cabinet this evening," Churchill then replied, "I found them also very much disturbed at the apparent possibility of a wide difference opening between the British and United States Governments on such a subject and such a time." The matter had become grave, for the Americans insisted on their oil, despite the alliance and common wartime suffering.

On March 4, 1944, Churchill sent a message to Roosevelt almost unique among those the heads of the major Allies exchanged, one that defined the most fundamental interest and policy of the British state before the onslaught of American pressures:

> Thank you very much for your assurances about no sheeps eyes at our oilfields in Iran and Iraq. Let me reciprocate by giving you fullest assurance that we have no thought of trying to horn in upon your interests or property in Saudi Arabia. My position in this as in all matters is that Great Britain seeks no advantage, territorial or otherwise, as result of the war. On the other hand she will not be deprived of anything which rightly belongs to her after having given her best services to the good cause—at least not so long as your humble servant is entrusted with the conduct of her affairs.[41]

Two days later Churchill suggested that the British would be glad to publicly announce the opening of the conference on a technical level, but the following day, March 7, the State Department unilaterally released a press statement reporting Hull would head the American delegation at the planned oil talks. The British could now repudiate the Americans or co-operate—they were left with no other alternative. Three days later Roosevelt requested Hull to demand that the British send their ministerial delegation within ten days of the opening of the discussions between experts that ostensibly would begin shortly. The British did the minimum amount necessary to avoid a public break with the Americans on the issue. Their technical delegation arrived in Washington only in mid-April, there to confront the American governmental experts and the ten representatives of the United States oil industry appointed to aid them.

While the heads of state quibbled at the highest level and their assistants at the lower, America defined its oil policy with a new precision that could be the basis for making proposals to the British. In mid-February the State Department alerted a number of the American embassies to the fact that "we are actively engaged in developing a firm postwar foreign oil policy," and that the department, from Hull on down, was meeting with the heads of the oil industry to obtain their views. In the meantime the United States demanded equal rights with other foreign nationals to explore and develop foreign oil. Given United States power, such a position implied America would demand control over the future development of foreign oil. By this time the State Department's policy completely identified the national interest with that of American oil firms operating abroad, not merely because numerous former oil industry executives occupied key posts in the department, but primarily due to the traditional synthesis of private and public interest which had been the functional basis of American foreign economic policy for decades. As further illustration of this practical unity of interest Stettinius notified the embassies:

> . . . if the occasion arises, you should render all appropriate assistance to the representatives of American oil companies who may be seeking petroleum concessions. . . . This assistance should include such introductions by you as may facilitate proper contacts between the companies' representatives and government officials. . . . To the maximum extent appropriate, in the light of the foregoing policy, you should indicate an interest in the matter to government officials.[42]

Such a combination, he might have added, would be irresistible. And when the Americans talked of such Open Door principles they adamantly insisted on excluding other foreign interests from Saudi Arabia and anywhere else they had the power to do so.

Such attitudes prejudged the final United States policy which emerged on April 11 as the "Petroleum Policy of the United States." The document deserves close attention, for it vividly illustrates the specific nature of American war aims for the world economy, aims which they labeled internationalist, but which revealed a classic pursuit of national self-interest, and in this case, an aggrandizement of the welfare of the American oil industry.

The policy demanded "equal access" and "equal opportunity for American enterprise in exploration" as one might expect. It also called for "a broad policy of conservation of Western Hemisphere petroleum reserves" in the interests of "hemispheric security," which meant "Curtailment, in so far as practicable, of the flow of petroleum and its products from Western Hemisphere sources to Eastern Hemisphere markets." Given United States consumption of the vast majority of Western Hemispheric output, this meant in effect a United States monopoly of nearly one-half the known world reserves at that time. If America cited depletion fears for this policy, the European nations might use the same justification. For the policy also called for meeting increased world oil demands out of Eastern Hemispheric, mainly Middle Eastern, output. To attain these objectives it would be necessary to use "diplomatic assistance" and "To arrive at an international understanding concerning the development of Middle Eastern petroleum resources. . . ." This actually meant an end to the prewar agreements involving the output and marketing of oil. Nor would the United States open its existing privileges to allow equal opportunity for other nations.

> Furthermore, and of greater importance, United States policy should, in general, aim to assure to this country, in the interest of security, a substantial and geographically diversified holding of foreign petroleum resources in the hands of United States nationals. This would involve the preservation of the absolute position presently obtaining, and therefore vigilant protection of existing concessions in United States hands coupled with insistence upon the Open Door principle of equal opportunity for United States companies in new areas.

Given the already predominant position of the United States in the world oil economy, the Open Door in these terms meant near American monopoly over the most critical natural resource in the world—precisely what the British suspected. And although Hull for years inveighed against bilateral trade and economic agreements, the instrument for attaining this policy would be a "bilateral understanding with the United Kingdom" which they then might present to other nations for multilateral agreement.[43] Such is the stuff from which noble words are made.

To this policy, which American conduct over the past years revealed to them in detail, the British could hardly agree. When they arrived in Washington they insisted only that any American proposal provide for British military, industrial, and commercial well-being. The American delegation piously replied that such assurance "would be in conflict with our established commercial policy." Not surprisingly, the draft agreement was vague, with suitable references to the Atlantic Charter to satisfy the rhetorical desires of both nations, but it in no way revealed their true intentions. For the fact remained that by mid-1944 the power and capability of each side to impose its will on the other would determine the outcome. The British had no illusions about this, for now every agreement they signed with the United States on postwar economic relations was suitably larded with escape clauses. To show their disdain for the decisions of the experts the British again inordinately delayed in sending a ministerial delegation to sign the agreement in Washington, that irritating symbol of the shift in world power. ". . . the situation is becoming embarrassing," Roosevelt cabled Churchill in early June. At the end of the month, when they heard nothing more from the British, Hull sent Winant press accounts of British procrastination being based on lack of enthusiasm for American plans, and insisted on forcing "departure without further delay."[44] Finally, Lord Beaverbrook led a British delegation to meet on July 25 with the considerably outranking American delegation including Hull, Ickes, and Forrestal. Together they designed their official communiqué to conceal the now public conflict and to enunciate a few general principles for the regulation of the world oil economy, and they also created the purely advisory Anglo-American "International Petroleum Commission." All the two nations then had to do was have Parliament and the Senate approve the agreement. The conference, *Business Week* commented, was "as vague as expected."[45] Surely the two Allies could agree on at least this much.

The Escalation of the Stakes

While the American and British governments negotiated a settlement of the Middle Eastern oil situation in theory and principle, the diplomats moved to determine the outcome in fact. Throughout 1944 the Saudi Arabian and Iranian chessboards saw innumerable British and American moves and countermoves, until the crisis of Anglo-American relations escalated to involve a third Great Power hitherto a mere observer to the imbroglio—the Soviet Union.

In Saudi Arabia there were many inseparably intertwined elements: a king who sought greater rewards for his favors and oil; Aramco, as the American oil concessionary was called after January 1944, anxious to increase official support for its plans; and the remnants of a pipeline scheme that was little more than a part of the official policy to obtain oil and exclude the British from Saudi Arabia. Aramco at the end of 1943 notified the State Department "that the best efforts of private American companies, without the assistance of their government, might not be successful in reaching a satisfactory and secure arrangement in the face of possible opposition in which other governments took an active part." It especially sought aid in getting a pipeline constructed, and in January 1944 the State Department assured Aramco that it could expect that "this Government will assist you in every appropriate way with other governments" in regard to the oil and pipeline questions.[46] This in fact included not merely opposition to Ickes' plans for a government-owned pipeline in Saudi Arabia, which he correctly insisted did not compete with the private oil industry but merely aided it, but the persistent effort to reduce British power over Saudi Arabian financial affairs.

King Ibn Saud saw every reason to make the most of the Great Power rivalry for his sole natural asset. In February he initiated a long series of complaints to American officials concerning their insufficient material and financial support, and they watched every British delivery of silver or arms to Saudi Arabia with mounting apprehension. Rumors of intrigues to remove American advisers and influence were cited as evidence of the need to remove the British from the scene. "If Saudi Arabia is permitted to lean too heavily upon the British," Hull explained to Roosevelt in early April, "there is always the danger that the British will request a *quid pro quo* in oil." It would be necessary, he urged, "to extend additional financial and economic assistance to Saudi Arabia in order to safeguard adequately the American national interest in the great petroleum resources of that country." The British, however, were remarkably solicitous of American opinion on their provision of advisers and supplies to Ibn Saud, and readily acceded to the American request to share equally in providing the Lend-Lease subsidy to Saudi Arabia. Nevertheless the American diplomats still suspected the nefariousness of their intentions and let their imaginations enlarge the motives and power of the British to absurd proportions. "Saudi Arabia is rapidly becoming an active battle ground in the implementation of two systems of foreign policy," the American minister to Egypt, Kirk, reported in late April; the British "aimed to make countries in which they are interested dependent in perpetuity," the Americans wished "to help backward countries to help themselves. . . ." "Needless to say," he added, "a stable world order can be achieved only under the American system." Since the issues went "to the essence of post-war action" by the two nations everywhere, the United States had to resolve it for the ultimate welfare of the underdeveloped world by providing for that of Aramco immediately.[47]

Officials in Washington were unanimous in this view of the Saudi Arabian problem and the need to obtain its oil. Hull triumphed over Ickes' approach to the pipeline problem and defined basic oil policy with the full support of Forrestal, Leahy, and other military leaders. The OSS completed in February a detailed examination of the British treaty position in Saudi Arabia, Kuwait, and Bahrain, assuming all of the Arabian Peninsula would interest the United States after the war. By April the American resident minister in Jidda was urging Hull to eliminate all vestiges of British presence, from antilocust experts to the financial mission, and to take over the entire subsidy to Ibn Saud's regime. But the meeting of Anglo-American experts in Washington eliminated the need for immediate action along this line, for in fact the British now only desired to maintain the status quo—respect for their interests in Iran in return for a passive British role in Saudi Arabia. In early June the British refused to acknowledge the preponderant American interest in every phase of the Saudi Arabian economy, as Hull had demanded, and their refusal only brought the matter to the boiling point.

To hedge against future contingencies in Saudi Arabia, Leahy in June obtained Roosevelt's approval for the construction of an air base in Saudi Arabia, ostensibly for military purposes but actually, as Leahy recounted, "so that we, particularly our Navy, would have access to some of King Ibn Saud's oil."[48] Given this intense and obvious American interest, Ibn Saud could hold out for more and more Lend-Lease aid, aid which by August far exceeded the country's immediate needs and led Ibn Saud to initiate a stockpiling program that had no conceivable wartime or economic, as opposed to political, purpose. Now Saud increased his pressure in a manner calculated to make the most of his advantage. It seems, as the new American minister, William Eddy, reported Saud's thought in early September, that the United States was "content to have its economic activity in Arabia reduced and defined by its ally," a twit intended to bring results. Perhaps the Americans would lose interest, in which case, "Without arms or resources, Saudi Arabia must not reject the hand that measures its food and drink." As if to add point to his message Saud permitted the British to delay the contemplated American base at Dhahran, which the State Department let London know was an "unfriendly act": "There was no law in heaven or earth," Assistant Secretary of State A. A. Berle, Jr., growled at the British counselor in Washington, "which entitled anybody to interfere with our building an airfield for legitimate purposes in Saudi Arabia." "A covert contest which begins to assume unpleasant proportions in prevailing over airfields in the Middle East," Hull warned Winant on October 17. He should inform Eden that the affair "has made an extremely painful impression here." It was, he added, "a reversion to a dog-eat-dog policy which, if continued, has possibilities we are not presently able to appraise."[49] Ominous words indeed, but for oil they would be repeated frequently in subsequent years.

Ibn Saud did not have to prod Washington and the baksheesh was forthcoming, to the advantage of all. Forrestal and Stimson in late October urged Hull to draw up a list of American demands, involving an air base at Dhahran and contemplated oil concessions, "at the same time informing the King of the nature of the assistance that can be given. . . ." Aramco added to the pressure by reporting the king's "displeasure and possible disgust" at American penury, one that might affect the company's profits.

Washington soon so sufficiently reassured Saud that he was willing to permit a survey to begin for purposes of building the much-sought-after Aramco pipeline to the Mediterranean, which Wallace Murray, head of the State Department's Office of Near Eastern Affairs, understood as "a further indication that the King is disposed to play ball with us in everything that pertains to the development of our great oil concession in his country." They could now strike a deal, one that would eliminate the British menace once and for all, extend the American monopoly over Arabian oil, and allow the Americans to build their base in the name of a conflict against the Axis which was in fact a result of the conflict with England. At the end of 1944 Stettinius, with Forrestal and Stimson's concurrence, asked Roosevelt to approve a long-range assistance program to Saudi Arabia, one that would leave that nation "independent" and which if the United States did not provide the aid it would "undoubtedly . . . be supplied by some other nation which might thus acquire a dominant position in that country inimical to the welfare of Saudi Arabia and the national interest of the United States." Such a disinterested defense of weak nations would cost only such sums "to the extent deemed necessary by the Secretary of State," and an Export-Import Bank loan "for the improvement of economic conditions and living standards in Saudi Arabia."[50] Washington duly notified the king of the new American altruism, and for the next several decades he responded in kind. The United States had defeated British imperialism in the Near East.

Iran: From Controversy to Crisis

At the beginning of 1944 as British and American oilmen, with the backing of their governments, scrambled to win concessions from the Iranian government for its largely uncommitted oil lands, new elements arose to complicate the two-way battle that the Anglo-Americans were duplicating at the same time elsewhere in the Middle East. The Iranian government cultivated the American desire to obtain concessions, but now came under growing internal pressure from forces opposed to the preponderance of the United States in Iranian affairs. The Millspaugh mission was decreasingly interested in Iranian opinion, and in fact unilaterally revised a Soviet treaty with Iran in a manner that shocked even the pro-American Foreign Minister, Mohammed Saed, who by February was complaining that Millspaugh had proven a dismal failure and Washington had best remove him. According to Saed, he refused to hire qualified Iranians, employed too many incompetent Americans, and Saed now attributed personal faults of every variety to the American. ". . . a composite of Iranian-British-Soviet thought," the American chargé reported back to Hull.[51]

As Washington mapped out the remaining Iranian oil concessions in infinite detail it ignored the growing pressure against Millspaugh, a task made more difficult when Saed became Prime Minister at the beginning of April. Though pro-American, Saed could hardly avoid internal political pressures or the fact that Britain too opposed the ever more audacious Millspaugh. During the first half of 1944 as well the State Department energetically backed the claims of the American oil company representatives then in Teheran, insisting that the two American firms—Sinclair Oil and Standard Vacuum—do everything possible to obtain the concessions. In April, as oil-concession matters moved into more advanced stages of negotiation, Millspaugh arranged for Herbert Hoover, Jr., and A. A. Curtis, two well-known consultants to the United States oil industry, to define Iran's interests in talks with Anglo-Iranian Oil, Standard Vacuum, and Sinclair Oil. By April, Millspaugh, who was now synonymous with American interest in Iran, became the main subject of Iranian politics, causing, according to the American embassy, an alliance of extreme nationalists, led by Mohammed Mossadegh, profiteers, and the pro-Communist Tudeh party to align themselves against Saed.

Throughout the first third of 1944 Washington's deep interest in Iran continued, and the reports of Patrick Hurley, Roosevelt's special representative in the Middle East, reiterated the future importance of the area. Hurley's saucy observations appealed to Roosevelt, over whom he exercised a powerful influence, for his categories of explanation and logic, and his frankness, were remarkably like the President's own impulsive mannerisms. Hurley associated Britain's presence in Iran and the Middle East in general with "the principles of imperialism, monopoly, and exploitation."[52] Evoking this belief, he appealed to Roosevelt to work for the principles of "liberty and democracy" by obtaining important oil concessions, maintaining a mission to straighten out Iran's internal affairs, and breaking the economic hold of the British. Millspaugh, he could also report, might not after all be the perfect man for so intricate and important a function, for his manners alienated far too many Iranians.[53] Hurley convinced Roosevelt of Iran's importance, and in January the President told Hull: "I was rather thrilled with the idea of using Iran as an example of what we could do by an unselfish American policy."[54] As usual Roosevelt left the critical details of implementing such a policy to others, and when the results came back he invariably endorsed them.

Hurley's persuasive talents meshed well with Hull's own objectives. Hull appreciated the importance of the area and Millspaugh's acknowledged deficiencies, and removed Ambassador Dreyfus in the hope of finding someone more capable for the magnitude of the responsibility. But "Regardless of the individuals concerned, the Department intends fully to support the [adviser] program, which constitutes an important implementation of an American policy supported by the highest authority in this Government." Besides, as the American chargé reported, the British too were also secretly attempting to destroy the adviser program, despite their public praise of it. At the end of June, Saed stripped Millspaugh of a major part of his economic powers, which caused the American to submit his resignation. Saed, for reasons probably connected with his desire to maintain American interest, refused to accept Millspaugh's resignation, which compelled the American chargé to admit "it is difficult to see how Saed government could remain in office and still enjoy the confidence of the Majlis and the people."[55] Saed would take his chances, for he wished explicitly to reassure the American government of his good will.

In this atmosphere of growing crisis and controversy over American power in Iran, the State Department now had to formulate a basic policy on the country consistent with its larger Middle Eastern strategy. In mid-July, Richard Ford, the American chargé, stressed the need for "a strong stand here both now and in the future," one oil and the potential "market for American goods" justified, and the State Department sent its reply at the end of the month for his guidance. "While our position in Iran prior to the war was relatively unimportant," Stettinius wrote, the war's "exigencies" altered that fact. Iran came to America for assistance, and Roosevelt decided that it would serve "as something of a testing ground for the Atlantic Charter and the good faith of the United Nations." ". . . a strong and independent Iran" was the goal of United States policy, and now the United States had national interests there which "includes the possibility of sharing more fully in Iran's commerce and the development of its resources. . . ." The first three expressions of this new commitment were a continuation of the adviser program, "Close interest in the present negotiations for a petroleum concession in Iran," and air-base rights.[56] The State Department mentioned no other sustained, tangible instruments of policy. The very same month Hoover and Curtis arrived to represent Iran at the advanced stage of the oil-concession negotiations with the American firms.

By August the inflammable ingredients of Great Power conflict came to a head. Millspaugh provided additional fuel with an off-the-record interview in an Iranian newspaper suggesting that only the United States could save Iran from Soviet or British infractions of its independence. Rumors of the oil-concession negotiations were also officially confirmed during August as more and more Iranians asked how Americans could be sitting on both sides of the negotiating table. ". . . to gain this rich prize for American interests will require quick action," Ford wired Washington at the beginning of August.[57] It seemed likely that the American companies might now beat the British, despite mounting Iranian counterpressures. Then everything stopped as the Russians entered the scene. What originally had been an Anglo-American conflict now became a three-way crisis among the major Allies.

Other than complaints about the rigorous provisions of Soviet-Iranian wartime economic agreements, until September the crisis developed without serious thought of possible Soviet interest in the affairs of their formerly pro-German neighbor to the south. That the Anglo-American concession race broke the British-Soviet understanding scarcely caused a ripple, and even when the Russians in a statement to the press in February briefly revived an old concession to northern Iranian oil rights, the Americans thought nothing more of the matter. With hindsight Millspaugh in 1946 admitted that ignoring the Russians had been a mistake.

In early September the Assistant People's Commissar for Foreign Affairs, Sergei I. Kavtaradze, arrived in Teheran with a delegation of experts. He concealed the purpose of his visit for only a short time: he came to obtain five-year oil-concession rights to an area in Russian-occupied northern Iran, covering the five northern provinces. The first response of the new American ambassador to Iran, Leland Burnette Morris, was to suggest that the Iranian government announce that it would postpone concession grants to any nation for six months to a year. Two days later, on October 9, Saed announced he would defer all concession negotiations until the end of the war. Shortly thereafter Morris informed the Iranian government that the United States had no objection to removing Millspaugh, and a few months later the latter resigned. But Kavtaradze stayed on in Teheran through October, making public statements on the Saed government's hostility toward the U.S.S.R. By the end of the month Tudeh party agitation throughout Iran for an overthrow of the Saed government reached a pitch, with Russian funds amply aiding their efforts. On November 8, a day after Saed ordered the arrest of the leaders of the Tudeh party, a new government scarcely more popular replaced the wobbling regime. On December 2 the Majlis passed a law making it illegal to open discussions on foreign oil concessions without its consent. The author of the measure was Mossadegh, and Iranian nationalism triumphed over both the Americans and the Russians, with the British yet to pay their debt in the eventual loss of their concession. The Russians were furious, and Morris advised the Americans to proceed with utmost caution. They gladly accepted the postponement and contented themselves in the meantime with efforts to obtain postwar airplane landing rights in Abadan and elsewhere, notifying the Iranians that they expected the government to inform them when they resumed concession discussions.[58]

American intervention in Iran was an excellent example of how the pursuit of national objectives provoked the redefinition of a regional situation and created the basis for international crises. It was primarily the struggle over oil and the extension of American control over Iranian affairs that caused the Russians to intervene not only for oil, but to establish the principle that affairs along their borders could no longer be determined without regard to Soviet interests and security. Soviet references to the

Iranian crisis in the fall of 1944 were for the most part critical of the
growth of American power and influence there and the ability of the United
States to define Iranian-Soviet relations. Kennan perceived this immediately, and warned Washington that "The basic motive of recent Soviet
action in northern Iran is probably not the need for the oil itself but
apprehension of potential foreign penetration in that area. . . ."[59] The
response of the Russians to Saed, who permitted himself to become an
American pawn, was an example of the probable Soviet reaction to the
traditional leadership willing to play this game.

By the end of 1944 the United States had won its struggle to monopolize
Saudi Arabian oil concessions, but Britain and Russia had foiled its plans
in Iran. In the wake of its limited success it had to consider a whole new
host of problems, not the least of which was the ability of the Russians to
cause the downfall of an admittedly weak Iranian government. On the need
to resist the growth of Soviet power the Americans and British could find
some basis for a common Iranian policy, at least for the moment. When
the Foreign Office suggested that they raise the problem of Soviet pressure
on Iran at the forthcoming Yalta Conference, Stettinius concurred and
told Roosevelt that the matter would test "the Dumbarton Oaks plans for
postwar collaboration."[60] In assessing the Iranian situation for the President in January 1945 the State Department played up to Roosevelt's
project for making Iran a testing ground for Allied cooperation, American
adviser program and all. Nowhere did it mention that the United States
government was in any way responsible for the crisis.[61] Again Washington
construed Soviet noncooperation with American objectives as an example
of Soviet expansionist tendencies.

Britain: The Rewards of Cooperation

Britain lost in Saudi Arabia, and although it had stymied the Americans at least for the time in Iran, the new character of Iranian politics
sharply undercut British power in that nation. All the British could do
now was to hope that their tortured, laborious negotiations with the United
States which produced the Anglo-American oil agreement of August would
win Senate approval and perhaps become an instrument of their much-
desired stability in the Middle Eastern oil situation.

The State Department sent the agreement to the Senate Committee on
Foreign Relations in August for the necessary approval, and the chairman
of that body was Tom C. Connally of Texas. Connally had a long record of
working for the interests of American domestic oil producers, who fought
foreign imports and the giant international firms in the name of anti-
monopoly and free enterprise, which ill fit the carefully and happily regulated American oil industry and the millionaires who owned it. Connally

was not going to disappoint his most important constituents, who flooded him with mail describing the agreement as everything from a cartel to a tool of socialism. The international oil companies supported the agreement, for they knew, as Hull explained, that the State Department designed it to deal only with Middle Eastern oil. But one other aspect of the treaty disturbed some Senators: the basic premise of equality of power and control that the treaty posited. It implied that a commission composed of non-Americans might define American policy and regulate its industry. There was much Senate interest in oil and the Open Door to British oil in the Middle East, but it was based essentially on the same motives as State Department policy—the United States did not seek equality, but hegemony under its control. The words of the Anglo-American agreement in no way revealed this, though this was clearly its intent. On January 10, 1945, with the agreement still bottled up in the Senate, Roosevelt heeded the advice of Stettinius and requested that the Senate return the agreement for "whatever revision appears to be necessary. . . ."[62]

The British negotiated a number of commodity agreements on rubber, cotton, and other goods during 1944, but no issue compared to the oil controversy, which unlike Bretton Woods did not deal with abstract future structures but real power, the basis of British economic and political strength. The United States was depriving them of that, and what little faith they had in American promises the Senate now undermined, for it might do much the same to any one of the numerous postwar economic and political agreements then under discussion. Caution, more than ever before, became the watchword. They had lost much and would lose no more if they could prevent it. For by early 1945 the only thing that bound the United States and the United Kingdom together was a mutual fear of Russia and the Left in the postwar world and the necessity of fighting a common enemy on the same front.

No other raw material could arouse such decisive action in Washington as oil, which caused the geopoliticians, especially those around Forrestal, to throw all caution to the winds. He based his passionate concern for the commodity on a seemingly sophisticated realpolitik which hardly succeeded in a world far too intricate to ignore the remaining interests and power of other states. Iran demonstrated how many uncontrollable elements existed to be brought under control, but what Washington learned from the experience only whetted American ambitions. Forrestal explained his views to Stettinius in December 1944:

> The prestige and hence the influence of the United States is in part related to the wealth of the Government and its nationals in terms of oil resources, foreign as well as domestic. It is assumed, therefore, that the bargaining power of the United States in international conferences involving vital materials like oil and such problems as aviation, ship-

ping, island bases, and international security agreements relating to the disposition of armed forces and facilities, will depend in some degree upon the retention by the United States of such oil resources.[63]

These international obligations the Americans based on something far more than domestic prosperity, but a new imperium of global obligations which, if successful, would permit the United States by the logic of For-restal's realpolitik to define the course of the world. To implement this policy he urged an energetic expansion of American oil holdings in the Mesopotamian Basin and Persian Gulf. In fact Forrestal knew that oil, bases, and the accoutrements of power he envisioned for the United States in the postwar world involved not merely a powerful Navy, which he advocated, but one superior to that of Britain's, and this too he calculated.

For a moment, in December 1944, Washington discussed the question of what would happen in the Middle East should British power be removed, and concluded with the War Department that "the continuance of the British Empire in some reasonable strength is in the strategic interests of the United States," which to the State Department specifically meant the exclusion of Russian power.[64] In fact the United States did not want Britain to be either too strong or too weak, but applied its best energies in a manner designed to weaken it, for even beyond a modicum of British power it preferred American omnipotence, in oil most of all, and this was the only permanent basis of British strength or interest in the area. Better yet was a Great Britain integrated and dependent on American leadership, and in fact American policy, whether intended or not, led directly toward that end. If the British Empire and Bolshevism should disappear, operational policy in the Middle East implied, "independent" states such as Iran and Saudi Arabia, two of the most reactionary nations of the world, might flourish. [For the United States saw underdeveloped areas primarily as a problem of raw-materials supplies,] and that misery and stagnation would be the basis of such an American-led world was of no consequence in American planning for peace.

Since the Americans could not define the critical point at which British power was neither too great nor too weak, but could only clearly define their own objectives, they laid the basis for Britain's defeat in the Middle East. If the United States was willing to assume merely Britain's oil holdings, and not the imperialist strategic and political obligations which are the overhead charges of economic imperialism in the modern world, a power vacuum that a weakened Britain would not be able to fill would result. Could the United States protect its oil under such circumstances? And would it create the new imperium?

PLANNING FOR PEACE, III: THE REINTEGRATION OF GERMANY AND RUSSIA

GERMANY'S POSITION in the postwar world was also a problem of future relations with the Soviet Union, and beyond this the character of the world economy that would emerge from the chaos of war. At first the Anglo-Americans saw it only indirectly in this light, but as the war proceeded the men in the United States and England who thought of these matters soon appreciated the interrelatedness of the future of Germany and Russia; since many were also profoundly preoccupied with postwar economic planning, the vision of the future soon became a unified one. The seeming vacillation in American policy on Germany from 1943 until well after the war reflected the unpredictable nature of the two key variables—the role of Russia and the condition of the postwar world economy—and the need to hedge against a firm commitment that might later preclude a more appropriate and firmer policy.

The basic problem of planning for Germany's future in the postwar world was not administrative or organizational, as most American writers on the problem have suggested, but involved questions of fundamental political, economic, and military policy that the purely administrative questions merely reflected. One should neither dismiss nor make too much of interagency rivalries, many based on relatively petty personal jealousies, for behind these surface animosities, which soon became petulant, were the central political issues of postwar planning. What is more significant than such vendettas was the fact that no single policy line triumphed intact, and Washington retained elements of all the major schools, many contradictory, in such American policy as was to emerge. A weak Germany could not serve as a balance to Soviet power in Central Europe. A high level of

German reparations available to Russia and the world would significantly exclude the United States as the major source for the reconstruction of the world economy, especially in the form Washington wished to see it. A loan to Russia might be a critical lever for defining postwar Soviet policy and bringing it back into the fold of the Western world, and American planners intimately related this matter to Germany, the only other possible major external source of aid to Russia. With ever-growing clarity the policy-makers in London, Moscow, and Washington understood the intertwined character of the problem of Germany, Russia, and the postwar world.

First Thoughts on the German Problem

If Germany was the heart of the war from a military viewpoint, from the political perspective of Washington until the end of 1944 it assumed a considerably lower priority than the immediate inter-Allied political controversies over Eastern Europe, Italy, much less the practical consequences of the occupation, actual or impending, of North Africa, France, or Italy. The seriousness and depth of American thought on the future of Germany increased during the course of the war and with the movement of Anglo-American troops across France, but Washington never defined a policy that firmly excluded other options in the near future. Hence the story of American planning for Germany is a series of twisting, tortuous controversies which led to a posture permitting full freedom to the United States after the war.

By 1943 planning for Germany in the postwar world proceeded in several forms in Washington and as a by-product of Anglo-American discussions on the invasion of Europe, either in the form of Operation RANKIN or OVERLORD. Perhaps more consequential than abstract plans still on paper was the emergence of a series of fundamental policy attitudes on the part of Roosevelt, Hull, Stimson, and others, and the fact that Germany was the one area of postwar planning that the President chose to give some basic guidance, an element that introduced considerable wavering and revealed much about Roosevelt's qualities as a leader.

Roosevelt felt a special responsibility for German affairs because his long stay in that country as a youth and his presumed knowledge of the language and the people gave him self-confidence he did not have in the discussion of other complex problems of postwar policy, where the role of his advisers was more obviously preeminent. When his advisers decided his ideas were impractical they sought to cajole and subtly persuade him to accept their views, a task that was never too difficult if only for the moment. For this reason Roosevelt became the object of the interagency controversies over the future of Germany, the final arbiter of such American policy as there was.

The State Department since early 1942 had assigned a committee of experts the responsibility of preparing specific postwar plans for Germany. But before their recommendations could be received, both Hull and the American military leaders moved toward some more concrete positions, the latter regarding the avoidance of British domination of German civil affairs as a prime objective as well. When Eden arrived in Washington in March 1943 to consider the overall political problems of the war, Hull and the President revealed the direction in which their minds were turning. The British had yet to formulate a clear policy of their own, and Eden urged Hull and Hopkins to reach Anglo-American agreement before discussing the difficult subject with the Russians, a position Roosevelt accepted quickly. This united front to the Russians on the matter was virtually the only specific agreement possible between the two nations at the time, for they were then only able to communicate their joint uncertainties to each other. Yet from the very beginning a fear of Russia set the tone for future discussion of the German problem. At this time, on the assumption, as Hopkins phrased it, that "It will, obviously, be a much simpler matter if the British and American armies are heavily in France or Germany at the time of the collapse," the Americans pressed for the implementation of OVERLORD as soon as possible and began the preparations for RANKIN. If the Americans and British could not agree, and then present a plan for Germany to the Russians for their consent, "one of two things would happen," Hopkins predicted: "either Germany would go Communist or out and out anarchic state would set in. . . ."[1] They explicitly rejected a Germany too far to the left or too weak. Even if they could not define a positive program, early in their deliberations on Germany both the United States and Great Britain resolved what they would not tolerate in Germany. Between the poles of Communism and anarchy, however, there was much room for ambiguity.

Eden's visit permitted the American leaders to formulate a few general attitudes. Everyone acknowledged that the Versailles settlement had solved nothing, if only because German power was quickly reconstituted, and was a poor model to emulate. Roosevelt at the beginning of his meeting with Eden on March 15 then suggested that they should not arbitrarily divide Germany, but encourage separatism which was always a latent factor in German public opinion. Turning from a soft line to a hard one the President agreed with Eden, according to Hopkins' notes, that should spontaneous splits not occur, "under any circumstances, Germany must be divided into several states," Prussia being at least one of them.[2] Lord Halifax, who saw dismemberment as a possible cause of resurgent German nationalism, contradicted Eden on the spot, and Sumner Welles reinforced the Roosevelt-Eden consensus by defining a tentative State Department view for dismemberment, including international control of the Ruhr. This lack of a considered and firm State Department policy was reflected in the fact that on July 27 the department's special committee on Germany strongly advised against dismemberment and for as much decentralization short of partition as was possible, a policy the committee was to maintain the remainder of the year.

In the months after Eden's visit, and prior to the Quebec Conference of August 1943, the Anglo-American military leaders took up the question of the occupation of Germany as a part of planning for RANKIN and OVERLORD. The British, under Lieutenant General F. E. Morgan, prepared a first draft for discussion. They defined three zones on a tentative basis, each being roughly equal, and now a specific set of plans around which they might make definite decisions existed to plague the uncertain policy-makers of both nations. Given the anticipated physically separate position of the British and American armies after OVERLORD, the Anglo-American military defined separate zones of occupation as an operational premise, a decision that their superiors never seriously challenged. When the political and military leaders of Britain and the United States met in Quebec, definite, critical premises for future Anglo-American policy already existed, not the least of which was their desire to exclude Russia and Communism from as much of Germany as possible. In light of the West's failure to invade Western Europe at this time, these premises, adopted without consulting the Russians, are more important as presuppositions than as proposals they were capable of implementing.

At Quebec the Combined Chiefs of Staff approved the British recommendations for German zones, set in the context of the RANKIN plan for a quick descent on Germany in case of a sudden termination of the war before OVERLORD. The political leaders could agree with equal ease on a formula of maximum decentralization without imposed dismemberment, a retreat from one of Roosevelt's earlier vague formulae. Roosevelt with relative ease reversed himself once more on October 5, shortly before Hull left for the Moscow Conference. Invoking his authority and knowledge as a former traveler and student in Germany, but not his powers as President, Roosevelt at the beginning of his discussion informed Hull that partition of Germany into at least three states was the solution, though by the end of the talk Hull swayed him sufficiently to elicit the admission that many mistakes would be made in Germany, possibly including partition.[3] With such vagueness from his superior Hull felt free to add details while in Moscow, for what Roosevelt thought was leadership was a major source of confusion to his chief aides, which the United States could hardly afford indefinitely.

At Moscow, Hull proposed on his own initiative that the Three Powers must occupy and disarm Germany within the context of the maximum decentralization compatible with essential federal unity, though he still paid obeisance to the possibility of spontaneous political divisions into separate states. Hull accepted the principle of reparations, mainly in goods and services, but with two critical reservations. "Reparations should not be relied on as a major instrument of control over Germany's military power," and the victors should levy them only to the extent that "they may reasonably be expected to contribute to the strengthening of the post-war world economic and political order."[4] Since the American gave no figures and referred to a proposed commission that they never created until Yalta, the magnitude and purposes of reparations were open to extremely wide interpretation. Perhaps no other position on Germany was so fraught with dangerous implications to postwar world affairs, for if the United States saw a strong Germany as crucial to the kind of postwar world order Hull believed so essential, the resurrection of German power too was possible within his definition of the problem. If the War Department objected to Hull's position when they saw it the following month, it was in part because they felt it impinged on their responsibility for civil affairs in Germany, made no reference to military government, and stressed disarmament far more than they thought desirable. They said nothing, however, concerning the critical economic principles of the State Department policy, and eventually supported them when they became the central focus of the controversy over Germany.

At Moscow, during the last months of 1943, when friendship and mutual need were never greater among the Allies, the Foreign Ministers did not discuss pessimistic possibilities. All delicate questions of implementing general policies the three nations referred to the European Advisory Commission which they organized there, though both Hull and Eden knew that body would exist without real power or freedom to give form to such decisive political matters. Molotov, perhaps aware of the still-deep ambivalence among the British and American governments on future German problems, agreed to the American proposals as a minimum program, asking for further discussion on every matter, especially dismemberment, with no public statements until they had defined a common program. Again they assigned to the projected EAC the responsibility for continuous study of such problems. In fact the Russians were not yet anxious to begin detailed discussions on the problem of postwar Germany, which they sensed would be a highly divisive subject, and deferred only to the most general principles, insisting, as Donald Nelson, chairman of the War Production Board, reported after a mid-October conversation with Molotov, "that the first task was to defeat the Germans thoroughly . . . and then . . . formulate a common program on how to deal with Germany."[5] Until the Western Allies reentered the Continent through France and relieved Soviet military burdens, the Russians were not anxious to reveal possible disagreements.

Yet in July 1943 Russia embarked on a course vis-à-vis Germany that met with mixed reaction among American policy-makers, raising the apprehension of some. That month the Soviets organized the Free Germany Committee among captured German soldiers and German Communist refugees in Russia and elsewhere. Its program was innocuous enough, promising full democracy in the context of a non-Communist postwar Germany, and its weekly paper featured the black, white, and red colors of the pre-World War I Kaiser. Standley in Moscow advised Hull that the movement was for propaganda purposes only and merely intended to sow defeatism in German ranks, but Hull was less certain and feared it might reflect "the Soviet attitude towards the future of Germany," which is to say, their desire to control it.[6] The total effect reinforced that already substantial wing in Washington seeking a hedge against allegedly aggressive Soviet plans for Germany.

Serious concern for British policy, especially on the part of Roosevelt and the War Department, inevitably matched anxiety over Soviet intentions. On his way to the November meeting with the British in Cairo, before the Teheran Conference, Roosevelt reconsidered the zonal occupation plan that the Combined Chiefs of Staff approved at Quebec, assuming a roughly equal division of Germany, with the British obtaining the northwest third. Freehand he drew the map to allocate to the United States the bulk of Germany, including Berlin, leaving Britain with the southwestern area on French borders. Each zone would become the basis of an independent German state. Needless to say the British did not welcome the revision, even after the Pentagon scaled it down somewhat, and both governments referred the entire problem back to the European Advisory Commission, despite universal American suspicion that it was a British tool. This task was the only serious responsibility the EAC assumed and implemented, though it merely confirmed the basic decisions of Quebec.

Roosevelt therefore arrived at Teheran with many notions on Germany utterly contradictory to the American position at the Moscow Conference, and the Russians immediately perceived the universal confusion that prevailed among the Anglo-American policy-makers. Stalin attempted to obtain further details of Anglo-American views on the control of Germany, expressing his fear that after its defeat, perhaps within fifteen to twenty years, Germany would be able to fight again. The Germans, he insisted, were industrious and able, and might rearm unless the Allies took positive action to restrict their manufacturing capacity. Stalin expressed his lack of faith in the German working class as the future deterrent to emergent nationalism, but could offer no aid in providing specific control measures, preferring to sound out Roosevelt and Churchill. His only proposal, made half in jest, was to shoot the fifty thousand most important German military leaders and technicians, a statement that infuriated Churchill and caused him to leave the room until the Russian leader reassured him the comment was made in levity. By the end of the conference no one had presented a mutually agreeable plan for Germany.

Roosevelt then suggested creating five autonomous German states, plus

United Nations control of the Ruhr, the Saar, Hamburg, and the Kiel Canal, a new position devised for the occasion. Churchill in turn recommended detaching southern Germany and incorporating it into a Danubian Confederation, which Stalin discouraged by suggesting that Germany would only dominate such a confederation. The Russian maintained that they could not trust any Germans, whether the country was partitioned or a part of a confederation, but despite his skepticism of all the proposals made he had none of his own to offer. It was understood that the entire discussion was preliminary, and they left that issue unresolved.[7] In referring these questions to the impotent European Advisory Commission the heads of state assured that they would do nothing to solve these basic problems save by conventional diplomacy, probably as a result of another meeting, one that they were not to convene until February 1945. In the interim, time and advancing armies helped to resolve the myriad questions that they would confront.

By the end of 1943 the leaders of Washington had not yet formulated the American position save in regard to certain critical essentials involving a fear of the Bolshevization of Germany, the desire not to completely break the back of German economic strength as the victors had done after Versailles, and the understanding everyone shared, save Roosevelt, that a dismembered Germany might open the Continent to the overwhelming power of Russia.[8] The State Department had its line, the War Department in drawing up military and occupation plans became deeply involved in the most critical political questions and sought to guard them as its own prerogative, and the President shifted from one position to another, and from time to time defined new ones. Since the end of the war was not in sight they could afford such floundering for the time being. After all, the British seemed quite as divided among themselves, and the Russians had nothing specific to propose.

The German Dilemma

During the first half of 1944 planning for Germany centered about the specific question of occupation zones and similar organizational matters that were relatively easy to solve. Then the far more complicated and significant issue of Germany's basic economic and political role in the postwar period emerged, a matter which they subjected to interminable debates and maneuvers without reaching a final solution.

The zonal problem was primarily one of Roosevelt's advisers convincing him to agree with the basic divisions agreed upon at the Quebec Conference and which he had unilaterally discarded. That plan allotted the Russians 40 percent of Germany's 1938 territory, 36 percent of its productive resources, and one-third of the population, not an overly generous share given the War Department's assumption that the Russians would conquer Germany as far as the Rhine. However, the Allies assigned the EAC the responsibility of drawing up a formal Allied agreement on this subject. Roosevelt's insistence on a larger American zone comprising 46 percent of prewar Germany and half its population, and one in the northwest of Germany as well, the State Department's mistrust of the very concept of the EAC, which they regarded as a tool of the Foreign Office, and the War Department's desire to retain as much responsibility for occupation affairs in American military hands as was possible seriously tangled the EAC's task. Yet neither the State nor War departments shared Roosevelt's desire for a northwest zone, much less a zone encompassing most of Germany. Eisenhower called for a combined Anglo-American administration of the western zone until the spring of 1944, when Washington unceremoniously informed him it was not his affair.

The first EAC meeting in January convened to discuss this zonal question, considering only the Quebec division, and the following month the Russians formally accepted it. Thereafter the question of zones and the occupational structure became an issue of internal disputes in Washington, and given the refusal to grant Winant, the American representative, power or directives to settle the matter or even to present Roosevelt's alternatives, it was not until February 1945 that they reached a final settlement along the lines of the Quebec agreement, a controversy that hardly involved the Russians at all. The State and War departments never permitted the EAC to deal with the far more significant issues of reparations and the postwar control of Germany. The EAC also considered the problem of surrender terms that the Allies were to offer Germany and a rudimentary Three Power control structure. The only other question of consequence pertaining to Germany that the West submitted to the Russians during 1944 was that of a common occupation currency, and here everyone understood that unless the United States furnished common printing plates to the Soviet Union the Russians would be compelled to print their own currency, thereby creating an immediate and irreparable division in the German economy. Agreement on this issue was no problem.[9]

In the meantime the War and State departments could pressure Roosevelt into relinquishing his plans for administration of the northwest zone of Germany. Roosevelt premised the design on the belief that American troops would want access to ports for a speedy withdrawal from Germany after the war, and that American presence in the south would inevitably involve it in Balkan and French politics. Stimson, Leahy, and others, with tortured reasoning and patience, ultimately prevailed over the President, though not before he obtained special port and access rights in the British zone. They could not, however, force Roosevelt to relinquish, at least in principle, the concept of unconditional surrender, which by the spring of

1944 only Roosevelt among the leaders of the entire Allied camp favored.

The debate over the much larger policy issues concerning the future of Germany was far more consequential. Here the controversy involved the English as well as the various key factions in Washington, and the Russians were not asked to comment on the still unresolved Western views until Yalta. The divisions among the men of power in both London and Washington were approximately the same and mutually reinforcing. The Foreign Office and the United States War Department both felt limited retribution against the Nazi leaders would be the main penalty the Allies would impose on Germany, though they did not abjure reparations if they did not interfere with their greater desire for administrative efficiency in the military occupation of Germany.

On a political level Stimson, Forrestal, and others also shared Foreign Office fears that Draconian penalties against Germany would create a vacuum into which Russian power might move, and "that a stable peaceful Europe requires a prosperous stable Germany. . . ."[10] The State Department for its part set up the attainment of its postwar economic and political objectives as the prime goal, against which it measured all proposals for Germany. The State Department always considered the German question as part of the larger problem of foreign economic policy, and in June 1944 presented the Committee on Foreign Economic Policy, an inter-Cabinet body excluding only the military, with policy drafts making the reintegration of Germany into a liberalized, which is to say Hullian, world economy the ultimate and overriding objective. Control of economic means essential to future aggression they accepted in principle, though the level and types of control were left vague save that they would not be "enduring," but their critical goal was to remove the economic causes of war. "The effectuation," as the final policy statement phrased it, ". . . of a fundamental change in the organization and conduct of German economic life which will integrate Germany into the type of world economy envisaged by the Atlantic Charter." This required a reparations program that did not conflict with this repeatedly stated goal, which would run a maximum of ten years but preferably closer to five, and which aided European reconstruction without pauperizing the Germans. The State Department fully understood that reparations were "artificial and necessarily different from normal trade. The longer it continues the longer is deferred the full resumption of regular multilateral trade and the desired integration of Germany into the world economy."[11] The time limit was imperative, and the United States would oppose all attempts to predetermine amounts. This explicitly meant, among other things, preventing the collapse of the German economy, which might spell disaster for American efforts to normalize the European economy, and even temporary use of existing German economic and political machinery. If the War Department failed to endorse these proposals immediately, it was only because it regarded occupation affairs as a purely military question, and it wished to protect military jurisdiction. In fact this meant that the State and War departments formed an essentially united bloc in Washington.

Churchill and Roosevelt were both flexible in the debate over Germany, shifting their weight in various directions during its course. Churchill in public statements assured the Germans that they would not be "enslaved or destroyed," but neither would they qualify for those rights specified in the Atlantic Charter.[12] It is significant that with the exception of a small group of socialist intellectuals and Labour party members, no one of political consequence in either the United States or England advocated a far-reaching democratic social and economic revolution in Germany designed to destroy the critical alliance between the Nazi party and big business and to make German imperialism impossible. The strengthening of the German Left as a counterbalance to reaction, which not even the Russians openly suggested, Washington implicitly rejected. The Free Germany Committee caused Hull much apprehension, and the OSS in mid-1944 anxiously charted the growing influence of the German Communist party, utilizing its conservative United Front strategy, and allegedly having the strongest underground in Germany.

Lord Robert Vansittart, the Conservative, bitterly anti-Russian English political leader, advocated the most punitive occupation philosophy to receive public attention in 1944. He called for the total destruction of German industrial power, extensive trials of large numbers of German leaders, and a prolonged and stringent occupation. Many have erroneously identified Vansittart's widely discussed opinions with the views of Henry Morgenthau and Harry Dexter White of the United States Treasury Department, and in their common conservatism and specific control measures there is some truth to this analogy. Beyond that, however, it breaks down.

The Morgenthau-White view of what the Allies should do with Germany is the most interesting, the most complex, and surely the most misunderstood plan. Historians have called it anti-German, which is an accurate label but grossly misleading unless placed in its much-ignored context. It was in a most integral fashion also a plan for de-Bolshevizing Russia and of reintegrating it into a new capitalist world economy which Morgenthau, White, and the State Department discussed during 1943 and 1944. In this sense the Morgenthau plan was opposed to Communist internationalism—an abstraction which existed only in a few Leninist tracts and the minds of frightened Western politicians—and in favor of the creation of a world economy modeled after the ideal American image. The destruction of the German economy was not an end in itself or joined to a relatively isolated debate, but a part of a much larger and more ambitious design, a plan that can only be comprehended when the specifics of the Morgenthau-White proposals for the postwar role of the U.S.S.R. in the world economy are analyzed and the pre-1944 position of White and Morgenthau on Russia considered in greater detail than has hitherto been the case.

Both Morgenthau and White were among the more anti-Russian executives in Washington, and their record in this regard extended back to at least 1940, when the Treasury Department froze funds of the Baltic nations in the United States in a manner that the Russians thought singularly unfriendly. White, for his part, suspected in October 1940 that the Russians would soon damage United States interests in the Far East by signing a nonaggression pact with Japan, and several days after the German attack on Russia Morgenthau refused to initiate any steps to aid the U.S.S.R. ". . . I am in no hurry to do anything about Russia," he informed his assistants. "It is six of one and seven of another, as far as I am concerned. One day it is the Ogpu [GPU] and the next day it is the—what is the German police?"[13]

At the end of 1943 the Russians assigned Eugene Varga, one of their most important economists, the special task of publicly attacking the White plan for the postwar world financial structure. As we shall see, Morgenthau's plans for Germany seriously challenged Soviet postwar interests in that country, for the Russians hoped for large-scale reparations from Germany, reparations the Treasury Department's proposals would have made impossible.

After D-Day it was increasingly apparent that the Allies' failure to chart the future course of Germany might result in disaster for the West in the event of a sudden collapse of German resistance, an event that the Anglo-Americans did not consider improbable after the initial smashing Allied victories of the summer campaign on both fronts. The State Department's definition of economic policy and the War Department's planning for specific occupational control they had yet to transform into a firm policy for guidance, and now something definite was overdue. While the State Department privately favored the principle of unified Three Power control of Germany, by August only the Russians had presented a specific plan to implement it, and Washington did not permit the American members of the EAC to give it their approval. "Unless we can get some papers through the JCS," Philip Mosely of the EAC warned the State Department in early September, "our situation here is going to be desperate. As it is SHAEF has to go ahead planning for the first two months of joint Anglo-American occupation without any agreed tripartite policy to base its work on." As it was, Mosely complained, the Russians endorsed the policy of Three Power cooperation and wished American concurrence before getting to the administrative details. "After all," he warned, "tripartite policy with regard to

Germany is the real touchstone of Allied post-war cooperation."[14] In reality Washington had yet to define a policy on cooperation on Germany and its very future vis-à-vis the Soviet Union.

The War Department authorized SHAEF (Supreme Headquarters Allied Expeditionary Forces) in London to prepare a "Handbook of Military Government for Germany," a draft of which it had not yet approved when one of his former Treasury employees now assigned to SHAEF brought it to Morgenthau's attention. Washington had completely stymied the EAC in its work for reasons already mentioned and Morgenthau now became the catalyst for a further definition of United States and British policy, one that was long overdue and probably would have occurred in any event in much the same form.

The State Department's direction did not impress Morgenthau, who regarded it as too lax. The War Department's military handbook he dismissed as the product of technicians arrogating critical functions to themselves. The reparations proposals also struck White as a means of maintaining German industrial capacity and giving it a central role in European reconstruction, a role both White and Morgenthau assigned to the United States at Bretton Woods. During the second week of August, while the two men were in London, they gave their attention to the problem of Germany for the first time. Their crudely devised proposals reflected their hasty manner, but were nevertheless compatible with their views of the postwar world economy. It is in this larger context of the extent to which existing plans for Germany were also directed toward the containment of Russia that one must consider the plan that Morgenthau, White, and aides improvised over the following weeks.

For some time prior to September 9, when the British Chiefs of Staff submitted a formal memo to Eden, important British leaders debated the possible postwar reintegration of the non-Soviet zones of Germany into a Western European bloc that might be critical in the event of postwar Russian hostility or aggression. While the Foreign Office rejected the reasoning and the British military retreated somewhat by merely offering the suggestion as an option, the British also rejected the dismemberment of Germany, preferring a Germany that would be neither too weak nor too strong for the time being. Such thoughts existed in Washington as well. When they met on August 13, Eden filled Morgenthau in on the details of this controversy. He described three major factions: his own, in favor of a harsh peace; a second group, which included at least the military, "desiring that Germany should constitute a bulwark against possible spread of communism"; and Churchill, somewhere between the two.[15] The Foreign Secretary also complained of the serious lack of planning and a clear policy among the Allies, the disappointing failure of the EAC, and stressed that Russia would watch Anglo-American policy toward Germany as the critical test of postwar cooperation. Morgenthau, a novice in these matters, was horrified and returned to Washington resolved to take the matter in hand in a way compatible with his postwar financial plans. The same month Winant wrote Roosevelt directly, stressing the need for a policy on Germany and reparations which took into account its impact on postwar relations with the U.S.S.R.

When Morgenthau arrived in Washington he asked White and several aides to draw up a comprehensive plan for Germany, stressing reeducation as much as the economy, and initiated a campaign to arouse Roosevelt's interest in the matter once again, expressing surprise that no one apparently contemplated dismemberment any longer. He also pressured Stimson and McCloy, and Stimson agreed only that it was now time to define a firm policy. On August 25 Stimson convinced the President to organize a Cabinet-level committee, composed of Stimson, Hull, and Morgenthau, to outline a policy. He appealed on a humanitarian and pragmatic basis that they avoid dismemberment plans, that the Allies penalize only guilty individuals rather than the nation, and that they employ German resources in European reconstruction. Roosevelt, or so it seemed at the time, was unreceptive.[16] For the very next day he chastised Stimson for the still unofficial SHAEF handbook on Germany, and it appeared as if Morgenthau had made a strong impression. But a few days later Roosevelt added Hopkins to the Cabinet committee on Germany, giving Stimson an important ally. On September 1, or less than two weeks after first considering the issue, Morgenthau held the first draft of his plan for Germany.

Morgenthau's scheme was not entirely original and merely applied in an extreme fashion proposals others had considered and rejected during 1943 and early 1944. It was a preliminary draft, one he deliberately made strong with the knowledge it would be watered down, and later modified several times, but as it first stood it called for total German disarmament and the destruction of all arms industry and related manufacturing facilities, allocation of East Prussia, the Saar, the area north of the Kiel Canal, and various Rhine areas to Germany's neighbors, and the remainder divided into two independent states. The Allies would make the Ruhr an international zone and not permit it to trade with Germany, and later Morgenthau added a proviso for the nearly total destruction of its plants and mines. The Draconian aspects of the plan, which White and lesser Treasury officials clearly had qualms about, Morgenthau always restricted to the Ruhr, with the enhanced export market for England serving as a major rationale for the scheme. He would permit Germany itself to maintain consumer goods and light industries. Reparations could not come out of current production, but only through dismantling and forced labor, and the occupation authorities could assume no responsibility for economic regulation, which would be left to the Germans themselves. No effort would be made to prevent chaos and famine. The plan demanded total denazification. The memo said nothing about what such a plan implied for future United States-Soviet relations, but it was obvious that the Russians could expect substantial reparations only if it came from current production, for it is in the nature of modern industry that machines in the hands of experienced men reproduce their own value many times over. The Russians would have to seek alternatives, and this, as we shall see, Morgenthau and White already clearly understood.

The State Department immediately reacted with near horror, not merely because, as Hull recalled, it "was a plan of blind vengeance," but because "in striking at Germany, it was striking at all of Europe."[17] There would be no recovery on this basis, and the door would be opened to Communism and closed to American plans for economic reconstruction. The State Department wanted spontaneous partition, Hull insisted, but opposed imposing it in a form that would encourage nationalist irredentism. For the next several weeks there followed inconclusive, shifting debate among the Cabinet committee members, Roosevelt himself vacillating unpredictably. To Stimson, McCloy, and their allies, a subsistence economy in Germany would create new tensions, for the "speed of reconstruction is of great importance," Stimson wrote at the time, "if we hope to avoid dangerous convulsions in Europe."[18] Permitting Russia to share in the international control of the Ruhr caused McCloy to be "alarmed at giving this addition to Russia's power."[19] Stimson for his part saw the plan as giving Russia or Poland too much of East Prussia and Silesia. Morgenthau wisely sought out Roosevelt at Hyde Park, away from the counterbalancing pressures of the President's other advisers, and won a momentary endorsement by adopting the President's suggestions regarding a stronger policy on the Ruhr, and prohibitions of parades, uniforms, and airplanes, all of which struck Roosevelt as important. At the same time he had his staff prepare arguments on why his plan would help save the postwar British economy. The last word was yet to be heard.

On September 11 the Quebec Conference opened and Morgenthau was present while Hull, recovering from an operation, was not. Stimson too was absent. Churchill arrived on the scene after both the War Cabinet and Hull had strictly enjoined him to resist the Morgenthau plan. At this very time, in addition, the British were deeply worried about their future export position and earnings and were attempting to obtain a relaxation on Lend-Lease restrictions interfering with certain critical exports. The matter of Germany, which after the implementation of the Morgenthau plan would no longer exist as a British competitor, was set in this context, and according to Hull, Morgenthau threw out the bait of possible postwar credits totaling over $6 billion. Churchill at first reacted violently, but soon saw the logic, and according to his memoir he agreed, without first consulting

Eden, to "consider" the plan. On September 15 he and Roosevelt initialed a significantly watered-down version which reduced the question to the metallurgical, chemical, and electrical industries, the "war-making industries in the Ruhr and in the Saar," and the conversion of Germany "into a country primarily agricultural and pastoral in its character. . . ."[20] Eden was furious at this concession, but when they returned to London the War Cabinet rejected the plan outright. Hull saw Morgenthau trading away Lend-Lease and important levers for British acceptance of his trade program. Stimson now bitterly complained that the plan was irrational, and Morgenthau "so biased by his Semitic grievances that he is really a very dangerous adviser to the President at this time."[21] But Roosevelt, so it seemed, had been firmly converted to the Morgenthau plan.

Morgenthau regarded the Quebec meeting as "the high spot of my whole career in the Government," a complete triumph.[22] In fact it only forced Hull and Stimson to intensify their efforts and led to an even more acrimonious renewal of the controversy. Stimson immediately drafted a memo to Roosevelt, pitched on the highest level of morality, and in the meantime the Cabinet continued to haggle. Hull, who claimed "stupefaction" over Roosevelt's decision, joined with Stimson to ask how he might arrive at such critical decisions before consulting the Russians, a consideration that had not occurred to them prior to that time. Reinforcing this line was the fact the British were still deeply divided among themselves on the issue of Germany, and in fact remained split at least until Yalta. A firm American policy, therefore, would be in the nature of a unilateral decision damaging to the alliance. Hull then directed his appeal to Roosevelt along these lines, also lecturing the President on the responsibility of the State Department, especially after years of effort on this question, for the conduct of foreign policy.

Meanwhile, on September 22 the Joint Chiefs of Staff sent Eisenhower JCS 1067, a draft directive for the occupation of Germany in case it suddenly collapsed along the lines of RANKIN C. It was essentially organizational, avoiding the drastic assumptions of the Morgenthau plan. As vague as it was JCS 1067 was the only formal policy that the United States had at the time, but it too underwent constant revision both in Washington and in the hands of the English, who refused to endorse it. What was most interesting about JCS 1067 was its strictly unilateral character and not what it proposed, for despite its numerous revisions the Americans found it impossible to implement. The Americans no longer sought to negotiate a common occupation policy with the Russians and now with the British as well, but rather to impose whatever they might devise, a policy that led to disunity and spheres of influence in all the other conquered Axis nations. This fact greatly embarrassed Winant, and he hesitated to present it to the EAC for fear of jeopardizing the agreement on zones and a common

German control council that was now ready for Three Power signatures. JCS 1067, Winant warned Roosevelt, not only affected the principle of Three Power agreement on broad policy, which appeared to be successful insofar as the EAC was concerned, but it threatened to break Germany into separate and divided economic and political units along the lines of the artificial military zones, ending German unity before the three Allies could consider such matters. Washington, needless to say, ignored Winant's point.[23]

Roosevelt was naturally unable to resist the combined pressures of his advisers. Added to this, on September 24 the press described an exaggerated version of the Morgenthau plan and the Cabinet split, strongly supporting Hull and Stimson. Two days later Roosevelt dissolved the Cabinet committee and on the 29th publicly described the problem of Germany as still under study. On the 29th the President also wrote Hull that "No one wants to make Germany a wholly agricultural nation again," much less completely eradicate the industry of the Ruhr and the Saar, but he insisted that they did not have to consult the British nor, especially, the Russians regarding the issue, for "In regard to the Soviet government, it is true that we have no idea as yet what they have in mind, but we have to remember that in their occupied territory they will do more or less what they wish."[24] The same day the Cabinet committee informed Roosevelt that they did not endorse the Morgenthau plan, that the United States should postpone all decisions on the partitioning of Germany, and that other than the destruction of military industry incapable of reconversion, basic economic objectives in Germany should be to reintegrate it into the world economy by eliminating self-sufficiency, preventing rearmament, and reducing the power of the large industrialists and landowners. They took no firm position on reparations, save to argue that the United States itself had no desire to collect any. Thus challenged, Roosevelt backed down altogether. He only signed the Morgenthau memo, he now insisted, to prevent the British from going bankrupt. On October 3 Stimson saw Roosevelt and noted he appeared "very tired and unwell."[25] The President admitted that the provisions of the plan, to which he had not given "much thought," had "staggered" him. "Henry Morgenthau pulled a boner," the President observed in burying the scheme.[26] But Roosevelt erred as well, and from this point on he carefully heeded the as yet not altogether unified proposals of his other advisers.

During October the President moved apprehensively in the field of planning on Germany lest he create a new storm. He intended avoiding "too much detail and directives at the present moment" he told Hull on October 20, for everything would be "dependent on what we and the Allies find when we get into Germany—and we are not there yet."[27] Even Morgenthau, who had been eclipsed from the scene, now agreed with this generalist position. In lieu of other guidance the State Department continued preparing its own memorandum for circulation in official circles. Also for the first time they attempted to use the EAC, where the Russians were entirely cooperative, to define at least a few common bench marks with the British, who now largely restricted their discussions with the Americans to debates within SHAEF on JCS 1067, which they refused to accept in its existing form. Perhaps the most important development in this entire period, one everyone largely ignored at the time, was the State Department's functional, unchallenged definition of United States reparations policy in the Rumanian and Hungarian armistice negotiations, a critical precedent for the German problem that one cannot overestimate.

In effect in Hungary and Rumania the United States permitted the principles of its postwar economic goals to set the limits on its political strategy. During November the State Department moved to apply these principles to the German situation, dealing with its economy and reparations in a much larger setting than had hitherto been the case. The EAC was amicably settling the final zonal structure of Germany at the time, as Roosevelt agreed to take a southern German zone in return for an American-controlled enclave and post in the northern Bremen-Bremerhaven region. In mid-November Stettinius sent Roosevelt two general summaries of the critical economic problem the United States might expect in Germany. "Complete identity of objectives and methods in the several zones is unnecessary and unobtainable," he admitted, but in certain economic areas the Allies had to obtain a common minimum program. The prime British objective was to restrict German export competition, the Russians wanted large reparations, which could only come from current production. Both nations therefore favored close economic control and opposed extensive deindustrialization for their own reasons. American policy, in contrast, was rather different in certain regards and required a mediating role in others. "In the long run, we should look forward to a German economy geared into a liberal world economy on the basis of efficient specialization. This will imply equitable German access to export markets, abolition of German self-sufficiency, and abandonment of instruments of German economic aggression. . . ."[28] Sweeping deindustrialization would defeat this objective, and the occupation government would be called upon to prevent economic chaos debilitating to these goals. Reparations might be heavy, but short, and not used as a pretext for rapid industrial expansion that might create more problems than it solved. On November 15, and again on December 4, Roosevelt endorsed this formulation, which was merely a reiteration of the traditional State Department position. "We are against reparations," he notified Stettinius in a rather oversimplified note.[29]

Yet the President was not able to provide additional direction beyond this, and so, despite the efforts of Morgenthau and the Treasury to make policy sterner, the State Department then set the dominant tone. There was so much ambivalence in the department on a specific economic control and reparations policy—and a fear the Russians would not endorse the larger policy it had in mind—that Stettinius kept deferring basic policy discussions of German occupation problems within the EAC. This continued delay embarrassed the American delegates to the EAC because in November the Russians were showing "a cordiality and flexibility . . . seldom shown before."[30] Failure to present a policy, or insisting on presenting the unilaterally defined JCS 1067, Mosely warned the State Department, would suggest to the Russians that the West was organizing a Western European bloc against the U.S.S.R.

On a less dramatic level a State-War-Navy Coordinating Committee, organized at the beginning of December, addressed itself to the revision of JCS 1067 in a manner that hardly altered its basic ambiguity or unilateral character, and it underwent many such revisions. The State Department hoped to refine JCS 1067 to a point where they might present it to the Russians and English via the EAC, but Washington failed to get this far and never fully permitted the other Allies to understand the basic dimensions of American policy on Germany. United States officials themselves hotly debated these premises in Washington offices. The temperature of the debate rose as Morgenthau increasingly understood that the basic cleavage within Washington debates reflected the same controversy over the future of Germany as a barrier to the expansion of Soviet power that had entered British controversies over the same months. He and White, though willing to moderate their plan, now attempted to exploit this factor in the same manner that Hull had earlier relied on lack of consultation with Russia in his effort to stymie Morgenthau. "The real reason in support of a strong Germany," White wrote, "is a desire to maintain a strong enemy of the Soviet Union in Europe. . . ."[31] Morgenthau transmitted similar arguments to Roosevelt before Yalta, relying on them with far greater frequency than he had in August and the several months thereafter, when the British had revealed their own discussions in this vein.

There is no doubt that Hull, Stimson, Forrestal, and most of official Washington feared that chaos in Germany and elsewhere would open the door to Bolshevism, and this was hardly a well-kept secret.[32] There was a direct correlation between those advocating leniency in Germany and fear of the spread of the Left. The State Department's desire to save Germany for a renovated world capitalism reinforced this position. Yet surely there was nothing radical or pro-Soviet about the Morgenthau plan. On January 20, 1945, Maisky and Harriman discussed Germany's future. Though the Russian stressed security as their first consideration, which they might attain by an overall 25 percent reduction of Germany's industrial capacity, far less than most of Washington's estimates, much less Morgenthau's, he emphasized the extent and form of Soviet reparations demands in far greater detail. The Morgenthau plan, for reasons indicated below, would have deprived Russia of the level of reparations it had in mind and later presented at Yalta. The basic psychological assumptions of Morgenthau and White on Germany were entirely conservative, stressing the irredeemability of German character in a manner any radical, seeing the critical role of a reactionary social system in the formulation of politics, would have rejected. In fact the Treasury group shared the prevailing view in Washington that one had to control the effects and consequences of a moribund social order rather than restructure it to prevent both chaos and the re-emergence of reaction. The Morgenthau plan would merely have introduced new dynamics for destabilizing Europe, and only Roosevelt's personal susceptibilities made such hastily devised proposals possible in the first place.

By January the policy on Germany followed at Yalta reflected the predominant views of the State Department, which Stimson and his advisers essentially supported, for the War Department preferred to content itself with the details of occupation governments. More important was the fact that Roosevelt permitted State Department representatives, but no Treasury officials, to go to Yalta. The elements in State-War policy were not internally consistent, however, embodying as they did their desire to purge the existing political order of its leaders, purify it, and return to a revised pre-Nazi Weimar Republic that had, after all, proven fragile enough during its tenuous, brief existence. In this view the United States would retain German power and redefine it according to American principles and interests, integrated into an ideal world order excluding both the Left and Nazism. Disarmament, the elimination of Nazism and frenetic nationalism, reeducation, and political reconstruction were necessary, but imposed dismemberment "would carry with it an unnecessary decline of the European, as well as the German, standard of living." Political decentralization should therefore not be "more sweeping than that acceptable to moderate groups." ". . . the assimilation—on a basis of equality—of a reformed, peaceful and economically non-aggressive Germany into a liberal system of world trade," was the final goal. Before then, United States policy assumed, the Allies would require reparations, and while it defined no figures, it imposed important limiting conditions in advance. First, the occupation must maintain a "minimum" standard of living, whatever that might mean after the deluge of war. After that they could permit reparations, mainly in kind and within ten years at the most, the shorter the duration the better: "The longer reparation lasts . . . the more strongly is Germany likely to become entrenched in the markets of the claimant states" and to interfere with normal world trade.[33] Above all the United States would not finance reparations in any way, and would make the first charge on the German economic surplus to defray relief and occupation costs. It was now unclear what its devastated Allies might expect.

What was important about American planning for Germany in the postwar world was that they considered and evaluated all the essential options for Germany's future before Yalta, even if they resolved nothing definitively. Germany might be weak or strong, disarmed or fit into a military alliance. It might have a chaotic or a capitalist economy. It could be independent or integrated, on a political or an economic level, into the West. Since no one in Washington agreed on any of these alternatives, anything was possible, and since so many other issues complicated that of Germany, Roosevelt refused to submit these questions to the other major Allies until at least Yalta. In no area of major importance to the other Allies was United States planning so ambivalent and potentially so divisively dangerous. Germany alone could be the shoal on which the wartime Allies might crash apart, yet there were so many others as well.

Russia: Trade and De-Bolshevization

The United States confronted the question of postwar economic relations with the Soviet Union in three forms: first, the possibility of future Soviet-American trade, trade which might require credits and reconstruction loans; second, the possible role of the U.S.S.R. in attaining the kind of world economic order which consumed Hull and the State Department; third, the function of reparations, mainly from Germany, in offering a supplement or even an alternative to trade and economic cooperation with the U.S.S.R. All of these questions impinged on the most essential political and ideological issues, for all schemes had to confront the obvious reality that Russia was not a capitalist economy modeled on Western lines, and in any event credits obviously might have political conditions or provide political leverage to the non-Communist world. For both Russia and the West the issue of reparations involved the most sensitive security problem of the power and role of Germany in the postwar world.

The U.S.S.R. had never been important as an international trader, in part because the capitalist world's hostility had early compelled it to embark on a policy of self-sufficiency. Its trading techniques, however, were not unlike those common to the state-sponsored bulk-buying tactics that had sprung up throughout the world during the 1930's and especially during the war. Such massive buying power by a single agency could lead to price concessions in return for vast and assured markets and potentially enormous leverage over the prices and policies of private foreign exporters. In the even more significant case of England, Hull demanded a quick termination of bulk buying and threatened to retaliate in kind if cooperation was not forthcoming. If there was nothing unique about Soviet practices in this regard, and indeed if many American industries had their own purchasing associations to attain the same result during the interwar period, it contradicted Hull's objectives for a new world economy.

The Russians on the other hand offered a partial solution for the problem of the large unused industrial capacity that many expected to exist in the United States after the war, and the Russians were keenly aware of their leverage in this regard. The Americans had to confront both the possibility and value of normal commercial relations with the U.S.S.R., and on this question the experts disagreed. The State Department in 1942 assigned a committee the responsibility of estimating the ability of Russia to engage in world trade, and it concluded that long-term credits capable of repayment should not exceed $200 million, a minute sum. The Russians simply had very little the United States needed, and the matter was essentially a political proposition. Despite this bearish judgment, during the last months of 1943, Hull, Donald M. Nelson, and others in Washington began thinking seriously about the dilemma of postwar economic relations with Russia.

During mid-October, Nelson discussed the issue with Molotov and Stalin in Moscow, not in an official capacity but as a "business man," as he chose to call himself at the time. The United States, he told the Russian leaders, would emerge from the war with a massive industrial capacity, the Russians with an immense need. Both Molotov and Stalin agreed, and Stalin submitted a preliminary list of requirements. The critical question, they both asked, was whether they might find suitable means of credit to attain a mutually beneficial arrangement, and again in his private capacity Nelson suggested that the United States could do it, proposing the immediate creation of a joint commission to deal with the question. Stalin agreed, and in general struck the Americans in the room as being "greatly interested."[34]

Later that month Hull arrived for the Moscow Conference and the subject came up in a rather different form, involving not trade but agreement on principles for the "solution of post-war problems," a discussion that included not merely "the best methods of including the Soviet Union in line with our general commercial policy on a mutually profitable basis," but the future of the Comintern and religion in Russia as well.[35] In this context the impulse was toward the reintegration of Russia into the ideal liberal capitalist world Hull hoped to create—"The necessity," as Stimson jotted the following year, "of bring Russian orgn [sic] into the fold of Christian civilization."[36] What Hull had in mind, and he had asked the Moscow embassy in September to raise the question with Molotov before his arrival, was "the discussion of economic objectives referred to in Article VII."[37] At Moscow he pressed the Russians on the urgent need to think ahead on such larger issues, and they showed real interest only in those passing references Hull made to American aid in Russian reconstruction, including immediate preliminary discussions of the topic.

For the rest of 1943 this pattern repeated itself. The Russians were annoyingly slow in sending experts to Morgenthau's preliminary discussions of the White plan for postwar international financial reform, a plan they publicly attacked at the time, and their persistence in delaying and in raising questions on the proposed Article VII discussions only revealed their reticence. On the question of normal trade and reconstruction credits they moved authoritatively at the highest levels, indicating full readiness to do business immediately and to repay. But save for inconclusive conversations between Hopkins and the Soviet Purchasing Commission in Washington, the two nations resolved nothing. For, as Harriman reminded Hull:

> Our participation in reconstruction is an important and integral part of our diplomatic dealings with them and it is therefore in my judgment essential that the negotiations be handled under the direction of those dealing with our overall relations with the Soviet Union and not by a new independent agency or group.[38]

Economic power in this view, as with Britain, would become a political instrument.

It was therefore easier to stress the desirability of Soviet acquiescence to the abstract principles Washington defined rather than make premature bargains, and so the United States emphasized the discussion of Article VII for the time. In December, Hull supplied Harriman with a vast list of basic issues to raise for clarification, ranging from the need to reduce barriers to trade, abolish export restrictions and subsidies that were by this time integral to planned economies, and the need "To harmonize commercial interests of state-trading and private-enterprise countries," and to guarantee import quotas at prices that "commercial considerations" defined.[39] In brief the Americans delayed the issue of postwar economic collaboration with Russia, short of the improbable Soviet abandonment of Bolshevism, until they could carefully evaluate the political factors. In the meantime Washington and Moscow dickered over principles and details, each offering ample excuse for procrastination.

Roosevelt himself took no position designed to contradict this trend, and after returning from Teheran, where no one raised the topic, he merely asked Harriman to continue exploring the issue and to make recommendations. At the end of 1943, however, the Foreign Economic Administration sent a revised estimate of the potential volume of Russian postwar trade to Hopkins, suggesting the Russians might be able to sustain as much as $1 billion a year in foreign trade. In short, many now understood that it might not be entirely to United States self-interest to consider the matter as purely political and risk depriving itself of a potential, needed market. By the beginning of 1944 a note of ambivalence crept into Harriman's reports of intense Soviet desire to obtain credits, for "orders from the Soviet Government for reconstruction can be of considerable value in easing dislocations to our own employment problems. . . ." He now endorsed a loan of $500 million, at 2 to 3 percent interest, but only if "our relations are developing satisfactorily in other directions." At the beginning of February, Anastas Mikoyan submitted a request to Harriman for an initial $1 billion loan at one-half of one percent interest, in what was obviously a first bargaining position from Russia's most famous trade expert. Harriman now shifted responsibility for the decision to Washington, with somewhat greater emphasis on a potentially useful competitive advantage and markets. He also warned that "Vague promises excite Soviet suspicions," strongly implying it was now time "to offer a definite credit program. . . ."[40]

Roosevelt immediately responded to the Russians in the form of a personal plea to Stalin at the end of February for greater Russian cooperation in achieving the larger postwar economic objectives for which Hull was so energetically proselytizing. But as a whole spectrum of delicate political questions intruded into the American view of relations with Russia, especially in Eastern Europe, Harriman now shifted back to a more reserved posture and reminded Hull, who scarcely needed prodding, "that economic assistance is one of the most effective weapons at our disposal to influence European political events in the direction we desire and to avoid the development of a sphere of influence of the Soviet Union over Eastern Europe and the Balkans." Here the matter rested in a desultory fashion until June, Harriman taking an ambiguous position between the purely political and trade alternatives despite Soviet desires to discuss the matter and a new State Department estimate doubling its own previous evaluation of Soviet export capabilities. In Moscow during mid-June, Eric Johnston, head of the United States Chamber of Commerce, discussed the trade issue with Molotov and Mikoyan. He then announced to the press that the Russians would buy "many many billions of dollars worth of goods on credit terms mutually advantageous to the two countries."[41] Very significantly he added that the precise volume of Russian purchases might depend on the extent of German reparations which they might receive. The two issues were now joined publicly, even though Washington had always been aware of their intimate connection. As if to make the Russian market even more enticing to the Americans, at the end of June, Stalin himself invited Johnston for an interview and reiterated the Soviet's strong desire to trade and obtain American credits. Coating the proposition, Stalin assured him that Russia would not become an export competitor to its allies, but merely provide them with markets. He designed the package to be appealing.

It is a measure of the naïveté of Soviet assumptions concerning the nature of the capitalist orientation of their allies, as well as a reflection of their strictly pragmatic accommodation to wartime exigencies, that the Russians seriously expected postwar aid that would strengthen them economically and politically vis-à-vis the West. There can be no doubt that the Russians correctly perceived the West's desire for postwar markets and full employment, for Nelson had stressed the point and the theme pervaded numerous official statements, a fact that the Russians attempted to turn to their advantage by demanding large discounts and low interest terms. But to assume that the West did not realize the relatively limited potential of the Russian market at the time, much less the political consequences of economic policy, postulated a crude economic determinism in the definition of American foreign policy that failed to differentiate short-term economic interests that the Chamber of Commerce might impose from the longer-range conditions of ultimate survival. Indeed, during the spring of 1944 the Russians presumed, with some slight justification, that they might even turn Anglo-American rivalries for postwar export markets to their own advantage by implying they might throw their orders to one side or the other. Well after it was apparent that the Americans would concede only after long and arduous discussion, if at all, the Russians supposed that they were bargaining from a position of strength, overestimating their own power and minimizing the capability of their allies to engage in prolonged and cynical debate. For all their superficial realism, the Russians now lost contact with reality and believed that coexistence was possible on equitable terms.

If Stalin intended his rather obvious plea to evoke a response the Russians were to be disappointed. During the next several months the Russians attempted to strain the Lend-Lease negotiations then taking place in Washington in a manner designed to produce postwar credits at modest interest rates and significant discounts on American goods. The hard bargaining began to leave a bitter taste and resulted in only a minimum of agreement before Yalta, for the Americans did not destine Lend-Lease to become a substitute for a postwar loan. By the fall of 1944, when Feis published his book on foreign economic policy, it was apparent to the Russians, as the key State Department adviser observed, that "It will be relatively easy for the United States to build a sound economic relationship with the USSR if the policies of that country . . . bring reassurance."[42] What did such procrastination mean in the light of Harriman's admonition that vague promises would only arouse Russian suspicions?

The attitude of the United States toward a loan could only force the Russians to consider other possible sources of support to aid them in the reconstruction of their frightfully devastated nation should the Americans be unwilling to grant credits of considerable magnitude. American economic experts in the State Department knew that without external aid Soviet recovery would be much slower and more painful, the result of a national effort from a people already intensely weary and wounded. If the United States did not provide aid, only Germany could. "One major Russian objective of economic control. . . ," Stettinius wrote Roosevelt in considering the future of Germany, "will be energetic exploitation of the German economy for Russian reconstruction and development."[43] The reticent United States loan policy, therefore, made the question of Germany and reparations extremely critical to Russia. Here the Russians had little cause for optimism. Official American policy relegated the issue to that of a tool for larger United States postwar economic objectives. In Italy, Hungary, and Rumania the Russians ran up against solid Anglo-American opposition on this question. In the wings Morgenthau advocated a reorganization of the German economy along lines that would automatically have excluded reparations on the scale the Soviets envisaged and needed. American policy appeared to be aimed at reducing both options for major external aid.

At the end of October the Russians informed Washington that they would soon submit a proposal for a long-term credit, but before Molotov could formally hand the Soviet request to Harriman, Morgenthau on January 1, 1945 preempted the focus of the issue in Washington.

Morgenthau and White always understood that a major defect in their plan for Germany was the low level of reparations it would make available to the U.S.S.R. In hastily devising their scheme they left this matter hanging. At the same time both men had a view of a world economic order quite as sophisticated and interested as Hull's, and their roles in this regard were complementary. The result of the White plan, both in intent and consequences, would have been the creation of vast markets for American exports and the hegemony of Washington over the world financial system. For this reason the British compelled its drastic modification and ultimately prevented its implementation. Unlike the project for Germany, Treasury officials had very carefully thought out the White plan and had fully considered its possible impact. And also unlike the scheme for Germany, Morgenthau's next proposal on a Russian loan had been in gestation for nearly a year.

Morgenthau and White became the most important and sophisticated advocates of the reintegration of the U.S.S.R. into the capitalist world economy on a basis which economists have dubbed as neo-colonialism in recent years when Western states have made similar proposals elsewhere. In March 1944 White gave Morgenthau a memo on the relationship of United States future raw materials needs to a loan to Russia. Existing supplies of manganese, chromium, mercury, lead, and other vital minerals were weighed against existing reserves and consumption, and White concluded that a five-year credit of $5 billion, with repayment guaranteed in needed raw materials over a thirty-year period, would solve numerous

American problems in a most advantageous manner and restructure the relations of the U.S.S.R. to the world economy. He intended the plan to achieve Hull's ends, but by more practical means than a plea to an American-defined morality.

Morgenthau now half-heartedly presented a modified version of the scheme to Roosevelt, increasing the size of the loan to $10 billion at 2 percent interest, the Soviets to repay in raw materials or cash over thirty-five years, with an American option on either means of repayment. In the course of the subsequent discussions that month he offered the additional observation that the loan would solve economic problems at home as well as improve relations with the U.S.S.R. Neither the global vision nor the pursuit of national interest was lacking, nor were Morgenthau and White ever to lose sight of them. But the Treasury Department preferred not to press its scheme immediately, acknowledging State Department supremacy in the matter. The foreign-policy leaders immediately judged the plan economically unfeasible and politically undesirable.

On January 3 Molotov submitted a Soviet request for $6 billion, to be repaid over thirty years at 2¼ percent interest, with one-fifth discounts on purchase orders placed before the end of the war. Harriman accepted the *aide-mémoire* with the dampening observation that Congress had authorized discussion of the next Lend-Lease protocol only, the terms of which were still mired in interminable negotiations. Along with their requests the Soviets forced official Washington to consider its policy on the Russian loan problem in the context of two proposals, both of which met the same response. Harriman sent the Russian request along, and a few days later advised Stettinius of

> my very strong and earnest opinion that the question of the credit should be tied into our overall diplomatic relations with the Soviet Union and at the appropriate time the Russians should be given to understand that our willingness to cooperate wholeheartedly with them in their vast reconstruction problems will depend upon their behavior in international matters. I feel, too, that the eventual Lend-Lease settlement should also be borne in mind in this connection.

Leo T. Crowley, the Lend-Lease administrator, endorsed Harriman's view, suggesting they first iron out the sticky Lend-Lease negotiations under way for many months. ". . . from a tactical point of view," the State Department then told Harriman, it could accept neither the Russian nor the Morgenthau proposals. At the same time Acting Secretary of State Grew urged the *New York Times* not to reveal that the Russians had requested a loan. The department's official policy before Yalta was that "Postwar credits to the USSR can serve as a useful instrument in our overall relations with the USSR."[44] They had yet to bring that instrument to bear.

Such a strategy could control Russian policy, as Washington hoped, or help formulate it. When the Yalta Conference opened the Russians understood that their allies were not at all inclined to aid their reconstruction save if the Soviet Union acquiesced to Western policies on political and economic controversies as vital to Russia as to its allies. The Russians had to view the problem of Germany in the light of very limited options, its relative importance increasing as other alternatives disappeared. The Russians could not force the Americans to grant aid, but they had earned their rights to restitution from the Germans on the long and bloody battlefield from Stalingrad to the very borders of Germany. What the West would not give, the Russians might take, and take what they regarded as infinitely less than their due.

BOOK TWO

FROM YALTA THROUGH POTSDAM AND THE END OF THE WAR

CHAPTER

14

THE YALTA CONFERENCE:
THE EFFORT TO FORGE A
POLITICAL ALLIANCE

WHEN THE three Great Allies met at Yalta at the beginning of February 1945, the war in Europe was coming to an end and the contours of the main political and economic problems in Europe were apparent to all. For Roosevelt, Stettinius, Hopkins, Byrnes, Harriman, and the other American leaders gathered in the southern Crimean resort, the critical challenges on the political level now seemed obvious, and the course for meeting them, while obscure in a few dimensions, they had also defined in outline.

First there was the question of Russian intentions. Next the Americans confronted the problem of the Left, the nascent civil war within a world war in the form of masses in revolt throughout the globe, masses that had suffered through a tragedy of historic enormity and unparalleled personal sacrifices. Lastly was the troublesome problem of Great Britain, the reticent ally seeking to carve its own peace and place in the world. Over all these deeply complex issues and forces the United States hoped to establish control or evoke cooperation for the attainment of a set of war aims, mainly economic in content, now spelled out in an increasingly precise and coherent form.

The heads of state had not met since November 1943 and the political problems of the war had multiplied without any serious diplomatic effort by the United States at any time to confront them before they became insoluble. Indeed, until the end of 1944 Washington hoped that by postponing discussions and confining conferences to specific American political and economic postwar objectives, such as the United Nations or a reform of the world economy, it might more easily handle the immediate, pressing questions. British efforts to meet the problem of Eastern Europe head on, in the form of Churchill's strange meeting with Stalin in October 1944, could not succeed so long as the United States refused to show its hand. By the time of the Yalta Conference most American leaders seriously doubted the premise that the American position would be stronger rather than weaker after delay, for now that the adhesive of common military danger in Europe had worn loose, the need for mutual collaboration on a political level had grown thin as well. For the Russians, Western aid in the form of a second front came late, perhaps much later than it was truly needed, and Soviet troops managed consistently to defeat German land power well before D-Day. The war with Japan mainly concerned the American military leaders, who insisted that Russian intervention into that war was necessary to bring it to a relatively quick conclusion, a need which operated in favor of the Russian diplomatic position.

The United States had always been suspicious of Bolshevism and Russia, but the mutual exigencies of the war compelled the Americans to subdue this fear, and for a time the American leaders hoped Russia might in some manner be reintegrated into the world system which the United States projected as a key war aim, and in effect de-Bolshevized. These two beliefs went hand in hand, for Russian cooperation meant ipso facto the end of its revolutionary proselytizing. By the end of 1944 whatever American optimism had existed along this line after Teheran had virtually disappeared. Both Eastern Europe and the emergence of a new, regenerated Left elsewhere inevitably shattered their hope.

Eastern Europe consistently disappointed the American leaders, who regarded no question as important as that of Poland, which they saw as the prime index of Russian intentions. The London Poles' political strategy did not overly trouble the United States, though before Yalta, Washington deemed it wiser to hedge on the American wartime opposition to the Curzon Line and any discussion of border matters, a policy that encouraged the London Poles up to that time to oppose not merely the Russians, but the advice of the English as well. Now that the Russians recognized the Lublin Poles, Mikolajczyk resigned from the London government, and the English openly accused Washington of aiding intransigent Polish nationalism, the State Department was willing to reconsider its policy in the belief that it was not too late to undo the damage resulting from its traditional position. Yet American diplomats were convinced that the Polish situation had arisen because of Russian ambitions, not their own or Polish faults, much less the lack of options from which the Russians might choose. They did not juxtapose Poland against the very different conditions that were emerging in Czechoslovakia, Finland, or Rumania mainly because they could not accept the neutralist and left-oriented logic of Beneš' politics, much less see Soviet policy in those nations as an example of Russian conservatism within the internal structure of postwar Eastern European society.

Not the evidence of Soviet pluralism but the irritating Russian insistence that they apply precisely the "Italian pattern" to Rumanian, Hungarian, and Bulgarian occupation governments caught United States attention
and raised its gravest alarm. Yugoslavia represented the Eastern European
future the Americans most feared, for here the Russians, British, and
Yugoslav Communists collaborated to exclude American influence altogether, in large part because American support for Mihailovic's Chetniks
proved a disaster. They had not heeded British pleadings that they seek to
control Tito by working with him on the basis of his nationalism. However,
a synthesis of Communism and nationalism was a subtle concept with no
place in Washington's definition of the Left in Eastern Europe or anywhere
else for that matter. Rather than adapt itself to the universally anti-
Bolshevik realism of the British or the conservatism of the Russians, Washington contented itself until Yalta with thwarting the ambitions of both its
allies as best it might and evolving long-term goals in Eastern Europe,
overwhelmingly economic in character, rather than formulate immediately
relevant political strategies.

Eastern European developments caused much apprehension over Russian intentions and a general hardening of United States policy toward the
Soviets. Even more urgent was the rise of the Left, for which the Americans were certain the Russians shared a heavy responsibility. In France,
Italy, Belgium, and virtually all of Western Europe they had stopped the
threat of the Left only because military control of civil affairs permitted a
suspension of normal civil liberties that might lead to the transformation
of the Old Order. Such rule would sooner or later have to come to an end,
with the concomitant question of what the Left would do at that time. In
France the British were convinced that they had found their answer in De
Gaulle, whom the Americans opposed with unabashed hostility until the
very months before Yalta, when their posture became one of watchful
reserve. In Greece the British used the club and knout to stop the Left.
Since the Russians understood that they would assume responsibility in the
eyes of their allies for any revolution in the Western sphere of influence,
and their national interests might suffer because of the acts of foreign
revolutionaries, the Soviet Union by 1945 energetically attempted to help
the United States and England check the tide of revolt. The British understood and appreciated this fact in Greece, and thought it a part of their
spheres-of-influence agreement they believed they had won from Stalin in
October 1944, but neither the English nor the Americans perceived its
significance elsewhere to the extent of incorporating it into their overall
assessments of the future of European politics. They continued to hold
Russia accountable for each rash editorial, each riot, each hungry crowd
seeking to bring an end to the miseries and leaders of the Old Order, an
order both England and the United States in their own ways were deter-

mined to preserve and stabilize via arms, or at best, modest reforms.

The Americans never understood that the Communist parties by virtue of Russian influence were safest in politics, and the only group capable of aborting the Left by deluding it. The Anglo-Americans considered it sufficient to stop the Left by dictating to small nations, friends and foes alike, the form of internal social and political systems they preferred, a precedent the West began and the Russians immediately accepted as the Allies divided Europe into spheres of influence.

To the United States, especially in its postwar economic objectives, Britain posed a monumental question that Americans hoped to resolve through both diplomacy and the manipulation of levers of power via Lend-Lease and possible postwar financial credits. The entire war had revealed a frightful, exacerbating dispute between the two Western Allies on almost every major issue. They continuously disagreed over military strategy, and in Italy and France they intrigued over who should rule. The British scored decisively when De Gaulle emerged triumphant and threatened to bring France into a planned Western European political, economic, and military bloc frankly intended to counter overwhelming Russian and American power in Europe. In Eastern Europe the Anglo-American differences on political strategy were sharp and continuous, with no consoling victories for the American position, but only a series of defeats for the British, save in Greece, where the United States supported the ruthless and bloody English suppression of the ELAS.

Yet Anglo-American rivalries were sharpest in the economic sphere. The Americans wanted Great Britain to come out of the war neither too weak nor too strong, but receptive to United States objectives. Continuous haggling over Lend-Lease and dollar balances, then export markets, and England's obligations under Article VII of the Lend-Lease Agreement were dissolving all trust and mutual confidence in an alliance built on common language and necessity. The frightful crises over Saudi Arabian and Iranian oil, escalating in the latter case to a source of serious dispute with the Russians as well, ultimately caused the English to suspect the worst concerning postwar American ambitions and to refuse to stake much on the disinterested quality of American goals. By Yalta the vital unity between the two nations depended largely on their mutual enemies and the common Anglo-American fear of Russia and the threat of the Left.

The United States was fully aware of all these frustrating and difficult elements but hoped to compensate for them, confident that it would emerge from the war preeminent on the political and industrial level and able to define the structure of the postwar world. However, it had not yet resolved all the steps toward this end, and it still had to formulate Germany's role in the future. But in essence the American vision of the future, as the English well understood, was clear. On a political level the United States hoped to become the center of the contemplated United Nations, with a special status among the Great Allies on the Security Council equal to its real power in the expectation the United Nations would become an instrument in the attainment of American political objectives. Washington had heavily loaded the membership of the United Nations to favor American control of the forthcoming San Francisco Conference and the contemplated General Assembly.

Such political vision was broad, but on an economic level the goals were even broader and the instrumentalities for their attainment much more specific, for Hull and American planners had allocated a special place to foreign economic war aims. They saw the structure of the postwar economy as a key lever in determining the nature of the peace, and America would employ its economic power for the mutual benefit of the common weal as well as to provide needed outlets for a vast industrial capacity at home. Bretton Woods, Hull's trading goals, and the like were the key means for constructing a common world economic structure. Washington envisioned a "normal" world economy at this level of planning, one that had not existed since 1914 but which the United States might create, one whose basic problem would be surplus and abundance rather than scarcity. It uncritically assumed these objectives were entirely attainable rather than mere aspirations. The English, however, knew the Americans were advocating policies for others but not for themselves, especially when they examined how the Americans translated such principles into an oil or tariffs policy. After hard and bitter experience many skeptical Allies suspected that the American brand of economic internationalism was synonymous with American hegemony over the world economy.

American definitions of war aims postulated an ideal world order that would emerge from the chaos of the war, one not wracked by social and economic disorder, hunger, and radical changes in the conditions that had defined the prewar world. In developing constant objectives and desired structures on the economic level the planners in Washington did not anticipate radical frustrations in the immediate postwar realities, did not sense the possibility that after a decade of sustained violence and terror it might be altogether beyond American capabilities to restore and reform the era of the late nineteenth and early twentieth century—to undo the social impact of two world wars. Above all it had yet to convince allies essential for the success of the undertaking that the new internationalism it advocated was something more than American power and domination masking itself under a new label. United States leaders regarded Soviet and British skepticism toward this grand American vision and their reticence on numerous specific political and economic matters as evidence of their possible unwillingness to cooperate in the postwar era.

It is true that unilateralism had by 1945 become the major characteristic of the alliance, on an immediate level in Italy, Poland, France, and Greece, and most assuredly in the American initiatives and insistence on postwar economic and political goals. No structure had existed for the resolution of such matters, save conventional diplomacy which the United States always used as a tool of delay, but the lack of a continuous diplomatic forum reflected a conscious desire on the part of the Americans to wait for time and circumstances to evolve to their favor. By Yalta, Washington seriously doubted the success of this wartime policy as the accumulated problems remained unresolved, and the conflict between the Allies was now well under way. Normal channels of diplomacy had been fruitless and deliberately weakened. Now hopefully the meeting of the heads of state could resolve not merely the weaknesses inherent in the two competing social systems, but also control the revolutionary social dynamic emerging from the war. Above all the United States could confront its two allies with the spectrum of American objectives that had accumulated since the superficial political discussions at Teheran fourteen months earlier, and ask them to respond. Their failure to endorse the American goals might define the future of Allied cooperation and therefore the political and economic nature of the postwar world. At the very late hour of February 1945 the leaders of the United States regarded the meeting at Yalta as an effort to tie together and solve the unwieldy and divisive political and economic issues of the past two years, a desperate final attempt to turn the military Allies into a political and economic alliance as well.

Roosevelt the Leader

Roosevelt went to Yalta with a battery of State Department and military advisers in addition to Byrnes, Hopkins, Leahy, Harriman, and others —in brief, save for Stimson and Morgenthau, the men who had the greatest influence on him by virtue of their positions and appointments. Yet the critical quality of the President as a world political leader to this day still befuddles commentators who attempt to suggest that the illness that took Roosevelt's life two months later significantly swayed the decisions he made at Yalta. Such an interpretation, which the personal memoirs of the event hardly support, ignores both the specific decisions made at Yalta and the peculiar Roosevelt style that characterized his leadership of foreign affairs throughout the war.

As a leader Roosevelt was a consistently destabilizing element in the conduct of American foreign affairs during the wartime crises, which were intricate and often assumed a command of facts as a prerequisite for serious judgments. Roosevelt was highly impressionable, and although there is no direct evidence of his insight into this personal shortcoming, his advisers beat him down on so many points that it seems likely he soon became aware of his own weaknesses and his dependence on the skills of others. Problems arose when someone got to Roosevelt first, which compelled the major advisers to work out their disagreements among themselves. His susceptibility to men of extremely limited talents and strong impulses, who gave him consistently inaccurate advice on many questions, compounded this difficulty. Leahy, Patrick Hurley, and Morgenthau were examples of this breed, men who were inevitably taken in rein but who introduced unknown surprises via the President throughout the war.

Churchill himself was often able to convert Roosevelt to his projects, and in casual comments Roosevelt assigned England leadership for Italian and French political affairs over which, when the events themselves transpired, the United States had no intention of relinquishing at least an equal voice. Roosevelt, until the State Department took him in hand, first based his conception of a postwar United Nations structure on Churchill's scheme for dividing the globe into three large areas of responsibility which the British defined to give themselves a central role in the direction of the postwar world. His notions on Germany, the one subject on which he felt fully competent, were idiosyncratic and he soon bowed to the advice of the men around him, though not before creating a useless crisis over the Morgenthau plan that colored all that followed. In the case of Iran and the Middle East he asked Hurley to provide a plan for servicing America in the name of Iranian welfare in a manner which the other Allies regarded with only ill-concealed cynicism. In no major area of postwar planning from 1943 onward did the President assume the basic responsibility for the definition of American objectives.

Roosevelt did not lead or define American foreign policy during World War II, and it soon developed that his advisers (with more effort than they frequently thought necessary, but inherent in the lack of firm, central direction from on high) hammered out that policy for the nation. In doing so they evoked precedent and a clear sense of American interests in the world, interests they understood as a result of their ties with men of power in American society and also because of their very long service in government, a fact that provided continuity in the broad outlines of policy in numerous areas, not the least of which was foreign economic policy and relations with England and Russia. The President himself had difficulty in grasping complex and involved issues, much less in carrying them through over sustained periods of time. If he might throw out colorful, often daring proposals that were obviously impractical, his advisers could invariably get him back to their level of definition and discourse. Although genial, Roosevelt was not a man of vision, not a Woodrow Wilson with a unique personal mission. Indeed he was in no sense either by training or instinct an intellectual or a technician, but rather a well-born patrician in politics. He preferred to procrastinate on critical decisions rather than to make them, but despite this quality of mind, in the last analysis he always came down on the side of the considered opinion of his advisers. "Mr. Roosevelt's policy," Stimson tells in his memoir, "was so often either unknown or not clear to those who had to execute it, and worse yet, in some cases it seemed self-contradictory." Stimson's effort to find redemption for the fact that "Franklin Roosevelt as a wartime international leader proved himself as good as one man could be—but one man was not enough to keep track of so vast an undertaking," in no way moderated this harsh judgment.[1] "Harry Hopkins said that the President was inept," Churchill told Lord Moran, his personal physician, at the Teheran Conference after the President's most intimate adviser had reason to realize that fact well. "He was asked a lot of questions and gave the wrong answers."[2]

His most generous contemporaries, especially those who knew him the shortest time and were not used to his overall manner, thought perhaps Roosevelt was ill. There was slight medical basis for this belief before 1945, but significant was the general consensus on Roosevelt's lack of native ability—for whatever the reason. "Ed Stettinius told me the President was far from well," Eisenhower's chief aide noted in April 1944, "and that he is becoming increasingly difficult to deal with because he changed his mind so often."[3] In reality Roosevelt was not merely unequal to his abler advisers, some of whom were men of very great talent in their milieu, but inferior in subtlety and comprehension of facts to Churchill and Stalin. That was the danger Yalta posed, for even earlier, when his health was unquestionably excellent, he committed his nation at conferences with Churchill or Stalin and others only to return to Washington to discover his advisers would not share or endorse his commitments. Roosevelt was always a weak man at a conference, and Yalta was the most important he attended.

What was even more serious, Roosevelt had great confidence in his power of personal persuasion, a talent that had won him the affection of the American people four times, but in no way was sufficient to cause Stalin and Churchill to abjure their interests any more quickly than America would relinquish its. He did not adequately appreciate that Stalin and Churchill were rather different objects of his attention and that the mere convocation of a meeting would scarcely change realities. His advisers had fewer illusions, and never permitted the matter to get out of hand. Still, as usual, Roosevelt the man was a complicating factor, and although the State Department later was pleased that he relied on its briefing books in numerous areas, it could not know this in advance. Roosevelt, if only for a moment, was an unpredictable factor. It had always been so.

Yalta: An Overview

The British, Russians, and Americans based their coalition on mutual military needs rather than political sympathy, and from the military viewpoint the position of the U.S.S.R. had rarely been stronger vis-à-vis its allies than when the statesmen met in the touchingly refurbished Tsarist palace to discuss the future of the world. The Russians still had much to give to the Anglo-Americans, and at no time was that Western need more apparent than in the days before Yalta. There was the promise of aid in the future for the defeat of Japan, aid the United States military leaders, for reasons discussed in Chapter IX, thought especially critical. But at the beginning of 1945 the role of the Russians in the war against Germany was not merely indispensable—it was still the major ingredient of military victory.

In the north of France and in southern Belgium the United States Third Army had begun to lose the military initiative during the fall, in part because of their caution in risking an advance across the Rhine in winter, but also because of a critical gasoline shortage at least partially the result of the vast black-market operations of American soldiers themselves. Neither the British nor the Russians faced the same problem, but the British alone, irrespective of their impressive successes, could not hold the northern front in the West. Despite overwhelming American and British superiority in arms and men, on December 16 the Germans struck at the surprised American forces in the Ardennes region of Belgium and began a quick assault that for a time threatened reconquest of a substantial portion of liberated Belgium. Anglo-American forces during the last weeks of December were being routed, while in the East the Russians made final preparations for a tremendous winter campaign.

On December 24, for the first time in this fashion, both Roosevelt and Churchill appealed to Stalin for information on when the Russian winter offensive might begin and when distracting relief would be provided against German pressure. "Our confidence in the offensives to be of the Russian army," Churchill half pleaded, "is such that we have never asked you a question before and we are convinced now that the answer will be reassuring." To emphasize the importance of the request Churchill dispatched Air Chief Marshal Tedder to Moscow with details of the situation, but he became weatherbound in Cairo until mid-January. In the meantime the British leader described the heavy battles and on January 6, on behalf of Eisenhower as well, stressed the "need to know in outline what you plan to do, as this obviously affects all his and our major decisions." The next day Stalin sent his welcome answer: despite poor weather and incomplete preparations, "in view of our Allies' position on the Western Front" the Soviet offensive would begin not later than the second half of January. Churchill found himself "most grateful to you for your thrilling message," and described the "heavy losses" of the Americans in "The battle in the West [which] goes not too badly." More than true to their promise, the Russian offensive opened on January 11, for which Roosevelt sent his heartfelt thanks a week later.[4]

The crushing Soviet campaign swept the bulk of the German army from its path, taking Warsaw, then the capital of East Prussia, crossing into Silesia and the main portion of the German homeland itself, a hundred miles from Berlin. By Yalta the Russians had advanced up to three hundred miles, destroyed forty-five German divisions, and removed approximately 400,000 German soldiers from the war. Also by Yalta the Germans had shifted sixteen divisions from the western to the eastern front, had five more in transition, and the Russians expected them to shift thirty to thirty-five toward the East—where in effect they would fight the remainder of the war. The Germans withdrew from the Ardennes, where they had stalled the West, for in the East the Russian hordes cut through all their resistance. What had been Russian military succor to the West now threatened to change the political results of the war. The West asked the Russians to make a commitment in blood, and the meaning of this to the discussions at Yalta was clear. "There can be little doubt that the changing chessboard of war influenced Stalin's political moves," Eden recalled in his memoirs. "At Yalta the military situation was still conspicuously in his favour."[5]

The British Chiefs of Staff assessed the military perspective at the end of January and concluded the war in Europe would end by late June at the earliest, unless "as a result of the present Russian offensive, Germany may be defeated by the middle of April." Two other possibilities existed, though the Anglo-Americans had not yet based primary strategy on them: the Germans might "denude the West as to make an Allied advance comparatively easy," one that Eisenhower did not otherwise expect to cross the Rhine until late March; or the war might continue to November 1945, in which case Russia still had much to offer, a fact which at the beginning of 1945 pushed aside the frustrating political disputes which had dominated Western attention during 1944. The political implications of a campaign in Germany were now apparent even to the British, who finally accepted the American assessment of the political consequences of strategy and agreed definitely to abandon the Balkan strategy that had been their wartime mainstay and redeploy as many Mediterranean forces to the western front as possible "to seek a decision in that theater."[6]

The military prestige of the Russians was never greater than at Yalta, and the Americans and British there listened with deference and awe as Stalin described the fire power and speed of the Red Army in the East, for which Churchill, on behalf of the Americans as well, expressed his "gratitude."[7] Although the political significance of this military relationship is intangible, the historian should not minimize it, for while the West was failing, the Russians were winning because of their stark power.

Given this Russian military advantage, in one sense the West had nothing to lose if the decisions of the Yalta Conference were as general as seemed compatible with progress—unless the English and Americans could get what they wanted at the time—with the details to be filled in when the relations in power became more favorable to the West. Their continued need for Soviet military resources in Europe and the Far East, however, limited this strategy.

Roosevelt, Churchill, and their aides met at Malta from January 30 to February 2, and the conference at Yalta extended from February 4 through the 11th. At Malta the Russians' proximity to Berlin explicitly impressed both Stettinius and Eden, and they resolved immediately to iron out the zonal problem in Germany and the last Anglo-American disagreements that had obstructed the ratification of the EAC plan for German zones. On February 1 Stettinius wired Winant from Malta that the United States should finally sign the protocol on the division of Germany into three power zones, a document that had been ready in final form for two months and in principle for much longer. Only five days later they were relieved to receive formal Russian approval. If possible the three Allies would accept the principle of a unified political and economic policy in Germany. In effect they would ask the Russians to forego the power military victory gave them in lieu of an agreement. Germany at this point had an especially urgent status by virtue of imminent Russian conquest, and hence the Americans and British agreed at Malta that their objective at Yalta was to settle those pressing issues which Russian occupation might solve unilaterally, and defer the remainder by referring them to postconference commissions. They mentioned the impotent EAC at Malta by name. The planned objective at Yalta for the Anglo-Americans was to avoid a comprehensive and detailed solution on the future of Germany.

If one only reads the debates at Yalta, the initial impression is that the three Allies were divided on Germany, and surely the Russians must have left with a sense of Anglo-American disunity. Disagreements that the Anglo-Americans expressed were not contrived, but nevertheless the end result was to table the critical questions until the West might reestablish the balance of power in Europe and lessen the need for Russian military aid. When Eden, Molotov, and Stettinius discussed Germany the first day Eden merely suggested that the entire subject required further study, and while Molotov admitted that the other Allies had apparently given more attention to the matter than the Russians, he said the Russians hoped to obtain German reparations and, significant in this context, long-term American credits as well. Stettinius expressed willingness to discuss reparations, now or later. Molotov was to test him, for the Soviet Foreign Minister was really bluffing, and within several hours the Russians presented the most detailed reparations scheme to the heads of state that anyone had hitherto submitted. The Russian plan called for $10 billion reparations to the U.S.S.R. that they would withdraw over a period of ten years by shipping dismantled plants to Russia and from current production. The Russians proposed reducing heavy industry by four-fifths, abolition of arms and arms-related industries, and continued Allied control over the German economy beyond the reparations period. The Soviets would define reparations for all countries in accordance with contributions to the war effort and losses suffered, a criterion that would have excluded, for all practical purposes, Western Europe. Churchill balked instantly, called the sum "fantastic" and its distribution unfair. Roosevelt said he favored maximum reparations compatible with avoiding starvation in Germany, a position that required no commitments to numbers. The Russians rejected the assertion that the figure was too high, and Stalin pointedly stated that France deserved to collect nothing. Two days later the Russians submitted extremely detailed calculations on how they reached their figure of $20 billion reparations to all the Allies, the only technical calculations any of the Allies had presented up to that time. Stettinius agreed to study it, as well he might, for the Russians now suggested that they form a reparations commission to deal with the specific technical problems after Yalta, their immediate desire being only to determine guiding principles for its work. As an additional inducement the formal Russian proposal submitted on the 7th contained an allocation of $8 billion for the United States and England which they might distribute as they saw fit.[8]

The question of German reparations was intimately linked to the problem of German dismemberment, which came up at the same time, for Germany's ability to pay would reflect the question of postwar control of its disputed and rich border areas. Without the Ruhr or the Saar, for example, it would be impossible for the West to accept the Russian case at face value. Stalin therefore brought up the problem by reminding Roosevelt that at Teheran the President had expressed a desire to split Germany into five or more states, as had Churchill in a rather different fashion, but they had discussed nothing more since then. What, Stalin now probed, was the present American position? The time had come to formulate a policy, though he would not reveal his own. Roosevelt instantly expressed a preference for a discussion of the final occupation zones, a rather different matter, and Churchill refused to commit himself to a definite plan, merely advocating further study of the issue. But Roosevelt now seemingly warmed up to the principle of dismemberment, which the State Department repeatedly rejected, and Stalin asked for a decision on principle, agreeing with Churchill that a commission iron out the details, including the number of states to be created.

The three leaders next gave the Foreign Ministers the subject of Germany in the hope that they might find a way around Churchill's objections. There Eden at first refused to accept even a contingent American statement proposing dismemberment "to the degree necessary to safeguard the peace and security. . . ."[9] They ended the matter by referring it to the EAC. Having tabled dismemberment by sending it to a committee without power, where Roosevelt expected it to die, the Allies returned to the more vital problem of reparations. Stettinius then accepted the principles of the Russian position, or so it seemed, but he refused to accept their figure and merely asked that they submit the entire question and technical means for its implementation to the Moscow commission that all agreed would continue with the issue. He agreed $20 billion might be a "basis" for discussion, as might half of all reparations collected to go to the U.S.S.R., but the British refused to consent to this nebulous formula, frankly stating that they did not believe Germany could pay anywhere near that sum, and that they should not expect it to do so for as long as a decade. Maisky expressed real disappointment at Eden's responses: "Its whole spirit was to take from Germany as little as possible."[10] Stettinius was more practical: he simply reminded Eden, in front of the Russians, that all they were agreeing to was discussion, not actual figures, which might be very different indeed. Eden still refused to approve, for England would not refer a figure to the Moscow reparations conference, but only the principle. The final protocol on the problem reflected the American position, but it was clear from the terminology that the discussion would be open and in no way binding. At their last technical discussion Stalin, according to the Yalta minutes, "emphasized the unsatisfactory nature of the reparations question at the conference."[11] Roosevelt and Hopkins also explicitly understood that they had made no commitment to the Russians.

The Allies resolved only one question pertaining to Germany at Yalta, and that was France's role in the occupation. The British wished to give the French part of the Anglo-American area as an occupation zone in Germany, and Roosevelt supported them on the grounds that it was problematical how long Congress would approve American ground forces remaining in Europe—perhaps only two years after the war—but he first wished to see France excluded from the projected Allied Control Council for Germany. Stalin was skeptical: France had done nothing to defeat Germany, had opened its doors to the Axis and collaborated, and in fact was weak. Stalin was reluctantly prepared to let the English and Americans assign France an occupation zone, to which it had less right than Poland or Yugoslavia, but he too refused to grant it a seat on the Control Council. By the end of the conference Roosevelt indicated readiness to have France on the Control Council, and so Stalin also relented, unwilling to thwart his allies.[12]

On Germany, therefore, the Yalta Conference resulted in a substantial accomplishment for the Americans and English, who alone obtained tangible concessions, if only on France, and above all secured Russian approval to the formal postponement of a German problem which, unlike the issue of the United Nations or Poland, was neither abstract nor beyond redemption. In brief, the Russians agreed not to run Germany unilaterally despite every indication of an imminent military victory that would permit them to do so. They did not trade this leverage by withholding their final signature from zonal divisions in return for specific concessions on reparations or American credits, which they saw as interrelated questions. Germany represented a success for the English and Americans, the most anxious question before them during their weeks of defeat prior to Yalta.

Poland

If the Russians gleaned an ambiguous compromise for their efforts in regard to Germany, the West received the same on Poland, for here the divisions between the United States and Britain worked to aid the Russians. Britain had always favored the Curzon Line and was much more concerned about the political integrity of postwar Poland. The Americans had shown patience and sympathy for Polish claims and ambitions until the very eve of the conference. Therefore the Americans had more than the English to concede to the Russians, who by now occupied most of Poland. The issues were twofold: Polish postwar borders and the nature of the government that would rule the nation.

At Malta the British and Americans attempted to work out a common strategy on the Polish question, and Stettinius emphasized the importance of the matter by suggesting that an unacceptable outcome might prejudice United States entry into the United Nations. They agreed that they could not recognize the Lublin government and that it was now too late to reform the London exiles, much less hope for a fusion between the two. Perhaps they could ask for a new interim government, composed of Mikolajczyk, Witos, Romer, Bierut and a number of non-Communist prewar figures, to run the nation until it might organize free elections. The two Allies would submit the proposal, which Mikolajczyk first originated, to Stalin, but clearly such an interim government would base its authority on the decision of the three Great Powers, not the Russians alone. On territorial matters the agreement was less obvious. The Americans still insisted that Lwow Province go to the Poles, and that they follow the Curzon Line in other areas to define postwar Polish boundaries in the East. In the West the British now backed away from their promise to Mikolajczyk of the previous October to support the incorporation of German territory into Poland up to the western Neisse River. The Americans were categorically opposed to border changes along the Oder, much less the western Neisse, but they left all this to future bargaining, for a concession on the political structure of Poland might alter the indefinite English and American views.

The heads of state discussed Poland at seven of their eight plenary meetings, and probably allocated more time to it than any other question at the conference. It was the only subject which caused Stalin to drop his cool pose and make an impassioned statement of the Russian policy. At the very first meeting Roosevelt, Churchill, and Stalin presented the essentials

of their positions and solutions, and from that point onward they jockeyed
for illusory compromises that really sacrificed no principles. To the Russians, as Stalin explained immediately, Poland was a question of both
honor and security, and no one could now ask "that we should be less
Russian than Curzon. . . ."[13] Military security dictated that they could not
permit a London-exile-supported underground to shoot at the Soviet rear,
and Stalin defended the Lublin government on these grounds as well as its
being as representative as De Gaulle's Provisional Government—an assertion that was a good debating point but both false and irrelevant, since like
the Russians the English and Americans were less concerned with democratic politics than friendly nations.

At this juncture, on February 6, Roosevelt sent Stalin a letter proposing a temporary government along the lines he had discussed with Churchill both at Malta and Yalta. Within a few hours after receiving it Stalin
asked the leaders of the Lublin government to come to Yalta, and on the
7th Molotov offered a package arrangement for Poland: the Allies would
accept the Curzon Line, with minor modifications in favor of Poland in the
east, the Oder-western Neisse in the west; the Lublin government would
add "some" democratic "émigré" leaders, which thus enlarged would obtain Anglo-American recognition; "as soon as possible," Poland would
hold general elections and a Three Power commission would consider the
enlargement of the Lublin government and submit recommendations to
their governments.[14] Roosevelt found the proposal interesting, as did
Churchill, and both asked for time to evaluate it, though Churchill resented
the Russians' use of the word "émigré" and commented "it would be a pity
to stuff the Polish goose so full of German food that it got indigestion."[15]
Stalin assured him the Germans were fleeing the Red Army advance and
the western area was deserted.

The following day Churchill tried to link Poland to the "lamentable
consequences" failure to reach a common agreement would have on world
opinion and the future of the alliance. It was "frightfully important" they
reach agreement in a signed form. Stalin deprecated the situation Churchill
described as not being "so tragic," and then countered Churchill's ardent
advocacy of democracy for Poland by asking "what was going on in
Greece." It would, Churchill replied, "take a great deal of time to explain.
. . ." Roosevelt, more to the point, wanted to know how long a delay Stalin
expected before the elections he proposed, to which Stalin answered one
month, depending on the military situation. But now the Americans proposed their modification of the Russian package of the 7th: they would
accept the Curzon Line as proposed, but the western boundary only on the
Oder and eastern Neisse, a difference of 8,100 square miles; they would
agree to Three Power discussions on the future Polish government to create
a Government of National Unity of democratic elements in and outside

Poland under a presidential committee of three, of which Bierut, the Communist, would be the only representative of the Lublin Poles. When the Poles formed such a government, the Allies would recognize it, and it would hold elections as soon as conditions permitted. Molotov suggested that the plan, with a few slight modifications, might be acceptable if the United States dropped the proposal for a presidential committee.

The next day Stettinius accepted this change, meanwhile threatening American refusal to participate in the United Nations should the Allies be unable to agree on Poland. After a few minor quibbles over terms, Russia accepted the revised American proposal. The critical question in the compromise was not who would rule Poland for the time being, for the agreed statement was vague on this point and merely referred the matter of reorganizing the existing Polish Provisional Government to the Poles themselves and a commission of Molotov, Harriman, and Clark Kerr that was to meet in Moscow. Rather it was the issue of the nature of the elections ultimately to be held. The agreement specified "free and unfettered elections as soon as practicable on the basis of universal suffrage and secret ballot," with all "democratic" parties free to run.[16] But the means for implementation were obscure, and as everyone knew, this might be critical. All details on the western Polish frontier they left equally vague; the peace conference would settle that question. In the East, however, the Anglo-Americans unequivocally accepted the Curzon Line in the final conference protocol. In effect, the Allies tabled Poland for time and future events to make their decisions on that nation contingent on relations between the Allies everywhere.[17]

Eastern Europe

The discussion of Poland was the overwhelming focus of the Yalta debates over Eastern Europe, but other problems of the region arose intermittently, if only because the United States was not ready to accept the Stalin-Churchill agreement of the previous October, such as it was, and also due to joint Anglo-American irritation over Soviet control of the Hungarian, Rumanian, and Bulgarian control commissions and the allegedly rough handling of Western oil properties in Rumania. At Malta, Eden and Stettinius consoled each other with the hope that they might accomplish something during the following days.

There was not sufficient time at Yalta for the leaders and their assistants to cover the numerous phases of Eastern European affairs, and the Americans attempted to meet this physical limitation by advancing a blanket policy in the form of a draft "Declaration on Liberated Europe," a document they circulated in advance but which did not come up for discussion until February 9, when numerous other Eastern European matters were approaching final agreement. Other than Poland, Greece and Yugo-slavia commanded a prior claim on the attention of the rulers of the victorious alliance.

Greece was by now a joint Anglo-American millstone that Stalin threw back when Western moralism waxed hot. At Malta the American Chiefs of Staff agreed to a British request that they release equipment to arm 60,000 Greek troops, troops with which the British intended to suppress the sole popular movement in Greece. The Americans only admonished the British not to permit the flow of equipment to detract from the more critical campaign in northwest Europe. Stalin for his part understood the British optimistically felt they had reached an agreement the previous October, and by evoking it in regard to Greece he might establish his claims else-where. He therefore held Greece up to the British, but also made it repeat-edly clear, according to the Yalta minutes, that "he had no intention of criticizing British actions there or interfering in Greece," a fact which caused Churchill, who as much as admitted he would keep the EAM out of the government, to indicate he was "very much obliged to Marshal Stalin for not having taken too great an interest in Greek affairs."[18]

In Yugoslavia mutual Anglo-Soviet interests were quite as easy to rec-oncile as the Russians showed growing discomfort over Tito's diplomacy. The Tito-Subasic agreement was now beginning to bog down, and the king, despite British pressures, still refused to accept a regency. Churchill indi-cated readiness to bypass the king, but he wanted Russian aid in getting Tito to agree to a revision of the original agreement with Subasic. It was time to implement the original agreement, but also to broaden the member-ship of Tito's antifascist parliament to include noncollaborationist elements of the prewar parliament; all acts of this reformed parliament were to be subject to review when the Yugoslavs elected a new Assembly after free elections, at which time the existing government would relinquish power. ". . . two words to Tito," Churchill assured Stalin, would settle the matter. Stalin was not quite so certain, for he described Tito as "a proud man" who "might resent advice." Churchill mocked the statement, and Stalin "answered that he was not afraid."[19] A remarkable dialogue, and the British had reason to suspect Stalin could not help. British policy still hoped at this time to turn Yugoslavia into "a sort of neutral area between British and Russian zones of influence."[20] The Americans wanted nothing to do with the logic, since neutralism was a political category their moral-ism could never admit.

Stalin and Molotov tried to renege on the two words almost immedi-ately, and then suggested implementing the existing agreements without complicating amendments of the sort the British advised. Now Churchill posed as a democrat, claiming all he asked was that the future legislature review the acts of the temporary authorities, or else Tito would be a dictator. A dictator? That Stalin would not admit, but he conceded the present "national committee" was not a government, "and this is not a good situation."[21] But Stalin would not, when pressed, go back on his initial pledge to aid Churchill, and agreed to send a joint telegram proposing the amendments after Tito immediately put into effect the original Tito-Subasic agreement. All of the British proposals, with Soviet concurrence, the Allies now sent to Tito. Roosevelt at first had been unwilling to sign the Yugoslav statement, perhaps reflecting the traditional American hostility toward British, Titoist, and Russian policy, but the final declaration was tripartite. Not for the first or last time, Tito ignored them all.

WITH the exception of Poland, the United States preferred defining its Eastern European policy on the broadest level of principle, a policy that would cover the many issues that the "Italian formula" created when applied to the control of the three Axis collaborators as well as emerging Russian influence. The original draft of the "Declaration on Liberated Europe," dated February 5, applied to the pro-German nations alike, and pledged "mutual agreement to concert the action of their four governments in assisting the peoples liberated . . . to solve by democratic means their pressing political and economic problems."[22] In short, the United States hoped to terminate the pattern of wartime unilateral initiative and dissolve the accumulated liabilities of Anglo-American policy. The West would ask the Russians to forego the rights battle and victory made available, triumphs that made them the ultimate beneficiaries of the "Italian formula." Amidst references to applying the principles of the Atlantic Charter, emergency relief, and the like, was the critical substitute designed to eliminate the Allied Control Commissions and attain the objectives the State Department first set out in the plans for an Emergency European High Commission to rule Europe. In carrying out the lofty goals of the declaration the four governments, including France, would consult in "matters of direct interest" via their respective ambassadors closest to the areas involved, and the Four Powers would meet quarterly via their foreign ministers. The structure, modeled on the Holy Alliance, in fact would dissolve the Control Commissions.

But it was quickly apparent that the entire proposal on an administrative level was so bizarre that the Americans dropped the references to Four rather than Three Powers, as well as the question of "appropriate machinery," save to indicate the creation of a structure which implicitly meant the elimination of the control commissions. They retained the essential spirit, however, with a few minor literary revisions, in the draft they handed to Stalin and Churchill on February 9. Stalin did not oppose the statement itself, but asked only for an amendment to include "support will be given to the political leaders of those countries who have taken an active part in the struggle against the German invaders." With this addition, he stated, he would approve it immediately. Churchill agreed so long as all understood that "the Atlantic Charter did not apply to the British Empire."[23]

Eden and Stettinius opposed the Russian amendment as interference in the internal political affairs of other countries. So confronted, Molotov insisted that the critical American phrase on the "joint responsibilities" of the Three Powers be turned into "mutual consultations."[24] Both Eden and Stettinius readily accepted the change, and Molotov, with a pointed reference to its value in preventing events such as those in Greece, dropped the Soviet amendment. In this form the declaration became Allied policy. As such it could mean nothing unless the West was also ready to prevent the resurgence of the prewar anti-Russian social forces that had collaborated with Hitler. The Soviet criterion would have required an alliance between the West and the Eastern European Left, the only group in Eastern Europe that had not yet shown in practice contempt for the civil libertarian rhetoric of the declaration. No such unity was imaginable.

The United Nations and the Future

The United Nations was a peculiarly American project, and several times at Yalta, Stettinius and others intimated that its future was contingent on a successful agreement on the Polish issue. In fact in the months preceding Yalta the Russians and British alike continually rejected the American contention that the veto principle in the Security Council could not apply to discussion, but only to contemplated measures involving concrete actions and penalties, and the Allies were now to confront these issues again.

The subject came up the first evening of the conference, and Stalin reiterated the Soviet position that he could cooperate with the British and Americans in joint operations, but that he would never agree to permitting the small powers to judge Russian actions. Churchill too felt everything depended on the unity and cooperation of the three Great Powers, and all else was secondary. In effect each restated his traditional position. It was left to American ingenuity to devise a compromise to convince everyone they could attain their goals, a task to which Stettinius, who had virtual control over the entire matter, directed his main energies. Several days later he presented the formula: Security Council votes on procedural topics would require a mere majority of seven votes, and a permanent member could veto other matters save on issues to which it was a party. Stettinius readily admitted that the proposed compromise was identical to Roosevelt's suggestions to Stalin and Churchill of December 5. Though skeptical before, Churchill now accepted the proposal, but Stalin agreed only to study the document once more, dropping the matter with the observation that the primary purpose of a world organization was to prevent disunity among the three Great Powers. The Soviet Union still recalled, he pointedly added, that the League of Nations, at the instigation of England and France, had expelled Russia and used the League to mobilize world opinion against the U.S.S.R. Roosevelt correctly observed the veto would apply only to discussion in the Security Council if the American plan were rejected, but nothing could keep members from using the General Assembly in the same propagandistic manner as the League. In fact this realization focused attention on the question of General Assembly membership, and made the veto even more precious. It also meant that there was ample room for horse trading on two important factors: the veto and United Nations membership.

The United States proposal was extremely complex, and in addition to a long exposition by Stettinius on February 6, the Americans gave the Russians and English a detailed memorandum designed to break through the confusion of precisely what a member of the Security Council could veto. The United States proposed each of the Five Powers in the council could veto decisions involving action or sanctions, and this the Three Powers had always desired and understood. The central issue therefore was which procedural issues and topics of discussion they might veto or ban for Security Council deliberation, and it was this question that plagued the Allies later. Stettinius itemized a total of eleven categories of situations, some with four subsections. All membership questions were subject to a veto, as well as a variety of "threats to the peace" and means for supressing them—a distinction that later plagued the Americans.[25] Arms control and various regional arrangements were subject to a veto, plus five categories of threats to the peace to which none of the Five Powers was a party, in which case they might decide not to consider such problems. Stalin thought he understood the intricate formula, and no one challenged his interpretation: the veto applied to any dispute involving sanctions, even if one of the Five Powers was a party to the dispute; in regard to "conflicts which could be settled by peaceful means . . . the parties in dispute would not be allowed to vote."[26] Therefore it was implicit that if the dispute was something more than potentially peaceful the veto would apply, even on discussions and on issues which involved the U.S.S.R. or another permanent Security Council member. Since the interpretations did not go into the much shorter resolution that the Americans submitted, these critical meanings were implied but certainly not made explicit.

The Russians claimed the veto question had not been clear before. They now accepted the American package on the following day, and in the same breath asked for the admission of White Russia, the Ukraine, and, hopefully, Lithuania into the General Assembly. The Russians raised this issue before at Dumbarton Oaks, and as at that time, the British immediately supported the Russian claim on the grounds the British Empire afforded them many more than one vote in the General Assembly. Roosevelt for his part was prepared to oppose two more votes for the U.S.S.R., and prior to arriving at Yalta had informed various leaders in Washington that he might ask for forty-eight votes for the United States if the Russians persisted in their demand. But as Stalin pointed out, under the existing understanding all nations that had declared war against the Axis, including at least ten South American nations that had not fired a shot, would be represented at the forthcoming San Francisco Conference. And even more nations were preparing to declare their belligerency. Implicitly these were mere puppets of the United States, and in fact Washington since Dumbarton Oaks encouraged such declarations of war to pile up votes at the founding conference on the United Nations and in the Assembly. Churchill supported Stalin, and Roosevelt could only ask for time to study the issue, perhaps through the Foreign Ministers and hopefully at the forthcoming San Francisco Conference itself.

Since the British and Russians saw the membership issue in exactly the same light, they compelled Stettinius on February 8 to endorse a strange compromise which referred the question of two additional Russian votes as well as the original membership of the United Nations to the San Francisco Conference on April 25. However, White Russia and the Ukraine could not sign the United Nations Declaration until then. There was no certainty that the conference itself would admit them, although Britain and the United States pledged to do so, especially if those attending the conference were ready on their own or with prompting behind the scenes to oppose the Russian request. Therefore, the critical question was: who would be qualified to attend the founding of the United Nations?

Roosevelt admitted to Stalin and Churchill that the State Department had for some months been urging many South American nations to declare war on Germany, and that in the meantime they had aided the war effort only with their raw materials. Churchill could hardly conceal his cynicism toward this tactic, but he and Stalin agreed, in deference to the Americans, that all nations declaring war against the Axis before March 1 could attend the United Nations Conference. Even this compromise did not please other members of the American delegation, especially James Byrnes, and on the following day he and Alger Hiss convinced Roosevelt that the best alternative was to convince Stalin to permit the President to withdraw from his commitment to support three votes for the U.S.S.R. On the 10th Roosevelt sent Stalin a letter suggesting that one vote for the United States and three for the U.S.S.R. might cause him serious political difficulties at home, requiring him to ask for two additional votes as well. Stalin replied the next day, offering officially to endorse additional votes for the United States, but he would not release the Americans from their pledge. He had

successfully called their bluff.[27] The Russians obtained their only real
concession on the problem of the United Nations, one that was purely
ceremonial and in no way challenged the United States' definition and
control of the postwar political organization.

Roosevelt raised one other significant area of postwar political planning at Yalta in the course of the United Nations debate, the issue of
trusteeships. He first presented the matter to Stalin in the context of postwar international control of Korea and Indochina, trusteeships that were to
last as long as thirty years, and at least in the case of Korea were not to
involve the stationing of foreign troops. The combination was unwieldy, for
trusteeship without an occupation was patently impossible, and even ignoring the strong British opposition to removing French control in Indochina,
it was clear that the United States had something else in mind. In fact the
debate over creating bases in the Pacific was still raging in Washington, and
at Yalta the Americans hoped to clear the ground for possible acquisition
of the former Japanese islands, and perhaps more as well. The three heads
of state gave their attention to the matter only on February 9, when the
Foreign Ministers recommended that the five permanent members of the
Security Council consult on the "territorial trusteeship and dependent
areas" problem before San Francisco, when the conference would consider
the topic again. Despite the fact that the proposal included both France
and Britain, both certain to defend their colonial empires, Churchill "inter-
rupted with great vigor" to denounce the very concept of "fifty nations
thrusting interfering fingers into the life's existence of the British Empire."[28] After much excitement and reassurances Stettinius made it clear
that it was not colonialism but the Japanese mandated islands he had in
mind, and with this the final conference document agreed to lay the basis
for a transfer of enemy territories, and more remotely, mandates that the
League of Nations had distributed after World War I. The Americans were
now legally free to acquire Pacific bases if they chose to do so and could
convince the United Nations.

Russia and the Future of China

At Yalta the Americans linked their intense efforts to get the Russians
into the war in Asia to their deep concern on the question of China. Within
China itself the Americans hoped there would be cooperation between
Chiang and the Communists, but they also insisted Chiang retain the right
to define the terms of collaboration and internal reform. Stalin had already
spelled out to Harriman the previous December the political demands that
the Russians would make as a price of entry into the war, and when the
subject finally came up on February 8, Stalin's rather modest claims to the
American ambassador became the immediate term of reference, and for
this reason, as Leahy recalled and the minutes record, "the entire matter

consumed relatively very little time."[29] What the Russians gave in return was far more consequential.

There was never any question that the victors should return Lower Sakhalin and the Kuriles to Russia, but they had yet to resolve the issue of whether Dairen and Port Arthur should be free ports or leased. Stalin was rather clear in placing entry into the war as a price for concessions on these points, ostensibly because the Russian people would not otherwise understand the reasons for the struggle. He was closer to the mark when insisting on access to the Chinese Eastern and the South Manchurian railroads; he referred to the fact that the Tsars had also used the stretches. But he almost immediately conceded on making Dairen a free port. The discussion finally turned to Chiang's political problems, and Stalin observed that Chiang needed some new associates and that the Kuomintang included people who might satisfy the requirement. Roosevelt admitted that Chiang's failure to win the cooperation of the "so-called communists" was largely Chiang's fault.[30] Stalin only referred to the earlier United Front and expressed bewilderment at Chiang's abandoning it. He did not mention that the Communists had been liquidated as a result of following his advice in this strategy, nor did he plead their case. Although Roosevelt and Stalin had yet to settle the final details, the meeting of minds was obvious from the inception. The question of Chiang's views on these matters came up, but it was obvious Soviet-American agreement was the critical prerequisite. Stalin thought immediate unanimity among the Big Three—Churchill was not present at any of these talks—was sufficient for the moment, and observed that Soong was coming to Moscow in April.

At Yalta the Combined Chiefs of Staff reiterated their desire to obtain Soviet entry into the war against Japan as soon as possible. When Marshall and King asked Soviet General A. I. Antonov about Soviet plans the day after the heads of state discussed China, the Russian merely repeated that "There is no change in the intent" behind Stalin's statement to Harriman the previous October that approximately three months after the war with Germany ended the Russians would attack Japan.[31] Yet this comment had been almost offhand, and was in fact not at all binding. Nothing that Antonov said firmly obligated the Russians to their three-month schedule.

On the last working day of the conference Molotov gave Harriman a draft of "Marshal Stalin's Political Conditions for Russia's Entry in the War Against Japan," specifying a return of its lost islands, maintenance of the status quo in Outer Mongolia, leases to Dairen and the former Tsarist base of Port Arthur, a restoration of Tsarist rights to the northern railroads, and full Chinese sovereignty over Manchuria. In return they added, apparently unsolicited, the following new clause: "For its part the Soviet Union expresses its willingness to conclude with the National Government of China a pact of friendship and alliance between the USSR and China in order to render assistance to China with its armed forces for the purpose of liberating China from the Japanese yoke."[32] Russia would work for the Kuomintang against the Communists.

Stalin and Roosevelt immediately considered the proposition, and while the Russian then agreed to make Dairen a free port, he also successfully won the insertion of a clause acknowledging the "preeminent interests" of the U.S.S.R. there as well as on the joint Chinese-Russian commission that was to run the northern railroads. Harriman then introduced a new clause requiring Chiang's concurrence to all that they had agreed upon. Stalin left that task to Roosevelt, indicating only that to prevent a preemptive Japanese blow he did not wish Chiang to be informed before he had an opportunity to move his troops to the Far East. Since everyone knew there were no secrets in Chungking and that all information could be purchased, this was critical.[33]

The Americans and Russians informed the British of their agreements only on the final day of the conference, and Eden was so angry at being excluded that he urged Churchill not to sign the protocol, but was unsuccessful. The three states treated the understanding with the greatest secrecy, if only to keep the Japanese from learning of the contemplated Russian move via the Chinese, but in fact the Russians had yet to formally commit themselves to enter the war, for the KMT Chinese might refuse to support the protocol. Yet its validation was entirely in the interest of the United States and Chiang, for as Leahy correctly perceived it, the United States won "Stalin's agreement to support the Chinese Government of Chiang Kai-shek. . . ."[34] The Russians were amazingly cooperative because they did not view a strong China as being in their interests, and all they demanded predicated a weak government as the price of reestablishing the nineteenth-century Tsarist privileges in China. The protocol also fixed a limit on the privileges the Russians might take once entering Chinese territory and liberating it for the Kuomintang. It meant Russia would continue to oppose Chinese Communism in its struggle to transform and restore China to greatness.

GERMANY, Poland, the United Nations organization, and Eastern Europe were the major topics the Allies discussed and acted upon at Yalta. Yet the three leaders gathered at Yalta broached and then dropped numerous smaller issues that divided the alliance, only to emphasize the distance that they had to travel before true tripartite political agreement was possible. Indeed, the case of the Turkish Straits and the Montreux Convention of 1936 governing its use raised a new issue of potential controversy where none had existed before. The State Department hoped the question would not come up because the convention "has worked well," but on the last day of serious discussion at Yalta, Stalin said that a revision of the treaty was most desirable. Time was short, Stalin had no specific alternatives to offer, Churchill agreed that revision was overdue, and the Americans were silent throughout. Stalin's statement that "it was impossible to accept a situation in which Turkey had a hand on Russia's throat" made it clear that he expected Turkey to relinquish something.[35] They left the matter hanging, with no agreement on the precise arrangements for further conversations.

The three nations considered Iran rather more carefully, for the material promise of oil was more pressing and the immediate frustrations of Russia having thwarted them in obtaining oil concessions was still much on the minds of Anglo-American diplomats. At Malta, Eden indicated that it was more important than ever to get Russian troops out of Iran after the war, as they had agreed in their 1941 treaty, and so the two Western nations stressed this theme at Yalta, maintaining that they too favored oil concessions to Russia when the Iranians were ready to resume negotiations. Molotov said the Iranian oil question was not urgent, and accepted Anglo-American solicitude for Russian oil rights without a note of sarcasm. Later the English submitted a note suggesting Allied troop withdrawals even before the end of hostilities, and a mutual self-denial pledge in regard to oil concessions. The subject came up again, but the Allies only referred it to normal diplomatic channels for agreement.[36]

What did the wartime Allies resolve at Yalta? It would be false cynicism to say nothing, incorrect to claim that the conference accomplished a great deal. For a time the mood of the conference created its own criterion, for the men gathered there at times appeared capable of lowering their guards and responding to one another as individuals. The dinner meetings were often extremely cordial and personally friendly, so much so that Stalin and Churchill uttered effusive words equal to the occasions again and again, with Roosevelt making plainer, less eloquent homilies by virtue of his more limited oratorical talents, but also imbibing the atmosphere of good will. Churchill, who fought Bolshevism everywhere and had in prior weeks advocated the suppression of the Left by bullets and blood, could now talk of "Stalin's life as most precious to the hopes and hearts of all of us," pledging "We shall not weaken in supporting your exertions." Stalin could reply in kind, even more expansively, toasting "In the history of diplomacy I know of no such close alliance of three Great Powers as this . . . ," an alliance for "lasting peace."[37] ". . . the atmosphere at this dinner was as that of a family," like the relations between our countries, the less verbally agile Roosevelt could chime.[38] Yet these words were not merely those of cunning men. The leaders believed the elegant phrases, at least for the moment, as they temporarily forgot the past and the reality amidst cooing and compromise.

To the Americans, Yalta was a great event. "We really believed in our hearts that this was the dawn of the new day we had all been praying for and talking about for so many years," Hopkins recounted. "We were absolutely certain that we had won the first great victory of the peace. . . . The

Russians had proved that they could be reasonable and farseeing and there wasn't any doubt in the minds of the President or any of us that we could live with them. . . ."[39] Their one fear was that if Stalin were to die, he might be replaced by someone less sensible. For their part the Russians immediately heralded Yalta

> as a memorable milestone on the road to the complete defeat and extirpation of the brown plague of fascism, on the road to ensuring world peace and security in the interests of all the freedom-loving nations, big and small. The Soviet public is unanimous in its appraisal of these decisions and regards them as unquestionable proof of the growing mutual understanding between the Allies.[40]

Well might the Americans and English regard Yalta as an encouraging test of Soviet intentions, for the Russians came in a position of tactical military superiority and with a vast credit of blood and aid to the West, both of which they failed to exploit fully. The military realities on the western front in the weeks before Yalta had eclipsed the profound political and ideological divisions of the alliance. The Russians did not exploit their advantage on the German question despite the West's out-of-hand refusal to discuss, much less accept, for obviously political reasons, their unusually detailed technical arguments on reparations. The Americans and English chose to postpone the details of agreement in regard to Germany, the American plans for the United Nations were patently obvious to all, and only in Poland and Eastern Europe did the Russians hedge their commitments to give themselves options in the future—they might well have taken much more and dealt with existing conditions realistically. In brief, Stalin played a conservative game at Yalta just as the Communist parties were then attempting to do throughout Europe. He was prepared naïvely to grant more to Western interests than he asked in return. For this reason the Americans could depart elated, full of hopes and illusions.

The "betrayal of Yalta" that some have referred to since the war was really a deflation of the illusions cultivated, not in the results obtained. Quite intentionally, in the hope that subsequent power balances would be more favorable, the United States and Britain left the final accords subject to much further clarification and agreement, an obscurity that could lead to immediate agreement and subsequent dispute. Perhaps as critical as the topics discussed and broad agreements reached were the subjects they did not consider, which were quite as important to the United States' assessment of Russian intentions and war aims. They hardly referred to the problem of the Left, and unless the Western Powers could contain the Left, not merely in Greece but everywhere, the United States could not attain that single prerequisite it had fixed as its goal—stability of the world economic and political order. Conflicting economic objectives set traps for all three nations at every turn, and they had not even alluded to them. Stability was not for the Russians or anyone else to give or deny, for the war had shaken and shattered the world, and before anyone could chart its new course much would yet occur. For the war was the beginning of a world revolution which one could see everywhere, and the diplomats could not bargain over that, but simply hold one another responsible for the chaos they themselves helped to create.

Yalta was the first and last truly political meeting of the heads of the three Great Powers during the war against Germany, a meeting that came when the end of the war was in sight and mutual need, and therefore the pressures for true compromises, about to come to an end. The speed with which the fragile, unformed political alliance masking a military coalition could now disintegrate was virtually uninhibited.

Pell-mell to Cairo

As the toasts were downed and the warming words uttered, one small incident more than any other revealed that Yalta would be only a momentary respite before the basic conflicts between the three Great Powers again defined the main thrust of world politics. The Russians compromised a great deal during the sessions, and indeed the conference is significant in one sense mainly as an indication of how conservative Stalin had become. But they had much more to do, many unresolved issues to clarify, and late in the evening of February 10, the night before the conference was formally scheduled to disband, according to the American record, Stalin "then said he thought more time was needed to consider and finish the business of the conference." To this Roosevelt "answered that he had three Kings waiting for him in the Near East, including Ibn Saud."[41] Stalin could wait, but Churchill was dumfounded.

Even later that same night the "flabbergasted" Churchill sought out Hopkins, "greatly disturbed and [he] wanted to know what were the President's intentions in relation to these three sovereigns," including Farouk of Egypt and Haile Selassie of Ethiopia. Hopkins assured him it was "a lot of horseplay," for the President enjoyed pageantry.[42] Churchill saw it as a plot to destroy British influence, and his aides immediately asked the three kings to remain in Cairo after Roosevelt's departure. For Roosevelt and Ibn Saud discussed at least the Zionist question, and probably much else besides. When Churchill saw the Arabian potentate, he made a striking gift of a bulletproof Rolls-Royce, and whereas the Americans had brought the Arabs to Suez on a destroyer, Churchill returned them on a cruiser.[43] Roosevelt had found eight days for Stalin and Churchill and three for his assorted kings. It was again politics as usual.

CHAPTER

15

GERMANY AND
THE END OF ILLUSION

I N THIS HIGHLY CHARGED environment of instability and competition within the Allied alliance obvious to all with eyes and will to
see, the Nazis attempted to mold their tactics to the existing political
factors of the war in the hope of minimizing, even avoiding, defeat. They
sought to create an anti-Bolshevik alliance with the English and Americans, and to make Germany an integral part of it. Given the nature of the
Allied tensions, the Anglo-American response to the temptation was less
than unequivocal, but the Nazis discovered they were both too late, and in
1945, too premature. Less bellicose Germans were later to carry the strategy to a successful conclusion, for there were many in England and the
United States even in 1944 who did not wish to see Germany, in one form
or another, collapse as a barrier to Russian power.

During the summer of 1944 Hitler had roughly disparaged the argument some of his generals advanced that Germany attempt to relax or
surrender in the West to play the Allies off against one another. Then his
objective was to fight well everywhere. By September, however, there was
no option but to take their advice and at least experiment. Hitler ordered
the withdrawal from Greece in the hope "we can kindle and fan strife
between Communist and nationalist forces," and he might well have congratulated his new perspicacity as substantial numbers of British troops
were thrown into the fray as well. By December 1944 the actual and even
larger impending civil war in the Allied camp encouraged German military
and political strategy geared entirely to the object of dividing and joining.
All that was necessary, as Hitler explained to his generals in December
1944, was to convince the Anglo-Americans that they could not expect
surrender or an easy victory, and indeed they might fight on the western

front while the Russians threatened to conquer Europe for Bolshevism from the East.

> The following must also be considered, gentlemen. In all history there has never been a coalition composed of such heterogeneous partners with such totally divergent objectives as that of our enemies. The states which are now our enemies are the greatest opposites which exist on earth: ultra-capitalist states on one side and ultra-Marxist states on the other; on one side a dying empire—Britain; on the other side a colony, the United States waiting to claim its inheritance. These are states whose objectives diverge daily. And anyone who, if I may use the phrase, sits like a spider in his web and follows these developments can see how hour by hour these antitheses are increasing. If we can deal it a couple of heavy blows, this artificially constructed common front may collapse with a mighty thunderclap at any moment. Each of the partners in this coalition has entered it in the hope of achieving thereby his political objectives . . . either to cheat the others out of something or to get something out of it: the United States' object is to be England's heir, Russia's object is to capture the Balkans, to capture the Straits, to capture Persian oil, to capture Iran, to capture the Persian Gulf; England's object is to maintain her position, to strengthen her position in the Mediterranean. In other words one day—it can happen any moment, for on the other side history is being made merely by mortal men—this coalition may dissolve. . . .[1]

In planning his vast counterattack against the Anglo-American armies in Belgium in December, Hitler intended to impress on his Western foes, in the most overwhelming manner possible, that for them the war would be a disaster even if they defeated his armies.

Hitler's logic was too precarious, the timing being all important, for if the defeat he was seeking to avoid came in the East, the disintegration of the alliance would hardly save the Nazis, though it might lead to an Anglo-American revival of Germany without him. On January 12, 1945, as the Russians smashed across the German lines and toward the Oder to relieve their beleaguered allies, Hitler and Goering at first gloated, even considering, as Goering suggested on January 27, "we will get a telegram [from the English] in a few days."[2] The obverse side of this proposition is that the Russians alone would defeat and penalize Germany with a vengeance that rumors from the East and Soviet journalist Ilya Ehrenburg's ferocious declarations during the months before made seem awful indeed. The telegram did not arrive, and working within the same strategy of dividing the Allies, the Nazis decided to move their forces to fight the war on the eastern front.

The Russians reported the flood of German troops from the West toward the East at Yalta, at which time there were as many German divisions on the central Polish front alone—eighty—as faced all the Anglo-American armies on the entire western front. But in that month the Germans shifted as many as thirty-five additional divisions to the East. The British Chiefs of Staff thought that if the war ended before July it would be a result of the Russian offensive, for they had not scheduled the Western offensive to begin until after the end of March. The Germans confounded them, and by March 25 only twenty-six German divisions remained on the western front as opposed to 170 on the eastern front, and most of this small number held the northern German ports so that the Germans could evacuate to them and be free to surrender to the Anglo-American armies. For the Germans decided to hold fast in the East and to relax, though by no mean entirely, in the West. From February 1 to May 6 the Western armies moved 250 to 300 miles across Germany on a broad front, while the more powerful Russian armies were in many areas limited to twenty-five miles, and to less than 125 miles in the major regions. During the last three weeks of the war, as the Germans disintegrated in the West, in some places Anglo-American forces covered over 150 miles, and in only a few locations did the Russians equal half that distance. Two American armies crossed the Rhine north of the Ruhr with the loss of fourteen men. Along most of the eastern front the Germans fought to hold critical points with an intensity the Russians at times grudgingly respected, and lost 300,000 men killed on the central front alone, but only 86,000 captured.

The terror of the war was never greater than in the spring of 1945, and the irrationality of the Nazi leaders, with a timetable based on political assumptions over which they had no control, was never greater than as they burned up the German people. In Berlin itself rich and aristocratic Germans lived neat lives amid the chaos, while everywhere else the black market became rampant, teen-age prostitution common, and the signs of disintegration, which are the hallmark of a lost war the rulers have yet to acknowledge, were everywhere. Reality for the German leaders became identical to wish fulfillment and conventional wisdom that was mad was still believed in the hope that they might skirt defeat. Amidst the chaos there was still order.

For the political and military leaders of the West the German strategy created new opportunities, for to the extent that diplomacy was a substitute for power, and the alliance based on military convenience rather than political consensus, the collapse of German armies on their front opened to the West the possibility of vast political gain. The question arose: which military strategy was best designed to attain paramount political objectives?

Every move now had political meaning, and all the diplomatic nerves of friends and antagonists alike were sensitive to each gesture and word. As Hitler's dreams became more unreal, German officers now moved to exploit the chaos to define their own objectives, some with the agreement of Berlin, others alone. In January, Hitler knew that his highest officers were anxious to sign an armistice in the West to fight in the East. "War is a political instrument," Field Marshal Montgomery, the head of British forces remarked in his discussion of the period; "once it is clear that you are going to win, political considerations must influence its further course."[3] While some German officers believed "the sense of military duty . . . to fight on," others were now not so sure.[4] Never was it easier for generals to surrender, and in the process mask political victory in military considerations.

Everyone in London and Washington save Roosevelt opposed the principle of unconditional surrender, and in fact the Allies had not applied it to any of the Axis peace treaties signed before March 1945. On March 1 Roosevelt took some of the claws out of the doctrine by publicly defining it in greater detail than ever before. It did not mean permanent occupation, and "We do not want the German people to starve, or to become a burden on the rest of the world." The American objective was peace—"That objective will not harm the German people."[5] He had cast the bait, and given the virtual autonomy of the German generals in the anarchy of defeat, their only inhibition was their sense of duty. To some this was not much. For during March the United States and England had to make two critical military decisions with the most obvious political implications: how to fight the war in Germany, given the minimal German resistance; and on what terms to accept surrenders.

The decision on the best manner to fight the war was a subject of intense dispute between the English and Americans. Conventional interpretations suggest that the British strategy of sending Montgomery's 21st Army Group into northern Germany as fast and as far as it could go, hopefully to Berlin, was political in motive while the Americans naïvely planned to fight the war along a broad front beyond the Rhine. In fact, of course, during late March the Western forces did cross the Rhine according to Eisenhower's plan, but this approach was hardly less political in intent or outcome than that of the British. The Americans first suggested the concept of RANKIN, and Roosevelt and Hopkins very much favored taking Berlin. In February 1945, however, German and Western strength in the West was still equal, and the Germans had not yet stopped the momentum of the Russian offensive, then less than a hundred miles from Berlin. The Americans had to consider whether there was not some more critical objective they could more likely attain than Berlin, for the Russians and their allies had just divided postwar Germany into zones, Berlin included. Hence they already had the right to a share in the control of Berlin; they could not keep the Russians out of the capital even if the Western troops took it, and certainly the Soviets could then move toward some other strategic objective if Eisenhower took the great risk of a rush to Berlin. Eisenhower, during 1944, wanted very much to capture Berlin before the Russians, but by the end of March 1945 it was "nothing but a geographical location" to him.[6] His officers appreciated the political dimension but thought the military gains from the certain house-to-house combat too insignificant to warrant the bloodshed. "In the light of the political decisions already reached to dispose of central Germany," Eisenhower wrote later, "it was futile . . . to expend military resources in striving to capture and hold a region which we were obligated, by prior decision of a higher authority, to evacuate once the fighting was over." On the other hand, there was a higher political logic that even the British admitted had much weight. "Being unfettered by political decision as to other areas, I directed troop advances toward Denmark and Austria."[7] But Eisenhower ordered Montgomery to reach Lübeck, on the eastern coast of the Schleswig-Holstein state and Danish peninsula, thereby stopping any Russian advance from obtaining access to the Atlantic coast should the agreed zonal boundaries later be disregarded. They eventually won that race with the Russians with only six hours to spare.

Churchill also very much favored a southern drive to prevent Hitler from reaching an Alpine redoubt and prolonging the war from there. But he argued that Berlin had important political and symbolic value, for it was certain the Russians would also take Vienna, thereby giving the impression "they have been the overwhelming contributor to our common victory. . . ."[8] He was especially furious when he discovered that Eisenhower, at the end of March, wired the outlines of his military plans to Stalin, plans that were still sufficiently general to be altered in important aspects, but were essential to prevent direct competition with Russia and a catastrophic duplication of Allied military efforts along common fronts. In effect, therefore, Eisenhower agreed to go as far as the river Elbe in the central part of Germany, but to strike across northern and southern Germany in an ambitious manner that still also assumed that the Western advance would be far more extensive and faster than that of the Russian forces. Despite Churchill's bitterness toward the American for taking such decisions without consultation, Eisenhower's plan seemed optimal in terms of its goals, and hardly a modest military objective. As he patiently explained to Churchill on April 1, "The only difference between your suggestions and my plan is one of timing. . . ." There was only a limited number of troops and time was short, and it was necessary to allocate priorities, Lübeck having a political significance that Churchill readily agreed was more than symbolic. Resistance might stiffen everywhere, but "if at any moment collapse should suddenly come about everywhere along the front we would rush forward, and Lübeck and Berlin would be included in our important targets." Therefore, Eisenhower emphasized priorities, not objectives, and Churchill then typically urged on April 2 that "I deem it highly important that we should shake hands with the Russians as far to the east as possible. . . ."[9]

For obvious political reasons, at the very same time that Churchill and Eisenhower disputed such matters, Stimson and Marshall informed Eisenhower that, military factors being equal, they wished to avoid inflicting damage on the Ruhr, so important, as the official history paraphrases Stimson, to "the economic future of Europe."[10] Eisenhower agreed, and he noted strategic bombing of the Ruhr had already stopped, and told Marshall that his forces would bypass the Ruhr as much as possible. Still, despite an essential consensus on the political dimensions of military strategy, the bickering Western leaders had to confront the fact that German resistance, though far less in the West than the East, was still prevalent. In the Ruhr pocket at the beginning of April the Western armies surrounded some one-third of a million German troops, but they could not entirely ignore them to race on to Berlin, and not until the last three weeks of the war did the German armies in the West disintegrate almost at random. In the meantime, despite German resistance in the East, after initial hesitation the Russians decided to pay the frightful price asked for Berlin, one the West too would have paid, for Hitler controlled the forces there and unlike his outlying generals was not ready to surrender. He gave the order to defend Berlin from an American advance during April. The Russians decided to encircle the city and also to attack it directly, despite Stalin's assurances to Churchill that the city was of lesser interest to him. By April 21 Russian troops were engaged in three weeks of storm and fire on the Berlin front and sacrificed 305,000 dead, wounded, and missing men, half again as many as the English and Americans lost during all of 1945.[11]

The Italian Surrender Crisis

How to accept the surrender of the Germans was far more aggravating to relations with the Russians during March than any other factor of the many exacerbating the alliance. Despite the recent account of the affair by Allen Dulles, head of the OSS at the time, the precise circumstances around the attempt of the German military forces in northern Italy to surrender in March 1945 are still not known. But the consequences of the affair were very great, and the historian can now point to new dimensions of the incident. The initial impulse for these negotiations originated in early February with the OSS in Berne under Allen Dulles, which was anxious to stimulate surrender moves among German army leaders on the western front. While the first American initiative bore no fruit, it is critical to the affair to understand that its genesis was "a result of our own initiative," in Dulles' words.[12] But by the end of February acquaintances of the head of the SS in Italy, General Karl Wolff, contacted OSS agents in Berne, for

Wolff was interested in arranging a separate surrender of the German forces in Italy and was unable to communicate in any other manner. The intermediaries for the two sides met in Lugano at the beginning of March, at which time the Germans set the discussion in the context of a surrender that would permit the Allies to take northern Italy before the Communist-led Resistance might do so. Despite Dulles' initial effort to claim all he sought to do was prevent German destruction of northern Italian industry, or the persistent Russian allegation the negotiations were to free troops for the eastern front, much less the official American version that there was nothing to the affair save a desire to secure unconditional surrender and innocent misunderstandings, there can be no doubt about certain vital contextual facts.

For many months the question of the Communists in northern Italy had been the central, almost obsessive, problem of the area to the Anglo-American leaders, and this was as important as any factor in leading to their willingness to pursue the matter. Dulles and the American military leaders were concerned that Tito's forces might reach Trieste and even northern Italy before the Anglo-American armies, or that the Communist-led Resistance would drive out the Germans: "thus, prior occupation of this area by Communist-dominated forces might well determine the zones of postwar influence, or even occupation."[13] The Berne incident and the Italian surrender were preeminently political affairs to keep the Communists out of power, and the Germans were the instruments of that policy. The Germans could not readily redeploy the bulk of their troops in Italy to the eastern front, and in a political sense their quick evacuation was not to the political interests of the United States or England. It was more important that they remain, under defined circumstances.

When Wolff saw Dulles on March 8 he flatly rejected negotiations on unconditional surrender, and in fact the West had nothing immediate to gain from it. The war in Italy was stalemated, and Allied occupation of the north was likely to increase Anglo-American troop commitments in that nation. Then why did they proceed to consider a surrender, since the official Anglo-American strategy was to decide the war in Germany, and it was approaching its obvious conclusion on that front? In fact the greatest political threat to Anglo-American interests was precisely the sudden German withdrawal the Russians later said was the object of the discussions. Suffice it to say, when the OSS informed the Allied command at Caserta of the talks, and both British General Terence S. Airey and American General Lyman Lemnitzer went in disguise to Switzerland in mid-March, they pressed their Italian agents and various trusted Resistance leaders that they brought there for information on the strength of the Communists in the north and the chances for a repetition of events in Athens. On March 19 Wolff returned to Switzerland once more. But Wolff's authority to execute a surrender was in doubt, and even the possibility of his or his family's surviving treason charges for the little he had done was in question. By this time the affair was well on its way to becoming the cause of a major crisis within the Allied camp.

The following month Wolff justified his actions to Nazi leader Heinrich Himmler by claiming that he was attempting to divide the Anglo-Americans from the Russians, an undertaking by the same means to which many other Germans, including Himmler, were committed. Whether intended or not, Wolff succeeded far more brilliantly than he could realize.

The British informed the Russians of the Berne discussions on March 12, for Churchill was most anxious to avoid giving the impression of negotiating a separate surrender, and much to Harriman's irritation unilaterally invited the Russians to send a representative after Molotov insisted on it. After all, Molotov observed, Russia was "bearing the brunt of the war."[14] The concession was a reluctant one, and certainly over American objections, for on the 15th the Americans informed the Russians that Alexander's representatives, Lemnitzer and Airey, were already in Berne (but not that Wolff would arrive four days later) and it was an obvious hint to the Russians not to attend. At the same time the Combined Chiefs of Staff told the Russians that while they could send observers, only Alexander as head of the theater was free to negotiate and make decisions. The Russians took the advice as they intended it, and on March 16 Molotov informed the British that inasmuch as the Anglo-Americans were excluding them, they insisted that their allies terminate the Berne discussions and that all future German surrender negotiations include all three Allies. These "bombshells," as Stimson interpreted them, warranted strong replies, and Washington treated the matter as gravely important.[15]

The issue did not die, for on March 22 Molotov answered a British effort to dismiss the affair with a scorching letter stating "the Soviet Government sees this matter, not as a misunderstanding, but as something worse."[16] To Churchill a storm was obviously brewing with the Russians, and since the discussions in Berne came to a temporary end and the British had little to lose by continued German occupation of the north for a while longer, he thought the best course was to maintain silence. The West and Germany would resume surrender negotiations elsewhere, "in a far more vital area than Italy. In this military and political questions will be intertwined. The Russians may have a legitimate fear of our doing a deal in the West to hold them well back in the East."[17] Since Churchill was quite ready to negotiate or take any step to contain Russia in the East, he saw no point in squandering the single opportunity by arousing Russian suspicions over a peripheral area. In fact it would have been difficult to permit the Russians to participate in discussions that considered at the very least, and perhaps exclusively, the containment of the Italian Left.

On March 24, with the backing of his aides, Roosevelt chose to ignore Churchill's reasoning and sent Stalin a message on the affair, assuring him the Berne discussions had been purely technical, to determine the authority of the Germans involved, but had "no political implications whatever." They would continue such discussions in the future if circumstances justified it, Molotov's wishes or not. Four days later Stalin replied in what was perhaps to become the sharpest expression of mutual distrust of the entire war, for he simply did not believe the President. Under no circumstances, Stalin insisted, could the Allies allow surrender talks to ease an enemy's position or permit the maneuvering troops to enter other areas. The West had not encircled the Germans in northern Italy as the Soviets did in Poland, so the reasons for their surrender were obviously not military, and Stalin implied that this was the reason the West excluded his representatives from the talks. Roosevelt replied, stating "the matter now stands in an atmosphere of regrettable apprehension and mistrust." There was no question of permitting Germans to shift their troops, and Himmler and the SS were using the affair to sow distrust among the Allies.

Now Stalin retorted by turning to the entire European military situation, exposing Soviet fears of concealed negotiations while "Anglo-American troops are enabled to advance into the heart of Germany almost without resistance. . . . the Germans on the Western Front have in fact ceased the war against Britain and America." Then in the worst blow of all he claimed that the negotiations at Berne ended in an agreement with Field Marshal Albert Kesselring to permit the Anglo-American troops to shift eastward in return for easing the armistice terms. Roosevelt, with Marshall's aid, wrote on April 4 "with astonishment," denying the allegation with something less than convincing candor. They did not hold negotiations in Berne, "The meeting had no political implications whatever," the United States would conform to the principle of unconditional surrender in any negotiations, and the Russians "would be welcomed" at any future meetings on surrender, though he did not specify their rights. "Our advances on the Western Front are due to military action," an assertion that avoided the thrust of Stalin's argument. "Finally I would say this, it would be one of the great tragedies of history if at the very moment of the victory, now within our grasp, such distrust, such lack of faith should prejudice the entire undertaking. . . ." These professions did not move Stalin, who defended his informants and cited the "strange and unaccountable" behavior of the Germans, with 147 divisions on the eastern front, fighting for every foot of land while freely surrendering major cities in the West. It was "absolutely necessary," he insisted again, to enable Russians to participate in every surrender discussion.[18]

There the matter might rest for a brief period while the negotiations with Wolff resumed, even as the Allies exchanged hot words, and now moved toward fruition, but the Germans asked for surrender terms that the Americans and British refused to meet. By April 12, when Roosevelt sent Stalin his last message, he dismissed the Berne incident as a "minor misunderstanding," one that served no useful purpose. By that time too he assured Churchill that while "I would minimize the general Soviet problem as much as possible," and this included much more than Berne, but the continuation of the entire spectrum of difficulties of the past two years, "We must be firm however, and our course thus far is correct."[19]

The Berne incident reflected the weakness and ambiguities within both the German and Allied camps. The decision of the Combined Chiefs of Staff to ask the Russians to send observers rather than equal negotiators to future meetings with the Germans, though talks would continue whether the Russians were present or not, scarcely minimized the significance of this division to the alliance. Whatever the motives of the West, any separate surrenders by the Germans in a major theater of war would have enabled Anglo-American troops to fill in the vacuum, political as well as military, that the German collapse was bound to create. Everyone involved in the Berne incident understood this, and the temporary lull in the affair was due only to its seeming lack of promise and was not a rejection of separate surrenders as a source of division in the alliance with the U.S.S.R. as well as a source of political gain. Roosevelt's coyness and feigned innocence did not convince Stalin, and it was entirely logical, despite the inaccuracy of some of the Russian's allegations and the obscurity of relevant facts, for Stalin to suspect the worst. In reality Churchill and the Americans considered every political advantage they might gain from alternative military strategies and the Nazi policy of shifting the rewards of the land war in Germany to the West.

The Soviet Problem—Once Again

The Berne surrender crisis touched on many sensitive political issues approaching the boiling point, and one now aggravated another. In a sense the sharp words Stalin and Roosevelt exchanged in their last letters were also discourses over other topics, primarily the continued deterioration in overall United States-Russian relations. The question of Poland and Eastern Europe, and also the impending United Nations Conference, were foremost among these. In the context of the war with Germany the alliance was strained as never before.

Everyone in Washington understood this by the end of March, and on April 2, addressing a State-War-Navy meeting of Cabinet heads, Stettinius covered what Forrestal noted as the "serious deterioration in our relations with Russia." The Soviet mood was increasingly tough, and on April 4 Harriman began sending a long, detailed series of reports from Moscow confirming the worst fears. ". . . we now have ample proof that the Soviet government views all matters from the standpoint of their own selfish interests," and his first critical evidence was the role of the Western European Communist parties in exploiting economic and political difficulties. The United States and England necessarily had to "adopt an independent line" to prevent "Soviet domination in Europe. . . ." This meant economic aid and the re-creation of economic stability to prevent the Soviet desire to establish "totalitarianism." "The only hope of stopping Soviet penetration is the development of sound economic conditions," and the United States could establish friendship with the U.S.S.R. "on a *quid pro quo* basis."[20]

In fact, Harriman's first telegram assessed conditions in Western Europe, for which he held the Russians responsible to a critical degree, but two days later he followed with a more direct critique of the overall objectives of Soviet foreign policy, objectives with direct bearing on the rapidly evolving situation in Germany. The Russians were now determined to create a security ring of friendly states around their borders, penetrate the other European countries through their Communist parties, and cooperate with the United States and England elsewhere if only to prevent "a close understanding among western nations," something "they fear more than anything else. . . ." A "generous and considerate attitude," such as the United States adopted until then, the Russians interpreted as a sign of weakness, and now it was necessary for the United States to be ready "to go along without them," cement relations with other allies, and let the Russians know that if they wished help it could be only on American terms. Harriman broached the issue of Germany in a blunt fashion: "Up till recently the issues we have had with the Soviets have been relatively small compared with their contribution to the war, but now we should begin to establish a new relationship." To interpolate, the Russians, who gave much to defeat Germany, were now attempting to collect on the political consequences, and nothing more, military or political, could accrue to the West by continuing such an alliance. Harriman saw no point in believing, as some in the State Department had counseled, that they could avoid independent German policies, for the Russians would take what they wanted from Germany in the form of reparations, and an agreement on this subject was a long way off. He continued to urge the use of postwar credits to Russia as a political tool, "dependent upon a reciprocal cooperative attitude of the Soviet Government in other matters."[21]

By the time Roosevelt died on April 12, therefore, Washington increasingly set the question of Germany in the context of overall relations with the U.S.S.R. and some considered it a part of the problem of the expansion of Communism. Whether conscious or not, nothing was to be lost by permitting the German surrender strategy to unfold as the Nazis had planned, for all save the Russians acknowledged anti-Bolshevism as a common denominator. In this context the Berne discussions were both a cause and reflection of the rapid disintegration of even the semblance of an alliance against Germany.

An underlying consensus on these subjects existed in Washington by the time Roosevelt died, and the President had willingly permitted himself, as always, to share in this mode of diplomacy, for he was neither inclined to, nor capable of, defining an alternative. Harry S. Truman retained all of Roosevelt's key advisers, who by and large continued to direct policy for the rest of the war. "I shall count on you for all the help I can get," he told them minutes after he was sworn in as President.[22]

Still, the former Senator from Independence, Missouri, provided a personal ingredient that should be neither underestimated nor exaggerated. If the content was the same, the style and pronunciation were different, but since Truman had, in his own words, "always fully supported the Roosevelt program—both international and domestic . . . ," the outcome was predictable despite the very great initial apprehension of Churchill and Halifax that there might be a radical shift in American policy.[23] Truman's instincts and intellect were comparable to Roosevelt's, and Eden quickly assured Churchill he would be a "loyal collaborator."[24] Leahy, the strongest advocate of a tough policy toward Russia, was on hand to provide the continuity and play on the same penchant for the dramatic and absurd, and Stimson was within the week pleased with Truman's responsiveness and efficiency. The day after taking office the State Department gave Truman an overall assessment of world problems and diplomacy with Russia, which had "since the Yalta Conference . . . taken a firm and uncompromising position on nearly every major question that has arisen in our relations."[25]

The major distinction between Roosevelt and Truman was their phraseology in achieving the same ends, for Truman had none of Roosevelt's grace and bearing, and was blunt where Roosevelt could be diplomatic or at least pleasant. It was, after all, Truman whom the press quoted in June 1941 as declaring, "If we see that Germany is winning we ought to help Russia and if Russia is winning we ought to help Germany and that way let them kill as many as possible, although I don't want to see Hitler victorious under any circumstances."[26] Others had expressed the same reasoning in different form in subsequent years, but it was this very question of German and Soviet power that was relevant when Truman took his oath. Yet the style was unquestionably Truman's own. Molotov came to see the President on April 23, and Poland was the main subject of conversation. Harriman and Leahy were also present and the President took Harriman's posture toward the Russians, "Using blunt language unadorned by the polite verbiage of diplomacy," as Leahy described the session.[27] In the context of the Polish and United Nations problem he warned Molotov that the future of postwar collaboration was at stake. "I have never been talked to like that in my life," Molotov told the President when leaving. "Carry out your agreements and you won't get talked to like that," Truman rasped back.[28] It was the same policy, but in another coating.

The Nazi Surrenders

April 1945 was a month of tension and profound doubt for United States-Russian relations, and in this context the final defeat of Germany took place under circumstances which unavoidably reflected the condition to which the Allied coalition had fallen.

The death of Roosevelt encouraged the desperate Hitler to believe that "the turning point of this war will be decided" to his favor, and until he destroyed himself on April 30 in his bunker beneath the raging storm in Berlin, he was certain the Anglo-Americans and Russians would soon be fighting each other. By that time the Nazi empire had become so decentralized that the heads of each of the unconquered regions prepared to arrange their own fates as best they might, only the concept of discipline exercising sufficient restraint to prevent total chaos.

For the Nazis the end was near, and while they laid their final plans for surrender and defeat, the Allies during April reconsidered their military strategy. The Americans drew up the zonal agreements for Germany when it appeared most unlikely that the Anglo-American forces would capture the three-fifths of Germany allocated to them, and the Russians might reach the Rhine, and Churchill and Roosevelt were delighted to get the final Russian approval of the treaty when the military factors of the war were still in favor of the Red Army. At the end of March, Eisenhower and Churchill debated military strategy, assuming that the zones would not limit troop advances, and implicitly, that the West might not respect them. After initial disagreement on a Berlin campaign they decided to thrust toward Lübeck and the south on an optimum prediction of their speed, which by mid-April proved to be too conservative. But the Germans were fighting only in the East, and opened new options to the Anglo-American forces to consider.

Churchill wished to get as far to the east as possible, and at the beginning of April he informed Eisenhower that since the Allies had not yet arranged zonal divisions for Austria, and the Russians seemed likely to take most of it, it would be inadvisable to withdraw from those zones of Germany allocated to the Russians but now likely to fall into Western hands. The matter was political, not military, and he then asked Truman to countermand Eisenhower's orders permitting Army commanders to withdraw to the EAC-defined zones at will. The Allies "rather hastily" drew up the zones, he wrote Truman on the 18th, and although he was willing to agree to them, they should not withdraw until the Anglo-Americans and Russians settled certain complex questions involving food supplies after V-E Day.[29] To Eden, in Washington at the time, Churchill confessed that Eisenhower was entirely correct in concentrating on the conquest of Lübeck before the Russians, for Russian access to Denmark would open a Pandora's box of problems. He now granted that the Russians would not easily take Berlin; nor could the American troops scattered over a relatively wide front. The south German region too was now more important.

Truman was amenable, also agreeing that they make the zonal partition of Austria a contingency to what could then be optional troop withdrawal to agreed zones, and after slight dickering, with all the political implications in mind, Churchill on April 27 sent Stalin a telegram making the as-yet-unsigned agreement on Austrian zones the precondition of troop withdrawals. Truman wired the Russian a supporting cable, and on May 2 Stalin sent a vague reply leaving the matter to the mutual agreement of the commanders in the field. Churchill had won the point. Most disturbing of all to Truman during these final days was the alleged Russian refusal to permit British and American representatives to go directly to Vienna to gather information on possible zonal divisions, despite their initial invitation on April 13. In the meantime this permitted the Russians to organize a provisional Austrian government under the leadership of Karl Renner, an Austrian Socialist with a strongly anti-Communist background.

While these anxious problems were moving across the desks of the leaders of England and the United States, they had also to make the final decisions on where to fight the war on the basis of a far greater weakening of German forces than they could predict at the end of March. On April 25 the Russian and American armies met on the river Elbe, which was as far as Eisenhower had thought it possible to go in central Germany by the end of the war, but he was ready to move as quickly as possible elsewhere. The British regarded the matter as purely political, and the United States Chiefs of Staff concurred. Marshall at first was "loath to hazard American lives for purely political purposes," for obviously the Russians could capture the remaining area, but he had no sooner made the statement than he forgot it.[30] For he and Eisenhower had made such political decisions throughout the war and most certainly in regard to Lübeck. Eisenhower notified the Russians of his plans for a general advance in March, and while Churchill warned Truman on April 30 "if the Western Allies play no significant part in Czechoslovakian liberation that country will go the way of Yugoslavia," Eisenhower already had informed the Russians of his plans to move beyond the Austrian Redoubt and well into Czechoslovakia along a line running from Karlsbad—Pilsen—České Budějovice.[31] The Russians endorsed the new advance.

But on May 4 the way appeared clear to thrust even farther into Czechoslovakia than had seemed possible only the week before, and Eisenhower asked for Soviet agreement to move to the west bank of the Elbe and Moldau rivers, or to Prague itself. During the following days both the State Department and the German High Command urged the Americans to advance. Now the Russians balked, recalling that they had honored a recent American request that they stop their advance on the lower Elbe along a line Eisenhower designated. Moreover, they pointed to a "possible confusion of forces."[32] There was nothing to prevent the Americans from taking Prague, which under the leadership of the Left soon rose in revolt against the Germans, but they honored the Russian request and the city fell to the Red Army on May 9.

As these events transpired the German generals prepared for their end, but in a manner designed to soften the impact of a catastrophic military defeat. The Germans fought hard in the hope that the Allies might turn on one another in time, but during April for many of their military leaders it was essential to use the time to evacuate as many Germans as possible from the East to the West before the final deluge. The Germans intended their resistance in the West mainly to protect Hamburg and an area along the northern Elbe capable of receiving and holding millions of German refugees escaping by sea and land from the Soviet advance. When Hitler appointed Admiral Karl Doenitz his successor on April 30, the new leader made this his final task, to which surrender or struggle became a mere instrument, "to save German territory and the German race from Bolshevism." Everything else was futile, and so the Germans on the fronts other than the East and northern Elbe were essentially free to reach separate surrender agreements. As Doenitz recalled:

> Although I had publicly declared in a broadcast on May 1 my intention of continuing to resist in the west only for so long as was required for the implementation of my plans in the east, I fully realized that I could only put an end to hostilities against the British and the Americans by means of an actual surrender on the field of battle. But whether, in view of the "unconditional surrender" slogan, we should ever succeed in persuading them to accept a separate and partial capitulation, I did not know. But I had to try—not, however, openly, because the Russians would undoubtedly, if they knew what was going on, intervene and spoil any chance I might have of succeeding.[33]

Doenitz soon learned he could have his arrangement with the West only by making it appear that he was surrrendering in the East as well, for on April 25 Heinrich Himmler, working via the Swedish government, offered to capitulate only the western front. The effort was too crude, and after Churchill and Truman discussed the matter by phone they insisted on a simultaneous surrender on all fronts and immediately informed Stalin of Himmler's effort. For the first time in weeks the Allies exchanged thankful words on important matters. On April 24 Wolff again appeared in Switzerland with power to surrender the German army in Italy, a subject which he discussed with Dulles throughout April after the controversial exchanges of the prior month. Churchill duly notified Stalin two days later, and on the 29th, with the Russians present, Wolff signed an unconditional surrender for Italy. Stalin approved of both actions by his allies, and now relaxed somewhat.

The hitherto secret details of the Italian surrender revealed how fully political the last events of combat had become, as well as the ideological basis of the Berne negotiations and those that followed. The victors ordered the German soldiers to "stay-put" in their existing positions and hand over their arms *only* to those forces General Alexander designated to receive their surrender; which was to say, they would not surrender to the Resistance or transfer power to it. Until the Anglo-American armies arrived the Germans would "Maintain in operation all public utility and essential civilian services," and with the aid of the CLNAI, provide for "'The general maintenance of law and order."[34] If the Anglo-American forces could not stop a possible Communist takeover they would rely on the Germans to fend off the Resistance as best they could.

When Himmler made his offer to surrender to the West he attached an additional proposal which the two Allies did not tell Stalin, one that the United States accepted with the clear understanding that such an agreement would save Germans from Russian capture. Himmler suggested that the German troops in Denmark and Norway surrender and be interned in Sweden for the duration of the war. The Swedes accepted, his officers explained the problem in all its dimensions to Truman, and no later than the 27th he approved the idea. Only the speed of events elsewhere prevented the scheme from coming to fruition, but it defined an important principle. As a result SHAEF informed Army Group commanders they could immediately accept the surrenders of troops facing their fronts. Now the Germans could obtain their ends by surrendering to the West piecemeal.

On May 2 Montgomery's troops took Schleswig-Holstein, giving him control of the main escape route for German refugees from the East. Doenitz then ordered Admiral Hans von Friedeburg to arrange immediately for the surrender of northwest Germany, and when the West accepted, to offer the rest of the western theater to Eisenhower. The following day he authorized Field Marshal Kesselring to surrender his sector on the southwest front to the Americans, and specially instructed Friedeburg and his aides not only to offer to surrender the troops directly facing Montgomery, but also three German armies retreating from Berlin and vast numbers of fleeing civilians. Montgomery formally refused to take the surrender of these three armies, but he added that "if any German soldiers came . . . with their hands up they would automatically be taken prisoner."[35] After the German troops surrendered, Montgomery added, the adversaries could then discuss the best way of handling the civilians. This arrangement Montgomery stated in a manner designed to make it appear as if the West was accepting no separate surrender of troops actually on the Russian front. But in reality, as Montgomery wrote in a memo to Doenitz, "All members of the German armed forces who come into the 21 Army Group front from the east desiring to surrender will be made Prisoners of War."[36] On the afternoon of the 4th the Germans surrendered their northern forces, covering Holland and Denmark as well, and approximately 2,500,000 Germans, three-fifths of whom were soldiers, fell into British hands. As Doenitz correctly describes it, "the British had accepted my offer of separate surrender. . . ."[37] Also on May 4, waves of women and children accompanied by about 100,000 German troops, all escaping the Russians, offered to surrender to the Ninth United States Army on the southern Elbe. Since such an organized surrender was a violation of the agreement with the Russians, the Ninth Army permitted the human mass to cross the river, and by the 7th they had surrendered individually to the Americans. At the same time massive German armies under Kesselring and the southern generals were surrendering as best they could. At that moment Doenitz decided to execute his final mission, for he now felt certain he could succeed. "The German plan is now becoming pretty clear," Macmillan noted on May 4. "It is to obtain *de facto* what they failed to obtain *de jure,* viz., a surrender to the British and Americans instead of to the Russians. They are now making and will go on making these piecemeal surrenders—holding the Eastern line with rearguards and trying to save their men, not their territory."[38] Conscious of the German strategy, the Anglo-American leaders were ready to play their advantage.

Friedeburg arrived at the forward SHAEF headquarters in Reims at about 5:00 P.M., May 5, and Eisenhower asked the Russians to send an officer immediately, assuring them he would insist on a simultaneous German surrender to the Allies facing them on all fronts.

When Friedeburg arrived he informed General Walter Bedell Smith that he had authority to surrender on the western front alone, and Smith told him that they would insist on a total surrender. In the twenty-minute conversation, however, Friedeburg declared he would need forty-eight hours to communicate any surrender that they might arrange to the outlying commanders. The Americans permitted Friedeburg to relay the conversation to Doenitz, who told him General Alfred Jodl would arrive in Reims the next day to aid him. Doenitz instructed Jodl, who had the power to sign any treaty, that if the Americans refused to sign a separate treaty outright he should attempt to arrange a simultaneous surrender on all fronts with a period as long as possible between the end of hostilities and the formal end of the war, during which time German soldiers would be free to move and surrender on any front. Given Anglo-American policy during the preceding days, Doenitz had every reason to believe that he might thereby succeed in avoiding unconditional surrender. When Jodl arrived he offered the proposition. Eisenhower recalled:

> To us it seemed clear that the Germans were playing for time so that they could transfer behind our lines the largest possible number of German soldiers still in the field. I told General Smith to inform Jodl that unless they instantly ceased all pretense and delay I would close the entire Allied front and would, by force, prevent any German refugees from entering our lines.[39]

Throughout the evening of the 6th negotiations continued.

Eisenhower's statement if analyzed carefully meant that the Anglo-Americans would keep the western front open if there were no further German delays, in effect reducing the haggling to the time allowed for the period of grace. Smith supported the German request for forty-eight hours free mobility, but they wished it to go into effect forty-eight hours after signing the treaty, which if they delayed for any reason might give them many more than two days. The stratagem was obvious, and Eisenhower angrily informed the Germans via his aides that forty-eight hours from that midnight he would close his lines to the movement from the East whether they surrendered or not. Thus confronted Jodl and Friedeburg wired Doenitz for his authorization, and it came back almost immediately. At 2:41 A.M., May 7, with a Russian general hurriedly flown in from Paris, the Germans surrendered. They had forty-five hours grace. "The hour that would decide the fate of the German armies on the eastern front and of the refugees streaming westwards had now struck," Doenitz writes.[40] Some fell behind, millions of others succeeded.

It was a bitter ending for the Grand Alliance against Germany, with both timing and motives in open disarray. The EAC had worked on a German surrender document for many months, and the Americans did not even consult it once at Reims, ostensibly because Smith "suffered a rare lapse of memory" despite a telephoned reminder from Winant on the 5th.[41] When Eisenhower wired Truman about the situation on May 6, he also informed him that the purpose of the German forty-eight-hour strategy "is to continue to make a front against the Russians as long as they possibly can in order to evacuate maximum numbers of Germans into our lines."[42] The West it appeared could only gain, and on May 6 the Russians raised objections, ostensibly to arrive too late, and "Early on the morning of May 7 . . . ," asked General John R. Deane, the American military attaché in Moscow, to make certain changes (to conform to the EAC draft) in the surrender, which the Allies should sign in Berlin rather than Reims.[43] Now they informed the Americans their representative at Reims was not qualified to sign—Eisenhower knew this at least two days earlier—and the entire affair, the Russians implied, was an obvious German feint. Deane claims that the Russian telegram, dated May 6, crossed news of the surrender. Broadcasts from Doenitz's headquarters urged troops on the eastern front to resist to the end, even though these were made before Doenitz empowered Jodl to surrender in the East. The Germans would have to sign the surrender a second time. Eisenhower anticipated the possibility of such a move by the Russians, perhaps even knew of it, and deliberately inserted a clause in the surrender requiring another act of surrender should one of the Allies deem it necessary. It was.

While it is true further delay in signing a treaty would have given the Germans more time, without Western cooperation in permitting their troop movements toward the West that delay would have been less consequential than the impact of the sordid end of the war on relations with the U.S.S.R. Two additional days would hardly have altered the outcome of the war if the Anglo-Americans considered only military factors, and whatever the American intentions in departing from their principle of unconditional surrender, the ill-considered haste achieved nothing. Given the entirely political basis of Anglo-American military strategy at the time, and the general relations with the U.S.S.R., such hard facts as exist point unmistakably to a tawdry effort by the United States and England to wring something out of the surrender for themselves.

From this point onward the event only magnified ill feelings. Eisenhower at first assured the Russians that he would be happy to sign another surrender in Berlin, but on the advice of his staff and Churchill he withdrew the offer. At Berlin itself there was a difficult dispute over protocol between the French, English and American generals gathered there, delaying the signing for several hours. Then the heads of state failed to coordinate their release of the news to the world, Stalin insisting on May 7 that they make no announcement until it was certain fighting on the eastern front, still raging as intensely as ever, actually stopped. But by that time American newsmen, to Churchill's pleasure, had leaked it all over the world. And lastly, on May 10 Eisenhower ordered Doenitz to stop the fighting still continuing on various sectors of the eastern front, especially Czechoslovakia.[44]

The war with Germany ended in an ignoble maze of obvious intrigue and jockeying for advantage.

POLAND AND EASTERN EUROPE, 1945: REALITIES VERSUS OBJECTIVES

AT YALTA the United States sought to stop the drift in Eastern Europe toward a radically new order that the war, the breakdown of the traditional social systems, and the physical presence of the Red Army all made possible. In the case of Yugoslavia and Poland the Americans depended on the ability of personalities such as Subasic and Mikolajczyk to introduce a political relationship within which America could relate to Eastern Europe in attaining its postwar political and economic objectives. But no one could predict what the future held in Eastern Europe, save if the U.S.S.R. was ready to define it over the wishes of the masses, and whether Eastern Europe would willingly reintegrate into the larger European system and permit a restoration of traditional internal and external relationships, or whether the options the United States and Britain offered were any more acceptable than those the Russians presented. The Czechs, perhaps even the Yugoslavs, rejected the hegemony of Russia and the West alike, and had not defined the alternatives the United States could endorse. In this complex reality, over which it had virtually no control and made no effort to confront and define, the United States retreated increasingly to diplomatic dispatches that only colored overall relations within an alliance tottering over a whole spectrum of insoluble issues, and contented itself with the definition of basic principles which constituted the hard core of real American interests in Eastern Europe. In relying on men rather than social forces the United States was doomed to failure, for the forces of the Old Order were either dead or too compromised to succeed after generations of excess. As was the case throughout 1944, the United States had an Eastern European policy that only created obstacles to the attainment of Russian and English objectives and assumed that the passage of time would smooth over consistent failures and frustrations.

Poland, February-May 1945: The Drift Toward the Russian Orbit

After interminable haggling at Yalta the Allies produced an agreement on Poland vague enough to leave the impression of formal unity where in fact there was none. Each Ally read into it what it chose, with equal justification, but the long sessions on the topic when no consensus appeared possible exposed their original intent. The Russians unequivocally stated that they would regard the Lublin government as the basis for any modest alterations in the existing administration, the Americans said that they would prefer a government *de novo*. It was precisely this point, and not the even vaguer question of free elections or borders, that was to plague the commission authorized to meet in Moscow to consider the implementation of the Yalta decision.

The commission members—Harriman, Clark Kerr, and Molotov—first met on February 23, and immediately returned to those very disagreements that divided the heads of state at Yalta. The final text on Poland stated that "The provisional government now functioning in Poland should be reorganized on a broader democratic basis with the inclusion of democratic leaders from Poland itself and from those living abroad." To effect this extremely variable directive the commission in Moscow was "authorized to consult in the first instance in Moscow with members of the present provisional government and with other democratic leaders from within Poland and from abroad with a view to the reorganization of the present government along the above lines."[1] The Yalta statement now became an embarrassment, for it could mean anything. Molotov insisted that they take it literally, that it meant they could not invite outside Poles to Moscow without the agreement of the Poles ruling Warsaw. This free interpretation resulted in initial Soviet agreement to invite only one outside Pole, even excluding Mikolaczyk, whose persistent refusal to endorse the Curzon Line and Yalta agreement greatly embarrassed the Anglo-Americans. Harriman and Kerr, on the other hand, insisted that the so-called Lublin Poles might be a part, but not the core, of a new Polish government. In fact all three powers were anxious to violate the sense of the agreed Yalta text in order now once more to advance their views for that nation's future. By early March the discussions were stalemated and Harriman and Churchill were angry, not the least because Molotov had first invited the two Allies to send observers to Poland and then withdrew the offer.

Churchill urged Roosevelt to join him in sending Stalin a strong dispatch on the subject which also went far beyond the obvious Russian violation of the meaning of the Yalta communiqué by asking them, among other things, to suspend any further "fundamental" legislation from Warsaw—an assumption that transgressed the Yalta statement in turn by assuming the Poles in Warsaw were no government at all.[2] Both Kerr and Roosevelt doubted the wisdom of the strategy, which they thought premature, and while the President reassured Churchill the American objectives were the same, indicated it would be better to ask the Russians to declare a "political truce" between the various Polish factions.[3] Roosevelt and Churchill devoted much time to this issue throughout March, but they allowed their subordinates to communicate with the Russians, and toward the end of March, Molotov submitted a so-called compromise which only further froze the positions of both sides. In fact both the Russian distortion of the Yalta agreement claiming to give them or their Lublin underlings the right to veto unacceptable Poles, and the Western position that the Provisional Government was not to form the kernel of a new government, were responsible for a total stalemate. But since the Russians controlled Poland, time worked to their advantage.

Both the Anglo-Americans and the Russians claimed that the government and leaders the other side championed were unrepresentative of the true sentiments of the Polish people, but privately they were all quite uncertain who represented them. In fact no one really knew. Moreover, although the West dismissed the public Russian claim that only a friendly Polish government in Warsaw could control the problem of terrorists and an anti-Soviet underground, Churchill was especially concerned that any failure in quickly improving the Polish government "might give the Russians and Lublin ground for this contention," for the right-wing NSZ section of the former Home Army had already shown signs of implementing the oft-made threat to fight the Russians.[4]

Russian claims for backing their puppet government were shrill and unconvincing to all. Actually they understood that they had to broaden the base of support for the government, and at the end of March they indirectly and unsuccessfully approached Mikolajczyk and his followers in London to return to Warsaw to join the government without the sanction of England and the United States. At the same time they tolerated profound factions within the Communist party in Poland itself and permitted numerous other political parties to function with a relatively high degree of freedom. They did not challenge the Catholic Church in any way, and exempted its estates from redistribution; land that the government divided it gave to small holders rather than collectives, thereby winning powerful new supporters for the regime. At least some confidential British reports indicated the Warsaw government was developing significant popular support, and the OSS in March concluded no one "knows fully what changes and shifts have taken place in the political sentiments of the Polish population. . . ."[5] The experts by no means excluded radical changes, though their leaders sought means of minimizing them. The prewar officer class was virtually liquidated or in exile, and in destroying the Jews the Nazis eliminated a critical part of the commercial class.

In all probability neither the Russians nor the Anglo-Americans represented the dominant moods among the Polish masses, but since the Red Army occupied the country it was obvious to all which way the wind was blowing. In the bitter, hard environment of deprivation, wartime membership in the Communist party was a considerable asset in obtaining jobs, housing, and food, and this certainly is an important factor in explaining the rise of CP membership from 20,000 in 1944 to 235,000 by the end of 1945. But this mundane element by no means fully explains the reality, for the Communists had a very real and important mass following beyond the opportunists who were especially strong among prewar civil servants and surviving intellectuals. Many prewar conservatives, especially in the army, and certain prewar social rightists with Falangist and Catholic tendencies, were certainly ready to work with the regime in return for its toleration of their views. General Rola-Zymierski, head of the Polish People's Army and himself a prewar anti-Communist with a compromised record, in April publicly welcomed all former officers into the new army, and was proud of the many who had already accepted the offer. "We are ready to include in the new Government," Bierut declared the same month, "the widest circles of opposition which fully share the decisions of the Crimea Conference. . . ."[6] If this contingency excluded the xenophobic Polish nationalists prominent before the war, there is no reason to believe that at the time the proscription went beyond them.

Ultimately, returning exiled political leaders, of whom Mikolajczyk was the most important, were ready to work within the regime for opportunistic reasons or, if one prefers, for love of country. Lastly, many prewar militant Socialist party members, including Edward Osóbka-Morawski, Jozef Cyrankiewicz, and other prominent figures, were very much in favor of a United Front with a CP willing to work with them. The CP itself remained split between a genuinely nationalist wing under Gomulka and a slavishly pro-Moscow wing under Bierut. The Poles did not consider the CP ipso facto a Russian puppet. The party had considerable standing quite apart from its control of power, the Russians tolerated its diversity, and many Poles believed it was dedicated to long-overdue changes. Nationalization, for example, was unquestionably a popular plank for all parties, but hardly found favor in the West. Even the bitterly anti-Russian underground advocated far-reaching nationalization of industry, land reform, and social welfare. It seems most unlikely, therefore, that many Poles would have welcomed the success of the Anglo-American aims for Poland. Yet during the early spring of 1945 the leaders of the successful alliance did not worry about such niceties.

By April, Washington viewed the Polish question within the framework

of the whole range of problems with the U.S.S.R., from the Berne surrender controversy to the United Nations, but also in itself dangerous to
the "entire peace of the world," as Stimson phrased it at the beginning of
April.[7] In the context of Eastern European affairs it was even more disturbing, for it suggested a pattern that would follow the Russian armies
everywhere. "Surely," Churchill pressed Roosevelt at the end of March,
"we must not be maneuvered into becoming parties to imposing on Poland
—and on how much more of Eastern Europe—the Russian version of
democracy?"[8] Roosevelt replied that he shared his "anxiety and concern,"
and the time had come to take a stand, and on April 1 he sent Stalin a long
message on Poland, which Churchill backed with one of his own. They
urged a political truce that would require the Poles in London and
Warsaw to "cease any measures and counter-measures against each other,"
and to allow the Moscow commission to continue its work without permitting the Lublin Poles to veto any names. They conceded only that the
Lublin Poles could play "a prominent role" in a reconstituted government
—a phrase that skirted the critical issue. On a speedy and fair solution of
all this Roosevelt staked a great deal, even "the successful development of
our program for international collaboration. . . ."[9] Poland had now become
the single most important source of tension with the U.S.S.R.

Stalin's reply thawed the Russian stand somewhat, and although both
sides cited the Yalta agreement as authority, apparently they were all ready
to add critical compromising amendments on matters the heads of state
could not agree upon the previous February. Each in fact had already
moved well beyond Yalta to the substantive issues avoided or in dispute
there. Now the Russians were willing to invite five Poles from Poland and
three from London to consult with the commission on the basis of the
"reconstruction," but not the abolition of the Warsaw government, which
would remain the "core." But the Allies had first to invite the Provisional
Government's representatives, asking only those who respected the Yalta
decisions in regard to the Curzon Line and friendship with the U.S.S.R.[10]
Stalin conceded on the veto question, but not on the essential issue of the
overall character of the Polish government that was really the primary
concern of Washington and London. To Churchill, Stalin indicated his
willingness to urge the Warsaw Poles to include Mikolajczyk in the government if he endorsed the Curzon Line. While not contented, the British
regarded these concessions as a sign that the Russians wished to pursue
the conversations. Churchill immediately began his by now typically "painful" discussions with the Pole, and on April 11 urged Roosevelt to take no
further action on Poland without prior consultation.[11] This then was the
melancholy state of the Polish problem when Roosevelt died.

As usual, it was not easy for Churchill or Stalin to deal with Mikolajczyk, for the man was both weak and strong. He was politically ambitious, and for this reason he resigned from the London exile government

and flirted with the Lublin group, but he was somehow convinced that Stalin needed him as a more attractive alternative to the Polish Communist party, and that he could still exact his price. Mikolajczyk unquestionably realized that for the Americans and English he was the only plausible political option. However, he remained an ardent nationalist and was reluctant to concede what he did not own: the disputed eastern territories. Eden and Churchill cajoled and then threatened in their familiar fashion, and Mikolajczyk responded on April 15 with a statement accepting the "Crimean decision," of which there were several, on Poland, but pointedly ignored the Curzon Line. When Churchill sent Stalin the declaration the Russian immediately pointed to the omission, and after some delay the Pole issued a circuitous acceptance of the Curzon Line as the fiat of the Great Powers, mentioning that he would personally have preferred the Lwow Province as well.

While the British extracted the dutiful words from the reluctant Pole, on April 14 Truman proposed to Churchill a joint message to Stalin on Poland to which he immediately assented. Truman's proposal followed Harriman's urgings to refuse to "accept a whitewash of the Warsaw regime." The real issue, they told Stalin four days later, was "whether or not the Warsaw Government has the right to veto individual candidates for consultation . . . ," a procedure that the Yalta decision did not warrant.[12] The actual proposal, however, revealed the President's far greater concern over the nature of the Polish government, for it suggested that of the eight Polish invitees to confer with the commission in Moscow, not more than three be pro-Warsaw government. The Warsaw Poles could be the first to arrive, but the collective group would then suggest the names of other Poles they would invite, and until the new group met, the American and British governments would not commit themselves to the balance or composition of the new Polish government.

Molotov and Eden were in Washington by April 22, on their way to the United Nations meeting, and several days earlier Harriman arrived for a series of Cabinet meetings on overall relations with the Soviet Union, in which Poland played a critical part. Harriman returned on his own initiative to sound the tocsin on the menace of Russia. To Forrestal he talked of the need for firmness, and advised him not to worry about the Russians' attempt to use the fear of Germany to justify their creating Communist states along their borders. Communist expansionism, he explained, would engage in "an ideological warfare just as vigorous and dangerous as Fascism or Nazism."[13] He told Truman much the same, and since the Russians needed aid for reconstruction and were ultimately dependent on United States help, it was necessary to stand firm to a "barbarian invasion of Europe," especially Eastern Europe, that brought with it secret police and the end to all freedom in any nation that they controlled. To Truman he confided that he had rushed back to tell him "that Stalin is breaking his agreements."[14] Poland was the prime example of this. The President promised to be blunt with Molotov, and he linked American participation in the United Nations to a satisfactory solution of the Polish question.

There was a pallor of gloom throughout the highest ranks of Washington when Molotov arrived on the 22nd, for Leahy, Forrestal, Eden, and Harriman had reinforced their mutual pessimism in conversations and the Russians conceded too little on Poland to alter it. When Molotov saw Truman that evening the conversation was civil, but inevitably turned to Poland, and the Russian contented himself with the observation that Russia had a more vital interest in Poland since it was contiguous to its borders. Poland, Truman responded, was a symbol of the future. They resolved nothing.

The following day Truman met with his key war advisers to discuss the larger issue of relations with the U.S.S.R. and the Polish problem in particular. Stettinius, Harriman, Leahy, and Forrestal spoke of the necessity for a decisive stand on Poland, even at the risk of a break. Poland's importance to the future of all Eastern Europe was self-evident in the eyes of the group. To Marshall, however, Poland was not worth possible Russian refusal to enter the war against Japan, and Stimson had grave reservations about the obvious thrust of American policy toward Eastern Europe. Stimson, thinking as a military rather than a political strategist, felt throughout the emerging crisis over Poland that the matter did not justify the strain, for "in the big military matters the Soviet Government had kept their word. . . ."[15] It was, he now felt, too late to work out the postwar political settlement, and he was not surprised or overly chagrined that the Balkans might become a Soviet sphere of influence, much less that they would not hold free elections there, since only the Anglo-Americans "have a real idea of what an independent free ballot is."[16] On this day, however, he alone believed Poland did not warrant a major crisis, even though Leahy felt it inevitable that Russia would be the dominant but not the exclusive power over that nation.

By the time the Cabinet adjourned Truman was in something of a rage. He had already warned Eden he would tell Molotov "in words of one syllable" what he thought of a whole spectrum of Russian policies; on the United Nations, Truman announced, he planned to tell Molotov the Russians are "to join us [or] they could go to hell."[17] The confrontation was unusual, and Molotov listened while the President vaguely threatened to cut off economic aid and berated him mainly on Poland, leaving him with a curt note for Stalin on the question. It was at this meeting that Molotov protested the rude lecture Truman gave him, bringing the conversation to an abrupt end.

The icy note Truman handed Molotov claimed the Yalta decision committed Russia to the creation of a "new" government, and the United States would not proceed on any other basis. He reiterated his request on a new Polish government of the earlier week, made together with Churchill, and informed Stalin that a failure to implement the Yalta decision on Poland "would seriously shake confidence in the unity of the three Governments and their determination to continue the collaboration in the future as they have in the past." There was nothing in this approach likely to succeed, for Truman had not only conveniently misinterpreted the Yalta agreement, ignoring the most obvious area in which Russia openly violated its admittedly vague terms, but he and Churchill asked Stalin to agree to a procedure for a new government that not merely violated Yalta but required a fundamental revision of Soviet policy.

On April 24 Stalin sent a cold reply to the joint demand. He started with the Anglo-American misinterpretation of the Yalta agreement on the nature of the future Polish government, and then passed to the heart of the matter: the need for a friendly Poland on its borders to insure Soviet security. ". . . the Soviet people's blood freely shed on the fields of Poland for the liberation of that country" warranted this assurance; and most directly he suggested that both Greece and Belgium were examples of what Russia sought to do in Poland. "The Soviet Government was not consulted when those Governments were being formed, nor did it claim the right to interfere in those matters, because it realises how important Belgium and Greece are to the security of Great Britain." He suggested that they use the Yugoslav situation as a model for the future of Poland. The issues were now reduced to bare essentials—security and spheres of influence—and he rejected the Western plan for Poland merely by ignoring it. Churchill could only reply to Stalin by reiterating his plan for a new Polish government, rejecting the Yugoslav model outright because "Marshal Tito has become a complete dictator," and defending British policy in Belgium and Greece and the legitimacy of a British interest in Poland, for whom Britain had gone to war.

> There is not much comfort in looking into a future where you and the other countries you dominate, plus the Communist parties in many other States, are all drawn up on one side, and those who rally to the English-speaking nations and their Associates or Dominions are on the other. It is quite obvious that their quarrel would tear the world to pieces. . . .

In this context, as Churchill wrote Stalin, of "serious difficulties which, if they continue, will darken the hour of victory," the Allies took the German surrender and Churchill urged Truman not to remove troops from their easternmost positions.[18]

By the end of April relations with the U.S.S.R. had therefore reached a total impasse, with no new dimension added to the acrid correspondence and discussions between the Russians and their allies. Time, however, was with the Russians, and they used it to their advantage throughout the debate. On April 21 they signed a treaty of friendship with Poland, in the name of a barrier against Germany, which also required the Poles to stay aloof from any alliance or coalition directed against the U.S.S.R. The previous month, however, the Russians arrested sixteen major leaders of the ostensibly disbanded Home Army for concealing arms and radios, and Stalin later confided, working as espionage agents for the British. Churchill claimed they had been invited to Moscow, but Stalin denied it. There was nothing surprising about the event, for Churchill feared the NSZ underground and various dissidents would do as they had threatened for several years: resist the Russians. In fact resistance had already begun on a small scale, and by 1946 cost the Polish Communists many thousands of lives, perhaps even the 15,000 they claimed. Even if the Russians exaggerated the importance of the movement to serve their own purposes (for as yet the underground was small and isolated), it is unquestionable that the essential charges were accurate if relatively minor. The Russians sentenced thirteen of the group to terms of from eighteen months to ten years in prison after a brief trial during June which consisted of factual confessions the Russians embellished to meet their own immediate needs by making it appear the convicted truly represented the London émigré elements.

But given the delicate state of the discussion over Poland, the petty event was merely more fuel for controversy. Churchill and Kerr inquired about the arrested Poles and on May 4 Stalin blandly repeated the allegations against the sixteen men and made no attempt to apologize, and turning to the larger issue, he coldly informed Churchill that the Anglo-American refusal to deal with the Warsaw Provisional Government as the basis of a new administration "precludes the possibility of an agreed decision on the Polish question."[19] After being unable to devise a compromise to the larger Polish problem Eden and Stettinius, on the evening of May 4, informed Molotov that their governments could not continue the interminable discussions on the subject. That very same day Stalin dispatched a message to Truman and Churchill, received May 5, which came to the same conclusion. They had reached a complete impasse, and now Harriman and the British informed Washington that there would be no solution to the Polish problem until the heads of state could meet, and the sooner the better, for time was of the essence.

In this setting Washington chose to apply pressures on the Russians via a manipulation of the Lend-Lease program, a policy Harriman had been urging and with which Joseph Grew agreed. They carefully considered the move, but not exclusively to convey a message to the Russians, for it also involved the English, and it is this at least equally important dimension which writers on the period have ignored. Truman claims that when Leo Crowley, the Lend-Lease administrator, came to his office on May 8 to ask him to sign a cutback order, he hardly looked at the document. The order stopped all further shipments of Lend-Lease goods and recalled ships already on the seas. England, not Russia, was hardest hit, and the public outcry over the action was instantaneous. Three days later Truman modified the order somewhat to permit goods at sea or on the docks ready for loading, or for Soviet participation in the Far Eastern war to continue, and postponed announcing a firm policy. On May 12 the Russian chargé in Washington called Grew and asked him if there was any truth in the rumor that the Administration was discontinuing Lend-Lease and Grew denied it, failing, however, to tell him that America's key leaders were considering permanent, substantial cutbacks that very day.

Insofar as the discussions concerned the Russians they were set entirely in the context of pressuring them along lines Harriman advised. Grew thought it all "full of dynamite."[20] Truman approved the final policy, and according to Grew he realized that the Russians would be unhappy about it. There was a limit to the extent of the pressure, however, since the leaders in Washington still very much desired Russian participation in the war against Japan. They resolved their ambiguities with a decision to continue all materials Russia could use in the Far Eastern war. But other than the above-mentioned exceptions, and a concession to permit the Soviets to purchase supplies needed to complete industrial plants already initiated with Lend-Lease aid, the United States cut off Russia aid to the extent of well over half of their requests for aid. The American decision did not cite Russian policy as the public reason for the slashback; it did not éven mention Russia by name, and indeed the English dimension of the affair is no less significant. Stimson saw such actions as far more meaningful than continued debates: "The Russians will understand them better than anything else. It is a case where we have got to regain the lead and perhaps do it in a pretty rough and realistic way. . . . They can't get along without our help and industries. . . ."[21]

Stimson's endorsement of this strategy of direct pressure points up a critical fact among Truman's key advisers in Washington: none of them advocated the kind of far-reaching détente with Soviet power as had Churchill the prior fall. Along with Roosevelt they based their attitude toward cooperation with the U.S.S.R. on a clear appreciation of United States need for Russian military assistance, first in Europe and later in the Far East, concomitant with their desire to create a permanent basis of real power capable of containing Russia. This attitude compelled them to be ambivalent about the future of Germany—Stimson more than any other— the need to stop the Left, and the full panoply of measures on the political and economic level designed to transform the world in a manner that presumably benefited both the United States and the remainder of the globe at the same time. They did not rely on "trust," and to the extent they considered postwar cooperation with the U.S.S.R. it was with the explicit assumption Russia would cease to be Bolshevik, which inferred expansionism, and adopt American canons of behavior and belief. In brief, while there were differences in emphasis on specific points, the key Washington advisers had no deep-rooted disagreements on the basic objectives and means of United States foreign and military policy during the spring of 1945. Within the framework of this essential consensus on United States-Soviet relations Truman decided to send Harry Hopkins to Moscow as his special representative to talk to Stalin in May.

The Polish question was the foremost reason for dispatching the gravely ill Hopkins on so long a voyage, and on this dispute Truman was quite firm. The American policy on all critical political questions throughout the war was to postpone consideration of those difficult controversies for which there was no acceptable answer, and this approach delayed the Yalta meeting in the belief that the American power to dictate the peace at the end of the war would be greater by virtue of its economic and political strength—its capital resources and its United Nations organization. Washington still accepted the logic of this position in May 1945, but it was also obvious that it could not resist the intense pressures from the British and Harriman to convene a conference of the heads of state indefinitely. Hopkins' voyage represented a preliminary high-level conference, but there was no shift during this time in the reliance on power—economic, political, and military—as the ultimate arbiter of international affairs. Since diplomacy within the alliance had virtually terminated and armies stood amassed, Truman saw nothing to lose by trying to present the American position directly to Stalin, not to reach a modus vivendi but to convince the Russian to accept American objectives. During the same period he moved to arrange for a direct meeting of the three heads of state, one ultimately scheduled for Potsdam, and I consider this parallel event below. There was another reason for a face-to-face meeting at that time: the belief Harriman and Charles Bohlen, Stettinius' assistant, propagated, that Molotov and Stalin stood for two different factions—hard and soft respectively—within the Kremlin, and that Stalin was both under pressure and misinformed. A tough position by the United States, so Bohlen explained, would weaken Stalin's standing at home, and an American refusal to talk to him at a Three Power meeting would lead to even greater Soviet belligerency.

When Harriman returned to Washington at the end of April he suggested that Truman send Hopkins to see Stalin, and so one of the leading advocates of a tough line toward Russia originated the idea of the conference. They did not design a new political strategy or concession for the occasion, and so Hopkins was both expected and inclined to work within the constituted policy. On May 4, over the objections of the State Department and Byrnes, Truman asked Hopkins to return to Moscow with Harriman, and on the 26th the two men saw Stalin. After the amenities Hopkins explained to the Russian leader that the deterioration of relations with Russia in the past six weeks, in particular over Poland, was the main reason for his leaving his sickbed to make the voyage. He also reiterated "that the interests of the United States were world wide and not confined to North and South America and the Pacific Ocean," and for this reason Poland was of intimate concern. Soon Hopkins implied Russia had interfered with the implementation of the Yalta decision on Poland, but also assured him that the United States wished to see friendly states on Soviet borders rather than the cordon sanitaire which Stalin asserted Britain was then attempting to reconstitute. In that case, Stalin replied, "we can easily come to terms. . . ."[22]

In the course of the conversations these men held until June 6 Stalin talked freely, yet said little that was new: Russia did not want a weak Poland as an open corridor to yet a third German invasion, and it scorned the possibility of an unfriendly government similar to those of earlier years. Russia did not wish to interfere in Poland's internal affairs, since Communism was not exportable, but the nation had to be "democratic," and the Lublin Committee qualified. The appearance of Russian unilateralism, he suggested, was due to Western refusal to extend understanding to the Russian position, based as it was on considerations of vital political and military security. The British had done no less in Greece. He then offered to advise the government in Warsaw to accept four names for their eighteen to twenty ministries from a list submitted by England and the United States. Mikolajczyk was immediately acceptable and asked to come to Moscow at once. Generalities over, the bargaining began.

Truman reported to Churchill that he found Hopkins' news "very encouraging," and after some debate they agreed not to link the general Polish question to the release of the sixteen Polish underground leaders, for whom Hopkins also pleaded. Among other things Hopkins insisted that the Russians introduce fundamental civil liberties into Poland, to which Stalin immediately assented—in theory. Yet the core of the arrangement was the list of four names, which exchanges with Washington and London eventually resolved with the Russians. Churchill saw this as only a starting point, not a final formula, and as a first step toward getting the Poles to solve their problems by negotiating among themselves. But each side interpreted the meaning of the arrangement to suit its own convenience; nevertheless, for the first time, they brought the various Polish factions to Moscow to talk to each other.[23] Russia retreated on the right to veto names, but prevailed on the overall political balance in Poland.

Hopkins reiterated the importance of Poland as the great symbol of the possibility of friendly future relations between the Soviet Union and the United States, but he raised numerous other questions—the Far East, the United Nations, Russian Marshal Georgi Zhukov's membership on the German Control Council—on which he had received so much satisfaction that he ignored the equivocal nature of the actual Polish settlement in the euphoria of seeming success. Stalin had been extremely agreeable for the most part, but he was openly bitter on the way the United States had cut off and then partially restored Lend-Lease. "If the refusal to continue Lend Lease was designed as pressure on the Russians in order to soften them up then it was a fundamental mistake," Stalin is paraphrased as saying. Hopkins feigned hurt innocence "that he [Stalin] believed that the United States would use Lend Lease as a means of showing our displeasure with the Soviet Union."[24] This dialogue was the true measure of the appearance and realities behind the words of the men gathered in Moscow, and indeed at every similar conference that year, for words now meant nothing and true discourse had failed, not simply because objectives were fundamentally incompatible, but because they had nothing to trade to make actions and realities meaningful in terms of rewards as well as penalties. At no time did Washington offer Russia the option of Anglo-American aid in building an Eastern Europe based on the neutral Czech pattern, not merely because that option did not exist in Poland, but also because the United States could not tolerate the left nationalist alternatives the Czechs and Yugoslavs were groping toward. The developments in these nations appeared no less ominous than the events in Poland.

Harriman for his part was so delighted with Stalin's concessions that he thought the meetings "more successful than I had hoped," even though "I am afraid Stalin does not and never will fully understand our interest in a free Poland as a matter of principle." Yet he was certain the results confirmed the prime justification for the direct confrontation with Stalin in the first place: his misleading information from the much more intractable Molotov, who "is far more suspicious of us and less willing to view matters in our mutual relations from a broad standpoint than is Stalin." Dealing with the Soviet dictator directly "was a great help," and Harriman urged more such meetings.[25]

Throughout the first three weeks of June the Poles from London and Warsaw met in Moscow and on June 21 reported the creation of a unified government to Kerr, Harriman, and Molotov. They established a Presidium of the Polish National Council with Bierut as chairman and Witos, close to the Communists, and Stanislaw Grabski, a colleague of Mikolajczyk, as members, and announced twenty ministries, with Osóbka-Morawski as Prime Minister and Mikolajczyk and Gomulka as his deputies. The Communists ostensibly held only five ministries, plus the army, but these were all critical and in fact they were well placed in all ministries. Fourteen of the twenty-one Cabinet members therefore were what was termed "Lublin Poles." The new government extended invitations to members of prewar parties for support and to reconstitute their parties, and many Peasant, Socialist, and Liberal-Conservative leaders in Poland endorsed it. Their reasons were manifold. The basic political strategy of the Communists in Eastern Europe was to work with any centrist group ready to collaborate on their terms, and since the Gomulka faction had a high standing among some Polish nationalists this was not difficult. Moreover, there can be no doubt that the Communists sought desperately to strengthen their mass support by working with Mikolajczyk, who stayed in the government for two years. As Polish nationalists they distinctly understood that the Allies at the forthcoming Potsdam Conference would not consider claims to the Oder-western Neisse area if they came from a Communist government. For reasons of national solidarity and expansion the unification was urgent. Beyond this, in addition to its popular land reform, the government initiated a dynamic reconstruction program in housing that begrudgingly won much respect, and for all these reasons many Poles who considered rehabilitation a more pressing task than internecine civil war supported a program based on national political unity, social reform, and reconstruction.[26]

Despite much reticence both the English and American leaders welcomed the new turn for Poland, and Churchill now kindled the hope that at Potsdam he might consolidate Polish independence. Even Mikolajczyk was pleased. Bierut assured Harriman that he would maintain close and friendly relations with the United States and permit Americans to travel freely. Poland, he stressed, would welcome American economic aid. Though the Foreign Office wished to delay, official Washington now pressed for recognition, and on July 5 the two governments extended it. The operational assumption in the State Department, however, was that the new government was Communist-dominated and almost in the Soviet orbit, and by appointing Arthur Bliss Lane, heretofore Ambassador to the London exiles, it embarked on a hostile policy from the inception. The State Department knew that Lane was bitterly critical of the Yalta agreements and the new Warsaw government, and he made no effort to conceal this antipathy. His subsequent career in Poland was to have the greatest consequences in shaping Polish-American relations, and this was fully predictable by July 1945. Lane apart, however, in the weeks before the Potsdam Conference it was essential for the State Department to define systematically its ideal objectives and policy for Poland, and this it did with new clarity. It wished, of course, to implement the Yalta Agreement regarding free elections under international supervision, which meant that while Washington might tolerate a predominant Soviet influence—and this it had not yet conceded—"neither would it desire to see Poland become in fact a Soviet satellite and have American influence there completely eliminated."

What this meant in structural terms soon became explicit, for the only inflexible objective of American policy was now defined in economic terms: "In assisting through credits and otherwise in the physical reconstruction of Polish economy, we should insist on the acceptance by Poland of a policy of equal opportunity for us in trade, investments and access to sources of information." Bierut had impressed Harriman with the extremely strong desire of the Poles to obtain reconstruction credits, and Harriman saw it as the key to future Polish politics: "Aside from the humanitarian aspects and the value in connection with developing future markets for American equipment . . . ," aid via UNRRA and an Export-Import Bank loan "will have a far-reaching and permanent effect on the influence of the U.S. in the political scene in Poland . . . ," particularly free elections. On the basis of these urgings Lane went to Poland with the promise of UNRRA aid, the possibility of a loan, and a request to purchase Polish coal immediately for dollars, and with the sale of Army surplus trucks to carry it to Western Europe. In return the United States expected the "Reestablishment of private trade between the United States and Poland . . . ," as soon as possible.[27] There was still hope of using American economic power to reintegrate Poland into the West by one means or another.

This was the only firm aspect of United States policy, for on politics and the future of Poland's western boundary there was much room to maneuver. On May 8 the United States informed the Russians that it would not recognize the unilateral Soviet transfer of the Oder-Neisse region to Poland, and in fact the State Department strongly preferred border adjustments in Poland's favor less than two-thirds the size of the Oder-Neisse boundary. But since Churchill conceded much more to Mikolajczyk the prior October and then recanted, they decided not to be absolutely unbending on the issue should the British and Russians insist on the Oder or Oder-Neisse.[28] They did not consider that for purely nationalist reasons any Polish government, Right or Left, would orient itself toward those powers supporting their borders and claims against German destruction of six million Polish lives and the lifeblood of the economy, much less that the Poles could justifiably ask the Germans to sacrifice admittedly all-German lands for the past ravages. And no one suspected that the Poles would come to Potsdam as one man to entreat the West to permit a destitute nation to collect blood money, nor that one of their spokesmen would be the leader for whom the West had gladly risked ripping apart the wartime alliance.

The Former Axis Nations: The Russians and the Conservatives

Overall Russian conduct in Eastern Europe had been diverse, and local political conditions defined it as much as a general Soviet policy that was faltering and by no means monolithic, for there was still no single coherent pattern of Soviet behavior at this time. The West was convinced that the Russians were Bolshevizing Eastern Europe, even if the means employed seemed externally democratic. The Americans went to Yalta determined to undo the existing Allied Control Commissions structures modeled on the Italian precedent, and came away with an amorphous Declaration on Liberated Europe that satisfied no one and solved nothing. The problem of Eastern Europe, other than Poland, reemerged in even more aggravated form within weeks of the end of Yalta.

Rumania

The Rumanians had partially stabilized their political situation at the end of 1944 around the Radescu government, but within the country the basic problems of politics and society remained unsolved. The Russians had supported Radescu and King Michael, to whom they awarded the Order of Victory, because they hoped that they could provide both administrative tranquility and reparations. It was widely known that the Russians were responsible for holding down the far more radical local Communists and their allies in the National Democratic Front.

The fundamental collapse of Rumanian institutions frustrated both the Russian desire to attain stability in Rumania and the American effort to obtain a greater share in the direction of affairs via the Control Commission. The problems of Rumanian society and the impact of the war precluded the possibility of forestalling the growing pressures engendered in a decaying society. The Radescu regime maintained the existing civil service largely intact, both to rule and to sustain important political allies, thereby leaving a large prewar fascist element in office. The OSS reported to Washington that Radescu was "exceedingly slow in getting down to the tasks of apprehending war criminals. . . ."[29] Anti-Semitism was rampant everywhere and fighting common in northern Transylvania, where the right-wing Rumanians associated the Jews both with the Hungarian minority and the Communists. The government did nothing about land reform. Nevertheless, despite its character, the Russians continued to sanction the regime.

The local Communists had a minority position in the government but were in fact increasingly circumscribed and unhappy, both with Radescu and Russian policy. In January, Ana Pauker and Gheorghiu-Dej went to Moscow to convince the Kremlin a change was urgent or larger disorders, perhaps even civil war, would result. They did not exaggerate their forecast, for both the Right and the Left had already initiated violence, and the peasants themselves had begun to redistribute the land. Both military security and principle fully convinced the Russians that a change in Rumania was essential, and by early February they were openly criticizing the Radescu government as too reactionary—a fact that was incontestable. Radescu for his part began publicly and violently attacking the Communists in terms that struck directly at their heavily Jewish and Hungarian origins, for Pauker was Jewish. Now the Communists attempted to assume the functions of the Interior Ministry and fanned the controversy over reform and epuration of Iron Guardists and fascists, some of whom had been welcomed into the ranks of the Communists as well. A pitched riot between left-wing workers and right-wing elements in Bucharest became the cause of a vast leftist protest demonstration on February 24, and at that time shooting began—the Left claimed Radescu's police were responsible—and many demonstrators were wounded and two killed. At this point Radescu called on the aid of the Rumanian army, which was mainly on the front, and the Red Army immediately intervened to disarm Radescu's supporters.

While the Russians may have had ideological reasons for what followed, in fact their southern supply lines went through the country and the Soviet offensive was at the moment meeting stout resistance, a justification for intervention they carefully explained to Michael. They had other military reasons as well, for Radescu had called the army back into politics, and that group had only recently transferred its allegiance from Hitler to the Allies. Vishinsky arrived in Bucharest several days later and ordered Michael to create a new government, and after much storming and threatening from the Russians, the worst of which Michael ignored, on March 6 Petru Groza of the Ploughman's Front became Premier.[30]

Groza was extremely close to the Communists, and formally gave them only three ministries, Justice, Public Works, and Interior, but all were critical. More interesting was the Vice-Premier and Minister of Foreign Affairs, Gheorghiu Tatarescu, who, in 1936 as a member of an earlier government, had sentenced Pauker to ten years in prison. It is unquestionable that with this appointment, which both angered and embarrassed local Communists, the Russians intended to reassure the Rumanian conservatives and West insofar as that was possible in a political situation that had moved into the streets. Still, one must conclude that although factors over which they had slight control imposed limits on Russian conduct, they catered much to local conservatism and nationalism from the fall of 1944 until the spring of 1945, after which time Western pressures removed the relative freedom of action. Soviet editorials on the question after the February crisis stressed the opposition to Radescu from minority elements within the National Tsaranist and National Liberal parties, "the clergy, of business circles, the army, etc."[31] In fact this was wishful thinking, but it indicated Russian refusal at this time to isolate the Left and rely solely on the Communists, who permitted numerous "reformed" prewar fascists to enter their once meager ranks. On March 9, catering to nationalist sentiments in the country, the Russians returned north and east Transylvania to Rumanian administration, and during the same month Groza finally took action on land reform and a purge of fascists in government. It was essentially this government that ruled Rumania for the remainder of our story.

The State Department knew a crisis over Rumania was brewing, and even on February 24 the State Department instructed Harriman to call for an "orderly course" of the problem, hopefully via the Control Commission or the three Allied capitals.[32] The events of the day made the note belated, and in fact the Americans received no satisfaction, for they continued to believe that the prewar Peasant and National Liberal parties, which they admitted were right-wing and closely associated with the prewar regimes, had the largest popular following and deserved to control Rumania. Only the OSS felt most of the nation was uncommitted to any party. But the American Cabinet discussed on March 2 what to their mind was a more disturbing development in Rumania: the refusal of the Russian occupation authorities "to let down the bars for American [oil] businessmen to enter Rumania."[33] Throughout the crisis of February and March the Russians merely ignored the Americans and British. To Churchill the question of Poland was far more important, for he had given Stalin predominant control over Rumanian affairs the previous October, and the Russian's loyal regard for British rights in Greece still impressed him. The British so notified the Americans in early March, and left it to them to carry the cudgels for the prewar parties. Harriman, without much success, urged the State Department to downgrade the Rumanian issue.

The Americans sent several notes to the Russians on the Rumanian crisis, especially complaining about the failure to consult with Burton Y. Berry, the American political representative in Bucharest. The Russians rejected the American notes outright, first referring to their need to establish order behind their rear lines, but ultimately ending with the oft-cited "situation in Italy where on no occasions have the Allied representatives . . . informed the Soviet representative of important measures undertaken. . . ."[34]

Hungary

The Russians had complete physical control over Hungary, the most reactionary of Hitler's Eastern allies, and they were quite as free to impose a local equivalent of the Groza, much less Bierut, governments. Yet they did not do so; this the leaders of the West understood, but they ignored the significance of Hungary to the roots and motives of Russian policy in Eastern Europe during 1945 for more deductive and pessimistic conclusions, for although Hungary was acceptable politically to the United States, it was moving the Czech way as well.

Russian policy in Hungary was unquestionably to work primarily with the prewar centrist, even right-wing, elements ready to abandon the expansionist and anti-Soviet foreign policy of that nation during the interwar years. Various Soviet political advisers addressed themselves during the war to the task of creating a political alliance in Hungary based on the conservatives, and they found it difficult to obtain the support of those genuine prewar radicals who favored long-overdue reforms in the most retrograde of Eastern Europe's nations. In December 1944 the Russians permitted General Bela Miklos to create a Provisional Government, and the Communists busied themselves helping the Social Democrats, the Small Holders' party, and other groups reconstitute themselves so that they might organize a United Front along by-then familiar lines. Miklos remained head of the five-party government throughout the period covered in this book, and the State Department described him as "a conservative."[35] "The Communists, as well as the ex-Horthyites, considered left socialism as the greatest danger," Michael Karolyi, the leading Hungarian democrat, records, and they vied with each other to wear the mantle of extreme nationalism that had plagued Hungary before the war.[36]

The CP itself, like all others in Eastern Europe, was deeply split between a nationalist, principled wing and those primarily oriented toward Moscow. The Communists were powerful in the trade unions and were certainly the most important single party during early 1945, but they left the Interior Ministry and many critical posts to others and never exercised the very real option they had to take total power in that deeply divided nation. Reform was slow save in land, and there was a consensus, to quote Hugh Seton-Watson, that "the communists were far from having complete control."[37] Many members of the old ruling classes found the adjustment to the new order remarkably tranquil, for the Russians welcomed their aid. In early July the State Department, despite many complaints regarding economic affairs and the Allied Control Commission, concluded that "The Soviet Government has not attempted to install a purely leftist regime as in Rumania."[38] Given the intense American suspicion of virtually every Soviet action in Eastern Europe at this time, the relative confidence in the Hungarian situation was due to the fact that Hungary was returning to the traditional Center, and to advance the story, by the fall the Small Holders' party was running on an anti-Russian and antisocialist program that won them 57 percent of the vote in the November national election—admitted by all observers to have been free—while the Communists received only 17 percent. Given their earlier triumph in the Budapest election, the Russians watched the opposition's growth with almost no alarm, for Soviet strategy assumed that Communism need not be exported unless external military and foreign considerations demanded it.[39]

Bulgaria

Among the Eastern European nations, the United States had the least interest in Bulgaria, but events there appeared only to confirm the view that the Russians sought to impose their will on their neighbors. They considered the Communist control over the popular Fatherland Front alliance as virtually monolithic, and they were convinced that the front would triumph in the projected August 26 elections. Maynard B. Barnes, the American political representative there, and General John A. Crane of the

Allied Control Commission, painted the darkest possible picture of the internal political situation, indicating also that the local opposition was depending wholly on ultimate Anglo-American intervention on their behalf. In fact the opposition withdrew from the political orbit, boycotted the national elections, and failed to explore such possibilities as existed, leaving a total vacuum for the extremely aggressive local Communists to fill. Relief from the West was never to arrive. Given the American representatives' main emphasis on the limited powers that the Soviets permitted them, the central issue in United States policy toward that nation became the formal structure of the Allied Control Commission, and questions of abstract principle.[40]

IT is not altogether clear why the United States thought it might advance its aims in Eastern Europe by calling for the implementation of the vague provisos of the Declaration on Liberated Europe concerning political democracy. In fact the parties the United States favored were not democratic, nor had the prewar order fulfilled the criteria the United States now presumably wished established or, implicitly, restored. They could merely imply the theme of restoration, for to admit that democracy was still an alien political experience for Eastern Europe was to reveal the essential American goals, goals which were the core of American policy and had much to do with larger considerations of political-military strategy and economic objectives but precious little with principle. Therefore the Americans were as ready as anyone to sacrifice "democracy" in Eastern Europe as an abstract entity if their more concrete needs and interests were satisfied on a tangible level.

The Russians were impatient with all the Western solicitousness for Eastern European democracy, which they regarded merely as a ploy for the re-creation of the cordon sanitaire and economic expansion. They dealt with the question publicly in mid-April, in a widely circulated article on "Democracy" in *War and the Working Class,* published in three languages. Summarizing the interwar history of Eastern Europe country by country, the Russian author pointed to the need for political unity within these nations to create the preconditions for eventual democracy and the immediate defeat of fascist forces that had directed internal politics for decades. As justification it recalled the Yalta Declaration on Liberated Europe, a striking example of what the American document meant to the Russians. Moreover, in citing the events in Greece and the colonial world the author wanted to know what really motivated the Allied concern for democracy. In a kind of distorted logic which only unpredictable events later proved correct, the Soviet view was that

it would be quite hopeless to demand that democracy should be built
up in all countries of Europe on the British or American model. This
would be a totally unwarranted attempt to interfere in the internal
affairs of other peoples. . . . Such an attempt would, of course, have no
chance of success, because it would contradict the very spirit of
democratism, would contradict the indisputable right of the people "to
create democratic institutions of their own choice."[41]

[In brief, the Russian might have stated more directly, Eastern Europe
had been fascist and it would not become democratic overnight according
to Western lights, and in any event Russia would not permit it to become
reactionary *and* anti-Soviet again.] Eastern European democracy was such a
frail reef, and Soviet security interests so much more important, that they
would choose the needs of security before protection of the delicate and
unpredictable party structure that emerged. Pressure from the outside to
make Eastern Europe a cockpit of world politics would lead to the extinc-
tion of what little freedom existed.

The reports of the American representatives on the Allied Control
Commissions in Hungary, Rumania, and Bulgaria, colored with woeful
tales of personal indignities and restrictions placed on them, made Washington determined to try once more, as prior to Yalta, to shatter the Italian
precedent imposed on the ACC's as a step toward neutralizing Russian
hegemony. At the beginning of May, Truman was even willing to withdraw
the American representatives from the Bulgarian and Rumanian commissions, but with little difficulty Grew dissuaded him. The issue was complicated in the extreme, for they had fewer complaints about the conditions in
Hungary than in the other two nations. Moreover, the problems of recognition and peace treaties were soon intertwined, and perhaps above all, the
British refused to share the American approach to the Eastern European
problem.

At the end of May, Stalin asked Truman to recognize the Rumanian
and Bulgarian governments, with Hungary perhaps to follow later, but
Truman answered by making it plain that he would not recognize those
governments until they became democratic. To this Stalin replied by citing
Italy as an instance where the West was just as firmly in control of affairs,
but where the Russians had recognized the government. In effect he asked
for a quid pro quo. If nothing else the exchange resurrected the principle of
recognition as a means of indicating approval of internal affairs and threw
it into the Eastern European cauldron.

The situation was complex and became increasingly so in the weeks
prior to Potsdam as alarming reports still poured in from the capitals of the
three former Axis nations. In mid-June, Grew recommended that the
United States take its stand on advocating an equal share in the three

Control Commissions and the implementation of the Declaration on Liberated Europe as well. At the beginning of July, Washington duly notified the British of American intentions, including a delay in diplomatic recognition and the conclusion of peace treaties pending satisfaction on these issues. After some debate the three American representatives to the Control Commissions endorsed this strategy. Yet the United States understood the basic problem to be the creation of friendly governments in those nations, for which the commissions were means but not ends. At the end of June the State Department prepared a resolution to offer at Potsdam calling for "the reorganization of the present governments in Rumania and Bulgaria, and, should it become necessary, in Hungary. . . ," and the postponement of peace treaties and diplomatic recognition until Russia effected the change.[42] There was only one thing wrong with such a position: it not only failed to define the nature of the reorganization desired, but it neglected to mention Western concessions for Italy even on the Control Commission level. It was not likely to work, and the Foreign Office said so in direct terms. By the time of the conference at Potsdam the British were ready to conclude peace treaties with Bulgaria, Rumania, and Hungary, with no political strings attached, and on a reiteration of the Declaration on Liberated Europe, in which the United States had more faith than the British, they would trail behind.[43]

For the former Axis satellites of Eastern Europe, therefore, the political policy of the United States floundered until Washington was uncertain what the essential political objective had become, much less the political means required to implement it. As it had prior to Yalta the American government realized again that economics, not democracy, was its central concern.

The Czech Experiment in Suspension

The Czech government in London hoped to find its way in Eastern Europe by maintaining a policy of neutrality and friendship with Russia and the West, and in December 1943 committed the country to that course in its treaty with the U.S.S.R. Washington's response to the audacious undertaking had never been cordial, and by the spring of 1945 it increasingly put Czechoslovakia in the same category as Poland and Rumania in illustrating the thrust of Soviet expansionism. During the spring of 1945 it became obvious that the Czechs' ability to succeed in their precarious effort would depend on a stable European environment with a minimum of pressure from either side, pressure that might push them too far into one camp or the other. There were ominous indications that they would fail.

In the Western view the Czechs not only moved too close to Russia, either willingly or by necessity, but their plans for a postwar domestic

economy and political life Washington and London found extremely unat-
tractive, and this became the basis of future difficulty with the Americans
in particular. During April, when his government was reorganized, Beneš
agreed to give an important minority position to the Communist party, led
by Clement Gottwald, in the form of seven of the twenty-five projected
ministries. It was sufficient that Gottwald was a Communist, and no one in
Washington really knew what kind or asked. In fact the Bolshevik was a
mild man who had become cynical and flexible as a result of the twists and
turns of Soviet policy in the 1930's, and who had concluded Communism
of the Russian variety would not suit the Czechs. Beneš had a high opinion
of his patriotism. During Beneš' visit to Moscow during mid-March,
Stalin again reassured him that he had no desire to Bolshevize the Czechs,
and again that the Communist party would remain loyal to Czech interests
first of all. On an economic level all in the Czech London government
united in advocating extensive nationalization of the mines and heavy industry, agrarian reform, and advanced social welfare legislation. On April
5, shortly after the Provisional Government returned to its country in the
wake of the advancing Russian troops, it adopted a program at Košice
which pledged the nation to far-reaching structural changes, and also to
"the closest alliance with the victorious great Slav power in the East," and
"particularly close friendship with the United States. . . ."[44] The Russians
welcomed such superlatives and only the month before had pledged to
rearm ten Czech divisions, and later did so.

Yet later in April the gregarious and delightful Czech Foreign Minister,
Jan Masaryk, was at the San Francisco Conference and during one of the
early sessions the Russians, greatly outnumbered and jockeying with the
Americans on numerous issues, found that they needed someone to propose an invitation to the Polish government. Molotov approached Masaryk, who hesitated, leading the Russian to observe that the treaty between the two nations made no sense without his aid on this subject.
"Masaryk almost collapsed under this threat," his aide recalled, and Eden
noted he appeared "a depressed prisoner of the Russians," passing the
observation along to Stettinius.[45] The moral of the story was simple:
should international conflicts force the nations to line up on one side or
another, the Czechs would be compelled to join the Russians, and it was
precisely this point that Beneš attempted to make in Washington in 1943
when arguing for a new course with the Russians in Europe. But the Anglo-
Americans expanded the purely personal response of Masaryk into the
view that the Czechs were acting as the reluctant captives of the Russians.
Masaryk's reaction, however, as Beneš warned Bruce Lockhart and others
well before this time, was based in large part on a long personal history of
cycles of elation and depression under pressure.

It was only several days after this incident that Churchill urged Eisenhower to march on to Prague; the general first hesitated and then decided to cross into Czechoslovakia, and finally on May 5 agreed to a Russian request that he not extend his forces all the way to Prague. Later writers erroneously interpreted the story as a sign of American weakness toward the Russians, but a closer look at all the circumstances involving the Czechs at this time reveal new and interesting political dimensions of the last days of the war in Czechoslovakia. In fact in February 1944 the Czech government in London had strongly stressed the importance of the Czech troops fighting with the Anglo-American armies participating in the liberation of their country, and they renewed the request at the end of April 1945. But during the first week of May 1945, Eisenhower had them around Dunkerque on the English Channel, and other events were to intrude into Eisenhower's thinking on Czechoslovakia. For on the morning of May 5 the people of Prague spontaneously and without organization, as in Paris, began to liberate themselves. They disarmed German garrisons, many glad to hand over guns as they began or continued their flight through the city toward the American lines, and that night the Czechs set up barricades as the revolt spread. That night too, as in Paris, the Communist party's Resistance units joined the people in the streets and began providing both direction and political coloration. Soon liberated prisoners of war of many nationalities, and even a large group from the Vlasov Army, anti-Soviet Russians that had fought for the Germans, joined them. Despite this polyglot, and the largely decentralized character of the now bloody engagement, the Communists' control of the radio gave the impression that they had the affair firmly in hand. Then the revolutionists sent radio appeals to the American troops in Pilsen, only a short distance away. They never received an answer. What had happened?

Eisenhower knew of the uprising on May 5, and the following day entreaties for aid began pouring in from Prague. Czech diplomats in London also appealed on May 6 to SHAEF for aid, but by the time the proper bureau received the requests on May 7 the Anglo-Americans had already signed the surrender at Reims and responded to the Czechs in London that the war was over. Yet the Germans fought for Prague because many of their escaping armies had to pass through the city to reach the American-held areas, despite the fact that a United States escort brought a ranking German officer to Prague the evening of the 7th to inform the German commander of the surrender. That evening Churchill again asked Eisenhower to press on to Prague if possible, and if the Russians had not yet reached the city. In fact, on May 5, perhaps before they knew of the uprising, the Russians asked Eisenhower not to advance beyond Pilsen. The Americans therefore ignored or rejected the continuous Czech appeals from Prague and London ostensibly because of the Russian request, even to the extent of refusing to send requested dive bombers which would in no sense have violated the understanding with the Russians not to advance. SHAEF contented itself with forwarding all Czech requests to the Russians, whose first units were only able to reach the city on the 9th. On the following day, as the battle raged beyond the city and the war was now officially over, Eisenhower took two steps to end it in fact. First he told Doenitz to broadcast an order to the German troops to lay down their arms; next he removed their incentive to fight by setting up roadblocks to stop the Germans' flight, turning them back to the Russians. The battle of Czechoslovakia ended only on May 12. American popularity among the Czechs was never lower.

The Americans' refusal to save Prague, even by making the gestures of May 10 some days earlier, either reflected a literalism which kept them from approaching the Russians once again about entering Prague or a deeper hostility toward the Czechs. In fact they would have lost nothing by asking the Russians if they objected to American liberation of the city, as Churchill again asked, and politically much was to be gained if the Soviets refused. At the very least one may conclude that there was probably no desire to aid what the Americans understood to be a Communist-led uprising. But it is important to note that during April there was a minor political crisis within the Czech government involving a Cabinet shift that, according to the official United States Army history, caused "leading SHAEF officials to conclude that a housecleaning aimed at individuals who had been close to the Western Allies was in progress." The American and British ambassadors that month attempted to join the Czech government at Košice, but the Czechs pleaded accommodations were short at the moment, and since Beneš "had held several meetings with the Soviet Ambassador," the connection appeared suspicious enough to conclude that he was acting on orders from Moscow.[46] Relations were bad, but the Czechs permitted the American and British ambassadors to go to Prague at the very end of May, and so the State Department concluded in mid-June that "With respect to Czechoslovakia, the situation is now somewhat improved."[47] This was the general state of relations with the Beneš government when Prague asked for American aid and planes. The historian can only refer again to the highly charged political mood of early May, and the reader must draw his own conclusions on American indifference toward the Prague uprising in lieu of final evidence.

Beneš wished to be neutral in the East-West conflict, and in June he wanted the Russian and American troops out of his country. The Russian troops had not ingratiated themselves with their aggressive behavior toward Czech goods and women, but Stalin had pleaded with Beneš "to comprehend that the army is not composed of angels. Grasp this and forgive them."[48] This was easier to do, however, if they left the country. Taking hints from Czech leaders, and measurably reassured by large Soviet evacuations, Washington decided in August to withdraw American troops only in proportion to Soviet reductions, and immediately recalled two-thirds, the rest to linger until the end of the following November. But the Russians evacuated Prague completely at the beginning of June, and the American ambassador, Laurence Steinhardt, much to his surprise, found none of the difficulties he had anticipated, and indeed that he could "function without restraint."[49] By mid-June the State Department had not decided whether to raise the Czech issue at Potsdam, despite its most profound suspicions, for the disparity between facts and theory in regard to Czechoslovakia disarmed its complaints.

Beneš had one other reason in the early summer of 1945 to maintain excellent relations with Russia, for the Soviet Union was the key to the delicate, potentially dangerous Polish-Czech relations. The Polish Communists made no secret of their desire to retain the prewar imperialist acquisitions of Beck in the Teschen area after Munich. Only the Russians, the Czechs felt, could get Teschen back, and at the end of June, Zdenek Fierlinger, the Prime Minister, went to Moscow and received assurances of Russian support for the pre-Munich Czech borders.[50] The traditional character of Eastern European politics was still very much alive.

Yugoslavia: Tito Goes His Own Way

The discussion of Yugoslav affairs at Yalta had been all too brief, but the British attempted to continue their role as international overseer of Yugoslav internal affairs by strengthening the Tito-Subasic agreement which they had so laboriously constructed over American opposition. Churchill had chided Stalin into supporting his proposed revisions, clearly to the dictator's discomfort. On the final day of serious discussion at Yalta, Eden submitted a note to Stettinius and Molotov on the hitherto neglected problem of the Venezia Giulia region, including the city of Trieste, an area that the victorious Entente had awarded to Italy in 1919. But Roosevelt insisted on disbanding the conference the following day, and so they left Eden's memo to subsequent consideration via conventional channels.

Eden warned what Tito had already publicly stated: there would be trouble over the Trieste area unless the Allies recognized Yugoslav claims. His Partisans already controlled much of the region, and when the Allied military government entered, two armed forces would face each other. All Yugoslavs, including Subasic, ardently laid claim to the entire disputed area. To avoid a clash Eden proposed a provisional demarcation line for the area based on ethnic distributions, with Tito in control of his region, with a separate agreement to arrange Allied communications through it. From a strictly military viewpoint, as Field Marshal Alexander, commander of Allied forces in the Mediterranean argued, only control of the ports of Trieste and Pola, the area to the west of it, and lines of communication to Austria was necessary for him. Alexander hoped to present this demand to Tito at the end of February when they were to meet, but for political reasons the State Department rejected the proposal as leaving too much of prewar Italy in Yugoslav hands, and the Americans demanded total control of the disputed region. The result was a vague oral agreement which would permit Alexander to have final jurisdiction in the Trieste region, though local Yugoslav civil authorities would remain but would not prejudice the final disposition of Trieste. This might mean almost anything, as Alexander himself felt and as everyone soon learned.

In March, Alexander still thought the Allies and Tito should divide the region into two operational zones, with Tito controlling all but the port of Trieste, the port of Fiume, and lines of communication to Italy and Austria. But Washington categorically opposed recognizing any unilateral changes Tito might impose on any part of the disputed area, and insisted that the Allied military government control the entire region. The initial British impulse to compromise was squelched. Equally complicating was the fact that when they asked the Russians the same month to endorse the Anglo-American position on the problem, the Soviets did not even bother to reply. By April, therefore, no agreement on the future of the area existed and the question was now how to establish control should Tito interpret the vague February understanding in his own favor. The crucial details of the matter were never settled, but had Washington accepted Eden's plan it would have awarded Tito most of the disputed area, with the exception of the city of Trieste itself, for most of the region was Slovene and Croatian. But political passions at the time were hot, and circumstances compelled Tito to wait several years before a settlement awarded him the large majority of the land he claimed.[51]

Tito regarded the Yalta agreement on Yugoslavia and the Russian approval of it as a great betrayal. And since Subasic was merely one man without a party or army behind him, the appointment of a Regency Council and the formation of a new Provisional Government in March hardly concealed the fact that Tito and his Partisan national assembly, AVNOJ, were continuing to consolidate power and create the most advanced socialist economy in Eastern Europe. If the Americans ever needed proof of the nefarious intentions of the U.S.S.R., the man Washington unanimously considered Moscow's obedient agent in Yugoslavia provided their evidence. During early March, Churchill informed the Foreign Office he was now finally prepared to abandon the strategy of wooing Tito out of the Russian orbit, advocating that they spend their energy instead on saving Italy from Communism. Eden rejected the advice, insisting that Britain continue the effort to make Yugoslavia "a sort of neutral area between British and Russian zones of influence."[52] By the following month that policy collapsed, for the very reasons Eden had predicted in his memo on Trieste and because the Americans insisted on avoiding a negotiated settlement.

The failure to solve the Trieste problem meant that the one question on which Tito might conflict with the West was now brought to the foreground, and expressions of British sympathy formerly shown for his claims to Trieste were now discarded as the West, largely due to American pressure, made Tito a symbol of the necessity to resist the Russians, who scarcely controlled the Yugoslav any more than the British did. The course of the controversy compelled Tito to move closer to the Russians than he had ever been, and the British strategy on Yugoslavia failed—but only for a time.

At the end of April the German forces in northern Italy began to withdraw from their positions, and on the 29th they formally surrendered, opening the way to entry into Trieste, which they insisted on surrendering only to Alexander's forces. The official reasons for taking Trieste have always been obscure, though Churchill later said it was essential as a supply port for future Western zones in Austria. He based this proposition on the belief that the Russians would solve the Austrian zonal question amicably—in April this was by no means certain—and that the Yugoslavs would allow their territory to be used as a supply line, an even more doubtful proposition. They also considered Trieste a major lever to future Eastern European affairs, particularly economic, and Churchill convinced Truman of this on April 27: "that there should be an outlet to the south seems of interest to the trade of the many States involved."[53] Such an option might someday prove useful. It appears most likely that many Anglo-American leaders by April regarded Trieste as an important place to resist Communism, for the Austrian justification was scarcely mentioned during the hectic weeks that followed, and the end of the war removed military considerations. Churchill was angry at Tito, and what the British once regarded as a legitimate claim they now saw as part of a grand Soviet design for all of Europe. The debate over Yugoslavia and Trieste during early May was virtually identical to the issues considered at the very same time in the context of Germany and Central Europe: how to stop the thrust of Russian expansion. And British hopes for cultivating Yugoslav independence of the U.S.S.R. were shattered on the shoals of Yugoslav state interests.

On April 27 Churchill, ignoring his advisers' caution, wired Truman that they must immediately authorize the Anglo-American forces under Field Marshal Alexander to occupy as much of Venezia Giulia, and especially the port of Trieste itself, as was possible—most certainly before Tito's forces arrived. "Possession is nine points of the law," he reminded Truman in regard to what he termed "political-military operations." The

State Department, Joint Chiefs of Staff, and Stimson agreed on the following day, and with American consent London ordered Alexander to move on the entire Venezia Giulia and Trieste area "even before Soviet and Yugoslav agreements have been obtained."[54] They could seek approval later, the Anglo-Americans concluded as they now ignored the initial British plan of March. This position might risk armed conflict with Tito, even though the Joint Chiefs instructed Alexander to consult with them before taking military action, and perhaps even with Russia, and on the 30th the angry Churchill wired back, discussing the entire problem in the context of the advances on Berlin, Vienna, and separate surrenders, but also indicating that Alexander ought quickly and secretly to take the port of Trieste alone, preferably by sea rather than land. The fate of the rest of the region they then might discuss with the Yugoslavs. He suspected and later confirmed that Tito perhaps already controlled the area.

Now Truman, Grew, Stimson, and Marshall thought again about their order to Alexander and its implication, and they decided to retract it. Armed conflict with Russia over Trieste might cause the U.S.S.R. to stay out of the war against Japan. Stimson observed he never wished to go into northern Italy in the first place—entering the eastern Mediterranean and Balkans was part of the British strategy—and they might just as easily settle the issue of Venezia Giulia at a later peace conference. Truman decided he too did not want American troops fighting in Yugoslavia, "nor did he wish to become involved in Balkan political questions."[55] Truman immediately informed Churchill that he should notify the Yugoslavs of the imminent arrival of Alexander's forces and that Tito's troops would come under the Englishman's command. They would not ask Tito's consent, nor that of the Russians. If the Yugoslavs refused to cooperate under Alexander's authority, Truman now insisted that Alexander take no action before consultation with the United States Joint Chiefs of Staff. On May 1 Alexander informed Tito of Anglo-American command over Yugoslav troops in the Trieste region, but he also warned Churchill to move very carefully before asking his troops "to fight an Ally" for whom they had much admiration.[56] The following day the forces of Alexander's army began pouring into the region by sea and land to discover that Tito's men had beaten them by some days and had begun to create their own government.

During the first three days of May the gyrations of their own policy bewildered Stimson and others, and they were confused as to British intentions; their only relief was that so far only British troops were involved in the dangerous situation. It was unclear whether the British wished to work with or against Tito's forces, and whether the Americans were opposing or aiding Alexander. Late on May 2, Washington discovered American troops were also in the area, and for two additional days Tito's and Alexander's troops glared at each other, neither able to create their occupation governments. Confusion as to actual United States policy was in large part a result of the State Department's desire to carry through with the strong political assumptions that had stimulated the crisis in the first instance. Clearly, by May 7 the State Department wished Alexander to take over as much of the controversial region as possible, even at the risk, as Stimson thought, of "an open clash of arms with Tito. . . ."[57] During these same days Churchill stiffened the British position to reinforce that of Grew's. Alexander now thought that the original agreement with Tito of the prior February was acceptable as a basis of a settlement if the West assured Tito that the Allied troops would eventually evacuate the area. However Churchill irately told Alexander to hold his position should "Tito, backed by Russia . . . push hard . . . ," and not to make any agreement which implied recognition of Yugoslav territorial claims. ". . . it would be wise," he added, "to have a solid mass of troops in this area, with a great superiority of modern weapons and frequent demonstrations of the Air Force. . . ."[58] During these very same days the Allies negotiated the German surrender.

After some ambivalence both Washington and London returned to their original impulse to show a strong face to the Russians and their presumed agents. On May 10 Grew saw Truman and explained that the Russians were behind the Trieste invasion "with a view to utilizing Trieste as a Russian port in the future. . . ," but also as a part of their general plan of expansion.[59] He produced a memo from Kennan warning of the growth of Soviet expansionism in Eastern Europe. Grew persuaded Truman, and he told the Acting Secretary of State to reverse his position, that the solution to the Trieste problem was to "throw them out."[60] During these same days Tito told Alexander that he had entered the area for political reasons, but that was no less true of the reasons for Anglo-American intervention. Stimson was unable to win Truman over, and on May 12 noted Truman had decided Tito "will require a sharp rap over the knuckles."[61] Truman's decision was in part based on his fear that Italian Communists were fanning nationalist aspirations for the region by blaming Allied weakness for Tito's imperialism, a weird assumption suggesting that Communist machinations produced virtually all the problems of the region. Moreover he saw Tito as a great expansionist, with designs not merely for small sections of southern Austria as he was just then claiming, but Greece and Hungary as well. On May 12 Churchill received "a most welcome and strong message" from Truman to this effect, noting that "we should uphold the fundamental principles of territorial settlement by orderly process against force, intimidation or blackmail."[62] Truman made no effort to measure this standard against the initial reasons for Alexander's entry into the largely Yugoslav region.

With eyes set on Moscow, British and American policy was again in step, as Western and Yugoslav troops faced each other over loaded guns. Eden was in the United States at the time, and on the 14th and 15th discussed the question with Grew. "It was generally agreed," Grew's notes read, "that Tito was not very sure of himself and it was not believed that Stalin would give him unlimited support." Hostilities appeared likely, even necessary, given Yugoslav control of most of the area, and represented less of a risk than "to allow ourselves to be pushed around," Grew cited Eden as observing.[63] But Truman made the decision at this time to authorize American troops only to return Yugoslav fire, a concession to Stimson and the military, who were now much concerned about the possibility of a new war in Europe that would delay the resolution of the Pacific conflict with the original enemy. On the 15th Truman also instructed the Joint Chiefs of Staff to alert air, sea, and armored power for a descent on northern Yugoslavia should that be necessary, and to draw up military plans for fighting Tito. Over the next several days, as Yugoslav sentries restricted Alexander's troops from moving into their areas, alarm signals began pouring in, and on the 16th Stimson prematurely thought it likely Tito would "back down."[64]

But the Americans and British also decided not to withdraw ambassadors from Belgrade, perhaps to stress reliance on diplomacy rather than force. They had not consulted Tito directly during the early days of the crisis, and a few days before May 15 the American ambassador in Belgrade asked him to withdraw his troops to an unspecified extent, east of a line giving the Allied military commander control of Trieste, the northwest approaches, and the rail lines to Austria. Within that region his troops were to place themselves under Alexander's command. Churchill preferred expelling Tito's men from this undefined area, by force of arms if necessary, but Truman now insisted that military action await Tito's fire. Given the deteriorating conditions after the 16th, and Tito's subsequent rejection of the United States note, both sides had reached an impasse and raised the stakes.

The West saw the way out in a message to Stalin and a massive show of force to Tito, and on May 21 London and Washington approved both and sent the cable requesting the Russian's assistance. Stalin replied immediately, observing that the Yugoslavs not only predominated in the area but had also driven the Germans out. He nevertheless suggested a jointly-agreed-upon line of demarcation very much like that the British proposed earlier in March and the United States finally accepted in mid-May. Stalin suggested that the Yugoslavs in the Allied Area be placed under Alexander's authority, but that they administer the other disputed regions. Truman did not care for Stalin's defense of the Yugoslav actions, but both sides finally began negotiations on territories and the relative powers of Yugoslav civil and military authorities. Tito was quite anxious to discuss matters on these terms. When Subasic visited Truman on May 29, American officials informed him that if Belgrade reached no settlement the Americans would meet Tito "with overwhelming force. . . ."[65] The comment was gratuitous, for Tito had already accepted the essential principles of the Anglo-American position, which Subasic reminded Grew the next day, and on June 9 the West signed an agreement with the Yugoslavs for which Truman held Stalin's moderating role responsible. The West received the port of Trieste and nearly all the land leading to it—precisely what it had asked for.

The agreement with Tito on Trieste continued in an atmosphere of mutual recriminations and distrust, and Washington authorized the American commander in the Trieste area to use whatever force was necessary to implement it. Words raged, and Stalin protested when Alexander publicly compared Tito with Hitler. Tito on June 22 declared, "We were forced to submit to this great sacrifice with a heavy heart," and it is probable most of the force came from Stalin.[66] The West found problems in the administration and interpretation of the June 9 agreement, but it prevailed. The United States and the British were confident that they had successfully resisted the Russians rather than the Yugoslavs.

The controversy over Trieste deeply colored the American view of Soviet intentions in Eastern Europe, for it saw Tito as an ardent expansionist in the hands of Russian power, not only toward Bulgaria, where he advocated a Yugoslav-Bulgarian federation, but Macedonian Greece as well. The United States decided to hold the line on Trieste, for rather typically the American chargé in Belgrade defined Yugoslavia as a "totalitarian Communist regime" of the first order. It had created a completely nationalized economy, extending even to American firms, violating the State Department's belief that "American interests are entitled to nondiscriminatory economic and commercial treatment."[67] Behind Tito stood Russia, and though American economic interests were not the prime concern in Yugoslavia, the State Department saw that country as a model of Soviet plans elsewhere in Eastern Europe. For this reason alone the Trieste confrontation, staking the possibility of battle with a vast and powerful Partisan army, Washington regarded as worth the risks. In resisting Tito one was resisting Stalin.

But what made Tito dangerous to the West in 1945 would make him equally ominous to the Russians several years later, for he was not only able to shatter the traditional control of Western Europe over the Balkans, but the hold of Russia as well. Only Tito, Stalin perceived in 1945, stood for nationalism and autonomy, and only he could prevent the fulfillment of Soviet objectives for stability and security in Eastern Europe. With an independent mass base and a nationalist line Tito threatened to checkmate both Russian and American ambitions.

The Meeting at Potsdam

The breakdown within the alliance over Poland, perhaps most of all, but also the entire range of European questions, caused Churchill on May 5 to conclude that "Nothing can save us from the great catastrophe but a meeting and a show-down as early as possible at some point in Germany which is under American and British control. . . ," and he communicated this thought to Truman.[68] Harriman had already been urging such a face-to-face meeting as soon as possible, for time was working for the Russians, and for this reason Truman dispatched Hopkins to Russia at the end of the month.

Truman at first wanted Stalin to take the initiative for convening the meeting, and in any event, he told Churchill and later many of his advisers whom he didn't have to bluff, that he could not leave Washington before the end of the fiscal year, June 30. The ambassadors, the President hoped, would induce Stalin to propose a meeting. And while Churchill had hoped to arrange the meeting for mid-June—for he had an election the following month—he now shifted his timing drastically, and also urged Truman to join him in sending an invitation to Stalin for a date after "the early days of July," at which time he invited Truman to come to England and they would proceed to Germany together.[69] Was there grave significance to their timing of the conference?

Stalin was not so eager to hold the meeting as to initiate its convocation, and when Hopkins went to Moscow he was authorized to ask Stalin to meet in Alaska or Berlin. There is not much question that Truman thought the matter of protocol important, but such an attitude was consistent with delay as well, save insofar as it shifted the initiative in timing to the adversary, who presumably would have thought he had something to gain from a speedy meeting. In fact neither Truman nor Stalin thought the question of timing to be overly crucial. The division within Washington on this line was not one of disagreement on policy toward Russia, for Harriman wanted a meeting as quickly as possible and Stimson wished to see it postponed for a time.

Stimson's papers contain a number of interesting but cryptic passages pertaining primarily to the long-term relationship of the atomic bomb to future problems of foreign policy, and some observers have interpreted the alleged American desire to develop and bring the atomic bomb into play as a reason for the delay of the Potsdam Conference. While I will deal with this problem in much greater detail in Chapter 21, suffice it to say that the development of the atomic bomb existed not as a cause of basic United States policy, but as a contingent element no one could ignore. To postpone the Potsdam meeting mainly for reasons of completing a weapon, a political as well as a military tool, was not irrational, but it is plausible as a primary explanation only if the Americans hoped to keep Russia out of the war against Japan, only if they knew the full power of the bomb, only if the Russians were unfamiliar with its development and, most important, only if the United States was ultimately willing to employ it against a recalcitrant U.S.S.R. None of these factors prevailed.

On June 6, well after Truman had fixed a date to suit many conflicting schedules, Truman told Stimson that he had postponed the Potsdam meeting to July 15 in order, Stimson obscurely interpreted him as implying, to allow more time to drop the bomb on Japan, which in fact was still planned for August, or *after* the conference. But in the same conversation they discussed the possibility of sharing the atomic bomb with Russia in return for quid pro quos in Eastern Europe and Manchuria. Stimson opposed all conferences after Yalta, San Francisco included, in line with his preference for realism and realpolitik, one which long predated the bomb. Churchill was the strongest advocate of a showdown strategy, but he and Harriman thought maintenance of armies in fixed positions and not the atomic bomb was the key to its success. More important, they expected the United States to emerge from the war with overwhelming economic and political power —sufficient to shape the contours of the postwar world. And Truman sent Hopkins to Moscow with rather different assumptions concerning Soviet intervention into the Far Eastern war, for this was a major objective of his mission. When Hopkins saw Stalin, he asked him to agree to a conference on July 15 in Berlin, and the Russian quickly accepted the proposal. It was quite simple, and relatively innocent, as much as anything could be with the politically sensitive Truman.[70] If the bomb was a factor there were many others as well—the general problem of Europe, especially Eastern Europe, weighing far more heavily in American plans and timing.

The Eastern European Policy of the United States

The United States found it extremely difficult to fix on a firm political line for Eastern Europe, and slowly but surely it began to shy away from the question of internal political structures, both because its interests were not deeply involved in whether or not there were free elections in, say, Rumania, and also because it was increasingly apparent that such a posture was historically and immediately irrelevant. By staking its commitment on the careers of certain personalities to save the old political structure of Poland and Yugoslavia, to name but two states, the United States drifted away from the dynamics of real politics to a reliance on messianism, unlikely to succeed in the most ravaged nations of Europe. When Mihailovic failed it supported Subasic until events made the strategy of United States policy irrelevant. Yet even where it could not object to the internal political life of a nation, as in Czechoslovakia or perhaps even Hungary, the United States resisted Russian policy toward those countries, dismissing their significance to understanding the nature of Soviet intentions, because in the last analysis internal democracy did not concern those men in Washington who thought about Eastern Europe.

There were at least some officials in Washington and London who had a full understanding of the war's impact on the future of Eastern European society. However, while the United States was modestly flexible on the future of Eastern European politics, it hoped to re-create the traditional economic relationship between Eastern Europe and Western Europe and the world, which meant restoring the prewar economic status quo. To do this, to carry the political necessities one step further, ultimately meant resisting the apparent aims of Russia and the internal forces of change they tolerated, which in turn required aid to those local forces of the Old Order who stood for the prewar economic and political status quo.

At the end of April 1945 McCloy gave Truman a report on Central Europe, Germany included, which grasped the magnitude of the war's impact on the region.

> There is complete economic, social and political collapse going on in Central Europe, the extent of which is unparalleled in history unless one goes back to the collapse of the Roman Empire, and even that may not have as great an economic upheaval. . . . In this atmosphere of disturbance and collapse, atrocities and disarrangement, we are going to have to work out a practical relationship with the Russians.[71]

By "practical" McCloy meant a considerable toleration of Soviet presence, but not at the cost of excluding American participation, and Washington based that participation, as we shall see, on certain structural assumptions which were in fact limiting factors in the inevitable change predicted for the region. Soon the United States held the Russians responsible for what it once perceived as the effects of war, for the very breakdown of a society that had gladly participated in the bloodletting of over a century. The policy-makers soon forgot the portent of McCloy's analysis, save perhaps on the level of food relief, which was a temporary rather than a permanent solution for the ills of the region.

The British in the spring of 1945 undertook a similar analysis, with more far-reaching conclusions, and the official British history of the period records the Foreign Office's speculations as follows:

> The facts were not encouraging. Our own form of democracy had never established itself in central or south-eastern Europe outside Czechoslovakia. The population of these areas was now so much exhausted and impoverished—one might say, "proletarianised"—by the war that they wanted secure and stable government even at the cost of political and private liberty. They were unlikely to fight for parlia-

mentary institutions. If we tried to enforce our own form of democracy upon them, we should endanger our policy of cooperation with
the U.S.S.R. over an issue which was not vital to our interests in
Europe, but which the Soviet Government regarded as essential to their
security.[72]

Clark Kerr offered much the same thought at the end of March when
he advised that Britain concentrate on strengthening Western Europe, but
Churchill resisted the tentative assumptions of both analyses, and though
he stood alone and ultimately prevailed, it is still something of a fiction to
assert the fashionable view that Britain advocated a harder line toward the
Russians than did the United States. For the problem of Communism in
Eastern Europe was to some critical extent a by-product of Russian military movements across the region, but the menace of the Left in Western
Europe was not, and for this too the West held the Russians responsible. In
brief, the Eastern European social, political, and economic structure could
not break down without dramatically affecting the future of all Europe,
unless the West decided to take some strong steps to prevent what appeared to be the imminent success of the Left everywhere. In its own way
the United States alone appreciated the interrelated character of revolution
in Europe, for it soon became apparent that the political forces of change,
which the United States would at best only tolerate, necessarily would
bring with them far-reaching economic upheavals of much greater consequence for the rest of Europe, and these changes were unacceptable.

The United States defined its ends in Eastern Europe in such a manner
that if the Russians had total control over those tattered nations they could
easily have established a working détente with American capitalism, for
American core objectives were economic. The United States never became
specific on the level of political goals, save for their desire to contain the
Left and Russian influence.

A significant number of the American complaints on Eastern Europe
dealt with the minuscule American property holdings there, especially in
the oil industries of Rumania and Hungary. The only redeeming feature
Washington saw in the utterly politically ineffectual Control Commissions
was the fact, as General Cortland T. V. Schuyler in Rumania put it, "by
timely intervention with Soviet ACC authorities, we have at times been
able to afford some measure of protection to American firms and American
commercial interests in the country." Indeed, for this reason alone Schuyler
could advocate a continuation of the hobbled ACC structure as preferable
to nothing at all. The Americans repeatedly strove to prevent the use, much
less the dismantling, of their property in reparations arrangements, the
shipment of oil from American-owned wells to Russia, and to end the
restrictions imposed on the immediate return of American businessmen to

Eastern Europe. Above all else they opposed nationalization. The United States considered retaliatory measures against Russian policy in the Eastern European oil industry because it thought the "Rumanian-Hungarian oil picture is but one aspect of a world problem . . . and may require appropriate adjustments in policies of this Government. . . ," to quote Grew at the end of June 1945.[73] They were persistently unable to accept the breakdown of traditional European economic relations, for the United States wished to see Eastern Europe returned to the essentially semicolonial status of the prewar period.

In defining United States economic policy in Eastern Europe prior to Potsdam the State Department decided that "Early restoration of the economic life of the countries of Europe is vital to the establishment of a durable peace," which meant the revival of European production. Historically Eastern Europe had been critical to the entire European economy, and this was no less true in 1945. If the United States was to avoid the "critical situation in Western European countries"—with its threat of social and political upheaval—Harold Ickes warned at the end of July, it would have to tap the excess Eastern European oil. The extension of Soviet power over Eastern Europe, which by June had come to mean the triumph of the local Left and Communist alliances, threatened this reintegration in the most fundamental manner, and before Potsdam, Washington determined that "assurance should be sought that the Soviet Government does not pursue the aim of making exclusive economic arrangements with these [former Axis] countries and cutting them off from economic relations, on a basis of equal opportunity with the rest of the world."[74]

The Americans considered that a critical means for attaining this end was an inland waterway system, especially incorporating the Danube River states, which, as Truman explained in May 1945, would "help unify Europe by linking up the breadbasket with the industrial centers through a free flow of trade"—which was to say, the restoration of the larger, traditional European economy, one that ultimately required a powerful Germany as its keystone. In the weeks before Potsdam the State Department carefully thought through this project, whose ultimate objective was "the reestablishment of the international character of the Danube waterway and the eventual reestablishment of a permanent international Danube authority representative of all nations interested. . . ." The Anglo-Americans were in the process of organizing a European Inland Transport Conference, and in fact it met at the end of the year with many of the Eastern European states absent. The United States now saw itself as a legitimate member of such a Danubian organization, along with the riparian states, and it expected the large number of illegally removed Eastern European inland watercraft in the American zone of Germany to be "a strong bargaining point in securing an adequate organization. . . ."[75]

The United States was especially alarmed that the Russians, via reparations agreements and joint companies, would establish a monopoly position in the former Axis satellites. The American position implied that these nations could still sell their raw materials to their prewar markets, which meant Germany. The removal of Germany, on which Eastern Europe depended for its prewar trade, meant a total revolution in traditional trade patterns; until the Allies decided the character of the postwar German economy it was patently irrelevant, even from a capitalistic viewpoint, for the United States to talk of a restoration of the traditional economy, save if America expected Eastern Europe to accept a depression to allow the West to retain an option on the future organization of the European economy. The State Department decided to argue to the Russians at Potsdam that this kind of exclusive commercial penetration

> is at variance with the general commercial policy of this Government, which looks toward the expansion of trade and investment on a multi-lateral, non-discriminatory basis. The United States has a strong interest in the preservation of conditions in the countries of Eastern Europe which will permit the continued operation of such multilateral trade, and accordingly sees a necessity for maintaining not only its own trading interests and position in those countries, but also the trading interest and position of other countries which were importers to, and exporters from, Eastern Europe before the war.

Soviet security interests, American planners decided, could not result in "any interference with American property or trade in these sovereign countries."[76]

If American policy was vague on political demands for Eastern Europe, it was remarkably precise in its economic goals. If the Eastern European nations decided to embark on any radically new economic course, it would in some critical manner impinge on American objectives, and this was as true of democratic Czechoslovakia as it was of Communist Yugoslavia. By this criterion the Americans were to have much cause for complaint.

The Americans never translated their nominal recognition of the social and political breakdown of Eastern European society into realistic economic terms. The Americans wanted a return to the old economic order, not just the creation of independent states free from Russian control, for the United States was unable to accept the economic and revolutionary consequences of the war for Eastern Europe. The Russians, on the other hand, easily assimilated every tendency in Eastern Europe—fascist included—willing to tolerate a degree of economic exploitation and diplomatic hegemony.

Even in summer 1945 one could discern the elements of all the later

Eastern European crises in outline form, and the ability of the United States to reimpose a satisfactory solution on that tortured region was no less elusive. The leaders of the most powerful nation of the earth had very little optimism on the Eastern European picture as a whole when they prepared to confront the Russians at Potsdam.

THE EUROPEAN LEFT, 1945:
THE POLITICS OF
REVOLUTIONARIES

THROUGHOUT 1945 the collapse of the European social order and the responses of the masses to the condition of their lives engendered continuous, ominous realities that were beyond diplomacy and the bargaining table, but nevertheless defined the intrinsic value of all agreements the West and the Soviet Union might reach. The revolutionary upheaval simmering beneath the surface of Europe seemed imminent, and ultimately the critical danger facing the West. The question was not merely how to contain the threat and keep it from coming to fruition in the hands of the Resistance of France, Greece, or Italy, but what this danger said about Soviet intentions for Bolshevizing all of Europe. For the Americans considered the relationship of the Russians to the Left critical, and they never fundamentally differentiated the revolutionary ideology of the U.S.S.R. from the national interests and foreign policy of Russia. Behind Soviet promises was the problem of covert Russian encouragement of the Left, and the Americans would ultimately hold the Soviets responsible for the behavior of the Left. And just as the United States made no distinction between the action and ideology of the U.S.S.R., it made scarcely any for the behavior and ostensible ideology of the left parties of Western Europe and Greece.

Greece: Reaction and Revolution

The Greek ELAS was the only Resistance in Europe to fight an Allied army, and it embarked on that desperate course, divided within its own

ranks, only after British intransigence and the Greek conservatives removed the options for peaceful reintegration into Greek life. To the British
the sheer size of the EAM and its military arm, the ELAS, required a trial
by arms to reduce its power and prevent its triumph as the likely majority
party in any real democracy. The EAM, after virtually possessing most of
Greece and besting the British forces in combat, willingly surrendered its
arms and staked its future on the reliability of British promises and their
small and anxious local allies. This abdication was possible only because
the Communists in the EAM dictated it over a movement they could barely
control.

In the Varkiza agreement of February 12, 1945, the EAM and the
Communists finalized an earlier truce pact to hand in their arms and relinquish control of a vast part of Greece, and in return they were promised
amnesty and freedom from reprisals at the hands of the Greek right-wing
groups in the Security Battalions and "X" bands that the English and
rightists organized out of former collaborationist groups and royalist elements. Yet there could be no respite, Varkiza or not, for to legitimize the
power of the Left would simply mean a continuous threat to both British
and rightist interests, and there was no substitute for repression and terror
to attain a definitive solution for the conservatives' problems.

The terror that ensued was ruthless, and ultimately self-defeating. It
began immediately after the January 1945 truce and mounted in intensity.
Government-organized National Guard units recruited all willing anti-
Communists, including a large number of former collaborationists, and the
Plastiras government set out to reimpose control over the pro-EAM regions. In early February, Grew reported that "Observers in Athens consider that trial and sentencing of EAM members during peace talks was
mistake, particularly since no action has yet been taken against collaborationists."[1] That mistake continued, for the British considered collaboration
a lesser crime than radicalism, and they quickly gave rightist pro-
monarchical elements exclusive command of the reorganized army. As a
result of the political purge of the army, Plastiras resigned as Prime Minister on April 7. The British wished to place prewar royalist officers in
command of the army, but Plastiras preferred his political allies, conservative but also mildly republican in sympathy. The change resulted in a more
pliable and even more reactionary government under Admiral Peter Voulgaris, who spent his time furthering the repression and advancing territorial
claims for lands that figured prominently in past nationalist aspirations.
The British approved of Voulgaris, who called himself nonpolitical and
attempted to meet Greece's problems by irredentism.

The regime systematically purged the army and political bureaucracy of
pro-EAM elements. There was casual terror of random assassinations and
beatings, and systematic repression by security committees and courts-

martial that simply arrested EAM supporters and detained them without trial. The government tightly controlled trade unions, and charged former EAM underground government tax collectors with robbery and looting. The regime now judged ELAS executions of collaborators as murder. Outside the Athens area the government-proclaimed martial law lasted until August. The police and their supporters beat up EAM and Communists newsvendors, even arrested purchasers at random, and shot leftist reporters. Right-wing bands roamed many districts, doling out retribution at will. When the British Parliamentary Legal Mission visited Greece at the end of the year they reported that wholesale terror filled the filthy, crowded jails with a very minimum of 50,000 prisoners, and by comparison the excellent, even comfortable, prisons for some of the worst fascists were comparatively empty.[2]

The British hoped not merely to suppress the EAM, and this they encouraged with enthusiasm and relative success, but to build a viable alternative government, and it was their inability to find an effective rightist regime capable of successfully assuming both tasks that ultimately destroyed the British position in Greece, and the Right as well, for the result was very expensive. Indeed it proved more than Britain could bear.

The British could perfect the organs of repression, but they found it virtually impossible to make the Greek elite take advice on a painfully overdue and obvious reform of the economic and administrative structure, and they were unwilling to risk undermining the politically acceptable government by pressing it too hard on this count. Various economic and legal missions failed to remedy the deficiencies of the rightist regimes, which now wallowed in mounting corruption, cronyism, and reaction. Nearly half of all UNRRA aid to Europe by the end of May 1945 went to Greece, but the personnel UNRRA sent with the program served only as observers. Their reports were nearly unanimous in describing pervasive corruption and inefficiency, for much of the UNRRA aid ended up in the black market, to the profit of civil servants and politicians with rightist political connections. In the words of the official historian of UNRRA, who tried his best to be charitable when discussing "chronic incompetence," "mediocre officials," and the like, "it still remains true that the Government was frequently one of the obstacles which UNRRA had to overcome."[3] The result was a rampant inflation and social misery, which only opened the door wide to the eventual triumph of the Left via normal political processes and made repression the essential precondition to prevent the total collapse of the Old Order in Greece. Yet that breakdown too would have occurred, save that the Greek Right knew that by internationalizing their internal deficiencies they might retain some hope for survival, for they increasingly saw themselves, like most of the Right in Eastern and southern Europe, as too impotent to stem the tide without the aid of the English and Americans. In this course they laid the basis for future international crises.

The Greek Left's response to the failure of the Varkiza agreement reflected precisely those same divisions that wracked the EAM and the Communist party throughout the war and especially at the end of 1944, for the Communists desperately tried to restrain the Greek Left from responding to the repression, and to play a make-believe political game which in no manner accorded with the realities of Greek life.

The British-sponsored government formally allowed the Communists to maintain headquarters and a press in Athens, although they found life increasingly difficult amid the repression. The EAM in mid-March presented a long list of grievances to the Allied representatives in Athens, but with no effect. During this same time the EAM split along much the same lines as before. The Macedonian group aside, many of the military leaders of the ELAS, especially Aris Veloukhiotis, felt the nonimplementation of the Varkiza agreement left them no alternative but to return to the hills. This position was not merely political, but the logic of necessity, and during the summer of 1945 a number of small groups reappeared in the mountains, largely dissolving in the autumn. "There is evidence," as a British Parliamentary delegation later reported when the bands reemerged, "that amongst these bands are many Left-wing supporters who have fled to the mountains to escape terrorism exercised by the extreme Right."[4]

In late May, Nikos Zachariadis, the secretary of the Communist party, returned to Athens after spending the war in a Nazi concentration camp. He immediately conducted a comprehensive purge of the party, including the militant wing, and attempted to reintegrate the KKE into a Greek political structure that the Communists now wished to pretend was democratic by virtue of their legal existence. On June 5 Zachariadis wrote a long editorial in the KKE paper defining a friendly policy toward British strategic interests in Greece and the eastern Mediterranean, which he formally recognized. In return, however, the Communist asked for British noninterference in Greek internal affairs, which he hoped they would now permit to develop in a democratic and peaceful fashion. The KKE now advanced Greek national claims to the Dodecanese islands, Turkish Thrace, Cyprus, and disputed southern border areas, while other EAM leaders called for maintenance of the Macedonian nation within Greece, about which the Communists were silent. The KKE and its political allies in the EAM were now seeking entry into Greek politics on a democratic basis, certain that they could win at the polls what the field of combat denied them. To make this point as clearly as possible, on June 16 the party leadership expelled Veloukhiotis from the KKE as a former "Metaxas agent," and two days later right-wing soldiers exhibited the impaled heads of the hitherto elusive Veloukhiotis and another ELAS leader in the town square of Trikkala.

These grisly deaths rather than the beleaguered KKE office in Athens revealed the quality and possibilities of Greek political life in mid-1945, and there was no possibility for Voulgaris and the British to heed the

Communists' offer to become just another party, for the potential debacle of Greek society was so pervasive that to the British and the Right a KKE victory at the polls was too probable to be tested. For the rest of the year, therefore, as the government mounted the repression and terrorized the Left, ultimately into self-defense, the KKE trailed behind by proclaiming a neutral foreign policy, with friendship for Britain and the United States as well as Russia and Yugoslavia, and even supported the short-lived Sophoulis government at the end of November.

The Communists, along with two other EAM parties, revealed their wholly political and peaceful strategy in their June request to reverse the Varkiza agreement's provisions concerning a plebiscite on the monarchical question to be followed by general elections. With this they also asked, however, that the Four Powers supervise the election to assure its honesty. The naïveté of this tactic was twofold: first, that the British would agree to a KKE or EAM triumph at the polls as a result of an honest election; and second, that the Russians would cooperate in the undertaking, an assumption which supposed the Russians were concerned with their fate. In fact the Russians later refused to help supervise the affair for fear of setting an unwelcome precedent for Eastern Europe, and after initial opposition the British agreed to rigged elections for the following year.

The Russians made a deliberate decision which made the policy of the KKE during 1945 explicable. Stalin had been utterly indifferent to the fate of the Greek people, and repeatedly assured the English that he regarded the nation as within their sphere of interest and vital to their security. In April he reiterated this position, and wrote Churchill and Truman that he would not interfere in affairs there—expecting that they would do no less in Poland. In mid-June, *New Times,* the successor to *War and the Working Class,* printed a report on the repression in Greece, likening conditions to the situation under the Germans, an analogy the British government protested as hostile. In fact, by early July neither British nor American experts found any evidence of Soviet material aid to the KKE and, furthermore, whatever Russian intervention occurred actually helped to save British power in Greece by taming the KKE and EAM. Yet this task was beyond even the power of the Russians and their obedient and purged Greek KKE, for they could not control the intolerable repression which drove men back to the hills and safety, nor could they save the Greek society and economy from utter disintegration, much less stem the independent winds of nationalism blowing from the north.[5]

Macedonian Nationalism and Greek Expansion

The classic Balkan disputes revived quickly, masked now in ideology but revealing the same qualities that had bloodied the region for centuries.

Indeed, by wrapping an ideological garb around their age-old aims, both Greeks and Yugoslavs might hope to make expansionist objectives emerge ennobled, or in the case of the Greeks, win new and important support from Great Powers who might deliver to them what they could not obtain themselves. For the Greeks the internationalization of their historic aims was essential to their attainment and for the survival of a moribund, corrupt Greek society choking on its accumulated failures.

The Greek conservatives were passionately expansionist, and they spent much time throughout the war advancing their demands for northern Epirus, the Dodecanese, territory on the Bulgarian frontier, and elsewhere, At the beginning of 1945 the Ambassador of the Greek government again presented all of these claims fo the United States. "At the end of the war in Europe," the semi-official Greek history of the period reads, "Greek foreign policy, more than ever before, was chiefly concerned with two great problems—the peace settlement and getting aid for economic recovery."[6] Since the border issue was one that appealed to all Greeks, and the economy was seemingly plagued by failure, the Greek government stressed its territorial demands above all others, and on June 30, 1945, Voulgaris officially made them the most important task facing his government, with northern Epirus being the prime target. A week later the Greek government submitted a list of claims which included not only the traditional objectives, but the Italian colony of Cyrenaica as well, and the Greek Foreign Minister on July 9 visited the State Department and courted American support, especially against Bulgaria. "It must be borne in mind," an American embassy analyst reported at the beginning of July, "that Greek newspapers of the Right constantly speak of frontier revisions, and of a Greek-British campaign against Sofia."[7] For the time, at least, it was easier to make claims against the Communist nations to the north than the Turks.

There was another dimension to the expansionist enthusiasm that even the KKE encouraged—the pattern of repression against Macedonian elements in northern Greece, a sector of the nation that had been active in the ELAS for nationalist reasons and was to suffer for it. The repression against this minority was especially severe, and on grounds of physical survival, and also nationalism, several thousand escaped over the border to Yugoslavia, where a smaller number of Greek members of the ELAS joined them. Their fate was a mixed one, for the Yugoslavs kept them under military discipline in quarters many thought were essentially concentration camps. At the same time the Chams of Epirus, who escaped Greek persecution by fleeing to Albania, formed another potentially anti-Greek force.

The Yugoslav response, which Subasic shared with Tito, soon followed. Tito had already shown an interest in creating a Macedonian state within Yugoslavia, and the Greeks were certain that he coveted their section of Macedonia as well. Tito gave formal assurance that Yugoslavia harbored no such intentions in April, but no one in Athens believed him, in large part because Tito continued to express solicitous concern for the welfare of persecuted Macedonians in Greece. By mid-1945 all sides regularly created petty border incidents which erupted into a small crisis at the end of June. On July 8 Tito delivered a broadcast discussing the flow of refugees to the north, the persecution of Macedonians in Greece, and the numerous skirmishes between border guards. It was hardly a threatening statement, but it did refer to the Athens regime as reactionary. Voulgaris immediately brought the seemingly grave threat to the attention of the British and American ambassadors, and replied four days later in another radio broadcast to advance once more Greek claims against Yugoslavia.

The Yugoslavs were obviously concerned about the freely publicized Greek expansionist designs, and while they unquestionably had their own regarding Macedonia, they could not move to advance them for fear of clashing with the Bulgarian-oriented Macedonian groups, and at this time Tito was primarily concerned with achieving a federation with Bulgaria. "No intensification of the autonomous Macedonia agitation in Greece has been detected," the American embassy informed Washington at the end of June, "as might be expected if Tito intended immediate aggression against Greece."[8] Over the following months, however, the Yugoslavs criticized the Greek government much more strongly on the Macedonian issue. During the summer of 1945 the Greeks were content to direct English and American attention to the Yugoslav and Bulgarian response to their statements and actions as evidence of Communist expansionism. Given the mood in the West there was a propensity to mistake the allegations for the reality, but in fact the Greeks were busy attempting to internationalize a local affair.

The Yugoslavs and Bulgarians soon realized that a less belligerent government in Athens would lessen their age-old problems with the Greeks, though it was not until March 1946, when the number of armed bands composed of men fleeing government persecution substantially increased, that the Yugoslavs decided to give them aid. In the meantime the Yugoslavs became involved in a situation including groups isolated from the conservative Greek KKE, each with their own nationality problems and strategy, and not in the least responsive to Moscow's leadership. Here too the legacy of Balkan history planted the seeds for an independent Communism.[9] The Greek Right stirred up the sparks of old controversies, and in conjunction with the prolonged, if temporarily dormant, civil war in Greece, they began to brew the ingredients for a major international crisis available for whatever other purposes their protectors might choose to define.

.   .   .

THE Greek Right had yet to find its final patron, but that it would need one was unquestionable, for the price of maintaining such a government inevitably proved far too great for an economically exhausted Britain. The British found the Greek government entirely exasperating and cynical. "The hesitation of each successive Greek Government to tackle their economic, financial and administrative problems was their besetting sin," Reginald Leeper recalls. "They always excused themselves for doing nothing by saying that nothing could be done without a foreign loan."[10] For the next year and a half the British complained about this ineptitude, but in fact such procrastination was the basic political strategy of the Greek conservatives. Despite massive aid after liberation, the economic condition of Greece became the most desperate in all Europe as corrupt and incompetent Athenian officials left virtually untouched the vast misery of the war. They used foreign loans and aid to enrich what the British Parliamentary delegation later described as "a small class of wealthy people chiefly residing in and around Athens. Members of these families live in great luxury."[11] The needs of this class were such that Britain alone could not compensate for their direction of Greece.

Athens wished to obtain United States loans as well, and unsuccessfully attempted to do so at the end of 1944. United States policy had always left Greek affairs to British initiative, and in fact Washington endorsed the broad outlines of England's direction over the nation. Yet the United States supplied 70 percent of UNRRA aid, and by May the Greeks were in Washington with a special economic mission. At first Donald Nelson, the foreign aid adviser, wished to send an economic mission to Greece to study its needs, but Grew and Truman were apprehensive because, in Grew's words, UNRRA operations "were going very badly."[12] Washington, for the last time, was happy to pass off the problem as England's area of special interest, warranting detachment until England approved. The English, however, were not loath to have the Americans aid the desperate Greek economy with "loans" that were not likely to be repaid to England in any case.

At the end of June the State Department attempted to redefine a policy toward Greece, and concluded that "To take an active and benevolent interest in Greece at this time offers one of the most practical means of demonstrating this Government's determination to play an international role commensurate with its strength and public commitments." A Great Power had to have a policy on Greece, and this the United States would certainly have. An active policy toward Greece, the Administration now understood, would make the United States important in both the Near East and the Balkans. Yet the State Department knew relatively little about the complexities of the area, for it decided that Greece uniquely in the region was not "characterized by xenophobia." Moreover, the Greek government indicated a desire to come closer to the United States. Now Washington determined to ask the Greeks to have an election before a plebiscite, and even "to indicate our belief that a republican form of government offers more possibility for a peaceful future than the return of a monarchy already stigmatized by totalitarianism." Further economic aid, including loans, would be forthcoming. And the United States would inevitably "encourage Greece to an early reconciliation and the development of good relations with her neighbors by supporting the reduction or removal of commercial, financial, social and cultural barriers."[13]

By the end of July the Americans promised loans and aid, and the beginning of a long and increasingly serious relationship began out of the modest but sedulous Greek cultivation of American concern. Yet so long as the money disappeared as quickly as it was received, the Greek government could not hope to survive, for the masses of that starving land saw none of the succor. To contain the Greek people would ultimately require military might in the name of order and freedom—and a role commensurate with strength and power.

Italy and the Collapse of the Resistance

During December 1944 the leadership of the Italian Resistance in the occupied north agreed to subordinate itself to the future Allied military government and to act merely as the military representative of the Bonomi government in the north. Yet for the Anglo-American leaders the "Protocols of Rome" were merely a starting point for containing and ultimately destroying the threat that the potentially revolutionary "Winds from the North" posed, and they laid plans for occupying and holding the region as quickly as the Germans permitted. From February, as the Allies prepared their spring campaign, they decided to instruct the Resistance to restrict its activities to sabotage and protection of vital utilities and transport rather than organize its mass forces for tactical fighting. More important, the arms supplied were suitable only for the more limited purpose. Now the Americans and English could only wait and anxiously speculate as to what might evolve in the coming months, and take steps to prevent a repetition of a Greek-style crisis.

Despite the Anglo-American policies and German repression, by the beginning of the spring of 1945 the Resistance numbered perhaps 150,000 men, supplying themselves with growing stocks of deserted or captured fascist and German weapons. Success was imminent, and men joined. Then, on April 16, with Nazi armies melting away before them, the CLNAI issued its directive for a general uprising, a "national uprising," "the people's long campaign for freedom." "The interests of the workers coincide with those of the entire nation," the manifesto to the Italian proletariat in arms declared.[14] Italian conservatives and Western military leaders alike were fraught with anxiety, while the Left forgot that Marx once declared the working class has no nation of its own.

The workers of Milan, some 60,000 of them, revolted on the 24th, with slight bloodshed, assigning control of the factories to workers' councils and meting out justice to the fascists. Then in Turin, against heavy German opposition, they swiftly took the city. Throughout northern Italy the Resistance was in control everywhere, and quickly shot approximately 20,000 fascists or alleged collaborators. The Resistance was triumphant and in power. Was Italy on the verge of revolution?

The Allied military wasted no time in finding out. They knew it was necessary to disarm the Partisans and take over local governments. Disarmament, as the files of the military government reveal, the Anglo-Americans executed "with astonishing success."[15] They organized parades throughout northern Italy at the end of April and May, with bands and banners, speeches and toasts, and retrieved vast stores of arms. At least 60 percent were in hand by the end of June and the Anglo-Americans had broken the military back of the Resistance. Establishing political control was no more difficult. The military made all CLNAI decrees and appointees subject to military approval, and military government ruled the north until the end of the year, long after Rome governed the south and center. The occupation made the workers' councils inconsequential somewhat later, and in short order northern Italy was safe again. "The CLNAI," an occupation authority reported to headquarters on June 1, "has lived up to the agreements made prior to occupation and has cooperated insofar as possible. . . ."[16] A week later the Resistance organization officially dissolved itself.

With red banners and power in hand 150,000 armed men disappeared in a moment, and the almost morbid fears of the English and Americans proved entirely chimerical. Why?

The American attitude toward the Communists never relaxed, and the Chief Commissioner of the Allied Commission in June 1945 discussed the imminence of horrendous anarchy that might lead to a Communist takeover by force. But facts remain even when no one generalizes upon them or fits them into a realistic assessment, for there is no question that the Communists saved the Old Order in Italy. As if by reluctant necessity the Americans gradually acknowledged the conservative role of the CP when it was useful to do so, and ignored it when it violated more convenient preconceptions. When disarming the Resistance the Anglo-Americans made the decision "to secure the confidence of the Partisan commanders and conduct disarmament through them. . . ."[17] They then recognized that "An important factor in determining the attitude of the Allied officials will be the ability of the resistance leaders to maintain discipline among their followers."[18] In both cases the leaders were willing to cooperate, primarily because the majority were Communists.

By stressing the political goal of unity above all else, even if that alliance meant cooperation with fascist collaborators, the CP became the party of transcendent nationalism, a nationalism that submerged class goals and vetoed the triumph of the Left in a period of considerable, but by no means irresistible, revolutionary possibilities. The radical Italian masses had the illusion that the CP was a radical party, not a bureaucratic accretion of Russian foreign policy and a mere rhetoric monger. But so long as it was responsive to Soviet desires it was at its core a non-Italian party that could assume the mantle of nationalism because of the socially reactionary character of traditional Italian nationalism after World War I. The CP's phenomenal growth and political success were based on its nationalism, its activism in leading the struggle against the Nazi invaders and their fascist puppets, and its alleged social radicalism. The radical aspect of its general reputation was least consequential to the needs of the U.S.S.R., which wanted to defeat Nazism at any price, even as part of a world coalition that welcomed the disaffected Right. Litvinov, in a conversation with the American representative to the Italian Advisory Council in September 1944, admitted that "We do not want revolutions in the West, but if they happen we must approve."[19] But they would not happen if Soviet policy defined events, at least in Italy, because when the Russians recognized Badoglio they also issued a clear warning to the Communists not to grasp for the power that was almost theirs.

The Italian CP leadership instead preferred to enter the intrigues of Cabinet politics, secure posts for themselves in Rome, and stress their new role as the party of all Italians, irrespective of religion, class, or philosophy, who lived by their own labor. They attempted to cling to that role until the spring of 1947, when their former friends unceremoniously threw them out of the government. More significant was the Socialists' decision under Nenni to follow their lead, in the hope that a United Front of the two parties of the workers might succeed at the ballot box. From early 1945 on, both the Socialist and the Action parties elected to return to the government, and when the Bonomi government fell in June 1945 both were glad to enter the new Parri Cabinet as Allied military authorities supervised its organization. For the Action party the step was fatal, and soon its quarter of a million members passed to other groups, from Left to Right. Yet Nenni admitted one other factor caused him to shift from the strategy of the street back to the intrigues of parliament. "When the North fell it was impossible to take direct action for a republic with the Allies in Italy. It would have meant risking a conflict with the Allied occupation armies which could have ended only unsuccessfully. Therefore all energy was concentrated on the Constituent Assembly."[20] That too ended unsuccessfully, but there was no way out of the dilemma, for the Allies would not permit the Left to win, and they had made that decision before Yalta. Only the Communists, however, appeared to try to make a virtue out of this necessity, even to deny its existence, and not once did Togliatti utter an extraparliamentary manifesto.

France: The Party of Production

In France both the political strategy and ideology of the Communist party, the largest single party in France, was remarkably unified as the Communist leaders sought to define a theory suitable to their restrained, even conservative behavior. Despite apprehensions among American analysts, and especially the fear of the embassy in Paris that the prewar French leaders, most of whom had collaborated with Vichy, would not again take over the leadership of France, the Communists hewed to a nonrevolutionary course. In the process of pursuing a social-democratized political line the CP gave the defeated and discouraged French industrial and financial leaders the critical breathing spell necessary for their lives.

The Communists entered the government, and remained there until May 1947, on the basis of a United Front strategy and a desire to see French power restored at home and abroad. Given their relationship to the working class, only they could extract the indispensable precondition for the restoration of the Old Order—production. The Communists became the party of production, even the party of the speedup. Their leaders, Maurice Thorez and Jacques Duclos, despite the unhappiness among the militant faction prominent in the Resistance, defined a political line which above all else stressed the necessity of a United Front even at the cost of drastically blurring the identity of the Left, of which the Communists were indisputably the leaders in 1945.

United Front above all, and with everyone: workers, peasants, the middle classes, even priests. Indeed, as Thorez reminded the party in February, the Soviet Union permitted full freedom of religion, and he strictly forbade members to raise the question of theology and distract the nation from the united pursuit of the war. "The priests were with us," and the Catholics too had spilled blood in the common struggle against the Nazis, Thorez told the Tenth Party Congress in June.[21] Even after the war ended, when they could no longer evoke the exigencies for the defeat of fascism, the Communists persisted in their call for national unity, which was also the precondition of their incorporation into the mainstream of governmental and political power. Above all the Communists sought a share in that power, at any price.

The Communists in fact had no binding ideology, and their willingness to cooperate with the other centrist groups, even on the others' terms, reinforced their willingness to minimize the importance of Marxism in the party's definition of the world. Marxism was a science, not a dogma, Thorez informed the party—not a final revelation, but a continuous method of inquiry. The class struggle existed and was a fact, but in practice this struggle was one against the "trusts," not capitalism as such, and by mid-1945 nothing in Thorez's or Duclos' speeches cultivated the illusion of the Communists as the party of the armed resistance or militant working class. This purely reformist aspect of the party's ideology to some large extent explains its vast growth during 1945, much to the chagrin of the older, more ideologically committed militants, and the ambiance of a fraternal association spread throughout the ranks of the party—so much so that the tone of the organization took on that of an extended family. Indeed this successful organizational dimension that Duclos especially cultivated made the growth and durability of the CP a phenomenon that transcended foreign-policy crises and domestic prosperity to make the Communists a permanent dimension of the French order, especially in those regions in the central and southwest areas of France where the prewar party vote had been relatively light. For there, rather than the industrial centers of the north, the strength of the party grew by phenomenal percentages.

The political formula was so successful that despite the unhappiness of the militant wing of the party, and the opposition of the Americans to any Communist share in political power on any terms, it permanently hewed to a reformist line. The diverse expressions of this strategy deserve some attention. Perhaps no less important than the policy of the Communists in the government was their very willingness to abandon the party itself to the logical conclusion of the United Front policy—a new French workers' party based on organic unity with the Socialists. To some extent the proposal which Thorez first made in June and Duclos later advanced was akin to the now common tactic of the Communists of formulating a program to win votes rather than a program that was specific and negotiable. In reality the Communists could still hope in 1945 to become *the* party of the Left, maintaining their rate of growth by conveying the impression of reasonableness, which became their sole concern. Since the Socialists under Léon Blum stoutly resisted all such advances, the overture is meaningful only insofar as it revealed the willingness of the Communists to submerge their identity further on terms which functionally brought them yet closer to respectability.

To the Socialists, the Communists' prime obligation was to prove their independence of the U.S.S.R., and since the Communists were unlikely to confess subservience the preliminary talks soon mired on the point. Although the CP still paid lip service to the writings of Stalin and Lenin, ideology apart it was in fact the party of the constituted order, and more significantly its action rather than verbiage helped define the condition of a vulnerable French order that might have fallen had past ideology and existing practice been one and the same.[22]

The French Communists were quite willing to talk of submerging their identity via unity on the Left, but not to dissolve, for no successful politician ever gracefully passes from the scene—or opts for a new and untried course. Unity of the Left may have been on Communist terms, for the party had achieved a great deal and was not obligated to concede much, and its success—and survival—was based on the reality that it was playing an entirely nonrevolutionary game while purporting to represent the vague ideals of the Left. Duclos conveyed essentially this fact during April in his now famous article in *Cahiers du Communisme,* a document that the State Department carefully studied and misinterpreted then and thereafter as a sign of Communist and Soviet truculence. Virtually every word Duclos uttered before and after the article meshed with the line of Thorez and the party, and indeed Duclos was the prime implementor of the conservative strategy that Thorez propounded and Moscow unquestionably authorized as well. It fully revealed the very modest ambitions the party had set before itself. And in responding critically to it the American government and those who later shared its premises revealed that what disturbed them was not the practice Duclos advocated, but the more significant fact that they considered the mere existence of a powerful Communist party, on any terms, as a threat to United States interests. For Duclos made one critical point: the Communists would pursue a moderate line, but they would not dissolve themselves, and for hostile observers, implicitly, their sheer size and potential power might later lead them to consider new options more threatening to the constituted order.

The Duclos piece was in fact nothing more than a casual survey of the policy of the American Communist party in formally transforming itself into a nonpolitical association in May 1944. Four-fifths of the text consisted of a faithful summary, mainly via long quotations, of the position of Earl Browder for the dissolution of the American party. Duclos might object to the dissolution of the party, but nothing more. He asked only that the Americans not translate the postwar peaceful coexistence between the Allies, confirmed at Teheran and Yalta, into a rigid dogma for internal as opposed to international affairs. Yet Duclos insisted no less strongly on maintaining the struggle for "national unity," to which the French party was totally dedicated, and he praised the American Communists' endorsement of Roosevelt in the 1944 election. In America, as in France, the Communists should direct the internal struggle only against the "trusts," a vague epithet that revealed nothing specific and still allied the Communists with the constituted order.[23] In a public statement on March 30 Duclos was more definite in making it clear he believed the directors of British and

American business were of a radically different breed than the French industrialists, for the Anglo-Americans too were patriots. In the context of a United Front policy this was a gesture of cooperation toward international capitalism. The use of the term "the conquest of power" disturbed Washington several months later, yet any reading of the larger context of Duclos' article, much less the conduct of the French Communists or even their ambiguous but essentially favorable policy toward nationalization, reveals that these words expose only the interpreters' fears of French democratic politics rather than the realities of French Communism. Duclos nowhere implied, in this article or in speeches of the period, a violent seizure of the state. The Communist party, however, despite American wishes, would not disappear, but it would do everything by strictly parliamentary means to opt into a modernized version of a conservative French order.

In defining the major tasks before the French party in June 1945, Thorez specified the need to reconstruct the French economy, its imports, exports, and output; he hoped to see political reform via a new and powerful National Assembly and Constitution; and, lastly, he set a high priority on the creation of a unified French workers' party. Political reform would not involve the use of the local Committees of Liberation as a substitute for local administrative authorities constituted in the perfectly conventional manner, and this point Thorez never tired of making after the liberation of Paris. The committees should aid the local administrators, but nothing more, and it was patently obvious that this was a mere sop to the Resistance elements who felt their organizations should somehow become the core of government. In fact both Thorez and Duclos continuously reiterated their belief that the Communists would function in a perfectly constitutional manner, and not by violence, sectarianism, or a "revolutionary line," and privately Thorez assured his political allies in the other parties that they might ignore the factious sections of his party and the occasional sectarian words with which he might have to placate them. Political reform, he made it perfectly plain, meant a sovereign National Assembly, but neither a revolutionary nor an unstable government.

The policy of the Communists toward the sensitive questions of French colonialism and the future of the army revealed the extent to which they were unwilling to depart from the premises of French politics. On colonialism their stance was for all practical purposes one of "Progressive Empire" and at no time during 1945 did they advocate immediate colonial independence. On Indochina they maintained a discreet but obvious silence. On Algeria they referred to the desirable growth of democratic freedoms, but always they made it clear in the context of all North Africa that their objective was a progressive union with France, not independence.[24] During mid-1945 the Communists severely condemned the first postwar stirring of the independence movement against French control in Algeria as "fascist" uprisings.[25] The Communists' policy toward the future army was also moderate, despite the early demands among the rank and file of its Resistance adherents in the FTP for a "democratic army." Thorez could not dismiss this impulse altogether, but reconciled it with the politics of a United Front with the Center by calling for the incorporation of the qualified former Resistance members into an army that the nation ultimately would base on technical competence and classic military discipline. Since it was impossible to apply such a formula to everyone's satisfaction, their policy on military credits in the National Assembly and the manner in which Charles Tillon, former head of the FTP, ran the Ministry of Air assigned to him, revealed the true Communist commitment.

The Communists wanted a modern, mechanized, and powerful army during the war, and strangely persisted in this desire long after its conclusion, when it was apparent that any war France engaged in would only be against its colonial states or the U.S.S.R. They let the traditionally antimilitarist Socialists take the lead in the National Assembly in opposing the pretensions of the officers and cadres around De Gaulle. They voted the military funds necessary for the return of France to its empire through 1945, and it was Tillon who stoutly resisted all efforts to reduce support for the military aircraft industry which he founded. When the Communists ultimately went along with the Socialists in reducing a military budget which had no relationship to France's needs or resources, Duclos insisted that the act had no political meaning, save as a sign of confidence in the Socialists. The assimilation of the former FTP and Resistance members into the regular army, which the Communists had advocated since 1944, the French generals implemented in a manner that caused many, when not assigned as guards of prisoners or other menial tasks, to wonder whether they had not in fact been placed in "concentration camps" to make them harmless. Wherever possible the government gave former Resistance troops integrated into the army older, poorer weapons, and studiously restricted them to a disproportionately small section of the officer corps of the new army. In fact the army assimilated the Resistance to neutralize it. In this task the Communists cooperated fully.[26]

More important than their objectives on a political or military level, the French Communists played a critical role in disciplining the working class and ultimately making it possible for capitalism as an institution to survive and profit in France. Above all the Communists were the advocates of production, for they above all others could make the workers toil.

Although the Communists were occasionally reticent, and ambiguously defined the significance of the development, they supported the extensive nationalization of industry which followed in the wake of the war, especially of the property of pro-Vichy business elements. Nationalization was as much a penalty for collaboration as a scheme to reconstruct industry, and the Communists correctly insisted it was rather distinct from ideal socialism. Indeed the Communists sensed that "economic reform" would result in a strengthening of capitalism by taking over a small part of it to buttress the rest. Still, they voted for it, pointed to its distinction from what they favored, and in a larger sense their insistence on production at all costs made the existing reform program a logical outcome of their policy. "We are for the revolution, tomorrow," Thorez confessed: "while waiting, today, we wish the capitalist system to function according to its own laws. . . ."[27] During the war period the Communists were the most ardent advocates of increased production, and Thorez saw the value of rationalizing industry to enlarge output, and so while the party begrudgingly advocated the nationalization of monopolies, with adequate compensation within the context of a capitalist society, they also asked for greater worker participation in management, though not to the extent of endangering output, and after the war, reconstruction. Social idealism never supplanted technical criteria.

The extent of this commitment, which continued almost to the time they were ousted from the government and eventually endangered their trade-union base, was nothing short of compulsive. Indeed, the Communists took genuine pride in their role in the economic recovery of France, which they helped administer in the Industrial Production and Labor ministries. They expressed true satisfaction in their accomplishments even as late as September 1947, when the Yugoslav Communists attacked Duclos' report at the first Cominform meeting, which the militant Yugoslavs found entirely reformist and compromising even though the Soviet Union endorsed it. Throughout 1945 the party called upon the workers, and especially the coal miners, to overcome their "deficient psychology," avoid strikes and absenteeism, and produce. In this context they also called for the technical rationalization of French industry—along American lines. Thorez's most famous discourse on this theme, delivered July 21 to the Waziers coal miners, laid upon the backs of the miners, "in great measure," the obligation to make possible the renaissance of France. Curiously, during the same weeks the State Department's analysts reached largely the same conclusion about the relationship of coal to recovery in Europe and the prevention of revolutionary upheavals. At Waziers, Thorez again excoriated the "psychological deficiencies" of the miners, the use of medical certificates to take off work, even designating as "inadmissible" the conduct of a group of young miners who left work early at six in the evening to attend a dance.[28] If he condemned the policy of the mine owners, the indisputable leader of the Communists could also urge the miners to send their wives and daughters into the pits to increase production.

During the critical period in the history of French capitalism the major party of the Left took upon itself, with the guidance of the Soviet Union, the responsibility of managing and restoring a tottering system during its moment of greatest danger. It would be idle to suggest that the Communists alone saved French capitalism, for the Socialists pursued essentially the same line, and, as in Italy, the Anglo-American armies left few options, but the historical connection between the salvation of French capitalism and the Communists is a vital and scarcely perceived one, and common to other European areas at this time. Yet within a few years, despite the united efforts of all major French parties, the workers eventually grew tired of the toil and abnegation the Communists urged upon them, and created a new crisis for French capitalism and the United States—and forced the Communists to follow their initiatives, but from a distance. They would not risk the international consequences of a revolution in the West, and their chronic parliamentarianism ultimately became an established aspect of French life—safe and quite conservative.

The United States and the Threat of International Communism

Throughout the war the United States had been aware that the success of the Left might deprive it of the political and economic victory it hoped to attain. Washington never doubted the intimate, direct connection between the European Left and the Communist parties and the Soviet Union, and frequently warned the Russians that it, in effect, would hold them responsible for the conduct of the Communist parties. The United States would not permit the Russians to deprive the West of its share in the direction of world political affairs that the diplomats accepted in principle, and the Russians knew that their allies would hold them accountable for the behavior of the European Communist movement. Therefore the Russians consistently attempted to control its leadership and prevent the Communists from capitalizing on the immense possibilities inherent in the profound weakening of European capitalism. Thus, the restoration of capitalism, at least in Western Europe, became the prerequisite of stable diplomacy.

The former ruling classes of Europe appealed to the United States and England to save them from Bolshevism, and in doing so they appealed to the West's self-interest, their hatred and fear of Bolshevism. Where the Anglo-Americans could impose occupation governments they resolved to preserve the outlines of the prewar order, perhaps modestly reformed, by force of arms if necessary. And while this presented a short-term solution, the long-run prospects of a permanent military presence were less attractive. But at no time did they regard the U.S.S.R. as an equally counterrevolutionary force outside Eastern Europe, as an ally in disguise, and hanging over formal diplomatic relations and agreements was the pallor of the alleged connection between Russia and the European Left.

The worried thought the Anglo-Americans gave to this problem was never greater than in the spring of 1945 and the days before Potsdam, and soon they made the Left quite as responsible as the consequences of the war itself for the political and economic difficulties confronting the Americans. "The Communist Party or its associates," Harriman warned at the beginning of April in his widely studied reports, "everywhere are using economic difficulties in areas under our responsibilities to promote Soviet concepts and policies and to undermine the influence of the Western Allies." The result was the possibility of "Soviet domination in Europe." When Harriman returned to Washington at the end of the month he reiterated his fear that "half and maybe all of Europe might be communistic by the end of next winter . . . ," as Forrestal recorded it.[29] Harriman's prodding was superfluous, for by that time nearly all of official Washington at the highest level was convinced that the Russians were bent on Bolshevizing Europe. To the West, anxious to get the lid back on the chaos and disintegration the war created throughout the world, this explanation was convenient and reinforcing, if inaccurate. The American leaders devised a suitable mythology—the Red Scare—to buttress the rationally conceived desire to restore and strengthen the structure of an older, more responsive order.

The prospective "chaos" likely to result from "pestilence and famine throughout central Europe during the following winter," one that might lead to "political revolution and communistic infiltration," deeply beset Truman and the State Department by May.[30] Grew at the beginning of June dolefully reported, "I am deeply concerned over conditions in Western Europe and the possibility that serious disorders may develop during the coming months."[31] Truman communicated these anxieties to Churchill at the end of June, but the Prime Minister had already emphatically reported his own thoughts along these lines, and now a general consensus existed as a basis of joint policy. They linked up the entire question of Russia to this danger, for as Stimson phrased it in a reflective moment, "It also becomes clear that no permanently safe international relations can be established between two such fundamentally different national systems. With the best of efforts we cannot understand each other."[32] To Stimson the only solution was for Russia to de-Bolshevize its internal regime, to change its ideology.

The leaders of the United States never perceived the operational relationship of the Russians to the world Communist movement, save that a degree of discipline existed between the two, and this was considered sufficient cause for concern. They rarely discerned within an overall context the nationalist, essentially social democratic nature of the orthodox Communists in 1945, and revolutionary internationalism became a permanent object of Western fear and propaganda, one that justified in the last analysis working with the Right everywhere in Europe as Washington reached the implicit conclusion that America had fought the wrong war with the wrong country. "Averell [Harriman] was very gloomy about the influx of Russia into Europe," Forrestal wrote in summarizing this mood during July. "He said that the greatest crime of Hitler was that his actions had resulted in opening the gates of Eastern Europe to Asia."[33]

At the beginning of June the State Department completed a top-secret study of the "Possible Resurrection of the Communist International, Resumption of Extreme Leftist Activities, Possible Effect on United States," and Grew sent it to Truman for his careful consideration before Potsdam. The document, embellished with extracts and carefully doctored quotes which assumed rhetoric and action were one and the same, the author designed to reinforce the most paranoid anxieties on the subject. It concluded that "The transition to a more radical policy had already begun, however, as presaged by the attacks on the administration. In Western Europe all communist parties have recently reverted to their original formula of radical solutions of political and economic problems preliminary to their 'conquest of power.'" It admitted the Communists played a more moderate role at the beginning of 1945, but regarded this as a mere ploy to make themselves acceptable to the people and obtain freedoms which would permit them to attain their true ends. These were allegedly specified in Duclos' article in *Cahiers du Communisme,* which the department considered "instructions originating in Moscow" and grossly distorted in Washington's interpretation. Here it made no distinction between the Communists' criticisms of conservative nationalization and their actual support for it, much less the strictly rhetorical quality of all their mildly radical utterances, like Fourth of July orations, and their more modest actions. "The smoothly-functioning, experienced and disciplined communist machine has been demonstrated," the State Department concluded to its own satisfaction as it referred to the "Ascendancy of the Communist machine" in Loyalist Spain, the "Mutiny of crew of cruiser *Sven Provincien* in Netherlands East Indies 1933," and "1931 espionage New York City." In the context of the destitution and chaos, much less the impact of German economic measures on the European economy, conditions would "facilitate the growth of communism, for it is an herculean if not impossible task to unscramble the mixup and find the original owners." In considering this dismal picture the department memo offered Truman only one encouraging word of advice: "Decisive action against the American Communists would be a convincing demonstration to Stalin of the inherent strength of this country and would strengthen relations between the two countries."[34]

The jerry-built logic of the State Department in favor of a Red Scare at home to cope with dangers abroad was both premature and misplaced, but in any event the urgings were unnecessary. By July the State Department assumed the Comintern, using the French party as a cover, had been reconstructed for advancing revolutionary objectives under Soviet orders. The United States resolved not to permit revolution to sweep the globe, and the image of America as the new center and regulator of world power reinforced this determination. The Left was in fact expansionist for reasons having nothing to do with Russian policy, but intimately connected with the impact of the war on the Old Order, and here there was much that the United States could and would do to stop or redirect the tides of change sweeping the world. In the case of anticolonial movements the strength of the Left in each nation determined the index of American support or opposition, so that the United States endorsed a Japanese collaborator in Indonesia and opposed the anti-Japanese movement in Indochina. In Europe the occupation governments offered more hope and leeway, and hence the tendency was to relax the plans for a stern peace for Germany, and especially Italy, and reincorporate them into the Western world.

Washington decided Italy's future course well before the State Department's June warnings. It would not permit a left revolution or Resistance takeover in Italy. "This Government should support, by force if necessary," the State Department advised at the beginning of 1945, "any truly representative Italian Government during such period as Italy continues to be a theatre of combined Anglo-American military responsibility."[35] The question by mid-1945 was how long that responsibility might last. At the end of June, Admiral Ellery W. Stone, the American member of the Allied Commission, summarized the doleful conditions of economic chaos, political divisions, and arms still in the hands of the Resistance: ". . . the rapid growth of the seeds of an anarchial movement fostered by Moscow to bring Italy within the sphere of Russian influence. Already there are signs that, if present conditions long continue, Communism will triumph—possibly by force."[36] By force or otherwise, the United States could not permit it. Instead the United States advocated the restoration of sufficient Italian military and police power, and perhaps even the retention of the colonies as part of a nonpunitive peace, but until the Italians could handle the problem themselves it urged that five Allied divisions remain in the country.

Churchill first advocated the maintenance of Western troops in Europe to prevent a Soviet advance or Communism, and Washington merely sidestepped the issue for the moment. By the beginning of June, Grew admitted, "I can foresee disturbances of such serious consequence as not only to involve conflict with our troops, but to imperil gravely our long-term interests." On this assumption the United States would in fact act to stop the Communists by force if necessary, and at the beginning of July the State Department formally recommended that "As regards Italy, it is essential to retain Allied troops during the interim period," and "subversive elements" with "partisan arms" seemed justification enough. At the same time they recognized and extended the logic of their earlier willingness to use troops against "disturbances," to require the placement of at least "token" American troops everywhere they might be needed.[37] McCloy reinforced this decision the following month when he visited Italy and canvassed military opinion on the scene and discovered that the large majority of key American personnel "feel that to remove all American troops from Italy would encourage violent outbreaks," and some felt "we would simply be selling out and abandoning the Italian peninsula to purely British policy."[38] Clearly the political imperatives required a far-reaching military commitment of indefinite duration, and by July 1945 the United States had made that choice in principle. The United States would do what circumstances required to preserve the conditions for the achievement of its long-term objectives.

If the American assessment of the actions and intentions of the European Communist parties appears crude and misinformed to the reader, he should recall that in the final analysis Washington's function was not to understand the character and needs of Russian policy but only the interests of the United States, and the large majority of American leaders considered it better to attain them crudely than not at all. Indeed, if the actions of occupation governments in Western Europe provided the Russians with precedents for Eastern Europe, Americans could pass over the irony in righteousness. But implicit in American policy, given the political and ideological quiescence of the Communists in the areas they controlled, was the need to stress solutions to economic chaos in the hope that political stabilization would follow, for with the exception of Greece there had been no overt revolutions, and Washington hoped there was still time. Now the focus was to pass imperceptibly to economic instability, the need to restore production and undo the consequences of war, and along with the will to maintain power via arms came a much greater emphasis on the need to reconstruct European capitalism, not in the context of surplus, which had been the operating premise of American planning before 1945, but scarcity and famine. In effect, given the immediate political instability and dangers of the situation, to attain their economic objectives in Europe the Americans had to confront the expensive weaknesses of traditional European society. Perhaps for the first time American planning began to shift toward a realistic assessment of the war's devastating consequences to the new world order it hoped to reconstruct within the structure of the old.

Such thoughts were possible only because the Russians and Communists chose a political course that gave the West a breathing spell and time to recuperate. The leaders in Washington never appreciated this precious development, but it may have saved them from total disaster. The Russians came out of their prewar shell after the anti-Bolshevik passions of the post-

World War I period, and they hoped to encourage a modicum of stability for themselves within the world community, even at the sacrifice of the Left. The West focused only on the internal character and ideology of the Russian state rather than its capabilities and intentions, and only on that aspect of the international Left which the Russians found themselves unable to control and discipline. Yet the West had nothing against totalitarianism per se, and was quite willing to cooperate with it and indeed encourage that phenomenon in preference to either left totalitarianism or left democracy. Russian ideology was based on a theory of revolutionary internationalism and mass action, but the Russians no more rested their behavior on their stated beliefs than was the West committed to democracy in Greece, Italy, or China. In fact the United States never grasped the critical distinction between Russian ideology and Soviet foreign policy. Russian foreign policy was in reality founded on the premise that states deal with states and that Russia would not attain its interests by encouraging the revolutionary movements of the world, but by reconciling the objectives of nations on a quid pro quo basis. Hence revolutionary ideology never described Soviet foreign policy, and if the Left expanded its power in at least a few areas it was over the resistance of Russia and only because the war caused total disintegration throughout vast regions of the globe. If the Russians had not given the West a respite, in fact Washington may have realized its worst fears everywhere in 1945. For only Russian conservatism stood between the Old Order and revolution.

The Typology of the Left

The threat of the Left and the Resistance during the last half of the war appeared so real and ominous that it should not come as a surprise that the United States and England could not afford to assess it too conservatively or else risk total political disaster because of overconfidence. They had to treat the Left for what it represented potentially rather than in fact, for the realities had yet to evolve and they could not adequately predict the path the European masses might take. No one knew that the Left's leaders and premises condemned them to passivity, or what the critical ingredients were that made men revolt.

The European Left was nationalist perhaps as much as any of the other political tendencies, and the mere thought that the Communists were agents of Moscow struck the ever-growing following of the CP as sheer demagogy. In France, Italy, Belgium—everywhere the CP became the key leader in the Resistance—it did so in behalf of patriotism and the nation, and everywhere it successfully minimized the social content of its program to attain a broad United Front with as many groups as possible. The total effect of this policy was that the Communists sacrificed their prewar

ideological identity more than any other political party, in large part because such a dilution was also consistent with Russian diplomatic strategy
toward the West.

The basic political commitments of the new rank-and-file supporters of
the European Communists were not necessarily more radical than those of
the leadership, though the historian cannot preclude this because it was
never tested, save in one nation—Greece—where the CP never firmly controlled the EAM and ELAS. There were a number of more or less common
ingredients in all revolutionary movements and situations in Europe
throughout this period, and by examining their relative importance one can
construct an elementary but usable theory of revolution appropriate to this
period. These must include the extent and power of *nationalism* and that of
social and economic radicalism. It is also critical to examine the nature of
the radical movement from the viewpoint of the extent to which the Communists *disciplined* it and the degree to which the Communists were united
in being responsive to Moscow. Then one must evaluate the extent of
terror from the Nazis and indigenous Right, and the *political options* to
violence seemingly permitted within the regime.

We know that it was a combination of peasant nationalism—an admix-
ture of patriotism and reform—and the Nazi and Japanese-imposed terror
that created the mass resistance in Yugoslavia and north China, for they
gave men no options for survival save to flee to the countryside and prepare to fight. The critical question, however, is what factors caused men to
fight or cooperate after the defeat of the Axis.

In the case of Poland, nationalism included a deep-rooted anti-Russian
sentiment that seriously complicated the direction radicalism might take,
for a substantial element chose to waver between resistance to the Nazis or
Russians, and ultimately to resist neither very effectively. Everywhere that
seemingly viable political alternatives to revolt existed the Left exercised
them, even where these options were patently contrived and precluded true
victory at the polls. Men chose the ballot box in preference to bullets save
where there was no alternative, as in Greece, or where they were too
isolated from the masses to choose to challenge manipulated structures, as
in Poland. But in Germany, Italy, and France, the Left, from the Communists to the Social Democrats, in fact relinquished the euphoria and visions
of wartime and returned to the well-known ways of parliamentarianism—
and capitalism.

The appeals of Communism transcended economic issues and therefore
meant the Communists would survive both repression *and* prosperity, and
few have acknowledged this critical nationalist dimension to Communism.
The Communist parties based their claims on their role as nationalists *and*
reformers, and their seemingly true patriotism in the moment of wartime
crisis as well as their social program gave them the backing of not merely

the prewar working classes that had always voted Communist or Socialist, but of new peasant and rural groups that had once been the backbone of conservatism. If one looks more closely at the men and women who joined the Resistance everywhere in Western Europe, one sees why the rank and file followed its leadership back to parliamentarianism—unless, as in Greece, repression and corruption shattered all possible illusions concerning the state—relinquishing de facto control of society in much of Europe during the final days of the war.

The Resistance in France, Italy, and Western Europe consisted of a passionately dedicated and brave hard core that was too politicized and a mass following that was too variable and did not and would not act until liberation and victory seemed imminent. When the circumstances required action many men were galvanized into motion, staking their very lives against initially overwhelming odds to revenge the humiliation of the occupation when victory seemed possible. Only one urban uprising—the Warsaw Ghetto of 1943—was an act of true desperation without any hope of success. Paris, Prague, Warsaw, Milan, Turin, and Bucharest were fired only when liberation by Allied troops was imminent and success appeared almost certain. These were revolts, not revolutions, in intent and consequence. This belief in success was always the catalyst to action, and revealed an instinctive cautious impulse, or perhaps fear of suicide, among the Resistance leaders and followers. The Resistance could not attract a mass following until the last months of the war, save where the conditions of unusual Nazi terror forced men into the liberated areas, as in Yugoslavia.

Before the fall of 1943 the Resistance in Western Europe was hardly more than a sectarian phenomenon built around underground political parties. This late emergence indicated that without hope of success only a hard core of dedicated men would evidence great bravery under conditions of almost certain defeat. Surely the fluctuation in the membership of the Resistance groups was proof of a propensity toward caution when the choice went beyond fighting or, as in Yugoslavia or occupied China, dying as a result of the sheer terror and externally imposed pressures of the invaders. In Italy and France, for example, one could be an *attentiste* and wait, secure in the knowledge that the powerful Anglo-American armies would soon defeat the Nazis. Hence men fought under conditions of sheer terror or impending victory. In Italy and France they were content to arrive late and leave early, amidst bugles and flowery speeches, rather than fight their well-armed liberators. They were also, one must note, quite willing to show their defiance in the future by voting Left, a small act that changed nothing because events never broke the illusion of the Communists as a radical party.

The role of the Communists in the leadership of a Resistance movement was a critical factor in determining whether it would take an independent line. This control was meaningful only in light of objective conditions of terror and internal means of communication. Nazi-imposed desperation or the terror of the British and Right, the existence of minority protest movements, or the divisions within the Resistance leadership—all as in the case of Greece—encouraged indigenous separatism and action. Decentralization increased local initiatives, and to some extent the industrial level of a nation dictated the limits of possible centralization. The French Resistance was highly decentralized, but radios and communications permitted some contact. In Greece such coordination was often nonexistent. For the most part the Communists dominated the Resistance leadership to a degree sufficient to veto the more ambitious and radical impulses of the other Resistance parties, especially in Greece and Italy, even though the Communists could not succeed in their alternatives in Greece and prevent the return to the mountains.

The very hesitancy of the Western European Left to act until success appeared imminent led to their undoing, for at the very moment success became possible the presence of Anglo-American armies transformed local revolt into an affair of international politics, and the imperatives of the conflicts within the Allied bloc stalemated the possibility of success after the victory of a battle. Indigenous groups no longer had the power to determine their own destinies on the basis of their relative power among the population of one nation. Each of the major Allies actively prevented the most powerful local organizations from imposing political hegemony wherever they were inclined or able to do so, which was no more often the case in Eastern Europe than in the West. The Anglo-Americans were determined not to permit the Resistance to win in the field or in politics, and they were willing to support effete conservative, even neofascist, elements in order to prevent the triumph of forces aligned to the U.S.S.R. or the Left. To succeed, in other words, Western policy would have compelled the Resistance to revolt well before the Allies controlled the final outcome, but then German victory would have been possible, the masses reluctant, and there was no option to their tragic dilemma. Only in Yugoslavia was the risk both taken and imposed, and here the West and the Russians both lost control.

Above all, the Great Power element in the definition of the internal affairs of various states became the primary fact in the new Europe emerging from the chaos of the war, shaping the postwar settlement and the future relationship between the former Allies. Italy served as the precedent, and all sides followed the example elsewhere time and time again. This reality, and not the promises and formulas of diplomacy, determined the nature of the peace.

. . .

LATER the Communists in Western Europe cited the example of Greece to explain why they did not take to the streets before their Resistance forces melted away, but this was an afterthought, for they had defined the basic policy not to exploit the immense power available to them well before Athens and Brussels. The simple matter is that wherever leaders of the Old Order incorporated the Left into a modernized, reformed capitalism, the Left willingly assumed the role assigned to it. Where the occupation forces repressed it and brought the naked power of reaction to bear, the Left reluctantly fought, and lost, and this was the true lesson of Greece. Yet for reasons having nothing to do with the initial impetus, it is unquestionably true that a policy of repression and violence by Anglo-American authorities and their local allies would have met any effort on the part of the Italian or French Resistance to act. The British and Americans also took this decision before Athens and before they even remotely understood the truly conservative character of the Communists.

The United Front strategy was the key to Communist political policy everywhere from 1943 through 1946, and well beyond then in France and Italy as well. This strategy was a response to the cause of the failure of the Left in the 1930's as well as the needs of Russian global interests. Despite the occasional historic rhetoric which so frightened the West, or the much-misunderstood Duclos article of April 1945, the ancient rhetoric did not indicate what the Communists planned to do or in fact did. The only time the Left posed a true threat to Anglo-American interests occurred when the Russians did not fully control it or when the breakdown of the local social order was so complete that even the Communists could not prevent a sharp response from the masses.

After the war, many of the militants in the Communist movement who directed the leadership of the Resistance found official conservatism uncomfortable, and the pattern of internal purges within most postwar Communist parties followed the division between the bureaucratic conservatives and ex-Resistance militants, often depending on who spent the war in Moscow or in the home country. In Western Europe the Communists worked for elements of stability that reinforced the Old Order: no strikes, high production, and the like, and in fact took genuine pride in their very substantial administrative aid in restoring the Old Order in a refurbished form. Capitalism survived only where the Communists and Social Democrats were instrumental in reforming it. Elsewhere upheaval and collapse ensued and the Anglo-Americans and their allies had to apply sheer force against the revolutionary response of the people. In this sense the Left became the savior of Western European capitalism, and had the political preconditions for such an amalgam existed in Eastern Europe it is likely the Russians would have been willing to encourage such reform in the context of neutralism in foreign affairs.

If Moscow directed the Western European Communists, which appears likely in many but by no means all issues, including national claims abroad, then during the critical period of 1944–1947 the Russians gave the Western European social system a reprieve during which to consolidate its power. The Russians wanted a respite from the war to obtain their own breathing spell, and if this required stability for their former allies, the Russians were willing to provide it if at all possible. Succinctly, the Russians were as committed to revolution as the West was to democracy, and they both opposed a radical transformation of Western Europe and its long-range consequences threatening instability for the entire face of the globe. Without such a Soviet policy, without a form of Communist internationalism which meant a form of Moscow control, no one can predict with confidence what the social outcome of the war in Western Europe might have been in the hands of local, self-guiding left parties. The Americans not merely overstated the hegemony of the Russians over the world Communist movement, which existed perhaps most extensively in Western Europe, but they ignored the separatist tendencies that existed in every Communist party and most especially in Eastern Europe and Asia. Yet such a simplistic analysis was also rational in the sense that it was not Moscow control or separatism that disturbed the West, but the prospect of revolutionary change from any direction. More important was their failure to comprehend that the Moscow-oriented Communists were also the least dangerous—indeed, they were allies in disguise.

The United States feared the emergence of the Left long before the U.S.S.R. gave it any cause for specific complaints. The power vacuum in Europe was a reality that Washington could easily perceive, and it appeared to the West as if the Russians, via the Communists, could move into it. But in fact the Russians chose not to do so save where, in Eastern Europe, the intractable representatives of the prewar system left no options. It was logical for the United States and Britain to attempt to fill the vacuum by preparing to suppress the Left, and looking at the Left's capabilities for action rather than intentions, they feared the worst. This meant, as well, that the West would tolerate the viable segments of the prewar social orders, even though compromised, in the hope that they could fill the vacuum before it was too late. It was less important that the Communists were serving as a bureaucratic safety valve, and the Americans and British considered it simply sufficient to attempt to prevent the triumph of the radical Left everywhere in the world it seemed possible to frustrate it, and only in China did this task immediately appear too formidable. The United States did not postulate its policy, therefore, on the nature of Communist or Soviet conduct, but only on the character and possibilities of the political and structural facts and options themselves—and American needs.

Given the political and, above all, the economic peace aims the United

States set before itself as its objectives, it was necessary to reshape those threatening global realities, to limit the capabilities as well as the intentions of the Left and Russia—which might change for the worse—to set out on the difficult, if not impossible task, of undoing the consequences of World War II on every thread of the social and economic fabric of civilization. To contain the Left, even if the Russians and their satellite parties agreed to cooperate momentarily, was now the task before the Americans. By the middle of 1945 containment and reconstruction moved to the center of American planning, and that reality defined the limits within which the left movements would exist and seek the possibilities for their success, and in large measure this context determined the outcome and character of post-1918 socialism throughout the world.

THE UNITED NATIONS AND AMERICAN GLOBAL INTERESTS

WHETHER THE UNITED NATIONS organization would be a neutral structure, so constructed as to aid the pacific settlement of disputes among nations, or an instrument of the policy of one nation was the central issue to the future and purpose of the new body. As a neutral forum, however, it would have postulated the possibility of reason and majority rule triumphing over the goals of one nation or another, and since rather less altruistic considerations and real power govern international relations, this alternative was not probable in the last year of World War II. The question, therefore, was how far its organizers would permit the future United Nations mechanism to go in the direction of service to the United States and whether its evocation of international ideals would in fact mask national interests.

The United States had no great illusions concerning this dilemma, and by the beginning of 1945 Washington resolved to define the organization in a manner which sacrificed little American freedom of action, and opened new modalities for attaining its objectives. The United States determined to oppose its other allies' creating blocs and spheres of interest, but also to shape the future United Nations in a manner that acknowledged not just great power among the members of the Security Council, but also the distinctive role of the United States as the most powerful nation on earth. The membership of China on the Security Council, an ultimate veto, the overall composition of a General Assembly constituted largely from states likely to respond to United States desires, the tentative position the United States had shown at Dumbarton Oaks in regard to its own Western Hemispheric regional bloc and Pacific bases—all these indicated a conservative realism which suggested that the United Nations could operate successfully only if prior political agreement existed among the Allies. Both the British and Russians felt such prior understanding obviated the necessity of a United Nations, with which they were willing to go along to a limited degree in order to placate the Americans, but they did not see it as a substitute for conventional diplomacy and traditional means of reconciling interests. The Americans, for their part, by 1945 tended to envision the United Nations as a forum within which they might more easily obtain international political agreement, since it introduced other, more responsive voices into international deliberations. The United Nations was to be an instrument of a just peace, a place to obtain war aims and regulate the peace in a manner acceptable to the United States. Washington clearly marked out the thrust of American thinking in this direction before 1945, but during the months prior to the San Francisco Conference the American leaders had to resolve their last remaining ambiguities.

The Western Hemisphere and the United Nations

The American government left nothing to chance. If the role of the United Nations in regulating affairs in Europe and Asia, for which Washington largely intended it, were possibly to fail in the future the United States did not wish to relinquish its control over its own hemisphere. It saw this Latin American alliance, in turn, as a tool for extending a measure of control over Eastern Hemispheric affairs via the General Assembly, where the vote of Haiti would weigh as heavily as the vote of Belgium or Hungary. After Dumbarton Oaks the United States began urging the neutral Latin American states to declare war on Germany in order to qualify as founding members of the United Nations, and during early February, United States diplomats bent all effort to enroll as many of their southern neighbors in the war as possible before the March 1 deadline imposed at Yalta for determining who might qualify to attend the United Nations founding conference. Six were to do so.

More complex was the question of the relationship of the United Nations to regional organizations, for with the exception of Stimson, who saw diplomacy as based on power alone, no important adviser in Washington early in 1945 was willing to see a Soviet or English bloc emerge as a preeminent factor in European politics. The British made no secret of their intentions in this regard, and their desire to base the world political structure on regional blocs; and at the beginning of February the Russians published an article on the same theme, and calling for the division of the General Assembly into four regional sections, which Grew and the State Department very carefully analyzed. The dilemma was obvious: if the

United States treated the Western Hemisphere and the Pacific as its sphere of influence the English and Russians would do the same elsewhere. It was therefore crucial for the United States, already well on its way to creating a much more unified hemispheric system, to define its functions so that it could both attain its objectives and make them appear compatible with a world organization and global relationships such as America advocated for others.

This tension was not easy to resolve, in part because Hull and State Department planners always considered that a separate Pan-American system "did not infringe on the powers we thought should reside in the world-wide association of nations," though Hull thought primarily in economic rather than political terms. That new world association would be responsive to United States desires also, since the Pan-American bloc would control it, and so it was not necessary to waver publicly from their assertion that the Pan-American system and the United Nations were complementary. A regional bloc could not replace the Security Council or take action exclusive of it—though they might take action in lieu of United Nations agreement—much less restrict its freedom to intervene in the affairs of every section of the world. But by February the United States was determined that within this public limitation and justification it would have its own hemispheric structure parallel to, but not in place of, the United Nations. Yet they believed this relationship in the Western Hemisphere to be something exclusive, not for Britain or Russia to imitate elsewhere because unlike other powers, as Hull explained it, the United States "had exercised economic and other self-restraint."[1]

This was their public justification, and the explanation that they offered to the other Allies. In fact everyone knew better. The United States was creating a bloc, not only within the hemisphere, but within the United Nations. It did not have to exercise the power such a bloc afforded, but the power was there nonetheless should it be necessary.

The United States at the end of 1944 initiated the groundwork for an Inter-American Conference on War and Peace which was then held from February 21 through early March in Mexico City. George Messersmith, the United States ambassador to Mexico, worked together with the State Department to organize the conference along lines reflecting the United States' view of its immediate international and long-range Latin American needs, making the meeting both political and economic in character. Messersmith, by late 1944, had become the key architect of United States policy toward its southern neighbors, and in particular on the delicate Argentine question which Washington treated publicly as a question of Argentine pro-Axis sentiment, but in fact reflected a deep fear of British economic penetration in the nation, and through it, the southern Latin American region. Messersmith wrote Washington in November 1944:

It is so obvious that in any world security system this hemisphere will have to act as a unit and that this is in the interest of world security. ... it is incredible that the British, who are so much interested in establishing certain spheres of influence, should not realize that it is undermining their own situation and world security to disrupt American unity.[2]

At the end of the following January, as he laid final plans for the Mexico City Conference, Messersmith thought that "it is in our grasp not only to consolidate the unity of the twenty Republics in the political and economic field," but also "to establish a situation which will bring about the appropriate changes in the Argentine and bring her back into the fold." The Russians intended doing the same elsewhere, and England was "not only bent on maintaining the Empire and Empire preferences but extending their field of influence over a good part of Western and Northern Europe." The Latin Americans wanted such unity, he avowed, and "This, I believe, means that we while not abandoning in any way any of our real principles, must in practice consider the realities . . . and I think when we get down to those terms we will realize that in the postwar world if we have this whole hemisphere behind us we are in a position to make a real fight for these principles for which we stand." There were pressing economic reasons for doing so as well. "After all, in many respects the Far East and this hemisphere will be the principal outlet in the years immediately following the postwar period for our goods." This did not mean an exclusive United States market, but Messersmith implied the United States could make this choice as well, and his displeasure over British control of Argentina revealed the thrust of his concern. "We are planning to keep the markets of this hemisphere open to all. Russia and Britain are planning economies which will be open only to those whom they choose to admit."[3]

This conception of the Mexico City Conference prevailed in the Act of Chapultepec, and as Messersmith elatedly reported at its conclusion, "There is no doubt that the fear of Soviet Russia and England hung like a pall over these Latin States. . . ."[4] Stettinius arrived with San Francisco in view, and in the words of the official history of the United States and the founding of the United Nations, "The Secretary was primarily interested in achieving a common front at the conference in support of the proposed world charter."[5] The economic dimension was more difficult, and this made William Clayton the most important man at the conference, and at its conclusion he was able to have the conference pass an economic resolution which met all the United States criteria—by now goals that Washington knew by heart. These included equality of access to trade and raw materials, lower tariff barriers and the elimination of economic nationalism, the promotion of private investment, and the like. On a hemispheric military level the conference recommended the creation of a general staff of the American republics for "closer military collaboration."[6] A foreign state's attack against one of the hemispheric nations they would consider an act against all, and the resolution suggested a series of collective measures on an economic and military level. Messersmith, Stettinius, and Clayton received virtually everything they asked for, but even Hull, who favored regional exceptionalism in principle, thought the entire conference too grossly obvious, especially its military aspect, and was much distressed: "Once we had agreed to this new position on intervention, Russia had more excuse to intervene in neighboring states, and we had less reason to oppose her doing so."[7]

The British and Russians were no less observant than Hull, and the Russian chargé in Mexico immediately asked Messersmith what the Act of Chapultepec meant. The Foreign Office knew, and in late March prepared a memo noting that nineteen Latin American and nine European nations would be represented at the San Francisco Conference. Messersmith was also certain that "they know very well what we have been doing," and he advised Roosevelt that "if our British and Russian friends become difficult, we shall have to tell them some plain truths, and I think we have to be just as realistic as they."[8]

These realities were ill-concealed beneath the veneer of polite diplomatic verbiage.

The Vandenberg Thesis

The United States policy-makers wrote their definitions of the future structure of the United Nations with the basic interests of the United States as a world power foremost in mind, but they paid much attention to the moods of the Senate leaders of both parties, for the Senate had once buried the League of Nations and the State Department vowed to avoid the same fate. The ranking members of the Senate Foreign Relations Committee were in essential agreement with the Dumbarton Oaks proposals, and never doubted their virtue. The ranking Republican, Arthur Vandenberg, had sought and received the State Department's support for the proposition that the United Nations would serve not merely as a formal instrument of world organization, but also as a means for attaining United States foreign policy objectives in specific instances, Poland being the most pressing to Vandenberg. He had not cajoled the State Department into endorsing his view, for Washington universally accepted the concept of the United Nations as a vehicle for attaining an American-defined just peace, even though Stimson was less certain that it would succeed in accomplishing what diplomacy had failed to achieve.

Vandenberg's views were well known, and on January 10, 1945, he made the most important speech of his career, one that the world press widely quoted and studied. The Michigan Senator inveighed against the United States' continuing as a "silent partner" in the Allied alliance while "Moscow wants to assert unilateral war and peace aims which collide with ours," or "when Mr. Churchill proceeds upon his unilateral ways to make decisions often repugnant to our ideas and our ideals." It was time to reassert, he urged in carefully phrased words, the "basic pledges" of the Atlantic Charter, to cooperate with the Allies, but only "consistent with legitimate American self-interest. . . ."⁹ While failing to mention Poland and Eastern Europe, there was no doubt that Vandenberg had that region foremost in mind. In mid-February the State Department informally announced that the Senator would be a delegate to the forthcoming San Francisco Conference dedicated to creating a structure within which the nations of the world, England and Russia included, would presumably seek to cooperate.

Vandenberg refused to accept immediately, and after he heard of the Yalta settlement on the Curzon Line and the future of Poland his reluctance grew. "I cannot go to this conference as a stooge. If my instructions would bind me to Dumbarton Oaks 'as is' I certainly could not go at all." "I expect [the President] to say I am a free agent," he wrote on February 20. "In that event I shall accept. . . . it is a question whether the American people will ever sanction a Peace League which permanently stratifies the palpably unjust decisions made at Yalta. . . ." Eight days later Roosevelt formally requested him to become a delegate, and now he presented his reservations directly to the President. Roosevelt accepted them, as he had in any case after Dumbarton Oaks, and the decision was sealed. Vandenberg was determined to go to San Francisco to secure for Poland and the "little states" the "justice" that they had not obtained before. The United Nations would become the means for attaining the "just peace." It was not feasible, he argued, to differentiate between a peace-making and peace-keeping organization, for "I strive for the principle that permanent peace can succeed only on the basis of justice and that any injustice—past, present or future—should therefore be within the jurisdiction of the Peace League's review and recommendation."

Continuous meetings with the State Department during March gave him ample opportunity to hammer home his views, but the department required no conversion. As he learned more about the Allies' agreements on voting procedures in the United Nations made at Yalta he became angrier and made more and stronger suggestions. By the time he left for the conference he had reached a thorough meeting of the minds with the State Department: "We are getting along famously. The only cloud on the horizon is Russia (and Yalta). Russia continues to be irksome."¹⁰ "I am trying," he concluded a week before the event, "to write the concept of 'justice' into Dumbarton Oaks. . . . The American Delegation and the State

Department have *accepted* every demand I have made along these lines. It remains to be seen what happens when we collide with London and Moscow."[11]

Vandenberg and/or Molotov to San Francisco

The Russians and English had been openly skeptical of the American vision of the nature of a United Nations organization. At Yalta, Stalin reiterated his belief in Three Power cooperation as the precondition for any stable world order, and he believed that this was what the United Nations should seek to attain. The Russians had already published highly critical comments on the projected Western European bloc around Great Britain, but they were now willing, after the rejection of their 1943 proposal for a political-military commission, to formalize the bloc system as part of a global cooperative scheme in which the three Allies, in effect, would manage the postwar world. Such an arrangement Washington would never accept. Churchill never made any attempt to conceal his preference for regional blocs which would leave England with the empire and a predominant position in a united Europe. At the beginning of April he reiterated that "I have never been at all keen on this Conference," and that the one thing that would change his mind would be a Russian effort to keep it from being held.[12]

On March 1, *War and the Working Class* published a long attack on "Senator Vandenberg and His Scheme," concentrating mainly on his speech of the prior January, but also referring to numerous other statements which indicated that Moscow had intensively scrutinized the Michigan Senator. It was not merely an attack on Vandenberg, however, but a barely subdued condemnation of the thrust of United States planning for the United Nations. The article denied Vandenberg's specific judgments of the U.S.S.R., and considered that "his criticism of the 'dictatorship of the Great Powers' is a mask to conceal his pretentious claims for the establishment of the dictatorship of one Great Power over all the other powers, great, medium and small." It cited the conference at Mexico City, and the desire of the United States for bases in the Pacific was juxtaposed against the ostensible American rhetoric of internationalism. Then it posed the question:

> But where has it been decreed that the other powers, big and small, including the Powers who have borne the full brunt of the struggle against Hitler Germany, must now pay the United States for its participation in world affairs by renouncing their independence in policy making? Is not this participation primarily in the interests of the United States itself.[13]

Now Vandenberg was going to San Francisco.

One other event must have filled the Russians with suspicion of the American view of the nature of the United Nations. On March 1 the Big Three and China sent invitations to all the nations at war with Germany, except the Ukraine and White Russia, to attend the San Francisco Conference. The United States agreed at Yalta to vote for the permanent membership of these two Soviet states and they agreed to invite all nations at war with the Germans. The United States reiterated an official decision to oppose their actual participation in the conference itself. Gromyko notified the State Department of their composition, but not that of the U.S.S.R., in mid-March. In the most literal sense the United States position was correct, but it was such a subtle distinction to say that these delegations could not attend, though at war and later eligible for American backing, that the U.S.S.R. took the matter as the United States intended it. About a week later the State Department received the list of the Russian delegates to the San Francisco Conference, and Molotov's name was not on it.

If the Americans could indicate their intentions by sending one delegate, Vandenberg, the Russians could reveal theirs by withholding another. Gromyko would make the trip from Washington as the highest-ranking Russian there. It was an obvious, intentional downgrading of the United Nations. Stalin himself made this very point when Roosevelt immediately dashed off a letter to the Russian telling him the absence of Molotov "will be construed all over the world as a lack of comparable interest in the great objectives of this Conference on the part of the Soviet Government."[14] On the day before he dispatched the cable to Stalin, Gromyko asked that the United States agree to invite the Polish Provisional Government to San Francisco, and it flatly refused. Now it was Stalin's turn, for the impotent Supreme Soviet was to convene a session in April and he considered Molotov's attendance imperative. Stettinius then again told the Russian ambassador what he already knew: they would not invite the delegations from the Ukraine and White Russia to the conference.

There the matter rested when Roosevelt died. The next day Harriman saw Stalin, and the Russian expressed his sorrow and reiterated his desire to work with the new President. Harriman interjected that Molotov's presence at San Francisco, with perhaps a visit to Truman first, would be the best way of showing his resolve. Stalin agreed on the spot. It was after this that Truman prepared his one-syllable speech for the Russian Foreign Minister and told his Cabinet, as Forrestal recorded it, "He intended to go on with the plans for San Francisco and if the Russians did not wish to join us they could go to hell. . . ."[15]

The Pacific as an American Lake

It was no secret throughout the war that the United States planned to obtain control of a large number of postwar bases in the Pacific, and as early as March 1943 Sumner Welles was compelled publicly to deny it was United States policy that "the Pacific should be a lake under American jurisdiction. . . ."[16] In fact, the statement was premature because Washington had yet to reach a final decision. There was division, not on whether the bases should go to the United States, for on that goal there was unanimity, but rather on how the United States should acquire them and whose authority might transfer them. The War Department and especially the Navy advocated outright United States ownership, even at the cost of America's being charged with imperialism, but the State Department thought the technique a frightful precedent for other Allied nations, and instead urged that the United States arrange to obtain the islands under United Nations authority as trusteeships. But other than the question of tactics, Stimson spoke for the government in June 1944 when he told a Congressman that "you're dead right in believing that after this war's over the sentiment of the people will be in favor of having what the government thinks will be enough to maintain our power in the Pacific."[17] The United States at Dumbarton Oaks had excluded trusteeships from the agenda because it had yet to formulate its final position, and both the Russians and British expressed surprise over the omission. Obviously they could not delay a final policy much longer.

The British were fully aware of the split in Washington, and they saw it as useful leverage for obtaining American backing for their desire to retain their colonial possessions in return for supporting American ambitions. Despite the fact that the Russians had asked that their allies include them in any conversations on the disposition of the colonies of Axis Powers, and had been assured that this would be done, at the beginning of 1945 the British and Americans held informal talks on the subject. It is likely that the British stood on the position, as Churchill wrote Eden at the time, "If the Americans want to take Japanese islands which they have conquered, let them do so with our blessing and any form of words that may be agreeable to them. But 'Hands Off the British Empire' is our maxim."[18] At Yalta the Americans discussed the topic informally with the British, and then officially with the Russians present. On both occasions the British understood that, verbiage aside, it was not British colonialism but Japanese bases that the Americans had in mind, and the quickly considered final policy statement at Yalta on trusteeships applied mainly to conquered enemy territories, and more obscurely, mandated areas that the League of Nations had distributed. In effect, an operational agreement existed whereby the British would support American claims in return for silence on the empire. The British were pleased, and now the Americans had to decide how best to use the new options open to them.

Stimson viewed the problem without illusions. When he considered the problem of the Pacific he saw it in the same context as Soviet ambitions in Eastern Europe, and he wished to solve all these issues before Yalta and certainly outside the auspices of the projected United Nations. The State Department felt it sufficient to create a general trusteeship mechanism with defined principles, and not worry about the actual allocation of territories until the end of the war, at which time, its position implied, United States power in the United Nations and at the peace table would decide the fate of the islands. It was this position that Roosevelt endorsed, fully committed, as was the State Department, not to relinquish desired bases. At the end of March, Forrestal and Stimson determined to make an effort to redefine official policy on the question before San Francisco, when the United States, Stimson feared, might make "quixotic gestures" that might risk sacrificing the hard-won islands. Their general line was now to stress the islands' importance to United States security and as "a trust on behalf of world security," one the United States would define unilaterally.[19] The State Department balked immediately when the War and Navy departments showed their rephrased position to them at the beginning of April, and Ickes and others pointed out that unilateral confiscation of Pacific bases might lead the British to take Middle East mandates with oil in the same manner, damaging American interests. This dispute was one of the first items of business submitted to the new President. By this time the debate drew the delegates to the forthcoming United Nations Conference into the consideration of the question.

The State Department's viewpoint was entirely functional: the United States would hold the islands at the end of the war, when it could, with some assurance, expect the United Nations to legitimize the conquest. Should the United States simply take them outright, however, it would set a crucial precedent for Russia, and perhaps England, to do the same elsewhere. To Forrestal the "retention of power by the United States was not inconsistent with the work on and the hopes for a world peace organization," but neither Stimson nor Forrestal could override the persuasive logic of the State Department and now they unsuccessfully pressed for not bringing the issue up at San Francisco.[20]

The policy of trusteeships the United States took to the founding conference of the United Nations stressed the form of control rather than the substantive allocation of territories. The categories of trusteeships the Big Three defined at Yalta, Washington accepted, but the delegation was practically concerned only with United States base rights. The United States intended its proposed trusteeship system to attain, by agreement, "the maintenance of United States military and strategic rights . . . [and] such control as will be necessary to assure general peace and security in the Pacific Ocean area as well as elsewhere in the world. . . ."[21]

The assumptions of this statement hardly concealed the strategic objectives of the United States, for it was perfectly clear that the United States sought to advance its national interests in the guise of performing erstwhile international obligations, obligations which threatened to take it to every corner of the globe. That the other powers would respond skeptically to this policy, at the least, one might have predicted well in advance. If the United States intended to protect its interests, its allies would do so as well. For the English that meant the British Empire, and perhaps much else. For the Russians that was surely to mean at least Eastern Europe. Yet in assessing the course of the world in April 1945, these nations could find a precedent for the protection of strategic interests, a policy the United States defined with clarity and realism.

San Francisco: Toward a New World Order

The American delegation arrived in San Francisco on April 24, the day before the opening of the conference, and Stettinius gave the delegation what Vandenberg termed "a *thrilling* message" by reporting on Truman's bitter meeting with Molotov the day before. "*If you* had been talking about Poland to Molotov," he told the Senator, "not even *you* could have made a stronger statement than Truman did." The following day Vandenberg noted, "The Conference opens today—with Russian clouds in every sky. I don't know whether this is Frisco or Munich."[22] Tom Connally, the ranking Democratic Senator at the conference, observed that Vandenberg was "cussing. . . . Daily he complained and saw dark plots everywhere," and indeed Vandenberg employed the term "plot" at the time to describe various Yalta agreements.[23] This scowling mood set the context for the events of the first days, so bitter that it was obscure whether the Americans had met the Russians to cooperate with, or to chastise, them.

The delegates first fought over the presidency of the meeting, which the United States delegation thought belonged to Stettinius as the ranking representative of the host country. Molotov was not impressed, and asked for four rotating presidents. This petty question of protocol took two days to resolve by making four rotating chairmen with Stettinius as their chairman. Over the same days, however, the U.S.S.R. raised the more critical question of membership in the conference by proposing on the very first day the admission of the Ukraine and White Russia. With the exception of Vandenberg, the American delegation immediately voted to seat the two Soviet republics, and that evening the Latin American states indicated that they would insist the conference admit Argentina at the same time. The following day Molotov asked that the conference invite the Poles as well, and a day later Masaryk also moved their admission. The Americans quickly buried the Polish effort. By the end of April, therefore, petty peripheral issues had created a mood of competition and conflict over small matters, with no graceful gestures on trivial issues to the Russian position.

Even though the United States was prepared to support the entry of the Soviet republics, it agreed to postponing the matter until April 30, when the United Nations also admitted Argentina with United States support. Molotov, for his part, pointed to the presence of delegations from India and the Philippines, and juxtaposed the admission of allegedly pro-fascist Argentina to the exclusion of Poland. In fact, both Russian opposition and a desire to defer to the wishes of the Latin American nations for something more substantial in return colored the willingness of the United States to support Argentina's admission. It had been an inauspicious beginning. In effect the conference made membership of a nation in the United Nations contingent on the political approval or disapproval of the Great Powers, in this case by the one nation in control of the voting structure, an approach consistent with the United States' interpretation of the purpose of the organization.

Vandenberg found his desire to introduce "justice" and a review of former treaties far easier to implement. He had the term "justice" inserted three times into the Charter of the United Nations, since its meaning depended on one's viewpoint, and the Russians were most agreeable. Molotov quickly assented to the right of the General Assembly to "recommend measures for the peaceful adjustment of any situations, regardless of origin," phrasing Eden devised to satisfy everyone. Even the Russians treated the Atlantic Charter as one standard for such changes, and Vandenberg had no difficulty in this regard either.[24] In the make-believe world of self-justifying debate, abstractions began replacing realities.

The two major substantive issues before the San Francisco Conference did not, however, involve the petty issues over which the delegates consumed so much time and words, but rather the questions of regional pacts in the world political structure and, later, the nature of the Security Council veto. The regional issue did not come up until May 5, and it dominated the discussion for most of May. The Russians, like the United States, came with definite ideas on the questions, for in principle they had nothing against the real concept beneath it if they could claim the same right. Moreover, they wished to be free to exercise their bilateral treaties with France and others directed against Germany, including a resurgent Germany. Their interests temporarily coincided with rather different United States objectives.

By early May there were some second thoughts in Washington concerning the strategy of regionalism, and it impinged on the question of what real justification remained for a world organization if the principle of exclusive bloc or regional action were formally authorized. Since the United States was confident of controlling the Security Council and General Assembly, not a few State Department officials, Hull included, were ready to minimize the logic and excesses of the Mexico City Conference. American advisers at San Francisco increasingly realized that emphasis on regionalism and the Act of Chapultepec would give the impression of United States lack of interest in Europe and open the door to Soviet and British-led blocs. The right of self-defense still existed, as well as a veto in the Security Council, should any member seek to prevent United States action in the Western Hemisphere, and in the course of ceaseless debates the American delegates tended, with constant reference to Washington, toward making obligations under the United Nations Charter explicit and regional right of action only implicit. In brief, the American leaders gropingly concluded that they wished to use a Western Hemispheric system to back their role elsewhere, and not as a substitute or limitation on American global involvement. But the ambivalence among American leaders was deep, and in the agonizing process of defining the ultimate policy the American conception of the postwar political structure emerged in even greater detail.

Vandenberg was the only American on the United Nations committee dealing with this problem, and he wished to retain freedom of action for the Pan-American bloc in the future, but also subject to a measure of control possible Russian willingness to do the same. How to reconcile these two delicate and seemingly contradictory impulses took much imagination. Almost from the first day they met the Russian desire by permitting action, without any prior United Nations approval, against a former Axis power. The United Nations might intervene later, but this solved Russia's anxieties over Germany, and Vandenberg accepted it as entirely reasonable. Since it was not Germany but Russia that weighed most heavily on the minds of the Americans, this appeared to be a small concession.

The War Department and military that John J. McCloy represented at San Francisco strongly preferred classic spheres of influence, and did not wish to give up the Monroe Doctrine as a justification for United States regulation of hemispheric affairs. Stimson himself was most critical of the sentimentalism of the so-called Good Neighbor Policy for putting "serious obstacles in the path of the exercise of the Monroe Doctrine."[25] They not only preferred the original thinking behind the Mexico City Conference, but wished to retain a veto on action outside the hemisphere. Vandenberg thought he had the solution and proposed attaching an amendment to the United Nations Charter which explicitly exempted from a veto measures taken under the Act of Chapultepec signed at Mexico City. The State Department balked, but John Foster Dulles, Vandenberg's constant aide, hesitantly found justification for the rationale in that Dumbarton Oaks had not forbidden self-defense, and the Act of Chapultepec and the Monroe

Doctrine were merely that. The ingredients for a compromise now existed, and the American delegates had only to find the ingenious formula to reconcile their conflicting desires.

On May 8, as the American delegation searched for the appropriate resolution which would resolve both the appearance of global unity and freedom of hemispheric action, McCloy phoned Stimson to summarize the problems and seek aid in finding a solution, for the exemption of action against former Axis members in no way solved the needs of the United States. This conversation is so insightful in illustrating the mode of discourse and the clarity of central assumptions, the American hopes and expectations for the United Nations, that the historian does well merely to let it speak to the reader through extensive quotation.

> "*McCloy:* . . . the argument is that if you extend that to the regional arrangement against non-enemy states, Russia will want to have the same thing in Europe and Asia and you will build up these big regional systems which may provoke even greater wars and you've cut out the heart of the world organization.
>
> "*Secretary [Stimson]:* Yes
>
> "*McCloy:* That the whole idea is to use collective action and by these exceptions you would
>
> "*Secretary:* of course you'll, you'll cut into the size of the new organization by what you agreed to now
>
> "*McCloy:* Yes, that's right. That was recognized. . . .
>
> "*McCloy:* and maybe that same nation that had done the underhanded stirring up might veto any action by the regional arrangement to stop it—to put a stop to the aggression. Now that's the thing that they [Russia] are afraid of, but, and it's a real fear and they have a real asset and they are a real military asset to us,
>
> "*Secretary:* Yes,
>
> "*McCloy:* but on the other hand we have a very strong interest in being able to intervene promptly in Europe where the—twice now within a generation we've been forced to send our sons over some
>
> "*Secretary:* Yes
>
> "*McCloy:* relatively minor Balkan incident, and we don't want to lose the right to intervene promptly in Europe merely for the sake of preserving our South American solidarity because after all we, we will have England, England's navy and army, if not France's on our side, whereas the South American people are not particularly strong in their own right, and the armies start in Europe and they don't start in South America. However, I've been taking the position that we ought to have our cake and eat it too; that we ought to be free to operate under this regional arrangement in South America, at the

same time intervene promptly in Europe; that we oughtn't to give away either asset. . . .

"*Secretary:* . . . I think so, decidedly, because in the Monroe Doctrine and in—and that runs into hemispherical solidarity

"*McCloy:* Yes

"*Secretary:* we've gotten something that we've developed over the decades

"*McCloy:* Yes

"*Secretary:* and it's in, it's an asset in case, and I don't think it ought to be taken away from us. . . .

"*Secretary:* I think you've got to reserve, provided what will probably be the case, namely that Russia will rig up a situation there which she will tie up a pretty big region to herself, or run it herself, more or less

"*McCloy:* Yes

"*Secretary:* I think that it's not asking too much to have our little region over here which never has bothered anybody

"*McCloy:* Yes. . . .

"*McCloy:* . . . but you see we may be faced with these alternatives, we may find that if we press for that we will offend Russia—they'll just say 'No, we won't do that. Are you here for a world organization, or aren't you'; the exception is logically limited to enemy states. . . .

"*Secretary:* . . . Now that can be put in some way that she'll [Russia] see it, and if she is going to take these steps which she has been doing lately and which she is evidently going to continue, of building up friendly protectorates around her

"*McCloy:* Yes, yes

"*Secretary:* why she has no legitimate right to object to our hemispheral situation over here. That ought to stand by itself.

"*McCloy:* Now, she will say 'All right, we'll give you that, but give us that same thing in Europe and in Asia.' If we do that I do think there's an argument that we cut the heart out of the whole world organization—is it worth doing that? . . .

"*Secretary:* Well you don't think that Russia is going to give up her right to act unilaterally in those nations around her which she thinks so darned—are useful, like Romania and Poland and the other things —you don't think she's going to give that up do you?

"*McCloy:* Uh, no, she will, no—but there's no express provision in the Charter—the express provision in the Charter says that you cannot move under these regional arrangements without the authority of the Security Council except in the case of enemy states

"*Secretary:* Yes, I know,

"*McCloy:* Well, now the—she will cling to that veto power I think on this continent probably unless she gets something in return, and what

she would want in return would probably, if we suggested we wanted
to be relieved of that prohibition. . . .

"*McCloy:* she'd say she wanted to be relieved of the same prohibition
in the rest of Europe against non-enemy states, which would, in
effect, mean that you might have a great eastern European region and
a great western European region and an Asiatic region and an American region and we finally have a good big regional war one of these
days. And that looks as if it takes the meat out of the world organization

"*Secretary:* Yes. . . .

"*Secretary:* Well now exactly what is the issue which you want my
judgment on?

"*McCloy:* I want to know precisely this: Whether you would favor the
attempt—to make a further attempt, in the face of probably Russian
opposition, to come out, to get out from under the provision which is
now in Dumbarton Oaks that prohibits

"*Secretary:* I know that

"*McCloy:* enforcement action

"*Secretary:* yes

"*McCloy:* under the regional arrangement in this hemisphere even
though those, that enforcement action may be against non-enemy
states, because we've already got it so far as enemy states are concerned with the amendment that was made the other day.

"*Secretary:* Now let me think. . . . The only thing that you're thinking
of adding to is to

"*McCloy:* is an exception in favor of Chapultepec.

"*Secretary:* Yes; I mean is to, putting it in different language, giving
the United States the power to act unilaterally for the protection of
the hemisphere

"*McCloy:* Unilaterally or under the Act of Chapultepec which will be
multilaterally. . . .

"*McCloy:* . . . that would give her [Russia] sort of a free hand in
Europe which we therefore might not be able to intervene in time to
avoid a conflagration in Europe, although it is perfectly clear that our
interests are vital in Europe whereas she doesn't have anything to
fear from us in South America.

"*Secretary:* Well, the first part, the thing that we are asking for is first a
freer hand as a policeman in this hemisphere; and second, a little
freer hand in defending the hemisphere against any outside power
other even than the Axis

"*McCloy:* Yes

"*Secretary:* The first one is a little power in which we ought to be free
in because that will keep order here

"McCloy: Yes, because it is little.

"Secretary: Because it is little. The second one is a pretty big thing

"McCloy: Yes

"Secretary: Then there is this side. I think both those are important. Russia will, consider this, Russia will probably act that way anyhow no matter what the Dumbarton Oaks does

"McCloy: Yes. But I think you will have a great outcry of public opinion in the country against such a broadening of the regional arrangement. They will say that the Security Council and the World Organization has been defeated. And I'm not at all sure that it wouldn't be. . . .

"McCloy: The proponents of Dumbarton Oaks say 'Well, we will be free to act if there is any aggression against this continent.' We certainly will be free to send, as Hay did, send the fleet down there in spite of this provision because that comes under self-defense and the aggressor would be acting inconsistent with the provisions of the Charter itself if he set in motion the aggression against this continent

"Secretary: Well I think that's probably true and that may be a good reason for not insisting on the second thing; as for the first one, which may be very important in moderate interventions in this country, we have been a pretty active old Uncle Sam in stopping things, and I think we ought to continue to be. I think you ought to be able to prevent Russia from using that thing in her parallel, alleged parallel position. It isn't parallel to it. She's not such an overwhelmingly gigantic power from the ones which she's probably going to make a row about as we are here and on the other hand our fussing around among those little fellow[s] there doesn't upset any balance in Europe at all. That's the main answer. It doesn't upset any balance there where she may upset a balance that affects us. That's the difference. I think I would stand on that. I think you ought to maintain that, although it seems to be a little thing, it's been a pretty well developed thing and I think you can say that it isn't parallel to what she threatens to do.

"McCloy: Yes.

"Secretary: Well I've got to quit now.

"McCloy: That's all I need. That's the line I've been taking, but I wanted to check it with you because it is being looked upon here as the great issue in the conference and they are all very much concerned about

"Secretary: Well, on the other thing, if we had had the right of self-defense anyhow, as I think we would if we were attacked by a big power, why then we'd do it anyhow. . . ."[26]

The reconciliation of these dual impulses took the American delegation another week of "wrangling and re-writing." By May 12 the delegation, under McCloy's direction, prepared an article stipulating the right of self-defense existed whether or not the Security Council acted, and such action taken under the specifically mentioned Act of Chapultepec would be legal under the United Nations Charter. A nation would report their steps to the Security Council, which then might also take action. The concept did not exist in the Dumbarton Oaks draft, and the British rejected it, while the Russians vacillated. Intensive negotiations eventually led to a draft now known as Article 51 which stated the principle without reference to the Act of Chapultepec. Vandenberg accepted the compromise, but also had passed a delegation resolution to placate the United States Senate, and here spelled out the full intent of Article 51. On May 15 Vandenberg called on Stettinius and "I urged him to take hold of this problem with a firm hand. . . ." "Three hours later," Vandenberg records, "we had a meeting with the Latins . . . and Stettinius *told them* what we would do. . . . The Latins took it. The President gave Stettinius his O.K. . . . I announced it to the Regional Committee of the Conference at a meeting this evening." The following week it passed, after Gromyko received his O.K. from Moscow. ". . . we have found an answer which satisfies practically everybody."[27]

Article 51 became the basis of "collective self-defense" treaties of the United States over the following years. Another clause, Article 52, legitimized "regional arrangements" intended for the "maintenance of international peace," and this every major power could use. But Article 53 banned them all by stating, "But no enforcement action shall be taken under regional arrangements or by regional agencies without the authorization of the Security Council, with the exception of measures against any enemy [Axis] state. . . ." Although the Russians cited Article 53, the West only Article 51, in later years, the existence of the veto over Security Council actions meant in fact that the United States-sponsored regional system would be operative when the Security Council could not be, and perhaps even if it acted. No possibility of global unity and common action for peace via the United Nations mechanism ever existed, since the controlling power in the United Nations never intended it. The United Nations gave the partial division of the world into spheres of influence and competing blocs a formal legal structure, and thus the Great Powers both created and acknowledged reality.

The United States did not have to pass new amendments to the charter to convince the other Allies that the United Nations held out slight hope as a viable means of resolving world political and economic crises, for the "meeting with the Latins" had presaged the future quite vividly. Nelson Rockefeller, head of the Office of Inter-American Affairs and Assistant Secretary of State at the time, and also a powerful figure in the Latin economy, accompanied the delegation to San Francisco to maintain liaison with the Latin American delegates. "Several times, on close issues," Connally writes, "we told him, 'Look, get your people lined up right away.' "[28] Under the circumstances, and given the conservative, anti-Russian outlook of the leaders of these nations, the task was not difficult, and this possibility had been the objective of the enrollment campaign of the prior year and early 1945. At San Francisco and subsequently the appropriate State Department officials calculated the record of the reliability of various Latin American states on numerous issues.[29]

The Veto as the Last Protection

All this was plain to Russia and Britain, and the United States did not fail to press its control of the conference to the utmost, even on petty issues. The mood was such within the delegation as to brook no compromise, and Washington encouraged intransigence. By mid-May, Stettinius had ample reason to be pleased with his progress. The Russians, however, did not share his pleasure. Now they determined to interpret the veto privilege as broadly as possible, for if they could not hope to control or share equitably in the work of the United Nations they might deprive it as much as possible of its value as a club against themselves. Molotov stated several weeks after the opening of the conference that "the unanimity of the leading Powers is the basic problem of the post-war security of nations," and by the end of the month it appeared to the Russians that they were not likely to have it on acceptable terms.[30]

The veto agreement at Yalta was inordinately complex, perhaps more than any issue before the Allies, and there was ample opportunity for the Russians to interpret it flexibly to suit their own purposes. Everyone understood that the veto in the Security Council would apply to any affirmative action in regard to breaches of the peace, sanctions, and the like. In explaining the American interpretation to the Russians at Yalta, Stettinius listed six major categories open to the veto, many dealing with membership and organizational recommendations, arms control, and regional agreements, in addition to five categories involving the "peaceful settlement of disputes."[31] They also explained that the veto did not apply to the discussion of issues to which a nation was a party in dispute, though a veto could prohibit action. At the time Stalin added that he understood the intricate matter to mean that the veto would apply to questions in dispute which might not be resolved peacefully, implicitly even at a discussion level and by parties to the dispute. The Americans did not challenge his interpretation, and on this basis the Russians agreed to the obscure procedural categories subject to—or exempt from—a veto. In reality what appeared to be agreement turned out to be a postponement of a dispute over fine points, one which by no means represented a reversal in the Russian position—as the Americans insisted. Unfortunately the final Yalta Conference document had been much shorter than the explanatory American memos that went with it. On May 20 Vandenberg discovered that the Russians believed they could veto discussion of the disputes of other nations presented to the Security Council, and he in turn resolved to take the narrowest interpretation possible of the veto power, ignoring some of the actual rights accruing to the Russians and the subtleties in their position. For the Russians also stated that they would not expect the veto right to apply to the discussion of questions that peaceful means could clearly resolve. Gromyko insisted that discussion itself could become a political decision having tangible consequences that might trigger a chain of events—a view that the American conception of the Security Council as a bar of world opinion confirmed. In the subsequent melee the Americans ignored these distinctions. By the end of the month the controversy centered on what the veto actually permitted the Russians to do, and Gromyko, who was then alone in charge of the Russian delegation, insisted on waiting for orders from the Kremlin. The delay was "desperately irritating" to Vandenberg, more so when on June 1 Gromyko reported that he now upheld the right of any one of the Five Powers to veto discussion of any issue.[32]

The American delegation was furious, and on the morning of the following day Grew and Stettinius recommended to Truman that the United States threaten to refuse to join the United Nations on this basis, and to have Hopkins, then in Moscow, take the matter up with Stalin in these terms. Truman agreed, and Hopkins, on the evening of June 6, presented the matter to Stalin. Prior to that time, however, and contrary to the official American position that the inordinately complex matter had been settled at Yalta, Stettinius admitted to Harriman on June 3 that "The specific issue was not discussed either at Dumbarton Oaks or at Yalta, but was always taken for granted by us and the British." Now, despite the Secretary of State's observation that "the Russian Delegation had been extremely cooperative on all other issues which were under discussion," the Americans were prepared to threaten nonparticipation in the still unborn world organization.[33]

Stalin's reply reveals why the Russians withdrew their cooperation over an admittedly fine and weak point. Molotov noted that a distinction between vetoes being exercised in discussions of peaceful controversies or those potentially threatening to the peace had been drawn at Yalta, and Stalin dismissed it as insignificant and supported the American position. However, he gave a no less obscure prescription in favor of the veto's applying to discussions involving enforcement action, and then turned to what had obviously troubled the Russians. Stalin complained of the precedent— he did not mention the United States by name—of lining up the votes of small nations, and then he disparaged the tendency to rely on such blocs in place of Great Power agreement. But he accepted the American position, and this was all the triumphant Hopkins had heard. If the Americans were to grasp the moral of Stalin's words later, for the moment Vandenberg could hardly contain his jubilation: *"America Wins!"* ". . . the 'big battle' is over. . . ."[34] Truman was no less satisfied. Yet if the purpose was to win cooperation and not battles, the approach had been a failure.

The Future of the United Nations

During the debates on the more controversial issues of regional arrangements and the veto, committees at the San Francisco Conference dealt with the problem of the trusteeship of coveted base areas. The delegations submitted numerous drafts, but the Russian proposal was the most irksome and potentially dangerous, as it called for "early and full independent statehood" as the major goal.[35] The Americans found the Soviet "high-minded" position on colonial freedom, as Grew termed it, especially annoying given the belief Russia was "subjugating" Poland, but he also feared that Russia "may appear before the world as the champion of all dependent peoples."[36] And since the United States had the votes, it could assure that the United Nations would block the Russians. The United States proposal called for a trusteeship system dealing with those areas the Allies agreed upon at Yalta, but added a new dimension. The United Nations would divide these areas into two categories: strategic, over which the Security Council had jurisdiction, and a Trusteeship Council to deal with the remainder. Washington considered all American territorial objectives strategic, and its veto in the Security Council would assure absolute control over them. The British opposed this differentiation since their mandated areas were mainly populous and hardly of great strategic value. To meet this objection and unify the Anglo-American coalition, the Americans inserted an article in the charter stipulating it "the duty of the administering authority to ensure that the trust territory shall play its part in the maintenance of international peace and security," to cover whatever contingencies the British might seek to interpret to their advantage. The Security Council, and not the Trusteeship Council, would review these measures.

Having taken care of its own needs, the Anglo-American bloc made certain that the United Nations conservatively defined the objectives of the Trusteeship Council. The American delegation sought to detract from the Soviet championship of colonial independence, but also to take into account, as Stettinius phrased it, that "When perhaps the inevitable struggle came between Russia and ourselves the question would be who are our friends. . . . Would we have the support of Great Britain if we had undermined her position?" The result of these considerations was "a double formula," hopefully able to placate the colonial peoples but certain to satisfy the British.[37] To deny independence as a conceivable goal they considered too gross, and so the final United Nations Charter read "progressive development towards self-government or independence as may be appropriate to the particular circumstances . . . ," which the American delegate announced did not mean "any foreseeable future."[38] The delegates defeated an Egyptian motion that the United Nations allocate dependent peoples some share in administration, as well as proposals the General Assembly be able to send inspectors to trust territories or declare an area ready for some stage of self-government. But the American delegation inserted a clause for commercial equality in the trusteed areas, and the conference did not grant the Trusteeship Council itself any real power. Both the British and United States governments were pleased with the results.

The large majority of the smaller nations gathered at San Francisco chafed throughout the experience, for the Great Powers had ignored and manipulated them to their own convenience, and sporadic expressions of irritation in the form of resolutions were common. This was the case when the Latin American nations initiated the seating of Argentina. Where the United States found such independence useless, as in the case of the colonialism question, they squelched it. On the paramount matters the United State organized its bloc, but on the lesser ones it acceded to the wishes of the small nations. In early June the smaller nations attempted to win the right to discuss and recommend for the General Assembly, and several weeks later, as the meeting approached its end, Russia continued to insist that the conference delete this charter amendment. On June 18 Stettinius asked Molotov, then in Moscow, to break the deadlock, and the delegates passed a compromise solution permitting the General Assembly to discuss and recommend on an issue not already under consideration by the Security Council, much to the delight of the United States. This measure in effect strengthened the United States view of the relationship of discussion to the veto. The Russians relented once again.

All that was left was to give a ceremonial capstone to the new venture, one appropriate to its real character. The conference considered but waited until later to locate the United Nations' main headquarters in New York, a gesture symbolic of the United States' view of its role as the focus of world power in the future, a vision that had also resulted in placing the International Monetary Fund in Washington. The first considerations of the subject reflected Roosevelt's fertile imagination, and earlier he had informed Hull that he believed they should locate the Security Council in the Azores or Niihau, Hawaii—"the most interesting and heavenly spot . . . on earth" —away from the pressures of the world, and the Assembly might move to a different city each year to come in contact with people. In mid-1944 Hull records, "The President then spoke of the Black Hills, saying it was 400 miles in every direction from civilization; that there were two good hotels and trout streams available. . . ."[39] While dramatic, these proposals were not practical, and Roosevelt then mentioned giving the Empire State Building or the Pentagon to the United Nations Secretariat, the former as his personal memorial to the people of his home state. In mid-1944 he asked the State Department to prepare a report on the matter, and its committee by November concluded that Asia and the Near East were not sufficiently important political centers, Canada was too close to the British Commonwealth, and Latin America was too unstable. While they understood the liabilities attached to using the United States itself, the committee made no recommendation, but it was obvious which direction the American sentiment was beginning to turn.

The State Department did not resolve the issue until the San Francisco Conference, but there the American delegation informally cultivated support for an American site, which the General Assembly would choose later that year.[40]

And so the San Francisco Conference came to an end. Vandenberg was pleased: "We have finished our job. I am proud of it."[41] Even *Pravda* observed, "Perhaps the solution reached will not appear ideal to some, but it is the best possible at present. . . . The essential condition for the effectiveness of this organization is the joint, unanimous action of the mighty Great Powers. . . ."[42] This meant the Security Council.

"Power Politics Pure and Simple"

The United States regarded the United Nations as an instrument of power, but only one of many available, whose function would be to marshal opinion and the smaller nations in a politically useful manner, as a kind of "bar of world opinion," to cite Roosevelt, capable of regulating, to some measure, the direction of international political affairs. At no period during World War II did United States policy-makers intend to place as much reliance on the new postwar political organization as on the traditional tools of power based on time-proven diplomatic alliances and the existence of force in reserve. And at no time prior to Potsdam did the United States expect, or attempt, to solve any of its pressing, immediate political and economic problems via the new United Nations.

The United States did not scale its global political and strategic commitments to the capabilities and assumptions of its small prewar military establishment, and expecting to be the center of the postwar world system meant greatly enlarged military responsibilities. Its immediate willingness to continue troop commitments in Italy as long as the internal political situation required them, or to use them in the event of a revolutionary breakdown of the social systems of Western Europe, indicated United States readiness to remedy any lag in military planning to meet the political requirements of its new self-appointed role. The United States emerged from the war prepared and anxious to assume the most far-reaching responsibilities, and the instrumentalities for doing so it calculated realistically and never permitted to trail far behind.

The military services were divided on postwar force-level planning. During 1943 the Army supposed that its tasks would be global, but its manpower for the job restricted, and the War Department for its part aspired to a postwar military force of three million men, with emphasis on air power, a hope which realities soon forced it to pare down. In September 1944, Marshall issued a policy circular on postwar military planning which assumed a Regular Army of 275,000 men and a much larger Army Reserve. The Air Force always understood the plan to be contingent on an absence of serious international difficulties, and never accepted it. From 1943 onward the Navy calculated it would possess the world's largest fleet and maintain it everywhere. Several new military options looming on the horizon seemed quite compatible with a small professional army and great military power, however much they ran against the desires of Stimson and Forrestal. One was the atomic bomb, as yet not proven but an important and likely weapon with global possibilities. The other was universal military training, which might produce as many as 630,000 new trainees a year.

By the fall of 1944 Marshall, Stimson, and Forrestal were actively developing support from union leaders, Congress, and the like for this second alternative, and Truman endorsed the principle as soon as he became President. By June 1945, as the United States was obtaining bases and extending commitments utterly incompatible with a small military establishment, UMT became official Administration policy, and it initiated a campaign to pass necessary legislation. The State Department publicly endorsed the policy before Congress in the name of the United Nations' indefinite future needs and the United States' present requirements, which were geared to the larger political problems emerging from the war. In principle the State Department during June supported a confidential request from the military for permanent American air bases in Europe. Grew was ready to consent to future bases in Italy and France, but opposed reaching as far north as Norway—perhaps because its proximity to the Soviet Union made the purposes behind bases there all too crude. The following month, as the Potsdam Conference further corroded the political unity of the crumbling wartime coalition, the War Department hoped to retain an interim military establishment of two and a half million men for the "occupation" problems that it hoped would be temporary.

Washington revised and ultimately scrapped all such plans and expectations, for the conditions of international politics which had led to their formulation in the first instance were rapidly changing. By spring 1945 these factors caused the United States to increase its postwar military objective to a large extent and to attempt to bring closer together political needs and military planning. By June, Washington geared those plans not to German power, but toward the anticipated Russian capability and the threat of the Left.[43]

Prior to Potsdam other critical events indicated that the United States had no illusions concerning the potentialities that the United Nations offered, nor any faith in its value as a substitute for the application of power and conventional diplomacy. The United Nations Conference had just disbanded when at the end of June the State Department formally endorsed a plan proposing a Council of Foreign Ministers of the five major Allies to deal with the problems of the peace in Europe as a substitute for a formal peace conference such as the Entente had disastrously held at Versailles after World War I. While the State Department often cited the precedent and failure of Versailles as its justification, the belief that the United Nations Security Council structure was not viable for this purpose was implicit in such a council, in part because of the veto, but also because one of the pitfalls of Versailles had been the presence of the numerous smaller powers, each with their claims and inordinately long speeches. In effect the Great Powers would decide among themselves on an ad hoc basis, with power speaking to power without naïve formalisms concerning the equality of nations. However, they still had no illusion about the ability of the Five Powers to solve Europe's problems. The department studied the EAC experience, surveyed its dismal message, and decided to try to disband it. Perhaps more important, after Harriman proposed the Council plan to Molotov on July 7 the suggestion that they ask China to help define the future of Europe visibly surprised the Russian. Harriman could only reply that China was on the Security Council.

When the United States decided in June that it wished to settle the major political problems of the war outside a peace conference, no one juxtaposed the proposal against the basic assumption in the conduct of American diplomacy for most of the war. Until early 1945 Washington continuously postponed the consideration of a whole spectrum of pressing issues, especially dealing with Eastern Europe, on the premise that a future peace conference might solve them. In fact Washington based this strategy on the belief that overwhelming American political and economic power at the end of the war would permit the United States to define the final peace settlement more easily. Hence, the new American position in favor of a Council of Foreign Ministers also implicitly acknowledged the failure of the keystone of United States wartime political strategy.

Before Potsdam the liberal rhetoric of internationalism was not an obstacle to the United States' determined effort to attain its objectives for a postwar political and economic world acceptable to its interests; rather, that rhetoric was systematically integrated as a justification for the undertaking. With great clarity, at Mexico City the United States indicated that it planned to create a regional bloc isolated from the world and also as a means of intervening into Eastern Hemispheric affairs via the United Nations. The British had their bloc in the form of the empire, and they hoped to extend it to Western Europe as well. The Russians made it clear they would demand no less. Washington had always been split on this question. All the major advisers insisted on the Western Hemisphere and Pacific as an exclusive area under United States control politically and strategically, and Stimson was far more interested in extending American hegemony to the Far East than to Eastern Europe. As the consummate realist, he was certain that Russia would do no less, and that the better part of wisdom would be to stabilize the world order by dividing it. Unfortunately for the United States the U.S.S.R. could not provide stability, for it did not sufficiently control the Left's response to the grave crisis of world capitalism. Russia could not negotiate what it did not possess. By June, Stimson's tolerance of Soviet aspirations in Eastern Europe diminished, but many others in Washington now saw their prior opposition to the early British demand for its sphere of influence in a rather new perspective, one that the expansion of Soviet power imposed.

Throughout 1944 the United States criticized the projected creation of a Western European bloc along the lines Churchill and the Foreign Office desired. By June 1945 many in Washington concluded that the effect, if not the purpose, of British policy in Europe was to balance power on the Continent, which the growth of Russia and the collapse of Germany now threatened. They understood that they had based their early opposition to the bloc in part on its initiating a conflict between Russian and British power, one that might drag the United States into the turmoil with all its consequences. The State Department still paid obeisance to the hope the United Nations might provide some means of avoiding such blocs, but it was not relying on it:

> Spheres of influence do in fact exist, and will probably continue to do so for some time to come. Regional arrangements are recognized as necessary and legitimate features of international security, provided they are subordinate to the General Security Organization. In view of the actual Eastern European sphere and the Western Hemisphere bloc (Act of Chapultepec), we are hardly in a position to frown upon the establishment of measures designed to strengthen the security of nations in other areas of the world. However, such measures represent power politics pure and simple, with all the concomitant disadvantages.

Now the State Department was ready to admit that the United Nations structure was not likely to solve the problem of Russian power in the immediate future, and that the United States could expect the British to pursue their own self-interest without much justification for American complaints.

Antipathy toward the sterling bloc and exclusive economic arrangements historically stimulated the opposition to British or any other blocs. If Britain and Western Europe could overcome these negative features of the bloc system then they would qualify as acceptable partners in containing Communism. Before Potsdam the United States therefore altered its policy on the Western European bloc:

> . . . we should neither endorse nor oppose such *political* arrangements as are in fact subordinated to the General Organization. In the economic field, however, we should at all times strongly oppose any features which would place additional restrictions on trade and run counter to our announced principles of free access to foreign markets and raw materials.[44]

This decision anticipated much of the history of the postwar era, from NATO to foreign economic policy. The United States now grasped the concept of a politically and militarily cohesive but economically accessible Europe as a critical element in the global power struggle.

The United Nations was born without illusions and without sacrifices on the part of the United States. The new organization failed before it began, for Washington conceived it with exceptions and loopholes, in an atmosphere of suspicion and manipulation, not as a forum for agreement, but as an instrument in the Great Power conflict. The voting structure of the organization prejudged the outcome of its future decisions, and it was obvious to all that the Great Powers would proceed on a more realistic basis in attaining and protecting their vital interests. Now, however, there were two public standards for international conduct: one the United Nations defined on behalf of a seemingly idealistic internationalism, which described the motives and behavior of no important nation; the other, based on "power politics pure and simple." Moving behind the internationalist rhetoric of the new structure it fully expected to control, the United States hoped to define the basic thrust of postwar world politics in a fashion compatible with its national interests.

THE ECONOMICS OF
VICTORY

B Y THE SPRING of 1945 the main leverage the United States still
retained for achieving its war aims was neither political, ideological,
nor military, but, it was hoped, economic. The diplomacy of the United
States so far had failed to thwart the seeming movement toward the left
throughout Europe, the ideological offensive remained with the indigenous
forces of change, and militarily the Russian armies carried the brunt of the
land war and conquered the greatest part of Europe. Yet the remainder of
the world was starved and devastated, and only the United States emerged
from the war economically stronger than ever before, and believed itself
fully capable via its economic power of defining the political and ideological outcome of the war. The war had undermined capitalism everywhere except in the United States, and only the Americans could aspire to
resuscitate it globally.

The United States spent much time and thought prior to 1945 defining its economic war aims and creating the instruments to attain them.
After Yalta, however, it was apparent from the world's economic and
political condition that America would have to find at least a temporary
compromise between ultimate principles and immediate necessities, though
the principles would remain the ultimate goal toward which to direct
immediate policy. It was now even less an issue of quickly reforming the
world economic structure automatically to solve outstanding, accumulated
political problems as Hull and the State Department had hoped until the
end of 1944, but now also a question of utilizing economic power, as a
more immediate and direct instrument of political policy, for the political
prerequisites for the success of economic war aims were now vital. If the
Left triumphed everywhere, or if England retained its closed bloc economy,
there could be no thought of attaining an ideal world order. During the
spring of 1945, therefore, United States policy became less abstract and

more geared to pressing political needs and the relevance of economic power to current diplomatic tactics. Increasingly the objective of establishing an ideal and tranquil world order was deferred and sacrificed to the more urgent and obvious necessities, but deferred with the intention that the vision of the future might later become a reality. That vision was never to vanish.

The Reaffirmation of a Creed

The leaders in Washington never ceased to comprehend the nature and form of the world they hoped to attain. Almost ritually they refined their basic view of it and the assumptions underpinning their beliefs. But the economic impact of the war on the world economic structure increasingly divorced that reaffirmation from the unpleasant and complex limitations of reality. For throughout 1944 and 1945 the wartime pattern of trade restrictions within the sterling bloc, government bulk-buying and export controls, and all the accumulated economic controls that the United States was determined to dissolve, continued unabated. Dean Acheson commented during March that

> . . . the governments of the world have learned as they have never learned before, all the tricks of economic warfare. . . . If that situation were spread throughout the world, it would have a devastating effect upon recovery from the war. Probably the only hope of maintaining stability—social, political, and economic—in the world, in the face of the great post-war troubles, is to adopt measures which will lead to an expansion of production, consumption, and trade. . . .[1]

Political stability therefore became the central precondition for attaining the long-term interests of the United States.

The State and Treasury departments gave no less thought to this theme during the first half of 1945 than the preceding two years, and their solutions were the same. William Clayton emerged as the leading spokesman for the policy that Hull first defined and that each Administration endorsed. Both their public and private statements reflected this policy commitment. ". . . equality of opportunity," the State Department privately informed the French government during March in connection with its aspiration to rebuild a sphere of influence in Syria and Lebanon, "was high on our list of war aims and that we had no intention of fighting this war and then abandoning our objectives."[2] "Let us never forget," Clayton reminded high-tariff advocates, "that world peace will always be gravely jeopardized by the kind of international economic warfare which was so bitterly waged between the two world wars. Democracy and free enterprise will not survive another world war."[3] Clayton also watched, "very informally," over the policy of the United States toward the problem of cotton, one of the major beneficiaries of the contemplated foreign economic policy of the United States.[4] Again and again speeches and articles coming out of Washington stressed the need to implement the principles of Article VII, to prevent economic and trade controls from dominating the world economy, and to create a world economic structure open to American trade expansion. Even Morgenthau opened the door to a reintegration of former pro-Axis nations on a nonpolitical, "strictly business basis," so that they might create a restored world financial structure as a foundation for long-term world peace.[5] If stability and American prosperity were the objectives of an integrated world economy, the United States might have to make certain immediate political concessions.

Throughout the first ten months of 1945 the State Department busied itself with the outlines for an International Trade Organization, which attempted to achieve on a trading level what it had designed the International Monetary Fund to achieve on a financial plane; and while it advances our story to peer ahead at the ITO, it is important to note that the principles of the ITO finally published in November reflected the larger assumptions of policy during the remainder of the war. "To promote international commercial cooperation. . . . to avoid recourse to measures destructive of world commerce. . . . To facilitate access by all members, on equal terms, to the trade and to the raw materials of the world. . . . for the reduction of tariffs and other trade barriers, and for the elimination of all forms of discriminatory treatment in international commerce. . . ."—all these themes were now well-known premises of wartime discussions.[6] They had in fact become critical pillars in the definition of United States foreign policy.

Washington knew of course that wishes and statements of principle would not alter reality, and for this it was essential to apply American economic power. To the rest of the world the true meaning of these principles depended on the consistency with which the United States was willing to implement at home those principles of a free world trade system which it asked the world to endorse. When the Socialist-led Australian government in early 1945 proposed the convocation of a world conference on high employment and mass consumption the State Department was discouraging, for fear it would stimulate uneconomic production and trade barriers. Implicitly the department gave profit a higher priority than welfare. On the question of exports the United States had a predictably unequivocal position: it wished to sell. On the problem of what prices it would demand for its agricultural exports the situation was less clear.

The immediate key to industrial exports as well as to international agreement to American economic objectives was a large-scale program of credits, a program bureaucrats and bankers alike favored in principle. Only the revival of a lively export trade could head off economic nationalism and develop an important outlet for war-expanded industrial capacity. In the long-run, however, a drastic lowering of American tariffs would be critical to normal trade, and many formerly high-tariff industrial groups for the first time shifted behind the essentials of the Hull-Clayton foreign economic policy. The Committee for Economic Development emerged during this period as the leading big business supporter of such a policy, and the American Bankers Association, while opposed to the International Monetary Fund, supported a substantial expansion of the capital of the Export-Import Bank, which tied all its loans to United States purchases. Foreign nations could not find high-risk capital in private channels, and for this reason alone the Hullian program would require the government to finance the creation of a renovated world capitalist economy; an economy, they hoped, that private agencies would ultimately operate.

The problem of United States commodity exports was much more complex, for the nation was a major importer as well as exporter of agricultural commodities and it was obvious that foreign producers might use any plan casually designed to maintain prices for American farmers to justify higher prices for materials they sold to American industry. The dilemma required a delicate posture not easy to assume, and in fact the Americans never achieved it.

The Department of Agriculture nominally supported the trade and financial programs of the State and Treasury departments, but in fact worried far more about proposals designed to maintain American farm prices. The thrust of its concern in the spring of 1945, when it published its postwar trade program, was with the prospect of "many burdensome agricultural surpluses tending to depress farm incomes and prevent trade expansion."[7] In particular it worried about too much rice, wheat, cotton, fats, and oils. Even if there were a very large expansion of international trade, as even the State Department conceded, many of these goods would remain in surplus supply over the long run. Predictable trade required an international commodity control apparatus, one that included the consumer nations as well as the producers, for it was precisely such exclusion that had so irritated American industrial consumers prior to the war. The State Department was willing to accede to the Agricultural Department's plans on the matter because it felt that the collapse of American farm purchasing power or excessive surplus would impair its trade program and the United States market for foreign goods. In fact the support of the farm bloc in Congress would be critical to any comprehensive foreign economic program, and the State Department would have to defer to agricultural interests even at the expense of consistency. Both departments paid obeisance to each other's desires.

The Agriculture Department hoped to use international commodity agreements for products grown in the United States and likely to be in surplus, and beyond the usual means for increasing consumption, which it generally believed to be limited, it wanted minimum and maximum prices fixed for essential commodities and a buffer stock scheme for maintaining reserves and controlling prices. The inconsistency of such a plan with the nominal objectives of the Hull-Clayton program was not at all unusual by 1945, for this anomaly was only one of many to strike the rest of the world, especially the British, as a rather typical example of the self-serving character of American proclamations and intentions.[8]

Great Britain: The Key to the Future

The success or failure of United States foreign economic peace aims depended almost entirely on its ability to win or extract the cooperation of Great Britain. Throughout 1943 and 1944 the United States negotiated and argued these questions with the English, fully aware of the stakes involved as it tailored and controlled British export markets, dollar balances, and even concessions in Middle Eastern oil fields, with a view to implementing American economic objectives. It was crucial, in the American view, that Britain emerge from the war neither too weak nor too strong, but amenable to American direction on the larger issues. Above all Washington hoped to force Britain to dissolve the basic structure of the sterling bloc and the additional vast apparatus of wartime controls over its internal economy and foreign trade. Clayton and the State Department were fully aware that England alone would be the critical test of their ability to attain their economic war aims.

The British did not respond well to the merciless pressures that the Americans applied in various ways, and they were hardly inclined to view United States intentions as charitable or disinterested. In fact they reacted only to pressures and by early 1945 nearly every leader in Washington realized that the British were not likely to prove manageable without further efforts on the part of American policy-makers. It was a cause of much concern. At Yalta, Stettinius reminded Roosevelt that the British might take his lack of pressure on Article VII of the Lend-Lease Agreement as an example of a lack of American interest, and Roosevelt sent Churchill a letter urging that they appoint new delegations to further discuss the larger problems and reinvigorate progress on trade policy. The British failed to agree, and the following month the *Department of State Bulletin* freely and frankly discussed the dangers of the continuation of British exchange and trade controls, urging cooperation along the lines of the by now well-known Article VII, but also bluntly making the point that should the British continue bilateral and exclusive trading relations, "This is a game that two can play, and the natural reaction of many is that the American answer to such a threat should be higher tariffs against British goods and perhaps some exclusive trading arrangements of our own."[9]

By the spring of 1945 and in the weeks before the Potsdam Conference this general fear of the direction of British economic policy set the backdrop for the conduct of United States economic policy toward the British, and nothing involving Anglo-American economic relations at this time can be divorced from Washington's growing anxiety and desire to make England tractable to American objectives. Preparatory to Potsdam the State Department summarized the problem in its larger context, and concluded that "It is important to come very soon to definite understandings with the British on postwar financial questions. There is serious danger that otherwise Britain may not ultimately go along with our program to restore worldwide multilateralism in finance and trade." The Americans again asked Churchill to discuss implementing Article VII, and they correlated Lend-Lease and a postwar loan to practical means of pressuring the British for cooperation that otherwise might not be forthcoming. The department noted British political opposition to Article VII both from the Left and Right, and Keynes's declaration that the Bretton Woods Agreement was not incompatible with bilateral trading disturbed it. Department officials acknowledged that "The British were very reluctant to commit themselves to Article VII in the first place, and they have shown themselves equally reluctant to proceed with discussions looking towards its implementation."[10]

To bend this opposition and reluctance into cooperation became the main goal of American foreign economic objectives after Yalta. First the State Department took issue with all British restrictionism and plans to create a Western European bloc with attributes of a trading coalition, and then intended to wave the carrot of American economic aid in return for tangible endorsement of United States economic war aims. The British perceived that they held the important trump card for the Americans and that they had much to gain by promising neither too much nor too little, enough to pacify the Americans, but not so much as to invite perilous new economic risks.

The week before Potsdam, Churchill thought that he understood the temper of American feelings and aspirations when he decided to "expect the Americans in dealing with us to be more responsive to arguments based on the danger of economic chaos in European countries than to *the balder pleas about the risks of extreme Left Governments or of the spread of Communism.*"[11] In fact in American thinking these issues were intimately interrelated, but Churchill appreciated the vulnerable sensitivity of Washington and he was ready to make a gesture toward the American goals, for if England's consent would convince Washington that there would truly be universal prosperity, Britain could profit from the munificence resting behind the enormous cornucopia the Americans were anxious to open—in return for concessions. Only time would determine who would gain and who would lose.

The Problem of Britain: Lend-Lease

The impact of the war on British economic power was disastrous. Washington planners geared American policy to the expectation of Britain's leaving the war neither too weak nor too strong, and Lend-Lease and export policies were based on that fragile assumption, but the desperate statistics that the British dolefully confronted at the end of the war reflected the miscalculation. Britain fought a global war as a Great Power, but in reality ceased to be one as a consequence of the enormous financial and material sacrifices entailed in the venture. "If you had gone down like France," Truman confessed to Churchill at Potsdam, "we might be fighting the Germans on the American coast at the present time." The Allies of the United States, in brief, had sacrificed both blood and power while the Americans emerged from the war relatively unscathed, stronger than before, and the unrivaled center of the world economy. "This justifies us," Truman added for Churchill's solace, "in regarding these matters as above the purely financial plane."[12] The British hoped they would.

Between 1938 and 1945 British exports declined from £471 million to £258 million, and its imports increased over the same period from £858 million to £1,299 million. Its overseas debt increased nearly five times, to £3,355 million, and it liquidated over £1 billion in investments, thereby halving net overseas income from this source. By the following year its foreign indebtedness was far greater than that of all Western Europe combined, and excluding debts to the United States, three times larger than that of France. The British virtually dissipated the legacy and power of nineteenth-century imperialism.

By May 8, when Truman abruptly terminated Lend-Lease aid to Russia and England save for use in the Pacific, the specific Lend-Lease conditions had become the critical lever for controlling British dollar balances, and to a lesser extent, exports in competition with American goods. The planning regulating this program by fall 1944 had reached a high degree of sophistication, and in September 1944, when the controversy with England over these questions was especially unpleasant and defined temporary British willingness to endorse a version of the Morgenthau plan, Roosevelt warned General George Marshall that he should consider the contemplated reduction of Lend-Lease with the utmost care, impinging as it did on every major area of national policy. At Quebec, Roosevelt also promised Churchill that the United States would tailor Lend-Lease to permit some degree of British reconversion to civilian needs, and together they signed a pledge not to alter the program prior to consultations. The solution was in part a way of getting the British to lower their export campaign to regain their foreign markets from the Americans, and over the following months the British reduced Roosevelt's words to a formal understanding. Almost everyone of importance in Washington or London was aware of this fact in May 1945.

The United States nevertheless felt justified in slashing Lend-Lease to England because the British gold and dollar holdings of April 1945 were considerably above the gloomy forecasts upon which Roosevelt based his promise in September 1944. In fact the strategy of keeping Britain below a certain level of hard reserves was still operative when Washington cut back Lend-Lease, and the United States persisted in believing that the British financial situation was not at all as catastrophic as their exchequer claimed. When Churchill complained loudly and clearly to Truman about the cutback of May he also stressed the fact that all British reconversion planning was based on the American promises of fall 1944. Truman's response that Congress intended the Allies to use Lend-Lease just to fight the war was only partially correct, but since the United States desired only a very limited British involvement in the Pacific war Churchill found little consolation in this view. In fact Washington did not want Britain to reconstruct with free Lend-Lease aid, but via a loan, and before granting such a loan the Americans intended to extract a far-reaching quid pro quo on behalf of United States economic goals.

By June 1945 the State Department hoped to resolve the problem of Lend-Lease in the context of a comprehensive plan for implementing Article VII as the foundation of future economic relations between the two nations. The United States Treasury unsuccessfully opposed the loan as being unrelated to immediate British needs and plans, which experts could not determine until perhaps a year or two after the war, and the Treasury knew that the British were opposed to immediate negotiations. Before Truman left for Potsdam, where he was to assure Churchill of his noble intentions, the State Department told him that "it is probable that the British will be reluctant to discuss financial questions, particularly post-lend-lease credits. At the same time such credits will, in our opinion, be essential if we are to obtain satisfactory arrangements with them on trade and commercial policy." By this they meant not merely principles, but export competition, tariffs, the future of world oil, commodity agreements, and the entire spectrum of foreign economic questions. Such a resolution was especially urgent in light of Washington's suspicions that the British really did not share its enthusiasm for the new Hullian world modeled after Gladstone's nineteenth-century British imperialism of free trade. "The crucial problem," the State Department concluded, "is to arrest the British tendency toward exclusiveness and restrictionism before it grows strong."[13]

The United States could not grant a loan to Britain, and the British did not accept American economic objectives in a binding form until Lend-

Lease came to an end. When Churchill and Truman very briefly discussed the problem at Potsdam, Churchill remained vague and noncommittal, much more interested in whether the Americans would really cut their tariffs than in promising anything in return. When the Labour party came to power during the middle of the conference the danger of a noncooperative England, dedicated to state trading as well as the sterling bloc, posed altogether new dangers, far beyond a mere breakdown in world trade, but impinging much more directly on the future of capitalism. With a loan the United States might define the limits of British socialism as well, and neutralize it insofar as that were possible. By the end of July, Clayton considered all of these options and at the beginning of August, at the latest, he informed Keynes that they would have to make a "business-like" arrangement. Keynes, in all his naïveté, at this time was confident that he might obtain an interest-free loan or even an outright grant from the Americans by referring to the equality of sacrifice all the Allies had yet to make. The illusion was not to last long. He misunderstood the motives of American policy.

At the beginning of August, as an American plane dropped the first atomic bomb on Hiroshima, Clayton briefed the critical leaders in London on the impending financial crackdown. It was American policy, he told them, to tie any loan to the larger questions of commercial policy. He merely ignored earlier pledges not to end Lend-Lease in such a manner as to disrupt British recovery or planning. There would be no respite, for the British were altogether too slow in endorsing the American program. To anticipate the end of the pattern of wartime discussions on this matter and the beginning of a new phase in Anglo-American economic relations, the United States prepared to stop Lend-Lease altogether with the defeat of Japan, and on August 21 cancelled the program entirely save where foreign governments were willing to pay its full cost. "It was a great shock," Clement Attlee, the new Prime Minister, recalled. "The tap was turned off at a moment's notice. . . . We had not had a chance to reorganize ourselves on a peace-time basis." The British financial situation passed from bad to worse, perhaps even becoming critical. "It made quite an impossible situation. That's why we had to go and ask for an American loan right away."[14] The United States had intended precisely this result. Now it hoped it might finally obtain full British consent for the new world economy America hoped to create.

Britain: Practice and Principle, Once More

As the United States attempted to secure British agreement to its broader policy for the future world economy, the specific manner in which the United States tried to solve immediate problems of Anglo-American economic relations continued to impress the British, as it had earlier in the war. There were a number of smaller points of contention, involving export competition and commodity agreements, but as usual the essential point of disagreement centered on the oil resources of the Middle East. These issues could assume a significance far beyond their immediate dollar value because the United States was much more concerned about the strength rather than the weaknesses of the British economy, and its possible independent course. Indeed the possibility that England might be too weak to risk participating in postwar American plans was largely ignored on behalf of tendentious analyses of British reserves and overseas assets which struck State Department analysts as enormous.

The commodity problem must be deferred to subsequent volumes, but it is sufficient to say that the various "study groups" dealing with rubber, sugar, wheat, and the like continued to receive the sustained attention of various experts in Washington. More significant was their fear that England would so control its imports as to minimize trade with the dollar areas and to increase its exports faster than the United States might be able to do. It was one of Washington's basic policies that the "rate of reconversion in the United Kingdom is not disproportionate to that in the United States. . . ," which in practice meant only that America would not permit England to exceed United States reconversion and would in fact allow it to fall behind.[15] The British would not recoup their vast prewar export markets in Latin America, where British exports declined from 40 percent of the Latin American imports in 1938 to 8 percent in 1948.

With the end of Lend-Lease the United States scrapped all of its stated obligations for the recovery of Britain's export trade, for the Americans implicitly assumed that they could obtain all the advantages of an international economy immediately by taking over Britain's markets. Much to American irritation, by spring 1945 the British continued to resist this drastic trade displacement. Exclusionary British civil aviation policies designed to keep American aircraft out of the Middle East and to restrict the sale of American planes in the sterling area raised the trade and export issue again. The matter was the object of a sharp United States note during April, which the British blithely ignored until the end of June, by which time the State Department hoped Truman would raise the matter with Churchill at Potsdam.

Any problems involving oil and the Middle East caused the State Department to wince, but as a result of the transformation of the scramble in Iran into an affair involving Russia, the Middle East by mid-1945 presented a problem in two forms. First, in the Iranian situation an economic conflict turned into a political crisis, one involving Russia as well as internal political factions and incipient Arab nationalism. Before the British and Americans could resolve their own conflicts they had to eliminate the threat of Soviet power as their neutralizer. The other problem was a continuation of the interwar conflict between the United States and England for oil concessions, which sharply intensified at this time in Saudi Arabia. Although Iran and Saudi Arabia were the two major areas of rivalry, the United States made it plain that in principle it expected free access to any other Middle Eastern area that might eventually prove profitable. When the French suggested to the State Department in March that this in effect meant that the strong would vanquish the weak, the United States bluntly informed them that America would not accept a sphere of influence for any other nation. Henceforth some Arab factions seeking to neutralize British power were able to find a ready friend in Washington, and the Arab nationalists based their first expressions of opposition to the British on this implied American endorsement of the containment of British power, which was also the prerequisite of the American Open Door policy.

As had been the case since 1943, the American policy of equal access for United States investors also included the intention to monopolize the Saudi Arabian oil industry, excluding European interests. By the beginning of 1945 the British intensified their struggle as they realized that the effect of a successful American policy would drive them entirely from the Middle Eastern oil industry. Since Saudi Arabia represented future promise rather than present production, the basic United States policy simply continued to finance Saudi Arabia's demands, making it clear that the United States remained the ruling dynasty's most powerful and responsive friend. At their meeting in Cairo during the days following Yalta, Roosevelt recalled "that he had told Ibn Saud that essentially he, the President, was a businessman . . . and that as a businessman he would be very much interested in Arabia." As a potential enticement, over the subsequent months the State Department told Arab diplomats that the United States would not support Zionist claims on Palestine but would instead work to maintain the status quo, an assurance that linked Arab destinies more closely to American designs on oil.[16]

Forrestal especially actively urged continued good-will payments to Ibn Saud, and the implementation of plans to create a major base at Dhahran. Rather crudely but frankly, he noted in his diary in July after a conversation with Byrnes that "I told him I thought it was a matter of first importance; that we were spending and had spent millions in Saudi Arabia, and the British and not ourselves were getting the benefit of it. I told him that, roughly speaking, Saudi Arabia, according to oil people in whom I had confidence, is one of the three great puddles left in the world. . . ."[17] Less significant than the fact that the British had yet to obtain anything from Ibn Saud in the form of concessions, was the strong desire of such well-placed leaders as Forrestal to acquire such "puddles" and to define and shape American policy on the basis of that desire.

The other puddles were of no less interest to the State Department. While they continued to attempt to iron out a revised version of an Anglo-American petroleum agreement more acceptable to Congress and the American oil industry (they released a draft at the end of September and Congress ultimately defeated it), department analysts surveyed the world's oil resources and reemphasized the mineral's historically important role in American foreign policy. The dimensions of the problem, they acknowledged, would impinge on the whole spectrum of United States foreign policy. The fate of Eastern Europe's oil would be "the earliest and most significant test of this country's ability to understand and work with the U.S.S.R. in commercial matters. . . ." The trend toward state oil monopolies and socialism throughout Europe, "and the effect of such proposals upon legitimate property rights of American nationals," defined the response of the United States to the movements of change throughout the world, for "this Government must nevertheless recognize and proclaim that international commerce, predicated upon free trade and private enterprise (which is the conceptual core of United States economic foreign policy) is, in the long run, incompatible with an extensive spread of state ownership and operations of commercial property."

On this basis the United States sought to remold the direction of change throughout the world, on behalf of oil in the first instance only, and the role of the State Department in this undertaking would be at least as strong as before the war. The department staked out Ethiopia, Paraguay, Brazil, and Colombia for future penetration, and "In China there are great possibilities for the post-war period." The Americans took it for granted that they should control developments throughout the world, and that international conditions should conform to their needs:

> The desirability of control by American nationals over petroleum properties abroad is based on two considerations: (a) that the talent of the American oil industry for discovery and development is historically demonstrated so that results are likely to be better according to the extent to which American private interests participate, and (b) that other things being equal, oil controlled by United States nationals is likely to be a little more accessible to the United States for commercial uses in times of peace and for strategic purposes in times of war.[18]

The carefully formulated official policy of late 1944 in favor of creating a world economy involving American hegemony over at least this most critical mineral was still the objective. And so the rest of the world might resist long and hard.

The Americans' difficulties in applying their world oil policy can best be seen in Iran. There the Soviet responded to imminent Western oil concessions by actively intervening on behalf of their own economic and strategic interests in Iran and thereby threatened both the British and especially American hopes to obtain new concessions. How to remove Soviet troops and pressures as a deterrent to the restoration of a far simpler two-way rivalry perplexed the Anglo-Americans. At Yalta both the United States and England urged the Russians to advance the date for troop withdrawals, fixed at six months after the termination of hostilities, and accept a self-denying clause concerning oil concessions, one to which both the British and Russians had already agreed in 1941. The Russians de-murred, and insisted on standing by existing agreements, which in fact England had already violated when responding to American efforts to ob-tain oil concessions. By May the Iranian government again urged Washing-ton to pressure the Russians to leave as soon as possible, but now Churchill and his Chiefs of Staff thought some continued British military presence might be necessary, not merely for the Russians, but most probably for fear that the Iranians would deal only with the United States if permitted to do so.

To the United States, the continuation of its so-called independent advisory commissions in Iran was quite sufficient foreign involvement in Iranian affairs, and from 1945 on the United States consistently urged that foreign troops withdraw far more quickly than either the Russian or British governments desired. The United States could therefore represent itself as the disinterested advocate of Iranian national interests, a position circum-stances forced it to maintain after Potsdam, where Russia accepted only the principle of immediate withdrawal of foreign troops from Teheran, and during the sustained crisis over Iran that recurred repeatedly after the war. In this position the United States championed Iranian rights over British and Russian imperialism, and ultimately obtained a major share in the out-put of the Iranian oil industry.[19]

Food as an Instrument of Politics

The United States was ambiguous throughout the war on the role of food as a weapon of political and economic strategy. Convinced that it had to relate food and UNRRA to its fear of agricultural surpluses, the United States used the Hot Springs Food Conference as a forum for advancing American principles for postwar economic reconstruction. By the spring of 1945, though Washington was still chiefly concerned with the prospect of a long-run oversupply of food and an American farm depression, the rele-vance of food to the growth of the Left everywhere was too obvious to ignore. In this context the question was how to reconcile the anxiety over surplus with the dread of the Left and revolution, and also how to adminis-ter the existing food program to maximize political results for American interests. The Americans never resolved this vacillation and in the first eight months of 1945 they eventually opted for a policy of restricting food stockpiles, but also of using the remaining surplus food in as politically effective ways as possible.

Washington was extremely alarmed over the political and economic consequences of famine and starvation in Europe in the spring of 1945, but never discovered the methods for coping with the danger. Stettinius and especially Stimson warned Truman of the problem almost continuously, for the need to avoid excessive economic disruption in Europe ultimately shaped their view of the role of the German economy in aiding economic, and hence political, stability. As soon as he came to office the State Department beseeched Truman to act on the grave implications of the threat of hunger, which could lead to "internal chaos."[20] Stimson in May was convinced that Truman and most of official Washington agreed with his assessment of "the probability of pestilence and famine in central Europe next winter. This is likely to be followed by political revolution and Communistic infiltration. . . . It is vital to keep these countries from being driven to revolution or Communism by famine."[21] What action would be appropriate and sufficient?

There were some leaders in Washington who analyzed the entire danger of Soviet control of Eastern Europe as a problem of the breakup of traditional European economic integration and its implications for preventing famine and a subsequent move toward the left throughout Europe. The Russians, at the moment, possessed the traditional agricultural export areas of Europe, and both Stimson and the State Department were convinced that Russian cooperation in the reintegration of the European economy was vital to stave off chaos everywhere. For this reason they could not cut off the food-relief program of UNRRA from Eastern Europe for fear that the ultimate damage to Anglo-American–controlled areas would be the greater. They needed Soviet cooperation, therefore, for immediate objectives as well as for the longer-term goal of keeping Eastern Europe open to the world economy. The issue of Eastern Europe and European economic reintegration was critical as well, because by spring of 1945 it was not at all certain that the United States would be willing or able to meet or adjust to the full magnitude of hunger and chaos in Europe.

The basic dilemma that the United States confronted was its desire to prevent the Left from gaining among the hungry populations of Europe, but also to maintain high food prices, which in turn required avoiding surpluses at home. American estimates of the extent of the anticipated food shortage in Europe differed sharply, but during the spring of 1945 they were distinctly running in favor of a view that shortages would be temporary and short-lived, during which time the political dangers would be great, but thereafter the traditional food surpluses would plague the world. In this context the United States felt a deep responsibility to American farmers and national prosperity as well as to the ravaged peoples of

Europe and Asia. Every Department of Agriculture appraisal of the future published at this time reinforced the vision of "a constant pressure toward surplus acres and surplus production."[22] The relaxation of rationing in the United States in the fall of 1944 was politically motivated and also designed to reduce threatened surpluses, and the government further reduced 1945 agricultural production goals below those of 1944. Although aware of the grave consequences of an error, during the spring of 1945 Washington thought that most of the required food would have to come not from the United States but from Eastern Europe, and that the real problem was one of distribution rather than production. There was even some doubt in intelligence circles as to whether food-storage facilities could be found in Europe.

Until the late summer of 1945, when Washington finally realized that it had drastically miscalculated Europe's food needs and the extent of the 1945 harvest in the United States, the Americans thought only in terms of maximizing the political results of the existing food program. Until then, and indeed for all of 1945, United States food exports in every form declined below the 1944 level. Stimson was the key architect of this greater emphasis on the political uses of food, for as the ultimate head of the military occupation he had the largest responsibility for the problem. Moreover, there was an important precedent for the use of food as a political instrument, since Herbert Hoover had used a food-relief program after World War I in Central and Eastern Europe to thwart the Left in that area.

Early in May, Hoover went to see Stimson concerning the problem, and he urged that the United States shift its food program as far as possible to the American military authorities' political direction, and that they downgrade the relatively neutral UNRRA program. Stimson needed no prodding, for Hoover's

> ideas followed very much the line which McCloy and I had been fighting for. . . . If we could turn in to those [West European] countries 2 million tons of wheat per month for June, July and August, you could take the bread ration off that entire area. This would be good psychology. We could turn the tide of Communism in all those countries. Hoover stamped out Communism in this way in central Europe.[23]

UNRRA, Stimson complained, was obliged to distribute aid roughly according to need, which meant Eastern Europe, even Yugoslavia. But for various reasons they could not immediately discontinue UNRRA aid, for the United States did not entirely control the program; they still hoped and needed to reintegrate Eastern Europe into the entire European economy, and food, they believed, would prevent the voluntary defection of the

Eastern European masses to Bolshevism. Stimson was delighted to continue his discussion of the problem with Hoover over the following months, since he regarded the ex-President as "a real master" of the approach, and Hoover also urged Truman to emphasize the direct military administration of food distribution in Western-occupied areas.[24] Hoover's critical assumption was that the West had already lost Eastern Europe, that "Czechoslovakia was Communist controlled by May, 1945 . . . ," and that their prime task would be to consolidate American power elsewhere.[25] He was satisfied in early June when he learned that the United States would not permit UNRRA to control food in Western-occupied areas, where the relief program ultimately proved more extensive than that of an UNRRA serving a far larger and more devastated area. American military officers were also pleased, for they regarded UNRRA's international character as uselessly complicating, and in its own way, politically valuable to the Russians. As Stimson reminded Truman in late July, "a return to stable conditions" in Europe was critical to the survival of democracy, even to the extent of permitting Germany "to live and work." Such a program of rehabilitation had to "be channelled through one man and one agency," which meant an American.[26]

By the summer of 1945 United States Congressmen widely believed the allegation that Russia was using UNRRA to consolidate rather than reduce its power in Eastern Europe, and the shift in American emphasis was from this time on obviously in favor of a food program that served visible political objectives. Reconstruction, relief, and foreign aid, in this context, became even more an instrument of American political and economic strategy, a principle that was not new by mid-1945, but which they then applied systematically everywhere. Though China eventually emerged as the largest recipient of UNRRA aid, Poland, Italy, Yugoslavia, and Greece followed in that order of magnitude of aid, and the distribution of aid on the basis of need rather than political cooperation, as skewed as it was to nations in the Western orbit, especially Greece and Italy, became less useful than direct distribution in accordance with political cooperation. To foretell the end, Clayton himself in August 1946 formally withdrew future United States support from the UNRRA organization. America had developed more useful instruments of policy.[27]

The End of the Russian Loan

The principle of using economic aid as an instrument of political and economic policy, and above all as a means to introduce stability and stop Communism, meant a final shattering of the last shred of Russian hope for an American loan. In reality by Yalta the chances for such a loan were already extremely slim. When the Russians requested a $6-billion postwar credit in January 1945 no one in Washington was inclined to grant it to them save as part of a vast quid pro quo on global political and economic questions, and nothing that occurred in the following months changed American plans in this regard.

Despite the State Department's efforts, news of the Russian request found its way to the public and at least part of the business press rather favorably considered it. But on March 10 Grew formally notified the Soviets not to expect a quick positive response to their request. Since Washington did not intend to supply business with postwar markets in this form, the practical reconstruction relations with Russia, as with England, shifted to the nature and volume of Lend-Lease. The Russians, not unpredictably, now attempted to maximize the volume of Lend-Lease received in the form of industrial equipment that they might also use later for peacetime reconstruction, and the State Department, no less predictably, refused to cooperate and turned a more acerbic eye to alleged Soviet trans-shipment of Lend-Lease goods to its friends in Eastern Europe.

Harriman had become the most important adviser on the matter of a loan to Russia, and since he also advocated a stern political line toward the U.S.S.R. he meshed the policies into a unified approach. On April 11 he reported to Washington on Stalin's revelation that Russia planned to triple its prewar steel output within fifteen years, and that they had geared their request for a loan to this ambitious undertaking. By this stage of the war there was hardly anyone in Washington who felt that it was to American interests to see a strong Russia emerge from the war, and the idea of aiding it to do so was not at all attractive. Harriman opposed granting the Russian request, and thought "our basic interests might better be served by increasing our trade with other parts of the world," especially Western Europe.[28] Yet to refuse definitely to make a loan would sacrifice an important bait for Soviet acquiescence to American policies. Under no circumstance, Harriman advised, should the United States grant loans "without retaining to ourselves the power to restrict or reduce them as we see fit . . . bearing in mind our changing economic and political interests." If under improbable circumstances the United States granted a loan, Russian good behavior should be the price of its continuation. Best of all, Harriman thought, was a policy of feigning interest in granting a loan "dependent upon a reciprocal cooperative attitude of the Soviet Government in other matters."[29]

When the United States cut off Lend-Lease, and then restored it at a much lower level in May, all of the key leaders in Washington understood that they were applying economic tools for political ends, much as Harriman had urged for some months. Since nothing in the larger political relations with the U.S.S.R. justified a revision of this policy in Washington's eyes, in thinking of future wartime economic relations with the Russians it essentially had to determine what the Russians might first be willing to give in return for later aid. On an economic level this meant, prior to Potsdam, "Russian commercial policy questions, particularly such matters as export dumping, barter, restrictive bilateral agreements, and the use of the Russian foreign trade monopoly to obtain political objectives."[30] Tangibly, this included Russian, but especially Eastern European, participation in all-European economic bodies, especially coal and transport, the reintegration of Eastern European resources into the continental economy, and the United States' equal access to Eastern European trade and materials. These were essentially political questions involving the future of Eastern Europe, on which the Russians were not inclined to concede more than was imperative. They did not hesitate to reveal informally to American economic experts in the summer of 1945 that the principles of Article VII were not compatible with socialism or industrialization, and that they thought the United States understood this. When in August the Russians asked for a $1-billion loan they probably had no illusions about their chances or the ideological price involved. For its part the United States solved the problem by later claiming to have misfiled and lost the request, only belatedly to rediscover it in February 1946 after the Russians revealed that the United States had utterly ignored the application.

Because of the dismal loan prospect and their dire economic need, the Russians at the end of July also asked UNRRA for $700 million aid, and since that organization's charter required it to make grants according to need, and the United States could not exclusively decide the matter, the issue became uncontrollable. Grew attempted to get the Russians to withdraw the request, and Harriman pointed out the aid would only permit the Russians to maintain their army—and postpone meeting American terms in Eastern Europe. But the Canadian government insisted that UNRRA could not reject the Russian application without endangering Canada's future contributions, and Winant reminded Washington that Russia was fully qualified to receive aid under the terms of UNRRA. In the end a compromise was reached when UNRRA, over quiet American opposition, gave $250 million to the devastated regions of Byelorussia and the Ukraine.[31]

In fact, of course, any aid to the U.S.S.R. was incompatible with the now basic goal of strengthening world capitalism and the American position within it against the threat of socialism and the U.S.S.R. No one had any illusions about this objective, and by the end of the war the United States understood very clearly the relationship of functional and immediate economic policy to the attainment of a world order compatible with American war aims. It might apply that principle in various ways at different times, depending on the immediate exigencies and often at great temporary sacrifice and cost, but the Americans never forgot the reasons for it. After they had reconstructed and stabilized world capitalism, both politically and economically, the wartime leaders in Washington intended to create an international order modeled after the American dream dating back to Woodrow Wilson and amplified by Cordell Hull. In the meantime there would be twists and turns in a world the most destructive war in history had ripped apart, but ultimately they hoped to realize their final goal.

The assumptions of this policy were relatively optimistic, and have yet to prove justified. For when not just Bolshevism but also socialism and rapid industrialization in the context of national economic control became the enemy, the United States undertook to set its face against the universal trends in the world in the hope that its economic and political resources would be equal to the task. It would have to reconstruct not just the areas where the Left and Communists were triumphing daily, but the entire British Empire and capitalist Europe as well. By mid-1945 most key leaders in Washington fully understood the extent and consequences of this assumption and had already laid down the basis for America's postwar global role.

GERMANY: REVENGE
VERSUS REINTEGRATION

I N ANALYZING its policy toward Germany after May 8, the United
States had to evaluate the political and economic costs of a program of revenge and penalties, and this in turn involved an assessment of
the connection of Germany to the direction of relations with the U.S.S.R.
and the danger of instability in Europe threatening broader American objectives. All these factors were in flux and only time might tell whether it
was wiser to wreak retribution on Germany or reintegrate it into Europe
and the world, if not an anti-Bolshevik bloc. Indecision resulted in procrastination and the formulation of a policy which appeared vacillating and
ambiguous, but nevertheless permitted the United States and England to
retain options on a permanent policy for a strong or weak Germany.
Therefore the problem of Russia and the threat of the Left were the critical
factors in planning for Germany as the war ended.

Withdrawals into Zones

During the tortured final weeks of the war with Germany, Churchill
urged Truman not to permit the withdrawal of American troops back to
the EAC-agreed-upon zones until the Allies could solve important political
and organizational problems concerning the future of Germany and Austria, and Truman responded by making withdrawal contingent on the
"Military situation."[1] As the Allies were taking the final German surrender
under what at best were clumsy circumstances, on May 4 Churchill expressed to Eden his forebodings that

> the Allies ought not to retreat from their present positions to the
> occupational line until we are satisfied about Poland, and also about

the temporary character of the Russian occupation of Germany, and the conditions to be established in the Russianized or Russian-controlled countries in the Danube valley . . . and the Balkans. . . . If they are not settled before the United States armies withdraw from Europe and the Western World folds up its war machines there are no prospects of a satisfactory solution and very little of preventing a third World War.[2]

Thus, while he sent soothing words to Stalin and celebrated the common victory, Churchill transmitted blunter messages to Truman, and on May 11 sent a copy of the above message as well in the hope that the President would share his vision of now attaining by force of arms what prior Western diplomatic and military efforts had failed to achieve. Truman, now mindful of the war in Asia, was less hysterical, and merely assured the Prime Minister that he would "stand firmly on our present announced attitude toward all the questions at issue." Yet Churchill repeated the theme in subsequent messages and reminded Truman of the dangers of "inflicting severities upon Germany, which is ruined and prostrate . . . open[ing] to the Russians in a very short time to advance if they chose to the waters of the North Sea and the Atlantic."[3] He again clearly stated the options for Germany to the leaders of the United States, and by that time the overwhelming sentiment in the British War Cabinet was for as soft a peace for Germany as was compatible with British security, the greater immediate danger being the U.S.S.R.

The first weeks of the occupation of defeated Germany reflected this British conception in the bluntest fashion possible: the deliberate continuation of the Nazi government under Doenitz and his aides at Flensburg, a government Hitler himself designated. Under the supervision of the British, Doenitz issued orders to his officers and army and served in effect as the intermediary director of state. On May 16 Eisenhower discussed the embarrassing condition with Churchill, and then reported to Truman that

> Churchill stated that the Allies should not assume full responsibility for Germany but should take measures to prevent Germany from ever being able to start another war. German problems should be handled by Germans and some of the German generals now held by us might be employed for this purpose since they would be obeyed by the German people.[4]

The following day, as adverse criticism concerning the situation began appearing in the surprised press of the world, Eisenhower sent Robert Murphy to Flensburg. Doenitz's "remarks at Flensburg," Murphy wrote later, "could be interpreted only as an offer to join us in a crusade against the Bolsheviks."[5] The entire affair was crude in the most obvious manner, and although Eisenhower had the rump government arrested on May 23, the experience reflected the state to which the former wartime alliance had fallen.

While everyone noticed Flensburg immediately, most overlooked the other aspects of Churchill's intense desire to maintain German power for possible use against the Russians. On May 17 Churchill ordered his officers not to destroy any German planes before the Cabinet had reached a decision, and ten days later discussed the use of air power for "striking at the communications of the Russian armies should they decide to advance farther than is agreed."[6] The British kept approximately 700,000 German troops in essentially military formations in their zone at this time, and they disbanded them at the end of the year only because of Russian protests. By that time Churchill's martial ardor had subsided, and a new Prime Minister had taken his place.

These were some of the moods as the West considered the formal organization of the zonal structure with the Russians during May and June, a problem doubly complicated because at the time the Russians were as anxious as they were ever going to be to reassure the West of their amicable plans for Germany. During these months the Allies had to arrange for the final details of the control machinery and access to Berlin, and also prepare for the most complex issue of withdrawals—requiring an Anglo-American retreat of as much as 120 miles out of the zone the EAC allocated to the Russians. The EAC agreement gave each nation absolute control over the affairs in their zone save "in matters affecting Germany as a whole. . . ."[7] Such a definition left a broad area in which to maneuver. Churchill had linked the withdrawal problem to the still-pending Austrian zonal agreement, and as the State Department noted, "The United States Government agreed to go along partially with this. . . ," but in fact, one must add, Churchill wanted to remain in the existing positions and he may have expected the Austrian problem to be complex enough to permit it.[8] Once committed to this formula, however, he could not easily reject it.

When Stalin saw Hopkins on May 28 he assured the American he wished the German Control Council to develop a unified policy and to operate effectively, pointing especially to the danger of the Germans playing off one side against another to their own favor. Eisenhower at the same moment felt rather more sanguine about the possibilities of cooperation with the U.S.S.R., which had been most successful on a military level, though he was by no means ready to drop his guard. As military head of the Anglo-American forces he was in a critical position to test his impulses. Moreover, at the beginning of June the Three Powers virtually solved the Austrian zonal division, save for a dispute on zoning Vienna to give the United States an acceptable airfield. By mid-June, as well, after having disapproved of the way the Russians had installed the Austrian Renner government the prior April, the State Department also admitted that it was by no means a puppet of Russia, and was probably as good a government as anyone could devise at the time. The United States then contemplated recognition and opposed reparations from Austria.

On June 5 Eisenhower, Lucius D. Clay, head of the American occupation, and Robert Murphy, his political adviser, signed a series of far-reaching Control Council agreements in Berlin creating a council that through unanimous decisions would administer Germany above the zonal level as well as oversee the administration of the Four Power "Greater Berlin" area. If the occupying powers could not reach unanimity on some problem, the commanding general in each zone would be supreme on the matter in his own area of responsibility. Despite the invidious comparisons that the Germans might make on conditions and policies in various zones, and the opportunities for exploiting inter-Allied differences to their own advantage, the essential zonal and control structure was feasible, and its ultimate failure was based on larger political, rather than organizational, considerations. In June 1945 the United States still aspired to make the structure operate for all-German questions on a unified basis, always assuming it endorsed the common policy. Washington also deemed it vital to solve other problems first, and to prevent Germany from turning too far to the left or right. The United States saw Germany as a single problem, to be run as one economic unit, and it was not yet prepared to accept the British contention that they salvage the Western zones for a Western political sphere—though Washington admitted it was a possibility later—if only because no one was yet prepared to write off the Russian zone. There was slight tangible evidence that it would be necessary to do so.

The Austrian negotiations went well, and over Churchill's opposition Truman decided to begin to withdraw troops from the Russian zone on June 21. On July 4 the Allies concluded a satisfactory treaty for the Austrian occupation along lines that the British suggested. The Berlin access agreement was hardly more difficult. The original EAC treaty on Germany stipulated Three Power control of Berlin along agreed divisions, but it did not occur to anyone to insert formal provisions for access rights through the Soviet-controlled territory to Berlin, since the accord implied this. But on June 14 Truman asked Stalin to insert a provision for free rail, air, and road access for United States forces to Berlin. The Russian did not reply, but the matter seemed quite minor to everyone at the time, and when Clay asked Marshal G. K. Zhukov, the Russian military head of Germany, about it at the end of the month he immediately assented verbally to road, rail, and air routes. No one, not even Murphy, considered the problem more than a technical one; no formal document was signed at the time, and no one even thought of official minutes, and during the first ten days of July they ironed out the key principles of access routes along with vast numbers of other administrative details. During that time the Russians established another precedent concerning Berlin which the West later found useful, one which attracted far more attention and which also reinforced their access rights and position in Berlin. Approximately half of Berlin's prewar food supply came from the Russian-controlled zone, and now the Russians claimed that the economic disintegration in their zone was too great and the West would have to supply the food and coal for their sections of Berlin. Despite Clay's irritation, the West accepted the situation, and the Russians sacrificed their potentially most powerful tool for blockading the city. "The meeting went off smoothly," Murphy reported of one such discussion in early July. "The Russian attitude was conciliatory. . . ."[9] Such thoughts as blockades were not on anyone's mind at the time, and as late as November of the same year, as the Allies were arranging the formal details of air safety and access agreements for Western flights into Berlin, Clay and Murphy grandly consented to have Soviet military aircraft land on Western fields.[10]

On an organizational level, therefore, the first phases of Four Power control of Germany had gone all too easily, despite petty personal irritations and discomforts for the individuals assigned the tasks of administration. For the problem of Germany was never one of organization, and the men in the field were never more or less than the handmaidens of political policies determined with all of Europe in focus.

The Problem of the Left in Germany

The German masses had been either quiescent or patriotic throughout most of Hitler's terrorist rule, and if ever proof were needed for the proposition that even the most compromised, repressed, or manipulated of men can be galvanized into action for a new political course, Germany in the spring of 1945 serves that purpose well enough. Now, in rhythm with a Europe that wanted an end to war and capitalism, a significant group of the German working class joined the world-wide movement toward the left.

The Free Germany Committee in Russia had scored some measure of success among ordinary German soldiers, and the Russians permitted German Communist party refugees to prepare for a return in the wake of Russian troops. The Communist Resistance in Germany itself did very little throughout the war, though they did manage for a brief moment to make contact with a few of the plotters against Hitler's life. The German radicals educated on the anvil of wartime tragedy were neither organized nor disciplined, but they were deeply committed to a far more libertarian view of the Left than was compatible with Bolshevism. They descended,for the most part, not from Lenin and Stalin nor Kautsky and Bernstein, but from the tradition and mood of Luxemburg and the early Spartacists. As the Nazi machine collapsed and their troops surrendered and were defeated, the German antifascists moved to fill the vacuum.

Everywhere the Allied troops entered they found local Left committees—some called ANTIFA groups, many without names—running factories and municipalities which the owners and masters had deserted, via spontaneously created shop committees and councils. Some were old Socialists and Communists, many were new converts, but everywhere they moved to liberate concentration-camp prisoners, organize food supplies, and eradicate the Old Order. For the most part they scoffed at regular party doctrine and talked vaguely of new forms based on a united Left unlike that which had helped to open the door to Hitler. In the euphoria of liberation they talked of the unity of the proletariat, and even an old Social Democratic leader such as Kurt Schumacher could embrace the concept of the workers' revolution even if he could not allocate the Communists a share in it.

The Communists had to find a way of incorporating this new mood, for since 1941 they based their line both inside and outside Germany on a United Front strategy and the advocacy of parliamentarianism and civil liberties, making them the most conservative element of the Left. Insofar as there was a nonmilitary Resistance in Germany before 1945, the Communists were the strongest element in it, but in the spring of 1945 they were being swept along with a naturally radical stream that far exceeded their strength. The Communists and Social Democrats were the first to organize parties in all the zones, parties parallel to the ANTIFA committees, overlapping, but also in tension with them in terms of the basic assumptions and tactics of social change implicit in each. The dichotomy between direct action and legal reform was still dormant in the first days of freedom, but soon emerged in the conflict between newcomers anxious to cleanse Germany quickly of all vestiges of Nazism, and the society that created it, and the party regulars.

As the German Communist refugees arrived in the wake of the Russian forces they found local administrations largely in the hands of such indigenous committees, the leadership of which also often identified as new or old Communists. Some refugees found the new reality moving, even beautiful, and full of promise. But to the more bureaucratic party regulars, moving more and more to the fore of both the German Social Democrats (SPD) and Communists (KPD) as the weeks passed, and to the Russian and Anglo-American military, the local radicals were troublesome. The Russians believed in a United Front with the prewar bourgeoisie as a mechanical proposition, and their military administrators quickly shocked the new Left by removing them from numerous offices and arbitrarily appointing unknown and hitherto uncommitted bourgeois. After a brief period of giving their sex-starved troops freedom to rape and steal at will—denied to them across Poland—the Russian leaders in mid-April carefully and publicly differentiated between Nazis and Germans, a distinction they had not made earlier, and laid the basis for broad cooperation with most non-Nazi elements in Germany. Walter Ulbricht, the head of the German Communists, quickly moved to have the spontaneous organizations dissolved as illegal bodies, or assimilated and made harmless, and it soon became apparent that the German Communists would accept only a United Front from above and on their own terms.

In the very first months the Communists issued a program the party militants thought surprisingly reformist in its failure to mention Marx and in its recognition of private enterprise in the future. They strongly discouraged singing the "Internationale" or using "sectarian" phrases. When local KPD and SPD groups moved toward organic unity the Ulbricht faction, which served merely as a tool of Russian desires, stopped them. All parties in the Soviet zone, from the Liberal Democrats to the Communists, were free to take a nationalist posture and openly refuse to accept the Oder-Neisse frontier. After June 10 the Russians permitted other parties to form in their zone, and allowed trade unions to flourish, though not to strike. The unions often used the now-controlled organizations that the spontaneous workers' committees initially created, but the Soviets discouraged the smaller independent left parties that favored unity. In the mood of bewilderment and alienation that set in, the older SPD and KPD leaders began braking the more dynamic younger elements in the parties and trade unions, and it was the Social Democrats that emerged as the most important party in the Russian zone. The Russians had decided that there would either be a United Front from above or a return to the politics of Weimar.[11] In Germany, as everywhere else, conservatism was the hallmark of Russian policy.

The Russians could handle and redirect this radical political development because of their access to the German Communist party, and because their position on a transformation of the German social order was flexible rather than doctrinaire, but the Americans and British found all such trends frightful and potentially beyond control, for they had studied the development of the KPD and the German Resistance throughout the war and American OSS analysts had predicted trouble. And although in their wartime planning for Germany the Americans had assumed the existence of some form of German government at the end of the war, and even the Morgenthau plan posited it, Anglo-American armies immediately administered their zones at every level as much to keep the Left as the Nazis from power. In the first months of the occupation of Germany, therefore, such alarm led to far more political and civil liberty in the Soviet zone than in the West, and made organic zonal unity impossible. As usual, military occupation became the Anglo-American justification for redeeming the Old Order wherever they sent their troops.

The Americans and English dissolved the ANTIFA committees and workers' councils wherever they found them directing the affairs in their zones. Churchill for a time, during the most anxious month of May, was convinced that Russian parachutists were responsible for the Communist activities in his zone, and Montgomery shared his less paranoid fears on the subject. Throughout the Western zones the trade unions were either abolished or left entirely powerless, and their growth was far smaller than in the East. Here too, however, the militant leftists of the KPD and SPD were in tight control of the leadership of the working class, their future dependent not only on what the conquerors would permit them to do, but also on how they defined their relations to each other. In the Western zones the military occupation until July carefully restricted all printed matter to whatever it chose to release, but then began to license politically acceptable newspapers.

For the Americans the problem of the German Left was imposed on the larger context of the power of the Left throughout Europe, and these analyses often went hand in hand. They fully understood the strength of the Left in the Russian zone, and the invidious comparison between the relative freedom there and the total ban imposed on political activity in the West they immediately regarded as dangerous. "Any or most political groups we permit to organize in near future seem likely to become anti-American-Military Government. . . ," Murphy saw the dilemma at the end of June; but if the ban continued the Nazis and Communists would be the most adept in organizing an underground. In any event he saw the United Front tactics of the KPD merely as a preliminary to a "one party totalitarian political system of type already established in eastern Europe and Balkans." The result, Murphy predicted, would be that the Western political ban would permit German political activity to exist only under Russian auspices, which "will tend to overflow into our Zone, and when we finally raise the present ban . . . Communists may profit from a considerable head start. . . ."[12] Despite the prohibition, by early July, Clay had to admit that a hothouse of leftist parties and groups were functioning underground in the Western zones. Had the West permitted these groups to take action, it is likely that many Nazis would have been shot or imprisoned immediately.

Despite the fact that Washington vacillated on the future of German civil liberties, the purpose of the ban on the Left was explicable, for implicit in American policy was the assumption that the immediate, spontaneous destruction of the Old Order in Germany was less desirable than its continuation. At least the United States would retain the option of keeping the Old Order intact a while longer. The role of the individual in Germany could not be separated from the social structure in which he was compelled to exist and survive, and this was the gist of the recommendation an outside group of liberal academics asked to advise on future Germany policy gave to the State and War departments. ". . . the Germans themselves," the experts told them, "will attempt to carry through this change in a democratic direction, and . . . the occupation authorities should encourage these efforts." Washington ignored the advice. Perceptibly, the Americans played down the question of the social structure during the first months of occupation to stress "the mind of an individual or the mind of a nation," as if such "minds" could be reified like some racial concept divorced from environment. The way was open for the theme of "reeducation." "It is reeducation by the use of every means which can produce the change in German thinking . . . beliefs . . . psychology . . . character which we desire. . . . The Russians have no difficulty on this point. They propose to substitute Communism for Nazism." "We must be ready and willing to propagate ideas of liberty and justice and human dignity," concepts the State Department granted were difficult to translate into specific policies.[18] In the meantime the Left was growing in the East, struggling to do so in the West, and a program of reeducation would serve also as a sufficient basis of control until the Anglo-Americans might reach some more specific decisions.

JCS 1067—Again

By the time the war with Germany had ended, the official planning policy for control of the nation was still mired in conflict, but now the military and War Department moved to protect their interest in the problem against encroachment by the State Department. The State Department saw Germany essentially as a larger question of diplomacy, the military as a prospective administrative burden to be run as efficiently as was consistent with very minimal political objectives—and they put their emphasis on efficiency.

After the Yalta Conference the State Department decided that it required a more specific occupational policy for Germany than the amorphous JCS 1067, and it operated on the explicit premise that it now had exclusive responsibility from Roosevelt for such matters as postwar Germany and implementation of the Yalta decisions. Since November, Roosevelt, after his embarrassing affair over the Morgenthau plan, relied on the State Department for guidance on the issue, and on February 28 he reiterated its exclusive jurisdiction over the issue. As the unfortunate Stettinius and Grew soon discovered, apparently he had not told the other Cabinet members of his decision. The State Department based its new plan on the assumption that JCS 1067 erred in not giving the occupation complete authority to fix specific goals for the German economy and to establish the means to implement them. The EAC agreement to run Germany as an integrated unit, where possible, it only vaguely incorporated into its proposals, and it placed much less emphasis on reduction of German industrial power and much more on preventing economic chaos that would impede German and European economic recovery. It only partially heeded Winant's warning that downgrading Four Power cooperation would lead to the establishment of total Russian control in their zone.

Roosevelt approved the document on March 12, Stimson and Morgenthau resisted, and Roosevelt quickly withdrew his endorsement. Stimson and the War Department did not want unified control of Germany, and for administrative reasons preferred leaving maximum power with the American military government. Morgenthau wished minimum economic controls, which he felt would lead to drastic disorganization and an economic weakening of Germany. It was a measure of Morgenthau's increasing unimportance that no one told him of the critical details of the Yalta decision on Germany until mid-March, and all he could do in 1945 was to reinforce Stimson's desire for maximum zonal independence and the State Department's belief in minimum reparations. He regarded reparations, in particular, as a danger to the Bretton Woods agreement and to the establishment of a permanently weak German state. To the State Department, unnecessary weakening of the German and European economy via dismantling for reparations, or shipping goods toward the East, also coincided with a program of minimum reparations to the U.S.S.R. It still regarded the amount of the reparations to be extracted from Germany as an entirely open question, though it considered $20 billion to be much too high. Yet the vacillations in policy at this time reflected Roosevelt's increasing tendency to forget his commitments to various positions, and they should not be allowed to obscure the more significant fact of growing consensus in Washington on the topics of reparations and maximum zonal autonomy. After several months of additional haggling, during which time these men formulated a common policy, on May 10 Truman finally approved the seventh draft of JCS 1067 and kept it secret until October 1945.

In March the War Department appointed a top-flight military engineer, Major General Lucius D. Clay, to serve as its Chief of Military Government, and designated Robert Murphy to serve as both his and Eisenhower's political adviser. By instinct Clay liked to make things run, and the gist of discussions over JCS 1067 emphasized the critical role of diplomacy in working with three other nations, and in this area Clay had neither experience nor competence. For political and administrative reasons he was disinclined to side with Morgenthau on economic questions, and insofar as JCS 1067 was discretionary Clay could fill in many of its vital details over the next three years. Byrnes, now very close to Roosevelt, chose Clay for the task although he could not even speak German. The choice was both significant and deliberate, because it cut through much of the theoretical quibbling of the prior two years.

JCS 1067 was an open-ended document. Although it indicated "The principal Allied objective is to prevent Germany from ever again becoming a threat to the peace of the world," its economic provisions were entirely discretionary, avoiding specific figures and criteria entirely. The military government could estimate the standard of living "to prevent starvation and widespread disease," and JCS 1067 left the responsibility for attaining that level, vague as it was, to no specific authority. Most significant, the industrial provisions referred only to vague output levels, but specifically to "protect[ion] from destruction by the Germans" of large industrial plants, "prohibit and prevent production" of certain basic industrial materials, but no more than freezing these facilities. "Pending agreement in the Control Council," the Four Powers could individually make a final decision on their fate, a policy both the British and the Russians strongly criticized when they learned of it early in May. In short, United States policy would suspend, not destroy, German industrial power until the Allies might agree on a common program.[14]

When the State Department considered this approach it clearly understood that German industry had a vital role to play in European economic recovery. "But to ignore the existence of seventy-five or eighty millions of vigorous and industrious people," Forrestal chimed in an observation typical among many top leaders, "or to assume that they will not join with Russia if no other outlet is afforded them I think is closing our eyes to reality."[15] Above all, since JCS 1067 was only a secret unilateral American policy, its future, unless the United States were willing to shatter Four Power control immediately, depended on a host of subtle diplomatic problems which were its absolute prerequisite. Without their resolution JCS 1067 led, as Winant had warned, toward the partition of Germany.

Clay saw the document only at the end of April, just as he was about to leave for Germany, bewildered as to his responsibilities to either the State or War departments. He recalls that he was "shocked," and his financial adviser, Lewis H. Douglas, an important financier, exclaimed "This thing was assembled by economic idiots!"[16] Clay's economic adviser, William H. Draper, Jr., of Dillon, Read & Co., one of the major investment houses in the prewar German economy, also opposed the plan. Together they made known their criticisms of the plan to Washington and left for Europe to administer it as they saw fit. Draper's aides later wrote accounts of his strong sympathies for the German businessmen who had worked with the Nazis, and who had once cooperated with his firm as well. As the official history of the United States occupation government suggests, Clay interpreted the vague JCS 1067 very much as he thought best unless Washington specifically directed him to do otherwise. Eisenhower reinforced him, for "Clay and I were convinced that the rehabilitation of the Ruhr was vital to our best interests," and they told this to Truman immediately.[17]

Certain problems, such as the dismemberment of Germany into separate states, did not bother the United States occupation authorities. The idea first came up in Roosevelt's casual talks at the great wartime conferences, and the Russians only probed the American feelings on the topic without definitely committing themselves. They were no more explicit in the brief EAC discussions, but the corollary of dismemberment was the likely creation of an autonomous Soviet zone, and this Washington would not accept. In May the Russians reiterated both publicly and privately that they were not for dismemberment, and Stalin told Hopkins that he favored the reestablishment of Germany's consumer-goods industries as well as agriculture. By the beginning of the summer of 1945 there was widespread feeling in Washington that they should avoid dismemberment of Germany, and they made some effort to distinguish it from zonal control. It was still the official United States goal to treat Germany as a single economic unit. At the same time the State Department discussed favorably the "decentralization of the political structure and . . . [t]he German economy shall also be decentralized, except . . . to the minimum extent required for . . . the Control Council. . . ." If not contradictory, neither were these two positions easily reconcilable. In fact, however, the United States based its immediate opposition to economic or political dismemberment on its belief that "Any break-up of the effective unity of Germany at the present time would mean either a poor-house standard of living in the West with Communism the probable end-result or an elaborate relief program at American and British expense." If the key objectives were to stop Communism and prevent "an economic regression, not only for Germany but also for the whole of Europe," the grounds for accepting not merely decentralization but also permanent zonal divisions existed.[18]

Indeed, the policy toward the economic recovery of Germany might also be considered in this context, and in fact the dual menaces of Communism and economic depression became in Europe the lens through which Washington might study the future of Germany. The tensions in American policy, between an all-German economy or zonal control, high or low levels of output, therefore, did not reflect organizational conflicts and confusions, but a desire to maintain clear options on the most fundamental policy questions, the relevance of which time had yet to reveal.

Reparations—First or Last?

As the Allied troops swept into Germany they brought with them their customs and their vices, with the inevitable results for a cringing and fawning German nation now beginning to proclaim itself the most sorely abused victim of the war. The black market had been a common, tolerated institution among American troops since the landing in Italy, but in Germany it became a major institution as Germans traded their personal goods and often women traded themselves to eke out an existence amid the ruins. The Russian troops also engaged in this undertaking, both stealing and spending vast quantities of backlogged wartime pay in occupation currency identical to that the Anglo-Americans used in their zones. Soon a lively three-way black-market trade between Russians, Germans, and Americans was in operation for watches, cameras, and the like. What the Russians took the Americans bought, until the spoils of war became a common enterprise. In this the Germans sold what little merchandise and honor their men and women had left. Not for the first or the last time, Americans discovered that the misery of others could afford them the pleasures and luxuries of a society built upon chocolate and cigarettes if only one were willing to deprive the Germans of what small virtue they had retained. Given the currency regulations, United States troops could redeem the currency proceeds of black-market transactions in United States dollars, and in nearly five months the American troops in the Berlin area shipped out a sum six to seven times their total pay over the same period. The ultimate German overdraft in this form cost the United States Treasury an estimated $271 million before the military stopped it. Perhaps more important, such events introduced additional paralysis into the German economy even beyond that inherent in the destruction of wartime, for despite the very heavy damage to German buildings, the war destroyed not more than one-fifth of German industrial capacity and now these factories remained unused.

If ordinary Russian and American soldiers could cooperate in a manner that introduced important new realities into the German economy, their leaders fared much worse. The Yalta Conference agreed to certain reparations principles: an abstract $20 billion reparations figure, half of which would go to Russia, and instructions for a commission that was to meet in Moscow to determine how they might take reparations from the Germans in the form of plant removals, current production, and German labor. The British did not conceal their skepticism of the undertaking, the Americans explicitly declared they had made no definite commitments, and the Russians were determined to obtain German aid for purposes of their own recovery, either through diplomacy or immediate removals. During the spring State, War, and Treasury officials hammered out a coherent policy that postulated a much lower level of reparations than $20 billion, though authoritative reports from Germany convinced American experts that Germany's ability to pay reparations was still very substantial. By the end of April no one had any doubts concerning this policy, which they could not of course reveal to the Russians. Moreover, Harriman and his aides urged Washington to link reparations to American satisfaction on broader political issues. The United States was to stress dismantling rather than payment in output over a period of years, the occupation was to levy first charge on production to meet costs for required imports and to emphasize reparations in the form of raw materials rather than manufactured goods. They would discourage reparations in the form of re-exportable goods and reparations that might make a nation permanently dependent on German imports. Within these deliberately vague limitations the United States was then ready to discuss the critical issue.

The beginning was inauspicious, for the Three Powers could not agree on membership for four months as the Russians contended Yugoslavia and Poland deserved as much representation as France, whom the Americans and British first insisted on seating; yet they eventually conceded to Anglo-American intransigence. Edwin Pauley, an important oilman active in Democratic party politics, led the American delegation, but it was not until June 21 that he was able to present formally such American thoughts on reparations as the commission deemed worth discussing. In the meantime the informal realities in Germany moved to the fore in defining the future of that nation, and private but more pressing considerations continued to shape and alter American thinking on the economic future of Germany.

As the Russian troops entered Germany a large number of economic and industrial experts, directly responsible to economic ministries in Moscow rather than the local military, soon followed them with orders to dismantle and ship needed German industry back to Russia. The French later did the same in their zone, and in both cases the result was an even greater paralysis of industrial recovery in the occupied zones. The Russians gathered large quantities of material in this form and the policy continued more or less uninterrupted throughout 1945 until the local Soviet occupation authorities managed to stop it, for it complicated their own work and the civilian economic experts eventually appreciated that plant removals—many rusted away in rail sidings—were less efficient than reparations from current output. In Washington in the two months after the surrender many government officials concluded that quite irrespective of what the Soviets had formally agreed upon, they would unilaterally proceed to remove reparations, a conclusion that Soviet action until that time had fully warranted.[19] But since the Western zones contained over two-thirds of Germany's prewar industrial capacity, the Russians still had much to gain from a unified reparations policy, and the extent of their removals before July was not so great as to seriously affect total economic resources available for reparations.

The United States always regarded the problem of reparations, which was to say the future of Germany as a power, in the much larger economic and political context of European affairs and United States economic objectives. It never opposed reparations as such, and in principle favored them, but Washington always imposed a set of higher priorities to attain before extensive reparations might be possible, priorities which in the context of the type of world that was emerging doomed to failure reparations conferences such as those taking place in Moscow. These priorities, set in the background of shifting European political and economic events, made the United States appear ambiguous in its intentions, but were in themselves basic policy commitments whose eventual implementation determined the outline of postwar United States policy in Germany.

A critical consideration was the United States' need to aid the recovery of the European economy as the indispensable prerequisite to eliminating the threat of the Left, a factor that the leaders in Washington had comprehended during earlier discussion of Germany, but was now far more pressing. The State Department especially understood that what happened in Germany might intimately affect the future of, say, France, and it debated this while considering reparations. Grew wrote Stimson on June 8:

> I am deeply concerned over conditions in Western Europe and the possibility that serious disorders may develop during the coming months. If the people of that area, particularly those in France, have to face another winter without heat or without adequate food and clothing, I can foresee disturbances of such serious consequence as not only to involve conflict with our troops, but to gravely imperil our long-term interests. The outlook is at best a gloomy one. . . .

The possibility of such outbreaks, which caused Stimson much concern as well, would presumably mean the emergence of forces friendly to the U.S.S.R. No one was inclined, therefore, to weaken Western Europe by providing Russia with German reparations. This was equally true of Germany itself, where, although the Americans wished to extirpate Nazism by reeducation and the trial of leading war criminals, or even to decentralize the large cartels, they were unwilling to allow the Left to alter the basic structure of capitalism and society. Implicit, therefore, was the proposition that a strong Western Europe would need at least important elements of German resources, a situation that would also leave Russia weaker by denying it reparations. Both the State and War departments considered this question in the context of coal output, and on June 24 Truman and Grew asked Churchill and Eisenhower to concentrate on increasing German coal output to prevent "such political and economic chaos as to prejudice the redeployment of Allied troops and to jeopardise the achievement of the restoration of economic stability which is the necessary basis for a firm and just peace." "Unhappily, the creation of economic distress in Germany is not a policy which would be chosen if our sole interest were to convert Germany to our values and our outlook," Willard Thorp, a key State Department economics planner, warned in July, and it would make the now increasingly stressed theme of "reeducation" impossible in the midst of poverty.[20]

From a political viewpoint, and from the vantage of attaining United

States economic objectives, the reparations issue assumed the form of a double bonus or a double loss. To permit the Russians to collect would also weaken Western Europe, opening it perhaps to the growth of the Left; and conversely, to limit reparations would stop the dual thrust of Bolshevism via Russia and the Communist parties.

Events were to illustrate this proposition in other ways as well. If Russia might collect extensive reparations it would only be through an economically integrated German economy, as the Control Council and zonal treaties provided. Planning for German imports and exports, the formal United States position read during June and July, would have to be for Germany as a whole. Yet Germany was divided into four zones which, willy-nilly, the local occupation authorities could most easily administer if, contrary to the requirements of a balanced economy, they could check the movement of local resources to other zones while perhaps maximizing imports from them. Given the fact that the War Department expressed an antipathy for Four Power control when the matter arose during the spring in the revision of JCS 1067, for which it and Clay had an open disrespect as well as the duty to implement, it is not surprising that their initial tendency would be toward the zonal rather than all-German economic integration and recovery. And since the United States was certain that it could only definitely control its own zone, the natural inclination was to stress zonal recovery as best it might.

Occupation directives were sufficiently vague to make the opinions of the War Department and occupation authorities decisive in this regard. Eisenhower told Truman "of my belief that we should handle the German economy, and particularly the problem of reparations, in such a way as to insure Germans an opportunity to make a living. . . ."[21] "The Germans will suffer enormously anyhow," Stimson warned Truman at the beginning of July when asking him not to unnecessarily complicate his functional administrative problems.[22] Truman was receptive to this line of thought, for he had always opposed the Morgenthau plan and at the beginning of July, when Morgenthau had insisted on going to Potsdam to continue with foreign-policy questions, Truman extracted his resignation. Therefore the men in actual charge of Germany were not inclined to do more for the success of the reparations program or the creation of a single, integrated German economy than agreement with the U.S.S.R. absolutely justified or Washington ordered.

The immediate expression of this increasingly critical attitude was the "first charge" principle for German production, as well as the desire to minimize Germany's use of reparations to establish a premium, if artificial, export position for itself in the postwar economy, especially in capital goods. And, quite legitimately, if the Big Four were to treat Germany as a single economic unit for reparations, they would have to determine both its borders and existing resources, a political and technical precondition which now made reparations an extremely complex matter. While Pauley was in Moscow arguing with the Russians over aggravating preliminary questions, American officials were considering all of these factors in Washington and ultimately had to present them to the Russians as organizational rather than policy problems.

Grew informed Pauley in mid-May that the United States would oppose reparations in the form of compulsory labor save for judicially convicted war criminals. No later than the end of June the State Department decided American policy would now discard, once and for all, wartime consideration of the Four Power internationalization of the Ruhr. The reasons for this decision revealed the basic framework within which the United States would consider reparations and German policy. For one thing it would create "an extension of Soviet power and influence into the heart of Western Europe. . . ." For another, "Without the Ruhr's production of legitimate peacetime goods the German economy would be gravely impaired and . . . the national life could be put on a functioning basis only through the reintroduction of some form of autarchy, a development which it is to our national interest to forestall." While such a policy was also intended to bring Germany "through economic reform into freer and closer relations with European and world economy," a prime objective of American policy for every nation, it also meant that the West would retain for itself the industrial sector of Germany best able to provide reparations.[23] In brief, unless the Americans could receive satisfaction on numerous other counts, the Russians would not be able to collect reparations of the magnitude abstractly discussed at Yalta.

The key to the basic definition of the problem of Germany therefore rested with Western initiative. Perhaps for this reason the Russians took some pains to cooperate in creating Four Power control machinery for Germany that the United States at least was still reluctant to embrace as a basic mode of control for all of Germany. Since successful Four Power economic control meant control of the Ruhr as well, if only via the Control Council, the Western desire to isolate Russia from Western Europe might also be attained in permanent zonal divisions. And if any aspect of economic collaboration with the U.S.S.R. undermined larger United States economic objectives or opened the door to the Left, then Great Power competition might replace cooperation. The Americans considered and understood all of these dimensions.

While haggling with the Russians about the membership of the Reparations Commission, Pauley himself provided direction to the debate which further reveals the objectives behind the American policy. Pauley informed Stettinius that he was skeptical of $20 billion as a basis of reparations, and was instead concentrating on the definitions which would be percentages of things, as yet undetermined in value or amounts, rather than figures. He proposed dividing "whatever reparations may become available" in the form of 55 percent to Russia and the remainder equally shared by Britain and the United States, presumably each power to distribute as it saw fit. This arrangement prejudged none of the basic policy issues involving the size of reparations, and from the inception shifted the question to a technical level that the Americans intended to conceal critical policy reservations. These technical questions were quite crucial, but even had the reparations conference solved them—and it did not—the policy conflict would have spelled the long-term postponement, if not defeat, of a decision to permit the U.S.S.R. to extract large-scale reparations from the Western zones of Germany, and the United States understood this as well. Pauley's instructions were such that the State Department asked him to conclude an agreement that eliminated Germany's war-making capacity, while stressing that the agreement should also aid European recovery without fostering "dependence of other countries upon the German economy," a vague relationship which offered no specific guidance.[24] During the first two weeks of July, preparatory to the Potsdam Conference, American officials gave form to the meaning of this ambiguous combination.

First, the American delegation in Moscow told the Russians it would be necessary to take a physical inventory of German industrial and economic resources in order to determine what was available for reparations, especially in light of ongoing Soviet removals of war booty, though one must add that Russian removals were still a small fraction of existing German resources, most of which were in the Western zones. Then after much discussion the Americans told the Russians that they would first charge to the German economy occupation costs and the expense of essential imports before paying any reparations, a point that the Russians stoutly resisted.[25] Pauley explained that this new principle would not compel the United States to finance reparations indirectly by supplying relief to the German people. And implicit in this policy was the assumption that the prevention of the impoverishment of the German people, with a concomitant threat of a movement toward the left and fundamental changes in the social structure, was more important than Russian recovery; and these conditions in turn suggested that if no one could hold the Americans or Germans responsible for the costs of reconstruction after the war, the Russians could foot their own bill. Lastly, the American delegation in Moscow understood that until the Allies settled German territorial issues, and in particular the Oder-Neisse boundary with Poland, there could be no final basis for determining exact reparations. The issue of German land to the east of the Oder-Neisse, which Poland then administered, conveniently created for the Americans a somewhat larger problem than the primarily agricultural nature of the region actually justified.

All of these complexities made progress in Moscow impossible, even on a technical level, and all that the delegates agreed upon was a division of the as yet undetermined final figure on a ratio of 56–22–22, with the pious hope that the meeting at Potsdam might throw more light on the many issues, political as well as technical, that they had yet to solve. Yet before their departure for Potsdam, Grew made it plain to Pauley that all other issues aside, $20 billion was now excessive by at least $6 to $8 billion, and perhaps even more, and while Stimson avoided an official declaration to the State Department, he urged Truman to play down reparations for the many reasons already discussed.

The State Department, in perhaps the understatement of the period, concluded on July 12 that "There are indications that common agreement as to the American purpose in the occupation of Germany does not exist."[26] The American reparations experts who, bewildered about their functions, began arriving in a devastated Berlin that month, were utterly uncertain whether they were carpetbaggers, penalizers, or aides to the reconstruction of German power.[27] What was important about this seeming confusion was that the ambiguity was really over clear policies and clear alternatives, so deep and fundamental that they raised essential questions about the very purpose of World War II. They were the same critical propositions that came up in Washington and London as early as the summer of 1944, and on the existence of which Hitler and his generals had based their last desperate strategy. Would Germany be weak or strong, a barrier to Soviet power as part of a reformed, denazified, anti-Bolshevik alliance, hopefully integrated into a United States-led renovated liberal world economy, or a neutral area of cooperation between the West and Russia? Until the United States could definitely resolve that question there was no hope of solving the dilemma of Germany via commissions of experts.

The United States did not regard its reparations posture, JCS 1067, and the like as final policies, but rather as a postponement of a policy until it could better evaluate the larger direction of international and European affairs. In the meantime Americans in Germany, essentially hostile to collaboration with the U.S.S.R., made day-to-day policy—and with minimal reference to JCS 1067. The Americans would not destroy German power further but only suspend it, and they were clearly aware that they might later reintegrate and reemploy it to advance their own basic objectives in Europe and the world.

THE FAR EAST AFTER
YALTA: THE DILEMMA OF
CHINA AND THE FUTURE
OF JAPAN

B Y EARLY 1945 it was obvious to the Allies and to the Communists and Kuomintang that the United States had become the arbiter of the future of China. When Mao Tse-tung and his aides spoke to the leaders of the Kuomintang they knew that indirectly they were addressing themselves to the representatives of the United States in China, in the hope that they might convince them of what was beyond negotiation among the Chinese. At the same time, aware of the limits as well as the possibilities of American policy, Chiang saw Russia as the key to his future relations with the Communists. The prolonged negotiations between the Communists and Kuomintang, which never bore fruit, nor even ultimately served as a substitute for civil war, increasingly became a tangential factor in the future of China.

After some ambivalence and exploring the possibilities of working with the Communists, the United States by early 1945 determined that to sustain the Kuomintang government, that being the only option, was the basic objective of its policy throughout these interminable debates. Reaching this position had been painful for the head of the American forces in China, General Albert Wedemeyer, and for Roosevelt's political representative, Patrick J. Hurley. Chiang would not fight the Japanese, his regime was entirely corrupt, and the Communists not only accepted Hurley's program for the solution of China's political problems, but also agreed to place their troops, the only Chinese with military potential, under American command. At first with a heavy heart, but later with much passion as extraneous personal factors intruded, Hurley decided that the United States must support Chiang come what may, and permit him to define the limits of American diplomacy vis-à-vis the Chinese Communists. Yet despite this difficult choice, neither Hurley nor Wedemeyer throughout the remainder of the war, and despite several successful defensive Kuomintang actions, ever altered the extremely low esteem in which they held the military value of the non-Communist Chinese forces under Chiang and his associated war lords. Washington looked forward to the day the Soviet Red Army would drive the Japanese from China.

The American Policy in China after Yalta

It was during January that both Hurley and the State Department had formally settled that the continuation of Chiang in power was still the prime objective in China, and that any aid to the Communists would have to be through the Kuomintang and with its agreement. They also decided, while hedging their own military commitment, to try to mediate political unity and reform in China. To many Foreign Service and other officials working in China this policy was sound as a long-term goal, but they were also convinced the Kuomintang would neither change nor concede anything as long as it was convinced United States support would be forthcoming no matter what it did. Stilwell had made this point earlier, and the facts seemed to sustain it as Chiang's demands on the Communists increased. Individual officials serving in China had already sent such observations to Washington in January, but on February 14 Service and Raymond P. Ludden, representing a larger group in Chungking, communicated their recommendations directly to the State Department without Hurley's knowledge. On the 26th George Atcheson, the chargé in Chungking, sent a similar dispatch. Service, Ludden, and Atcheson also advocated giving arms to the Communists, who were likely to win without them and, implicitly, might also be converted to greater friendship for the United States rather than Russia. They all urged Washington to inform Chiang of this basic alteration in policy, and expected him to change with it.[1]

While there was nothing new in these observations and advice, the fact that his subordinates had circumvented Hurley was a breach in protocol. On February 15 Hurley called a press conference, publicly reiterated his unwavering support for Chiang, and notified the world he had compelled his entire staff to read a statement of his policy and sign a notice that they understood it. Perhaps with the knowledge of those in Chungking, the State and War departments during those very weeks were engrossed in formulating a policy on how to balance American support for Chiang against the military needs of fighting a war, and Grew recommended to Roosevelt that he favorably consider the views of Service and his circle. The reconciliation of these impulses was tortuous. The long-term American objective was to help develop "a united, democratically progressive, and cooperative China."[2] Chiang did not necessarily have to be its leader. It was politically impossible to arm the Communists, though this might later prove necessary should they have to increase the anticipated, hopefully low, American troop commitment in China and the Russians not enter the war. But beyond not giving aid to the Communists the American military believed that arms to the Kuomintang now had no real military advantage, and might even be reduced. The recommended policy coincided rather closely with the advice of Service, Atcheson, Ludden, and their friends. The State and War departments favorably considered, rather than accepted, the paper, for as we shall see, they were not overly friendly or optimistic about a powerful China in any event. When the piqued Hurley arrived in Washington at the beginning of March he had little difficulty persuading Roosevelt, with whom he was personally close, to reject the new policy direction that Hurley's staff and the State and War departments implied, however dimly. Moreover, he convinced Roosevelt to remove the dissenters from China, and henceforth his domination and ego were left unchallenged, with his influence on Wedemeyer growing after the general's more critical and sophisticated political officers were also in effect fired.

In this stormy context Hurley undertook to bring the Kuomintang and Communists together via negotiations and mediation, despite Chiang's full knowledge that there was no penalty in being obdurate and Hurley's virtual admission of that fact at his February 15 press conference. Also during this period Americans in Chungking reported that Hurley was now very friendly with T. V. Soong, whom they regarded as the most corrupt of the Chiang clique, and that Hurley had even shown Soong some of Service's policy memos. Among his staff, most of whom had more experience and competence, no pejorative was strong enough to describe Hurley, and they were convinced both sides in China saw through him and regarded the negotiations as farcical. It was apparent to most of them that Chiang was not going to give up one-party personal rule, and that Hurley would and could do nothing to alter the Chinese leader's dependence on ultimate salvation by American or Russian intervention.

The Communists originally accepted the five-point program Hurley drafted with Mao in November, and Chiang rejected it. Chiang's almost constant position was that the Communists should disarm and hand over their territory to his control, and the vague nature of the Kuomintang proposals to the Communists at the end of January, when talks resumed, left no doubt that Chiang was not ready to alter this stand. During these talks the Kuomintang further convinced Hurley that all the Communists

wished to do was to overthrow Nationalist rule rather than institute democratic collaboration. On February 20, several days after talks in Chungking
had adjourned and Chiang had advanced a vague, cynical plan for a Political Consultation Conference which he soon made plain would not require
him to relinquish power for an indefinite time to come, Hurley addressed a
sharp letter to Chou En-lai in response to his request to send a large
contingent as part of the Chinese delegation to the San Francisco Conference. "The Communist Party of China is not a nation. . . . It is one of the
political parties of China. The only difference from the ordinary political
party is that it is armed." He urged them to "unite with, be included in and
cooperate under the National Government in China."[3] This estimate egre-
giously ignored reality, for at the time the Communists controlled an area
at least as large as that under the full control of Chiang, and the war lords
and Japanese dominated the rest. The fiction of China as a state, with
Chiang as its leader, avoided unpleasant realities, but also made negotiations impossible for the remainder of the American presence there. By mid-
March talks broke off again after the Communists rejected Chiang's patently lopsided proposal for a future National Congress, to begin its vague
consultations the following November, with the Communists to give up
their arms and lands before receiving any binding guarantees.

The question of negotiations between the Kuomintang and the Communists is far less consequential than the premises of the United States as
mediator and the reasons the Communists tolerated the obviously fruitless
jockeying. Communist persistence in sharing the ludicrous assumptions of
the game, and their far greater degree of flexibility and compromise, reflected the fact that they understood the negotiations were not really with
the Kuomintang but with the United States, for the Communists considered
the United States to be the key to the problem of China. In their own
way the Kuomintang had the same view, ignoring the suspicion among
some in the American embassy that Chiang wished a conflict between the
United States and Russia to liberate China from the Communists. Having
won the Americans to his side, Chiang hoped to gain the support of the
U.S.S.R. as well—and to isolate Mao.

It was apparent no later than December—when the Communists
agreed to American military proposals, Chiang vetoed them, and the Communists invited direct collaboration—that Mao was determined to gain
American support, even to the extent of offering to visit Roosevelt in
person. The following January, General Chu Teh, one of the leading Communist military figures, requested a $20-million loan, and it was this se-
quence of beckoning gestures that caused the Foreign Service officers and
the OSS to consider direct lines with the Communists. For this reason, as
well, the Communists wished to win international recognition by obtaining
as large a place as possible on the Chinese delegation to the founding

conference of the United Nations, but only succeeded in getting one representative. The course of negotiations with the Kuomintang proved stormy, Mao told the Communist National Congress late that April, and a one-party dictatorship might continue, with the possible threat of civil war, but the "international and domestic state of affairs"—always in that order—opened up the possibility of a democratic, reformed China.[4] Mao could therefore endorse the creation of a United Nations and proudly cite the party's participation in its founding. Given his realistic assessment of Chiang and the KMT over the prior two years, there is no question that Mao believed only the Great Powers might give China direction leading to unity and democracy.

Once they chose to do so, Mao's program guaranteed full Communist cooperation on the basis of equality, and it is important to note that only the Communists had an ideological rationale for participating in political discussions such as those the Americans said they proposed without preconditions. In his famous April statement "On Coalition Government," Mao reiterated the United Front assumptions of his party's strategy throughout the war. Neither the dictatorship of the Kuomintang nor the creation of a socialist state was possible, for socialism was a maximum program and not appropriate to the moment. "It is not domestic capitalism but foreign imperialism and domestic feudalism which are superfluous in China today; indeed, we have too little of capitalism." Mao desired a democratic coalition of all parties and elements, formed initially around the need for unity against Japan, which meant the abolition of one-party dictatorship. Such "a united-front democratic alliance based on the overwhelming majority of the people, under the leadership of the working class," was admittedly vague, but to such a proposition Mao was prepared to sacrifice the identity of the Communist armies. The Communists tasted Chiang's concept of freedom, Mao bitterly recalled in describing the massacres of 1927: "The moment a new-democratic coalition government comes into being in China, the Liberated Areas of China will hand their armed forces over to it. But all the Kuomintang armed forces will have to be handed over to it at the same time."[5] No one ever tested the offer nor explored its truth or falsity and real intentions.

Paying for China

During the hiatus in mediation, and while Hurley was off to Moscow for infinitely more important negotiations than those possible in Chungking —of which I will say more later—Washington further tried to hedge against the losses it anticipated from its hopeless policy. The war in China never went well, even as the Japanese suffered defeats everywhere else and fell short of supplies, and the expense of the war to the United States mounted even higher amidst the deepening chaos in the Chinese economy. Given the inflation and exchange rates, at the beginning of 1945 the Americans estimated that it cost them over $1 per mile to supply fuel for an automobile, and the black-market activities of the United States troops in China became so extensive that in early 1945 a former chief of the Service of Supply was arrested for having increased his personal assets by $230,000 while on duty in China. Worst of all for the American government was the activity of the Kuomintang itself.

In February, Washington discovered that H. H. Kung and T. V. Soong, well-known as the largest speculators in China with American funds, wished to obtain the outstanding balance of the $500-million "loan" of 1942 to buy gold and cotton textiles. They ostensibly justified the request as a means to combat inflation, but the economic analysts in the Chungking embassy and the Treasury believed their proposals had no economic value. While Washington gave formal consideration to these requests, at the end of April the State Department summarized its policy toward China for the guidance of the new President. The United States would continue to support Chiang, for he still "offers the best hope for unification and for avoidance of chaos in China's war effort," but if "the possible disintegration of the authority of the existing government" occurred, the long-term interests of the United States in China warranted "flexibility to permit cooperation with any other leadership in China which may give greater promise. . . ." In regard to postwar military assistance, Washington decided in April that none would be forthcoming "until we are convinced that that government is making progress toward achieving unity and toward gaining the solid support of the Chinese people."[6] For the moment, the written position was again reticent.

What such hesitancy before the facts would mean to United States policy arose within several weeks, for Soong was in the country and on April 19 told Truman that he wished to use $200 million from his 1942 loan to buy gold to send to China. The Treasury staff soon produced statistics to prove that there was no relationship between the sale of gold in China and inflation—in fact such a sale would probably aggravate prices—and they recommended in effect that the United States ask the Chinese to leave the money in the United States, and add enough from their vast dollar holdings to create a reconstruction fund of $500 million. The staff also drew up a list of how Soong and his family and friends used earlier official loans for their private purposes, and Morgenthau planned to give it to Soong himself along with a refusal. However, two factors—politics and cotton—greatly complicated the problem of the gold. Everyone knew of the corruption of China, but in light of their final decision to maintain the Chiang government, it was not easy to justify new standards at that late date. Moreover, the Chiang circle could use cotton no less than gold to fill their pockets, and William Clayton, Assistant Secretary of State, in line with a policy he consistently applied while in that office, wished the government to grant cotton-textile loans. The policy would have to be uniform, and Clayton was for cotton, and quite apart from this, Washington was for Chiang. Morgenthau hesitated, then on May 8 suggested a $500 million currency stabilization plan to Soong without actually precluding the $200 million balance of the 1942 loan or cotton. He also complained about the use of earlier loans. Soong took the proposal, referred to China as "a volcano which may erupt any moment," hoping the Americans would consider the political options before making a firm negative decision. The following day the men met again and both were more candid. Morgenthau frankly reported the use Soong's family had made of the earlier part of the loan, and after Soong feigned surprise the Secretary told him, "I hope I will not be called before Congress to have to explain."[7] Soong then bluntly reminded Morgenthau that failure to give him the promised loan might weaken him, perhaps fatally, in his forthcoming talks with Molotov.

Morgenthau was not moved, for his staff had told him that the use of American funds in China might become a public scandal in Congress, as it already was in China. For the moment he stood firm. Morgenthau also was ready to present the matter to Truman for a decision, given the split between the Treasury and State departments, and since Soong on May 14 promised the President that the KMT would manage the remainder of the loan to exclude the possibility of future reproach, the mood began to turn in Chiang's favor. The justification for the loan was not economic, Harry Dexter White reminded Morgenthau—"it was going down the drain"—but political. ". . . we do want to maintain this particular government," Emilio Collado, Clayton's aide, reported on the sentiment in the State Department. "We don't want to have all the collapse that would be incident to the fall of that government." On the basis of Soong's promise to Truman of future good conduct, the Treasury withdrew its opposition to the release of the funds and Morgenthau merely informed Soong that fulfillment of the pledge would determine future American aid. Soong was happy, but not fully contrite, and added for Morgenthau's information that while he might have some criticisms of the disposal of past loans, "I did not say that we wholly disapprove."[8] He had ample reason not to berate the use of the money.

The political extenuation for continuing American aid to Chiang prevailed at a very high cost; Soong was happy, and Clayton was delighted to see American cotton textiles going to China. Hurley, irritated that no one had consulted him, thought the money would do no good in any form: ". . . until there is a radical change in the present policy little can be expected."[9] He predicted more speculation and inflation as a result of the Kuomintang's policies, and although Soong appeared to be on good behavior for about a month, during June, shortly after his return to Chungking, he again modified the gold policy in a manner permitting insider profits on gold sales and ever higher inflation.[10]

The End of Communist Patience with the United States

It was now apparent to all that the Americans would not penalize Chiang for his policies, even though he asked them to pay him handsomely for the privilege of trying to save him from disaster. In this setting of total practical support for the Kuomintang, Hurley again attempted to mediate and the Communists developed a growing hostility toward American designs in China. During mid-May the Kuomintang Congress promised a series of far-reaching political and economic reforms and reiterated its intention to convene a national assembly the following November. At the end of the following month the Communists agreed to a Kuomintang initiative that they resume negotiations, but Mao linked democratic reforms to progress in other areas, and on June 28 Communist General Wang Jo-fei called on Hurley and informed him that the five-point program of the previous November was still acceptable. Wang eschewed, as Mao had often done in public, the prospect of creating a Communist state in China in the near future, though that was their ultimate goal. Throughout the following weeks the two sides negotiated, hemmed, and pulled, both obviously suspicious and mistrustful of the other's purposes. Neither in fact had any confidence in, or illusions about, the other side. Both were convinced time was on their side: the Communists because they alone were benefitting politically from the deluge of chaos and corruption, the Kuomintang because it was allied with the two most powerful nations in the world.

During June, Mao strongly condemned American policy in China, and "the U.S. government's policy of supporting Chiang Kai-shek against the Communists." Yet he also made an important distinction "within the U.S. government between the policy-makers and their subordinates," which was between Hurley and Washington. The Communists excoriated the Ambassador and obviously they would suspect anything he did. On July 12 Mao issued a devastating press release on Hurley's position, still insisting on associating it with the man and a circle around him, and retaining hope for a change in United States policy, but also indicating that Hurley was in effect making it at the time. Roosevelt, he implied, had not been so unfriendly. This policy, he now indicated, openly endorsed the Chiang regime and made it more reactionary, "creating a civil war crisis in China."[11] Armed clashes between the Communists and Kuomintang already were increasing. Mao now revealed how he supported Hurley's five-point program when the American had visited him at Yenan, and how Hurley had then backed away from it. It was quite apparent that the appointee and close friend of Roosevelt was *persona non grata* among the Communists. The Americans could come to Communist China only if they signed an agreement, Mao then stipulated, and came to fight the Japanese.

By the time Mao first turned on the United States he knew Chiang would obtain the remainder of his $500 million from the Americans, and this practical reality made a much greater impression on Mao than any knowledge he may have had of a split between Hurley and Washington. In fact, by the end of the same month the Americans' shifting policy on the postwar condition of the Far East—in effect, from a primary reliance on China to a reconstructed Japan as the critical balance in the region—meant that preparatory to Potsdam the State Department's policy shifted on paper but not yet in practice. In articulating its policy for a memo, the department advocated a united China, but did not once mention the Kuomintang or Chiang. ". . . an effective and stable government" was all it hoped for, but one that would "safeguard the principle of equal opportunity for the commerce and industry of all nations in China. . . ."[12] Such a reformed China by necessity would not be truly Communist. Above all they emphasized concern for the protection of American rights in Manchuria, which led as we shall see to an agreement with the Russians that they take a neutral position toward Chinese internal affairs and politics during their occupation. The policy paper said nothing about China as the key power in the Far East. The State Department was clearly considering all the options and leaving its policy open—in theory if not in fact. How they would decide among the options they had yet to resolve. However, only one week later the War Department's Military Intelligence Division widely circulated throughout the military services and Washington a secret and uniquely detailed study of the Chinese Communists, pointing to their vast accomplishments and military power, but also concluding that Moscow entirely controlled them. This belief, if nothing else, made the victory of the Kuomintang imperative if the United States was to avoid political defeat in the Far East.[13]

The Russians and China, Spring 1945

After the Yalta decisions the issue of China had for all practical purposes appeared to move from the battlefield to the conference table. Chiang was convinced the American and Russian support could snatch victory for him. And the Americans, despite all their fatalism, thought some good would come from the large concessions the Russians made at Yalta to take little and support the Chiang government in return. The Russians, as later events revealed, also did their best for Chiang and his government. Even Mao had misunderstood the realities of China and courted the Americans in the belief that, in the last analysis, their support or even their neutrality was the key to his success. Events, however, confounded all their various efforts, for nothing could re-create the social structure that Chiang and the Japanese had shattered, and the elitism Mao retained from his fading Leninist legacy blocked a clearer view of the inherent dynamism bubbling beneath the apparent disintegration of China—an ingredient which only the Communists remained to direct.

Nevertheless, during the spring of 1945 the deliberations in the well-furnished rooms of the capitals of the world blinded Communist and capitalist leaders alike to the ultimately fundamental events which were taking place in the huts of suffering peasants. The vague nature of the Yalta agreement on China, and what had yet to be done to make it operative, perforce made diplomacy the prime focus. The Russians did not definitely commit themselves to enter the war against Japan, and their tentative timing—from two to three months after the defeat of Germany—was too vague for American military planning, for in battle one month's pressure on another front could make all the difference between an early victory and a prolonged war. The Americans, with Stalin's ready consent, made the Yalta accords contingent on Chinese approval, thereby giving themselves and the Russians a possible escape clause via Chiang's intransigence. Stalin did not balk at this condition because he believed he had something to offer the Americans which might also strengthen his diplomatic hand elsewhere. During the spring of 1945, as Stalin hesitated, the Americans had to decide whether they still wanted Russian assistance and, once they made that decision, how best to engage in grand diplomacy. For this reason, as never before, all the problems of the Far East merged into a unified issue, involving the status and future of both China and Japan, the defeat of Japan by means of surrender or military defeat, or both, and the role of Russia in the context of all of these factors once it entered the war. It would be necessary for the United States to confront all of these matters sooner or later. Parallel to these considerations was the question of the role and implications, military and political, of what was called "S-1"—the atomic bomb.

The Kuomintang and Russians had few secrets regarding their strategies toward each other, and during mid-February the Chinese rumored from Chungking that Chiang wished to send Soong to Moscow in a new attempt to consolidate Soviet support for his regime. The Russians for their part published a number of sharply critical accounts of conditions in the Kuomintang areas, still carefully differentiating Chiang from his grossly corrupt allies, but also calling upon him to purge his party and institute reforms as a step toward national unity. They gave no direct support to the Communists, but they most favorably mentioned their program of democratic political reform. Privately they hoped Mao would cooperate with Chiang to avoid civil war. The Russians apparently thought they were in a strong position in regard to the Chinese and the Americans. They could

define conditions, and they took this aloof posture in the Far East until
Potsdam. In fact their confidence was warranted, for during the months
after the Yalta Conference the American ardor for Russian entry into the
war against Japan remained warm. In mid-February, General Douglas Mac-
Arthur advised the War Department to delay the invasion of Japan until
they obtained Soviet agreement to invade Manchuria, hopefully sooner
than three months after the end of war with Germany.[14]

With this limiting factor in mind, Hurley went to Moscow from Washington in April, stopping first in London. There he was distressed to learn
that the British still had utter disdain for "the great American illusion," as
Churchill called it, regarding China.[15] Despite his natural suspicion of
British imperialist intentions, especially regarding Hong Kong, Hurley had
no illusions about China, and that was the reason for the trip to the
Kremlin. Although Hurley later recalled that he went to see Stalin to undo
the negative consequences of the Yalta accord on China, at the time
Roosevelt authorized him to discuss general Chinese affairs with Stalin to
obtain Soviet renewal of support for Chiang, and to consider when it might
be possible to tell Chiang of the Yalta agreement and win his consent to
it—a stipulation directly linked to Soviet entry into the war and a task that
was therefore of paramount and quite independent importance to the United
States. In Moscow, Hurley saw Stalin and Molotov on April 15 and was
delighted with the results. Molotov repeated his earlier jibes at the Chinese
Communists, and both confirmed that it was necessary to avoid civil war
by supporting the Kuomintang and Chiang, whom Stalin, perhaps cynically, called "selfless." Some internal reform, he implied, might aid a very
great deal. On this there was no disagreement. "In short," Hurley cabled
Washington, "Stalin agreed unqualifiedly to America's policy in China.
. . ."[16] Stalin first left it to the Americans to determine when to tell Chiang
of the Yalta agreement, but the Americans decided to delay, and Stalin
then asked, for military reasons, that they check with him again before
notifying the Chinese.

Both Harriman and George Kennan attended the meeting between Hurley and the Russian leaders, and they sent rather different reports to Washington. Kennan, as was his wont, spun phrases and ignored facts to make
pessimistic forecasts of Soviet designs to dominate north China, and dismissed Stalin's statements by indicating "that to the Russians words mean
different things than they do to us."[17] Harriman thought Hurley's report
was factually accurate but too optimistic, and that Russia would not only
support the Communists, but perhaps even seek to create a puppet state in
Manchuria and north China.

In fact what occurred in Moscow did not impress Harriman and many
other civilian leaders in Washington, because by mid-April they saw the
Far East in the context of European events, events that filled the American

leaders with dread of larger Soviet global intentions and caused them to envision the same threats and dangers in China as existed in Europe. But the important aid that the Russian troops might still provide impressed the American military leaders, and until they secured that aid they tended to place less weight on the political dimensions of Far Eastern strategy. In mid-April, Marshall described to Eden the frightful losses that he expected in a land war against Japan should Russia not enter the war, even though the Joint Chiefs of Staff were certain the United States would still win such a war—at a price they did not care to pay. Marshall was worried that the Russians would enter the war after "we had done all the dirty work."[18] But since April 5, when the Russians denounced their neutrality pact with Japan, and took no serious steps to conceal their vast troop movements toward the Far East, they thereby made entry into the war only a matter of time. Yet it was precisely this question of timing that the Americans found so critical.

On April 23 the Cabinet and military leaders met to discuss the larger pattern of relations with the U.S.S.R., and the issue of the war in the Far East arose after they had considered at length the poor state of affairs with the Russians elsewhere. Here Marshall expounded his conservative views, against dominant opinion, but Stimson took his side. General John R. Deane, the military attaché in Moscow, consoled them all by arguing that the Russians would enter the war in the Far East regardless of American policy elsewhere. Yet there were grave liabilities in risking the Russians' staying out of the war due to pressures over Europe, even though it was not certain that was any longer possible. Stimson remained deeply committed to keeping large United States forces off the Chinese mainland, and though the American leaders stopped to ponder the political implications, they only resumed their original course with greater determination afterward. When Stettinius wired Hurley new instructions the same day as the Cabinet meeting, he suggested that continued internal chaos in China would only later give the Russians options to exercise against the Kuomintang should it be in their interests to do so. His prime task was to impress upon Chiang the need to solve his internal problems and to strengthen his good relations with the Soviet Union.

May was a month for scurrying and consolidation, but not for a reversal in policy. Although the deterioration of Japanese economic and military power continued, the United States still feared its hidden reserves and resources, and Stimson at the beginning of May urged Marshall to postpone further heavy casualty involvements until they better understood the atomic bomb's potential. Even Churchill, shortly thereafter, urged Halifax to inform the Americans that while they should pay no large political price for it in Europe, "We desire the entry of the Soviets into the war against Japan at the earliest moment."[19] During these same days official

Washington gave careful, if belated, thought to the future of defeated Japan, and inevitably the Soviet role vis-à-vis the occupation and Japan's future power. The advantage of Russian entry into the war against Japan, unlike Germany, was that Russia would fight in Manchuria and north China, and Japan itself could be an uncomplicated occupation matter involving only American authority. From a political viewpoint the United States had to obtain Russian assurances on China, and more particularly on American interests there, for the guarantees Russia gave to Chiang would hardly suffice for American purposes, since they feared Chiang might fall. The Americans would have to deal personally with Stalin.

As the State and War departments began considering these matters, the question arose whether the United States should take care of its own future interests in China directly or via the Kuomintang, and more particularly, the interminably postponed Soong visit to Moscow. Although it did not preclude it as a supplementary device, the United States was reluctant to depend on Chiang to protect American interests in China. Soong had been in the United States since mid-April, but no one had officially informed him of the Yalta decisions, and hence he could not go to Moscow until he knew of them. Informally, however, Hurley after visiting Moscow exposed the substance of the Yalta agreement to Chiang and obtained his response to the specific provisions. He discovered that the Chinese were going to prove difficult on granting Port Arthur as a base and giving preeminent Soviet rights to the railroads and Dairen. In light of this Truman decided on May 10 not to reveal the Yalta accords to Soong formally—nor to permit him to go to Moscow until the Americans mended their own fences with Russia.

During these same days Washington hammered out an American strategy on the future of Russia in the Far East, one designed to serve American interests. On May 12 Grew and the State Department asked the War Department to comment on the political issues arising from Soviet entry into the war, and the need to obtain more definite assurances regarding the unification of China under Kuomintang auspices, the return of Manchuria to China, and the future of Korea, which was to become a Four Power trusteeship. In particular the State Department wanted to know whether the military agreed that they should work out the question of Chinese unity with Russia "before . . . any approach to the Chinese Government on the basis of the Yalta Agreement."[20] Grew was certain as to his own view of the matter, for during these very days he advocated an extremely stern line toward Tito over the Trieste crisis, and on May 19 penned a purely private memo on his innermost thoughts—one not circulated—prophesying Russia would annex all of the Far East once it entered the war. "A future war with Soviet Russia," he wrote, "is as certain as anything in this world can be certain."[21]

Before Stimson could send Grew an answer to his official memo Soong met with Truman, who told him nothing of the formal agreement at Yalta. When the Chinese asked for a plane to go to Moscow at the opportune time, Truman tabled the matter, implicitly consolidating the strategy of direct negotiations with the Russians first. Yet Soong also frightened Stimson during these very same days by giving the impression the Kuomintang wanted the Americans to make a commitment to fight in China—"the very thing," Stimson noted, "that I am resolved that we shall not do unless it is over my dead body. . . ."[22] There were only two means of avoiding this alternative: the Russians entering the Chinese mainland theater—". . . we think that will be all right," Stimson wrote—and S-1, the atomic bomb, yet to become a definite, predictable factor. Stimson's reply to Grew on May 21 reflected this informal opinion as well as certain obvious realities Grew chose to ignore. The concessions the West made to the Russians at Yalta were within Soviet military grasp whether or not they entered the war, which they would do as soon as it was to their interest, no later and probably not much sooner despite any political inducement the United States might offer. At the moment the Russians could easily take Manchuria, Korea, and north China, Stimson admitted, before American troops could do so. Therefore they could be of very great help to the war effort—if they entered the war in time. Toward the end of the war they would seize their objectives without having materially aided the American forces. While Stimson and Forrestal both agreed "it would be desirable to have a complete understanding and agreement with the Russians concerning the Far East," especially given the Chinese schism, they geared their entire analysis to the assumption that it was critical to get the Russians into the war to help the United States, and not at an almost certain later date of Stalin's own choosing.[23] Grew's pessimism could not overcome Stimson's fear of a war on the Chinese mainland.

In the latter half of May the Americans based their policy partially on their need of Soviet military aid, but also on the realization that China was nearly lost with or without Soviet entry into the war, and surely they would gain nothing by spilling American blood on behalf of Chiang's political future. Before sending Harry Hopkins to see Stalin at the end of May, Truman urged him to get from the Russian a commitment to enter the war as soon as possible. On May 28 Hopkins saw Stalin and covered the entire spectrum of Far Eastern questions from the American viewpoint. He asked Stalin about Soviet entry into the war, and the Russian responded again that his armies would be ready three months after the defeat of Germany —August 8—but the actual date of operations depended on confirmation of the political agreement made at Yalta, which in fact the Americans delayed by not officially revealing its contents to the Chinese, or so Stalin believed. Stalin now indicated that he wished to postpone the matter until "the first part of July," when he expected Soong in Moscow.[24] He approved the first American request in April to tell the Chinese of the matter, then agreed to the American delay. Now Stalin was in no hurry, ostensibly because the Chinese were talkative and might reveal Soviet intentions to the Japanese —intentions which were by then virtually public information. When Soong arrived they might resolve the political issues, and in the meantime the Americans could only wait—unsure of Soviet military plans.

On the substantive political matters Stalin was more cooperative. He reaffirmed everything he told to Hurley, leaving Harriman no doubt that his words were clear, whatever his actions might hold. Russia would support the unity of China under the leadership of Chiang, and he would return Japanese-occupied territory the Red Army captured to Chiang alone, and Chiang could send his representatives along with the Russian army as occupation authorities. Stalin would not aid China economically after the war, and merely left the Americans the task, accepting the principles of the Open Door policy and implying American economic primacy in the postwar period. He had no territorial claims, and stood only by the Yalta accord, including the trusteeship plan for Korea. Whatever else happened at Moscow during Hopkins' visit, both Hopkins and Harriman were "very encouraged," according to the former, and thought the conference "of real value" in the words of the more than skeptical Ambassador. Hopkins was convinced that the Russians would enter the war during August, and now urged Truman to get Soong to Moscow as soon as Stalin would see him, which he misinterpreted as "any time now" but was actually July 1.[25]

Having taken care of the American interests, the White House immediately informed Soong an American plane would take him to Moscow no later than July 1. Before Truman saw Soong on June 9 to reveal to him the exact contents of the Yalta Agreement, the Russian representative in Chungking saw Chiang and repeated the assurances Stalin gave to Hopkins, although not mentioning the specific commitment to enter the war or the precise terms of Yalta. It was probably about this time, as Mao revealed more than twenty years later, that Stalin warned Mao not to follow a revolutionary line and to cooperate with Chiang, for civil war would be the ruination of China. Chungking welcomed the news, and in conjunction with Hurley's information on the specific problems dealt with at Yalta the Chinese had ample time to assess all the factors confronting them. Soong did not respond to Truman's first official presentation of the Yalta Agreement, but after the meeting informed Leahy that he did not care for the section on the Manchurian railroads, and perhaps it might be best to wait until non-Russian forces were available to clear the area. "When do you think you would be in a position to do that?" Leahy asked. "Well," Soong replied after a moment's thought, "that might be any time in the next five hundred years."[26]

Several days later, in a private talk with Grew, Soong further complained about the vagueness of the provisions, and he thought the proposed ninety-nine-year Russian lease to Port Arthur too long, the principle of Dairen as a free port acceptable if Chinese sovereignty was explicitly recognized, and they would also endorse the agreement on the South Manchurian Railroad if no Soviet troops were stationed on it. On June 14 Truman met with Soong for the last time, and they covered points already revealed by Hurley and Grew and later discussed in Moscow. Truman revealed the added assurances Stalin gave Hopkins, and also informed the Chinese Foreign Minister of American priorities, at the end of which he frankly placed friendship with China. His "chief interest now," his "chief preoccupation at the moment," "was to see the Soviet Union participate in the Far Eastern war in sufficient time to be of help in shortening the war and save American and Chinese lives," Grew's notes record.[27]

Virtually all of Washington's leading decision-makers feared a Chinese effort to drag them into their morass and charge the United States vast amounts in blood and money in the process of doing so. Indeed, nothing in the dismal record of experience in China reassured the United States that Chiang would be above such tactics as a means of enriching himself. The Americans no longer premised their policy in June 1945 on China emerging from the war as the main American anchor in the Far East, nor did they gear their strategy to the need to satisfy Chiang Kai-shek. On the same day he saw Soong, Truman ordered the Joint Chiefs of Staff to formulate plans "as to exactly what we want the Russians to do" on a military level—the issue of their participation was not at stake—with the objective "of economizing to the maximum extent possible in the loss of American lives." This meant using both the Russians and the atomic bomb. The Joint Chiefs never had any doubt that they could win the war without the aid of either, and the Navy's King emphasized to Truman that "regardless of the desirability of the Russians entering the war, they were not indispensable and he did not think we should go so far as to beg them to come in."[28] But no one questioned the desirability, or the need for begging, but only the political price involved. Hopkins had largely obtained the desired political assurances. When Stimson later sought clarification on others he took it for granted that the Russians would enter the war when it was to their interest, and he kept American interests in Manchuria rather than Chinese aspirations in the foreground.

In fact Chiang did much during the last half of June to make Soviet neutrality an even more dangerous prospect for the United States. On June 15 he asked Hurley to seek American and British participation in any treaty he might sign with the Russians, even to the extent of sharing a joint base with them at Port Arthur. The United States almost immediately rejected the proposal, and Hurley argued that Chiang had everything to gain by the Russian agreement at Yalta to support the Kuomintang against the Communists. Chiang also knew he had nothing to lose, but little did he realize that during those very months the Russians were urging Mao to do everything possible to avoid civil war.[29]

The Atomic Bomb and Far Eastern Diplomacy

From the moment work began on the construction of the atomic bomb in 1941 until the Americans dropped it on Hiroshima on August 6, 1945, none of the American leaders involved ever had any doubt that they were building the bomb to be used. This assumption was axiomatic at the time, and it was only later revulsion that led to the artificial investigation of the relatively unimportant spring 1945 debate on the moral problems of using the bomb. The war and the mass destruction of civilians posed all the moral questions well before August 1945, by which time years of sustained murder and brutality had grotesquely distorted men's sensibilities.

The nuclear scientists of all the major warring powers were aware of the military potentialities of nuclear physics, and we now know the Germans conducted their own lethargic research program into the bomb throughout the war. At the end of 1944 and during 1945 both the Russians and special American units picked up German scientists as quickly as they could find them. We now also know that the Russians created their first laboratory to build a bomb in the summer of 1942, by which time they were familiar with the existence of programs in the United States and Germany, and that they accelerated their activity in February 1943. By September 1943 Stimson was certain the Russians were spying on the American program, and by the end of 1944 most of the executives connected with the project assumed this to be the case. Late in 1943 Peter Kapitza, the leading Soviet nuclear physicist, formally invited Niels Bohr, the great Danish physicist, to settle in Russia, where he would receive all the facilities he required. In July 1944 one of the French scientists working on the bomb project in Canada told De Gaulle of its development, and in late 1944 even Soong informed Ambassador Gauss of a vast American project devoted to producing a decisive secret weapon that would end the war. At the beginning of 1945 Jean F. Joliot, the Communist head of the French Government's research center, discussed possible French involvement in the atomic bomb project with British authorities. In brief, the only secret connected with the bomb was whether the United States had produced it, and how, and not in its anticipated construction.

When Stimson, who was the primary head of the atomic-bomb development, thought about the problem of the bomb in relation to the Russians it was always with the knowledge that the Russians knew the Americans were building such a weapon. To tell them officially merely created problems involving sharing technical knowledge, and from this viewpoint such discussion was unacceptable. At no time did the Americans believe they could surprise the Russians with a weapon that would cause them to cower, and at every stage in their diplomacy the Russians acted with full knowledge that the United States was likely to be the first to have an atomic bomb. At the end of 1944 Stimson thought the Russians were a long way from obtaining the secret of how to build a bomb, and he felt it unwise to tell them anything about the method until America obtained "a real quid pro quo" on diplomatic questions.[30] Roosevelt agreed.

As Major General Leslie R. Groves, the head of the Manhattan Project under Stimson, summarized the prospect for the bomb in December 1944, the first one would be ready about August 1 of the following year, with another before the end of the year. He expected it to be 10 kilotons, the equivalent of 10,000 tons of TNT. The implosion bomb also being developed would not be ready before late July and would be about .5 kiloton, and probably not exceed 2.5 kilotons for some time. Although the maximum prediction was for 18 kilotons, most of the scientists connected with the project thought until as late as May that the first bomb would be a relatively modest .7 to 1.5 kilotons. Given this timetable and this expected range of power, the military based their planning for the war on known, controllable, conventional weapons, weapons that were quite sufficient in the march toward victory in early 1945. Moreover, to both the Navy and Army the theory of strategic bombing inherent in the weapon was not very persuasive, and they consistently denied the premise that air power might win the war.

During November 1944 American B-29's began their first incendiary bomb raids on Tokyo, and on March 9, 1945, wave upon wave dropped masses of small incendiaries containing an early version of napalm on the city's population—for they directed this assault against civilians. Soon small fires spread, connected, and grew into a vast firestorm that sucked the oxygen out of the lower atmosphere. The bomb raid was a "success" for the Americans; they killed 125,000 Japanese in one attack. The Allies bombed Hamburg and Dresden in the same manner, and Nagoya, Osaka, and Kobe, and Tokyo again on May 24. The basic moral decision that the Americans had to make during the war was whether or not they would violate international law by indiscriminately attacking and destroying civilians, and they resolved that dilemma within the context of conventional weapons. Neither fanfare nor hesitation accompanied their choice, and in fact the atomic bomb used against Hiroshima was less lethal than massive fire bombing. The war had so brutalized the American leaders that burning vast numbers of civilians no longer posed a real predicament by the spring of 1945. Given the anticipated power of the atomic bomb, which was far less than that of fire bombing, no one expected small quantities of it to end the war. Only its technique was novel—nothing more.

By June 1945 the mass destruction of civilians via strategic bombing did impress Stimson as something of a moral problem, but the thought no sooner arose than he forgot it, and in no appreciable manner did it shape American use of conventional or atomic bombs. "I did not want to have the United States get the reputation of outdoing Hitler in atrocities," he noted telling the President on June 6. There was another difficulty posed by mass conventional bombing, and that was its very success, a success that made the two modes of human destruction qualitatively identical in fact and in the minds of the American military. "I was a little fearful," Stimson told Truman, "that before we could get ready the Air Force might have Japan so thoroughly bombed out that the new weapon would not have a fair background to show its strength." To this the President "laughed and said he understood."[31]

Early in 1945 Groves had asked Marshall for authorization to draw up detailed plans for use of the bomb, and the head of the Joint Chiefs merely passed the responsibility back to Groves. After Yalta, Stimson for his part still preferred "to tread softly" on discussing the existence of the bomb with the Russians and to wait "until we have some much more tangible 'fruits of repentance' from the Russians as a quid pro quo. . . ."[32] This attitude defined the very general plans for postwar atomic energy control that various officials raised during the spring of 1945, plans that dealt essentially with American development of atomic energy. The actual thought that went into the matter of the new genie was on how best to employ it against Japan. A group of scientists defined the principles of targeting, and in April, Stimson urged the new President to create a committee to advise him on the use and future of the atomic bomb. Truman appointed such an "Interim Committee" consisting of Stimson, Byrnes, Clayton, Ralph A. Bard of the Navy, and George L. Harrison, Stimson's deputy, and the scientists Vannevar Bush, Karl T. Compton, and James B. Conant, although it did not meet until the last day of May. He added a scientific panel of four to advise the committee, but all of the scientists were well known for their cooperative attitude toward Washington officials, and in fact were administrative scientists with declining personal interests in research. The committee excluded the younger and more liberal scientists connected with the Manhattan Project, who were now much alarmed at an American policy that might encourage a postwar arms race.

By the time the committee began to function the Allies had effectively defeated Japan and reduced its industrial capacity and manpower to nearly a last-stand posture. The Navy knew this and so argued, but from its strategic position and not convincingly. At the end of May, although Stimson had thought continuously about the problem during the prior weeks, the Americans now tried to weigh the atomic bomb both from the viewpoint of its use against Japan and its implications to future relations with the Soviet

Union. Stimson knew the bomb would influence many phases of postwar relations with the U.S.S.R., and he also reviewed the problem of Soviet entry into the war against Japan in this light. But one should not make too much of these thoughts or link them too closely, for once the Americans built and used the bomb they had to reconsider its relationship to the Russians and everything else, but such new reassessments are not the same as basic alterations in policy. In reality the issues are whether the United States would have dropped the bomb even if it had perfect relations with the Russians, and also what did its refusal to share the information imply about the American vision of its future power. The actual policy Washington adopted toward the Russians in the end, as events showed, reflected the same mechanistic attitudes that left unchallenged its decision to drop the bomb. One must remember that at no time did the Americans see the bomb as a weapon for defeating the formidable Japanese army in China, and at no time did they consider it desirable that the Soviets invade the Japanese mainland. The bomb did not reduce the importance of Soviet entry into Manchuria and north China, for the Chinese were surely not going to be able to eliminate the Japanese army there even after the United States had devastated all of Japan itself, and not for a moment did anyone in Washington think of using the atomic bomb in Manchuria. Since they knew the Russians based their diplomacy on premises which assumed the existence of the Manhattan Project, any American revelation—in whatever form— designed to effect Soviet diplomacy was superfluous.

Truman and Grew at the end of May finally suggested that other officials consider the issue of dropping the bomb in the context of a prior warning to Japan to surrender. On May 29 Marshall, McCloy, Elmer Davis, the head of the Office of War Information, and a group of leaders who were not all aware of the Manhattan Project, but only of the American prospect of doing "something worse" to Japan, rejected the idea.[33] In the context of a warning to Japan, or the mechanics of its use, and not whether the bomb should be used, the planning proceeded from the end of May onward. On May 31 and June 1 the Interim Committee met for the first time, and the scientists held forth first, estimating that a bomb would kill perhaps 20,000 people, or, to interpolate, less than many conventional attacks. Some pleaded for a continuation of the vast government appropriations for their labs, estimating the length of time it would take to construct a thermonuclear or hydrogen bomb. They considered the possibility of "a competitor" overtaking America in the field, to use the exact term in the official history, and all resolved that the United States should keep its atomic plant intact and develop it. The problem of telling the Russians of the project was really one of sharing knowledge, and on this the scientists disagreed; Bush and Conant, who had prepared a memo on the matter earlier, urged international control with inspection. Both Byrnes and

Marshall discouraged such talk, Marshall citing Russia's lack of cooperation, and Byrnes the need to stay ahead—even of the British—and to deal
with future relations with the U.S.S.R. on a political level. They always
discussed the question of using the bomb itself in the context of choosing a
target—Bard wished an advance warning, but this they hardly considered
—and after some debate they concluded that the United States would use
the bomb as soon as it was ready, against a military target surrounded by
workers' homes, and without warning.[34]

The committee immediately informed Truman of its decisions, and on
June 6 Stimson visited him for a more systematic discussion of the problems involved. One must remember that at this time Stimson opposed
diplomatic conferences with the U.S.S.R., including the one at Potsdam,
and Truman was well aware of his position. For reasons already mentioned
and having nothing to do with the atomic bomb, and over the objection of
Churchill and Harriman, the President delayed the Potsdam meeting, and
implied to Stimson additional time to develop the bomb *and use it* against
Japan was a reason. In reality, by July 15 and for several weeks thereafter
no one, including Stimson, expected the bomb to be ready for use, and obviously the statement was a sop to Stimson but inconsistent with all the
facts, for a delay of the conference for this reason should have been until
late July at the earliest. The two men decided that until they dropped the
bomb on Japan they would not tell the Russians of its existence, and later
they would deflect any questions about sharing information. Stimson agreed
to such cooperation only after the Allies established full means of preventing its misuse, and also in return for quid pro quos in Poland, Yugoslavia,
Rumania, and Manchuria—at that point the United States could release its
secrets. At no time did Stimson imply that the Russians should not enter
the war, and in fact no one thought that they were unnecessary by virtue
of the existence of a bomb which they expected to be less destructive than
the average fire raid. On June 18 Truman had authorized preparations for
the landing on the Japanese mainland on November 1, employing a million
and a half men. By that time the United States would have dropped several
bombs.

During these same days a committee of seven scientists chaired by
James Franck, but also representative of a much larger group, heard of the
Interim Committee's decisions and decided to issue a modest, contrite
protest. They confessed ignorance of military and foreign affairs, but they
urged that a demonstration of the bomb on a barren area or island serve as
a substitute for an attack on Japan, and that the United States make a
sincere attempt at international control. They gave their recommendation
to Stimson, who in turn passed it along to the scientific panel, which
promptly decided to leave the subject to the domain of those who knew
more about politics than they. In reality the proposal was rather too

modest to regard seriously, and no one ever did save those who favored it, for it failed to question any of the basic assumptions of United States policy. The top-flight scientists connected with the entire program were for the most part busy arguing for future funds to retain the new empires of big research in the postwar era.[35] In the last analysis, what the scientists said would worry the politicians less than what they refused to do, and none showed readiness to boycott a policy they opposed. The relationship established an important precedent, one that became mutually profitable in the future.

The question of the bomb was not so much an issue of diplomacy and the Russians as it was of power—American power. For that power involved not merely excluding the Russians from access to the secret of the bomb, but retaining a monopoly of power where possible, which meant barring the English as well. The British early in the war gave heavily of their scientific knowledge and resources to help build the bomb, and at Quebec the prior September the two nations agreed to share the knowledge in the postwar era and to use the bomb only after joint agreement. By June the United States had given the British nothing, and Truman decided to confirm his Interim Committee's decisions without reference to Churchill, to whom he finally presented the matter on July 4 after American plans were well advanced. In fact, every concerned American leader agreed by May 31 that they would keep not only the Russians out of the atomic club, but they would do nothing more to aid the English, whom Stimson even wished to see deprived of information of the first test. Later the British complained and protested, and developed their own bomb themselves.[36]

Throughout the period before Potsdam the decision to use a bomb to destroy 20,000 people posed no personal moral dilemmas to men who had already ordered far more destructive attacks on civilian populations. They continued to base their planning on the premises of a long war and a need for Russian aid. No one ever doubted that they would drop the bomb when ready. When Truman came to the White House he took the ultimate responsibility for the decision, but as Groves later assessed it, "As far as I was concerned, his decision was one of noninterference—basically, a decision not to upset the existing plans."[37]

The Future of Japan

Planning for the postwar role of Japan was never comparable to that devoted to Germany, and the views on the topic ebbed and altered with the changing conditions of China. Ultimately Washington saw the problem of Japan, even in 1944, as a larger question of the future of the Far East and the role of China. Viewed in this context Chiang himself created the major options for planning, which had only one constant assumption—that the

United States would emerge as the dominant power in the Pacific and preeminent in the Far East. To do so with a minimal commitment of resources would require an alliance with a major state of the region. This meant China or Japan.

The Presidents and their executives quickly recognized Joseph C. Grew as the State Department's leading authority on Japan, for he had spent many years there as ambassador; and Grew was rather typical of many Far East hands in believing that there was scant hope for the future of China. Throughout the 1930's this group found the faults of China so great that they advocated neutrality toward Japanese expansion there, which they did not condone, but which they understood. They also opposed a firm line toward Japan in 1940 and 1941, and until the last months before the war advocated continued negotiations with the Japanese when most of Washington thought it had fully revealed its imperialist course. Grew made no secret of his belief in 1943 that "To try to graft a democracy on Japan would result in chaos . . ." and his desire to see the Emperor remain on the throne and serve as the basis of "a healthy structure in [the] future. . . ."[38] The United States, he maintained, should not attack the Emperor and in any case should not blame him for Japanese militarism. As before the war, Grew insisted that there were "liberals" in Japan with whom the United States could work, and whom a policy of total rejection would only discourage.

In the spring of 1944 the State Department pushed ahead on planning for the postwar role of Japan in the Far East, and at that time Hull assumed China would emerge "at the center of any arrangement that was made."[39] The high-level statement of policy that the department prepared in early May suggested three stages of occupation: first, stern discipline, retribution, and disarmament; second, surveillance and relaxation, with the introduction of democratic forms and education to encourage the liberals; and lastly, Japan would become a responsible member of the family of nations, essentially disarmed, free "to share in the world economy on a reasonable basis." The Allies would avoid prolonged occupation, which would be centralized and unified rather than zonal, as they planned for Germany, and they would use ". . . much of the Japanese administrative machinery" under Allied control. They would reduce the power of the Emperor, but would maintain the institution unless the Japanese themselves chose to abolish it. The occupation would encourage the "liberals," specifically identified as the statesmen prominent in the 1920's and called the "Anglo-American school," Christian leaders, various educational and social reformers, and "a considerable sprinkling of business leaders whose prosperity was based on world trade rather than on the greater East Asia prosperity sphere."[40] Only this last-named group in reality held any power at the time. Within the context of this policy the State Department emphasized flexibility. We are going to give civil and military administrators "a wide latitude," Grew wrote in July, "in order to permit them to use whatever assets they may find available for the establishment and maintenance of order and security."⁴¹

In comparison to the projected policy for Germany, this directive was extremely lenient, and it reflected American priorities and definitions of the causes of the war. To Hull the emphasis on economic factors was critical, for he was sure that the United States could reintegrate Japan into a liberal world economy and that its reasons for imperialism in Asia would be eliminated as a by-product of the attainment of American economic war aims. Unlike Germany, they could identify cordial groups with whom to work. If they could eliminate the atavism, they could reintegrate Japan without Draconian measures. During 1944 Washington did not regard Japan as a substitute for the Chinese anchor of the United States in the Far East, but there was no principled reason against its becoming the alternative should events prove necessary. The willingness to retain the Emperor and work through many of the existing political organizations indicated the basic ambivalence and flexibility in American policy before the total collapse of China.

By the end of 1944 planning had not proceeded much beyond this stage, and what there was consisted of specialized projections on various problems. When Hull retired, and especially after Stettinius left Washington, making Grew the Acting Secretary of State, such ambivalence as existed in planning on Japan was left in Grew's hands for resolution. Some immediately understood the significance of the change and exaggerated its impact, for in the end the policy would have been the same had Hull remained. In the context of the growing stalemate in China, however, in postwar planning the State Department then saw Japan as a very real option in the Far East, and Grew was inclined in that direction from the beginning. Observers commonly see the split as one between those who favored a primary American orientation toward China as opposed to Japan, but in fact it was more complex. The so-called pro-China group was not well placed, and consisted mainly of China experts at the lower levels who had no illusions about the strength of China or Chiang, whom most criticized. They were not so much pro-China as anti-Japanese. Given this fact they had no real options other than Japan, and they never influenced policy. This group at its highest level included Harry Dexter White, perhaps Morgenthau, and, standing alone, Hurley. The other active element oriented toward Japan first consisted of Grew at the top, Joseph Ballantine, director of the State Department's Office of Far Eastern Affairs, and most of the State Department, but they were to gain other powerful friends as events moved China toward the abyss. Ultimately they were ready to use Japanese power as the critical balance in the Far East, and in Korea to permit Japanese interests to hang on to prevent chaos and Bolshevism, which they were convinced would accompany total independence there.

The Japan-oriented group's analysis of the north China situation before 1939 was couched in essentially these terms. They were not so much for Japan as against instability in Asia and an opening to Communism in its wake. In early 1945 they did not formulate a policy in these terms, but they wished to retain options for such a political arrangement, and in the meantime impose a mild peace and reform, and incorporate Japan and let fate take its course. Every month of chaos in China during 1945 strengthened their hand. One can see the shift in policy in the State Department's discussion of the future of China before Yalta as opposed to Potsdam, when they dropped the last frail illusion.

When Grew came to his new post, those aware of this division on grand strategy over the role of Japan and China in the future of power in the Far East reviewed the entire course of American policy. These were the men, one Treasury official wrote, who "believe that agreement between the U.S. and pre-war Japan was possible . . . that war with Japan was unnecessary and caused mainly by our 'sentimental' attitude toward China, and . . . desired a strong Japan and a weak China."[42] Naval Intelligence, certainly the most conservative group in the field, heard of these accusations, and Captain Ellis M. Zacharias, their major expert on Japan, later took pains to deny the allegation that Grew favored the industrial groups about the Zaibatsu monopolies. "Mr. Grew and his advisers had in the past regarded the Zaibatsu as the most trustworthy element insofar as Western orientation and pro-American policy were concerned, but now they regarded Japan as an enemy entity and made no differentiation between the various factions."[43] Only time was to tell whether the State Department would actually gear itself to the world trade-oriented industrial elements, Zaibatsu or other, but in fact it was constantly making such differentiations and they were the basis of occupation and postwar planning. Grew himself in June 1945 made his own attitude clear on these prewar debates, which had direct implications to postwar planning, when he confidentially gave Stimson a memo the American minister to China in 1935 prepared, one which laid the onus of responsibility for the war on the "wilful," "reckless," "provocative" Chinese and the refusal of the world to comprehend their offense to Japan, forcing Japan to "depend only on its own strong arm to vindicate its rightful legal position in eastern Asia." The memo "does not and cannot condone many things the Japanese have done subsequent to the period under reference," Grew cautiously added, but it was still "very significant."[44]

"I am certain that we could not graft our type of a democracy on Japan," Grew informed one newspaperman in April 1945, "because I know very well they are not fitted for it and that it could not possibly work."[45]

With this viewpoint, by spring 1945 the American policy toward the future of Japan did not change, and only the relative weight assigned China or Japan became the critical issue. "What is our policy on Russian influence in the Far East?" Forrestal asked Stimson in early May; "Do we desire a counterweight to that influence? And should it be China or should it be Japan?"[46] These questions moved toward resolution before Potsdam.

When Hopkins saw Stalin at the end of May he asked the Russian about the future of Japan, a topic never before broached to him. The Soviet leader suggested he had no specific plans in mind, but he did prefer abolishing the institution of the Emperor, and he expected an occupation zone in Japan for Soviet troops. The Russians now threatened to upset all the assumptions of wartime planning and to extend their influence to Japan as they had to Germany. Prior to Potsdam, Stimson reinforced the assumptions of the State Department by surveying for Truman the liberal potential among Japan's leaders, and the State, War, and Navy departments' committee on a Japanese directive hastened to formulate a united policy on occupation. When Morgenthau attempted to gain representation on it, Grew blandly told him he would not consult him until the others had agreed. The committee admitted that in theory the British, Chinese, and, after they entered the war, the Russians had the right to share in the occupation, and formulate policies for its guidance. But the United States "should insist on control over the implementation of these policies," and the government, as if to prejudge Allied collaboration, should be centralized and without zones. "The major share of the responsibility for military government and the preponderance of forces used in occupation should be American, and the designated Commander of all occupational forces . . . and the principal subordinate Commanders should be American."[47] Truman endorsed the policy.

The significance of this position was not lost on the Russians, who cited the American policy in Japan to justify later developments in former Axis nations in Eastern Europe. But what is most meaningful about the policy on Japan before Yalta was not merely its exclusion of the Soviet Union but of Great Britain and China as well, both of whom had fought Japan long and hard enough, at least in their own eyes, to warrant more than a ceremonial role. The elimination of British power in the central Pacific meant American hegemony over the region, and for this reason the United States excluded the British from the war against Japan in the area. By refusing to seat China in Japan, as Roosevelt had offhandedly suggested he might, the United States recognized that the facile myth of Chinese strength was no longer worth retaining, and that this might also implicitly make the role of Japan more critical in the future of the Far East.

The United States controlled that future, whether China or Japan was to become its major ally in the Far East, by virtue of its exclusion of all other nations. The events in China itself suggested that tortured nation's chance of fulfilling the necessary role in larger American planning was declining, and that Japan might indeed emerge as the key to future American strength in the region. This issue was not resolved in 1945, but by planning to take monopoly control of Japan the United States retained the options for all contingencies—or so it believed—and fully comprehended the fundamental alternatives in the attainment of American supremacy in Asia.

JULY 1945: THE WAR
WITH JAPAN AND THE
POTSDAM CONFERENCE

THE FAR EAST presented a series of delicate balances and intertwining factors during July 1945, with the future of Japan and China, the role of Russia in the Far East, and the atomic bomb all merging to create a patchwork of dilemmas and possibilities to confront the decision-makers in Washington. Soong, in Moscow, tried to test Russian intentions and to win political succor for his wobbling regime; the Japanese now actively sought a way out of the war; and on July 15 the leaders of the alliance against Germany met at Potsdam, near the capital of the vanquished Nazi state, to expose and hopefully also to resolve their profound disagreements on the problems of Europe, and in this context they also had to consider the far less controversial questions of Asia and the war against Japan.

Japan Seeks Peace

The internal power structure of Japan was divided and delicately balanced, as it had always been since the leadership of the Japanese army, in conjunction with large landowners, a small element of the navy, and powerful elements in the government bureaucracy, overcame the objections of the navy, important sections of industry, and members of the royal circle to force Japan into war against the United States. After the fall of the Tojo Cabinet in July 1944, a major political defeat for the army, roughly the same political configuration of 1941 reemerged around the question of bringing a quick end to the war. Given the intricate balance between the various Japanese factions, none could move quickly for fear of precipitating a coup and total disaster for a Japan already facing certain military defeat. As if in slow motion, the pro-peace Japanese leaders cautiously probed and tested the possibilities that their opponents at home and their enemies abroad offered. For its part the United States had to decide what it meant by surrender, and whether military power or political negotiations would end the war.

The Japanese peace elements were circumspect, so much so that they hardly gave the United States much assurance of their serious intentions, and slight cause for optimism. At the end of September 1944 representatives of "important civilian circles" approached the Swedish minister in Tokyo to contact the British concerning a peace in which Japan would abandon all its conquests since Manchuria. The British, with Hull's concurrence, decided not to respond, for the offer looked like an attempt to split the Allies.[1] The American policy on both Japan and Germany demanded unconditional surrender, which it understood to mean the right to impose terms on the vanquished. In fact the United States already had determined that it would neither force Japan to pay retribution, as it would the Germans, nor abolish the institution of the Emperor, nor impose a mock democracy.

By the end of 1944 the Japanese peace factions believed that the war was obviously lost and that defeat would follow defeat. They renewed their efforts to redefine Japanese policy, but until they could solve their internal problems they had nothing to offer the Americans. In February 1945 the Emperor himself, a mild man incapable of standing up to the army throughout the war, finally canvassed a large group of critical leaders concerning the future of the war. Most refused to take a definitive position for immediate peace, and Tojo and the army still thought partial victory possible. Though Japanese air and sea power had been largely destroyed by that time, and only a shaky structure of each of these services remained, the army was still intact and naturally convinced that the forces on the ground would determine the war. Others in Japan were now more concerned with the prospect of revolution than of military defeat, to which they were reconciled. The most important spokesman of this group was Prince Fumimaro Konoye, an intimate of Emperor Hirohito and former premier during 1937–39 and then again during 1940–41. "What we have to fear," he explained to the Emperor in February, "is not so much a defeat as a Communist revolution which might take place in the event of defeat." The longer the war lasted, the worse the deterioration of the condition of the masses, the more unpopular the West as opposed to neutral Russia, the greater the sympathy for Communism among the younger bureaucrats and officers. No less threatening to Konoye was the merger of secularism and Communism, which he insisted was attracting growing support. ". . '. with defeat staring us in the face," he warned, "we shall simply be playing into the hands of the Communists if we elect to continue a war wherein there is no prospect of victory."[2]

Many others in Japan, well aware of the growing radicalization of the Japanese masses, shared these thoughts. The Chinese Communists were successfully indoctrinating many of the Japanese prisoners they captured, who formed various organizations after early 1944 and operated radios and a psychological-warfare campaign against Japanese troops. The Japanese ruling classes were aware of all this activity. No less consequential was the fact that the Americans went to some trouble to explain that they based their concept of unconditional surrender on the principles of the Atlantic Charter. In an oblique way, in brief, the United States encouraged the Japanese to believe what was in fact the case: the Americans did not intend to destroy Japan, but rather to renovate and incorporate it. Given the option of Bolshevism, the alternative was most attractive to the peace elements in and around the Japanese navy and industrial groups.

This inducement came from United States Naval Intelligence, which assigned Captain Ellis M. Zacharias the task of making broadcasts to which the Japanese leaders paid much attention. During early March, Zacharias and a group of right-wing geopoliticians Forrestal had gathered together from among Austro-Hungarian émigrés plotted various ways of exploiting the fragile Japanese political divisions to trigger a surrender before the Russians entered the war. Objectively they were convinced that Japan was on the verge of military defeat, an assumption that the entire Navy shared. They now advocated an intensive psychological-warfare campaign to encourage the peace faction and to exploit all peace overtures, and even such American initiatives as sending captured Japanese General Oshima and a secret submarine voyage to Japan led by the swashbuckling hero of adventure movies, Commander Douglas Fairbanks, Jr. Forrestal and King approved the program, but everyone else rebuffed it.

During this period the Japanese government fell and a Cabinet under Admiral Baron Kantaro Suzuki replaced it at the beginning of April. United States Naval Intelligence fully appreciated the significance of this change, since the new Prime Minister represented the navy and sections of big business and finance. Although Suzuki actively sought ways to peace, he would not surrender unconditionally. In fact the ruling class was still so delicately balanced that the new government could not consider unconditional surrender, but since March had debated a number of schemes for opening negotiations, perhaps via China, and from April onward it was simply a question of time before they consented to confront certain defeat and meet the Americans. When Germany fell the surrender faction grew stronger.[3]

Premature initiatives, which helped build caution and skepticism among the Americans, frustrated the Japanese effort to surrender, and in

the long run interfered with serious undertakings. At the end of April the
Japanese naval attaché in Switzerland contacted Allen Dulles of the OSS,
but Dulles soon discovered that the man had no authority, and could not
obtain any from the navy. A month later, as Hopkins was telling Stalin "of
the desire of the Japanese industrial families to preserve their position and
save Japan from destruction," Grew determined to encourage these liberal
elements geared toward a world, rather than exclusively Asian, economy
compatible with American goals.[4] On May 28 he won the President's
support for a proposal to offer the Japanese surrender terms permitting
them to retain the Emperor if they chose, which in fact was the American
position since the year before. Grew proposed that the victorious Allies
announce to the Japanese that they intended only to disarm their military
establishment and occupy their homeland, but that America would not
enslave the people and in due time would end the occupation, permitting
Japan to return to the world economy as a peace-loving nation with a
political system of its own choice, probably a constitutional monarchy.
Everything revolved around the phrase "unconditional surrender," but before Truman authorized a public offer to the Japanese he insisted Grew
consult the Joint Chiefs of Staff, Stimson, and Forrestal. They agreed with
the surrender principle, but they thought the situation was not ripe for a
public change in policy. They dropped the matter, but only for the moment. At the same time the President and his key aides decided not to warn
Japan of the possibility of an atomic attack.

Fatally ambivalent, the Japanese through May and June did little more
than define principles, and they failed to take decisive action for a strong
overture for peace as their military machine tottered before disaster. They
were so evenly divided as to become ineffectual, and the minor surrender
efforts that they initiated via Sweden and Switzerland only lowered the
credibility of later, more serious overtures. On June 8 the Japanese Supreme
War Direction Council began its session (which would last for over two
months), and while it hammered out its differences, in effect it accepted the
army position to continue the war. In mid-June, Grew again unsuccessfully
urged Truman publicly to offer Japan surrender terms based on actual
American planning for that nation's future. Grew explained the proposal to
the President, Stimson, and the Joint Chiefs of Staff as a settlement with
"liberal-minded" Japanese.[5] The military at this point was convinced that
the war required ground forces to conquer the islands, with the aid of the
Russians and the bomb. They did not appreciate the value of public diplomacy, which they believed would lower the fighting edge of American
soldiers by building false hopes. Truman now only agreed to raise the matter
at Potsdam.

Then on June 20 the Emperor swung behind the navy and the Japanese
agreed to use Russia for exploratory peace discussions. The government

made its decision over army objections, and was dilatory, and furthermore the inquiry took the form of an effort to strike a large-scale diplomatic bargain with Russia in the Far East to keep it out of the war. At this time, despite a vast Soviet troop build-up to 1.6 million men in the Far East, the Japanese did not expect Russian entry into the war before September. The Russians refused to cooperate, and the clumsy maneuver cost the Japanese much time.

While the Japanese vacillated, Stimson and the State Department kept reflecting on the surrender question and further defined certain assumptions prior to meeting the Russians at Potsdam. Grew reiterated the State Department's desire publicly to offer the Japanese specific surrender terms, and he was resolved that the United States delegation would take up the matter at the forthcoming Potsdam meeting. By early July, Stimson, who shared Grew's optimism on the Japanese liberal elements' willingness to accept the American image of a future world order, was ready to support a new surrender offer at Potsdam, but *after* Japan had "been sufficiently pounded" by atomic bombs. Stimson saw no conflict between sustained military action and diplomacy, and no reason to think future Japanese peace gestures would be more substantial than those false alarms that helped to build American immunity to surrender overtures.[6] He predicted to Truman on July 2 that the war in Japan would be "very long, costly and arduous.....".[7] He did not expect the atomic bomb to alter that fact.

There the surrender question rested before Potsdam, the repeated false starts and the profound division in Japan itself having built up American immunity to surrender offers and the hope of a quick negotiated surrender. The Japanese leaders were in fact, as Washington comprehended, unwilling collectively to confront realities and act decisively. On July 7 they took firmer action and asked Konoye to go to Moscow to seek Russian mediation in the war, but the Emperor secretly asked him to negotiate peace on any terms. Four days later the Minister of Foreign Affairs, Shigenori Togo, raised the proposal to his ambassador in Moscow, Naotake Sato, and instructed him to inform the Russians that Konoye wished to come to Moscow to discuss mediation. Konoye would arrive after Stalin left for Potsdam, and Togo explicitly excluded unconditional surrender as a possibility. No one told Sato of Konoye's secret mandate, which the army may have refused to accept. Sato derided the false pretensions of his superior and the unwillingness of Tokyo to acknowledge realities and defeat. But on July 13 he duly notified the Russians that Japan wished their aid, and the Soviets seemed too preoccupied or uninterested to hold out much hope for a positive reply.

Since the Americans had cracked the Japanese code, they knew of the debates and the haggling, save for Konoye's secret instructions, and it only filled them with increased suspicion of Japanese motives. Togo was not

ready to consider surrender in the form the Americans had publicly demanded, but Forrestal thought it "The first real evidence of a Japanese
desire to get out of the war," and the words "first" and "desire" indicate
that the new departure was a possible option only. Until this time the
critical figures in Washington had ample reason to feel suspicious of Japanese sincerity, and Stimson himself thought them "maneuverings for
peace."[8] Whether they would materialize remained debatable. Grew himself was not ready to grasp at such overtures as Japan had made, and during
the first week of July he insisted that the bids up to that time had not come
from serious, responsible parties.[9] When Truman arrived at Potsdam on
July 16, his advisers did not expect an early Japanese surrender and they
were, as a result of repeated, empty Japanese gestures, prone to plan on the
basis of known, tangible factors. In mid-July this meant the atomic bomb
and the Red Army.

The New Secretary of State

When Truman went to Potsdam he took with him his new Secretary of
State as of July 3, James F. Byrnes. Byrnes was an old-fashioned South
Carolina politician who managed to become one of Roosevelt's favorites.
After long service in the House and Senate he moved to the Supreme
Court, but Roosevelt soon brought him to the White House as head of the
Office of War Mobilization. There he gradually replaced Hopkins as the
leading adviser to the President, and Roosevelt made no secret that Byrnes
was his first choice for the Vice-Presidency in 1944. The party decided
otherwise, much to Byrnes's disappointment, but Roosevelt continued to
use him for a growing variety of critical functions, even taking him to
Yalta. In 1948 Byrnes supported the Dixiecrat candidate for the Presidency, and Barry Goldwater sixteen years later. Roosevelt, as was his
wont, was attracted to the man on a personal basis and because of his
admitted efficiency, and he saw nothing incongruous about Byrnes's opinions and the roles that the President assigned to him. Although the former
Senatorial leader had little special interest or competence in foreign policy,
the Secretary of State's post was the highest political reward in the Cabinet.
When Truman took over the Presidency he determined to appoint the
politically powerful and experienced man to the post as soon as a graceful
opportunity permitted.

Truman told Byrnes of the contemplated appointment, and when Stettinius returned from the San Francisco Conference the President accepted
his resignation. The new Secretary did not have a precise mind, and Senator Tom Connally was convinced quickly enough that he "knew little about
foreign affairs."[10] During the month of July he revealed his weaknesses in
various ways, and Truman after the war realized that payment of a politi-

cal debt was not conducive to an effective foreign policy requiring some degree of subtlety that, even Truman was quick to perceive, Byrnes lacked. Yet Byrnes took the advice of his executive assistants in the State Department, assuring continuity in policy. Byrnes considered options, but he was incapable of defining a consistent policy to achieve his goals.[11]

The Far Eastern Patchwork and War

The intricate complexities facing the leaders of the United States at the beginning of July can only be seen in the larger context in which Washington regarded them at the time. One must distinguish between the global problems of the dismal relations between Russia and the West and the immediate tasks at hand in the Far East, and take into account potentially bloody costs to the United States if the Soviets did not enter the war or if the United States refused to use the atomic bomb. A continuation of the military coalition with Russia had its political dangers, and for these America sought political assurances that United States interests, being undermined everywhere else, would not suffer a similar fate in China; but to ignore the fact that the United States still thought it was engaged in a long and difficult war poses fatal traps for the historical record.

After the 15th no one in Washington or in Potsdam fully appreciated that an ever-growing number of Japanese rulers were desperately serious about surrendering. Had they really understood the depth of the urgency behind the Konoye-navy position, then unquestionably the United States would have explored this option, for surrender would have solved certain military problems, though not others, pertaining to China. During the first week of July both the OSS and the Combined Intelligence Committee assessed the probable course of the war. The agencies informed the various military branches that the Japanese were mobilizing their civilians to resist an invasion of the homeland, and while they acknowledged that the navy and air force were effectively destroyed, the army still possessed over four and a half million soldiers, over two million in Japan itself, and as many as one million in north China and Manchuria. As for the American demand for unconditional surrender, "There are as yet no indications that the Japanese are ready to accept such terms."[12]

The closer the Americans approached the homeland the greater their casualties became, so that by Okinawa they estimated their loss ratio of killed and wounded was almost as great as among Japanese troops. The military prospect of a war in Japan itself was frightfully bloody and grim, and indeed at the beginning of July the Japanese had 4,800 planes ready for suicide attacks against the invaders. On the opening day of Potsdam, Stimson was quite convinced, even though certain that the atomic bomb would soon be ready, that the Russian troops would still have much to do.

Truman shared his view, and in his memoir recalls that "There were many reasons for my going to Potsdam, but the most urgent, to my mind, was to get from Stalin a personal reaffirmation of Russia's entry into the war against Japan, a matter which our military chiefs were most anxious to clinch."[13] Their joint determination was only reinforced on July 20 when the OSS predicted widespread Japanese suicide defenses of the dangerous Kamikaze variety which had already cost many American lives, sunk 34 ships, and damaged 285 others.

Russian intervention remained very much in doubt, because regardless of American desires, from the inception the Russians irritatingly tied entrance into the war to Chiang's acceptance of the Yalta proposals on China. At no time did the Russians drop this posture, eliminate the need for the Americans to cajole them, or lose entire control of the initiatives. Even if not again invited, they could always enter the war when they were ready to do so, and the United States Joint Chiefs of Staff knew intervention would come when it was to the Soviet advantage. It was the timing, rather than the principle, that still interested the American leaders, and when they had to consider how far they wished to go in pleading with the Russians it was never with the belief that they could keep the Russians out of the war. Both sides acted with utter realism on this issue and merely sought to maximize their gains.

When Soong arrived in Moscow the last day of June he instantly discovered that the Russians felt they had the upper hand in the negotiations and would delay if necessary. Stalin and Molotov were willing to grant full recognition immediately to the Kuomintang as opposed to the Communists, and to allow a civil-affairs agreement which would permit Chiang's officers to take over Soviet-occupied territory; in return they wanted the imperialist prerogatives a weak China would concede in the form of a more than generous interpretation of the Yalta provisions on Manchurian railroads, one that would have given the Russians control of the railroads and a contiguous economic complex of factories and mines, and much more extended base rights to Dairen, Port Arthur, and the surrounding territories. Soong for his part retrenched on the Yalta Agreement by refusing to relinquish the Chinese claim on Outer Mongolia or to concede Port Arthur to Russian administration. China insisted on owning the Manchurian railroads on an exclusive basis. It was immediately apparent to Washington that the two nations were unlikely to agree, and on July 4 the State Department notified Harriman to inform Soong that the United States favored the status quo, which was to say, Russian control, in Mongolia. Several days later Harriman told him to make certain that any agreement between China and Russia protected equal American access to Dairen and the railroads in question—in brief, that they maintain the Open Door for future American economic interests. After some horse trading Soong and the Russians remained far apart on the control of the ports and railroads, and on July 10 Soong suggested that he would have to return to Chungking for further instructions. Stalin was no less adamant, and pointed out to Soong that the Soviet Union wished an agreement immediately so that it might fix the date of entry into the war against Japan. But the Russian gave nothing to make this possible, and several days later Soong returned to China, leaving Moscow on a cordial note. To Harriman, Soong confided his hope that the United States would win Russia to the Chinese position at Potsdam, and Chiang also sent such a plea on the 20th.[14]

Obviously the Russians were not overly anxious for an agreement, for they wanted a weak China to exploit, nor were the Chinese yet ready to abandon the hope that the Americans might add to their strength to confront Moscow. The question of Soviet entry into the war apart, the United States had no reason to welcome the breakdown in the talks, which Truman urged Chiang to resume on his own responsibility. Both Truman and Byrnes were too wise to risk American interests on a common front with Chiang. If Chiang failed to accept the Yalta accords the Russians were also free to support whomever they wished in China, and for the United States the larger political issue was at stake rather than the precise control mechanisms at Port Arthur. After long experience with Chiang the Americans had no reason to expect him to avoid a suicidal course by sacrificing the major point for a small one. Insofar as these lesser technicalities were concerned, it was not the Chinese interests in Manchuria and north China that the United States wished to protect, but its own. To protect these interests required a direct agreement with the Russians on the Open Door in north China, one which went beyond Yalta. Several days before Potsdam the State Department formally determined to go outside the limits of the proposed Yalta Agreement and obtain from both China and Russia separate, explicit agreements recognizing that "The United States has . . . an important practical interest in trade and commerce in Manchuria which should be safeguarded."[15] Since, as Stimson felt, "Manchuria has never been actually and really a part of China," only the Russians could grant equal opportunity.[16]

Truman had not formally invited Stimson to Potsdam but the Secretary of War determined to go anyway. Both he and Harriman were much disturbed over the possibility of a future Soviet trade monopoly in Manchuria, and he raised the question with Truman as soon as he arrived in Germany. Truman did not think the problem insignificant—quite the contrary—but it impressed him as weighing rather too heavily with his Secretary of War and for the next ten days he excluded Stimson from many critical meetings.

It is important to note that when the Potsdam Conference opened the overall political and military situation in the Far East and Europe had not altered over the preceding weeks, nor did it change throughout the conference. The Japanese military fought with ardor, and the Americans fully expected that the atomic bomb would explode and be available to do what conventional strategic bombing was inflicting with growing frequency. The situation in China gave no cause for hope, and the Americans still needed Russian aid there. Meanwhile every European issue filled Truman, Churchill, and their aides with growing frustration and anger over Soviet policies and intentions, until a sullen mood enveloped the gathering. Inevitably this attitude soon crept into their evaluation of Far Eastern problems and needs, and the impact of events in Europe influenced their assessment of the Far Eastern perspective. Yet the practical leaders of the United States could not ignore the very tangible military aid the Russians still might give, and what they said during the morose sixteen days was far less consequential than what they ultimately chose to do.

The question of Soviet entry into the war against Japan was not really one of whether the Americans wished their aid, but, as it had been for two years, whether the Russians would finally and unequivocally consent. When Stalin arrived at Potsdam he still felt that he had something to give the West, and therefore was in a position to ask for rewards in return. The Americans had to ask themselves how hard they wished to press the Russians. Because of Soviet insistence these problems were linked to Chinese ratification of the proposed Yalta accord. On the 16th and 17th Stimson urged Truman to interpret the Yalta Agreement in a manner that would not permit the Russians to sweep Manchuria into their economic sphere of influence. Although this was also Soong's view, Stimson obviously intended United States support to China merely to be a way of protecting "our clear and growing interests in the orient."[17] For the same reasons he urged a reiteration of the Four Power trusteeship agreement on Korea committing American troops to prevent a Communist takeover there. At no time did Stimson link the need for Soviet entry into the war to these issues.

During the evening of the 16th Stimson received a cable that "Babies satisfactorily born,"—the United States had successfully exploded an atomic bomb, and his aides were rushing the details to Potsdam.[18] Not until they arrived five days later did the American delegation realize that the bomb introduced a new factor into the conference. Until then they had conducted the discussion over the Far East on the assumption they still required Russian entry into the war, and after the next day they had already obtained in principle Soviet assent to the Open Door. On the 17th, when Stalin turned to China, Stimson had convinced both Truman and Byrnes of the importance of the Open Door. On that day Stalin made it plain that he would have to reach an accord with the Chinese before entering the war— mid-August being his most definite date for going to war—but he also thought agreement was not far off. After summarizing the issues Truman asked Stalin what implications the arrangement in Manchuria would have on American rights, and Stalin immediately described Dairen as a free port open equally to all foreign commerce; this, Truman responded, was the Open Door policy, and at the end of the conversation, the American reporter noted, both the President and Byrnes "indicated that the main interest of the United States was in a free port." During these comforting exchanges, among the few Truman heard, the President again asked Stalin when they might expect Soviet entry into the war, and he indicated his confidence in Russia's promise to aid its allies. Later that day Truman assured Stimson he had clinched the Open Door principle. Stimson was not so confident, and the next day forced Truman on the defensive by emphasizing "to him the importance of going over the matter detail by detail so as to be sure that there would be no misunderstanding. . . ."[19] Stimson, the President apparently thought, was becoming a nuisance.

As additional details of the atomic explosion at New Mexico arrived, the deliberations over the Far Eastern war continued. On the 18th the Anglo-American Combined Chiefs of Staff, with Marshall and King leading the American delegation, decided to pass along all operational and intelligence data to the Russians to improve their military efficiency when they entered the war—the unquestioned assumption being that they would do so. On the negotiations with China and protecting the Open Door, Harriman advised pressing for a definition of the Yalta accord in a way that would safeguard American interests and support Soong's position insofar as it aided the United States.

Churchill was the first to realize the bomb had political and military significance far greater than the first sodden response of the Americans appeared to suggest. Field Marshal Alan Brooke thought the Prime Minister's infantile enthusiasm bordered on the dangerous: "He was already seeing himself capable of eliminating all the Russian centres of industry. . . . He had at once painted a wonderful picture of himself as the sole possessor of these bombs and capable of dumping them where he wished. . . ."[20] He tried to communicate the fantasy to his associates, but they resisted it, and he urged Truman to dispense with the aid of the Russians in the war. Truman did not immediately respond to the idea, for when Truman saw Stalin on the 19th their conversation turned to a common shipping pool and the future sale of surplus boats. Russia, the President declared, would reenter the shipping pool as an equal when it declared war against Japan. "I added that we were eager to have Russia in the shipping pool with us," Truman noted of the renewed, if oblique, invitation.[21] On the morning of the 21st Stimson received the graphic details of the explosion and immediately took them to Truman and Byrnes. The bomb was 15 to 20 kilotons, much more than most had expected. It certainly might destroy a city. Truman, Stimson reported, was "pepped up," he had new confidence and, significantly, "thanked me for having come to the Conference."[22] Stimson notified Churchill the following day, and the English leader again urged that they consider it as a diplomatic lever on the Russians.

To advance the story, the American leaders had a week to debate the bomb's implications for their military and political strategy, and Churchill argued that it eliminated the need for Russian entry into the war. On the morning of the 23rd, as he listened to repeated, bitter complaints concerning Russian policy in Europe, Truman himself raised the question. Stimson then asked Marshall whether Soviet entry was still necessary, and the two men agreed to feel out the Russian intentions, intentions that were obscure in the sense that the Russians still linked entry, and especially a date, to a settlement with China. Marshall made several telling points as the President decided to suspend policy for the day. The Russians, he observed, were needed to hold down the Japanese army in Manchuria, and this they were already doing by their massed presence on the borders. Even if the United States could defeat Japan without Russian aid, the Russians were not now going to sit by idly because of questions of protocol and agreement with Chiang. They could still strike Manchuria after the Japanese surrendered, and in any event, the President and his advisers must have realized as Marshall spoke on, that they could not use the atomic bomb in China. On that same day the President wired Hurley to inform Chiang that he was no longer under American pressure to concede more than the Allies agreed upon at Yalta, whatever that meant in detail, and that Soong ought to return to Moscow—he did not indicate urgency—should disagreement with the Russians continue. Churchill, perhaps correctly, took this to mean "it is quite clear that the United States do not at the present time desire Russian participation in the war against Japan."[23] Stimson, to learn when he might use the bomb against Japan, wired his aide, Harrison, who answered possibly between August 1 and 3, that there was a good chance for the following two days, and almost certainly before August 10.

Should this reconsideration of policy be taken as a new policy itself, and was the dropping of the bomb a result of relations with Russia or a reflection of a desire to end the war before the U.S.S.R. could intervene? Inevitably the United States evaluated the impact of the bomb on its fixed policy, and necessarily came to the conclusion that the Russians could no longer be kept out of the war, were probably still needed, and the existence of the bomb would not pressure them on a political level. The Americans could compel the Russians into collaboration with them on American terms only if they were willing to use the bomb against the Russians themselves, and the historian cannot project the fact that such was the case some years later onto the conditions of July 1945. At the time only Churchill entertained the idea. The Russians in fact knew that the bomb would be available to the Americans, and they already based their diplomacy and conduct on certain constant factors—mainly centered about the recognition of American power and the preservation of Soviet security. To engage in an atomic war with Russia at the time, with Europe already starving and a massive battle-hardened Russian army intact, was a thought only a Churchill might entertain, and on July 24 he was defeated in the British general election.

The bomb itself was built to be dropped, no one ever had the slightest doubt America would use it, and Soviet coyness could not alter these facts. Truman wavered on Soviet entry but further reflection immediately brought him back into line, as he rejected the contemplated alternative. The Russians would hopefully succor the Americans in China as they had in Europe. The United States would obtain the political assurances needed for American interests in Manchuria directly from the Russians.

July 24 was a day of many irreversible decisions on the Far East, and Truman and his advisers confirmed and consolidated the main thrust of policy of the preceding week. Churchill departed the following day, and Stimson soon followed. The Secretary of War made something of an irritant of himself, despite his glad news of the new weapon. On the 23rd he complained to Truman that he was being excluded from many of the critical meetings, and when on the following day he repeated the grievance, Truman coolly told him he might leave anytime he chose to do so. On that same day, with Stimson's hardy concurrence, Truman, Churchill, and the Combined Chiefs of Staff met and reiterated the policy to "Encourage Russian entry into the war against Japan."[24] At the same session the Americans finally officially excluded Britain from the definition of the grand strategy of the war against Japan. They agreed that the military situation still necessitated an invasion of Japan, requiring perhaps a million or more men. They did not expect the bomb to alter that fact. That afternoon, when the Anglo-American generals met with Antonov, he persisted in tying entry into the war, now perhaps for the last half of August, to the resolution of the China question. The Russians still believed they had something to offer and might expect a price in return. Even after the bomb the Americans were still compelled to consider how they might induce the Russians to enter the war.

On the same day Truman sent instructions to the Air Force to drop the first bomb as soon as it was ready, and weather permitted, "after about 3 August," and to deliver the rest on four target cities "as soon as made ready."[25] Nothing had changed; the Americans would implement their wartime plans.

At the beginning of the month, Stimson again raised the question of whether and when to inform Stalin of the new weapon, and he urged the President to be as vague on the matter as possible to avoid a confrontation over the future of the bomb and international control of it. On July 18 Truman asked Churchill his opinion, obviously already determined to tell Stalin something about a powerful new weapon while skirting specifics as to its character. To this Churchill assented. All of the versions of the observers present on the evening of the 24th confirm the basic facts. Truman ambled up to Stalin, and mentioned that the United States had developed a new and unusually destructive bomb that they were soon to use against Japan. Stalin seemed pleased, expressed hope that they would put it to good use, and asked no questions. Truman never used the word "atom" and Stalin showed no surprise. Positions during the subsequent days hardly altered, and clearly Stalin already understood enough to know before the end of the conference that the superbomb was the very weapon the Russians were seeking to develop or win for themselves.

Stalin, during a genial banquet several evenings earlier, had toasted the next meeting of the gathering in Tokyo, and spoke of the imminent Russian intervention on a massive scale, but the Russians had been so persistently elusive in the past that the Secretary of War felt impelled, before returning home, to tell Stalin on July 25 "that I hoped that the combination of the forces of the Soviet Union, the United States and the United Kingdom, would bring speedy victory—not only complete but short." "Stalin," Stimson recorded several times in various ways, "said that Three Power intervention in the Pacific would surely speed up victory."[26]

Once the Russians seemingly dropped their annoying reserve, the American leaders responded emphatically to the promise of their aid, for no one wished to confront the monumental dangers Japan still appeared to pose to American lives. They only had to guard against damage to American interests in Manchuria—directly with the Russians if possible—and to encourage the Chinese to drop the reticent stand Truman and Byrnes had authorized on the 23rd, to remove that cause for Russian delay in entering the fray. On July 28 Harriman advised Byrnes that "Although it may not be desirable for us at this time to show any concern over the question of Russia's entry into the war against Japan," they would lose nothing by having the Chinese sign an agreement with them that did not sacrifice the Open Door. Above all a direct Russian reaffirmation, one which put Stalin's verbal assurances in writing, might best protect the principle of the Open Door in Manchuria and would give the United States the opportunity "to deal with the Soviet Government directly," rather than via a weak China not likely to prove persuasive.[27] The Americans prepared a draft protocol and the same day Byrnes cabled Soong to arrange to go to Moscow as soon as Stalin returned. Over the next days the United States pressed the Chinese, so much that Harriman warned Byrnes of the dangers of Soong's sacrificing Dairen as a free port, a matter central to keeping the Manchurian door open to American trade. The other problems, he now thought, were capable of quick resolution. Then on July 29 Molotov asked Truman if the Allies would prepare an invitation to the U.S.S.R. to join the war, one that might give them a formal excuse to intervene—but again he made intervention contingent on the painful matter of prior agreement with the Chinese.

Molotov's request offered the Americans both a possibility and a problem. As of that late date the Russians still refused to make an unequivocal commitment on entry into the war and the time that they expected to do so; though the Americans generally anticipated August, nothing was binding. The Americans had successfully tested the bomb and would drop it within days. Another would be ready shortly thereafter. The Russians gave Americans oral assurances on the Open Door in Manchuria, but so far nothing was on paper and Soong had yet to find evidence of Russian willingness to relinquish the Tsarist patrimony in China. The Japanese were probing, not for the first time, the possibility of surrender, although they were fighting for every inch of the islands approaching the homeland. Now the Russians themselves offered the United States the option of keeping the Soviet Union out of the war and ending the affronts concerning their political price.

Only Byrnes among the senior members of the American delegation favored trying to end the war before the Russians entered, and Truman now stood firmly with the military leaders, though he resented the tone of the Soviet request and their continued exploitation of the assumption that they were the key to victory in the Far East. Truman told Byrnes to draft the request to the Russians, and to give an aloof, legal justification to permit the Russians to violate the nonaggression treaty that they still had in force with the Japanese. Byrnes some years later suggested that Truman authorized the legal coolness of the letter as part of an attempt to avoid the Russian request, but deep regret then colored his memory. No one considered the option of prolonged delay at the time and, save for Byrnes, everyone understood they needed Russian aid and that they could not avoid it at the moment the Russians chose to give it. The critical question was still when they might expect it. Working late into the night with Benjamin Cohen, his lawyer, Byrnes drafted the invitation on the basis of Russia's obligations under the United Nations Charter. On July 31, after much haste so as not to appear indifferent, Truman gave the statement to Stalin, who expressed his great appreciation to the President. It is worth noting that Truman offered Stalin the option of delaying the American request at his own initiative until after he concluded his talks with Soong, as Stalin told him would be necessary, but Truman assured him the invitation would be instantly forthcoming on demand. He also suggested that Russia might prefer basing its entry into the war on some other grounds than those given in his letter, and clearly Soviet entry was not contingent on Byrnes's cool formulation or in any way discouraged.[28]

The Potsdam Surrender Offer

Stimson and most especially Grew were very much in favor of offering the Japanese the opportunity to leave the war after issuing an Allied proclamation, but the Secretary of War planned this act to follow the dropping of the atomic bomb, and he suspected that the overture would not do much good. A few days before his departure for Potsdam, Grew handed Byrnes a draft of such a proclamation and asked him to consider and act upon it. Byrnes immediately noticed the clause mentioning the policy of retaining the Emperor, which Grew and Stimson endorsed and was in reality American policy for the postwar nation. Still feeling insecure in his new post, he decided to consult Hull, and his most distinguished predecessor warned him that it would appear as a retreat from unconditional surrender. It would be best, he advised, to wait until Japan had been fully bombed and the Russians entered the war. Byrnes agreed, decided to recommend that they revise the statement, and if possible, postpone it altogether. When Stimson arrived at Potsdam he was anxious to issue a proclamation to the Japanese, but he found Byrnes opposed and claiming Presidential backing for his stand, even after the first bomb had been tested and reported successful. Stimson won support from the Joint Chiefs of Staff, who on the 18th informed the President that they favored a proclamation, but with no commitments or explicit references as to the future structure of Japanese politics. Truman was now prepared to support the proclamation.

While the Allied leaders sat in Potsdam, Sato in Moscow and Foreign Minister Togo still continued their acerbic cables on what Sato considered to be the clumsy and unrealistic efforts of Japan to surrender. Since the United States had cracked the Japanese code, they knew the contents of the cables immediately and the Pentagon kept Stimson, at least, aware of them. Stalin, shortly after the conference opened, told Churchill and Truman of the Japanese approaches. Meanwhile both the Japanese and the American press suddenly became aware of the broadcasts of Zacharias promising the provisions of the Atlantic Charter to a defeated Japan, and it created so much attention that some proclamation was essential if only to deny what in fact was the secret American policy. When Truman asked Churchill about the matter on the 24th, Churchill urged him to issue a milder proclamation which permitted the Japanese to retain their "military honour," a phrase which caused the President to bridle and respond that they had none.[29] But the English leader took the draft for comment without illusions as to its consequences for the course of the actual war, and now, according to Truman, "Churchill was as anxious as I was for the Russians to come into the Japanese war."[30] On the same day Stimson urged Truman to break with the position of Byrnes and the Joint Chiefs and insert some reassuring words into the proclamation concerning the future of the dynasty, for they might be critical in actually stimulating surrender moves. Truman promised only to consider it, and the following day Stimson left Potsdam.

Had Truman or Byrnes seriously thought there was any way of keeping the Russians out of the Far Eastern war, much less that it was desirable, ending the war by permitting the Japanese to surrender quickly would have been entirely consistent with such a viewpoint. In that case they would have supported Stimson's advice. Byrnes would have preferred Russia's staying out, but he was so unsure of himself at this stage, and so unaware of the inconsistencies between his desires and action, that he chose to take an incompatible hard-line toward both the Russians and Japanese.

The British made a few minor modifications in the American-proposed draft, and although Truman told Stalin his staff was preparing it, the Americans did not show the Russians an advance copy. The final text, dated the 26th, only once called for unconditional surrender, and it avoided all mention of the future of the Emperor, implicitly leaving it to the Allies to determine whether he remained or not after surrender. It threatened frightful destruction of the armed forces and homeland, but did not specify the means. The Allies would disarm the military and deprive Japan of its imperial conquests. The proclamation also specified that the Allies had no intention of enslaving Japan, and would welcome it back into the world economy on the principle of equal access of all nations to raw materials. The victors would encourage "democratic tendencies," including civil liberties. Ultimately the occupation would end after the Allies had accomplished their objectives and the Japanese had chosen "a peacefully inclined and responsible government." But to qualify Japan had to surrender unconditionally, and "The alternative for Japan is prompt and utter destruction."[31]

The Americans showed Molotov a text of the final draft after they had released it to the press, and he immediately asked for a two- to three-day delay, which of course was already too late to grant. If the Russians now thought the Americans were attempting to end the war before they joined it, they surely did not end their delaying tactics at Potsdam, and their later haste in advancing their entry was unquestionably based on other factors. For it was rather apparent at the time, to the Americans no less than the Russians, that the Japanese were not going to accept the offer, and both Stimson and Grew were sure the proclamation fell short of what they hoped would be its real purpose. To Grew, it had been drained of its potential value in strengthening the Emperor against the army.

Togo on July 25 informed Sato that while he would consider a peace based on the Atlantic Charter, "it is impossible to accept unconditional surrender under any circumstances. . . ."[32] This information was available to the Americans almost as quickly as to Sato. Then, when the United States issued the Potsdam Proclamation via every radio station in the American network, they submitted no formal text to the Japanese via a neutral country, and reduced the matter to psychological warfare. The Suzuki government was interested in conditional surrender, and one must understand all that followed in the context of the procrastination and delicate power structure which by late July had reduced the leaders of Japan to a diplomatic impotence that Washington fully comprehended. At his afternoon press conference on July 28 the reporters asked Suzuki about the Potsdam Declaration, and the American translation had his comment read, "As for the Government, it does not find any important value in it, and there is no other recourse but to ignore it entirely and resolutely fight for the successful conclusion of this war."[33]

Stimson and Truman thought the answer unambiguous because they did not know Japanese, though another translation of the reply was slightly different, but for practical purposes "ignore" is all that counted. The critical Japanese word, *mokusatsu,* from which they extracted "ignore," under certain circumstances can also mean "no comment," perhaps even "pending further information."[34] The subtle distinction, which made a difference but would not necessarily have changed the paralyzing division in Japan once the information was forthcoming, was immediately grasped by the Japanese hard-line factions around the army and turned into a serious issue. They demanded an unequivocal statement, and on the 30th Suzuki gave it to them in a reiteration of the first statement, as the Americans had understood it, in sharper form. Such semantic haggling made no difference in actual policy, for on these very days Togo was still pressing the Russians to welcome Prince Konoye to Moscow to explore means for ending the war without unconditional surrender and with Japan's "honor and existence" preserved.[35] The Americans knew all of this, and Harriman and Forrestal were distressed that the Russians had become the link to ending the war with Japan. While they were not at all optimistic about the chances of success on the terms the Japanese appeared to be considering, the triangular arrangement obviously made peace all the more difficult.

Mechanism prevailed. No one seriously explored any of the options—neither Japanese surrender, nor delay, nor withholding the bomb. The leaders of the United States considered, and for a moment rethought, but in the end they did not alter their course, not merely because there was no effective way of preventing the Russians from doing what they had been asked to undertake for several years, but because the United States still felt the Russians had something left to offer that might save time and American blood. In fact the leaders of the United States decided to continue the war on the basis of known and predictable factors: they took a conservative position and would not risk the alternatives of possibly fighting the war in China. Any realistic assessment of the objective conditions of the Japanese during those weeks might have convinced a reasonable group of men that significant alternatives to prolonged war existed, but the Japanese leaders themselves were incapable of confronting their defeat and acting accordingly. The United States would take no chances. For precisely the same reasons of mechanism and conservatism, which the Japanese in their own desperate way shared, the Americans decided to use the bomb as a known and now predictable factor of war, an economical means of destroying vast numbers of men, women, and children, soldiers and civilians. Well before August 1945 they had reduced this to a routine.

The United States could have won the war without the Russians and without the atomic bomb.

THE POTSDAM CONFERENCE: THE FUTURE OF EUROPE AND THE END OF A COALITION

TALK AND COMPROMISE could not resolve the mutual disagreements and the burdens of years of seething conflicts the United States, England, and the Soviet Union brought to Potsdam, for they were based on antagonisms between social systems and tangible vital interests. More fundamentally, unforeseen revolutionary change was undermining the entire pattern of prewar political and economic relations both within and between nations. That crisis in the Old Order would only grow, and the causes of it—the weakening, even collapse of much of world capitalism and colonialism—were such that the three nations gathered near Berlin could not, despite their intentions, put together what over three decades of war and crises had undone. In fact much of the rest of the world, oblivious of the desires of the high and mighty, had already begun to move to shape their own destinies and thwart the stabilizing efforts of the men at Potsdam.

The alliance had been a purely military arrangement, bound together only by mutual necessity, and Potsdam was only the second truly political conference of the heads of state, one that they called into being because the gap in mutual aspirations had become too great to ignore totally. Yalta had solved nothing, but perhaps—though the hope was dim—it was not too late for a new accommodation.

Germany and the Future of European Power

Treated as a purely technical problem of reparations or zonal authority, the question of Germany at Potsdam—surely the most important of all the problems considered—appears inordinately complex. In fact it was painfully simple to all concerned, and the bargaining and tugging between the former allies at Potsdam should not conceal the basic reality that for the United States the German question was essentially whether Germany should be weak or strong in the postwar period—or a balance between the two—and a barrier to the expansion of Communism and Russia toward the Atlantic. A harsh peace, with heavy reparations, would require that the Germans, rather than the battered Russians, pay for a substantial part of postwar Soviet reconstruction. To the Russians, now probably quite certain that they would not obtain loans or credits from the United States, German reparations meant potentially great capital imports in one form or another and the elimination of a powerful nation with which they had twice gone to war in twenty-five years. For this reason alone they had in the months prior to Potsdam energetically attempted to make the Four Power Control Council in Berlin a successful example of the future, for unless they collected reparations from the Anglo-French-American zones, comprising two-thirds of the nation's wealth, the U.S.S.R. could hope to obtain little.

To the State Department, and most especially to the War Department, Germany's excessive weakness would open the door to chaos in all of Europe, greatly compound the administrative problems confronting the military occupation authorities, and perhaps shift a vast relief burden to the backs of the American taxpayers—for they would not permit Germany to starve. And on general principle the United States opposed reparations of a magnitude that would finance postwar European reconstruction, interfering with the "normalization" of trade and American loans. Lueius Clay, Stimson and, increasingly, the State Department favored a significant measure of German economic recovery and the reintegration of a democratized and peaceful Germany into a world modeled on American-defined trade and political principles, principles quite incompatible with either the triumph of Communism or the resurgence of Nazism. The Americans had yet to clarify the precise means for attaining this delicate end, for the policy statement JCS 1067 really gave Clay's military government a number of options in implementing policy. But since they expected the Russians to do as they pleased in their zone, or in any event would pose the greatest immediate political threat, the Americans now regarded a maximum of zonal autonomy as the desirable means of reconstruction. By mid-July such a policy appeared to hold the greatest promise of attaining the not altogether consistent United States objectives in the homeland of its former enemy.

The visual impact the ruins in Germany made on Truman and those American leaders who had never before seen the sights of war reinforced the American impulse to write a mild peace, and they quickly forgot that the destruction in Eastern Europe and Russia was far greater. As Truman drove through Berlin on July 16 he saw "piles of stone and rubble," and "the long, never-ending procession of old men, women, and children wandering aimlessly. . . ."[1] The same day Stimson urged the President to avoid any further destruction of existing resources, and to use the remaining German power to "enable her to play her part in the necessary rehabilitation of Europe."[2] This would require some decentralization, in the form of a dismembered Ruhr, but not enough to weaken Germany and, with it, Europe.

The reparations issue, amiably suited to horse trading as well as a large degree of deception, impinged centrally on the question of the future control of Germany and the amount of power the Allies would permit it to retain. That reparations became the most complicated and central issue at Potsdam reflected the ambiguity in United States plans and the total lack of consensus among the Russians and their former collaborators. It immediately subsumed the question of the future of the Four Power Control Council, the status of the Ruhr, Poland's western boundary, and ultimately, the still unspoken aspirations of the Anglo-Americans for Germany.

The Reparations Commission in Moscow created as a result of the Yalta Conference ended in an impasse, the Americans insisting that they fix no dollar size on quantitative amounts for final reparations, and that the United States would follow the first-charge principle to pay for imports into its zone before reparations. In effect the Americans would permit the Germans to trade before going hungry to meet their obligations to their former enemies, and the Russians quickly pointed out at Potsdam that this principle would encourage the Germans to prove their need to import, and allow them to end up, as after World War I, powerful traders while paying small reparations. To the Americans, anxious to see the restoration of a world economy based on "normal" trading principles, the first-charge principle was inviolable, and as Byrnes told Molotov on July 23, "There can be no discussion of this matter."[3] In fact, implicit in this doctrine was self-contained zonal economic autonomy rather than a Four Power economic control mechanism which balanced the total needs and priorities of Germany.

From the opening of the conference the Russians urged the creation of effective Four Power control over the German economy, which took for granted a lower than prewar German living standard. At the same time they pressed for international control of the Ruhr, a proposal the Americans tabled by agreeing to study it without commitment. In fact Stimson opposed the plan for fear it would extend Soviet power into Western Europe and weaken Germany, and official Washington shared his assumption. To the Russians the question of international control of the Ruhr, or the precise powers of the Control Council, were in the long run less important than the acquisition of a definable amount of reparations for their own reconstruction. In the last analysis they were even quite ready to sacrifice the principle of treating Germany as a single economic unit—of which they were the strongest advocate—if they could get something in return. The objective of economic aid was far stronger than their desire for Four Power economic control, which they did not fully trust, and Russia advocated continuing the veto within the council on economic directives. Byrnes for his part almost initially favored placing the emphasis on zonal economies, which implicitly involved the partition of Germany.

For one thing, Byrnes was concerned, as were most Americans, with the quantity of German goods the Russians had already taken out of their zone, an action that might alter the overall amount available for reparations. Moreover, since the Russians handed over the land east of the Oder-Neisse rivers to the Poles, the total sum available for reparations was reduced to some extent, and both sides rather hotly debated its importance at the time. On the morning of the 23rd, as Byrnes and Truman were feeling especially impatient toward the Russians, the Secretary of State, with the approval of William Clayton and Edwin Pauley, proposed to Molotov that since Russia allegedly had about one-half of Germany's wealth in its zone, perhaps it would be best for each country to take its reparations from its own zone and maintain trade for mutually needed goods. The Russians immediately rejected the idea, and Molotov offered to reduce their reparations claim of $10 billion if they could formulate an overall plan. Byrnes was skeptical. Later that day, as they continued haggling and Byrnes referred to existing Soviet removals, Molotov chopped $1 billion off the Russian claim, later cutting another billion if the Anglo-Americans would agree to grant Russia $2 billion in reparations from the Ruhr. Amidst unpleasant innuendos, neither Eden nor Byrnes would make the commitment in dollars or quantities that the Russians so desired. As if to test their intent, Molotov ended the session by implying the U.S.S.R. was less interested in an internationalized Ruhr than aid from it. The Russians now accepted the first-charge principle for certain minimum imports. Now the Americans would have to define a position which truly revealed something more of their plans.[4]

Whether or not the Russian claims were true or false, the Americans did not have to agree to anything new at Potsdam concerning Four Power economic control, for the existing occupation machinery left the zonal commanders supreme in their area except when the Control Council made a unanimous decision, and Byrnes's aides quickly pointed this out. Rather than Russia's possessing one-half of Germany's "existing wealth," as Byrnes insisted, his aides also confidentially informed him that the entire Soviet zone contained only 31 percent of Germany's movable manufacturing facilities and 35 to 39 percent of the total prewar manufacturing and mining, and 48 percent of the agricultural resources of Germany. Despite this information, Byrnes persisted in telling the Russians they held one-half of Germany's industrial resources. The area Russia ceded to Poland contained only 6 percent of the prewar manufacturing assets, and since the Anglo-Americans also accepted the principle of territorial compensation to Poland in the west, the small fraction attributable to Soviet unilateral action was of very minor consequence.

The extent of the destruction in this region no one could estimate, but everyone also knew the heaviest fighting occurred in the East. Even granting Russian removals, which most probably were less than the $1 billion the Russians had cut from their reparations demands, it was apparent to Byrnes and the American delegation that the failure of the reparations negotiations would leave the Western zones stronger in potential industrial assets. What the Americans and English would take from the Western zones reflected a political decision involving the strength of the local social system under enforced lowering of living standards. At Potsdam, Pauley estimated that removable direct war potential in the Western zones amounted to a scant $1.7 billion—the Russian estimate was four to five times higher—and since "the mere mention of this figure at this time would preclude any agreement being made at all," Pauley advised Byrnes to avoid figures altogether and persist only with percentages of unknown quantities.[5] In fact the West planned to give the Russians almost nothing. Neither war booty nor Poland's movement into the east German region substantially altered the economic balance in favor of the West, even ignoring the fact that the American troops took over 10,000 loaded freight cars, plus much rolling stock, from the zone allocated to the Russians but which the Americans temporarily occupied.

The dispute was not centered on technical issues, but on basic policy concerning the larger question of Germany in Europe. "He said," one of Byrnes's aides recorded the next day while the Secretary angrily attacked the Russians before his staff, "England should never have permitted Hitler to rise, that the German people under a democracy would have been a far superior ally than Russia. . . . There is too much difference in the ideologies of the US and Russia to work out a long term program."[6] "We intended," Truman recalled of the conference, "to make it possible for Germany to develop into a decent nation and to take her place in the civilized world."[7] A renewed and denazified Germany as part of the non-Communist world and a stable Europe was a far more desirable objective to the United States than reparations and Four Power control which would only strengthen Russia in the postwar era.

British anxiety over their own economic problems at home and the fact that their zone of Germany historically had a vast food deficit profoundly colored their view of reparations. They would have to pay to feed their zone if reparations impaired German economic recovery and exports. For this reason they had a greater interest than the Americans in seeing the German economy reintegrated and the food basket of eastern Germany again made available. When their representative to one of the subcommittees on economic questions proposed that all the zones of Germany draw their food from the regions that had traditionally provided them, thereby precluding any territorial concessions to Poland, the Americans gave their support—though they did not press the point thereafter. It was critical, Churchill told Stalin on the 25th, that the Ruhr's goods be traded for food. Four Power economic control was compatible with this plan, the Byrnes suggestion as it stood was not. To keep the British from depleting their meager hard currency to maintain their zone in a potentially divided Germany would require a compromise.

On July 27 Byrnes found a solution to the Russian demands, the British needs, and the American designs. The Russians would draw their reparations from their own zone, but perhaps they would trade $1.5 billion in western German equipment over five or six years for food and coal. Polish administration of the territory along the eastern Neisse—they already held the much larger territory bordering on the western Neisse—the Big Three would accept until the final peace treaty. The same day, however, Byrnes granted Molotov no more satisfaction when he again brought up the Soviet demand for some firm reparations figure. The Russian was openly irritated that the Anglo-Americans now saw the $20-billion figure fixed at Yalta as nothing more than a "basis for discussion" that Byrnes declared "impractical." Molotov insisted on some figure, but Byrnes demurred on behalf of his zonal reparations plan. Later that evening Byrnes finally presented his package including the food exchange, and when Molotov asked "would not the Secretary's suggestion mean that each country would have a free hand in their own zones and would act entirely independently of the others?," Byrnes replied "that was true in substance. . . ."[8] Molotov thought the plan lopsided and accused Byrnes of really opposing reparations to the Soviet Union altogether, for the Ruhr could still provide vast reparations for all compatible with a program of disarmament of Germany. Byrnes, for his part, refused to agree.

By the end of the month it was quite apparent to the Russians that they were not going to obtain reparations from the intractable American and British leaders, and to the Americans it was equally clear that the Russians would not give up the eastern German regions transferred to the Poles. For various reasons discussed below, the United States could not avoid the pressure to make a gesture in the direction of the Poles, and on July 29 Byrnes offered Molotov his consent to the de facto Polish administration of the western Oder-Neisse region, until the final peace settlement, in return for their acceptance of the American zonal reparations scheme. One-quarter of the total Ruhr equipment available for reparations they would trade for food and coal. Molotov persisted in asking that they produce some dollar or quantitative figures or else they might get nothing, but Byrnes refused to concede, and soon they were quibbling over Byrnes's sedulous claim that the Soviet zone contained half of Germany's wealth. At best, he now suggested, they could trade 12.5 percent of Anglo-French-American zonal reparations for goods, but Molotov's persistence in asking for quantitative measures led nowhere. The Russians now understood that there would be a partition in fact, and when Molotov raised this with Byrnes the American claimed Four Power economic control could still continue in finance, foreign trade, and transport. How, of course, he could no longer say.

The following day, with the conference drawing to a close, the bitter and elusive reparations question entered the final stage of bargaining, with only one side holding control of the dominant stakes in the German indus-trial economy. Byrnes now offered to trade one-quarter of the Ruhr capital equipment the United States determined to be available for reparations, and also to give the Russians an additional 15 percent outright. In all cases the zonal commander would have the right to veto any proposals on repara-tions from the Four Power Control Council or Reparations Commission. Molotov, unimpressed, again asked for figures and international control of the Ruhr. To this repetitious demand Byrnes could only reply that the Russians would have to rely on Western "good faith."[9] The concession on Polish control, Byrnes suggested, already represented a major Anglo-American compromise. Molotov was again unimpressed. In fact the final agreement on the major issues in Germany would reflect the existing physi-cal control of the land, and the Anglo-Americans would not take the risks, or the rewards, to attempt cooperation with the U.S.S.R. on Germany.

On July 31, the last full day of the conference, Stalin reluctantly ac-cepted the American plan including a modification that 15 percent of available reparations from the three Western zones be traded for Eastern zone food and coal, with 10 percent granted outright to the U.S.S.R.—a figure that was reached after bitter haggling. They assigned a time limit but no quantities, and in effect the reparations each nation might obtain it would extract from its respective zone, and the Americans fully under-stood they avoided binding reparations commitments to the U.S.S.R. The Ruhr was not internationalized, despite French support for the proposal. In effect the Russians received nothing tangible from the Western zones in reparations, and assumed the responsibility for the Polish claims.

The representatives of the three nations found it easier to draw up a list of common and obtusely vague principles for the administration of the German economy, but what was more important was the functional structure of control and the zonal autonomy they allocated to each of the four nations. The British delegation immediately split on the significance of the Byrnes reparations plan, as Sir David Waley of the Treasury pointed out that the Americans no longer treated Germany as an economic unit, since the Russian zone would remain on a lower standard of living—for the Russians would collect as much as they could from their own zone barring reparations from the west. The British found Byrnes's more general economic proposals on Germany no less suggestive of zonal economic partition, but since these principles remained vague the American representatives did not press what was obviously their clear intention. That the Americans understood the consequences of this zonal policy was evidenced in the State Department's prediction shortly prior to Potsdam that "If each zone is set up as a separate and distinct political or administrative unit of its own, the prospective result will be the creation of partite states having diverging political philosophies and the termination of inter-zonal commerce. . . ." "There appears to be an unfortunate tendency," Clayton complained immediately after the meeting, "to interpret the reparations operating agreement as an indication of complete abandonment of four power treatment of Germany." The United States military especially shared this doleful view. For Clayton, always interested in saving all of Germany for his carefully elaborated economic goals, believed the United States might present "at least some common policies" to the Russians via the Control Council.[10] In fact the conference laid the structure and foundations for German partition and the United States created the basis for a truncated Germany's return to world power.

Poland—Once More

The relations between the United States, England, and Russia over the Polish question had been painful every step of the way, and the accumulated disagreements of the war caused a total impasse on the question by early May. For this reason, more than any other, Hopkins went to Moscow at the end of the month, and obtained Stalin's assurances that Poland would include men such as Mikolajczyk and Grabski among its leaders. For the moment Washington found less cause for complaint about Polish affairs and proceeded to think through its plans for Poland in a manner that assumed there might be some opportunity for American capital to help define the future politics and economic structure of that nation. In the weeks prior to Potsdam the Poles in Warsaw assiduously cultivated an image of reasonableness on political and economic matters. Even Churchill thought there had been "great improvements" in Poland since the end of the war.[11] He and the Americans were resolved to encourage their continuation.

At Potsdam the Polish question impinged on the future internal political structure of that country, especially elections, the western border problem, and the relationship of the territorial question to Germany and the nature of the peace settlement imposed on that defeated nation. To the Americans, not prone to inflict too harsh a peace on Germany, much less concede more land to a state likely to become a Soviet ally, the fact that Polish centrists such as Mikolajczyk were no less adamant in demanding land compensation in the west complicated the question of territorial adjustments. To fail to aid them in some manner would simply be a warning to all Poles, anti-Communist nationalists included, that their only hope for German retribution after the war rested in an alliance with the U.S.S.R. Conflicting impulses tore American policy throughout the conference.

The British Foreign Office wanted to avoid excessive meddling in Polish internal affairs, and instead of going over the details of Cabinet composition as in the past, sought to obtain assurances of future free elections with international observation. Reports from Mikolajczyk himself that he and his Peasant party were not meeting difficulties in their work encouraged them in this effort. And throughout July the Russian-backed groups were out to do everything possible to placate openly the anxieties of the Anglo-American leaders.

The Polish strategy made only a slight impression on Truman, who later recalled in connection with this issue that "I was getting tired of sitting and listening to endless debate on matters that could not be settled at this conference . . . and on a number of occasions I felt like blowing the roof off the palace."[12] In fact he refused to settle the Polish border question, and reneged on clear commitments that the United States made at Yalta "that Poland must receive substantial accessions of territory in the north and west." On July 21, during the first top-level extended discussion of the matter, and well after his experts had calculated that the disputed area contained a maximum of 7 percent of Germany's industrial and mining output, Truman complained "how reparations or other questions could be decided if Germany was carved up." He was particularly irate that Russia already passed control of the territory as far as the Oder and western Neisse to the Poles, and he was not impressed by Stalin's only partially exaggerated claim that nine million Germans had already fled the area. Ignoring the Yalta Agreement on territorial compensation, Truman now insisted that the border adjustments were "a matter for the peace conference."[13]

What he did not reveal was that Washington already had made the decision that there probably would not be a peace conference on Germany. Churchill restricted himself to pointing to the vast flow of Germans into the occupation zones and the problem of feeding them, the difficulties facing the two and a half million Germans he insisted were still in the contested area, and the dangers to the peace if Poland took too much territory. To

Stalin it was less important to spare the Germans than to help the Poles, and leave Germany weak. Truman would make no commitments, but contented himself only with demanding free elections observed by the world press. This subject visibly irritated the Russians because Byrnes freely confessed that the Russians had placed no restrictions on Western newsmen already admitted to Poland. The reasons for this complaint about the press were therefore obscure. There was still much room for bargaining on the entire question of Poland.

The American and now British insistence that they defer the boundary question to some indefinite peace conference made it apparent that the Poles had only the Russians to defend their claims. Truman sulked throughout the debate. "The Bolshies have killed all of them," Leahy whispered into his ear during an argument on the fate of the German population in the region. Truman entirely ignored the commitment at Yalta, and he recalled, "they [the Russians] were now trying to compensate Poland at the expense of the other three occupying powers. I would not stand for it, nor would Churchill. I was of the opinion that the Russians had killed the German population or had chased them into our zones."[14] By July 23, with Truman unwilling to concede anything and the conference at an impasse, Stalin suggested that they call in the Poles themselves for consultation. All accepted the idea.

Stalin cleverly conceived the move, for he knew that while Truman and Churchill could refuse the demands of Poles friendly to Russia, they could hardly ignore the pleas of the former London Poles now associated with the new government. When the delegation including Bierut and Mikolajczyk arrived at Potsdam on the 24th to meet with the leaders of the West, each in their own way said what was necessary to win support for their border claim. Their performances were brilliant. Bierut for his part advanced the demand for the disputed area, but broadly hinted at other Polish concessions in return—though Truman was still unmoved on the 24th. The following day Bierut saw Clayton and expressed great enthusiasm for accepting American loans and future economic cooperation, perhaps even coal sales to Western Europe. To Eden he argued that he did not wish to create a Communist Poland, but one modeled after Western European democracies, with full civil and religious liberties. He had softened the ground.

Mikolajczyk was more blunt: the condition of his party was fragile, and without the support of the West, Polish democracy would flounder. Between the optimistic report of the conditions of Polish democracy at the opening of the conference and the 24th there had been a dreadful turn for the worse in Poland, a change that had occurred in ten days according to the Pole. While in the presence of Bierut he argued for the Polish border claim, but on the 24th he handed Harriman a memo linking the border issue to the need for speedy elections, the withdrawal of Soviet forces, and the full restoration of civil liberties. When he saw Eden the following morning he made the demand more direct: there would not be elections or a Soviet withdrawal without the recognition of the Polish border claim first of all. He had cleverly shifted the burden of the matter to the Americans and English.

On July 29 Byrnes presented Molotov with the American package compromise on the Oder-Neisse dispute and German reparations. In it the American agreed only to Polish administration of the region, the final delimitation to await the "peace settlement."[15] The following day Miko-lajczyk repeated his warning to Attlee and Foreign Minister Ernest Bevin concerning the fate of elections and Polish democracy should the West ignore the legitimate border demands. Bierut for his part agreed to elections no later than early 1946, with normal press privileges for Western newsmen. On the 31st the Anglo-American leaders handed back the entire matter to Stalin with the explanation that Soviet troops would have to leave the disputed territory and the Polish government would have to hold free and secret elections based on the 1921 Constitution by early 1946. Stalin agreed to the withdrawal save for communication lines leading to Germany. To the West, the Russians conceded something tangible only if Poland did not become Communist, and perhaps their gesture might prevent that fate. The Allies achieved an arrangement, but not a final solution.

In ironing out the definitive wording of the Polish protocol the Americans and English revealed their emphasis on the contingent nature of the border statement they offered in return for a clear and unequivocal pledge to hold free elections. The British stressed that they were by no means committed to support the Polish claim at a final "peace settlement" which would make the final judgment—in fact they revealed they would not. Byrnes was no less specific. The Polish government would simply administer the region "pending the final determination of Poland's western frontier."[16] The conference ceded no fraction of the territory permanently to the Poles. They also agreed that Poland, Czechoslovakia, and Hungary would transfer their German populations to Germany, but since the region east of the Oder-Neisse was still legally German, a strict interpretation hardly warranted the implication that the Poles might deport the remaining Germans and further establish de facto control of the region.

Nevertheless the United States government did not expect or want a final German peace conference, and what it meant by "settlement" is unclear. By reneging on an explicit pledge made at Yalta the Americans and English left an ambiguous condition which created a vast irredentist sore to plague the future of European affairs. The Poles warned the Americans of this obvious point, but what they did not state was that the major source of friction with Germany, which the vague legal status of the question inevitably created, would surely compel all Polish nationalists to align themselves with whatever power backed their claim. This too was obvious, but by August 1945 the Americans found it less important to attain equity and stability in Europe than to arrest Russian power in every way possible.

The Former Axis Powers

The American government brooded for months about the exclusion of its representatives from political supervision of Hungary, Rumania, and Bulgaria via the Allied Control Commissions, and prior to Potsdam planned to sink firmer roots into Eastern Europe, all of which, including Czechoslovakia, Truman felt Stalin was subjugating with an "iron-heel policy."[17] The United States still had to protect existing American economic interests in these nations, and to encourage the establishment of others. Yet always hanging over the American plans for the former Eastern European satellites of Germany were the complex and embarrassing problems of Italy and Greece, and the Soviet's ability to give no more than the West had granted to it.

The Soviets exercised nominal control in Hungary, and conservatism and anti-Semitism continued as the hallmarks of the internal politics in that nation. On July 12 the Russians proposed that they reorganize the Control Commission in Hungary greatly to increase the participation, but not the powers, of the American and British representatives, and four days later made the same offer in Rumania. Although the American representatives split on the significance of the proposal, which would have covered Bulgaria as well, and Grew thought it inadequate, the Russians neatly defined the basis for the Potsdam discussion of the question of the former Eastern European enemy states.

On the first day of Potsdam the U.S. delegation circulated a statement saying that, in effect, Russia had not fulfilled the Yalta Declaration on Liberated Europe, that it should reorganize the governments of Bulgaria and Rumania to conform to its provisions, and that the three Great Powers assist these nations and Greece to hold free elections. The United Nations could then recognize the new, reorganized governments. Though the American draft referred to "other countries" in general, it registered no specific complaints concerning Hungary, for there was little the United States wished to object to there.[18] Not only the Russians, but the leader of the conservative Rumanian National Peasant party, Iuliu Maniu, whom the United States favored, objected to the proposal. On July 20 the Russians formally rejected the American scheme, demanded Washington immediately recognize the governments of the three ex-Axis Powers and Finland, and circulated a scorching note on the "terrorism" in Greece. Eden denied the charges on Greece, and with finality Molotov turned to the situation in Italy. Despite the longer period of occupation the Italians had not held free elections, the Russian observed, and only Greece was making warlike speeches about the territory of its neighbors. Byrnes in response offered to include Italy and now Hungary in any international supervision of elections. Over the following days it became apparent that the Russians would press only for immediate diplomatic recognition of the former Axis states, reject the American plan, and persist in the theme "that conditions in Italy constituted a model for the control commissions in Rumania, Bulgaria, and Hungary."[19] Molotov was quite ready to modify any agreement to imitate formally the Italian pattern everywhere. With this strategy the Russians always maintained the upper hand on the question, for no one could refute their arguments.

The Russians insisted on linking the questions of Eastern Europe to Italy, Greece, and even Spain, and at one point Truman reacted against the complex interaction by threatening Stalin "that if they did not get to the main issues I was going to pack up and go home. I meant just that."[20] He had ample reason to be angry, for the Russians saw no room for further concessions along their borders, merely offering to recognize Italy if the Americans would do the same for the other Axis satellites. Truman received no satisfaction, but he remained at Potsdam, despite the fact that his cause for complaint increased in his own eyes.

For one thing, the Russians hardly responded to his proposal that the Allies turn the Danube into an international waterway, a plan designed to reintegrate the Eastern European economy into its traditional prewar relations. Then, as the leaders of the Great Powers were meeting in Germany, reports arrived that the Communists were trying to rig the Bulgarian elections, set for August 26, to assure the success of the Fatherland Front, presumably Communist-controlled, and Prime Minister Kimon Georgiev's Zveno party, an old-fashioned rightist party ready to deal with the Russians. Perhaps the treatment of American oil properties in Rumania aggravated the United States most of all, for the topic took an inordinate amount of time and attention and revealed the economic roots of American policy in Eastern Europe. The British were no less concerned.

For some months before July both the British and Americans had insisted that the Russians return their Rumanian oil equipment and protect their property. Ignoring the implicit assumption that the preservation of such holdings predicated the restoration of traditional prewar interests and capitalism, the fact that the subject was a "trifling matter," to quote Stalin, and the removals of equipment attributable to the confusion of the war impressed the Russians more.[21] Despite this, the State Department pressed the issue and Byrnes indicated that the United States defined the oil in the ground as American property and demanded compensation for the removal of any of it. In the end the conference settled this "irritant," as Byrnes called it, by creating joint commissions to examine the facts.[22] What Byrnes did not tell the Russians was that one of the purposes for raising the matter was the American fear of Russian trade monopolies in the former Axis countries "which deny to American nationals access, on equal terms, to such trade, raw materials and industry."[23]

The final agreement on the former Eastern European Axis satellites contained slight consolation for the American government, for the Russians accepted only a few minor words that hardly altered the status quo. Ultimately, maintaining this status quo everywhere was the critical hallmark of the entire conference. The Allied Control Commission structure remained intact, and the United States made contingent on a host of optional preconditions the question of the diplomatic recognition of the Eastern European Axis. The final resolution hardly implied the semblance of common agreement. The communiqué indicated that the three governments "have no doubt" as to the full press freedom to report on the future events and elections in the former Axis countries—words that scarcely concealed the total rupture of objectives that existed.[24] All that Russia granted the United States was the statement that hopefully Italy might become the first Axis nation to be welcomed into the United Nations.

ITALY could receive some slight measure of prominence because at Potsdam the United States chose to set itself against the other two members of the conference by championing the rights of the nation over which the Americans were quickly establishing predominant influence. For although the Russians attempted to use Italy to extract equal concessions for the other Axis satellites, in fact the Italian question at Potsdam was chiefly a matter of controversy between England and the United States.

On July 15 the State Department notified the Foreign Office that the United States would announce two days later that the United States was going to recommend the admission of Italy to the United Nations, and invited Britain to support the American initiative. The Foreign Office was furious at this obvious attempt to undercut British influence and prestige in Italy, the unilateral nature of the recommendation, and also, to a lesser extent, its political implications for a peace treaty. It asked for a delay, and Byrnes at first agreed. On second thought, as Grew phrased it, immediate recognition would help "build a sound democratic pol[itical] and econ[omic] order," which insinuated, since it would not be done within a day, one independent of both England and Russia.[25] They obviously intended to appeal to Italian nationalist sentiment. Beyond that, the United States would spare Italy the future costs of having joined the wrong side in the war.

On the 17th, when Truman proposed a declaration on the admission of Italy to the United Nations, Churchill rose to the challenge by recounting

Italy's attack long before the Americans entered the war, and the losses it inflicted on Britain. The next day the British embassy in Washington formally objected to the admission of Italy preceding the peace treaty, and dismissed press rumors the Russians would take up the Italian cause first. Molotov then tried to postpone the issue. The Americans now scrapped their original proposal, which promised Italy "political independence and economic recovery," and even vaguely hinted at the restoration of colonies, for a more modest declaration promising the quick conclusion of a peace treaty and subsequent admission to the United Nations.[26] The British won their point, and from this time on the Soviets insisted on linking Italy to the diplomatic recognition of Bulgaria and Rumania, which effectively killed the issue.

However, the United States was able to prevent its allies from imposing a punitive peace upon Italy. American experts estimated that the nearly total paralysis of the Italian economy would require vast United States relief expenditures to prevent starvation and Communism, and while Washington was willing to pay the price it would not for a moment consider Italian reparations to the U.S.S.R., money all were convinced would ultimately come out of American pockets. At the beginning of the conference, when Molotov insisted that the question of Italian reparations was appropriate for discussion, Byrnes tried to sweeten the pill by suggesting that after they had concluded a peace treaty the topic "might" be germane.[27] In the meantime the United States would not indirectly pay Italian reparations. They repeated the dialogue in various forms later in the conference, but always with the same conclusion as America pleaded Italian poverty. Undoubtedly American economic calculations were correct, given their determination to avoid the economic preconditions for the growth of the Left and achieve a stable capitalist economy. The Russians had suffered frightful destruction at Italian hands and did not care if the Italians shared some of the postwar deprivations, even if the United States did not pay for Italian relief. What is more significant about the American argument than its unquestionably valid calculations was the premise that the Anglo-American forces' mere possession of Italy gave them the right to veto an equal Russian share in the determination of that nation's economy. They applied that principle on a political level via the Allied Control Commission, and the Russians imitated it elsewhere. Now the United States had extended it into the economic sphere as well.

The Greeks and Yugoslavs

Who stood for democracy at Potsdam? No other region revealed more of the nature of the Anglo-American commitment to that institution than Greece and Yugoslavia, and events in Eastern Europe spoke for themselves as Russia, England, and the United States worked with anyone who would further their objectives, a pragmatic principle that belied the moral claims of all.

In Yugoslavia the English and Americans confronted an increasingly complex situation, which they ultimately preferred to avoid at Potsdam. The vague Tito-Subasic agreement had not satisfied the British, and the Yugoslav Communist party was in total control of the nation. The Trieste and Venezia-Giulia crisis had made Tito the paragon of dangerous Bolshevism for the Americans and English. On July 11 the head of the British delegation in Belgrade sought out Subasic for his estimate and advice. The ambitious Subasic, who always appreciated his own weakness as a personality without a party and was grateful for the deference that he received from Tito, suggested that he favored a United Front coalition of parties rather than classic political democracy, which might quickly degenerate into a war of nationalities. Although he expected the Communists to dominate such a coalition, all he asked for was more power for the cooperative non-Communist parties. He believed it would be helpful if the Great Powers reminded Tito that he had once signed such an agreement, but Subasic was totally discouraging on the possibility of a change in the regime. The alternative was civil war, but implicitly the domestic opposition would be rather meager, and would require "foreign armed assistance."[28] The British had lost their last foil to Tito, and their last feeble hope of defining Yugoslav affairs.

Early in the Potsdam Conference the British presented a statement calling for fulfillment of the Tito-Subasic agreement, and Stalin suggested that they confer with the Yugoslav government as an indispensable step in resolving the problem. Stalemated, the Americans and British during the next days considered further action on Yugoslavia and Trieste behind the scenes. On July 25 the War Department forwarded to Potsdam a British military proposal that Yugoslav committees of liberation in the Venezia-Giulia region be "eradicated" and "firmness should be used to sweep away Yugoslav system."[29] The State Department had already approved the proposal, but the War Department thought it crude and possibly dangerous in wording. On the very same day Tito and Subasic wrote Truman about the reimposition of Italian fascist governmental institutions in many sections of the contested region, and suggested instead that the Anglo-Americans organize democratic elections to create a civil government in the disputed areas. Such a step would have left Yugoslav nationality parties in control of the larger part of the region, and for this reason both the British and American diplomats strongly advised against agreement. On July 30 the Russians at Potsdam proposed free and democratic elections along the lines Tito and Subasic had proposed. The following day Ernest Bevin suggested they drop the subject of Yugoslavia altogether, to which Stalin and Truman immediately assented.

Greece was an even greater embarrassment to the democratic pretensions of the English and Americans, and Stalin and Molotov did not tire of throwing it in the face of opponents when they waxed especially righteous about political freedom in Eastern Europe. For in July 1945 there was no greater example than Greece of naked repression and nationalist jingoism in all Europe.

On the opening day of the conference the American ambassador in Athens, Lincoln MacVeagh, sent Byrnes a detailed report, carefully prepared by his staff, which admitted "the deficiencies of present Greek regional administrative and judicial procedure . . . for the civil liberties of leftists and Slavophones [Macedonians]." The existing police mechanism, in particular the National Guard, was especially guilty, "and many of them have served as Gendarmes under both Metaxas and the Germans." The instability of the nation would require foreign troops "to maintain peace and order inside the country," both to support and restrain the existing government. "With regard to Greek expansionism, it need only be said that the naturally receptive state of mind of the public is being exploited and stimulated to the utmost by public leaders and editors as a tactic of internal politics," one that they might use against the EAM, but would also stimulate a response in kind from the northern neighbors. While British officers in the north discounted the possibility of an invasion toward Greece, the American embassy in Albania several days later attributed most of the difficulty of that region to British officers and "the Greeks who started propaganda campaign on frontier problems and persecution."[30]

In this factual context the Big Three debated the subject of Greece at Potsdam. On July 19 Byrnes sent Molotov a letter asking Russian participation in Four Power supervision of the forthcoming Greek elections. The following day Molotov cited the repression and repeated Greek expansionist statements and submitted a brief note calling for the implementation of the Varkiza agreement of the prior February. To Byrnes he sent a refusal to supervise elections, unquestionably because the American immediately linked the proposal to election supervision in the Eastern European Axis satellites. Eden furiously denied all the charges and attributed Greek responsibility for the border problems to fantasy. Several days later Churchill circulated his rebuttal to the Russian memo, simply attacking the EAM-ELAS for the December 1944 crisis and offering two reports by Field Marshal Alexander and Sir Walter Citrine, the trade-union leader, as proof —obliquely in fact vindicating the Soviet charge. In reality the Russians had little interest in Greece, and they encouraged the Communists to enter a representative coalition government which had no relationship to the realities and possibilities of the actual Greek situation. They used Greece only to twit the British when they complained about Eastern Europe.

Meanwhile the Foreign Office worried about an impending crisis between Tito and the Greeks over the northern borders. On July 30 it suggested that the conference issue a statement against "violent and unilateral action" against neighbors by any nation in southeast Europe, and also vaguely endorsing the Varkiza and Tito-Subasic agreements.[31] On the same day the Russians proposed a common statement for the restoration of public order in Greece, the broadening of the government to include democratic elements, the implementation of the Varkiza agreement, and a British message to the Regent embodying the conference recommendations. It was with a measure of relief that Stalin and Truman accepted Bevin's recommendation the following day that the conference drop these conflicting memos and the entire subject of Greece along with Yugoslavia. Secretly, however, Attlee sent the Regent of Greece a message containing almost all of the substantive points in the Russian proposal. The British too were worried that the excesses of the Right would create a profound crisis which might turn repression and irredentism into civil war and international discord.

A Spectrum of Difficulties

The Council of Foreign Ministers

In a deeper sense the American position implied that American power, either alone or via direct settlements with the other Great Powers, would become the determining factor on the postwar diplomatic scene. The State Department during June decided that a peace conference would not formulate—as after the tragic failure of Versailles—the major political settlements of the war. Yet Washington also had few illusions about the value of the United Nations as a viable political instrument, an opinion its two great allies always fully shared. For these reasons the United States delegation arrived at Potsdam reasonably confident that the Russians and English would consent to the creation of a Council of Foreign Ministers which would meet regularly to consider a host of unsettled political differences, though by no means all of them.

It was the easiest of all issues to settle, for the Russians were interested in diplomacy and raised no basic objections when the United States on the first day of the conference proposed a council based on the five permanent members of the Security Council. Both Stalin and Churchill questioned the participation of China, and Truman readily agreed to exclude it. As the American proposal explained, the preparatory work of the council, which would draw up the peace treaties for Italy and the other Axis satellites in that order, was merely a prelude to "a full formal peace conference" to deal with the major Axis Powers.[32] In reality the United States intended no such conference, even though the Russians suffered from the misconception—which American vagueness cultivated—that the Allies would eventually organize one.

The following day the Foreign Ministers quickly approved the plan, and Molotov himself proposed including China on questions of interest to it. Functional membership might slide to three on certain issues, and they would invite other states to participate, but not to vote. Their main concern would be the European peace settlement, but the final text drawn up and ratified on the 20th postponed the entire German peace settlement until the Germans created an "adequate" government.[33] That might be a short or a long time.

Turkey

The Turks spent the better part of the war sounding the tocsin for the need to create an alliance—even with Germany—against the Soviet Union, plotting cordons sanitaire and building their military power. They were profoundly alarmed when their fear that Russia would emerge preeminent in Eastern Europe and the Balkans materialized. They continued to seek Anglo-American support for their views on the necessity to contain Russia, a Russia that at Yalta received Anglo-American assurances that the Allies would modify the Montreux Convention of 1936 governing the use of the Black Sea Straits to meet Soviet interests.

On June 7 the Turkish ambassador in Moscow visited Molotov to request the Russian views on a new treaty of friendship to replace that of 1925. The Russian suggested that they would first have to settle to Soviet satisfaction the outstanding border dispute over Kars and Ardahan, and the larger question of the Straits. After World War I the Turks picked up the disputed, largely non-Turkish provinces, which had belonged to Russia and which nearly all Armenians especially wished returned to it, when Lenin was anxious to consolidate power internally by discarding many Tsarist holdings. Rather than cautiously probing the meaning of Molotov's reference to Montreux without comment, the Turk asked whether the Russian was asking for bases. Molotov naturally answered in the affirmative.

The Russians were quite willing to permit the status quo on their borders to remain, but they saw little point to ratifying it formally. They simply answered questions the Turks put to them, but the Ankara government considered the Soviet response as a grave threat and immediately attempted to extend their own hysteria to London and Washington. Quietly they mobilized their army reserves, and spread the word that the Russians were massing troops on their borders preparatory to a possible invasion. The Turkish ambassador in Moscow set the entire question in the context of global Soviet expansion "from Finland to China."[34] Both the Americans and British responded to the Turkish excitement with skepticism, for Turkey initiated the reopening of the matter, and Turkish exclamations that they were ready to fight and die did not move them. ". . . no concrete threats had been made," Grew reminded the Turkish ambassador in Washington on July 7.[35]

Though fully aware of their exaggerations, Grew assured the Turks that while making no commitments the United States extended "sympathy" to the Turkish cause, an assurance that they once also gave Russia on the revision of the Straits Convention.[36] Even at the end of June the State Department believed that the Montreux Convention was "outmoded," and that certain changes would be "advisable," though neither Turkey nor Russia were likely to accept them.[37] On the opening day of Potsdam the Joint Chiefs of Staff suggested to the State-War-Navy Coordinating Committee that the Russians were not likely to go to war over the issue, as the Turks claimed, but it was also in the interest of the United States to preserve the status quo and to postpone any discussion that might lead to freer Soviet access to the Straits or Kiel Canal. The State Department's experts then agreed, and suggested that the United States permit no change without Turkish consent, which was equivalent to declaring that there would not be any and that the Americans would not honor their commitment at Yalta. The United States followed this line at Potsdam mainly via utopian international waterway schemes involving the Straits and known to be unacceptable.

On July 22 the Russians circulated a note suggesting direct negotiations between Turkey and the U.S.S.R., as the two primary states bordering the Black Sea, to modify the Montreux Convention. They proposed to arrange joint bases on the Straits and made no mention of Kars and Ardahan. In explaining the matter Molotov reminded the cautious Churchill that the Turks themselves raised the subject, and that the U.S.S.R. would be equally willing to have the other Black Sea powers, Bulgaria and Rumania, revise the Montreux Treaty as well. The following day Stalin tried to assuage Churchill's fears concerning a Soviet invasion of Turkey. Truman for his part began his exposition, often repeated in subsequent years, on the need to internationalize all waterways. Leahy on the 24th clearly defined for purposes of the United States delegation that the proposal's main function was to oppose the Russian claims on the Straits and their desire for bases. The same day the conference discussed the matter for the last time. Truman indicated American willingness to implement his international control scheme in the Black Sea Straits by sharing in a supervisory organization. Molotov asked Churchill if he would be prepared to grant the same right to Suez fortifications in British hands, and after he declined, Stalin suggested that they drop the matter altogether, for Russia had not felt the same intense concern as others over the issue. In fact Stalin still preferred the status quo to Great Power intervention.

The final protocol of Potsdam stated only that the Three Powers "recognized the need for revision of the Convention on the Straits," via Three Power and Turkish negotiations, without indicating the content of the revision that they were never to effect. During the actual conference the British and American representatives privately informed the Turks "to keep their heads," but in fact the Turks were no less excitable about American plans.[38] What disturbed them was the possibility of demilitarization of their own bases on the Straits and Turkish failure to get the Russians to renew their guarantee of Turkish eastern territory—a clear sign of Soviet imperialism to the passionately anti-Soviet Ankara government. In the end the Turks did not lose an inch or fight—or fail to win total American backing and an acceptance of their vision.

Spain and Democracy

While the United States maintained a hostile attitude toward Franco Spain during the war, like Britain it did not wish to see the civil war rekindled. The American ambassador to Spain, Carlton J. H. Hayes, warned that repeated public attacks on the regime would only result in a diverting civil conflict, and by early 1944 the Spanish government indicated a willingness to remain strictly neutral and settle outstanding differences with the United States. Despite strong public condemnation of the Franco regime, Washington carefully avoided breaking diplomatic relations or precipitating a crisis, even as Spanish troops fought on the Soviet front. The possibility of renewed civil war, especially by Spanish refugee members of the French Resistance, alarmed the Americans and especially the British. To both the United States and Britain the civil war threatened a Left, even a Communist, regime, and the Americans urged Franco to voluntarily mend his ways. In the days before the Potsdam Conference "our efforts to use Spain as a source of supply and a base for A. T. C. [Air Transport Command] operations" further tempered the American position. If some Allies undermined Franco via North Africa, American ambassador to Spain Norman Armour explained of the larger context, "by means of Communist penetration and unscrupulous use of Moroccan nationalist sentiment," Franco would be weakened. "Regardless of dismal view we may take of latter such activities would inevitably contribute to world instability at times when stability is at a premium."[39] For this reason too the West preferred to retain Franco.

On the very first day of the Potsdam Conference, Stalin indicated that he would raise the subject of the elimination of fascist Spain. Two days later Russia submitted a formal proposal condemning the Franco regime as an undemocratic and terrorist product of Germany and Italy, and proposed the Allies break diplomatic relations and give "support" to the democratic forces of Spain seeking to overthrow the dictatorship. The English and Americans then had the opportunity to test their commitment to democracy and freedom in Western as well as in Eastern Europe. Churchill did not like the suggestion, for although he expressed distaste for Franco to Stalin, he also indicated unwillingness to meddle, in violation of the United Nations Charter, in the internal affairs of a country. And, more frankly, he did not wish to see the civil war renewed. Truman too manifested no praise for Franco, and also his reluctance to start another civil war. Stalin retorted that the Spanish regime was not an internal affair but the outcome of Nazi aggression, and rather than advocating another civil war all he urged was a statement that made it clear to the Spanish people that this time they might count on the backing of the three governments should they act. In the course of the longer debate, during which both Truman and Churchill expressed willingness to tolerate the Spanish status quo, Churchill revealed that both "the valuable trade relations which Britain maintained with Spain" and the neighboring Portuguese dictatorship were also on his mind.[40] With Truman's consent the Big Three tabled the matter and they later only included a statement in the final protocol that the United Nations would not admit Spain by virtue of its close association with the Axis. The discussion revealed the full measure of the English and American dedication to democracy.

The Russians and Trusteeships

The United States and Britain several times consulted with each other on the disposition of the Axis colonies and League of Nations mandates, and together formed a coalition on the trusteeship question which deferred to their mutual interests. After an informal discussion at Yalta, British and American diplomats submitted a resolution, which the Russians also approved, that prior to the San Francisco Conference the Security Council members would discuss the question of trusteeships and in particular the Axis colonies. After the United Nations Conference these five states would decide who would receive the trusteed areas. The British attempted to hold the usual bilateral talks on the future of the colonies and mandates during April, but Roosevelt's death and the American split on the formal status of the Pacific bases cut the matter short. Neither ever consulted the Soviet Union.

This omission was aggravated by the fact that the British, as early as October 1944, implied that the Italians might very well receive Libya and Tripoli once again, and as the Americans courted Italian favor and attempted to soften the terms of surrender they too hinted that Italy might hope to see its former enemies restore its empire, at least in part. Several times during the San Francisco Conference, Andrei Gromyko informed the American delegation that Russia would like to acquire some territory under the United Nations trusteeship provisions, and now the Americans had to go beyond a polite but noncommittal acknowledgment and decide on its policy toward the expansion of Russian power by virtue of its contribution to the defeat of the European Axis or its evocation of general rules that were not, in the last analysis, meant for Soviet use. The Allies first confronted the problem in the Mediterranean over the international zone of Tangier.

After the fall of France the Spanish government occupied Tangier, and in spring 1945 it was ready to leave. Various Allies and Spain scheduled a conference on the matter in Paris for July 3, and they did not invite the U.S.S.R. Although the United States had not adhered to the Tangier Statute of 1923, the State Department decided that "The leading role which the United States has assumed in world affairs as a result of the war . . . makes it logical that we should assume a position in the International Zone of Tangier commensurate with our power and prestige." The British, French, and Spanish governments categorically opposed Russian participation, but the State Department decided that they must exclude the Russians by guile rather than on troublesome principle, and advised that they not invite the Russians but keep them informed—with the excuse they had never shown interest in Tangier. If the Russians pressed the matter, however, Washington was prepared to extend an invitation, but to discourage its will the participants notified Moscow of the conference only three days before it opened. On July 2 the astonished Russians sent protests to their European allies, and Gromyko sought out Grew to register an emphatic complaint. The defensive American could only respond that they had not thought that Russia was interested in the matter, although the Americans at the conference privately believed "the issue should be regarded in the larger frame of an expanding Russian interest in the Mediterranean." Over the next days the English and State Department searched for a formula—perhaps inviting a large number of additional states, or inviting the Russians only as observers. The American ambassador in Spain broached the danger of the Russians using Tangier as a base "to carry on activities designed to embarrass and weaken Franco regime."[41] Several days before Potsdam the participants suspended the Tangier conference until they might find a solution.

The Russians understood the Tangier affair exactly as their allies intended it, and they made no secret of their resentment of the way their allies had crudely and unilaterally excluded them from the affairs of Europe. Russia participated in the original Algeciras Conference of 1906 that created the Tangier zone, and in 1926 reaffirmed its rights in the matter. They refused to be precluded by oversight, and insisted on the deference their power and wartime role warranted. In this context one must regard the larger question of a reshuffling of Mediterranean colonies in July 1945.

On July 20 the Russians distributed a memo at Potsdam asking that the conference request the Council of Foreign Ministers to consider the problem of the Italian colonies in the Mediterranean and establish a trusteeship system under the various Three Powers, individually or jointly. The memo only implied Russian trusteeships. Two days later Molotov raised the question of what the Allies were to do with the Italian colonies in

Africa, which according to prior agreements no nation could unilaterally distribute. Merely raising the subject caused Churchill to tell the gathering that the British army conquered Libya, Tripoli, and Cyrenaica alone, and Molotov responded that Russia divided Berlin after conquering it. Churchill's aggressive tactics at first startled Stalin and he offered both to drop the matter and to remind the group of the Soviet request for trusteeships at San Francisco. More important, he urged that they create a cooperative system along the lines of the Russian memo to distribute the trusteeships. Still, the unpleasant exchange, both sides of which irritated Truman, had immediate results. The following day Britain advised its Moscow embassy to invite Russia to the renewed Tangier negotiations scheduled for August. When Molotov persisted on knowing whether colonies in the possession of the British army would give it the unilateral right to dispose of them, Eden agreed to the Soviet plan to refer the matter to the Council of Foreign Ministers. The American position differed from that of both Britain and Russia, and made no distinction between the problem of the disposition of the Italian colonies and the international procedures for future consultations on all trusteeship matters. It was the latter alone that might interfere with concrete American political and territorial goals. On the last day of the conference, Byrnes objected to referring the general trusteeship issue to the Council of Foreign Ministers and insisted that the Italian peace conference deal with the disposition of those few colonies. The final protocol included this proviso, but permitted the Council of Foreign Ministers merely to consider the topic the following September without power of decision. In reality the Americans won, and until the peace conference decided otherwise, Italy would retain its colonies.[42]

The Americans established the principle that possession was nine-tenths of the law in regard to the Italian colonies, and at Potsdam ignored all of their prior commitments. The assumption that its own vast power accorded it privileges denied others was a premise that anyone with power might attempt to apply elsewhere. The lesson was not lost.

The Future and Russia

The Potsdam Conference confirmed Truman's worst fears concerning the future of American-Soviet relations, fears that were seething and growing since 1943. Save for occasional moods of satisfaction, stimulated by the knowledge that the Russians would certainly provide succor for the war against Japan, Truman, as he later recalled, "was getting very impatient, as I had many times before in these sessions," and to his mother he wrote that the Russians were "pig-headed." "I hope I never have to hold another conference with them—but, of course, I will."[43] He did not.

Seemingly at every turn events frustrated American plans and aspirations for the world, and the confrontation with the Soviet Union at Potsdam underscored that reality. By reminding Churchill at Potsdam that British gold and exchange holdings were still too large for their pleasure, the Americans kept the British partially tractable, and elsewhere in Western and Central Europe they understood that the proper application of their economic power to reconstruction and relief, under American direction, might stop the triumph of Communism. But they could not co-opt the elusive Russians—only contain them. The Soviet Union might show readiness to join the various all-European economic bodies sanctioned at Potsdam, but they would not de-Bolshevize or aid in creating the type of world economic order which was a prime American peace aim. By Potsdam no one had any illusion about this fact.

Returning from Potsdam, Truman and his advisers attempted to formulate some redeeming words on the results of the conference, and they prepared five drafts of a speech, excising what they truly felt and intended. It is significant that in one of the earlier versions Truman and his staff asserted that "The most important accomplishment in Berlin—apart from the decisions about the Japanese war—was the establishment of the Council of Foreign Ministers." In a sense this meager estimate was entirely correct, and he might have added that everyone was completely aware that they had attained very little more. The Japanese phase of the discussion was the only one which truly pleased the American delegation. Yet to admit this was too indelicate, or to reveal that "the United States is going to get all the bases it needs in the Pacific for our complete and future protection. . . . We do not propose to give up what we have gained at such cost. . . ."[44] To state the goal so baldly was also to set precedents others might imitate. Instead Truman blandly summarized the conference communiqué, reduced the frank statements of American goals and sympathy for beleaguered Poles to a minimum, and added a few homilies to his radio address of August 9. Only once, when referring to the threat of hunger in Europe, did he reveal the profound fear that "Desperate men are liable to destroy the structure of their society to find in the wreckage some substitute for hope. If we let Europe go cold and hungry, we may lose some of the foundations of order on which the hope for world-wide peace must rest."[45] That foundation of order meant excluding the Left and Communism, and presumably Russia, from Europe, and it predicated the American obligation to accomplish that perilous and gigantic task.

Since, as Stimson confidentially phrased it, "no permanently safe international relations can be established between two such fundamentally different national systems," the United States would hold the secret of the atomic bomb until it obtained foolproof technical and political guarantees from Russia. Washington was unanimous on this point. Over the long run, despite the acknowledged fact that the Russians were war-weary and exhausted, Truman and his aides expected crisis and conflict with the Soviet Union.[46] For this reason, as Leahy accurately described it, "Truman had stood up to Stalin in a manner calculated to warm the heart of every patriotic American."[47] At Potsdam the Americans hardly did more on fundamental issues than "stand up" to Russia and maintain the world status quo without resorting to diplomacy or concessions. Both in fact and intent, as throughout the entire war, the American delegation arrived determined to receive, but not to give anything in return. On Germany they introduced a sleight of hand to create the illusion of some agreement, and while waxing hot on the condition of democracy in Eastern Europe, they conveniently assumed Spain, Greece, and Italy to be qualitatively superior by virtue of their submission or anti-Communism. Great Power intervention into the political and economic development of small states was formalized into a fact of international affairs, and sheer possession decided the outcome of the disputes over both the Black Sea Straits and the Mediterranean colonies. In brief, Potsdam left the status quo, undid many of the minimal obligations the former Allies entered into at Yalta, and continued a condition in the world in which nations would base the peace, such as it was, on power rather than diplomacy.

In reality there had never been effective diplomacy during the war itself, and there would be even less pretense over this fact once victory dissolved the binding necessities of war. To the United States, its sheer political, military, and economic might eliminated the necessity of accepting the existence of the lesser Soviet or British power, as substantial as that still might be. America was confident that it could write its own peace by dealing with each condition and nation directly. To succeed it would have to maintain and to extend its power in the wake of a war that gravely wounded the entire world order and left only the Western Hemisphere free of the ravages of bombs, blood, and revolutionary movements.

THE END OF THE WAR AND
THE REVOLUTIONARY
TIDE IN THE FAR EAST

THE POTSDAM CONFERENCE adjourned on August 1 amidst the dismal foreboding among the leaders of the United States and England as to the future of their relations with the Soviet Union and their ability to command the allegiance of the peoples of Western Europe and Asia. They now clearly defined the remaining tasks in the Far East and were sure of the means to accomplish them. The Americans would drop the atomic bomb and the Russians would enter the war, even if Soong's hasty return to Moscow proved fruitless. If the timing was uncertain, they could predict all of the remaining ingredients of the war against Japan with an iron certitude. No one had any doubts as to the outcome or what they had yet to do.

In China, and now throughout the Far East, the United States confronted the disappearance of any semblance of the prewar stability. The conundrum of China by August filled the leaders of the United States with the deepest apprehension, and led Washington to attain Soviet assurances directly for future American interests in north China and Manchuria, circumventing the Kuomintang government on the explicit premise that it would continue to disintegrate despite the most munificent American aid. Elsewhere in East Asia a vast upsurge of nationalist and revolutionary independence movements, of extremely diverse character, took over power in the wake of the Japanese collapse, posing another serious threat to the United States war aims in Asia.

Asia was aflame with revolution which transformed World War II in the Far East almost immediately from a classic international conflict into a civil war releasing a vast liberation movement that would eventually eclipse European affairs and define the larger destiny of world politics for the next generation.

The Defeat of Japan

The first bomb was ready for use on August 3, but the weather was poor and so the act was delayed until the 5th, 8:11 A.M. Tokyo time. "Results clear cut successful in all respects," the military notified Truman later that day, already about noon of the 6th, Washington time. Truman thought the event "the greatest thing in history," but neither he nor Stimson reflected for a moment on the more than 75,000 Japanese killed in the flash of death, and for the next week Stimson failed to perceive any immediate and grave political import in the event, for they had already pondered and fit the consequences of the bomb into the larger American strategy in the Far East. No one sentimentalized belatedly about lost lives: "We are now prepared to obliterate more rapidly and completely every productive enterprise," Truman warned in his announcement of the event to the world.[1] Invasion would follow the terrifying devastation, of which more would be forthcoming.

It took the Japanese leaders many painful hours to discover what was unique about the destruction of Hiroshima and why its cause, though not its effect, differed from other bombing attacks. They received a high-level report only the following day confirming that the Americans had used a single bomb to demolish most of the city, and for the most part the leading army men discounted this report even despite Truman's announcement of the new weapon, but the navy quickly appreciated that the Americans had used the atomic bomb "with which the enemy had been experimenting for a number of years. . . ."[2] The events of the next days were testimony to the irrationality and profound immorality of all leaders and the triumph of unwavering mechanism in the war between Japan and the Allies. The Japanese rulers associated reason with the denial of reality that upset conventional wisdom and challenged the basic assumptions and vested interests for which they justified vast outpourings of blood. The consequence of useful myopia was wholesale death, the essential element of the war everywhere. If the war appeared to justify the prerogatives of those defining the irrationality in the short run, the outcome of the war was also a decisive world-wide rupture between leaders and the led, one which accelerated the transformation of world politics in ever-growing areas from conflicts between states to conflicts between strata and classes aligned with states and dependent on them to various degrees for survival. In the days after Hiroshima the Japanese and American leaders exhibited all the consistency of men bent on saving the reasoning behind their monumental investment of the blood of millions.

The Japanese Supreme Command determined to minimize, even deny, the atomic bomb, and preferred to think that even if the Americans could build the bomb they would not dare continue to use it. Truman had already given the order to drop the bombs on the first selected targets in Japan as they became available, and this the Japanese could not know. On the 8th, however, they learned of the inevitable doom of their army in China at the hands of the Russians. The Russian entry into the war "dumbfounded" the Japanese leaders no less than the atomic bomb, for although the Japanese army in China was on twenty-four-hour alert during the prior week, the "abruptness" of the Soviet action, one major naval leader recorded, "has been quite a shock," perhaps because many Japanese officers believed that "The strength of the SOVIET UNION overseas forces and Air Forces is far superior to U. S. Forces."[3]

Incessant Russian delays and growing demands, the details of which follow later in the chapter, bogged down the negotiations between Soong and Molotov. But the American government knew the Russians would enter the war when they were ready to do so, and that further pleading on its part would not change the facts or remove the assets of such aid. Truman coupled his announcement of the first atomic bomb with the threat of an invasion because he still believed that it would be necessary. The Americans wanted to end the war quickly, but they had no alternative plan for defeating Japanese forces in China without Russian aid. Both Grew and Stimson on August 7 and 8 urged the President to press for an early peace, and Grew was especially anxious to avoid losing the Emperor's alleged support for the fragile peace faction lest the Japanese army in China and Manchuria and the Japanese people themselves continue the war with the Emperor's blessings.

Japanese Ambassador Sato, hoping to see Molotov as soon as he returned from Potsdam, was assigned the admittedly forlorn task of winning Russian mediation in Japan's plans for suing for a peace at something less than unconditional surrender. The Soviet Foreign Minister delayed the confrontation, and then late on the 8th met the Japanese Ambassador only to notify him that in the name of bringing peace the Russians would consider themselves at war with Japan the following day—precisely three months after the end of the war against Germany. Several hours later, without advance notice, the Russians gave both Harriman and Clark Kerr the news and reminded them of the initial Russian suggestion—it was hardly a pledge—that they would join the war three months after the German defeat. So as Soviet troops smashed across the Japanese lines in Manchuria that very day, the Russians entered the war fearing it would end too soon. In explaining to the Russian people, Stalin cited the defeats Tsarist Russia had suffered at the hands of Japan in 1904–1905, defeats they would now undo. On the evening of the 8th Stalin admitted to Harriman that the Japanese were looking for a way out of the war, a fact Sato made abundantly clear that day. Stalin also revealed the long-held Soviet knowledge of the atomic bomb and the problems involved, an awareness that Stimson and the responsible leaders in Washington always assumed. Truman did not bother wiring Stalin concerning the event, but contented himself with calling in the press and making "a simple announcement" of four sentences to the effect that "Russia has declared war on Japan. That is all."[4] Only Chiang Kai-shek sent the Russian leader an enthusiastic message of welcome, for now the Russians would liberate China.

During the morning of the 9th, Tokyo time, the United States dropped a second atomic bomb, this time on Nagasaki, without troubling to assess the impact of the first bomb or Soviet entry into the war on Japan's intention to surrender. The commander at the Tinian B-29 air base made the decision to drop another bomb on the 9th—his superiors originally planned it for two days later—but he had authority from Washington to do so. During these very same days the vast B-29 attacks on the civilian populations continued on an accelerated scale, reflecting Washington's belief that to defeat Japan would require much more than atomic bombs. While Stimson hoped this action would aid the Emperor in overcoming opposition to surrender, and he now urged delay in dropping the third bomb, in fact he and most of the leaders in Washington wanted to make surrender easier for Japan to keep the Russians out of the homeland of the enemy itself. This distinction was critical, and never altered. Soviet entry into the war itself was never contingent on American approval, and it could not be stopped. The Russians were fighting in their own self-interest, and this was the prevalent view in Washington. It was hardly necessary for the Americans to drop two bombs on Japan to exhibit the destructive power of the weapon to the Russians, and this was never their intention. They had attained a political quid pro quo with Russia in China and Manchuria. Now the political dimensions were paramount. The United States wished to restrict Soviet military activity to the Asian mainland and restrict British participation in the naval war, and impose exclusive American control on the Japanese islands. A quick surrender, within weeks if possible, would be the best means to accomplish this end. Few suspected that they would accomplish the task so easily.[5]

On the morning of the 9th the Emperor and Premier Suzuki decided to accept the Potsdam surrender terms, and when they presented their decision to the Supreme War Direction Council later that day the military leaders split evenly on the matter. The Emperor imposed his decision over the dissenters and the chronically ambivalent, and early the next morning relayed via the Swiss their decision to accept the Potsdam Declaration "with the understanding that the said declaration does not comprise any demand which prejudices the prerogatives of His Majesty as a Sovereign Ruler."[6]

The message arrived in Washington as Stimson was ready to leave for the airport on a vacation. Neither he nor anyone else in Washington expected the internal dynamics of Japanese society or the impact of the atomic bomb or Russian entry so to hasten the end of the war by compressing everything into a few short days. Too much cannot be made of this point, for it places Washington's own evaluation of the bomb and Soviet entry into the war in its proper context: for most American leaders regarded neither as likely to prove decisive in terms of shortening the war to a matter of days rather than weeks or even months. It was in this context, as well, that Stimson and his circle advocated a "quick surrender," for even a surrender within two months would have represented a drastic shortening of a war which planners still assumed might last over a year. The possibility of sudden collapse was hardly compatible with a long rest for the Secretary of War, but "That busted our holiday. . . ."[7]

Truman immediately convened a conference at the White House, and in effect agreed to accept something less than unconditional surrender by continuing the institution of the Emperor, a decision that had been made in principle well over a year before. The decision was now confirmed to freeze the bombing of Japan, and Truman authorized Byrnes to continue the negotiations when they received the official surrender offer. The next day the United States told the Japanese that the Allies would accept their terms with the explicit understanding that the Emperor would both authorize the surrender and thereafter be subject to the authority of the Allied Supreme Commander. While the Japanese leaders temporized over these terms, and ancient divisions and factions renewed their struggles to surrender or fight on, Harriman in Moscow confronted the Russians with the fast-changing developments and sought their endorsement of American political policy. The Americans felt that since the Russians fought the Far Eastern war for only two days they had little right to interfere with American leadership. The Russians for their part unquestionably believed that their sacrifices in Europe made possible in the first place the American diversion of manpower to the Far East, and that their heavy commitments to a presumably common cause required some measure of equality everywhere. While the Russians lost at least 8,000 men in the fierce two-week campaign against 714,000 Japanese troops, their fast assault, including parachute drops on Port Arthur and Dairen before the Americans might get to them, saved the Americans from the ominous prospect of mounting their own campaign in China.

On the night of the 10th, when Harriman sought Molotov's approval of the reply to Japan, the Russian expressed skepticism of Japanese surrender offers, as if, it seemed to the American, he were seeking time to advance Soviet troops even further into China. In fact, the Russian also indicated some disapproval of retaining the Emperor. He then sprung what the Americans feared most: the demand for a Russian voice in the choice of the Allied Commander and a share in the occupation government. This share, Harriman immediately insisted, was "absolutely inadmissible" from a nation that had been in the war only a few days. Molotov heatedly referred to the Russian burden in Europe and angered Harriman by insisting on delay. Within hours after Stalin was apprised of the matter the Russians withdrew their demand, much to the pleasure and surprise of Washington.[8] In accordance with the official policy of Washington there would not be a common occupation government in Japan. The occupation of Italy—or Rumania—rather than Germany would set the precedent for Japan, a fact the Russians did not forget.

On August 14, despite opposition and a minor abortive coup in Tokyo, the Japanese accepted United States terms for surrender. On September 2 the Japanese and Allies signed the formal documents in Tokyo Bay and World War II came to an end.

In the final weeks of the war with Japan, and especially after the cessation of hostilities in mid-August, the Americans developed with new clarity their determination to rule Japan without interference from their former comrades in arms, especially Russia. The American position on the Emperor, "the only symbol of authority," as Truman understood him, was by now a firm part of policy.[9] At Potsdam, Stimson reflected on the overall policy to exclude the Russians—and English as well—from the mainland occupation, and preferably to restrict them to the Kuriles. As part of the overall Far Eastern grand strategy that Washington was considering, he wished to see "a sympathetic Japan to the United States in case there should be any aggression by Russia in Manchuria."[10] Although by early August it had yet to define a larger occupation policy for the future of Japan in the world community beyond that of the earlier year—and in reality it retained options for its restoration—the United States intended to control the occupation so that the final determination would be strictly compatible with its interests.

In early August, Marshall reminded Truman that while they needed the help of the Allies, including Russia, to defeat Japan outside the homeland, and the Russians "should be asked to share this effort," perhaps even to the extent of supplying troop contingents in the occupation of the homeland itself, the United States must reserve mastery over the occupation government.[11] On August 11 the State, War, and Navy departments approved a policy memo, which Truman quickly signed, indicating that,whatever contingents the Allies sent to Japan, the United States alone would designate a centralized commander of a unified occupation government. Both the British and the Russians vainly expressed opposition to the arrangement.[12]

General Order Number I and the Tide of the Left in Asia

The surrender of Japan presented a monumental and complex set of problems for the Americans, for every place the Japanese conquered they shattered the Old Order of colonialism, or, as in the case of China, the tide of local Communist movements seemed irresistible. Everywhere in the Far East—China, Korea, the Philippines, the Dutch East Indies, Indochina—the necessity of fending off the Left and shoring up the stabilizing forces of the region appeared as a pressing task in the wake of the Japanese military collapse. Only Japan, firmly in the hands of the occupying forces, would emerge safely. Elsewhere the remnants of the Japanese army remained the last, thin barrier to the triumph of the anticolonialist Resistance movements, generally leftist in political identification. In north China the Russians had it within their power to determine the immediate political outcome in the Japanese-occupied areas into which they were advancing. To avoid political defeat in the wake of war and to counter the Resistance in Asia, on August 14 Truman promulgated "General Order Number 1," a far-reaching document the War Department drafted that in effect attempted to redefine the distribution of power throughout the entire Far East. For the moment only it was successful, but then the revolutionary momentum in Asia again moved irresistibly forward.

The Americans sent General Order Number 1 to Stalin and the British government for their information rather than approval. It defined the details and precise format for the surrender of the Japanese military establishment everywhere, and its political implications were so obvious that the pettiness of Stalin's objections revealed a willingness to accede to the American design for the Far East. Stalin restricted his initial complaints to the jurisdiction of Russian troops over the Russian territorial acquisition from Japan that the Americans promised to support at Yalta, hinted at the desirability of creating something akin to the Allied Control Council in Germany, and sought to achieve a degree of autonomy for Russian commanders in taking the surrenders of the Japanese in their theaters. The American document insisted that the Supreme Allied Commander—General Douglas MacArthur—alone retain absolute control over the Japanese surrender everywhere. The Russians quickly relented on the challenge to absolute United States control over surrenders and the occupation government of Japan, but the territorial ambitions of both the U.S.S.R. and the United States became the subject of a tense exchange between Stalin and Truman.

Stalin immediately asked for a share in the occupation of the Kurile Islands, which the Allies at the Yalta Conference had agreed to return to Russia. He also wished to see Soviet troops take the Japanese surrender in the upper half of Hokkaido, the northernmost of the four major islands of

Japan. Truman flatly refused the latter demand and linked the Kurile Islands request to the American acquisition of a military and commercial air base in the central area. Again Truman reasserted MacArthur's monopoly over the control and occupation of Japan. On the 22nd Stalin expressed surprise at the refusals, and reminded Truman that the Allies had not agreed upon base rights for the Americans on the Kuriles at Yalta. He expressed shock that Truman had framed the demand for base rights in a tone ordinarily reserved for the land of conquered states. After haggling and bitter innuendos, during which Truman made American support for the Russian claim to the Kuriles at least contingent on commercial air rights, the matter ended in a tone of strained correctness and the Russian consented to permit emergency landings on their airfields.[13]

In the largest sense, General Order Number 1 was a grand and sweeping American attempt to define the political outcome of the war in the Far East insofar as the military position of the forces of the various Allies would determine it. The Americans based it on their assumption that the Japanese would transfer in an orderly manner the control of Korea, the Philippines, the Dutch East Indies, and Indochina to politically acceptable military forces which MacArthur would designate in carefully defined regions. Everywhere the General Order commanded the Japanese to aid and assist the Allied takeover in the precise manner MacArthur dictated, and above all not to surrender to unauthorized local armed Resistance groups. Most important of all, Washington premised it on an American claim to a share in the control of areas likely to fall to the Russians or Chinese Communists first, and therefore on the belief that the Russians would consent to the American designs. In fact the General Order was a test of Russian intentions in Korea, Communist aspirations in China, and an effort to stop local leftist-led Resistance movements elsewhere and to channelize nonleftist independence movements where possible.

The Problem of Korea

Korea had been a troublesome question mark in gauging Russian intentions in the Far East after the war, and it also revealed American definitions of its postwar goals. In essence the problem was how to keep Korea from moving toward Communism and the Russian orbit and create a unique and perhaps dominant American presence there.

The first American impulse on Korea favored an international trusteeship, in which the United States would be an important member. When Eden was in Washington at the end of March 1943 Roosevelt mentioned the proposal with only China, the United States, "and one or two other countries participating."[14] He did not specify Britain or Russia. At no time during the war did the United States advocate immediate independence for the oldest victim of Japanese expansion, a fact that irritated Korean nationalist leaders in the United States. One of these, Syngman Rhee, early brought himself to the attention of the State Department as a deep friend of the United States, and he warned the State Department of the dangers of Russia's using Korean Communist divisions, then being trained in the Soviet Union, to Bolshevize his nation. When the United States went on record at the Cairo Conference as favoring independence for Korea "in due course," many American leaders immediately noticed the significance of the contingency and the exclusion of the Russians from the communiqué.[15] Hull thought it an important blunder. But it was also a necessary one, for by that time Gauss and the State Department feared that the Russians would create a puppet regime in Korea once they entered the country. By mid-1944 this evaluation became the critical factor in planning for the nation, so much so that in March, State Department experts recommended "the employment of technically qualified Japanese in Korean economic life . . . during the period of military government, to the extent that qualified Koreans or other suitable personnel are not available."[16] Given the long Japanese economic domination and the secondary role of Koreans in economic management, this policy was tantamount to the preservation of an economic dimension of Japanese imperialism.

By May 1944 the State Department formulated a postwar policy of Four Power trusteeship for Korea, preferably with a centralized administration. The United States took this policy to Yalta, along with the desire to "play a leading role in the occupation and military government," which together with China would have meant a dominant American role in Korea.[17] When Roosevelt first presented the idea to Stalin, along with the prediction that the trusteeship would last twenty to thirty years, Stalin acceded, but added that the shorter the trusteeship period the better. When Hopkins saw Stalin in May 1945 the Russian reiterated his acceptance of the American plan for Korea, leaving Washington free to pursue its course when the war ended. Without having a precise set of plans for the trusteeship structure, Stalin's endorsement of the contours of United States policy made possible the broad American vision of its future in the Far East, one involving world recognition of America's vast power and responsibility everywhere.

The American experts concerned with the future of that country still worried about the possibility of a Communist triumph in the hands of several divisions of Korean troops said to be in the Soviet Union. For this reason the official policy of the United States always favored Four Power trusteeship and joint occupation, but since the principle had never been reduced to an operational plan, in reality the Russians were not firmly committed. At the beginning of July, Molotov and Stalin informed Soong that they thought there were many details to settle in the unusual trusteeship proposal before it might be implemented, and in any event they did not want to see foreign troops stationed there—in effect rejecting a critical premise of the American plan. The first impulse of the War and State departments was to take the surrender of the Japanese in Korea as far north as possible, to preclude one nation's having sole responsibility for liberation, a goal that they predicated on the war's lasting longer than it did, giving the American forces an opportunity to make a landing and determine the outcome of events in lieu of a formal trusteeship plan. At the end of July the Joint Chiefs of Staff designated for conquest the Korean port of Pusan as second only to Shanghai in the event of a sudden Japanese surrender, but they were not prepared to take the port during August— another reflection of their belief that neither the atomic bomb nor Russian entry would end the war almost immediately. To patch up their miscalculation as best they might, the Americans in General Order Number 1 specified that Japanese troops south of the 38th parallel surrender to the United States, those above that line to the Russians. The 38th parallel was about an even division of the nation and gave the United States the ancient capital city of Seoul. Had possession determined the distribution of Korea, the Americans would have received precious little, for Russian troops entered Korea on August 12 and the first American forces did not arrive until September 8. When Stalin received General Order Number 1 neither he nor any of his subordinates rejected it save in those details already mentioned, and when the Americans arrived in Seoul and Inchon, deep in the American sector, they found the Russians in possession. The Red Army quickly withdrew north of the 38th parallel and acknowledged the American partition of Korea.

The American takeover of Korea vividly illustrated the principle of General Order Number 1 that the Japanese were to transfer power directly from their hands to authorized occupation forces, and until then prevent the local Left from intervening. On August 28 the Japanese commander in Korea wired MacArthur that "Communists and independence agitators are plotting to take advantage of the situation to disturb peace and order." Since Washington was opposed to both, the American replied immediately that "It is directed that you maintain order and preserve the machinery of government in Korea south of the 38th degree . . . until my forces assume those responsibilities. . . ."[18] Shortly thereafter the Koreans were told by American leaflets to respect the orders of the existing government—the Japanese—and not to participate in demonstrations of any sort, including those demanding immediate Korean independence.

Although the Americans did not first intend to consider the 38th parallel a final demarcation of the American zone of influence, they made no effort to arrange the details of the original plan with the Russians. The Four Power control of Germany was already, from the American viewpoint, an undesirable precedent they would avoid in Japan, and from the very inception Washington saw the problem of Korea in the context of forestalling a Communist takeover in the absence of any foreign troops. The Russian reluctance to accept unequivocally the basic assumptions of the American trusteeship plan made the northernmost demarcation line especially important if later they could not arrange unity in a manner that would permit Four Power control of the future political evolution of Korea. To accept possession as the basis of occupation was tantamount, in the American view, to accepting a totally Communist Korea. The unilateral decision to demand the division of Korea as far north as the 38th parallel was a successful test of Russian policy from the American viewpoint. It was also an artificial partition that the Koreans themselves in no way supported, and in that fact rested the seeds of future conflict.[19]

The Philippines and Controlled Liberation

The war in the Philippines was an extension of the near civil war in that nation inherited from the 1930's. The dominant trend in the island's agrarian economy, especially in the large central island of Luzon, was increasing land concentration, tenancy having doubled since the American conquest in 1898. In central Luzon the situation was especially critical, and during the 1930's agrarian revolts were common. The dominant class geared the rest of the nation's economy to the lopsided development of an extractive and agricultural raw materials industry serving the United States well, but by 1940 causing the agrarian nation to suffer a continuous major food deficit. For the masses the average standard of living was not above that of Southeast Asia. The export, import, and banking sectors were predominantly American-owned, and the local Filipino business groups, whom the Americans permitted to monopolize a nominal degree of self-government, were intimately associated with American interests as compradors. This small elite ran the Philippines with a corruption and inefficiency that was usefully self-serving. When the Japanese invaded the islands they found nearly all of the remaining local politicians quite willing to collaborate in their own self-interest, and they left the traditional ruling class in power. The exiled Osmeña government in Washington maintained relations with Manila throughout the war and the American psychological-warfare services never attacked the local collaborators.

To the Philippine peasantry the war was an opportunity to renew their opposition to the local landowning classes, and the weakening of a central authority and the relative scarcity of Japanese occupation forces led many landowners to flee to the city as the landless peasantry organized into armed bands, some based on local tribal groups who tended to war against one another, but the most important being the People's Anti-Japanese Army (the Hukbalahap), primarily Communist-led but also counting former liberal political figures among its directors. The peak strength of the Huks has been estimated at 100,000, and they controlled vast sections of the nation. This social revolution in the agrarian system, with the widespread elimination of tenancy, created new organs of self-government in local areas, and a radically new society. Although the Huks were eager to aid American intelligence and military operations, and killed over 20,000 Japanese and puppet troops, they functioned mainly as an armed peasantry seeking to end its misery. American officers assigned to work with them received cooperation in military matters, and soon grew to respect the Huks. Where possible, however, the United States attempted to create their own "nonpolitical" units, though these often clashed with the Huks. The American leaders were never ready to permit their own guerrilla units, much less the Huks, to become more than a useful convenience for the moment, and remained hostile to the guerrillas' ultimate intentions, a fact that the Americans in the jungles deeply resented.[20]

Washington was fully aware of the fact, as a Foreign Service officer authoritatively informed the State Department in November 1943, that "Under Japanese military occupation the Philippine Islands have been governed very largely under the same laws and by much the same men as under the Commonwealth."[21] And, no less significant, they appreciated the class basis of the opposition. In September 1943 Senator Millard Tydings introduced a resolution into the Senate to provide for Philippine independence immediately after the war, but it was vague enough when passed in June 1944 to leave open to further negotiations the question of future economic relations between the two nations and military base rights before the United States granted actual independence. Stimson insisted on base rights, for he saw the Philippines as a critical link in his postwar plan "to maintain our power in the Pacific."[22] What the American government wanted, therefore, only the conservative comprador elements, the very groups collaborating with the Japanese, were likely to grant. For this reason, despite the certainty that the Filipino people as a whole were bitterly anticollaborationist, the official American policy viewed the collaborationists with silent toleration, and many believed that prewar President Manuel Quezon, or even Sergio Osmeña in Washington, were not themselves unfriendly toward them.

Vindication of this suspicion came at the end of November 1944, when Osmeña landed on Leyte with MacArthur and immediately issued a statement exonerating those public officials who "had to remain at their posts to maintain a semblance of government, to protect the population from the oppressor to the extent possible by human ingenuity and to comfort the people in their misery."[23] The counterrevolution that followed in the wake of the American occupation laid the basis for a civil war that soon followed, and still has not ended, and to the large majority of the Filipinos the liberation was a more horrifying experience than the Japanese occupation. The indiscriminate American bombings certainly wreaked more physical destruction, and the black market and prostitution which followed in the wake of the American troops further ripped apart the already tottering social system. Petty speculation and corruption were the rule. Worse yet, however, was the American decision to undo the revolution that the Huks had brought to the countryside.

As the Japanese strength waned the Huks had grown stronger and bolder in implementing their essentially mild land-reform proposals; but they also began more widespread liquidation of collaborationists, many of whom were identical to the landowning class. By the beginning of 1945 all that stood between the Huks and a total transformation of the agrarian economy was the United States military, led by MacArthur. Although he approached the problem in his own manner, with a vast personal public relations staff and ample photos of himself attached to matches, bars of soap, and the like, MacArthur, in a manner the State Department found irritating and egocentric, implemented Washington's policy by speedily restoring the Old Order. He pressed the Filipino collaborationist police into the service of the United States, and the United States military authorities arrested and held the two major Huk leaders for seven months as security risks. During 1945 MacArthur increasingly used United States troops to break up Huk meetings, and the landlords then successfully agitated for the legal recognition of their former holdings. The occupation permitted Filipino authorities to use United States aid for private purposes, and gave them military equipment for use—it was obvious from the beginning—against the Huks. As successor to Osmeña, MacArthur singled out Manuel Roxas, whom the OSS most generously described as being "in the peculiar position of an exonerated collaborationist. . . ." In April 1945 MacArthur assigned Roxas to his staff with the rank of brigadier general, and the following June the Filipino publicly reentered politics and visited Washington to receive the further blessings of the Americans. Behind Roxas stood, according to the OSS, "some economically powerful groups," and it was Roxas who in April 1946 became the first President of the new nation.[24]

Throughout 1945 the United States' official specialists on the Philippines hoped the collaborationist-Resistance split would not define the future politics of the nation, and Osmeña himself favored a most generous policy toward collaborationists. But the even greater American desire for bases and the fear of the Huks prejudged the issue. They planned not so much to retain the Old Order as to restore it, and that exercise would eventually require a vast expenditure of men and blood. For after suffering numerous assaults and death, the Huks refused to give up their arms and land to the former collaborationist authorities.[25]

Southeast Asia: The Dutch East Indies and French Indochina

The American position on colonialism had always been equivocal and primarily a tactical lever for obtaining immediate access to raw materials. In fact and practice the United States had only a minor interest in Southeast Asia during the war, and as Hull recalled, "At no time did we press Britain, France, or The Netherlands for an immediate grant of self-government to their colonies. Our thought was that it would come after an adequate period of years, short or long. . . ."[26] It was the practice to see the problem of colonialism in the context of other areas where American interests might be greater, and so, for example, several times during the war Washington offered support for the postwar continuation of the empire as a quid pro quo for immediate French collaboration in North Africa, or demanded British support for United States Pacific bases as the price for tolerating their empire. When the OSS set up a priority of future problems in the Far East—one in which Japan ranked the highest, China next, but Southeast Asia fifth—its definition of limited American objectives in Southeast Asia included interest "in a number of industrial raw materials originating in these colonial regions as well as in actual or potential markets for U.S. manufactures and capital." Otherwise, as long as someone maintained "the political stability and orientation" of Southeast Asia along friendly lines the United States could remain indifferent to colonialism.[27] Support or opposition to European colonialism would depend on the extent to which the interested European nation respected American goals elsewhere, and the nature of the local opposition. If the Left led the independence movement, then the Americans would sustain collaborationists, if possible, or colonialism if necessary.

In the Dutch East Indies, Achmed Sukarno and Mohammed Hatta, whom the OSS considered "foremost collaborationist leaders," led the independence movement and their aspirations did not cause any alarm in Washington.[28] The Americans watched with indifference as the Dutch on August 11 ordered the Japanese to retain control of the islands until they could send in new troops; and Sukarno's flexibility on non-Dutch foreign interests later became the major attraction for winning tacit American support for his cause.

IN Indochina the situation was radically different, and in the final months of the war against Japan events laid the basis for the most sustained single foreign policy crisis of the postwar period. As the United States shifted, hesitated, and finally set its future policy for that area on a consistent course, it fully revealed the importance the political nature of the independence movement had in defining the American response to it.

Throughout 1943 Roosevelt believed Indochina should become a Four Power trusteeship after the war, with the United States and China among the four. At Teheran he repeated this position, which Stalin immediately endorsed, suggesting that eventual Indochinese independence might follow in two or three decades. Yet even by this time it was clear that a desire to penalize French collaboration with Germany and Japan, or De Gaulle's annoying independence, motivated American willingness to eliminate French control. For their part, anxious about the future of their own empire, the British made it clear that they would defend the French right to the restoration. Yet the critical element in the first American position was that ultimate independence for the Vietnamese would not be something they might take themselves, and at no time did Washington express a belief in the intrinsic value of freedom for the Vietnamese, but a blessing the world's Great Powers might grant at their own convenience. The seed of United States opposition to the independence movement that existed in Vietnam was implicit in this attitude.

In February 1944 the State and War departments proposed that the occupation and administration of liberated Indochina use French troops, presumably without prejudicing the final disposition of the country. Roosevelt stopped further consideration of this suggested policy, and in August the British made the same request, and when Roosevelt again rejected the principle they nevertheless went ahead to incorporate a French mission into the Southeast Asia Command under Lord Mountbatten. In fact Roosevelt was alone in his opposition, for Hull was in favor of French restoration with an immediate pledge to grant eventual independence, one he hoped the British and Dutch would imitate. During October the President revealed the ambiguities of his position by denying an OSS and State Department suggestion that they give arms to local Resistance groups to fight the Japanese, arms that they might also use to assure their own independence from the French.

At the beginning of November 1944 the President partially unwove these tangled and inconsistent threads when the OSS complained that the American military also approved British recognition of the French mission, and therefore the restoration of French colonialism. On November 3 Roosevelt outlined the form of future policy on Indochina, without giving it political substance, by insisting that the United States give no approval to the return of a French military mission to Indochina, since "We have made no final decisions on the future of Indo-China," and that the United States would have to review any French, English, or Dutch agreement on Southeast Asia.[29] But since this was not yet a policy, the British Foreign Office warned Stettinius that continued American vacillation would only lead to an awkward clash of positions.

Although Roosevelt at Yalta repeated his desire for a trusteeship, during March he toyed with the possibility of French restoration in return for their pledge to grant independence eventually, and by May 1945 the United States had no written affirmative directive on political policy in Indochina or Southeast Asia in general. In part due to the low priority assigned the issue, the gap also reflected growing apprehension as to what the future might hold for those countries as independent states. Meanwhile, others outside the conference rooms of Paris, London, and Washington were already determining that future.

The Japanese permitted the Vichy government in Indochina to rule the nation for them, but in early March 1945 they replaced it with a local puppet government under Bao Dai. No sooner did they do so than the major Resistance group, the League of Viet Minh led by Ho Chi Minh, inaugurated an active Resistance to create a new nation free of both French and Japanese control. Throughout this period the Viet Minh maintained contact with the OSS, who were well aware of its politics. A coalition of left and moderate forces formed the Vietminh in 1941, but Ho soon became its dominant leader. The Vietminh built its impregnable base on the peasant tenantry comprising some two-thirds of the agricultural population of all Vietnam—a country in which 3 percent of the landowners owned 60 percent of privately held land. For the peasants of Vietnam, ground down by high rent and exorbitant interest rates, the mild Vietminh agrarian reform giving land to the landless peasants, but carefully avoiding damage to "progressive" landowners, was the beginning of a new era. It made the triumph of the Vietminh inevitable. In relaying its program to Washington in July the Vietminh indicated that it wished independence within five to ten years, a democracy based on universal suffrage, and the national purchase of French economic holdings. The following month, when the Vietminh established the new republic, it modeled its new Declaration of Independence after the American version of the same name because, as Ho told a representative of the State Department shortly thereafter, "my people look to the United States as the one nation most likely to be sympathetic to our cause."[30] Never was a revolutionary leader more wrong. The American for his part found such sentiments mawkish, and "Perhaps naïvely, and without consideration of the conflicting postwar interests of the 'Big' nations themselves, the new government believed that by complying with the conditions of the wartime United Nations conferences it could invoke the benefits of these conferences in favor of its own independence."[31] From this viewpoint, even in 1945 the United States saw Indochina as the object of Great Power diplomacy and conflict.

At Potsdam, and again in the unilateral General Order Number 1, the United States had resolved its equivocation on Indochina by authorizing the British takeover of the nation south of the 16th parallel and Chinese occupation north of it, and this definitely meant the ultimate restoration of the French, whom the British loyally supported since 1943. One cannot exaggerate the importance of these steps, since it made the United States responsible for the French return at a time when Washington might have dictated the independence of that country. By this time everyone understood what the British were going to do.

The OSS worked with the Vietminh during the final months of the war to the extent of giving them petty quantities of arms in exchange for information and assistance, but they and the other American officials who went to Indochina during the heady first months of freedom were unanimous in believing that Ho "is an old revolutionist . . . a product of Moscow, a communist."[32] The OSS understood the nationalist ingredient in the Vietnamese revolution and they could not ignore the fact that Bao Dai enthusiastically endorsed the revolution, but they gave far more emphasis to the organized Communist dimension. These reports helped to consolidate Washington's support for the French. The first senior OSS Mission parachuted into Hanoi on August 22, shortly before the Vietnamese proclaimed their new republic, and during the same days the British landed to take the Japanese surrender and to restore French power. Over the subsequent weeks the United States Army Mission under Brigadier General Philip Gallagher arrived, ostensibly neutral, but also assigned the task of "preventing violence by Annamites on French nationals," Frenchmen who were there to restore the Old Order.[33] In the euphoria of red placards, manifestoes, and street meetings of seething masses of self-declared independent Vietnamese, the greatest of the postwar dramas began to unfold as the power of the Vietnamese clashed violently with the representatives of France, England, and the United States.

Until the summer of 1945 the American position had been against both French restoration and immediate national independence for the Vietnamese, and in the idea of trusteeship it had predicated an active American involvement in the determination of the future of the country and its control after the war. The option, which most of Roosevelt's advisers accepted, was in favor of a return of French predominance, perhaps with eventual independence. Considering the limited choices the next development in American policy was predictable.

Given the alternative, American support for the restoration of France to Indochina was a logical step toward stopping the triumph of the Left everywhere. Both in action and policy the American government now chose to gamble on the reimposition of French colonialism, as disagreeable as they once may have thought it to be. By mid-August, French officials were hinting that French restoration would fully open the Indochinese economy to the United States and England. At the end of the month, De Gaulle was in Washington, and on August 24 the conversation with Truman turned to Indochina. The United States, the President now told De Gaulle, favored the return of France to Indochina. He had made the final pledge to France, and it would shape the course of world history for decades.[34]

China: The Great Powers Endorse the Kuomintang

The Russians always retained the initiative on when to enter the war against Japan, and they exercised the discretion to their own interest despite the fact that Molotov had only returned to Moscow at the beginning of August and had not yet signed a final treaty with China. It was for Stalin to decide how freely to interpret the Yalta Agreement on China to regain all the Tsars had lost, and for the United States to see that China did not sign away rights which might impinge on the Open Door and long-term American objectives in Manchuria.

United States interests required that the Kuomintang not give away too much in its eagerness to obtain the backing of the Russians against the local Communists or their entry into the war. When Soong and Wang Shih-chieh, the new foreign minister, returned to Moscow at the beginning of August the American government told them it expected the KMT to consult with Washington prior to any formal agreement, and on August 5 Truman urged Soong not to make any further compromises on the truly international character of the port of Dairen, a precondition to the Open Door. This issue, rather than exaggerated Soviet demands on other points, most concerned the United States. As Molotov and Soong reduced the talks to finer matters of police authority and city-manager rights, Harriman jealously guarded future American prerogatives in Manchuria and tempered Soong's impulse to make further compromises. By this time, to the delight of the Chiang regime, the Russians entered the war and were sweeping into Manchuria. The American reticence, therefore, was not geared to keeping the Russians out of the war for lack of a treaty with the Chinese—something they never thought possible or desirable—but solely to keeping China open to future trade. The final Treaty of Friendship and Alliance between Russia and China pleased the leaders of the Kuomintang, who undoubtedly appreciated that an agreement with the Russians was indispensable before the Red Army entered much more of China, and might write its own peace; but Harriman, Byrnes, and much of official Washington retained their suspicions of its ultimate import. The wording might conceal rather different intent.

The Sino-Soviet Treaty essentially followed the terms of the Yalta proposals; the Soviet promise to give moral and military aid only to the Kuomintang government was its most important condition. The Red Army would immediately hand over the territory it liberated to the National Government for political administration. The Russians would lease Port Arthur as a base for only thirty years, while the Chinese would appoint the leading posts in the civil government. Dairen would become "a free port open to the commerce and shipping of all nations."[35]

The Kuomintang leaders were satisfied with the results, as was Hurley.

The treaty, Hurley wrote to Washington, "demonstrated conclusively that the Soviet Government supports the National Government of China. . . ."[36] This fact made it possible for the men around Chiang to attempt, with renewed vigor, to deal harshly with the menace of Communism at home.

With or without Russian and American support, China by August was moving irresistibly toward civil war and a test, by force of arms, of the strength of two Chinese systems. In this process the Japanese surrender and the presence of United States troops and aid to the Kuomintang became both a complicating and instrumental factor, one that gave Chiang the hope of winning a civil war. The treaty with Russia freed Chiang's hand, and the Americans put a gun in it.

At the beginning of July, Wedemeyer urged Marshall to try to get the Great Powers to coerce the Kuomintang and Communists to settle the incipient civil war. "I use the word coerce advisedly," he indicated in words remarkably like Stilwell's, "because it is my conviction that continued appeals to both sides couched in polite diplomatic terms will not accomplish unification."[37] He now proposed sending liaison teams along with the troops of the Kuomintang and Communists to gather intelligence and presumably to prevent them from turning their guns against each other. The collapse of the Japanese army, Wedemeyer understood, would leave a vacuum into which the two contending forces would rush and clash. In principle Chiang accepted the plan, and the American then submitted it to Mao for his consideration.

Mao at this time still hoped to avoid a civil war in the belief that such a policy was vital to winning the support of "world public opinion and the middle-of-the-roaders within the country," a classic bourgeois approach to social change.[38] He did not preclude the right of self-defense nor would he compromise the basic principles on which he would organize a coalition government. To Mao, Chiang held the initiative. Nevertheless, by this time he deeply mistrusted the United States' role in China, not merely because Chiang was using the vast Lend-Lease and economic aid within China and scarcely against Japan, but also because the United States Navy Group, intimately linked with Chiang's secret police, performed essentially political functions in helping to extirpate Communists. Communist complaints in June led Wedemeyer's command to create a secret investigation board, which largely sustained the charges. By August 2 such flagrant partiality compelled Wedemeyer to remind his officers that they were to avoid taking armed action on either side in the increasing clashes between the contending sides.

In this context of Communist suspicions of American actions and intentions, events and American policy by-passed Mao's opportunity to accept or reject the American liaison proposal. At the end of July the Joint Chiefs of Staff reiterated their long-standing desire to avoid becoming involved in the campaign on the Chinese mainland, but they also thought it necessary to occupy Shanghai and two northerly ports to permit the Kuomintang to return to north China before the Communists and Russians entered the vacuum. The policy set, Wedemeyer and Chiang immediately agreed that air flights of Nationalist troops to key centers would also supplement the program, the American promising not to collaborate with Communist troops insofar as that were possible. In short, as Wedemeyer asked Mao to consider steps toward peace, the Americans charted the means for helping Chiang to retake China while avoiding a massive commitment of manpower.

On August 10 the Americans reassured Chiang of American support when they combined all of these threads into a single directive for the Kuomintang's comprehensive reconquest of China, hopefully with limited American aid. Although Washington again directed its representatives to avoid taking sides in the civil war, it also made it explicit that American forces would give only the Nationalist Government the local political administration. The Americans in China understood that the end of Japan was near and that the existing plans would prove inadequate should the Japanese collapse suddenly. Both Chiang and Wedemeyer appealed to Washington for five extra divisions to move immediately into the Nanking, Peking, Canton, Shanghai areas, a decision they understood to be tantamount to support for a restoration of the Kuomintang against the Communists. Hurley endorsed the plea, and from Moscow both Harriman and Edwin Pauley urged similar lines of action. Above all, Hurley pointed out, the United States must prevent the Communists from taking the Japanese surrender, a step that would permit them to acquire arms and create a civil war.

To spread American forces throughout China for essentially hopeless political duties was not an attractive proposition in light of the past years of experience with Chiang. Still, it was policy to prevent Communism in China, and on August 14 General Order Number 1 ordered Japanese forces in China, excluding Manchuria, to return their conquests and to surrender them only to Chiang Kai-shek, the only Allied political figure mentioned by name in the entire directive. The War Department agreed to assign only two new American divisions to China, but not before it could find transportation for them. The department would and could not do more, for the sudden surrender left it unprepared for rapid movements into distant regions. The August 10 directive stood: the Americans would aid Chiang, but not with the commitment that he demanded. For this attitude Chiang himself was largely responsible. Wedemeyer now exploited all of his resources to transport Chiang's men to the critical centers of China.

The Communists claimed the right to take Japanese surrenders and occupy territory the enemy held, and Chiang's radio warned them not to move their units. On August 13, and again several days later, Mao replied that Chiang's policy was entirely political and self-serving, and the sacrifices of Communist forces in the field gave them the right to confront the enemy at the surrender table. From this moment civil war was inevitable. American troops were totally engaged in moving the Nationalists into Japanese-held areas, and the Americans instructed the Japanese to maintain order until they might arrive. The Russians too, despite some later minor assistance to the Communists, essentially respected their pledge to support Chiang against the Communists, and it was not until September that they came into contact with Communist troops. The Japanese held on to Shanghai, Peking, and Tientsin, and continued to clash with the Communists throughout the north. By the end of August both the Communists and Kuomintang forces, the latter with the aid of the major powers in Asia, were racing to fill in the military vacuum that the Japanese defeat had left.[39]

At the end of World War II Chiang had every military and diplomatic asset necessary for success in his plan to conquer China and extend his control to areas that had always eluded the Kuomintang. The support of the Allies, including small numbers of American troops, and the far more significant holding action of the Japanese and their puppets, meant that Chiang might hope temporarily to exercise control over China, and in fact he spread his troops far and wide to the major strategic points, later to find them vulnerable in their very dispersion. His army numbered almost three million, and his armament was far superior to that in the hands of 900,000 Communist troops and their militia of twice that size. Even economically Chiang had resources that were quite sufficient for the consolidation of power and the generation of internal reconstruction. The Kuomintang held vast foreign assets in dollars and gold, and the acquisition of Manchuria gave China a new, well-developed and largely intact industrial base that represented a potentially huge increase in Nationalist power. Given purely objective factors, Chiang was far stronger at the end of World War II than at the beginning, and these elements might have assured his triumph over the 100 million people in the much poorer Communist-controlled regions. The Communist party, moreover, had shown a willingness to abjure doctrine and work with almost any group willing to work with them, seeking to define broad terms on which to build a new society and relate itself to the world.

By August 1945 Chiang had the option of working with the Communists or wiping them out, and he might ultimately have succeeded in either course had his regime not been based on gangsterism. What to others would have been an opportunity to consolidate power was to Chiang a chance to enrich his clique. A more-or-less average army might have held the new areas and defeated the ill-equipped Communist troops. An economy based on something more than peculation and graft might have re-formed and reconstructed itself without challenging its own class basis in a renovated, modernized China. A moderately efficient capitalist and nationalist leadership might have directed the vast aid, military and economic, of the rest of the world toward these ends. In fact Chiang remained the critical element making inevitable the triumph of the Chinese revolution and China's subsequent entry into the twentieth century as a Great Power.

The Definition of American Objectives in China

Washington and the American embassy in Moscow watched the course of the Soong-Molotov negotiations in Moscow with the closest interest, and it was the clause on Dairen that primarily concerned the American government. On August 5 the State Department asked Harriman to try to induce the Russians to issue a public statement favoring the Open Door in Manchuria. By the middle of the month Molotov indicated that both prior undertakings and the new treaty would be sufficient, and by this time Washington decided that it would also ask Chiang for his assurances on the subject. He quickly granted them, but in word only. On August 22 Byrnes again urged Harriman to press the Russians on a joint Sino-Russian statement expressing their "adherence to the policy of the Open-Door, equality of opportunity and non-discrimination in matters relating to the management and operation of the railways and the free port of Dairen."[40] When the Ambassador asked Stalin about the question five days later the Russian agreed to separate but similar Soviet and Chinese statements on the subject, and accepted the critical principle. The failure to create such a public pledge came not at the hands of the Russians, but from the Chinese and Americans. In early September, Hurley pointed out to the State Department that since the entire idea originated before the signing of the Sino-Soviet Treaty, which now covered the matter and revealed assent to the American objectives, it was no longer necessary to obtain further pledges that might imply Chinese inability to implement the terms of the treaty. When the Russians asked for a draft of the Chinese pledge, the Chinese hinted that the new treaty was a sufficient guarantee for all concerned, and they never offered what the Americans had once so ardently desired. The State Department decided to table the matter. The debate was significant only for what it revealed of American goals and objectives in China. And by the end of the war against Japan everyone understood that there were more immediate, pressing problems than establishing an environment in which American businessmen might trade and prosper.

Yet these objectives were important in also exhibiting the limits of American alternatives in China, the reasons for their persistent support of the hopelessly corrupt Kuomintang, and the outlines of future policy. The idea of the Open Door was a standard part of the rhetoric of China policy, but by the end of the war the Americans redefined it to include reform within China itself, laying the basis for a liberal capitalism that might make American interests in China worthwhile and important in the long run. Most leaders in the War and State departments believed this goal beyond their immediate grasp, and thought the better part of wisdom was to rely on Japan, renovated and restored, to provide the major balance in the Far East—a Japan less predatory and compatible with a widespread American presence. During May, Truman appointed Edwin A. Locke, Jr., a banker who later became vice-president of the Chase National Bank, as his personal representative to China for economic affairs. Locke went to China with the rather typical belief that "We want a China with close economic, political and psychological . . . ties with the U.S." Reasonable American investments would have to industrialize such a China, perhaps over fifty years, "on a thoroughly practical and realistic basis," ultimately to create "a large, permanent and growing market for U.S. goods. . . ."[41] There was nothing new in this vision, but to attain it required a reform of the Nationalist Government—neither too much nor too little.

A China that developed into "a large scale market for American goods and capital," as the OSS defined key objectives in August, would have to solve the Communist problem.[42] By August, Locke was most pessimistic about the political preconditions of reform, but his plans for ameliorating China became a standard part of United States policy. He wished to see the Americans remain neutral in the imminent civil war that would eliminate the hope of Chinese economic development along lines compatible with American policy, a war that the Communists might very well win, despite inferior arms, because of the mass support of the people for their cause. Locke realized that the Communists no longer trusted Chiang or Hurley, and were not likely to give up their arms without solid assurances. Chiang, as of that moment, was committed to winning by force of arms.

Only the Great Powers, Locke warned Truman, might prevent the disaster in China, especially since Russia was not out to sweep the Communists into power. A Three Power advisory committee, with Kuomintang and Communist representatives, might recommend to Chiang a far-reaching plan of reform, one Locke thought Chiang himself would accept. To carry out the proposal the President's adviser presented a number of approaches, but the one that he preferred Washington implemented in modified form in the Marshall Mission to China several months later. "Remember," Stimson warned the former Chief of Staff, "that the Generalissimo has never honestly backed a thorough union with the Chinese Communists. He could not, for his administration is a mere surface veneer (more or less rotten) over a mass of the Chinese people beneath him."[43] Such realism was dominant among every American official working on

China at the time, but they had to deny the logic of its meaning—of remaining truly neutral—if they were to save China from Communism.

At the end of the war Washington believed that only the KMT could reform China in an acceptable manner, if reform were to come at all—which was to say, with the consent of the Kuomintang leaders. Locke thought Chiang would endorse reforms and Hopkins judged that "the new leaders in China, notably T. V. Soong . . . are quite prepared for the kind of economic reform that must come to China."[44] It was Soong who was the recipient of the advice the Americans gave on the nature of economic reform in the last moments of the war. Locke and Donald Nelson both urged him to take on American engineering and consulting firms to manage the vast new industrial complex in Manchuria, to train Chinese replacements for Japanese technicians, and in effect to preserve the existing economy and renovate it. And to glance ahead, when the United States issued loans and grants for specific economic purposes, it took care to make sure that they would not encourage state-owned industries in competition with American private firms in China.[45]

THE ultimate goals of the United States in Asia at the end of the war were rooted in its aspiration to see an intact region emerge from the war, one essentially like that which had existed between the two wars, and to slowly and cautiously reform it. This view of Asia precluded revolutionary movements seeking to attain too much too quickly. The dynamic forces of change clashed with the most basic American policies and premises as to the nature of an ideal world order and the proper relationship of Asia to the Western world. Starting from such an ideal assumption, the United States planned to renovate and reform Japan and, less hopefully, China, and via these nations to make American power and presence felt in all of Asia, to supplant European colonialism with paternal cords of economic relations which would profit the United States and permit prosperity in the new trusteeships. National independence would come gradually but inevitably, as nations matured over the decades.

Such a vision in no way corresponded to the realities or the possibilities of the new era, and despite the enormous economic and military power of the United States, Asia was too vast to occupy—the sole price of defining its future—and many in Washington appreciated this too at the time. Given United States objectives, by the end of the war it was actively aiding those forces of colonialism and conservatism seeking to restore the former condition of Asia which was a prerequisite for America's attainment of its designs. But the great masses of Asia heard nothing of the plans of Washington. They were hungry, and in arms. They would seek to write their own future. As the war came to an end they had already begun to do so.

CONCLUSION

THE COALITION against the Axis was born of necessity rather than deliberation or choice, and only the common need to defeat a common enemy bound it together. Great Britain, the Soviet Union, and the United States shared no single set of objectives other than this preeminent reality, no unifying political and economic peace aims—save, in the case of Britain and America, the negative one of containing Russia and the Left— and when Germany and Japan lay in smoking ruins the wartime Allies turned from a tenuous coalition to open conflict. That incipient struggle grew in importance throughout the war, until no later than the end of 1944 it necessarily became the defining obsession of the Western members of the coalition. That conflict has shaped the contours of modern world history, and we have yet to feel or know its full meaning and ultimate consequences.

No major power sacrificed less of its blood and material wealth during World War II than the United States. If one considers military potential in terms of overall industrial and technological capacity to sustain modern warfare over a period of time, in August 1945 only the United States had that power and only the United States emerged from the bloodiest conflagration in human history stronger than ever before. The war ultimately drained Britain more than even Russia, relative to its limited manpower and resources, transforming that small island into a power of the second tier. The United States was incomparably the greatest single nation in the world, with sharply articulated global political and, primarily, economic aspirations equal, even much more than equal, to the role.

The leaders in Washington were above all else fully aware of their own physical strength as well as their political and economic objectives, and they always viewed the problem of future relations with the U.S.S.R. or Great Britain, or the nature of the world, with these critical goals in clear

US had preponderant power

perspective. For how to advance its peace aims and apply its directing power to the inordinately complex and unpredictable realities of the broken, war-torn world colored every specific American response and assumption, and it was these expansive premises that were to define the postwar structure of relations—and conflict—between great states.

The problem of Soviet power gradually subsumed the other great wartime challenge to American diplomacy: the emergence of the Left and its threat to securing American economic and political war aims. In Eastern Europe, perhaps more than any other single region, American leaders found evidence of what they interpreted to be the dangers of Soviet expansionism that might undercut the attainment of their nation's largest postwar goals. The war utterly and finally destroyed the traditional Eastern European political and economic structure and nothing the Russians might do could alter that fact, for not the Soviet Union but the leaders of the Old Order in Eastern Europe themselves made that collapse inevitable. The Russians could work within that new structural limitation in a variety of ways, and in practice they did explore many political options, but they could not transcend the new socioeconomic reality. More aware than anyone else of their own weaknesses in the event of a conflict with the United States, the Russians pursued a conservative and cautious line wherever they could find local non-Communist groups willing to abjure the traditional diplomacy of the cordon sanitaire and anti-Bolshevism. They were entirely willing to restrain equally the militant Left and militant Right, and given the complex political admixtures of the region they showed neither more nor less respect for an unborn functional democracy in Eastern Europe than the Americans and British evidenced in Italy, Greece, or Belgium. For neither the Americans, British, nor Russians were willing to permit democracy to run its course anywhere in Europe at the cost of damaging their vital strategic and economic interests, perhaps also bringing about the triumph of the Left or the restoration of prewar clerical fascism. In fact we now know that the Russians lost control of the revolutionary forces in Yugoslavia and Greece, and that they had no intention of Bolshevizing Eastern Europe in 1945 if—but only if—they could find alternatives.

For the United States, Eastern Europe was a question of economic war aims to which political realities had also to conform to satisfy American aspirations, and quite apart from the local leaderships' policies toward Russia, that was hardly possible in nearly all the Eastern European nations. Even where the United States had yet to develop all of its objectives in specific detail, it was imperative that it prevent any Great Power from totally dominating Eastern Europe or any other region of the world for that matter, because the United States considered all political and economic blocs or spheres of influence that it did not control as directly undermining its larger political, and especially economic, objectives for an integrated world capitalism and a political structure which was the prerequisite to its goals. For this reason America opposed Britain's control over French affairs and set itself against an Eastern European reality which neither it, nor in the last analysis, the Russians, could fully shape according to a plan or desire.

Given the pervasive, chronic Russian conservatism on political questions during the war, one best reflected in the United Front tactics of accommodation which caused the Russian-disciplined Left to submerge its distinctive socialist character at all costs, the failure to reach agreement over Poland or Czechoslovakia—and Eastern Europe in general—reflected the effort of the United States to disengage Soviet influence in Eastern Europe and to create states ready to cooperate with a postwar economic program compatible with American objectives and interests. To the Russians during the war, Eastern Europe was a question of preventing the resurrection of traditionally hostile conservative leaders, and in this they had the total collapse of much of Eastern European society working on their behalf. To the Americans it was a matter of putting together a perhaps somewhat reformed version of the social and political sources of Eastern Europe's alliance with atavistic forces of imperialism and nationalism during two wars and reintegrating the region into a traditional prewar European economy in a condition of semicolonialism. That task was beyond the power of the United States or Russia, but it was a failure of American policy for which Washington was ultimately to hold Russia responsible. This exacerbation of world politics over Eastern Europe was a result of American expansion into the historically hopeless imbroglio and mire of Eastern European affairs.

In the last analysis both the Soviet Union and the United States could only partially control the uncontrollable—the Left—and could seemingly inhibit it only in Western Europe. For World War II brought to fruition a whole spectrum of internal crises inherent in the civil war in society, which was a by-product of different admixtures within each nation of industrial capitalism, World War I, and the continued weakening of world capitalism and colonialism after 1939. America, with some significant aid from Russia, might retard that collapse, yet it could not stay its irresistible momentum, and all the issues were joined during the period 1942–1945 that were again to break out with renewed force after the war to define the direction of modern world diplomacy and conflict. The Old Order of prewar capitalism and oligarchy with which the United States identified, with reservations, and which it hoped to reform and integrate into a transformed world capitalist economy, was dying in the colonial world and a dependent China; it committed suicide in Eastern Europe, and the United States could refurbish it in temporarily acceptable ways only in Western Europe. The impact of these changes on the conditions and structure of world power ultimately were to be more far-reaching than the Bolshevik Revolution itself, in part because—after 1947—the protective existence and support of Soviet power was a cushion between success and failure in many, but by no means all, socialist or revolutionary nations.

By 1945 the war itself delivered the *coup de grâce* to the prewar structure of European politics and economics, for which there was now but slight social backing, and therefore slight resistance to change. Only external intervention saved what remained of European capitalism, and it is this attempted unilateral Great Power definition of the internal affairs of other nations that became the defining fact of wartime and postwar politics. The Americans and British set the precedent in Italy, and formalized it in Europe when the United States also extended the principle elsewhere by preventing the emergence of a truly collaborative forum in the European Advisory Commission in the hope that occupation forces might contain potentially revolutionary changes via a controlled "democracy" whose limits and outcome the West might determine.

This larger instability in European economics and politics required the United States to aid the resuscitation of cooperative conservative elements of Europe and to attempt to prevent a total collapse of the Old Order in Europe and Asia that might open the door to Soviet predominance in a region or even the complete transformation of whole nations. For this reason the United States did not advance a truly permanent stern peace for Germany or Japan, since toward the end of the war many important American leaders accepted the need to reintegrate and reform German and Japanese power to create a balance to Soviet predominance and to advance American objectives. And this deliberate ambiguity, which permeated all their wartime considerations of the future role of the defeated Axis, implied that it was not the total destruction of Axis power, but the advancement of American global interests that soon became the preeminent concern in American planning. In this sense World War II was a tragic error to the American government in that even before the war was over it understood that perhaps a less imperialist Germany and Japan would be preferable to the U.S.S.R. as allies in the future.

Indeed, this perceptible shift in priorities ultimately became the basis of American postwar policy, reflecting a shift in tactical goals all along the line, one that also significantly downgraded initial American hostility to British political aims in Europe, and more particularly in France, on behalf of a far deeper commitment to the objectives of containment and stability —containment of the dual menace of the Left and the Soviet Union, and stability for the essential social and economic system of prewar European capitalism and colonialism.

Although the United States undertook a task that was insuperable in many places, it was still possible in much of Europe, and in any event the American government had no option but to resist as best it could those destabilizing political and economic conditions which brought revolutionary movements of every shape and variety into existence, and attempt to compensate for their subversive effect on American interests and postwar objectives by containing, redirecting, or destroying them. There was no other recourse for the United States but to undertake the difficult, and in many places, the impossible, for the consequence of inaction might have been the unchallenged triumph of the Left in numerous countries. Only the United States had the power to engage fully in international counterrevolution and sustain the forces of conservatism for prolonged periods of time, and it was this militant intervention into the affairs of literally every area of the world that set the pattern for postwar world politics. By 1945 Washington's decision to undertake that role was an unquestioned postulate in America's plans for the future of its power in the world.

The Russians understood the American intention and the risks of any covert aid to the Left, and they gave precious little of it during and immediately after the war, when they discovered that even an obviously conservative policy failed to blunt the American belief that behind all the world's social and economic ills, somehow, and in some critical fashion, a Russian plot and device existed. From this viewpoint United States policy-makers saw Russia and the Left as the cause rather than the reflection of the collapse of capitalism, and responsible for the failings of a system that began to commit suicide in vast areas of the globe no later than 1914. Still, it was Soviet conservatism on revolutionary movements everywhere that gave Western European capitalism the critical breathing spell during which it might recover, though the caution of the Western European Communist parties became a permanent and willingly self-imposed fact of political life. This desire to opt into the existing order where possible, and the correct realization that the American and British armies would certainly not permit a triumph of the Left either by the ballot or a takeover in the streets, shaped the political conduct of the Communist parties wherever there were Western troops. And the U.S.S.R. demanded and assiduously enforced this strategy where it controlled local Communist parties and, through them, the Resistance. It brought an end to the illusions of possibilities and national renovation that inspired the European Resistance. Yet where the Soviets could not control the armed opposition, or the Right was too rigid to absorb the armed Left—as in China, Greece, and Yugoslavia—the end result was revolution and international crisis.

These crises were not a by-product of Soviet policy, but reflected a lack of Russian control over the Left and the response of the British and, preeminently, the United States to the irresistible tides of change. Outside Western Europe the Americans could recognize, in moments of clarity, the total breakdown of existing societies, but they bent every energy—via dollars and ultimately force of arms—to avoid the political and economic consequences of a perceptible reality for which they could have no sympathy. In Western Europe both dollars and guns succeeded, but where the Americans could not undo disintegration resulting from the war and economic collapse, they often limited and shaped the character of change. American resistance to social and revolutionary upheavals from diverse sources and causes, whether Communist or revolutionary nationalist, polarized change in the world, denying pluralism and options which were natural to radical and humanist movements unable and unwilling to risk survival along with diversity and social exploration. Successful movements of social transformation, due in some degree to ideology but necessarily because of the external pressures, became monolithic and anti-American as a precondition to success. Counterrevolution in this manner defined the course of revolution and history for decades, and imposed on the remnants of the tortured men and women seeking to create a new life for themselves in Asia and elsewhere the American problem as the constant threat to social renovation and survival.

WITH each new success in confining British power in the Middle East or British financial freedom to pursue an independent course, or in its ability to define the future contours of the postwar world economy, the United States downgraded the relative importance it attached to bringing Great Britain into complete conformity with postwar American economic and political objectives. As time revealed the full extent of British weakness, and as the common denominator of anti-Communism made what the two states shared more important than ever before, the problems of the Soviet Union in the postwar world and the international movement of social change altered, but by no means eclipsed, the previous weight Washington assigned to its relations with the British Empire.

The initial Anglo-American rivalry was based on the interwar world economic experience, and on the basis of that period the United States defined its postwar economic objectives with an unusual precision unequaled in other fields. Nearly all important leaders in Washington assumed and hoped that the United States would revive and reform capitalism everywhere in the world, but preeminently in the British Empire, and that there would not be a collapse of world capitalism so deep or profound as to raise the fundamental question of the inherent viability of the system on an international level in any form. Only toward the very end of the war did the enormity and social impact of the event begin impressing many in Washington so that they understood that the needs of reconstruction in Europe might necessarily precede the creation of a liberal international

economy modeled after late-nineteenth-century British free trade. In the
meantime the Hullian theory of American economic objectives was less
significant than its specific goals, and these showed more practically what it
was the United States sought to attain for itself in its ideal world economy.
At least in the short run the accumulated privileges of the British in the
Middle East, and their unique challenge to United States hegemony over
the foreign trade sectors of other Western Hemispheric nations, presented
the major obstacles to attaining these goals. In the theory of a world
economy which Cordell Hull propounded on behalf of the government, the
United States would have enjoyed a competitive advantage over all the
other industrialized nations; in the practice of applying American power to
specific interests, in particular oil, the British were certain their wartime
ally was bent on a course of economic imperialism which might also result
in the eclipse, even demise, of British power. Rhetoric aside, expedient
references to the Open Door in the international economy functionally
meant American economic predominance, often monopoly control, over
many of the critical raw materials on which modern industrial power is
based. Oil revealed the theory and reality of American economic war aims.

The rivalry between the United States and Britain over oil and the
postwar world economic structure added to the inevitable weakening of
Britain during the war to create a vacuum in world power which the
Americans quickly and gladly filled in the Middle East and Latin America.
This new role was not unplanned or accidental, but was sought with a
compulsion and desire the British perceived as the creation of an American
equivalent of the form of spheres and blocs Washington attributed to the
British. The elimination of Britain's power in large areas of the world, and
the American entry into the wake, carried with it the enormous political
and strategic responsibilities which unavoidably befell those who wished
global profit, and that new burden was as much a by-product of an American desire for world economic expansion as it was a response to the emergence of the Left everywhere, much less the growth of Russian power. It
was inherent in the clear vision of the type of world order the Americans
wished to create, and inevitably the American defeat of Britain for predominance in the Middle East also predicated the task of policing ever-growing
regions of the world. America's foreign policy at the end of World War II
necessitated the ability and desire to employ loans, credits, and investments
everywhere, to create a world economic order according to its own desires.
In this the United States did only what was functional to its own needs and
objectives, as the British had done before it in an earlier era.

It is this deliberate quality, this articulate set of economic and political
goals which ultimately set the United States at the end of World War II
against the Soviet Union, against the tide of the Left, and against Britain as
a coequal guardian of world capitalism—in fact, against history as it had

been and had yet to become. That there was something accidental or unintended about the American response to the world is a comforting reassurance to those who wish to confuse the American rhetoric and descriptions of intentions with the realities and purposes of operational power, but given the society and its needs American foreign policy could hardly have been different. For the United States emerged from the war with a sense of vast power, and indeed, as the most powerful single state in the world, anxious to attain a highly organized world economic and political community as a precondition to the realization of its vital peace aims. But as strong as it was, the United States, even when the Soviet Union worked with it for its own reasons and toward its own ends, was too weak to mold the destiny of mankind everywhere on earth. It might limit and shape that fate, but it could not control the world by creating its desired political and economic order modeled after American aspirations.

At times the key decision-makers in Washington fully appreciated America's possible inadequacy and need for allies, as in their enigmatic attitudes toward the future of Germany in Europe and Japan in the Far East. Everywhere in the world America could deploy material power in various forms, and at the conference table it spoke with a weight beyond that of any other state. Estimating this strength in relation to that of other states, Washington fully intended that at the end of the war America could, and would, determine the basic character of the postwar world. For this reason Roosevelt and his aides throughout 1943 and 1944 opposed the desire of the British Foreign Office to meet Soviet aims in Eastern Europe at the bargaining table, for the leaders of the United States fully expected —and this was as true of Roosevelt as of Truman—to employ American power to define the political and economic outcome of the war when their allies were relatively weak. The problem, which it was impossible for anyone in Washington to sufficiently perceive and appreciate, was that the kind of world emerging from the war required power beyond the factory and army, the kind of resources and inspiration that only revolutionary movements in villages and mountains can possess and generate.

For insofar as world conflict was transformed from wars between states into ideological and civil wars for social transformation and liberation, the political arithmetic of insufficiency of numbers made it impossible for the Americans to be everywhere at once, and to employ vast technological power—in bases and ships the Americans planned to have throughout the world—against sheer mass. To succeed in that situation one had to be neither American, English, nor Russian, but to be present in every village in the hungry world, or, as in the case of the Russians, to endorse an inevitability that they could neither initiate nor prevent.

It was in this context of vast material might and yet greater ambition that World War II ended for the United States and defined the manner in which the postwar period began. There was nothing qualitatively unique about this goal or the tools that the United States employed, for the reliance on the state to attain the domestic and international objectives of private American business interests, or to advance a broader "national interest" on behalf of an allegedly new internationalism which scarcely concealed the imperial intent behind it, much less the consequences, was a characteristic of American life and had been for many decades. What was new was the vastly more destructive technology which now accompanied the expansion of states—of which the United States was both the most powerful and first after 1943—and the human consequences of international conflicts.

The United States has yet to construct the international political and economic system modeled after the images and goals which it carefully formulated during World War II, and to make its creation the test of a stable and ideal postwar order, or to compensate for the political and economic frustrations of only one nation of the world, set the stage for an endless series of international crises. In this sense the quality and purpose of modern American diplomacy—in principle and form—we may see in microcosm during the years 1943 to 1945. No nation could build such a world and the efforts of the United States to do so almost consistently revealed its weaknesses. It attempted to apply its strength while refusing to see the limits of American capabilities and ideology in a world that, given its inherently decentralized nature and problems, was moving beyond the mastery of any one nation or alliance of states. For nowhere were the long-term political and economic objectives that the United States formulated during World War II fully realized, save in the replacement of Britain in certain areas by a lesser American influence.

WORLD War II was a prelude to the profound and irreversible crisis in world affairs and the structure of societies everywhere which is the hallmark of our times.

For the war had come to an end, but the world was still aflame.

EPILOGUE

WORLD WAR I began as a "classic" struggle between states with traditional nationalist motives and aspirations. But once it became a protracted war of attrition on battlefields, demanding sacrifices in blood and resources, it was destined to affect profoundly the political consciousness of the masses within most of the warring countries. This added a new and crucial ideological dimension to international conflicts: the threat that contests between states would bring to the surface latent internal dissatisfaction leading to real or incipient civil wars within nations. World War I gave birth to the revolutionary Right of fascism in Germany and Italy and to Bolshevism in Russia.

By 1939, the ideological conflict between Bolshevism and fascism was far more important than traditional nationalist antagonisms in causing the next war. After 1919, the rapid growth of socialist ideologies in numerous places and regions projected the Left, defined here to include quite diverse forces in addition to orthodox Communists, into the mainstream of world politics in ways that were qualitatively more important than during 1914–1918. Fascism's demise by 1945 eliminated the principal prewar barrier to the Left's growth globally.

Modern wars retain, as before, their traditional military and diplomatic dimensions, but their outcomes are also defined increasingly in the changes they provoke in individual and national consciousness. This additional change obligates us to give far more consideration to a war's impact on social systems in the largest sense—their economies, the new moods they encourage among the people, and changing political and class structures. Historians' conventional methodologies, with their emphases on diplomatic and military matters, are less and less able to capture accurately the richly textured dimensions of the human experience in the modern era. In the twentieth century war telescopes "social time" within nations, quickly producing deep crises that in earlier periods might have taken many decades to gestate, crises that affect those individual values and commitments that are, above all, essential to mobilizing parties and movements of change and opposition. The social, economic, and ideological problems that emerged from World War II have produced the dominant legacies that shape, in some great measure, the postwar world as well.

Historians and social scientists have come to grips with these questions in piecemeal fashion at best, and since the publication of *The Politics of War* in 1968 there has not been an analogous effort to write a comparative synthesis that attempts also to portray the constraining social contexts throughout Europe and Asia within which United States foreign policy was compelled to function during 1941–1945. Since these constraints, at least as much as Soviet or British policies, were to define the political outcome of the war and the ongoing postwar challenges, particularly in Asia, the way history is written therefore has a bearing on our subsequent understanding of our own times. In general, most historians still regard differences between states as matters their leaders can resolve at a diplomatic level, provided only that they have the goodwill and desire to do so. In this book I have stressed that while there is clearly an important role for diplomacy to play in ensuring peace, we must not ignore those vital regions of social and ideological change that limit the power of leaders, even Great Power leaders, to decide the destinies of people. In all my subsequent writings I have argued that this loss of control has grown worse since 1945. The ability of the United States, either alone or even with the cooperation of the Soviet Union and China, to define in some global sense a political and social direction, notwithstanding those instances where they have been able to do so, is decreasing rapidly.

But if broad syntheses have not been attempted since 1968, there have been numerous important specialized accounts of countries, regions, and problems that provide valuable new information and insights into the issues of Soviet policy and conduct, Anglo-American relations, and the emergence of diverse leftist movements in Europe and Asia.

Comparatively little progress has been made on the question of the Soviet Union in terms of its policy-making and objectives, the role of Stalin, and Soviet-American relations. Soviet historians have contributed some relatively minor details to our knowledge, but to a large extent they have merely reworked American and British sources with which we are familiar, for glasnost has yet to affect their efforts. We now have confirmation that the Russians were indeed responsible for the Katyn Forest liquidations of Polish officers, yet we know little more than we did before

1968 about larger political issues of Soviet policy. Marshal Zhukov's memoir does scarcely more than confirm that a chastened Stalin was a good listener to his best generals after the near defeat of the U.S.S.R. in 1941, but it remains full of contradictory assertions. When *The Politics of War* first appeared, the *Moscow News* denounced it for its "anti-Communism" and as "calumnious," principally because of my account of the many ways in which Stalin stood ready to sacrifice numerous European and Asian Communist parties to British and American interests in return for favors. But there still is no Soviet effort, much less documentation, to disprove my basic contentions.

In fact, scholarship since 1968 has reinforced my thesis on Stalin's acquiescence to Anglo-American interests. Llewellyn Woodward's official five-volume version of *British Foreign Policy in the Second World War* (London, 1971–1976), using British sources, reiterates that Churchill's October 1944 understanding with Stalin evolved directly out of his efforts earlier that spring to contain the expansion of Communism in Southern and Eastern Europe, and Woodward stresses the putative accord's tentative character as owing both to United States opposition to premature political discussions and to British desires later to improve on its terms. Exegetical essays on the controversial Churchill-Stalin meeting continue to be written, but they do not alter our basic comprehension of the main facts regarding it.

On the contrary, excellent monographs on Soviet policy in Greece and on the nature of the Greek Communist Party, particularly those by John O. Iatrides, Procopis Papastratis, and Heinz Richter, document incontrovertibly that Moscow loyally sustained British interests and that the Greek Communists split as a consequence. In Yugoslavia, by contrast, Mark C. Wheeler's fine account, and essays that Phyllis Auty and Richard Clogg have edited, reveal how the British chose for military reasons to work with Tito, at the same time encouraging the rich potential within his spontaneous, broad movement for autonomy from Soviet influence. And Michael M. Boll's study of Bulgaria from 1943 to 1947, using new American and Bulgarian sources, treats Soviet political policy there as pragmatically subservient to their more immediate military needs as well as influenced in due course by trends elsewhere in Europe. More traditional defenders of United States policies in East Europe, such as Lynn E. Davis, adamantly decline to relate Soviet behavior there to contemporaneous events in Southern Europe, Spain, and Japan, where the British and the United States were implementing unilateral policies which reinforced their own interests and which, at least in Greece and Spain, sustained repressive regimes against the desires of their populations. Lawrence S. Wittner's *American Intervention in Greece, 1943–1949* (New

York, 1982) is the best effort to spell out the larger context guiding United States policy in that country, and James E. Miller's *The United States and Italy, 1940–1950* (Chapel Hill, 1986) is of the same high quality. Elsewhere in Europe, Maurice Agulhon of the Collège de France has analyzed a cautious French Communist leadership's policy and the Soviet influences on it, corroborating my interpretation.

While there has been a great deal of critical writing on the last phases of the war and American policy through this period, far too much of it has concentrated on the putative role of the atomic bomb as a decisive factor in shaping Washington's behavior and planning during the summer of 1945. Still, nothing has caused me to alter the substantially different interpretation contained in this book. On the contrary, there is a reductionist simplicity in many of these essentially monocausal accounts that ignores the larger global political and social context that affected United States thinking and planning, as well as produced those crises that increasingly exacerbated Soviet-American relations. Such works often display a certain provincialism, which accepts the differences between the Americans and Russians as having been quite small and, above all, potentially negotiable had there been a more flexible frame of mind among leaders, particularly Truman. Michael S. Sherry's excellent *The Rise of American Airpower* (New Haven, 1987) goes a long way toward minimizing the political reasons for the bomb's use and reintroduces and greatly amplifies the notion of technological fetishism regarding the use of the bomb and airpower in general, an interpretation I have sought to employ also.

Indeed, as Robert W. Tucker has noted in his often astute conservative critique, *The Radical Left and American Foreign Policy* (Baltimore, 1971), many so-called New Left historians are essentially liberals in implying that the United States policy toward the postwar world was based on mistaken notions that could so easily have been reversed had better individuals been in charge of policy. What these otherwise critical historians have minimized is the depth, nature, and breadth of American global interests, a fact that has led many of them—erroneously, in my opinion—to attribute to Roosevelt virtues and healthy instincts that might have altered significantly United States postwar policy had he lived. We still need more historians who seek to understand far more than the purely American context in which United States foreign policy emerged, though its domestic roots will always be crucial, historians who are tempted by the complexities of comparative studies and the social and political contexts in which such studies must be set. For it was the complexity of the world that in many cases frustrated Washington's attainment of its goals in numerous countries and caused it to hold the U.S.S.R. responsible for its failure. Such broadly defined causal explanations of these overseas challenges illuminate the appropriateness or inappropriateness of the United States's chosen methods of dealing with each, thereby explaining how and why these methods failed repeatedly after 1945. And the inclination to reduce America's principal goals to matters impinging almost exclusively on its differences with the Soviet Union still exercises a great, and misleading, attraction for many historians.

Writing on Anglo-American relations during the war has set a high standard of scholarship, but it has not produced any new conclusions. This was inevitable given its exemplary quality well before 1968. Woodward's multivolume history reconfirms that key British statesmen evisaged the creation of a postwar West European bloc independent of both Soviet and American control. And he documents how the United States effectively blocked the British Commonwealth from genuine participation in Japan's occupation, in effect subjecting Japan to an exclusively American political control (much as the Russians did to Poland). Christopher Thorne's *Allies of a Kind* (New York, 1978) exhaustively documents persistent American opposition to a British role in East Asia at the end of the war, concluding that "there is much truth in Professor Kolko's observation that 'the Anglo-American alliance was essentially a European coalition.' "

David S. Painter's superb *Oil and the American Century* (Baltimore, 1986), based on the fullest use of official sources so far, details the sustained, often bitter wartime Anglo-American rivalry for Middle East oil, which was to erupt in far more intense forms during the postwar decade. In conjunction with Miller's work on Italy, it too reveals how tenuous the Anglo-American alliance was outside Asia as well. Ironically, both Painter and Miller are full-time State Department historians with far greater access than most academics have to the sources, and their informed efforts have also been least compatible with the official version I criticize in this book. Compared to the multivolume work of Herbert Feis, who as official historian also had access to the documents and managed to exclude entirely from his books the issues of foreign economic policy on which he specialized for the State Department during the war, Painter's and Miller's works are far superior and, for practical purposes, nonideological. By contrast, Professor John L. Gaddis's *The United States and the Origins of the Cold War* (New York, 1972), whose neotraditionalist defense of Washington asks no critical questions and reiterates Feis's position, poses a few of the kinds of issues regarding public opinion that Feis left out, but nonetheless remains far less illuminating than the Feis work.

Much of the best writing on the larger context in which post-1941 American foreign policy has evolved has been done by those concerned with the linkages between society and political events, and they have often successfully captured the mind-set of crucial forces determining history: peasants, soldiers, members of the Resistance, and such. Detlev J. K. Peukert's *Inside Nazi Germany* (London, 1987) and Marlis B. Steinert's *Hitler's War and the Germans* (Athens, Ohio, 1977) are unusually successful efforts to probe the world of the working and middle-classes and their failure to resist, while Henri Michel's magisterial *The Shadow War* (London, 1972) describes how those relatively few under the Nazis who became part of the European Resistance evolved to a point where they were ready to assume great personal risks. Along with the work of Werner Rings, all these accounts provide precious insights into the complexities of the human condition in Europe during the war. Lloyd E. Eastman's *Seeds of Destruction* (Stanford, 1984) and Hsi-sheng Ch'i's *Nationalist China at War* (Ann Arbor, 1982) greatly deepen our comprehension of China's wartime political system and its interaction with the war and economy. If the books on Europe deal with individuals, either alone or in small groups, these studies of China move up the scale to focus on broader socioeconomic trends involving political power and policies and their meaning for peasants and soldiers. All greatly help to explain the difficulties and often insuperable barriers that prevented the United States's attainment of its political goals at the end of World War II and set the stage for the sustained post-1945 crises that continue to our own times.

NOTES

The following code abbreviations are used in the notes:

WLC Mss—William L. Clayton Papers, Harry S. Truman Library, Independence, Mo. (Record Group 108).

DDE Mss—Dwight D. Eisenhower Papers, Eisenhower Library, Abilene, Kansas.

JF Mss—James Forrestal Papers, Princeton University Library.

PG Mss—Brig. Gen. Philip Gallagher Papers, Office of the Chief of Military History, U. S. Army, Washington, D. C.

JCG Mss—Joseph C. Grew Papers, Houghton Library, Harvard College.

HLH Mss—Harry L. Hopkins Papers, Franklin D. Roosevelt Library, Hyde Park, N. Y.

JWJ Mss—J. Weldon Jones Papers, Truman Library (Record Group 81).

ABL Mss—Arthur Bliss Lane Papers, Sterling Library, Yale University.

LC—Library of Congress, Washington, D. C.

EAL Mss—Edwin A. Locke, Jr. Files, Harry S. Truman Papers, Truman Library (Record Group 3).

EAL-2 Mss—Edwin A. Locke, Jr. Papers, Truman Library (Record Group 48).

GSM Mss—George S. Messersmith Papers, University of Delaware Library, Newark.

RP Mss—Robert Patterson Papers, Library of Congress.

FDR Mss—Franklin D. Roosevelt Papers, Roosevelt Library.

SIR Mss—Samuel I. Rosenman Papers, Truman Library (Record Group 34).

LAS Mss—Laurence A. Steinhardt Papers, Library of Congress.

HLS Mss—Henry L. Stimson Papers, Sterling Library, Yale University.

DS—U. S. Department of State.

DSB—U. S. *Department of State Bulletin.*

FR—U. S. Department of State, *Foreign Relations of the United States* (Washington, 1861–). The year covered and the volume are also given in the citation.

AHV Mss—Arthur H. Vandenberg Papers, University of Michigan Library, Ann Arbor.

HDW Mss—Harry Dexter White Papers, Princeton University Library.

A footnote indicates the origin of each preceding quotation or series of quotations from the same source. Such citations frequently include references for nonquoted information following the prior footnote. Where there are no quotations, footnotes at the end of several or more paragraphs document the information preceding the footnote number.

Chapter 1: The Politics of Strategy in Europe

1. Anthony Eden, *The Reckoning: The Memoirs of Anthony Eden* (Boston, 1965), 368.
2. Nikolai A. Voznesensky, *The Economy of the USSR During World War II* (Washington, 1948), 2.
3. FR (1944), IV, 907.
4. *Ibid.*
5. Ministry of Foreign Affairs of the USSR, *Correspondence Between the Chairman of the Council of Ministers of the USSR and the Presidents of the U. S. A. and the Prime Ministers of Great Britain . . . 1941–1945* (Moscow, 1957), I, 21. Hereafter *Stalin Correspondence*. See also Ivan Maisky, *Memoirs of a Soviet Ambassador* (New York, 1967), 245ff.
6. *Ibid.*, I, 13.
7. *Ibid.*, I, 56.
8. *Ibid.*, I, 102.
9. *Ibid.*, I, 132. See also *ibid.*, II, 67–69.
10. *Ibid.*, I, 138. See also Llewellyn Woodward, *British Foreign Policy in the Second World War* (London, 1962), 241.
11. FR (1943), I, 657.
12. Winston S. Churchill, *Closing the Ring* [Bantam ed.] (New York, 1962), 319.
13. G. Deborin, *The Second World War* (Moscow, 1964?), 163. See also Voznesensky, *The Economy of the USSR*, 95–96.
14. *Stalin Correspondence*, I, 21, 24.
15. Woodward, *British Foreign Policy*, 157.
16. *Stalin Correspondence*, I, 93. See also *ibid.*, I, 51.
17. FR (The Conferences at Cairo and Teheran, 1943), 124. See also FR (1943), I, 634.
18. Churchill, *Closing the Ring*, 303. See also FR (Teheran), 174–75, 574.
19. Churchill, *Closing the Ring*, 244. See also *Stalin Correspondence*, I, 238; FR (1944), V, 893.
20. Churchill, *Closing the Ring*, 245. See also John Ehrman, *Grand Strategy: October 1944–August 1945* (London, 1956), 50–51.
21. Ehrman, *Grand Strategy*, 54–55, 86–87; FR (The Conferences at Malta and Yalta, 1945), 578 [hereafter *Yalta Papers*]; Winston S. Churchill, *Triumph and Tragedy* [Bantam ed.] (New York, 1962), 21; *Soviet News*, April 21, 1965; Chester Wilmot, *The Struggle for Europe* (New York, 1952), 621; Harry C. Butcher, *My Three Years With Eisenhower* (New York, 1946), 520–21.
22. Robert E. Sherwood, *Roosevelt and Hopkins: An Intimate History* (New York, 1948), 705–06. See also Alexander Werth, *Russia at War, 1941–1945* (New York, 1964), 622–27; U. S. Senate, Committee on Foreign Relations, *Hearings, Lend-Lease*. 79:1. March–April 1945. (Washington, 1945), 5–7.
23. Maurice Matloff, *Strategic Planning for Coalition Warfare, 1943–1944*

(Washington, 1959), 522. See also Werth, *Russia at War*, 935.

24. Lord Moran, *Churchill: Taken From the Diaries of Lord Moran—The Struggle for Survival, 1940–1965* (Boston, 1966), 23.

25. Matloff, *Strategic Planning for Coalition Warfare*, 9–10, 67, 134; Robert Murphy, *Diplomat Among Warriors* (Garden City, N. Y., 1964), 162–68; Elting E. Morison, *Turmoil and Tradition: A Study of the Life and Times of Henry L. Stimson* (Boston, 1960), 584–85; Herbert Feis, *Churchill-Roosevelt-Stalin* (Princeton, 1957), 47–53.

26. Stimson Diary, June 26, 1944, HLS Mss. See also Murphy, *Diplomat Among Warriors*, 186–88; Memo of Conversation, April 30, 1945, JCG Mss; Feis, *Churchill-Roosevelt-Stalin*, 105–06; Matloff, *Strategic Planning for Coalition Warfare*, 134; Stimson Diary, July 22, 1943, HLS Mss.

27. Stimson Diary, August 10, 1943, HLS Mss.

28. FR (Teheran), 65.

29. Henry L. Stimson and McGeorge Bundy, *On Active Service in War and Peace* (New York, 1948), 527.

30. Eden, *The Reckoning*, 370.

31. Churchill, *Closing the Ring*, 108–09.

32. Eden, *The Reckoning*, 371.

33. Roosevelt to Hull, March 23, 1943, FDR Mss, PSF, box 23. See also FR (1943), III, 26.

34. FR (1943), II, 346.

35. *Ibid.*, 347.

36. FR (Teheran), 65. See also *ibid.*, 35–39, 64.

37. For the entire issue, see Sherwood, *Roosevelt and Hopkins*, 696; Cordell Hull, *Memoirs* (New York, 1948), 1570–79; Memo from Hull to Roosevelt, December 22, 1943, FDR Mss, PSF, box 23; Churchill, *Closing the Ring*, 573–74; Feis, *Churchill-Roosevelt-Stalin*, 108–10; Butcher, *My Three Years*, 518.

38. FR (Teheran), 151. See also Churchill, *Closing the Ring*, 73, 286–89.

39. Arthur Bryant, *Triumph in the West: A History of the War Years Based on the Diaries of Field-Marshal Lord Alanbrooke, Chief of the Imperial General Staff* (New York, 1959), 47. See also Churchill, *Closing the Ring*, 260.

40. Churchill, *Closing the Ring*, 289.

41. Sherwood, *Roosevelt and Hopkins*, 780. See also, for example, Harry L. Coles and Albert K. Weinberg, eds., *Civil Affairs: Soldiers Become Governors* (Washington, 1964), 114–16; Bryant, *Triumph in the West, passim*; Butcher, *My Three Years*, 383–87, 442, 509, 718, 739; Murphy, *Diplomat Among Warriors*, 187; FR (1944), IV, 1014; Stimson Diary, October 29, 1943, HLS Mss.

42. FR (Teheran), 410. For the controversies over strategy, see Forrest C. Pogue, *The Supreme Command: The European Theater of Operations* (Washington, 1954), chaps. II, V; Matloff, *Strategic Planning for Coalition Warfare*, chap. XI.

43. Sherwood, *Roosevelt and Hopkins*, 737; FR (Teheran), 165, 175, 574, 691; Altemur Kilic, *Turkey and the World* (Washington, 1959), 90–101; Woodward, *British Foreign Policy*, 325–26; Eden, *The Reckoning*, 490–97; Moran, *Churchill*, 92; FR (1943), III, 317, 538; Stephen G. Xydis, *Greece and the Great Powers, 1944–1947: Prelude to the 'Truman Doctrine'* (Thessaloniki, 1963), 39.

44. FR (Teheran), 124, 151, 210; FR (1943), I, 644; Churchill, *Closing the Ring*, 335–36; Matloff, *Strategic Planning for Coalition Warfare*, 67; FR (1944), V, 814–17, 882ff.; Moran, *Churchill*, 157; Woodward, *British Foreign Policy*, 325–28; Hull, *Memoirs*, 1370–76.

45. Stimson Diary, October 28, 1943, HLS Mss. See also Matloff, *Strategic Planning for Coalition Warfare*, 215; Feis, *Churchill-Roosevelt-Stalin*, 128.

46. FR (1943), III, 26. See also Matloff, *Strategic Planning for Coalition Warfare*, 287–88.

47. Matloff, *Strategic Planning for Coalition Warfare*, 226.

48. FR (Teheran), 255.

49. *Ibid.*, 689; Warren L. Hickman, *Genesis of the European Recovery Program: A Study on the Trend of American Economic Policies* (Geneva, 1949), 148–49, 162; Matloff, *Strategic Planning for Coalition Warfare*, 226; William M. Franklin, "Zonal Boundaries and Access to Berlin," *World Politics*, XVI (1963), 6–7; Pogue, *Supreme Command*, 105–06; Sherwood, *Roosevelt and Hopkins*, 818; Cornelius Ryan, *The Last Battle* (New York, 1966), 120–23.

Chapter 2: The Problem of the Left and Allied Cooperation in Europe

1. All data from Branko Lazitch, *Les Partis Communistes d'Europe, 1919–1955* (Paris, 1956), *passim.*

2. FR (1943), III, 26.

3. FR (1944), IV, 815.

4. Dwight D. Eisenhower, *Crusade in Europe* (Garden City, N. Y., 1948), 318.

5. Arthur H. Vandenberg, Jr., ed., *The Private Papers of Senator Vandenberg* (Boston, 1952), 129–30.

6. R. H. Bruce Lockhart, *Comes the Reckoning* (London, 1947), 279.

7. Churchill, *Closing the Ring*, 621–22.

8. FR (1944), IV, 814.

9. *Ibid.*

10. FR (1943), III, 509. See also *ibid.*, 501, 530, 563; FR (1944), IV, 843–54.

11. FR (Teheran), 15. See also *ibid.*, 152–55.

12. FR (1943), III, 40.

13. FR (1943), I, 615–16.

14. FR (1944), IV, 816.

15. *Ibid.*, 997. See also *ibid.*, 902–10, 993–97.

16. FR (1943), III, 535, 529.

17. Louise W. Holborn, ed., *War and Peace Aims of the United Nations: January 1, 1943–September 1, 1945* (Boston, 1948), 757–58.

18. FR (1944), IV, 862–63.

19. Coles and Weinberg, *Civil Affairs*, 23–24, 146. See also *ibid.*, 23–24, 147; F. S. V. Donnison, *Civil Affairs and Military Government: North-West Europe, 1944–1946* (London, 1961), 21.

20. FR (1943), III, 556. See also *ibid.*, 26; Roosevelt to Hull, March 23, 1943, FDR Mss, PSF, box 23.

21. *Stalin Correspondence*, I, 149.

22. FR (1943), II, 384. See also *ibid.*, 383; *Stalin Correspondence*, I, 154, 162, II, 89.

23. FR (1943), III, 553.
24. FR (1943), I, 715. See also *ibid.*, 588, 597–98, 643, 707.
25. *Ibid.*, 609, 611.
26. Stimson Diary, October 29, 1943, HLS Mss.
27. See also *ibid.*, October 28, November 8, 1943.
28. FR (Teheran), 417–18.
29. FR (1944), I, 1. See also FR (1943), I, 812–14; FR (1943), IV, 420–22.
30. FR (1944), I, 3.
31. *Ibid.*, 15. See also *ibid.*, 11–14; George F. Kennan, *Memoirs, 1925–1960* (Boston, 1967), 165–66.
32. FR (1944), I, 25. See also *ibid.*, 20–22.
33. *Yalta Papers,* 155. See also FR (1944), I, 25–26, 30; FR (1944), III, 3–5.
34. FR (1944), I, 351.

Chapter 3: *Italy and the Restoration of Order*

1. Coles and Weinberg, *Civil Affairs,* 160. See also *ibid.*, 166; Hull, *Memoirs,* 1557.
2. Coles and Weinberg, *Civil Affairs,* 165–67, 274. See also *ibid.*, 271; FR (1943), III, 40.
3. Churchill, *Closing the Ring,* 44–45. See also FR (1940), II, 685–717.
4. Churchill, *Closing the Ring,* 86, 55–56.
5. For a general treatment, see Norman Kogan, *Italy and the Allies* (Cambridge, 1956), chaps. I–IV; Harold Macmillan, *The Blast of War, 1939–1945* (London, 1967), 464.
6. Stimson Diary, September 20, 1943, HLS Mss. See also *ibid.*, October 1, 1943; Coles and Weinberg, *Civil Affairs,* 236.
7. Churchill, *Closing the Ring,* 163–74.
8. *Ibid.*, 171; FR (1943), II, 426–27, 438–39; Kogan, *Italy and the Allies,* chap. V; Hull, *Memoirs,* 1552–53.
9. U. S. Office of Strategic Services, R. and A. Branch, "The Radical Trend in German-Occupied Italy." R & A 1681. (N. P., N. D.), 1. See also Charles F. Delzell, *Mussolini's Enemies: The Italian Anti-Fascist Resistance* (Princeton, 1961), 250–347, 371; Roberto B. Battaglia, *The Story of the Italian Resistance* (London, 1957), 32–65, 88–89; O.S.S., R. and A. Branch, "Contributions of the Italian Partisans to the Allied War Effort," R&A 2993 (N. P., 1945), 1–4.
10. Battaglia, *Italian Resistance,* 184–85.
11. Churchill, *Closing the Ring,* 426. See also O. S. S. "The Radical Trend in German-Occupied Italy," *passim;* FR (1944), III, 1000–05, 1019–20; Hull, *Memoirs,* 1553.
12. FR (1943), II, 444. See also *ibid.*, 437; Churchill, *Closing the Ring,* 167–68, 429–30; FR (1944), III, 1034–38; FR (Teheran), 309; William H. McNeill, *America, Britain, and Russia: Their Cooperation and Conflict, 1941–1946* (London, 1953), 309–10; Macmillan, *Blast of War,* 468–70.
13. FR (1944), III, 1040.
14. *Ibid.*, 1051, 1056. See also *ibid.*, 1044, 1047; Coles and Weinberg, *Civil Affairs,* 449.
15. FR (1944), III, 1065. See also *ibid.*, 1057, 1074–79; FR (1944), IV, 842; Pietro Badoglio, *Italy in the Second World War: Memories and*

Documents (London, 1948), 128–30; Stimson Diary, March 24, 1944, HLS Mss; Kogan, *Italy and the Allies,* 58–59.

16. Andrew Rothstein, ed., *Soviet Foreign Policy During the Patriotic War: Documents and Materials* (London, 1946), II, 67; *Stalin Correspondence,* I, 227, 230; FR (1944), I, 21–38; FR (1944), III, 1082; Churchill, *Closing the Ring,* 430–31; Churchill, *Triumph and Tragedy,* 61–62; Murphy, *Diplomat Among Warriors,* 202–03; Woodward, *British Foreign Policy,* 235–36.

17. Coles and Weinberg, *Civil Affairs,* 446. See also Aldo Garosci, "Palmiro Togliatti," *Survey,* No. 53 (1964), 141–42; Delzell, *Mussolini's Enemies,* 291.

18. Badoglio, *Italy in the Second World War,* 147.

19. Delzell, *Mussolini's Enemies,* 338.

20. Murphy, *Diplomat Among Warriors,* 215.

21. FR (1944), III, 1103.

22. *Ibid.,* 1114. See also *ibid.,* 1091, 1101, 1112–14; Coles and Weinberg, *Civil Affairs,* 447.

23. Coles and Weinberg, *Civil Affairs,* 619ff. See also Delzell, *Mussolini's Enemies, passim;* Kogan, *Italy and the Allies,* 90–98.

24. Coles and Weinberg, *Civil Affairs,* 435.

25. *Ibid.,* 439. See also *ibid.,* 438–41; FR (1944), III, 1005–30; C. R. S. Harris, *Allied Military Administration of Italy, 1943–1945* (London, 1957), 147.

26. FR (1944), III, 1037.

27. Coles and Weinberg, *Civil Affairs,* 147, 176–77, 186. See also *ibid.,* 145–46; FR (1944), III, 1053.

28. Coles and Weinberg, *Civil Affairs,* 386. See also *ibid.,* 195; Harris, *Allied Military Administration,* chaps. I, II; Holborn, *War and Peace Aims,* 9; Kogan, *Italy and the Allies,* 100; FR (1944), III, 1000, 1012, 1027.

29. Coles and Weinberg, *Civil Affairs,* 452. See also *ibid.,* 373, 384, 389; Harris, *Allied Military Administration,* 147–48.

30. Coles and Weinberg, *Civil Affairs,* 520. See also *ibid.,* 473.

31. FR (1944), III, 1129.

32. *Ibid.,* 1125–26. For the entire affair, see *ibid.,* 1123–34; Kogan, *Italy and the Allies,* chap. VII.

33. FR (1944), III, 1155. See also *ibid.,* 1153–54; Woodward, *British Foreign Policy,* 402–03; Hull, *Memoirs,* 1566–67; DSB, XI (October 15, 1944).

34. *Yalta Papers,* 269. See also FR (1944), III, 1151; Macmillan, *Blast of War,* 558–60.

35. FR (1944), III, 1161–62. See also *ibid.,* 1159.

36. *Yalta Papers,* 275. See also *ibid.,* 430–33.

37. *Ibid.,* 277. See also FR (1944), III, 1164; Stimson Diary, December 19, 1944, HLS Mss; Hull, *Memoirs,* 1569; Kogan, *Italy and the Allies,* 179–80; William Reitzel, *The Mediterranean: Its Role in America's Foreign Policy* (New York, 1948), 31–32; Hickman, *European Recovery Program,* 101–02; DSB, XI, 936; FR (1945), IV, 1250–51, 1283–84, 1305–12.

38. Coles and Weinberg, *Civil Affairs,* 532–35. See also *ibid.,* 532–37; O.S.S., "Contributions of the Italian Partisans to the Allied War Effort," March 13–14; Delzell, *Mussolini's Enemies,* 404–05; Harris, *Allied Military Administration,* 147–89.

39. Coles and Weinberg, *Civil Affairs*, 540, 542. See also Delzell, *Mussolini's Enemies*, 422-53; Battaglia, *Italian Resistance*, 223-57.

40. Delzell, *Mussolini's Enemies*, 464. See also *ibid.*, 399-470; Battaglia, *Italian Resistance*, 239-41; Coles and Weinberg, *Civil Affairs*, 540ff.

41. Coles and Weinberg, *Civil Affairs*, 544. See also *ibid.*, 542-43.

Chapter 4: France: American Policy and the Ambiguities of Reality

1. William L. Langer, *Our Vichy Gamble* (New York, 1947), 210. See also *ibid.*, 123-35, 161, 210-11; Woodward, *British Foreign Policy*, 103-07; William D. Leahy, *I Was There* (New York, 1950), 33, 74-75; Claude Paillat, *L'Échiquier D'Alger: Advantage a Vichy, Juin 1940-Novembre 1942* (Paris, 1966), *passim*.

2. Leahy, *I Was There*, 74.

3. *Ibid.*, 13, 167; Eden, *The Reckoning*, 410. See also Murphy, *Diplomat Among Warriors*, 115-17; Woodward, *British Foreign Policy*, 208-24; Paillat, *L'Échiquier D'Alger*, 369-91; McNeill, *America, Britain, and Russia*, 252-53; Coles and Weinberg, *Civil Affairs*, 33; Langer, *Vichy Gamble*, 369.

4. Coles and Weinberg, *Civil Affairs*, 35. See also Langer, *Vichy Gamble*, 299; Woodward, *British Foreign Policy*, 213-14; McNeill, *America, Britain, and Russia*, 258.

5. Coles and Weinberg, *Civil Affairs*, 47.

6. William E. Daugherty and Morris Janowitz, "The Darlan Story," in Daugherty and Janowitz, eds., *A Psychological Warfare Casebook* (Baltimore, 1958), 296.

7. Coles and Weinberg, *Civil Affairs*, 49. See also Murphy, *Diplomat Among Warriors*, 158-60; Jean Planchais, *Une Histoire Politique de L'Armée* (Paris, 1967), 51.

8. This account of Giraud is based on the definitive Henri Michel, *Les Courants de Pensée de la Résistance* (Paris, 1962), Pt. III; see also Alexander Werth, *France, 1940–1955* (New York, 1956), 212-13; Planchais, *Histoire Politique de L'Armée*, 38; Paillat, *L'Échiquier D'Alger*, 326-31.

9. Sherwood, *Roosevelt and Hopkins*, 683. See also Coles and Weinberg, *Civil Affairs*, 35.

10. FR (1943), II, 24. See also Murphy, *Diplomat Among Warriors*, 116-17; Michel, *Pensée de la Résistance*, 452; Paillat, *L'Échiquier D'Alger*, 329-30; Feis, *Churchill-Roosevelt-Stalin*, 141-43.

11. FR (1943), II, 27-28, 41.

12. Murphy, *Diplomat Among Warriors*, 173. See also *ibid.*, 171.

13. Eden, *The Reckoning*, 431. See also Murphy, *Diplomat Among Warriors*, 171ff.; Woodward, *British Foreign Policy*, 219; McNeill, *America, Britain, and Russia*, 259.

14. FR (1943), II, 111, 113. See also Julius W. Pratt, *Cordell Hull, 1933–1944* (New York, 1964), 551-93; Hull, *Memoirs*, 1216.

15. FR (1943), II, 116-17.

16. *Ibid.*, 155. See also Hull, *Memoirs*, 1217-23; Eden, *The Reckoning*, 447-50; Churchill, *Closing the Ring*, 150ff.

17. Churchill, *Closing the Ring*, 152.

18. *Ibid.*, 158. See also *ibid.*, 157ff.

19. Hull, *Memoirs,* 1233.
20. Holborn, *War and Peace Aims,* 457, 519–20.
21. Eden, *The Reckoning,* 395, 461. See also Woodward, *British Foreign Policy,* 222–23, 272, 463; Holborn, *War and Peace Aims,* 982–83.
22. Holborn, *War and Peace Aims,* 408, 499, 866. See also *ibid.,* 502, 868–70, 886.
23. FR (Teheran), 195. See also Charles de Gaulle, *Unity, 1942–1944* (New York, 1959), 212–13; FR (1944), III, 7.
24. Memo of Conversation, June 8, 1944, HLS Mss; Sherwood, *Roosevelt and Hopkins,* 712; *Yalta Papers,* 283, 305–06, 572; Eden, *The Reckoning,* 517–18; Woodward, *British Foreign Policy,* 463–64; Churchill, *Triumph and Tragedy,* 225; FR (The Conference of Berlin: The Potsdam Conference, 1945), I, 256 [hereafter *Potsdam Papers*].
25. Churchill, *Triumph and Tragedy,* 220.
26. Woodward, *British Foreign Policy,* 464–65; Charles de Gaulle, *Mémoires de Guerre: Le Salut, 1944–1946* (Paris, 1964), 385–86; FR (1945), IV, 675.
27. Michel, *Pensée de la Résistance,* 9, 56–64, Pt. I; Adrien Dansette, *Histoire de la Libération de Paris* (Paris, 1946), 28ff.; De Gaulle, *Unity, passim;* Werth, *France,* 209; Macmillan, *Blast of War,* 296.
28. Michel, *Pensée de la Résistance,* Pt. II, IV.
29. *Ibid.,* Pt. V; Jacques Fauvet, *Histoire du Parti Communiste Français* (Paris, 1965), 123ff.; Alfred J. Rieber, *Stalin and the French Communist Party, 1941–1947* (New York, 1962), 58ff.
30. FR (Teheran), 254. See also *ibid.,* 194–95, 255–56; FR (1944), I, 166, 182, 189.
31. Michel, *Pensée de la Résistance,* 62–63, 663; Dansette, *Histoire de la Libération,* 35; Martin Blumenson, *Breakout and Pursuit* (Washington, 1961), 599; Marcel Vigneras, *Rearming the French* (Washington, 1957), 300ff.
32. FR (1944), III, 669. See also *ibid.,* 670ff.; Vigneras, *Rearming the French,* 301ff.; Hull, *Memoirs,* 1429; Woodward, *British Foreign Policy,* 262–64.
33. Hull, *Memoirs,* 1431. See also Butcher, *My Three Years,* 473ff.
34. FR (1943), II, 143. See also FR (1944), III, 683, 692, 701–04; Woodward, *British Foreign Policy,* 53; De Gaulle, *Unity,* 57, 286–87; Charles de Gaulle, *Unity, 1942–1944—Documents* (New York, 1959), 11, 85–86.
35. Memo of Conversation, June 8, 1944, HLS Mss. See also FR (1943), II, 191; De Gaulle, *Unity,* 159–65; Milton Viorst, *Hostile Allies: FDR and Charles De Gaulle* (New York, 1965), 180–81; Fauvet, *Histoire du Parti Communiste,* 121–22.
36. Record of the Day, June 14, 1944, HLS Mss.
37. Memos of Conversations, June 20, 27, 1944; Notes of June 30, 1944, HLS Mss. See also FR (1944), III, 713.
38. Hull *Memoirs,* 1433.
39. FR (1944), III, 734. See also Memo of Conversation, August 18, 1944, from J. D. Lodge, JF Mss, box 19.
40. All information from Maurice Kriegel-Valrimont, *La Libération: Les Archives du COMAC (Mai-Août 1944)* (Paris, 1964), *passim.* This volume contains the official minutes of the tedious affair. See also Dansette, *Histoire de la Libération,* 22–42.
41. See Maurice Thorez, *Oeuvres* (Paris, 1960), XX, *passim.*

42. De Gaulle, *Unity*, 326.
43. Most important is De Gaulle's own discussion, *ibid.*, 324–27; see also Robert Aron, *De Gaulle Before Paris: The Liberation of France, June–August, 1944* (London, 1962), 231–32; Dansette, *Histoire de la Libération* [1966 edition], 76–122; Eden, *The Reckoning*, 519.
44. De Gaulle, *Unity*, 328. See also Dansette, *Histoire de la Libération*, 45–48, 76–78, 156–57; Pogue, *Supreme Command*, 240.
45. Kriegel-Valrimont, *La Libération*, 191. See also *ibid.*, 177ff.; Dansette, *Histoire de la Libération*, 164.
46. Blumenson, *Breakout and Pursuit*, 594–603, 623–24; Dansette, in *Le Monde*, November 9, 1966; Dansette, *Histoire de la Libération*, chap. III; Pogue, *Supreme Command*, 240–41; Stimson Diary, August 23, 1944, HLS Mss.
47. De Gaulle, *Unity-Documents*, 408. See also Pogue, *Supreme Command*, 241; De Gaulle, *Unity*, 333, 338–40.
48. De Gaulle, *Unity*, 340. See also *ibid.*, 343; Kriegel-Valrimont, *La Libération*, 216–23; Viorst, *Hostile Allies*, 213–14.
49. Stimson Diary, September 14, 1944, HLS Mss. See also Aron, *De Gaulle Before Paris*, 295; Viorst, *Hostile Allies*, 214–17; De Gaulle, *Unity*, 356–57; Dansette, *Histoire de la Libération*, 395–96; Kriegel-Valrimont, *La Libération*, 227–34; Coles and Weinberg, *Civil Affairs*, 758–70; Pogue, *Supreme Command*, 327–28; Woodward, *British Foreign Policy*, 96; FR (1944), III, 731–32; M. R. D. Foot, *SOE in France: An Account of the Work of the British Special Operations Executive in France, 1940–1944* (London, 1966), 421; Stimson Diary, September 9, 1944, HLS Mss; U. S. Senate, Committee on the Judiciary, *Morgenthau Diary (Germany)*. 90:1. November 20, 1967. (Washington, 1967), 774–75 [hereafter *Morgenthau Diary (Germany)*].
50. Eisenhower Memo to George C. Marshall, September 22, 1944, DDE Mss (1916–52, De Gaulle). See also Vigneras, *Rearming the French*, 319ff.; Planchais, *Histoire Politique de L'Armée*, 82–91; Pogue, *Supreme Command*, 328; Coles and Weinberg, *Civil Affairs*, 770.
51. FR (Teheran), 514. See also De Gaulle, *Le Salut*, 350–51; Georgette Elgey, *La République des Illusions: 1945–1951* (Paris, 1965), chap. I.
52. FR (1944), III, 723. See also *ibid.*, 666–67.
53. Charles de Gaulle, *Salvation, 1944–1946* (New York, 1960), 114.
54. *Yalta Papers*, 957.
55. Thorez, *Oeuvres*, 187–88.
56. Elgey, *La République des Illusions*, 23. See also *Recherches Internationales*, No. 44–45 (1964), 243–44.
57. Memo of Conference with the President, June 6, 1945, HLS Mss. See also Memo of November 26, 1945, JF Mss, box 100; entry of May 14 in Robert Patterson, "Note on Trip to European Theatre of Operations. . . . April 30, 1945–May 16, 1945." RP Mss, box 7; De Gaulle, *Le Salut*, 471; Memos of Conversations, February 19, 23, 24, 28, May 21, June 5, 8, 13, 25, 1945, JCG Mss; FR (1945), IV, 686.
58. *Yalta Papers*, 294, 300. See also memo of Conversations, June 13, 1945, JCG Mss; De Gaulle, *Salvation*, 242–43; *Potsdam Papers*, I, 252.
59. Coles and Weinberg, *Civil Affairs*, 809. See also *ibid.*, 803; O. S. S., R. & A. Branch, "The Belgian Underground." R & A 1999. August 19, 1944. (N. P. 1944), *passim*.

60. All Belgian data from Coles and Weinberg, *Civil Affairs*, 797–818; Pogue, *Supreme Command*, 330–32; Donnison, *Civil Affairs and Military Government*, 117–19. For Holland, see Donnison, *Civil Affairs and Military Government*, 139–40; Coles and Weinberg, *Civil Affairs*, 824.

Chapter 5: Eastern Europe, I: The Case of Poland

1. Samuel L. Sharp, *Poland: White Eagle on a Red Field* (Cambridge, 1953), chap. II.
2. Polish Ambassador to Hull, September 29, 1941, FDR Mss, PSF.
3. Werth, *Russia at War*, 636–39, 651; Edward J. Rozek, *Allied Wartime Diplomacy: A Pattern in Poland* (New York, 1958), 112–13; Churchill, *Closing the Ring*, 214–15; Woodward, *British Foreign Policy*, 191–93; Stanislaw Kot, *Conversations With the Kremlin and Dispatches From Russia* (London, 1963), 175–76; Rothstein, *Soviet Foreign Policy*, 40–41; Feis, *Churchill-Roosevelt-Stalin*, 657–59; DS, *Postwar Foreign Policy Preparation, 1939–1945* (Washington, 1950), 509; Maisky, *Memoirs*, 230–31.
4. FR (1943), III, 317.
5. FR (1943), I, 762. See also FR (1943), III, 15, 335, 470–71; Sharp, *Poland*, 286–87; Holborn, *War and Peace Aims*, 1058, 1071, 1073, 1083.
6. FR (1943), III, 359. See also *ibid.*, 316–17; Holborn, *War and Peace Aims*, 1058–59, 1074; Stanislaw Mikolajczyk, *The Rape of Poland: Pattern of Soviet Aggression* (New York, 1948), 265.
7. Sharp, *Poland*, 162.
8. FR (1943), III, 337, 470.
9. *Ibid.*, 358.
10. Sharp, *Poland*, 171.
11. FR (1943), III, 469. See also Sharp, *Poland*, 171–73; Rozek, *Allied Wartime Diplomacy*, 143.
12. FR (Teheran), 384.
13. FR (1943), III, 375.
14. T. Bor-Komorowski, *The Secret Army* (New York, 1951), 128. See also *Stalin Correspondence*, I, 120–25; FR (1943), III, 403; Feis, *Churchill-Roosevelt-Stalin*, 193.
15. FR (1943), III, 401.
16. *Stalin Correspondence*, I, 128.
17. Mikolajczyk, *Rape of Poland*, 265.
18. Rozek, *Allied Wartime Diplomacy*, 143.
19. Churchill, *Closing the Ring*, 309–10, 337–45; FR (Teheran), 603.
20. FR (1943), I, 542. See also FR (1943), III, 316–17, 335, 352, 356, 469–70, 482; DS, *Postwar Foreign Policy*, 498, 509–10; Hull, *Memoirs*, 1166.
21. FR (1943), III, 472, 487.
22. FR (Teheran), 384.
23. FR (1943), I, 622.
24. DS, *Postwar Foreign Policy*, 510. See also Vandenberg to Frank Januszewski, November 3, 6, 1943, AHV Mss.
25. Hull, *Memoirs*, 1169.
26. FR (1943), III, 364.
27. *Ibid.*, 435–36. See also *ibid.*, 372–73, 389.
28. FR (1943), I, 667.

29. Mikolajczyk, *Rape of Poland*, 270.
30. *Stalin Correspondence*, I, 182.
31. Holborn, *War and Peace Aims*, 764–65.
32. FR (1944), III, 1224, 1232, 1234. See also FR (1943), III, 731–32; Eduard Beneš, *Memoirs: From Munich to New War and New Victory* (Boston, 1953), 266–67; Holborn, *War and Peace Aims*, 465.
33. FR (1944), III, 1259, 1254, 1252. See also *ibid.*, 1248; Hull, *Memoirs*, 1438ff.; Woodward, *British Foreign Policy*, 279–84.
34. FR (1944), III, 1224, 1279. See also Sharp, *Poland*, 162–63.
35. FR (1944), IV, 839–42.
36. *Stalin Correspondence*, I, 207, 211.
37. FR (1944), IV, 873–74. See also Hull, *Memoirs*, 1442–43.
38. FR (1944), III, 1281–83, 1288. See also *ibid.*, 1274–86.
39. Hull, *Memoirs*, 1445.
40. FR (1944), III, 1284.
41. Soviet News, *Soviet-Polish Relations: A Collection of Official Documents and Press Extracts, 1944–1946* (London, 1946), 4. See also FR (1944), III, 1292–94, 1297, 1308–09.
42. Bor-Komorowski, *The Secret Army*, 201–03, 205.
43. *Ibid.*, 204. See also Sharp, *Poland*, 176–77.
44. Bor-Komorowski, *The Secret Army*, 212, 205. See also Michel Borwicz, "Sur la Pologne," *Revue d'Histoire de la Deuxième Guerre Mondiale*, XIII (1963), 93–98; Werth, *Russia at War*, 879; *New Statesman and Nation*, September 2, 1944, 147.
45. *Stalin Correspondence*, I, 249. See also FR (1944), III, 1308–09.
46. *Stalin Correspondence*, I, 254. See also FR (1944), III, 1312–13.
47. Bor-Komorowski, *The Secret Army*, 339–60; FR (1944), III, 1377; Sharp, *Poland*, 182–83; Mikolajczyk, *Rape of Poland*, 85–90; Churchill, *Triumph and Tragedy*, chap. IX.
48. FR (1944), IV, 1013; Wilmot, *Struggle for Europe*, 630; Werth, *Russia at War*, 872–82; Eden, *The Reckoning*, 548.
49. FR (1944), III, 523. See also *ibid.*, 521; Holborn, *War and Peace Aims*, 1035.
50. For the entire affair, see FR (1944), III, 521–23; West German Federal Ministry for Expellees, *Refugees and War Victims, Expulsion of the German Population from the Territories East of Oder-Neisse Line* (Bonn, 1960), IV, 151–58; Josef Korbel, *The Communist Šubversion of Czechoslovakia, 1938–48* (Princeton, 1959), 70–73; Jaroslav Solc, "Le Movement Slovaque de Partisans," *Revue d'Histoire de la Deuxième Guerre Mondiale*, XIII (1963), 61–78; Joseph A. Mikus, *Slovakia: A Political History, 1918–1950* (Milwaukee, 1963), 138–49; Eduard Taborsky, "Beneš and Stalin–Moscow, 1943 and 1945," *Journal of Central European History*, XIII (1953), 169; Ivo Duchacek, in *The Fate of East Central Europe: Hopes and Failures of American Foreign Policy*. Stephen D. Kertesz, ed. (Notre Dame, 1956), 199–200.
51. FR (1944), III, 1310–11, 1317. See also *ibid.*, 1308–14.
52. Rozek, *Allied Wartime Diplomacy*, 151, 178. See also O. S. S., R. & A. Branch, "Post-War Poland—Economic and Political Outlook." R & A 2311. March 9, 1945. (N. P., 1945), *passim; The Economist*, July 29, 1944, 136–37.
53. FR (1944), III, 1279; M. K. Dziewanowski, *The Communist Party of Poland* (Cambridge, 1959), 169–77.

Chapter 6: Eastern Europe, II: Diverse Paths to Security

1. Beneš, *Memoirs*, 240.
2. *Ibid.*, 276. See also Korbel, *Subversion of Czechoslovakia*, 78–81; Lockhart, *Comes the Reckoning*, 309.
3. Beneš, *Memoirs*, 241. See also Korbel, *Subversion of Czechoslovakia*. 80–81.
4. FR (1943), III, 670n.
5. Beneš, *Memoirs*, 194. See also *ibid.*, 193–96.
6. Holborn, *War and Peace Aims*, 1005, 1015.
7. FR (1943), III, 670n.
8. Beneš, *Memoirs*, 276.
9. FR (1943), I, 625. See also FR (1943), III, 677–78; Korbel, *Subversion of Czechoslovakia*, 81–82.
10. FR (1943), III, 719. See also *ibid.*, 677; Beneš, *Memoirs*, 243; Holborn, *War and Peace Aims*, 997–99, 1002–03, 1007.
11. FR (1943), III, 728–33.
12. Churchill, *Closing the Ring*, 386–87.
13. Holborn, *War and Peace Aims*, 1030. See also *ibid.*, 762; Taborsky, "Beneš and Stalin . . . ," 168–69.
14. FR (1944), IV, 870, 993. See also FR (1944), III, 515–20; FR (1944), I, 33.
15. FR (1944), IV, 143, 147.
16. *Ibid.*, 161. See also *ibid.*, 157–59.
17. Rothstein, *Soviet Foreign Policy*, 66.
18. FR (1944), IV, 186. See also *ibid.*, 172–73.
19. *Ibid.*, 236, 228. See also *ibid.*, 196, 209–11, 227; Holborn, *War and Peace Aims*, 515; N. Goldberger, in International Conference on the History of the Resistance Movements, *European Resistance Movements, 1939–45* (Milan, March 26–29, 1961) (New York, 1964), 191–223.
20. FR (1944), IV, 223.
21. *Ibid.*, 230.
22. *Ibid.*, 239–49, 275–76, 281.
23. Churchill, *Closing the Ring*, 397–98. See also *ibid.*, 400; Woodward, *British Foreign Policy*, 341.
24. Churchill, *Closing the Ring*, 407. See also *ibid.*, 398–401; FR (Teheran), 575; FR (1943), II, 1005; FR (1944), IV, 1331ff.; Woodward, *British Foreign Policy*, 1336–37.
25. FR (1944), IV, 1372. See also *ibid.*, 1335–55, 1369, 1411, 1415–16; Lockhart, *Comes the Reckoning*, 308–09; Churchill, *Closing the Ring*, 408.
26. FR (1944), IV, 1388, 1398. See also *ibid.*, 1392–93, 1403; Murphy, *Diplomat Among Warriors*, 221.
27. FR (1944), IV, 1378, 1387.
28. Vladimir Dedijer, *Tito* (New York, 1953), 232. See also *ibid.*, 178–81; Milovan Djilas, *Conversations with Stalin* (New York, 1962), chap. I; Macmillan, *Blast of War*, 534–35.
29. FR (Teheran), 575. See also Holborn, *War and Peace Aims*, 1109; FR (1944), IV, 1404–06; Evangelos Kofos, *Nationalism and Communism in Macedonia* (Thessaloniki, 1964), 115–18, 138–42; *The Economist*, February 11, 1950, 324.
30. Dedijer, *Tito*, 209. See also Eden, *The Reckoning*, 501.
31. Djilas, *Conversations with Stalin*, 73–74. See also FR (1943), II, 1005;

FR (1943), III, 732; Churchill, *Triumph and Tragedy*, 76.
32. Dedijer, *Tito*, 233.
33. *The Economist*, March 4, 1944, 298–99. Churchill, *Closing the Ring*, 340–42; FR (1944), III, 558.
34. Holborn, *War and Peace Aims*, 515. See also *ibid.*, 97ff.; Hull, *Memoirs*, 1577–80; *The Economist*, September 9, 1944, 345; FR (1945), IV, 598ff.

Chapter 7: Eastern Europe, III: "With Bow Against Bear"
(*October 1944 to January 1945*)

1. Churchill, *Closing the Ring*, 621–22. See also Eden, *The Reckoning*, 469–70; Woodward, *British Foreign Policy*, xlii; FR (Teheran), 130; FR (1943), I, 638–39; Moran, *Churchill*, 185.
2. Churchill, *Triumph and Tragedy*, 63, 65–66. See also Hull, *Memoirs*, 1454.
3. FR (1943), I, 639. See also *ibid.*, 762–63; Hull, *Memoirs*, 1457, 1640–41; *Stalin Correspondence* I, 238; FR (1943), III, 24, 335, 592, 601–02, 733; FR (Teheran), 847.
4. Moran, *Churchill*, 11. See also *ibid.*, 194 and *passim*; Woodward, *British Foreign Policy*, 454–55; *Yalta Papers*, 238.
5. Churchill, *Triumph and Tragedy*, 181.
6. Sherwood, *Roosevelt and Hopkins*, 834. See also *Stalin Correspondence*, II, 162–64.
7. *Stalin Correspondence*, II, 163.
8. Churchill, *Triumph and Tragedy*, 196–97.
9. *Ibid.*, 200–01. See also FR (1944), IV, 1007–10, 1016; Woodward, *British Foreign Policy*, 308.
10. *Stalin Correspondence*, I, 264.
11. FR (1944), IV, 1003. See also Moran, *Churchill*, 217–21.
12. Churchill, *Triumph and Tragedy*, 203.
13. FR (1944), III, 452.
14. Stimson Diary, December 31, 1944, HLS Mss. See also FR (1944), III, 452–460; FR (1945), IV, 149; *Yalta Papers*, 104–08, 159–60.
15. Mikolajczyk, *Rape of Poland*, 100.
16. Rozek, *Allied Wartime Diplomacy*, 280, 283. See also Moran, *Churchill*, 214–15; *Yalta Papers*, 202–03.
17. Churchill, *Triumph and Tragedy*, 208. See also *ibid.*, 203–08; *Yalta Papers*, 205; FR (1944), III, 1325–28.
18. *Yalta Papers*, 208.
19. *Ibid.*, 214, 212. See also *ibid.*, 209–14; FR (1944), III, 1331–36; Memo of Conversation with Roosevelt, November 20, 1944, ABL Mss, box 166.
20. Holborn, *War and Peace Aims*, 538, 542.
21. *Yalta Papers*, 218.
22. *Ibid.*, 227. See also *ibid.*, 230–34; *Stalin Correspondence*, I, 279, 282, 290–91; II, 175–76, 182–83; Arnold and Veronica M. Toynbee, eds., *The Realignment of Europe* (London, 1953), 224–25; Soviet News, *Moscow Trial of Sixteen Polish Diversionists, June 18–21, 1945* (London, 1945), *passim*; O. S. S., "Post-War Poland," 20–39.
23. FR (1944), IV, 1414. See also *ibid.*, 1006–14; Dedijer, *Tito*, 234.
24. FR (1944), IV, 1425. See also *ibid.*, 1417–18.
25. *Ibid.*, 1431. See also *ibid.*, 1423–45; *Stalin Correspondence*, I, 273; *Yalta Papers*, 253.
26. *Yalta Papers*, 256–57. See also FR (1944), IV, 1444.

27. FR (1944), IV, 1444. See also *Yalta Papers*, 264.

28. *Stalin Correspondence*, I, 296.

29. *Ibid.*, 297–302; FR (1945), V, 1175–91; Holborn, *War and Peace Aims*, 548; *Yalta Papers*, 260–65.

30. O.S.S., R. & A. Branch, "Current Party Politics in Rumania." R & A No. 2727. December 6, 1944. (N. P., 1944), 8, 12. See also Henry L. Roberts, *Rumania: Political Problems of an Agrarian State* (New Haven, 1951), 242ff.

31. FR (1944), IV, 255–56. See also Roberts, *Rumania*, 261.

32. FR (1944), IV, 259.

33. O.S.S., "Politics in Rumania," 12. See also FR (1944), IV, 259.

34. FR (1944), IV, 280–81. See also *ibid.*, 277–78; O.S.S., "Politics in Rumania," 5.

35. FR (1944), IV, 279–80; *Yalta Papers*, 246–48; O.S.S., "Politics in Rumania," 7.

36. FR (1944), III, 496. See also *ibid.*, 435–36, 487.

37. *Ibid.*, 481–96; *Yalta Papers*, 240–42; FR (1945), IV, 135–43.

38. *Yalta Papers*, 245. See also O.S.S., R. & A. Branch, "Political Hesitation in Hungary." R & A 2453S. September 22, 1944. (N. P., 1944), 1–2; FR (1944), III, 887, 890, 907, 915–18, 943, 952, 974.

39. *Yalta Papers*, 239.

40. FR (1943), III, 12. See also Notes for Talk with President, August 24, 1944, HLS Mss.

41. FR (Teheran), 155. See also FR (1943), I, 615–16; FR (1943), III, 13.

42. FR (1944), IV, 826, 855, 908, 910–11. See also Kennan, *Memoirs*, 224–25, 503–31.

43. FR (1944), III, 910–11. See also Walter Millis, ed., *The Forrestal Diaries* (New York, 1951), 14; Forrestal to Robert Strausz-Hupé, November 23, 1944, JF Mss, box 24.

44. FR (1944), IV, 993–94, 997. See also *ibid.*, 924.

45. Holborn, *War and Peace Aims*, 774, 776. See also DS, Office of Research and Intelligence, "Political and Social Implications of Recent Trends in Education in the U. S. S. R." No. 3079. February 26, 1946 (N. P., 1946); O.S.S., R. & A. Branch, "The Scope, Content, and Intent of Soviet Foreign Broadcasts." R & A No. 1146. September 4, 1943. (N. P., 1943); Isaac Deutscher, *Stalin: A Political Biography* (New York, 1960), 474–91.

46. FR (1944), III, 917, 923.

47. DS, Memorandum for the President: "Reconstruction of Poland," October 31, 1944, FDR Mss, PSF, box 134.

48. FR (1944), IV, 1025–26.

49. *Yalta Papers*, 235–37.

50. *Ibid.*, 100. See also FR (1945), I, 34.

51. *Yalta Papers*, 103.

52. U. S. Senate, Committee on Foreign Relations, *A Background Study on East-West Trade*. 89:1. April, 1965 (Washington, 1965), 1–2.

Chapter 8: The Greek Passion

1. André Kédros, *La Résistance Grecque (1940–1944)* (Paris, 1966), 90–93, 121–23, 362; Frank Smothers *et al.*, *Report on the Greeks* (New York, 1948), 24–25; Bickham Sweet-Escott, *Greece: A Political and Economic Survey, 1939–1953* (London, 1954), 21–24; L. S. Stavrianos, *Greece:*

American Dilemma and Opportunity (Chicago, 1952), 68–88; *Recherches Internationales,* No. 44–45, 257; Stephanos Sarafis, *Greek Resistance Army: The Story of the ELAS* (London, 1951), 198–99.

2. Kédros, *Résistance Grecque,* 290, 307, 387, 409; Stavrianos, *Greece,* 72; Woodward, *British Foreign Policy,* 352.

3. C. M. Woodhouse, *Apple of Discord: A Survey of Recent Greek Politics in Their International Setting* (London, N. D.), 65, 67. See also Smothers, *Report on the Greeks,* 20–25; R. V. Burks, *The Dynamics of Communism in Eastern Europe* (Princeton, 1961), 26, 47.

4. Woodward, *British Foreign Policy,* 355; Kofos, *Nationalism and Communism,* 120–28; Sarafis, *Greek Resistance Army,* 265–66.

5. International Conference on the History of the Resistance, *European Resistance Movements,* 111.

6. FR (1943), IV, 126, 133. See also *ibid.,* 131ff.; Reginald Leeper, *When Greek Meets Greek* (London 1950), 16; Woodward, *British Foreign Policy,* 354–55; Stavrianos, *Greece,* 79, 92, 103–04; Xydis, *Greece and the Great Powers,* 14–17, 61.

7. John Ehrman, *Grand Strategy: August 1943–September 1944* (London, 1956), 86–87; Churchill, *Closing the Ring,* 460. See also *ibid.,* 458–59; FR (1943), IV, 148–49; Sweet-Escott, *Greece,* 25; Stavrianos, *Greece,* 100.

8. FR (Teheran), 851.

9. FR (1944), V, 86. See also *ibid.,* 85; FR (1943), IV, 156–57.

10. Churchill, *Closing the Ring,* 463, 465–67. See also FR (1943), IV, 127.

11. FR (1944), V, 98–101. See also *ibid.,* 89ff.; Churchill, *Closing the Ring,* 470–71; Kédros, *Résistance Grecque,* 411–13.

12. FR (1944), V, 116. See also *ibid.,* 95–105, 115; Woodhouse, *Apple of Discord,* 189; Stavrianos, *Greece,* 106–12; *The Economist,* June 3, 1944, 742–43.

13. Eden, *The Reckoning,* 533. See also FR (1943), IV, 165; FR (1944), V, 105; Woodhouse, *Apple of Discord,* 112; *Stalin Correspondence,* I, 390; Sarafis, *Greek Resistance Army,* 223–25.

14. Woodhouse, *Apple of Discord,* 198–99; William H. McNeill, "The Outbreak of Fighting in Athens, 1944," *American Slavic and East European Review,* VIII (1949), 255; Kédros, *Résistance Grecque,* 423–26.

15. Churchill, *Triumph and Tragedy,* 93; Sarafis, *Greek Resistance Army,* 143.

16. FR (1944), V, 133–34.

17. Churchill, *Triumph and Tragedy,* 245. See also Macmillan, *Blast of War,* 574–76.

18. Walter Warlimont, *Inside Hitler's Headquarters, 1939–45* (New York, 1964), 471. See also L. S. Stavrianos, "The Immediate Origin of the Battle of Athens," *American Slavic and East European Review,* VIII (1949), 242–43; Woodward, *British Foreign Policy,* 357.

19. FR (1944), V, 135.

20. Stavrianos, "The Immediate Origin of the Battle of Athens," 243.

21. FR (1944), V, 136. See also Stavrianos, *Greece,* 125; Stavrianos, "The Immediate Origin of the Battle of Athens," 244–45; McNeill, "The Outbreak of Fighting in Athens," 254–55; Ehrman, *Grand Strategy . . . 1944–1945,* 61; Sarafis, *Greek Resistance Army,* 276.

22. Churchill, *Triumph and Tragedy,* 247.

23. FR (1944), V, 139. See also *ibid.,* 136–37; Ehrman, *Grand Strategy . . . 1944–1945,* 61.

24. FR (1944), V, 137. See also National Liberation Front (EAM), *White*

Book: May 1944–March 1945 (New York, 1945), 19ff.

25. Stavrianos, "The Immediate Origin of the Battle of Athens," 244. See also Kédros, *Résistance Grecque,* 472–73.

26. O.S.S., R. & A. Branch, "Political and Economic Outlook of the EAM on the Eve of the Greek Crisis (December 1944)," R & A No. 2821. January 5, 1945. (N. P., 1945), 3–4.

27. FR (1944), V, 140. See also O.S.S., "Political and Economic Outlook of the EAM . . . ," *passim;* Chris J. Agrafiotis, ed., *Was Churchill Right in Greece?* (Manchester, N. H., 1945?), 86–87; D. George Kousoulas, *Revolution and Defeat: The Story of the Greek Communist Party* (London, 1965), 201; Woodhouse, *Apple of Discord,* 96–97; Leeper, *When Greek Meets Greek,* 60.

28. Ehrman, *Grand Strategy . . . 1944–1945,* 61. See also FR (1944), V, 141, 148; Kédros, *Résistance Grecque,* 487–88; Sweet-Escott, *Greece,* 35–36; EAM, *White Book,* 41; Stavrianos, *Greece,* 130–35.

29. Churchill, *Triumph and Tragedy,* 249. See also Leeper, *When Greek Meets Greek,* 104; Kédros, *Résistance Grecque,* 494.

30. Holborn, *War and Peace Aims,* 531–32.

31. Sweet-Escott, *Greece,* 36.

32. Leeper, *When Greek Meets Greek,* 119, 136; Churchill, *Triumph and Tragedy,* 254. See also Leeper, *When Greek Meets Greek,* 117–20; *Recherches Internationales,* 278.

33. FR (1944), V, 150. See also *ibid.,* 145, 149; Churchill, *Triumph and Tragedy,* 255; Sherwood, *Roosevelt and Hopkins,* 840–41.

34. Churchill, *Triumph and Tragedy,* 610. See also *ibid.,* 252, 277; FR (1944), V, 170; *Yalta Papers,* 249–50.

35. FR (1944), V, 157. See also *ibid.,* 167; Kousoulas, *Revolution and Defeat,* 214; Leeper, *When Greek Meets Greek,* xvi; Woodhouse, *Apple of Discord,* 113.

36. Churchill, *Triumph and Tragedy,* 271, 273. See also Moran, *Churchill,* 228; Macmillan, *Blast of War,* 626–29.

37. Agrafiotis, *Was Churchill Right?,* 72. See also FR (1944), V, 174–77; Churchill, *Triumph and Tragedy,* 274–75; Leeper, *When Greek Meets Greek,* chap. IX.

38. Stavrianos, *Greece,* 443.

Chapter 9: *The Political Conditions of Military Strategy in the Far East*

1. *Forrestal Diaries,* 17. See also Matloff, *Strategic Planning for Coalition Warfare,* 9–10; U. S. Congress, Joint Committee on the Investigation of the Pearl Harbor Attack, *Hearings, Pearl Harbor Attack.* 79:1. (Washington, 1946), 1485–1550.

2. *Forrestal Diaries,* 18.

3. Charles F. Romanus and Riley Sunderland, *Stilwell's Command Problems* (Washington, 1956), ix.

4. *Forrestal Diaries,* 17.

5. Woodward, *British Foreign Policy,* 420.

6. Charles F. Romanus and Riley Sunderland, *Time Runs Out in CBI* (Washington, 1958), 159.

7. Churchill, *Closing the Ring,* 78. See also Romanus and Sunderland, *Time Runs Out,* 338.

8. Churchill, *Closing the Ring*, 79, 322–25, 350–52, 379–80; Romanus and Sunderland, *Stilwell's Command Problems*, 9; Ehrman, *Grand Strategy . . . 1943–1944*, 143–44.

9. Churchill, *Closing the Ring*, 494–96.

10. Churchill, *Triumph and Tragedy*, 143. See also *ibid.*, 125–26, 130–33; Sherwood, *Roosevelt and Hopkins*, 816.

11. Matloff, *Strategic Planning for Coalition Warfare*, 528. See also Ehrman, *Grand Strategy . . . 1944–1945*, 220; *Potsdam Papers*, I, 923; Bryant, *Triumph in the West*, 203–06.

12. Romanus and Sunderland, *Time Runs Out*, 369–71. See also *ibid.*, 382; FR (Teheran), 242.

13. Romanus and Sunderland, *Time Runs Out*, 242. See also *ibid.*, 371; FR (1944), VI, 95, 112.

14. Romanus and Sunderland, *Time Runs Out*, 11–12, 19, 242, 381; Lionel Max Chassin, *The Communist Conquest of China: A History of the Civil War, 1945–1949* (Cambridge, 1965), 43–46; Romanus and Sunderland, *Stilwell's Command Problems*, 291, 311.

15. George Woodbridge, *UNRRA: The History of The United Nations Relief and Rehabilitation Administration* (New York, 1950), II, 394; U. S. Senate, Committee on the Judiciary, *Morgenthau Diary (China)*. 89:1. February 5, 1965. (Washington, 1965), 1159, 1474, 1636–38 [hereafter *Morgenthau Diary*]; FR (1944), VI, 843.

16. Joseph W. Stilwell, *The Stilwell Papers* (New York, 1948), 316.

17. FR (Teheran), 242. See also Stimson, *On Active Service*, 532–33.

18. Romanus and Sunderland, *Stilwell's Command Problems*, 363–64.

19. O. Edmund Clubb, *20th Century China* (New York, 1964), 238. See also Memo from Stimson to General George C. Marshall, November 29, 1945, HLS Mss; Stilwell, *Stilwell Papers*, 124–25.

20. FR (Teheran), 265.

21. Chassin, *Communist Conquest of China*, 18.

22. Romanus and Sunderland, *Stilwell's Command Problems*, 308.

23. Hull, *Memoirs*, 1309–10.

24. Sherwood, *Roosevelt and Hopkins*, 779, 784, 792; Matloff, *Strategic Planning for Coalition Warfare*, 287ff.; Romanus and Sunderland, *Stilwell's Command Problems*, 365–66; FR (1944), IV, 943–44; Churchill, *Closing the Ring*, 620.

25. FR (1944), I, 699, 701, 703. See also Memo of Conversation, May 17, 1944, JCG Mss.

26. U. S. Department of Defense, *The Entry of the Soviet Union into the War Against Japan: Military Plans, 1941–1945* (Washington, 1955), 39, 41. See also FR (1944), IV, 1002.

27. *Yalta Papers*, 352. See also *ibid.*, 363, 367, 369, 389, 396.

28. Stimson Memo of January 23, 1945, in Stimson Diary, HLS Mss.

Chapter 10: The Epic of China

1. *Morgenthau Diary*, 133, 562, 695. See also *ibid.*, 720, 769–71, 780–82.

2. Stilwell, *Stilwell Papers*, 124. See also *Morgenthau Diary*, 920.

3. Stilwell, *Stilwell Papers*, 124–25, 215; Romanus and Sunderland, *Stilwell's Command Problems*, 3–6, 59–71.

4. Romanus and Sunderland, *Stilwell's Command Problems*, 74.

5. *Morgenthau Diary*, 1022.

6. *Ibid.*, 945. See also *ibid.*, 920–22.
7. Romanus and Sunderland, *Stilwell's Command Problems*, 302. See also *ibid.*, 79–80; DS, *United States Relations With China, With Special Reference to the Period 1944–1949* (Washington, 1949), 488–94; *Morgenthau Diary*, 1022–23; Herbert Feis, *The China Tangle: The American Effort in China From Pearl Harbor to the Marshall Mission* (Princeton, 1953), 122–23.
8. Romanus and Sunderland, *Stilwell's Command Problems*, 308, 363. See also *ibid.*, 310; *Morgenthau Diary*, 1133; Feis, *China Tangle*, 164.
9. Romanus and Sunderland, *Stilwell's Command Problems*, 386. See also *ibid.*, 374–77; Feis, *China Tangle*, chap. XV.
10. Romanus and Sunderland, *Stilwell's Command Problems*, 437. See also FR (1944), VI, 247–48; Memo of Conversation, August 14, 1944, JCG Mss.
11. Romanus and Sunderland, *Stilwell's Command Problems*, 445–46.
12. DS, *Relations With China*, 68.
13. Feis, *China Tangle*, 198. See also Romanus and Sunderland, *Stilwell's Command Problems*, 422–69.
14. *Morgenthau Diary*, 457–62, 878–79, 1049–50; Feis, *China Tangle*, 85–91; DS, *Relations With China*, 530–31.
15. Stilwell, *Stilwell Papers*, 316; Romanus and Sunderland, *Stilwell's Command Problems*, 302–06, 374–76; DS, *Relations With China*, 535–36, 564–66; FR (1944), VI, 518–19, 567, 600ff.; Feis, *China Tangle*, 142–50.
16. *Morgenthau Diary*, 1347, 1349.
17. DS, *Relations With China*, 561.
18. Romanus and Sunderland, *Stilwell's Command Problems*, 452. See also *ibid.*, 431–52.
19. FR (1943), III, 39. See also *ibid.*, 35–36; Tang Tsou, *America's Failure in China, 1941–50* (Chicago, 1963), 75; FR (1944), VI, 32–33.
20. Churchill, *Triumph and Tragedy*, 599.
21. Hull, *Memoirs*, 1282. See also *ibid.*, 1281; FR (1943), I, 1074; Feis, *China Tangle*, 96.
22. FR (Teheran), 264.
23. Woodward, *British Foreign Policy*, 450. See also FR (Teheran), 323–25; FR (1944), VI, 39, 1166.
24. Hull, *Memoirs*, 1586. See also Memo of Conversation, August 14, 1944, JCG Mss; FR (1944), VI, 232.
25. DS, *Relations With China*, 561.
26. *Yalta Papers*, 353. See also *Morgenthau Diary*, 1381.
27. Feis, *China Tangle*, 216. See also Romanus and Sunderland, *Time Runs Out*, 8–9, 16, 165.
28. DS, *Relations With China*, 75. See also *ibid.*, 74.
29. *Ibid.*, 76.
30. *Ibid.*, 574. See also *ibid.*, 572–75; Romanus and Sunderland, *Time Runs Out*, 73–75; FR (1944), VI, 600ff.
31. *Morgenthau Diary*, 1304.
32. *Ibid.*, 1380.
33. FR (1944), VI, 745. See also *Morgenthau Diary*, 1247–48, 1304–08, 1318–21, 1375, 1380; General Curtis E. LeMay, *Mission With LeMay: My Story* (Garden City, N. Y., 1965), 336–37; *Yalta Papers*, 349; Romanus and Sunderland, *Time Runs Out*, 75, 251–54; Feis, *China Tangle*, 205–06; FR (1944), VI, 19; DS, *Relations With China*, 76–82.
34. *Yalta Papers*, 950.

35. FR (1900), 290.
36. *Morgenthau Diary*, 7.
37. DS, *Relations With China*, 481, 513.
38. Stilwell, *Stilwell Papers*, 124; FR (1943), I, 1074.
39. Chiang Kai-shek, *China's Destiny and China's Economic Theory* (New York, 1947), 18, 197–231; *Morgenthau Diary*, 901–02.
40. *Morgenthau Diary*, 921–22. See also FR (1944), VI, 1008, 1043.
41. *Morgenthau Diary*, 1169.
42. *Business Week*, December 9, 1944, 112. See also FR (1944), VI, 263, 271, 276, 1051, 1060–61, 1066–67, 1072, 1078.
43. *Business Week*, November 11, 1944, 113.
44. FR (1944), VI, 1087, 1095. See also *ibid.*, 1082–86.
45. *Yalta Papers*, 357.
46. Barrington Moore, Jr., *Social Origins of Dictatorship and Democracy* (Boston, 1966), 214.
47. DS, *Relations With China*, 569–70.
48. *Morgenthau Diary*, 1341, 1345. See also *ibid.*, 1475, 1486–88; Chassin, *Communist Conquest of China*, 28.
49. Chassin, *Communist Conquest of China*, 26–36; Chalmers A. Johnson, *Peasant Nationalism and Communist Power: The Emergence of Revolutionary China, 1937–1945* (Stanford, 1962), chap. I; DS, *Relations With China*, 567–70; Theodore H. White and Annalee Jacoby, *Thunder Out of China* (New York, 1946), *passim;* Moore, *Social Origins*, 219–26.
50. *Morgenthau Diary*, 176. See also Harold R. Isaacs, *The Tragedy of the Chinese Revolution* (Stanford, 1951), *passim;* Charles B. McLane, *Soviet Policy and the Chinese Communists, 1931–1946* (New York, 1958), *passim.*
51. *Morgenthau Diary*, 212. See also *ibid.*, 91, 176–78, 189–92, 227, 233; Tsou, *America's Failure in China*, 183.
52. FR (Teheran), 376, 869, 891; DS, *Relations with China*, 564; Feis, *China Tangle*, 137–38, 141; FR (1944), VI, 786–89, 800; Memo of Conversation, May 17, 1944, JPG Mss; Romanus and Sunderland, *Stilwell's Command Problems*, 366; McLane, *Soviet Policy and the Chinese Communists*, 171–77.
53. Feis, *China Tangle*, 140. For another version see FR (1944), VI, 97.
54. Feis, *China Tangle*, 141, 150–51, 181; DS, *Relations with China*, 71–72.
55. *Yalta Papers*, 354. See also *ibid.*, 355–57, 378–79; Feis, *China Tangle*, 232–33.
56. DS, *Relations with China*, 73.
57. *Ibid.*, 92–94; *Yalta Papers*, 952–53.
58. Mao Tse-tung, *On the Tactics of Fighting Japanese Imperialism* (Peking, 1953), 17.
59. Mao Tse-tung, *An Anthology of His Writings*. Anne Freemantle, ed. (New York, 1962), 76. See also *ibid.*, 212, 137.
60. McLane, *Soviet Policy and the Chinese Communists*, 162–63.
61. Chassin, *Communist Conquest of China*, 30–39; Johnson, *Peasant Nationalism*, chaps. I and II; O.S.S., R. & A. Branch, "Political Techniques of the Chinese Communist Armed Forces." R & A 3217. July 30, 1945. (N. P., 1945), *passim;* Dougherty and Janowitz, *Psychological Warfare Casebook*, 844–50.
62. Mao Tse-tung, *On New Democracy* (Peking, 1960), 18, 20, 21, 27; *Selected*

Works (Peking, 1965), III, 15. See also Mao Tse-tung, *Problems of War and Strategy* (Peking, 1960), 19–20.

63. Mao, *Selected Works*, III, 114, 131–32. See also *ibid.*, 114–33.

64. *Ibid.*, 37. See also *ibid.*, 48.

65. McLane, *Soviet Policy and the Chinese Communists*, 163.

66. Mao, *Selected Works*, III, 117, 220, 195. See also *ibid.*, 192ff.

Chapter 11: Planning for Peace, I: General Principles

1. Holborn, *War and Peace Aims*, 192.

2. Hull, *Memoirs*, 81, 391, 518, 594, 746.

3. Richard L. Walker, *E. R. Stettinius, Jr.* (New York, 1965), 10.

4. U. S. Congress, Joint Committee on the Economic Report, *Hearings, Foreign Economic Policy*. 84:1. November, 1955. (Washington, 1955), 518; General Agreement on Tariffs and Trade [GATT], *Trends in International Trade: A Report by a Panel of Experts* (Geneva, 1958), 20–22.

5. Edward S. Mason, *Controlling World Trade: Cartels and Commodity Agreements* (New York, 1946), 26; Gabriel Kolko, "American Business and Germany, 1930–41," *Western Political Quarterly*, XV (1962), 713–28.

6. DS, *Postwar Foreign Policy*, 46.

7. Hickman, *European Recovery Program*, 66–67. See also Richard N. Gardner, *Sterling-Dollar Diplomacy: Anglo-American Collaboration in the Reconstruction of Multilateral Trade* (Oxford, 1956), 41–42.

8. Gardner, *Sterling-Dollar Diplomacy*, 45.

9. Hull, *Memoirs*, 975–76.

10. U. S. House, Special Committee on Post-War Economic Policy and Planning, *Hearings, Post-War Economic Policy and Planning*. 78:2, 79:1. (Washington, 1945), 1073.

11. Hull, *Memoirs*, 1153. See also Gardner, *Sterling-Dollar Diplomacy*, chap. IV; E. F. Penrose, *Economic Planning for the Peace* (Princeton, 1953), chap. II.

12. Holborn, *War and Peace Aims*, 277, 280. See also *ibid.*, 199, 235–39, 276, 280; Hull, *Memoirs*, 1177–78.

13. Stimson Diary, October 28, 1943, HLS Mss. See also Hull, *Memoirs*, 1303–04.

14. Stimson Diary, September 7, 1943, HLS Mss.

15. Penrose, *Economic Planning for the Peace*, 39–40; Gardner, *Sterling-Dollar Diplomacy*, 72–76; Hickman, *European Recovery Program*, 78–80; War Production Board, Bureau of Planning and Statistics, "War Production and Civilian Output After Victory in Europe." Part I, April 24, 1944 (Washington, 1944), 7, 9, 27, EAL Mss, box 11.

16. DS, *Postwar Foreign Policy*, 622. See also War Production Board, "War Production and Civilian Output," *passim*, EAL Mss; House Committee on Post-War Economic Policy, *Post-War Economic Policy*, 622.

17. Harry C. Hawkins, *The Importance of International Commerce to Prosperity*, April 2, 1944 (Washington, 1944), 4.

18. Holborn, *War and Peace Aims*, 291. See also DSB, December 10, 1944, 714; House Committee on Post-War Economic Policy, *Post-War Economic Policy*, 780; DSB, X (1944), 254–56, 275–76, 311–14, 468, 480.

19. House Committee on Post-War Economic Policy, *Post-War Economic Policy*, 1063, 1074. See also *ibid.*, 1085.

20. *Ibid.*, 1082. See also *ibid.*, 1092; Herbert Feis, *The Sinews of Peace* (New York, 1944), 118–24.
21. DSB, X (1944), 468, 255. See also Holborn, *War and Peace Aims*, 290.
22. Feis, *Sinews of Peace*, 215, 218.
23. House Committee on Post-War Economic Policy, *Post-War Economic Policy*, 861, 911–12, 929, 946–50, 985–87; Gardner, *Sterling-Dollar Diplomacy*, 76–79; Penrose, *Economic Planning for the Peace*, 45–52.
24. FR (1943), I, 1093.
25. Holborn, *War and Peace Aims*, 172. See also FR (1943), I, 1093–95; FR (1944), II, 34, 130.
26. Holborn, *War and Peace Aims*, 173.
27. U. S. Senate, Committee on Banking, *Hearings, Bretton Woods Agreements Act.* 79:1. (Washington, 1945), 6–8.
28. Feis, *Sinews of Peace*, 137–38.
29. FR (1943), I, 821, 830–31. See also *ibid.*, 824.
30. FR (1944), IV, 951. See also FR (1943), I, 835, 842–43, 929–32; Holborn, *War and Peace Aims*, 154.
31. James F. Byrnes to Roosevelt, August 30, 1944, FDR Mss, PSF 135. See also Bela Gold, *Wartime Economic Planning in Agriculture: A Study in the Allocation of Resources* (New York, 1949), 76, 427–29.
32. Feis, *Sinews of Peace*, 245–46. See also Roosevelt to Byrnes, September 1, 1944, FDR Mss, PSF 135; U. S. Commission on Foreign Economic Policy, *Staff Papers* (Washington, 1954), 168; D. Gale Johnson, *Trade and Agriculture: A Study of Inconsistent Policies* (New York, 1950), 4.
33. Hull, Memo for the President, June 2, 1944, FDR Mss, OF 5528. See also Mason, *Controlling World Trade*, 81; House Committee on Post-War Economic Policy, *Post-War Economic Policy*, 114–19, 929; FR (1944), II, 87–88; *Business Week*, February 26, 1944, 5; September 23, 1944, 15–16; DS, *Postwar Foreign Policy*, 359–60, 625.
34. DSB, X (1944), 720. See also Penrose, *Economic Planning for the Peace*, 191–92; Henry Chalmers, *World Trade Policies* (Berkeley, 1953), 324–25.
35. FR (1944), IV, 228.
36. FR (1944), III, 908, 917, 923.
37. DSB, X (1944), 690. See also FR (1944), III, 910; FR (1944), IV, 252.
38. W. L. Clayton to J. W. Fulbright, June 14, 1945, WLC Mss. See also *Business Week*, April 14, 1945, 18; Ellen Clayton Garwood, *Will Clayton: A Short Biography* (Austin, 1958), 22–24; DSB, X (1944), 690; and correspondence with Lamar Fleming in WLC Mss.
39. *Yalta Papers*, 327.
40. Holborn, *War and Peace Aims*, 249; Woodward, *British Foreign Policy*, 439–44; FR (1944), I, 627–28; FR (Teheran), 530–31; Sherwood, *Roosevelt and Hopkins*, 785–86, 792.
41. FR (1943), III, 39. See also *ibid.*, 35–39.
42. FR (Teheran), 264.
43. Churchill, *Closing the Ring*, 626. See also FR (Teheran), 242, 264–65, 323; Memos of Conversations, July 13, 24, 1944, JCG Mss.
44. FR (1944), I, 617. See also *ibid.*, 623ff.
45. Hull, *Memoirs*, 1662.
46. Ruth D. Russell, *A History of the United Nations Charter: The Role of the United States, 1940–1945* (Washington, 1958), 273–75; *Private Papers of Senator Vandenberg*, 41–45; Vandenberg to Thomas W. Lamont,

August 4, 1943; Vandenberg to Cordell Hull, May 3, 1944; Vandenberg to Wilbur Forest, May 23, 1944, AHV Mss.

47. Vandenberg Diary, May 11, 1944, AHV Mss.
48. Holborn, *War and Peace Aims*, 503. See also Tom Connally, *My Name is Tom Connally* (New York, 1954), 266; Hull, *Memoirs*, 1663–65; *Private Papers of Senator Vandenberg*, 101–05.
49. Churchill, *Closing the Ring*, 626.
50. *Yalta Papers*, 87. See also FR (Teheran), 530–31, 846.
51. FR (1944), I, 759. See also *ibid.*, 731, 737, 744, 765; Russell, *United Nations Charter*, 339; Hull, *Memoirs*, 1672–73.
52. Hull, *Memoirs*, 1679.
53. *Stalin Correspondence*, II, 159–60. See also FR (1944), I, 738, 742, 752, 765, 777.
54. Holborn, *War and Peace Aims*, 511. See also Hull, *Memoirs*, 1681, 1706; *Private Papers of Senator Vandenberg*, 120; FR (1944), I, 811–12, 819–20, 823, 836, 843.
55. FR (1944), I, 702.
56. FR (1943), I, 748. See also Hull, *Memoirs*, 1238.
57. Hull, *Memoirs*, 1599. See also Sherwood, *Roosevelt and Hopkins*, 718; FR (Teheran), 485.
58. Holborn, *War and Peace Aims*, 204.
59. Transcript of Telephone Conversation, June 13, 1944, HLS Mss.
60. *Yalta Papers*, 79, 84, 92–93. See also DS, *Postwar Foreign Policy*, 660; Hull, *Memoirs*, 1706.
61. Woodward, *British Foreign Policy*, 462. See also *Yalta Papers*, 49–56, 91.
62. *Private Papers of Senator Vandenberg*, 122. See also Woodward, *British Foreign Policy*, 460–62; *Yalta Papers*, 46.
63. *Private Papers of Senator Vandenberg*, 122–23.
64. *Yalta Papers*, 65. See also *Stalin Correspondence*, I, 173–79; DS, *Postwar Foreign Policy*, 337; *War and the Working Class*, January 15, 1945, 22–23.
65. Stimson Diary, December 31, 1944, HLS Mss.
66. *Yalta Papers*, 80.

Chapter 12: Planning for Peace, II: Great Britain in Theory and Practice

1. Hickman, *European Recovery Program*, 104–05; Penrose, *Economic Planning for the Peace*, 14–18, 66; FR (1944), II, 6, 11; Gardner, *Sterling-Dollar Diplomacy*, 24–31; Holborn, *War and Peace Aims*, 391–92, 396, 399.
2. FR (1943), III, 49. See also FR (1941), III, 20–53; John Gilbert Winant, *Letter from Grosvenor Square* (Boston, 1947), 157–60; FR (1943), I, 7–8; Stimson Diary, September 7, 8, 1943, HLS Mss.
3. FR (1943), III, 61–62. See also *ibid.*, 55, 58–59, 109.
4. *Ibid.*, 74. See also *ibid.*, 59, 65, 68–69.
5. *Ibid.*, 91. See also *ibid.*, 78, 83–84, 89.
6. FR (1944), III, 44, 46. See also *ibid.*, 35–48; FR (1943), III, 98–99, 104–05.
7. FR (1943), IV, 251, 259. See also *Business Week*, April 8, 1944, 111; O.S.S., R. &. A. Branch, "Curbs on United States Trade by the Government of India." R & A 3249. (N. P., 1944), *passim*.
8. FR (1943), III, 31, 107. See also FR (1944), V, 248–64.

9. *Business Week,* March 11, 1944, 15.
10. *The Economist,* April 15, 1944, 493.
11. Holborn, *War and Peace Aims,* 483–84.
12. FR (1944), III, 51–52. See also DSB, May 20, 1944, 468; *The Economist,* July 29, 1944, 138–39.
13. Feis, *Sinews of Peace,* 183.
14. FR (1944), III, 53–55.
15. *Ibid.,* 56.
16. *Ibid.,* 56–57.
17. *Ibid.,* 63–65. See also *ibid.,* 58–60; Stimson, *On Active Service,* 592–93.
18. FR (1944), III, 72. See also *ibid.,* 64–65.
19. *Business Week,* April 8, 1944, 111; DSB, July 23, 1944, 87.
20. Woodward, *British Foreign Policy,* 417. See also FR (1944), II, 78.
21. George S. Messersmith to Norman Armour, November 18, 1944, GSM Mss, box 3. See also Messersmith to Edward R. Stettinius, January 25, 1945, GSM Mss, box 3.
22. *Business Week,* October 28, 1944, 116.
23. FR (1944), III, 85, 78. See also *ibid.,* 77, 86; Hickman, *European Recovery Program,* 106–07.
24. Stimson Diary, November 27, 1944, HLS Mss.
25. *The Economist,* December 30, 1944, 858.
26. W. L. Clayton to James Dunn, January 11, 21, 1945; Lamar Fleming to W. L. Clayton, January 4, 1945; Lamar Fleming to William Rhea Blake, January [?], 1945, WLC Mss.
27. DSB, XIII(1945), 173.
28. FR (1943), IV, 857.
29. Hull, *Memoirs,* 1519. See also *ibid.,* 1517; Benjamin Shwadran, *The Middle East, Oil and the Great Powers* (New York, 1955), 308–09.
30. Patrick Hurley to Roosevelt, June 9, 1943, FDR Mss, PSF, box 16. See also J. P. Hurewitz, ed., *Diplomacy in the Near and Middle East: A Documentary Record: 1914–1956* (Princeton, 1956), 239–41; Shwadran, *The Middle East,* 310–31.
31. Woodward, *British Foreign Policy,* 395. See also FR (1943), IV, 887.
32. Harold B. Hoskins to Roosevelt, September 27, 1943, FDR Mss, PSF, box 16.
33. FR (1943), IV, 942.
34. Telephone Conversation of December 22, 1943, JF Mss, box 66.
35. Winston S. Churchill, *The Grand Alliance* (Boston, 1950), 485. See also Shwadran, *The Middle East,* 27–62; George Lenczowski, *Russia and the West in Iran, 1918–1948: A Study in Big-Power Rivalry* (Ithaca, 1949), 72–174, 328; N. S. Fatemi, *Oil Diplomacy: Powder Keg in Iran* (New York, 1954), chaps. VIII, XIII, XIV.
36. FR (1943), IV, 533. See also *ibid.,* 378–79; Arthur C. Millspaugh, *Americans in Persia* (Washington, 1946), 44–152, 221, 243; Hull, *Memoirs,* 1502–03; T. H. Vail Motter, *The Persian Corridor and Aid to Russia* (Washington, 1952), 433.
37. Millspaugh, *Americans in Persia,* 156.
38. FR (1943), IV, 625–26. See also *ibid.,* 625–28; Hull, *Memoirs,* 1505–07.
39. FR (1943), IV, 945. See also *ibid.,* 947; O.S.S., R. & A. Branch, "Survey of Iranian Oil Concessions." R & A 1981.1, 2. April–May 1944. (N. P., 1944), *passim.*

40. FR (1944), III, 95.
41. *Ibid.*, 96, 101–03. See also *ibid.*, 95–100.
42. *Ibid.*, 97. See also *ibid.*, 105–10.
43. FR (1944), V, 27–28, 30–31. See also DSB, June 15, 1947, 1170.
44. FR (1944), III, 111, 117–18. See also *ibid.*, 112–15.
45. *Business Week*, August 12, 1944, 112. See also DSB, August 13, 1944, 153; FR (1944), III, 119–21.
46. FR (1944), V, 9, 13.
47. *Ibid.*, 679, 690–91. See also *ibid.*, 25, 673ff.
48. Leahy, *I Was There*, 375. See also O.S.S., R. & A. Branch, "The British Treaty Position in the Arabian Peninsula." R & A 1653. February 4, 1944. (N. P., 1944) *passim;* FR (1944), V, 696–99, 712, 718–19.
49. FR (1944), V, 734–35, 664, 666–67. See also *ibid.*, 730–31.
50. *Ibid.*, 748, 751, 36, 757–58. See also Stimson to Stettinius, October 23, 1944, JF Mss, box 22.
51. FR (1944), V, 391.
52. U. S. Senate, Committee on Armed Services and Committee on Foreign Relations, *Hearings, Military Situation in the Far East.* 82:1. (Washington, 1951), IV, 2849. See also Fatemi, *Oil Diplomacy*, 229; O.S.S., "Iranian Oil Concessions," *passim;* FR (1944), V, 399, 445–52.
53. FR (1943), IV, 423. See also Senate, *Military Situation in the Far East,* 2848–49.
54. Hull, *Memoirs,* 1507.
55. FR (1944), V, 401, 414. See also *ibid.*, 406, 411–17.
56. *Ibid.*, 341, 343–44.
57. *Ibid.*, 452. See also *ibid.*, 424; Shwadran, *The Middle East*, 65–66.
58. Hull, *Memoirs,* 1509; Millspaugh, *Americans in Persia,* 233–47; FR (1944), V, 430, 461, 465, 477, 494–96; Shwadran, *The Middle East,* 65–68; Lenczowski, *Russia and the West in Iran,* 216ff.; *Yalta Papers,* 330–31.
59. FR (1944), V, 470. See also Shwadran, *The Middle East,* 66; Lenczowski, *Russia and the West in Iran,* 221; *Yalta Papers,* 334–35.
60. *Yalta Papers,* 339. See also *ibid.*, 336–37.
61. *Ibid.*, 340–45.
62. DSB, January 14, 1945, 63. See also FR (1944), III, 126–27; *Congressional Record,* 79:1, February 19, 1945, 1219–28.
63. FR (1944), V, 756.
64. *Ibid.*, 486. See also typed Memo on Premises of Postwar Navy, N. D., JF Mss, box 23; Vincent Davis, *Postwar Defense Policy and the U.S. Navy, 1943–1946* (Chapel Hill, 1966), 24, 29, 37.

Chapter 13: Planning for Peace, III: The Reintegration of Germany and Russia

1. FR (1943), III, 26. See also *ibid.*, 16; Hull, *Memoirs,* 1284–85.
2. FR (1943), III, 16.
3. *Ibid.*, 21–22; Paul Y. Hammond, "Directives for the Occupation of Germany: The Washington Controversy," in Harold Stein, ed., *American Civil-Military Decisions: A Book of Case Studies* (Montgomery, 1963), 318; DS, *Postwar Foreign Policy,* 558–60; Franklin, *World Politics,* XVI, 6–7; Hull, *Memoirs,* 1233–34, 1265–66.

4. FR (1943), I, 740. See also *ibid.*, 720–23.
5. FR (1943), III, 712. See also Hammond, "Directives for the Occupation of Germany," 321.
6. FR (1943), III, 603. See also *ibid.*, 572–74; Werth, *Russia at War*, 733–37; Daugherty and Janowitz, *Psychological Warfare Casebook*, 814–19.
7. Hammond, "Directives for the Occupation of Germany," 322–23; Churchill, *Closing the Ring*, 307–09, 319, 342–45; FR (Teheran), 513, 602–03; Sherwood, *Roosevelt and Hopkins*, 797–98.
8. See, for example, Stimson Diary, November 20, 1943, HLS Mss.
9. Philip E. Mosely, "The Occupation of Germany: New Light on How the Zones Were Drawn," *Foreign Affairs*, XXVIII (1950), 590; Mosely, *The Kremlin and World Politics* (New York, 1960), 167; Hammond, "Directives for the Occupation of Germany," 331–34; Franklin, *World Politics*, XVI, 13; FR (1944), III, 829–38; Kennan, *Memoirs*, 168.
10. FR (1944), III, 11. See also Matloff, *Strategic Planning for Coalition Warfare*, 431, 491; Memo of Conversation, June 8, 1944, HLS Mss; Walter L. Dorn, "The Debate over American Occupation Policy in Germany in 1944–1945," *Political Science Quarterly*, LXXII (1957), 481–83.
11. FR (1944), I, 279–80, 289. See also Hammond, "Directives for the Occupation of Germany," 342–44.
12. Holborn, *War and Peace Aims*, 465. See also *ibid.*, 466, 497.
13. *Morgenthau Diary*, 425. See also *ibid.*, 182, 190–92, 242; O.S.S., R. & A. Branch, "German Communist Party." R & A 1550. July 10, 1944. (N. P., 1944), *passim;* Dorn, *Political Science Quarterly*, LXXII, 485.
14. FR (1944), I, 331–32. See also *ibid.*, 299–300, 304; FR (1944), IV, 823.
15. Memo for the Secretary's Files, August 13, 1944, HDW Mss, file 22. See also Hammond, "Directives for the Occupation of Germany," 350; Woodward, *British Foreign Policy*, 469–71.
16. Penrose, *Economic Planning for the Peace*, 260–61; Stimson, Brief for Conference with the President, August 25, 1944; Memo of Conversation, August 25, 1944, HLS Mss; Hammond, "Directives for the Occupation of Germany," 355.
17. Hull, *Memoirs*, 1606; *Morgenthau Diary (Germany)*, 415–48. See also *Morgenthau Diary (Germany)*, 461–75, 485–95, 505–06, 518.
18. Memo in Stimson Diary, September 5, 1944, HLS Mss. See also *Morgenthau Diary (Germany)*, 517ff.
19. Stimson Diary, September 7, 1944, HLS Mss.
20. *Morgenthau Diary (Germany)*, 621. See also *ibid.*, 593–94, 601–02, 612–13, 619–20; Stimson Diary, September 5, 1944, HLS Mss; Stimson, *On Active Service*, 570–75; Hull, *Memoirs*, 1606–14; Woodward, *British Foreign Policy*, 472–73; Churchill, *Triumph and Tragedy*, 134; *Yalta Papers*, 135, 138.
21. Stimson Diary, September 14, 1944, HLS Mss.
22. *Morgenthau Diary*, 1234.
23. Hull, *Memoirs*, 1614; *Yalta Papers*, 130–33, 137, 143–54; Woodward, *British Foreign Policy*, 474–75; Hammond, "Directives for the Occupation of Germany," 371; FR (1944), I, 362ff; *Morgenthau Diary (Germany)*, 621–23, 627–28; FR (1945), III, 374, 396–98, 405–06.
24. *Yalta Papers*, 155. See also *Morgenthau Diary (Germany)*, 673.
25. Stimson, *On Active Service*, 580. See also *Yalta Papers*, 155–58.

26. Memo of Conversation, October 3, 1944, HLS Mss.
27. *Yalta Papers*, 158–59.
28. *Ibid.*, 166, 173. See also *ibid.*, 163–65; FR (1944), I, 371–84; *Morgenthau Diary (Germany)*, 770.
29. *Yalta Papers*, 174. See also *ibid.*, 170–72.
30. FR (1944), I, 391.
31. Manuscript in HDW Mss, file 22. See also FR (1944), I, 410ff; *Morgenthau Diary (Germany)*, 859–60, 876–77.
32. Forrestal to Robert Strausz-Hupé, November 23, 1944, JF Mss, box 24; *Yalta Papers*, 175; Hammond, "Directives for the Occupation of Germany," 405–06.
33. *Yalta Papers*, 187, 191, 195. See also *ibid.*, 176–78.
34. FR (1943), III, 710, 714. See also *ibid.*, 710–14, 722–23; Howard S. Ellis, "Bilateralism and the Future of International Trade," *Essays in International Finance*, No. 5, 1945, 15–16; FR (1944), II, 51–55.
35. FR (1943), I, 614–15.
36. Notes for Talk with President, August 24, 1944, HLS Mss.
37. FR (1943), I, 1111.
38. FR (1943), III, 789. See also *ibid.*, 782–83, 786–89; FR (1943), I, 635, 665–66, 739, 1098, 1016; FR (1944), II, 38.
39. FR (1943), I, 1122–23. See also *ibid.*, 1119–25.
40. FR (1944), IV, 1034, 1037, 1054–55. See also *ibid.*, 1041; Lauchlin Currie to Harry Hopkins, December 31, 1943, HLH Mss, box 2.
41. FR (1944), IV, 951, 967. See also *ibid.*, 958–60; *Stalin Correspondence*, II, 124–25.
42. Feis, *Sinews of Peace*, 31. See also FR (1944), IV, 958, 973–74, 1117–39; *The Economist*, August 26, 1944, 276.
43. FR (1944), I, 401. See also Penrose, *Economic Planning for the Peace*, 163.
44. *Yalta Papers*, 313, 323–24. See also *ibid.*, 309–11, 316–17; White Memo to Morgenthau, March 7, 1944, HDW Mss, file 23; White's Speech of October 18, 1945, HDW Mss, file 27; U. S. Senate, Committee on Banking and Currency, *Hearings, Bretton Woods Agreement Act.* 79:1. June, 1945. (Washington, 1945), 7–8; Memo of Conversation, January 24, 1945, JCG Mss; *Morgenthau Diary (Germany)*, 867–68, 881, 887–90, 907–09; FR (1945), V, 939–40, 966.

*Chapter 14: The Yalta Conference: The Effort to Forge
a Political Alliance*

1. Stimson, *On Active Service*, 563–64.
2. Moran, *Churchill*, 150.
3. Butcher, *My Three Years*, 518.
4. *Stalin Correspondence*, I, 288, 294–95. See also *ibid.*, I, 293, II, 184–85; Hickman, *European Recovery Program*, 166.
5. Eden, *The Reckoning*, 604. See also *Yalta Papers*, 582–83.
6. *Yalta Papers*, 478–80, 829. See also *ibid.*, 486.
7. *Ibid.*, 579. See also *ibid.*, 578.
8. *Ibid.*, 118, 498–99, 503–04, 609–10, 620–23, 702–04, 707.
9. *Ibid.*, 656. See also *ibid.*, 611–16.
10. *Ibid.*, 874–75. See also Sherwood, *Roosevelt and Hopkins*, 862.

11. *Yalta Papers*, 921. See also *ibid.*, 808–09, 822, 874–75, 901–03, 978–79.
12. *Ibid.*, 616–19, 710, 899–900, 937; Sherwood, *Roosevelt and Hopkins*, 862.
13. Byrnes, *Speaking Frankly*, 30. See also *Yalta Papers*, 499–500, 505–11; Churchill, *Triumph and Tragedy*, 313.
14. Churchill, *Triumph and Tragedy*, 319–20. See also *Stalin Correspondence*, II, 187–89; *Yalta Papers*, 711, 716.
15. *Yalta Papers*, 717. See also Churchill, *Triumph and Tragedy*, 320.
16. *Yalta Papers*, 778–81, 867. See also *ibid.*, 792–93, 803–07, 842–43.
17. *Ibid.*, 898–99, 905, 938.
18. *Ibid.*, 782. See also *ibid.*, 752–53, 849.
19. *Ibid.*, 781–82. See also *ibid.*, 821.
20. Eden, *The Reckoning*, 605.
21. *Yalta Papers*, 845.
22. *Ibid.*, 860. See also *ibid.*, 846, 849.
23. *Ibid.*, 848.
24. *Ibid.*, 873.
25. *Ibid.*, 662. See also *ibid.*, 589–90; Walter Johnson, "Edward R. Stettinius," in *An Uncertain Tradition: American Secretaries of State in the Twentieth Century*. Norman A. Graebner, ed. (New York, 1961), 216.
26. *Yalta Papers*, 666. See also *ibid.*, 663.
27. *Ibid.*, 711–14, 772–76, 857; Sherwood, *Roosevelt and Hopkins*, 856–57; Byrnes, *Speaking Frankly*, 40–41; *Stalin Correspondence*, II, 191–92.
28. *Yalta Papers*, 844. See also *ibid.*, 770; Byrnes, *Speaking Frankly*, x.
29. Leahy, *I Was There*, 318. See also *Yalta Papers*, 502, 950.
30. *Yalta Papers*, 771.
31. *Ibid.*, 835. See also *ibid.*, 768–71, 841.
32. *Ibid.*, 896. See also *ibid.*, 894–95.
33. *Ibid.*, 894–97, 984; Feis, *China Tangle*, 247; Byrnes, *Speaking Frankly*, 42–43.
34. Leahy, *I Was There*, 318. See also Eden, *The Reckoning*, 594.
35. *Yalta Papers*, 328, 903.
36. *Ibid.*, 500–01, 738–40, 819–20, 845, 982.
37. Churchill, *Triumph and Tragedy*, 310–11.
38. *Yalta Papers*, 798.
39. Sherwood, *Roosevelt and Hopkins*, 870.
40. *War and the Working Class*, February 15, 1945, 5.
41. *Yalta Papers*, 924.
42. Sherwood, *Roosevelt and Hopkins*, 871.
43. William A. Eddy, *F. D. R. Meets Ibn Saud* (New York, 1945), 14–15; Leahy, *I Was There*, 325–26; Churchill, *Triumph and Tragedy*, 341–42. Only Byrnes, in *Speaking Frankly*, 22, suggests Churchill knew of the meeting with Saud before February 10.

Chapter 15: Germany and the End of Illusion

1. Warlimont, *Inside Hitler's Headquarters*, 487–88.
2. William L. Shirer, *The Rise and Fall of the Third Reich: A History of Nazi Germany* (New York, 1962), 1425. See also Warlimont, *Inside Hitler's Headquarters*, 487–91.
3. Field-Marshal the Viscount Montgomery, *Memoirs* (Cleveland, 1958), 297. See also *Yalta Papers*, 479–80, 578, 583; Hickman, *European Recovery*

Program, 172; Ehrman, *Grand Strategy . . . 1944–1945*, Map 3, 162; Werth, *Russia at War*, 959–60; Hans-Georg Von Studnitz, *While Berlin Burns, 1943–1945* (Englewood Cliffs, N. J., 1964), 152, 167, 239–46.

4. Warlimont, *Inside Hitler's Headquarters*, 497.

5. DS, *The Axis in Defeat: A Collection of Documents on American Policy Toward Germany and Japan* (Washington, N. D.), 9.

6. Montgomery, *Memoirs*, 296.

7. Eisenhower to Mel Laird, September 12, 1961, DDE Mss, Post-Presidential file. See also FR (1945), III, 229.

8. Churchill, *Triumph and Tragedy*, 399. See also *ibid.*, 392; Montgomery. *Memoirs*, 297.

9. Churchill, *Triumph and Tragedy*, 400.

10. Pogue, *Supreme Command*, 439.

11. *Ibid.*, 472–73; Werth, *Russia at War*, 996; Deborin, *Second. World War*. 442.

12. Allen Dulles, *The Secret Surrender* (New York, 1966), 51. See also *ibid.*, 48–51.

13. *Ibid.*, 147. See also *ibid.*, 236; John Toland, *The Last 100 Days* (New York, 1966), 240; Churchill, *Triumph and Tragedy*, 379; Allen Dulles in National Foreign Trade Convention, *Report of the Thirty-Third National Trade Convention*. New York, November 11–13, 1946 (New York, 1947), 47.

14. Churchill, *Triumph and Tragedy*, 379. See also Delzell, *Mussolini's Enemies*, 497, 501; Macmillan, *Blast of War*, 670–88.

15. Stimson Diary, March 17, 1945, HLS Mss. See also *ibid,*, March 13, 1945; *Stalin Correspondence*, I, 397–98; Churchill, *Triumph and Tragedy*, 379–80; Byrnes, *Speaking Frankly*, 56–57; Feis, *Churchill-Roosevelt-Stalin*, 584–85.

16. *Stalin Correspondence*, I, 398.

17. Churchill, *Triumph and Tragedy*, 380.

18. *Stalin Correspondence*, II, 199, 204, 206–08. See also FR (1945), III, 726–53.

19. *Stalin Correspondence*, II, 214; Churchill, *Triumph and Tragedy*, 389.

20. *Forrestal Diaries*, 38–40.

21. Harriman to Stettinius, April 6, 11, 1945, JF Mss, box 24; Feis, *Churchill-Roosevelt-Stalin*, 597; *Forrestal Diaries*, 40–41.

22. *Forrestal Diaries*, 43.

23. Harry S. Truman, *Year of Decisions* (Garden City, N. Y., 1955), 12. Hereafter *Memoirs*. See also Churchill, *Triumph and Tragedy*, 410–11.

24. Churchill, *Triumph and Tragedy*, 414.

25. Truman, *Memoirs*, 15. See also *ibid.*, 18; Stimson Diary, April 12, 1945, HLS Mss; George Curry, *James F. Byrnes* (New York, 1965), 107, 343.

26. *New York Times*, June 24, 1941.

27. Leahy, *I Was There*, 351.

28. Truman, *Memoirs*, 82.

29. Churchill, *Triumph and Tragedy*, 440. See also *ibid.*, 437–41; Warlimont, *Inside Hitler's Headquarters*, 513; *New York Times*, January 12, 1966.

30. Pogue, *Supreme Command*, 468. See also Churchill, *Triumph and Tragedy*, 442–44; *Stalin Correspondence*, II, 224.

31. Churchill, *Triumph and Tragedy*, 433. See also Pogue, *Supreme Command*, 469.

32. Pogue, *Supreme Command*, 469. See also FR (1945), IV, 447–51.
33. Admiral Karl Doenitz, *Memoirs: Ten Years and Twenty Days* (Cleveland, 1959), 437, 450.
34. "Instrument of Local Surrender of German and Other Forces Under the Command or Control of the German Commander-in-Chief Southwest," Appendix A, in Modern Military Records Division, National Archives, Alexandria, Va. See also Dulles, *Secret Surrender*, 187; Churchill, *Triumph and Tragedy*, 450–53, 457–60; Truman, *Memoirs*, 88–93; Macmillan, *Blast of War*, 710–12; FR (1945), III, 760–65. Dulles' account excludes these critical details.
35. Montgomery, *Memoirs*, 300. See also FR (1945), V, 80–84; Doenitz, *Memoirs*, 453–57; Pogue, *Supreme Command*, 477; Memo of Conversation, April 27, 1945, JCG Mss.
36. Montgomery, *Memoirs*, 302.
37. Doenitz, *Memoirs*, 460.
38. Macmillan, *Blast of War*, 713.
39. Eisenhower, *Crusade in Europe*, 426. See also *ibid.*, 425; Pogue, *Supreme Command*, 481–82; John R. Deane, *The Strange Alliance: The Story of our Efforts at Wartime Co-operation with Russia* (New York, 1947), 166–67; Doenitz, *Memoirs*, 460–62; Butcher, *My Three Years*, 827; FR (1945), III, 777–78.
40. Doenitz, *Memoirs*, 464. See also *ibid.*, 463; Eisenhower, *Crusade in Europe*, 426; Butcher, *My Three Years*, 831–34; Pogue, *Supreme Command*, 486–87.
41. Murphy, *Diplomat Among Warriors*, 241. See also FR (1945), III, 283–97.
42. Truman, *Memoirs*, 205.
43. Deane, *Strange Alliance*, 168. See also Marlis G. Steinert, *Die 23 Tage der Regierung Dönitz* (Düsseldorf, 1967), 165–215.
44. *Ibid.*, 168–69; Pogue, *Supreme Command*, 490–91; Butcher, *My Three Years*, 824, 835; *Stalin Correspondence*, I, 348–52; Truman, *Memoirs*, 206.

Chapter 16: Poland and Eastern Europe, 1945: Realities versus Objectives

1. *Yalta Papers*, 867. See also *ibid.*, 806.
2. Churchill, *Triumph and Tragedy*, 364. See also FR (1945), V, 128ff.; Byrnes, *Speaking Frankly*, 53–54; Woodward, *British Foreign Policy*, 502–03; *Yalta Papers*, 99.
3. Woodward, *British Foreign Policy*, 504.
4. Churchill, *Triumph and Tragedy*, 366. See also *War and the Working Class*, March 15, 1945, 1–4.
5. O.S.S., "Post-War Poland," 18. See also Rozek, *Allied Wartime Diplomacy*, 364; Toynbee, *Realignment of Europe*, 233; FR (1945), V, 216.
6. Soviet News, *Soviet-Polish Relations*, 29. See also Dziewanowski, *Communist Party of Poland*, 192; Toynbee, *Realignment of Europe*, 233.
7. Stimson Diary, April 2, 1945, HLS Mss. See also Dziewanowski, *Communist Party of Poland*, 188–99; Mikolajczyk, *Rape of Poland*, 292.
8. Churchill, *Triumph and Tragedy*, 372.
9. *Ibid.*, 374; *Stalin Correspondence*, II, 202–04.
10. *Stalin Correspondence*, II, 211–13. See also FR (1945), V, 213.
11. Churchill, *Triumph and Tragedy*, 377. See also Woodward, *British Foreign Policy*, 508; *Stalin Correspondence*, I, 313.

12. Truman, *Memoirs*, 37; *Stalin Correspondence*, II, 216. See also Sharp, *Poland*, 193–95; Churchill, *Triumph and Tragedy*, 417–19; Rozek, *Allied Wartime Diplomacy*, 368–70; FR (1945), V, 222.

13. *Forrestal Diaries*, 47.

14. FR (1945), V, 232. See also *ibid.*, 231–33; Truman, *Memoirs*, 71–72.

15. FR (1945), V, 253. See also *ibid.*, 233, 252–55; *Forrestal Diaries*, 48; Truman, *Memoirs*, 76.

16. Stimson Diary, April 23, 1945, HLS Mss. See also Stimson, *On Active Service*, 608–09; FR (1945), V, 254.

17. Woodward, *British Foreign Policy*, 509; FR (1945), V, 253. See also Leahy, *I Was There*, 351–52; Truman, *Memoirs*, 77–79; *Forrestal Diaries*, 49–51.

18. *Stalin Correspondence*, II, 218–19; I, 330–32, 340, 343–44. See also Truman, *Memoirs*, 82; FR (1945), V, 256–58; Byrnes, *Speaking Frankly*, 61; Leahy, *I Was There*, 351; FR (1945), I, 384.

19. *Stalin Correspondence*, I, 348. See also Soviet News, *Soviet-Polish Relations*, 16–24; Dziewanowski, *Communist Party of Poland*, 194; Toynbee, *Realignment of Europe*, 224–25; Werth, *Russia at War*, 1009–14; Soviet News, *Moscow Trial, passim*.

20. Memo of Conversation, May 12, 1945, JCG Mss. See also Woodward, *British Foreign Policy*, 511; FR (1945), V, 844–45, 998–1003; Memos of Conversation, May 14, 15, 1945, JCG Mss.

21. Stimson Diary, May 14, 1945, HLS Mss. See also Memos of Conversations, May 12, 1945, JCG Mss; Truman, *Memoirs*, 228; FR (1945), V, 1026–30; Herbert Feis, *Between War and Peace: The Potsdam Conference* (Princeton, 1960), 28, 329–30.

22. Sherwood, *Roosevelt and Hopkins*, 889–90. See also Memo of Conversation, May 15, 1945, JCG Mss.

23. Sherwood, *Roosevelt and Hopkins*, 899–901, 906–10; Woodward, *British Foreign Policy*, 512–13.

24. Sherwood, *Roosevelt and Hopkins*, 894, 896.

25. *Potsdam Papers*, I, 61–62.

26. Toynbee, *Realignment of Europe*, 225, 233–35; Rozek, *Allied Wartime Diplomacy*, 388–98.

27. *Potsdam Papers*, I, 715, 786, 789. See also *ibid.*, 226, 717–19, 726–27; Churchill, *Triumph and Tragedy*, 498; Woodward, *British Foreign Policy*, 514; O.S.S., R. & A. Branch, "The Polish Provisional Government of National Unity." R & A 3180. July 17, 1945. (N. P., 1945), *passim;* FR (1945), V, 279–80, 346–55; Arthur Bliss Lane, *I Saw Poland Betrayed* (Indianapolis, 1948), 28ff.; Arthur Bliss Lane, Memo of June 1, 1945, in ABL Mss, box 166.

28. *Potsdam Papers*, I, 744–46, 750–54.

29. O.S.S., R. & A. Branch, "Progress of Epuration Under the Groza Government of Rumania." R & A 2957.1. May 29, 1945. (N. P., 1945), 14.

30. Hugh Seton-Watson, *The East European Revolution* (New York, 1956), 202–06; Byrnes, *Speaking Frankly*, 51–52; Roberts, *Rumania*, 262ff., Toynbee, *Realignment of Europe*, 289–91; *War and the Working Class*, February 15, 1945, 10–14.

31. *War and the Working Class*, March 1, 1945, 6. See also *ibid.*, March 15, 1945, 12–15; Roberts, *Rumania*, 264–71.

32. FR (1945), V, 478. See also Seton-Watson, *East European Revolution*, 206.

33. Memo of Conversation, March 2, 1945, JCG Mss. See also FR (1945), V, 478–517; *Potsdam Papers*, I, 371–73; O.S.S., "Politics in Rumania," *passim*.

34. FR (1945), V, 517. See also *ibid.*, 511ff.; Churchill, *Triumph and Tragedy*, 361–62; Roberts, *Rumania*, 268; Byrnes, *Speaking Frankly*, 50-52.

35. *Potsdam Papers*, I, 369.

36. Michael Karolyi, *Memoirs* (London, 1946), 309.

37. Seton-Watson, *East European Revolution*, 191.

38. *Potsdam Papers*, I, 367.

39. Seton-Watson, *East European Revolution*, 193; Karolyi, *Memoirs*, 309–24; Mark Ethridge and C. E. Black, "Negotiating on the Balkans, 1945–1947," in *Negotiating with the Russians*. Raymond Dennett and Joseph E. Johnson, eds. (Boston, 1951), 201.

40. *Potsdam Papers*, I, 362–66, 382, 401–03; FR (1945), IV, 162–254.

41. *War and the Working Class*, April 15, 1945, 14.

42. *Potsdam Papers*, I, 201, 317. See also *ibid.*, 169, 227, 399–400; Memo of Conversation, May 2, 1945, JCG Mss; Joseph C. Grew, *Turbulent Era: A Diplomatic Record of Forty Years, 1940–1945* (Boston, 1952), 1454–55; FR (1945), IV, 202–03.

43. *Potsdam Papers*, I, 320, 409, 417.

44. Holborn, *War and Peace Aims*, 1039ff. See also Eduard Taborsky, *Communism in Czechoslovakia, 1948–1960* (Princeton, 1961), 98–100; Hubert Ripka, *Czechoslovakia Enslaved: The Story of the Communist Coup d'Etat* (London, 1950), 26; FR (1945), IV, 427–31.

45. Korbel, *Subversion of Czechoslovakia*, 119; Eden, *The Reckoning*, 615. See also Taborsky, "Beneš and Stalin," 176.

46. Pogue, *Supreme Command*, 507. See also *ibid.*, 504–06; R. H. Bruce Lockhart, *Jan Masaryk, A Personal Memoir* (London, 1956), 42ff.; Victor L. Tapié, "L'Insurrection de Prague," *Revue d'Histoire de la Deuxième Guerre Mondiale*, XII (1962), 49–53; *Recherches Internationales*, No. 44–45, 394–411; Kennan, *Memoirs*, 254–55; FR (1945), IV, 30, 440–44, 450.

47. *Potsdam Papers*, I, 172.

48. Taborsky, "Beneš and Stalin," 179.

49. Laurence A. Steinhardt to Walton C. Ferris, August 7, 1945, LAS Mss, box 83. See also FR (1945), IV, 456–509.

50. *Potsdam Papers*, I, 172; Holborn, *War and Peace Aims*, 1044–45, 1086.

51. *Yalta Papers*, 888–89, 964; FR (1945), IV, 1109–18; FR (1945), V, 1201; Truman, *Memoirs*, 246; Harris, *Allied Military Administration*, 329–33; *Stalin Correspondence*, II, 235; Churchill, *Triumph and Tragedy*, 473; Memo of Conversation, May 15, 1945, JCG Mss; Yugoslav Embassy Information Office, *Trieste and the Julian March* (London, 1946), *passim;* Macmillan, *Blast of War*, 691–93.

52. Eden, *The Reckoning*, 605. See also Dedijer, *Tito*, 236; FR (1945), V, 1220–24.

53. Churchill, *Triumph and Tragedy*, 472. See also *ibid.*, 471; Truman, *Memoirs*, 243–45; FR (1945), IV, 1120–24.

54. Truman, *Memoirs*, 244. See also Stimson Diary, April 27–29, 1945, HLS Mss; Macmillan, *Blast of War*, 693–94.

55. Memo of Conversation, April 30, 1945, JCG Mss. See also Truman, *Memoirs*, 244–45; Stimson Diary, April 30–May 12, 1945, HLS Mss.

56. Churchill, *Triumph and Tragedy*, 473. See also Truman, *Memoirs*, 245.

57. Stimson Diary, May 7, 1945, HLS Mss. See also Memos of Conversations, May 2, 3, 7, 1945, JCG Mss; FR (1945), IV, 1139ff.
58. Churchill, *Triumph and Tragedy*, 473–74.
59. Grew, *Turbulent Era*, 1479. See also FR (1945), IV, 1151–55.
60. FR (1945), IV, 1154.
61. Stimson Diary, May 12, 1945, HLS Mss.
62. Churchill, *Triumph and Tragedy*, 474; Truman, *Memoirs*, 247.
63. Grew, *Turbulent Era*, 1481.
64. Stimson Diary, May 16, 1945, HLS Mss. See also Memo of Conversation, May 15, 1945, JCG Mss; Truman, *Memoirs*, 249; Harris, *Allied Military Administration*, 340; FR (1945), IV, 1157–60.
65. Truman, *Memoirs*, 252. See also *ibid.*, 248–49; Memo of Conversation, May 16, 1945, JCG Mss; *Stalin Correspondence*, II, 235ff., 299–300; Churchill, *Triumph and Tragedy*, 476–77; Harris, *Allied Military Administration*, 342; FR (1945), IV, 1167–78.
66. *Potsdam Papers*, I, 851. See also *Stalin Correspondence*, II, 245, 249; Memo of Conversation, May 30, 1945, JCG Mss.
67. *Potsdam Papers*, I, 827, 840. See also *ibid.*, 365, 667–68.
68. Churchill, *Triumph and Tragedy*, 430. See also Truman, *Memoirs*, 255; *Potsdam Papers*, I, 3.
69. Truman, *Memoirs*, 256. See also *ibid.*, 255; Grew, *Turbulent Era*, 1462.
70. Memo of Conference with the President, June 6, 1945, HLS Mss; *Potsdam Papers*, I, 4–13, 53–54; P. M. S. Blackett, *Fear, War, and the Bomb* (New York, 1949), chap. X; Gar Alperovitz, *Atomic Diplomacy: Hiroshima and Potsdam: The Use of the Atomic Bomb and the American Confrontation with Soviet Power* (New York, 1965), *passim*.
71. Truman, *Memoirs*, 102.
72. Woodward, *British Foreign Policy*, 517.
73. *Potsdam Papers*, I, 395, 426. See also *ibid.*, 425–32, 947; Woodward, *British Foreign Policy*, 517–18.
74. *Potsdam Papers*, I, 791, 189; II, 1386.
75. Truman, *Memoirs*, 236; *Potsdam Papers*, I, 330–31.
76. *Potsdam Papers*, I, 422–23.

Chapter 17: The European Left, 1945: The Politics of Revolutionaries

1. *Yalta Papers*, 960–61.
2. Great Britain, Parliament, *Report of the British Legal Mission to Greece, January 17, 1946.* Cmd. 6838 (London, 1946), 10–24; Toynbee, *Realignment of Europe*, 399–401; Great Britain, Foreign Office, *Report of the British Parliamentary Delegation to Greece, August, 1946* (London, 1947), 4–6; Sweet-Escott, *Greece*, 45–47; Woodhouse, *Apple of Discord*, 241–43; Leeper, *When Greek Meets Greek*, 157–66.
3. Woodbridge, *UNRRA*, II, 105. See also Gardner Patterson, "The Financial Experiences of Greece from Liberation to Truman Doctrine (October 1944–March 1947)" (Unpublished Ph.D. Thesis, Harvard, 1948), *passim*; Sweet-Escott, *Greece*, 43–47; Leeper, *When Greek Meets Greek*, 156, 180, 206–07.
4. Foreign Office, *Report of the British Parliamentary Delegation*, 4. See also Toynbee, *Realignment of Europe*, 401n.
5. Xydis, *Greece and the Great Powers*, 93–94; Kédros, *Résistance Grecque*,

518; Woodhouse, *Apple of Discord*, 243; Toynbee, *Realignment of Europe*, 401; Kousoulas, *Revolution and Defeat*, 222–27; *Potsdam Papers*, I, 653–59; Stavrianos, *Greece*, 163–71; *Stalin Correspondence*, II, 220; Dedijer, *Tito*, 293.

6. Xydis, *Greece and the Great Powers*, 96. See also Memo of Conversation, January 3, 1945, JCG Mss.

7. *Potsdam Papers*, I, 675. See also Memo of Conversation, July 9, 1945, JCG Mss.

8. *Potsdam Papers*, I, 668. See also *ibid.*, 667, 678–79; Toynbee, *Realignment of Europe*, 401; Kofos, *Nationalism and Communism*, 146–49; Xydis, *Greece and the Great Powers*, 95–96.

9. Kofos, *Nationalism and Communism*, 151–52; Kousoulas, *Revolution and Defeat*, 237.

10. Leeper, *When Greek Meets Greek*, 156.

11. Foreign Office, *Report of the British Parliamentary Delegation*, 13. See also *ibid.*, 9, 14.

12. Memo of Conversation, May 26, 1945, JCG Mss.

13. *Potsdam Papers*, I, 651–52.

14 Battaglia, *Italian Resistance*, 260–61. See also Coles and Weinberg, *Civil Affairs*, 526–28, 544–45; Delzell, *Mussolini's Enemies*, 479–80, 497; Macmillan, *Blast of War*, 670–88.

15. Coles and Weinberg, *Civil Affairs*, 564. See also Harris, *Allied Military Administration*, chap. XI; O.S.S., R. & A. Branch, "Political Results of the Liberation of North Italy." R & A 3099s. May 11, 1945. (N. P., 1945), *passim*.

16. Coles and Weinberg, *Civil Affairs*, 566. See also *ibid.*, 565; Delzell, *Mussolini's Enemies*, 547–51.

17. Coles and Weinberg, *Civil Affairs*, 548. See also *Potsdam Papers*, I, 688–89.

18. O.S.S., "Liberation of North Italy," 2.

19. FR (1944), III, 1149.

20. Kogan, *Italy and the Allies*, 122. See also *Recherches Internationales*, No. 44–45, 205–07; Harris, *Allied Military Administration*, 351–52.

21. Maurice Thorez, *Oeuvres* (Paris, 1963), XXI, 100. See also *Forrestal Diaries*, 77; Thorez, *Oeuvres*, XX, 202–23.

22. Thorez, *Oeuvres*, XX, 101, 177–78, 201–02; Fauvet, *Histoire du Parti Communiste Français*, 156–67.

23. Jacques Duclos, "A Propos de la Dissolution du Parti Communiste Américain," *Cahiers du Communisme* (April, 1945), 36–38.

24. Jacques Duclos, *Batailles Pour la République* (Paris, 1947), 36–38, 69–71; Duclos, "A Propos de la Dissolution," 37; *Potsdam Papers*, I, 227; Thorez, *Oeuvres*, XX, 79, 95–96, 187–88; Thorez, *Oeuvres*, XXI, 67, 103–05, 118, 123–27, 130–32, 138; Elgey, *La République des Illusions*, 28–30.

25. Elgey, *La République des Illusions*, 29.

26. Thorez, *Oeuvres*, XX, 167–71; Planchais, *Histoire Politique de L'Armée*, 82–120.

27. Elgey, *La République des Illusions*, 32. See also *ibid.*, 33–35; Duclos, "A Propos de la Dissolution," 37; Duclos, *Batailles Pour La République*, 36–38, 70–71.

28. Thorez, *Oeuvres*, XXI, 137, 160, 167. See also *ibid.*, 69–82, 159; Eugenio Reale, *Avec Jacques Duclos* (Paris, 1958), 76–81, 143–50, 176–77.

29. *Forrestal Diaries,* 39, 57.
30. Truman, *Memoirs,* 235–36.
31. *Potsdam Papers,* I, 628.
32. "Reflections of the Basic Problems which Confront Us," July 19, 1945, HLS Mss. See also Stimson, *On Active Service,* 606–07.
33. *Forrestal Diaries,* 79.
34. *Potsdam Papers,* I, 267–68, 270, 272, 278–80. See also FR (1945), V, 872–73.
35. *Yalta Papers,* 282.
36. *Potsdam Papers,* I, 689.
37. *Ibid.,* 628n, 704–05. See also *ibid.,* 691.
38. Coles and Weinberg, *Civil Affairs,* 625. See also Harris, *Allied Military Administration,* 236–57, 351–52; Kogan, *Italy and the Allies,* 113, 121–26; FR (1945), IV, 1020.

Chapter 18: The United Nations and American Global Interests

1. Hull, *Memoirs,* 1644–45. See also *Yalta Papers,* 952–55; Russell, *United Nations Charter,* 399.
2. George S. Messersmith to Norman Armour, November 18, 1944, GSM Mss, box 3.
3. Messersmith to Stettinius, January 25, 1945, GSM Mss, box 3.
4. Messersmith to Roosevelt, March 12, 1945, GSM Mss, box 3.
5. Russell, *United Nations Charter,* 556.
6. Holborn, *War and Peace Aims,* 1122. See also *ibid.,* 1128–29; Messersmith Memoirs, Vol. III, GSM Mss, box 8.
7. Hull, *Memoirs,* 1467. See also Holborn, *War and Peace Aims,* 1124–25.
8. Messersmith to Roosevelt, March 12, 1945, GSM Mss, box 3. See also Woodward, *British Foreign Policy,* 529.
9. *Private Papers of Senator Vandenberg,* 132–35.
10. *Ibid.,* 151–53, 157–58, 164–65. See also Memo of Conversation, March 23, 1945, JCG Mss.
11. Vandenberg to Frank M. Sparks, April 17, 1945, AHV Mss.
12. Churchill, *Triumph and Tragedy,* 640. See also *ibid.,* 520.
13. *War and the Working Class,* March 1, 1945, 21–22.
14. *Stalin Correspondence,* II, 197. See also *Yalta Papers,* 990–91.
15. *Forrestal Diaries,* 50. See also Memos of Conversations, March 23, 29, 1945, JCG Mss; *Stalin Correspondence,* II, 199; Truman, *Memoirs,* 26.
16. Holborn, *War and Peace Aims,* 204.
17. Telephone Conversation of June 13, 1944, HLS Mss.
18. Woodward, *British Foreign Policy,* 531n. See also *ibid.,* 530; DS, *Postwar Foreign Policy,* 660–62.
19. *Forrestal Diaries,* 37–38. See also Woodward, *British Foreign Policy,* 530–32; Stimson Diary, January 22, March 29, 30, 1945, HLS Mss; Stimson, *On Active Service,* 600–02.
20. *Forrestal Diaries,* 45. See also *Private Papers of Senator Vandenberg,* 169; FR (1945), I, 199.
21. Truman, *Memoirs,* 60. See also "Memorandum of Conference with the President, April 18, 1945," HLS Mss; FR (1945), I, 93, 122–23, 140–41, 198–99, 205, 210–14, 312–21, 350–51.
22. *Private Papers of Senator Vandenberg,* 175–76.

23. Connally, *My Name is Tom*, 280. See also *Private Papers of Senator Vandenberg*, 77.

24. *Private Papers of Senator Vandenberg*, 184–85. See also *ibid.*, 178–82; Soviet News, *Soviet Union at the San Francisco Conference* (London, 1945), 13–16; Truman, *Memoirs*, 281–82.

25. Stimson Diary, April 27–29, 1945, HLS Mss. See also FR (1945), I, 592–96, 632–39, 643–49.

26. "Telephone Conversation between the Secretary of War and Mr. McCloy in San Francisco, May 8, 1945," HLS Mss. See also *Private Papers of Senator Vandenberg*, 187–89; FR (1945), I, 643–44.

27. *Private Papers of Senator Vandenberg*, 192–93, 198. See also Stimson Diary, May 10, 1945, HLS Mss; Russell, *United Nations Charter*, 698–99; *Private Papers of Senator Vandenberg*, 192; FR (1945), I, 657–68, 672–77, 692–709, 723–25.

28. Connally, *My Name is Tom*, 279.

29. Norman Armour to Vandenberg, August 4, 1947, AHV Mss.

30. Soviet News, *San Francisco Conference*, 25. See also Memo of Conversation, May 9, 1945, JCG Mss.

31. *Yalta Papers*, 685.

32. *Private Papers of Senator Vandenberg*, 200ff. See also *Yalta Papers*, 661–63, 682–86; Byrnes, *Speaking Frankly*, 64; FR (1945), I, 1135.

33. FR (1945), I, 1136, 1089. See also Memo of Conversation, June 2, 1945, JCG Mss.

34. *Private Papers of Senator Vandenberg*, 208. See also *ibid.*, 204–06; Sherwood, *Roosevelt and Hopkins*, 910–12; FR (1945), I, 1190–1200.

35. Deborin, *Second World War*, 472.

36. Memo of Conversation, May 12, 1945, JCG Mss; FR (1945), I, 652.

37. FR (1945), I, 795–96. See also *ibid.*, 792ff.

38. Lloyd C. Gardner, *Economic Aspects of New Deal Diplomacy* (Madison, 1964), 193. See also Woodward, *British Foreign Policy*, 535.

39. FR (1944), I, 746. See also *ibid.*, 731; Woodward, *British Foreign Policy*, 534–35; Gardner, *New Deal Diplomacy*, 193; Truman, *Memoirs*, 288; *Private Papers of Senator Vandenberg*, 21–24.

40. Hull, *Memoirs*, 1681–82; Russell, *United Nations Charter*, 618–20.

41. *Private Papers of Senator Vandenberg*, 216.

42. Soviet News, *San Francisco Conference*, 3–4.

43. *Forrestal Diaries*, 15, 46; Stimson Diary, June 19, 26–30, 1945, HLS Mss; Major John C. Sparrow, *History of Personnel Demobilization in the United States Army* (Washington, 1951), *passim*; Michael D. Reagan, "Demobilization and Postwar Military Planning, 1943–1946," Unpublished manuscript, June, 1956; Davis, *Postwar Defense Policy, passim;* DSB, XII (1945), 1063; Stimson, *On Active Service*, 596–98. During the following September, Washington further articulated the political assumption behind a powerful American military establishment in the concept of the United States, rather than the still tottering United Nations, preserving world peace via its own power until the world organization might become a "living reality." See *Forrestal Diaries*, 97.

44. *Potsdam Papers*, I, 262, 264. See also *ibid.*, 199, 283–93; *Morgenthau Diary (Germany)*, 1441–42.

Chapter 19: The Economics of Victory

1. DSB, XII (1945), 470. See also Chalmers, *World Trade Policies,* 328–31.
2. Memo of Conversation, March 10, 1945, JCG Mss.
3. DSB, XII (1945), 982.
4. Clayton to J. W. Fulbright, June 14, 1945, WLC Mss.
5. Jack N. Behrman, "Political Factors in U. S. International Financial Co-operation, 1945–1950," *American Political Science Review,* XLVII (1953), 435. See also DSB, XII, 409–10, 459–75, 501–03, 593–99, 624–28, 933–38, 979–82, 1024–27; Senate, *Bretton Woods Agreement,* 7–8.
6. DS, *Postwar Foreign Policy,* 628.
7. U. S. Department of Agriculture, *A Post-War Foreign Trade Program for United States Agriculture* (Washington, 1945), 10. See also *ibid.,* 4–5; FR (1945), II, 1328–33; Calvin B. Hoover, *International Trade and Domestic Employment* (New York, 1945), ix; Raymond F. Mikesell, *United States Economic Policy and International Relations* (New York, 1962), 209; DSB, XII, 1024–27.
8. DSB, XII, 639; Department of Agriculture, *Post-War Foreign Trade Program, passim.*
9. DSB, XII, 503. See also *Yalta Papers,* 962–63.
10. *Potsdam Papers,* I, 810, 812.
11. Churchill, *Triumph and Tragedy,* 522.
12. *Ibid.,* 539–40.
13. *Postdam Papers,* I, 810, 814. See also *ibid.,* 806–08; Brookings Institution, International Studies Group, *Anglo-American Economic Relations: A Problem Paper* (Washington, 1950), 11–12; Miroslav A. Kriz, "Postwar International Lending," *Essays in International Finance,* No. 8, Spring, 1947, 9; Roosevelt to George C. Marshall, September 9, 1944, FDR Mss, PSF; *Morgenthau Diary (Germany),* 619–20, 628; *Morgenthau Diary,* 1679–80.
14. Earl Attlee, *A Prime Minister Remembers* (London, 1961), 129–30.
15. *Potsdam Papers,* I, 817.
16. FR (1945), I, 123. See also *ibid.,* 951–52.
17. *Forrestal Diaries,* 81. Raul Sosa-Rodriguez, *Les Problèmes Structurels des Relations Économiques Internationales de L'Amérique Latine* (Geneva, 1963), 118; *Potsdam Papers,* I, 817–22; Memos of Conversations, March 2, May 29, 1945, JCG Mss; R. Keith Kane to Forrestal, March 16, 1945, JF Mss, box 22.
18. John A. Loftus, "Petroleum in International Relations," DSB, XIII, 174–75.
19. Woodward, *British Foreign Policy,* 319–20; *Potsdam Papers,* I, 171, 950–58.
20. Truman, *Memoirs,* 45. See also FR (1945), II, 1085.
21. Stimson to Truman, May 16, 1945, in the Stimson Diary, HLS Mss. See also Truman, *Memoirs,* 236.
22. Department of Agriculture, *What Peace Can Mean to American Farmers: Post-War Agriculture and Employment* (Washington, 1945), 23. See also Stimson to Truman, May 16, 1945, in Stimson Diary, HLS Mss; *Potsdam Papers,* I, 180, 185, 189–90; Department of Agriculture, *Post-War Foreign Trade Program, passim.*

23. Memo of Conversation, May 13, 1945, HLS Mss. See also Gold, *Planning in Agriculture*, 434–53; Division of Naval Intelligence, Office of the Chief of Naval Operations, "International Developments of Naval Interest," May 12, 1945, 11, in JF Mss, box 25; *Forrestal Diaries*, 105–07; Herbert Hoover, *The Ordeal of Woodrow Wilson* (New York, 1958), 119ff.
24. Stimson Diary, May 11, 1945, HLS Mss; Herbert Hoover, *An American Epic* (Chicago, 1964), IV, 105.
25. Hoover, *American Epic*, 101.
26. Memo for the President, "The Rehabilitation of Europe as a Whole," July 22, 1945, HLS Mss.
27. Herbert Hoover, "Memorandum on the Organization of Foreign Relief . . . ," May 30, 1945; Herbert Hoover to Stimson, May 31, June 9, 1945; Herbert Hoover to Robert P. Patterson, February 9, 1948, all in HLS Mss; Penrose, *Economic Planning for the Peace*, 322–24; Mark W. Clark, *Calculated Risk* (New York, 1950), 474–75; Woodbridge, *UNRRA*, II, 46, 359, 428; Behrman, "Political Factors in U. S. International Financial Cooperation," 434.
28. FR (1945), V, 995. See also *ibid.*, 992; *Business Week*, March 10, 1945, 111; Feis, *Churchill-Roosevelt-Stalin*, 647; Memo of Conversation, March 3, 1945, JCG Mss.
29. Harriman to Stettinius, April 6, 1945, in JF Mss, box 24.
30. *Potsdam Papers*, I, 181. See also Memos of Conversations, May 12, 1945, JCG Mss.
31. Penrose, *Economic Planning for the Peace*, 112; McNeill, *America, Britain, and Russia*, 691; FR (1945), II, 1004–25.

Chapter 20: Germany: Revenge versus Reintegration

1. Truman, *Memoirs*, 83.
2. Churchill, *Triumph and Tragedy*, 430.
3. *Potsdam Papers*, I, 4, 9. See also *ibid.*, 6–7.
4. Truman, *Memoirs*, 300–01. See also Woodward, *British Foreign Policy*, 524–27.
5. Murphy *Diplomat Among Warriors*, 243–44.
6. Churchill, *Triumph and Tragedy*, 651. See also *ibid.*, 491; Pogue, *Supreme Command*, 498–99; Steinert, *Die 23 Tage*, 216ff.
7. U. S. Senate, Committee on Foreign Relations, *Documents on Germany, 1944–61.* 87:1. (Washington, 1961), 5.
8. *Potsdam Papers*, I, 435.
9. *Ibid.*, 639. See also *ibid.*, 51, 168, 178–79, 187, 266, 334–35, 342; Murphy, *Diplomat Among Warriors*, 255; FR (1945), III, 94–103, 136–38, 567–68.
10. Lucius D. Clay, *Decision in Germany* (Garden City, N. Y., 1950), chap. II; Manuel Gottlieb, *The German Peace Settlement and the Berlin Crisis* (New York, 1960), 22–23; Senate, *Documents on Germany*, 19–28, 41–53; Philip E. Mosely, "The Occupation of Germany: New Light on How the Zones Were Drawn," *Foreign Affairs*, XXVIII (1950), 601–04; Murphy, *Diplomat Among Warriors*, 261–63; *Potsdam Papers*, I, 234–39.
11. Shirer, *Fall of the Third Reich*, 1354–55; Woodward, *British Foreign Policy*, 264–67, 986–88; Wolfgang Leonhard, *Child of the Revolution* (Chicago, 1958), 299–338, 350–51; O. S. S., "German Communist

Party," *passim;* DS, Office of Research and Intelligence, "Status and Prospects of German Trade-Unions and Work Councils." No. 3381. May 27, 1946. (N. P., 1946), *passim;* FR (1945), V, 830; Gottlieb, *German Peace Settlement,* 43–54, 213; Raymond Ebsworth, *Restoring Democracy in Germany: The British Contribution* (London, 1960), 25–27; Lewis J. Edinger, *Kurt Schumacher: A Study in Political Behavior* (Stanford, 1965), 78–79; Beate Ruhm Von Oppen, ed., *Documents on Germany under Occupation, 1945–1954* (London, 1955), 59–64; FR (1945), III, 1042.

12. *Potsdam Papers,* I, 472–73. See also *ibid.,* 524; Churchill, *Triumph and Tragedy,* 461; Montgomery, *Memoirs,* 340; DS, "Status and Prospects of German Trade-Unions," 23–43; Daugherty and Janowitz, *Psychological Warfare Casebook,* 363–65; FR (1945), III, 1034–37.

13. *Potsdam Papers,* I, 484, 502–03.

14. DS, *Germany, 1947–1949: The Story in Documents* (Washington, 1950), 23–29. See also *Morgenthau Diary (Germany),* 974–76, 981–99, 1016–30, 1044–48, 1075–76, 1117; Hammond, "Directives for the Occupation of Germany," 414–15; Memos of Conversations, March 6, March 22 (2), 23, 1945, JCG Mss; FR (1945), III, 430–40, 455–72, 504–05.

15. *Forrestal Diaries,* 57. See also Hammond, "Directives for the Occupation of Germany," 425.

16. Clay, *Decision in Germany,* 18; Murphy, *Diplomat Among Warriors,* 251. See also Murphy, *Diplomat Among Warriors,* 249.

17. Eisenhower, *Crusade in Europe,* 442. See also Murphy, *Diplomat Among Warriors,* 250–51; Harold Zink, *The United States in Germany, 1944–1955* (Princeton, 1957), 94–95; *Morgenthau Diary (Germany),* 1542–43.

18. *Potsdam Papers,* I, 444–45, 439, 459. See also *ibid.,* 51, 439–47, 456–61; Kennan, *Memoirs,* 178, 258; FR (1945), III, 205–06.

19. Walter Rundell, Jr., *Black Market Money: The Collapse of U. S. Military Control in World War II* (Baton Rouge, 1964), 48–49; *Yalta Papers,* 982–83; Woodward, *British Foreign Policy,* 527; *Morgenthau Diary (Germany),* 1113, 1119, 1141–43, 1223, 1281–84; Leonhard, *Child of the Revolution,* 345; W. Friedmann, *The Allied Military Government of Germany* (London, 1947), 25–26; Gottlieb, *German Peace Settlement,* 47–49; Harriman to Stettinius, April 6, 1945, JF Mss; Division of Naval Intelligence, Office of the Chief of Naval Operations, "International Developments of Naval Interest," May 12, 1945, 9–10; Truman, *Memoirs,* 310; FR (1945), III, 437, 453, 1179–83, 1186, 1204–35.

20. *Potsdam Papers,* I, 628, 613, 504. See also *ibid.,* 469.

21. Eisenhower, *Crusade in Europe,* 442.

22. "Notes for Talk with the President," July 3, 1945, HLS Mss.

23. *Potsdam Papers,* I, 587, 589. See also *ibid.,* 446–47; Gottlieb, *German Peace Settlement,* 35; Memo of Conversation, May 19, 1945, JCG Mss.

24. *Potsdam Papers,* I, 511, 520.

25. *Ibid.,* 528, 537, 547.

26. *Ibid.,* 500. See also *ibid.,* 519–20, 526, 532, 543.

27. B. U. Ratchford and William D. Ross, *Berlin Reparations Assignment: Round One of the German Peace Settlement* (Chapel Hill, 1947), 9–47.

Chapter 21: The Far East After Yalta: The Dilemma of China and the Future of Japan

1. Romanus and Sunderland, *Time Runs Out*, 338; DS, *Relations with China*, 87–92, 575–76; *Morgenthau Diary*, 1413, 1417; Feis, *China Tangle*, 267–73.
2. Romanus and Sunderland, *Time Runs Out*, 337. See also Feis, *China Tangle*, 266.
3. DS, *Relations with China*, 577. See also Feis, *China Tangle*, 271–73; *Morgenthau Diary*, 1422–23, 1430, 1458–60.
4. Mao, *Selected Works*, III, 277. See also *ibid.*, 320; DS, *Relations with China*, 83–86, 576; *Morgenthau Diary*, 1460.
5. Mao, *Selected Works*, III, 283, 279, 296. See also *ibid.*, 306–07.
6. Truman, *Memoirs*, 102–03. See also *Morgenthau Diary*, 1427, 1431, 1435, 1461.
7. *Morgenthau Diary*, 1535, 1555. See also *ibid.*, 1511–12, 1522, 1526–27, 1541–42.
8. *Ibid.*, 1566, 1577, 1586. See also *ibid.*, 1557–58, 1584; Feis, *China Tangle*, 301.
9. *Morgenthau Diary*, 1631. See also *ibid.*, 1596, 1602–03, 1610.
10. *Ibid.*, 1631; Feis, *China Tangle*, 303.
11. Mao, *Selected Works*, III, 322, 335. See also *ibid.*, 333–36; DS, *Relations with China*, 100–05.
12. *Potsdam Papers*, I, 858.
13. U. S. Senate, Committee on the Judiciary, *Hearings, Institute of Pacific Relations*, 82:1, 2. (Washington, 1951–53), 2305ff.
14. *Morgenthau Diary*, 1418; *War and the Working Class*, March 1, 1945, 26–28; April 15, 1945, 15–19; *Le Monde*, March 11, 1967, 7; Department of Defense, *Entry of the Soviet Union*, 51.
15. Feis, *China Tangle*, 284.
16. DS, *Relations with China*, 95–96. See also Romanus and Sunderland, *Time Runs Out*, 339.
17. DS, *Relations with China*, 97.
18. *Forrestal Diaries*, 51. See also DS, *Relations with China*, 98; Eden, *The Reckoning*, 613; Department of Defense, *Entry of the Soviet Union*, 64.
19. Churchill, *Triumph and Tragedy*, 492. See also Feis, *China Tangle*, 304–05; Truman, *Memoirs*, 79; Leahy, *I Was There*, 351; Deane, *Strange Alliance*, chaps. XIII, XIV, XVI; Richard G. Hewlett and Oscar E. Anderson, *The New World, 1939–1946* (University Park, Pa., 1962), 350–51; DS, *Relations with China*, 98; Stimson Diary, May 10, 1945, HLS Mss; O. S. S., R. & A. Branch, "Japan: Winter 1944–1945." R & A 31128. May 18, 1945. (N. P., 1945), *passim;* Division of Naval Intelligence, Office of the Chief of Naval Operations, "International Developments of Naval Interest," May 12, 1945, 16.
20. Department of Defense, *Entry of the Soviet Union*, 69. See also *Forrestal Diaries*, 52; Romanus and Sunderland, *Time Runs Out*, 340; Stimson Diary, May 13, 1945, HLS Mss.
21. Grew, *Turbulent Era*, 1446.
22. Stimson Diary, May 15, 1945, HLS Mss.
23. Department of Defense, *Entry of the Soviet Union*, 71. See also Stimson Diary, May 15, 1945, HLS Mss.

24. *Potsdam Papers*, I, 42. See also Stimson Diary, March 16, 1945, HLS Mss; Stimson to George C. Marshall, November 29, 1945, HLS Mss; Truman, *Memoirs*, 264.

25. Sherwood, *Roosevelt and Hopkins*, 902–03; *Potsdam Papers*, I, 62.

26. Leahy, *I Was There*, 381. See also Truman, *Memoirs*, 265; *Le Monde*, March 11, 1967, 7; Feis, *China Tangle*, 312; *Peking Review*, September 20, 1963, 10.

27. Grew, *Turbulent Era*, 1468. See also Memo of Conversation, June 11, 1945, JCG Mss.

28. Department of Defense, *Entry of the Soviet Union*, 76, 85.

29. Feis, *China Tangle*, 314–15; *Le Monde*, March 11, 1967, 7.

30. Stimson Diary, December 31, 1944. See also Henry L. Stimson, "The Decision to Use the Atomic Bomb," *Harper's Magazine*, 194 (February, 1947), 98; *New York Times*, August 19, 1966; Stimson Diary, September 8, 1943, HLS Mss; Leslie R. Groves, *Now It Can Be Told: The Story of the Manhattan Project* (New York, 1962), chaps. XIII, XVI, XVII; Hewlett and Anderson, *The New World*, 334–35; Herbert Feis, *The Atomic Bomb and the End of World War II* (Princeton, 1966), 31–32; FR (1945), II, 2–3; Alice K. Smith, *A Peril and a Hope: The Scientists' Movement in America: 1945–47* (Chicago, 1965), 316–17.

31. Memo of Conference with the President, June 6, 1945, HLS Mss. See also *Yalta Papers*, 383–84.

32. Stimson Diary, February 13, 1945, HLS Mss.

33. Stimson Diary, May 29, 1945, HLS Mss. See also Hewlett and Anderson, *The New World*, 338–40; Robert Jungk, *Brighter Than a Thousand Suns: A Personal History of the Atomic Scientists* (New York, 1958), 181.

34. Jungk, *Brighter Than A Thousand Suns*, 182; Hewlett and Anderson, *The New World*, 338, 356–57; Herbert Feis, *Japan Subdued: The Atomic Bomb and the End of the War in the Pacific* (Princeton, 1961), 38.

35. Hewlett and Anderson, *The New World*, 358–60; Stimson Diary, June 6, 1945, HLS Mss; Memo for Talk With the President, June 6, 1945, HLS Mss; FR (1945), II, 13; Groves, *Now It Can Be Told*, 264; Jungk, *Brighter Than a Thousand Suns*, 183–86.

36. Feis, *Japan Subdued*, 46–47; Groves, *Now It Can Be Told*, 265; Hewlett and Anderson, *The New World*, 357; *Potsdam Papers*, II, 1371; Memo of Conference with the President, June 6, 1945, HLS Mss.

37. Groves, *Now It Can Be Told*, 265.

38. Grew to John S. Piper, November 30, 1943, JCG Mss.

39. Hull, *Memoirs*, 1587.

40. FR (1944), V, 1236, 1248, 1258–59.

41. Grew to "Long," July 10, 1944, JCG Mss. See also Hull, *Memoirs*, 1592.

42. *Morgenthau Diary*, 1394. See also O. S. S., R. & A. Branch, "North American Trade With China and Japan." R & A 2839. January 15, 1945. (N. P., 1945), *passim;* Edward R. Stettinius to Grew, November 11, 1944, JCG Mss; Dorothy Borg, *The United States and the Far Eastern Crisis of 1933–1938* (Cambridge, 1963), *passim.*

43. Captain Ellis M. Zacharias, *Secret Missions* (New York, 1946), 333.

44. Grew to Stimson, June 26, 1945, and attachment, HLS Mss.

45. Grew, *Turbulent Era*, 1420.

46. *Forrestal Diaries*, 52.

47. *Potsdam Papers*, I, 934. See also *ibid.*, 44; Sherwood, *Roosevelt and Hopkins*, 903–04; *Morgenthau Diary (Germany)*, 1592–93.

*Chapter 22: July 1945: The War with Japan and the
Potsdam Conference*

1. FR (1944), V, 1183–85.
2. U. S. Strategic Bombing Survey, *Japan's Struggle to End the War* (Washington, 1946), 21; Robert J. C. Butow, *Japan's Decision to Surrender* (Stanford, 1954), 49. See also FR (1944), V, 1276.
3. Daugherty and Janowitz, *Psychological Warfare Casebook*, 279–91, 846–47; Zacharias, *Secret Missions*, 336–41, chaps. XXXII–XXXIII; *Look*, May 23, 1950; Strategic Bombing Survey, *Japan's Struggle to End the War*, 12–13; Butow, *Japan's Decision to Surrender*, 67–69.
4. *Potsdam Papers*, I, 45. See also Butow, *Japan's Decision to Surrender*, 104–05.
5. Stimson Diary, June 18, 1945, HLS Mss. See also Grew, *Turbulent Era*, 1423–24, 1431–34; Memos of Conversations, May 28, 29, 1945, JCG Mss.
6. Stimson Diary, June 26–30, 1945, HLS Mss. See also *Potsdam Papers*, I, 891–92; Grew, *Turbulent Era*, 1435–38; Strategic Bombing Survey, *Japan's Struggle to End the War*, 13; U. S. Army, Forces in the Far East, *Study of the Strategical and Tactical Peculiarities of Far Eastern Russia and Soviet Far East Forces* ["Japanese Special Studies on Manchuria"] (Washington, 1955), 111–12; U. S. Army, Forces in the Far East, *Record of Operations Against Soviet Russia, Northern and Western Fronts (August–September 1945)* ["Japanese Monographs"] (Washington, 1954), 3; Butow, *Japan's Decision to Surrender*, 118–23. These and other contemporary Japanese documents released by the U. S. Army may be found in the Library of Congress.
7. Memo to Truman, July 2, 1945, in Stimson Diary, HLS Mss.
8. *Forrestal Diaries*, 74; Stimson Diary, July 16, 1945, HLS Mss. See also O. S. S., R. & A. Branch, "Japan—Conflicting Political Views." R & A 3216. July 23, 1945. (N. P., 1945), *passim; Potsdam Papers*, I, 874–83; Strategic Bombing Survey, *Japan's Struggle to End the War*, 13.
9. Memos of Conversations, July 5, 10–11, 1945, JCG Mss.
10. Connally, *My Name is Tom*, 289.
11. Truman, *Memoirs*, 23, 326.
12. Department of Defense, *Entry of the Soviet Union*, 87.
13. Truman, *Memoirs*, 411. See also Department of Defense, *Entry of the Soviet Union*, 79–87; Stimson, Memo for the President, July 16, 1945, HLS Mss.
14. O. S. S., R. & A. Branch, "Japan's Secret Weapon: Suicide." R & A 3302s. July 20, 1945. (N. P., 1945), *passim;* Feis, *The Atomic Bomb*, 192–93; Truman, *Memoirs*, 315–20; Feis, *China Tangle*, 317–20; *Potsdam Papers*, I, 862–64.
15. *Potsdam Papers*, I, 871. See also Truman, *Memoirs*, 320.
16. Stimson to George C. Marshall, November 29, 1945, HLS Mss.
17. Stimson, Memo for the President, July 16, 1945, HLS Mss. See also Stimson Diary, July 15, 23, 1945, HLS Mss.
18. Churchill, *Triumph and Tragedy*, 544. See also Stimson, Memo for the President, July 16, 1945, HLS Mss.
19. *Potsdam Papers*, II, 1587, 1224. See also *ibid.*, 1586; Stimson Diary, July 17, 1945, HLS Mss.
20. Bryant, *Triumph in the West*, 364. See also *Potsdam Papers*, II, 114, 1237–41.

21. Truman, *Memoirs*, 356.
22. *Potsdam Papers*, II, 1361.
23. *Potsdam Papers*, II, 276. See also *ibid.*, 1241; Stimson Diary, July 22, 23, 1945, HLS Mss.
24. *Potsdam Papers*, II, 1463. See also *ibid.*, 1373–74; Stimson Diary, July 23, 24, 1945, HLS Mss.
25. Truman, *Memoirs*, 420. See also *Potsdam Papers*, II, 345, 1464; Hewlett and Anderson, *The New World*, 393.
26. Conference with Generalissimo Stalin, July 25, 1945 . . ., HLS Mss. See also *Potsdam Papers*, II, 378–79, 396–97; Stimson Diary, July 3, 1945, HLS Mss; Churchill, *Triumph and Tragedy*, 547.
27. *Potsdam Papers*, II, 1244.
28. *Ibid.*, 476, 1245–47, 1333–34; Byrnes, *Speaking Frankly*, 208–09; Forrestal Diary, July 28, 1945, JF Mss, box 19; Curry, *Byrnes*, 121; Truman, *Memoirs*, 402.
29. Churchill, *Triumph and Tragedy*, 548. See also Hull, *Memoirs*, 1593–94; *Potsdam Papers*, II, 1252–59, 1266, 1269, 1273; Truman, *Memoirs*, 396; Stimson Diary, July 20, 1945, HLS Mss.
30. Truman, *Memoirs*, 387.
31. *Potsdam Papers*, II, 1476. See also *ibid.*, 1272, 1277; Truman, *Memoirs*, 387.
32. *Potsdam Papers*, II, 1261. See also *ibid.*, 449–50, 1284; Joseph Grew to Stimson, February 12, 1947, HLS Mss.
33. *Potsdam Papers*, II, 1293. See also *ibid.*, 1290.
34. *Ibid.*, 1293; Butow, *Japan's Decision to Surrender*, 145–47.
35. *Potsdam Papers*, II, 1298. See also Butow, *Japan's Decision to Surrender*, 148; Truman, *Memoirs*, 397; Stimson, *On Active Service*, 625.

Chapter 23: The Potsdam Conference: The Future of Europe
and the End of a Coalition

1. Truman, *Memoirs*, 341.
2. *Potsdam Papers*, II, 756. See also *ibid.*, 990–91.
3. *Ibid.*, 279. See also *ibid.*, 141–42.
4. *Ibid.*, 142, 183, 233, 275, 296–98, 810, 990, 998; Byrnes, *Speaking Frankly*, 83.
5. *Potsdam Papers*, II, 892. See also *ibid.*, 811, 863, 877–80.
6. Curry, *Byrnes*, 345. See also *Potsdam Papers*, II, 903–05.
7. Truman, *Memoirs*, 411.
8. *Potsdam Papers*, II, 429, 450. See also *ibid.*, 385; Woodward, *British Foreign Policy*, 547, 561; McNeill, *America, Britain, and Russia*, 612–13.
9. *Potsdam Papers*, II, 487. See also *ibid.*, 451–52, 472–75, 921–22.
10. *Ibid.*, I, 439; II, 938–40. See also *ibid.*, II, 512–18, 1505–06, 1564; Woodward, *British Foreign Policy*, 566.
11. Churchill, *Triumph and Tragedy*, 558.
12. Truman, *Memoirs*, 369. See also *Potsdam Papers*, II, 1108, 1112.
13. *Potsdam Papers*, II, 1580, 208, 210. See also *ibid.*, 842.
14. Truman, *Memoirs*, 369. See also *Potsdam Papers*, II, 193, 206, 249–52, 1123–24.
15. *Potsdam Papers*, II, 1151. See also *ibid.*, 332–34, 356–57, 404–06, 472, 1128–29, 1522–23; Woodward, *British Foreign Policy*, 544; Churchill, *Triumph and Tragedy*, 568–69.

16. *Potsdam Papers*, II, 588, 1509. See also *ibid.*, 518–19; Woodward, *British Foreign Policy*, 562–64; Byrnes, *Speaking Frankly*, 81.

17. Truman, *Memoirs*, 364.

18. *Potsdam Papers*, II, 644. See also *ibid.*, I, 405, II, 689–97.

19. *Potsdam Papers*, II, 230. See also *ibid.*, 150–55, 207, 228–32.

20. Truman, *Memoirs*, 360. See also *Potsdam Papers*, II, 232, 362.

21. Truman, *Memoirs*, 360. See also *ibid.*, 377; *Potsdam Papers*, II, 716–17, 728–30.

22. Byrnes, *Speaking Frankly*, 75.

23. *Potsdam Papers*, II, 742. See also *ibid.*, 234–36, 574, 738.

24. *Ibid.*, 1510.

25. *Ibid.*, 623. See also Woodward, *British Foreign Policy*, 550.

26. Truman, *Memoirs*, 346–47. See also *Potsdam Papers*, II, 53, 624–26; Woodward, *British Foreign Policy*, 531.

27. *Potsdam Papers*, II, 148. See also *ibid.*, 1088.

28. *Ibid.*, 1208.

29. *Ibid.*, 1213. See also *ibid.*, 127–28, 1209.

30. *Ibid.*, 1049, 1060, 1053, 1063. See also *ibid.*, 1056, 1214–22.

31. *Ibid.*, 1074. See also *ibid.*, 648, 1043–45.

32. *Ibid.*, 609. See also *ibid.*, 56–58.

33. *Ibid.*, 613. See also *ibid.*, 67.

34. *Ibid.*, I, 1030. See also *ibid.*, 1020ff. Woodward, *British Foreign Policy*, 540; George Kirk, *The Middle East, 1945–1950* (London, 1954), 23; Stephen G. Xydis, "The 1945 Crisis Over the Turkish Straits," *Balkan Studies*, I (1960), 7off.

35. Memo of Conversation, July 7, 1945, JCG Mss. See also *Potsdam Papers*, I, 1031–35.

36. Memo of Conversation, July 7, 1945, JCG Mss.

37. *Potsdam Papers*, I, 1014.

38. *Ibid.*, II, 1437. See also *ibid.*, 256–58, 302–04, 365–66, 1422, 1426, 1434.

39. *Ibid.*, II, 1408; I, 1002. See also *ibid.*, 1171; FR (1944), IV, 306, 338; FR (1945), V, 667–79.

40. *Potsdam Papers*, II, 1173, 124. See also *ibid.*, 122–26, 1175–76; Truman, *Memoirs*, 358–59.

41. *Potsdam Papers*, I, 982, 993, 1002. See also *ibid.*, I, 981–88, 993ff.; II, 239, 633–34, 1568; Woodward, *British Foreign Policy*, 531, 534; Memo of Conversation, July 2, 1945, JCG Mss; FR (1945), I, 1398–99.

42. *Potsdam Papers*, II, 282–83, 550–51, 632, 1409–17, 1493.

43. Truman, *Memoirs*, 402, 410. See also *Forrestal Diaries*, 78.

44. Drafts of Truman Speech of August 9, 1945, in SIR Mss, box 3. See also *Potsdam Papers*, II, 808–09, 1158–61, 1179–80.

45. Holborn, *War and Peace Aims*, 354.

46. *Potsdam Papers*, II, 1156, 1421–22. See also Truman, *Memoirs*, 423.

47. Leahy, *I Was There*, 427.

Chapter 24: The End of the War and the Revolutionary Tide in the Far East

1. Truman, *Memoirs*, 422. See also Stimson Diary, August 4, 6, 8, 1945, HLS Mss.

2. U. S. Army, Forces in the Far East, *5th Airfleet Operations* (*February-August, 1945*) ["Japanese Monographs"] (N. P., N. D.), 136. LC.

3. *Ibid.*, 137. See also U. S. Army, Forces in the Far East, *Outline of Operations Prior to the Termination of War and Activities Connected with the Cessation of Hostilities (July-August, 1945)* ["Japanese Monographs"] (Washington, 1952), 7, LC; Butow, *Japan's Decision to Surrender,* 150–52.

4. Truman, *Memoirs,* 425. See also *ibid.,* 426; Grew, *Turbulent Era,* 1439; Stimson Diary, Memo of Conference with the President, August 8, 1945, HLS Mss; Werth, *Russia at War,* 1038–40; Feis, *Japan Subdued,* 115.

5. Chinese Ministry of Information, *The Collected Wartime Messages of Generalissimo Chiang Kai-shek* (New York, 1946), II, 849; Stimson Diary, August 9, 10, 1945, HLS Mss.

6. DS, *The Axis in Defeat: A Collection of Documents on American Policy Toward Germany and Japan* (Washington, N. D.), 29. See also Strategic Bombing Survey, *Japan's Struggle to End the War,* 13; U. S. Army, *Outline of Operations Prior to the Termination of War,* 14–15.

7. Stimson Diary, August 10, 1945, HLS Mss.

8. Feis, *Japan Subdued,* 124. See also *ibid.,* 123–25; DS, *Axis in Defeat,* 30; *Forrestal Diaries,* 84–85; Deane, *Strange Alliance,* 278–79; *Stalin Correspondence,* II, 260; Werth, *Russia at War,* 1038–42; U. S. Army, *Operations Against Soviet Russia,* 267; U. S. Army, *Soviet Far East Forces,* 113.

9. Truman, *Memoirs,* 428.

10. *Potsdam Papers,* II, 1373. See also *ibid.,* 1323.

11. Feis, *Japan Subdued,* 148.

12. *Ibid.,* 149. See also Memo of Conversation, August 4, 1945, JCG Mss.

13. *Stalin Correspondence,* II, 1261–69; Truman, *Memoirs,* 443–44; U. S. House, Committee on Foreign Affairs, *Hearings, Korean Aid.* 81:1. June, 1949. (Washington, 1949), 118.

14. FR (1943), III, 37.

15. *Potsdam Papers,* I, 309. See also FR (1943), III, 1093–94; Hull, *Memoirs,* 1584.

16. FR (1944), V, 1229. See also *ibid.,* 1226–28.

17. *Yalta Papers,* 360. See also FR (1944), V, 1227, 1241.

18. Harold Isaacs, *No Peace for Asia* (New York, 1947), 94. See also *Potsdam Papers,* I, 309–24, 925–27; Truman, *Memoirs,* 316–17; Romanus and Sunderland, *Time Runs Out,* 389–91; George M. McCune, *Korea Today* (Cambridge, 1950), 47.

19. U. S. House, *Korean Aid,* 118–19, 141; Truman, *Memoirs,* 444–45.

20. George E. Taylor, *The Philippines and the United States: Problems of Partnership* (New York, 1964), 85–125; William J. Pomeroy, "The Unfinished Revolution in the Philippines," *Progressive Review,* I (1964), 59–60; Erich H. Jacoby, *Agrarian Unrest in Southeast Asia* (New York, 1949), 168–221; Monroe Hull, "Collaborator's Candidate," *Far Eastern Survey,* XV (1946), 73; Barbara Entenberg, "Agrarian Reform and the Hukbalahap," *Far Eastern Survey,* XV (1946), 245–46; John Keats, *They Fought Alone* (Philadelphia, 1963), 410–11; FR (1943), III, 1115; David J. Steinberg, *Philippine Collaboration in World War II* (Ann Arbor, 1967), *passim.*

21. FR (1943), III, 1108. See also *ibid.,* 1098–1101.

22. Record of Telephone Conversation, June 13, 1944, HLS Mss. See also Holborn, *War and Peace Aims,* 285–87.

23. Taylor, *Philippines and the United States,* 105. See also FR (1943), III, 1114.

24. O. S. S., R. & A. Branch, "Personalities in the Philippines Political Scene."

R & A 3220. July 30, 1945. (N. P., 1945), 1, 3. See also Keats, *They Fought Alone*, 410–17; Hull, "Collaborator's Candidate," 72; J. Weldon Jones to Manuel L. Roxas, June 21, 1945, JWJ Mss, box 14; FR (1944), V, 1307; Entenberg, "Agrarian Reform and the Hukbalahap," 246–47; Lawrence S. Finkelstein, *American Policy in Southeast Asia* (New York, 1950), 34; Taylor, *Philippines and the United States*, 110.

25. Memo of J. Weldon Jones, February 12, 1945, JWJ Mss, box 12; Memo of Meeting, April 19, 1945, HLS Mss; J. Weldon Jones to Sergio Osmeña, June 19, 1945, JWJ Mss, box 16; Jones to Manuel L. Roxas, June 21, 1945, JWJ Mss, box 14.

26. Hull, *Memoirs*, 1599.

27. O. S. S., R. & A. Branch, "Program of Geographic Work Fundamental to Far East Problems." R & A 3315. August 18, 1945. (N. P., 1945), 7–8, 5.

28. O. S. S., R. & A. Branch, "Transitional Period in Indonesia's Internal Political Situation." R & A 3232. August 24, 1945. (N. P., 1945), 5.

29. FR (1944), III, 780. See also *ibid.*, 773ff.; FR (1943), III, 37; FR (Teheran), 485; FR (1944), V, 1206; Hull, *Memoirs*, 1598.

30. State Department Report of October 15–28, 1945, in PG Mss. See also FR (1944), III, 783–84; FR (1945), I, 124; *Potsdam Papers*, I, 920; Jacoby, *Agrarian Unrest in Southeast Asia*, 143–48; Lê Châu, *La Révolution Paysanne du Sud Viet Nam* (Paris, 1966), 16–25, 54; Allan B. Cole, ed., *Conflict in Indo-China and International Repercussions: A Documentary History, 1945–1955* (Ithaca, 1956), 17.

31. Department of State Report, October 15–28, 1945, PG Mss.

32. Brig. Gen. Philip Gallagher to Maj. Gen. R. B. McClure, September 20, 1945, PG Mss.

33. *Ibid.* See also DS, Research and Intelligence Service, "Biographical Information on Prominent National Leaders in French Indochina." R & A 3336. October 25, 1945. (N. P., 1945), *passim;* State Department Report, October 15–27, 1945, PG Mss.

34. F. S. V. Donnison, *British Military Administration in the Far East, 1943–46* (London, 1956), 404–10; Finkelstein, *American Policy in Southeast Asia*, 10; Isaacs, *No Peace for Asia*, 147–60; De Gaulle, *Le Salut*, 467–68; FR (1945), IV, 704–05.

35. Holborn, *War and Peace Aims*, 802. See also *ibid.*, 799–810; Truman, *Memoirs*, 423–25, 433–36; Feis, *China Tangle*, 342–49; DS, *Relations with China*, 116–18.

36. DS, *Relations with China*, 120.

37. Romanus and Sunderland, *Time Runs Out*, 383.

38. Mao Tse-tung, *Selected Works* (Peking, 1961), IV, 49. See also *ibid.*, 13–50.

39. Romanus and Sunderland, *Time Runs Out*, 385–95; Feis, *China Tangle*, 336–37; Truman, *Memoirs*, 433–35; DS, *Relations with China*, 119; Mao, *Selected Works*, IV, 33–38; Chassin, *Communist Conquest of China*, 57; Isaacs, *Tragedy of the Chinese Revolution*, 320; McLane, *Soviet Policy and the Chinese Communists*, 198–99; Vice Adm. Milton E. Miles, *A Different Kind of War* (New York, 1967), *passim;* Henry I. Shaw, "United States Marine Corps in North China, 1945–1949" (unpublished official history in U. S. Office of Naval History, Washington, D. C.), 34–36.

40. DS, *Relations with China*, 119.

41. Edwin A. Locke, Jr., to Bob Carr, March 15, 1945, EAL-2 Mss, box 4. See also DS, *Relations with China,* 118–20; Feis, *China Tangle,* 349–50.
42. O. S. S., "Program of Geographic Work . . .," 4.
43. Stimson to George C. Marshall, November 29, 1945, HLS Mss. See also Memo, Locke to Truman, August 20, 1945, EAL-2 Mss, box 2.
44. Sherwood, *Roosevelt and Hopkins,* 925.
45. Donald M. Nelson to T. V. Soong, September 11, 1945, EAL Mss, box 8; P. W. Parker to James F. Byrnes, November 1, 1945; Emilio G. Collado to P. W. Parker, December 11, 1945, EAL Mss, box 7; Edwin A. Locke, Jr., to T. V. Soong, August 29, 1945, EAL-2 Mss, box 2.

INDEX

ABOUT THE AUTHOR

Gabriel Kolko is Distinguished Research Professor of History at York University in Toronto, Canada, and received his Ph.D. from Harvard University. Since *The Politics of War* appeared in 1968 he has published four books on United States foreign policy, including a highly acclaimed history of the Vietnam War, *Anatomy of a War* (Pantheon, 1986), and *Confronting the Third World* (Pantheon, 1988). He is currently writing a general study of war in the twentieth century.

347